T0325912

Advanced Methodologies and Technologies in System Security, Information Privacy, and Forensics

Mehdi Khosrow–Pour, D.B.A.
Information Resources Management Association, USA

A volume in the Advances in Information Security, Privacy, and Ethics (AISPE) Book Series

Published in the United States of America by
　　IGI Global
　　Information Science Reference (an imprint of IGI Global)
　　701 E. Chocolate Avenue
　　Hershey PA, USA 17033
　　Tel: 717-533-8845
　　Fax: 717-533-8661
　　E-mail: cust@igi-global.com
　　Web site: http://www.igi-global.com

Library of Congress Cataloging-in-Publication Data

Names: Khosrow-Pour, Mehdi, 1951- editor.
Title: Advanced methodologies and technologies in system security,
　information privacy, and forensics / Mehdi Khosrow-Pour, D.B.A., editor.
Description: Hershey, PA : Information Science Reference, [2019] | Includes
　bibliographical references.
Identifiers: LCCN 2018029248| ISBN 9781522574927 (h/c) | ISBN 9781522574934
　(eISBN)
Subjects: LCSH: Computer security. | Data protection. | Digital forensic
　science. | Computer networks--Security measures.
Classification: LCC QA76.9.A25 A353 2019 | DDC 005.8--dc23 LC record available at https://lccn.loc.gov/2018029248

This book is published in the IGI Global book series Advances in Information Security, Privacy, and Ethics (AISPE) (ISSN: 1948-9730; eISSN: 1948-9749)

British Cataloguing in Publication Data
A Cataloguing in Publication record for this book is available from the British Library.

For electronic access to this publication, please contact: eresources@igi-global.com.

Advances in Information Security, Privacy, and Ethics (AISPE) Book Series

Manish Gupta
State University of New York, USA

ISSN:1948-9730
EISSN:1948-9749

Mission

As digital technologies become more pervasive in everyday life and the Internet is utilized in ever increasing ways by both private and public entities, concern over digital threats becomes more prevalent.

The **Advances in Information Security, Privacy, & Ethics (AISPE) Book Series** provides cutting-edge research on the protection and misuse of information and technology across various industries and settings. Comprised of scholarly research on topics such as identity management, cryptography, system security, authentication, and data protection, this book series is ideal for reference by IT professionals, academicians, and upper-level students.

Coverage

- Network Security Services
- Telecommunications Regulations
- Security Classifications
- Computer ethics
- Internet Governance
- Privacy Issues of Social Networking
- Cyberethics
- IT Risk
- CIA Triad of Information Security
- Information Security Standards

> IGI Global is currently accepting manuscripts for publication within this series. To submit a proposal for a volume in this series, please contact our Acquisition Editors at Acquisitions@igi-global.com or visit: http://www.igi-global.com/publish/.

Titles in this Series

For a list of additional titles in this series, please visit: www.igi-global.com/book-series

Handbook of Research on Information and Cyber Security in the Fourth Industrial Revolution
Ziska Fields (University of KwaZulu-Natal, South Africa)
Information Science Reference • copyright 2018 • 647pp • H/C (ISBN: 9781522547631) • US $345.00 (our price)

Security and Privacy in Smart Sensor Networks
Yassine Maleh (University Hassan I, Morocco) Abdellah Ezzati (University Hassan I, Morocco) and Mustapha
Belaissaoui (University Hassan I, Morocco)
Information Science Reference • copyright 2018 • 441pp • H/C (ISBN: 9781522557364) • US $215.00 (our price)

The Changing Scope of Technoethics in Contemporary Society
Rocci Luppicini (University of Ottawa, Canada)
Information Science Reference • copyright 2018 • 403pp • H/C (ISBN: 9781522550945) • US $225.00 (our price)

Handbook of Research on Information Security in Biomedical Signal Processing
Chittaranjan Pradhan (KIIT University, India) Himansu Das (KIIT University, India) Bighnaraj Naik (Veer Surendra
Sai University of Technology (VSSUT), India) and Nilanjan Dey (Techno India College of Technology, India)
Information Science Reference • copyright 2018 • 414pp • H/C (ISBN: 9781522551522) • US $325.00 (our price)

Handbook of Research on Network Forensics and Analysis Techniques
Gulshan Shrivastava (National Institute of Technology Patna, India) Prabhat Kumar (National Institute of Technology Patna, India) B. B. Gupta (National Institute of Technology Kurukshetra, India) Suman Bala (Orange Labs, France) and Nilanjan Dey (Techno India College of Technology, India)
Information Science Reference • copyright 2018 • 509pp • H/C (ISBN: 9781522541004) • US $335.00 (our price)

Cyber Harassment and Policy Reform in the Digital Age Emerging Research and Opportunities
Ramona S. McNeal (University of Northern Iowa, USA) Susan M. Kunkle (Kent State University, USA) and Mary
Schmeida (Kent State University, USA)
Information Science Reference • copyright 2018 • 170pp • H/C (ISBN: 9781522552857) • US $145.00 (our price)

Security and Privacy Management, Techniques, and Protocols
Yassine Maleh (University Hassan I, Morocco)
Information Science Reference • copyright 2018 • 426pp • H/C (ISBN: 9781522555834) • US $205.00 (our price)

701 East Chocolate Avenue, Hershey, PA 17033, USA
Tel: 717-533-8845 x100 • Fax: 717-533-8661
E-Mail: cust@igi-global.com • www.igi-global.com

List of Contributors

Table of Contents

Preface

Advanced Methodologies and Technologies in System Security, Information Privacy, and Forensics is a single-volume major reference work comprised of 27 unique chapters focusing on some of the most advanced and innovative conceptual, methodological, and technical content available to scientists, researchers, and organizations worldwide. The concepts presented within these chapters are sure to support new research initiatives and various applications associated with securing information infrastructure, systems, and networks, while also aiding in criminal investigations.

This publication is aimed to serve the needs of libraries, corporations, research organizations, independent researchers, practitioners, scientists, policymakers, engineers, IT consultants, and instructors seeking advanced cross-disciplinary knowledge on a wide range of subject matter – from knowledge-based systems in forensic science to identity-based encryption algorithms.

Attention is also given to emerging topics including but not limited to intellectual property, cloud computing, information privacy, piracy, and the internet of things (IoT). The chapters within this publication are sure to provide readers with the tools necessary for further research and discovery in their respective industries and/or fields. Additionally, this publication could be extremely beneficial for use in coursework by instructors of various computer engineering and computer programming programs.

Advanced Methodologies and Technologies in System Security, Information Privacy, and Forensics is organized into four sections that provide comprehensive coverage of important topics in a variety of industries and fields. These sections are 1) Criminal Science and Forensics; 2) Cyber Crime, Cyber Bullying, and Digital Terrorism; 3) Cyber and Network Security; and 4) IT Security and Ethics.

The following paragraphs provide a summary of what to expect from this invaluable reference source:

Section 1, "Criminal Science and Forensics," is comprised of four chapters and opens this extensive reference source by highlighting the latest technological advancements used in digital forensic investigations and other types of criminal investigations. The first chapter in this section, "Forensic Investigations in Cloud Computing," authored by Prof. Diane Barrett from Bloomsburg University of Pennsylvania, USA, explores current forensic acquisition processes, why current processes need to be modified for cloud investigations, and how new methods can help in an investigation.

The second chapter in this section, "Internet-Facilitated Child Sexual Exploitation Crimes," authored by Prof. Keith F. Durkin from Ohio Northern University, USA and Prof. Ronald L. DeLong from the University of Dayton, USA, examines the characteristics of offenses, offenders, and victims. It also explores a multitude of issues related to the psychological assessment, classification, and treatment of the individuals who commit these offenses and strategies for the prevention of this behavior and the protection of minors online.

The third chapter in this section, "Knowledge-Based Forensic Patterns and Engineering System," authored by Prof. Vivek Tiwari from the International Institute of Information Technology Naya Raipur, India and Prof. R. S. Thakur from the Maulana Azad National Institute of Technology, India, outlines a devoted framework that can store forensic digital data patterns permanently and examines the issues, challenges, and conceptual multilayer framework for developing forensic pattern warehouse for the betterment of forensic prediction and forecasting.

The fourth and final chapter in this section, "Uncovering Limitations of E01 Self-Verifying Files," authored by Profs. Jan Krasniewicz and Sharon A. Cox from Birmingham City University, UK, describes the anomaly in the file format, discusses the implications for relying on the self-verification feature of the E01 file format, and concludes on methods to make any change to the file contents detectable.

Section 2, "Cyber Crime, Cyber Bullying, and Digital Terrorism," is comprised of three chapters and explores the use of digital technologies for bullying. The first chapter in this section, "Cyber Bullying," authored by Prof. Jo Ann Oravec from the University of Wisconsin – Whitewater, USA, analyzes research trends on cyberbullying as well as related concerns involving online harassment, online reputational damage, and cyberstalking. It includes reflections about the moral and personal dimensions of cyberbullying.

The second chapter in this section, "Cyberbullying Among Malaysian Children Based on Research Evidence," authored by Profs. Sarina Yusuf and Md. Salleh Hj. Hassan from the Universiti Putra Malaysia, Malaysia and Prof. Adamkolo Mohammed Mohammed Ibrahim from the Universiti Putra Malaysia, Malaysia & University of Maiduguri, Nigeria, investigates the level of cyberbullying among Malaysian children and contains a scale for measuring cyberbullying in Malaysian society.

The third and final chapter in this section, "The Nature, Extent, Causes, and Consequences of Cyberbullying," authored by Prof. Michelle F. Wright from Masaryk University, Czech Republic, describes the nature, extent, causes, and consequences of cyberbullying as well as cultural differences in these behaviors and theoretical underpinnings.

Section 3, "Cyber and Network Security," is comprised of five chapters and examines the latest academic material on new methodologies and applications in the areas of mobile and network security. The first chapter in this section, "Cyber Security Protection for Online Gaming Applications," authored by Prof. Wenbing Zhao from Cleveland State University, USA, examines the threats to online gaming applications and presents two strategies that can be used to build secure and dependable online gaming applications.

The second chapter in this section, "Piracy and Intellectual Property Theft in the Internet Era," authored by Prof. Shun-Yung Kevin Wang from the University of South Florida – St. Petersburg, USA and Dr. Jeremy J. McDaniel from Principal Financial Group, USA, elaborates on intellectual property theft and piracy in cyberspace. It also explores contemporary cases of intellectual property theft and piracy to illustrate the blurred line between victims and offenders, especially in the era of the internet.

The third chapter in this section, "Secure Group Key Sharing Protocols and Cloud System," authored by Profs. Vaishali Ravindra Thakare and John Singh K. from VIT University, India, provides details about secure group data sharing protocols available and how it will be applicable in healthcare cloud applications to share data securely over healthcare cloud.

The fourth chapter in this section, "Security of Internet-, Intranet-, and Computer-Based Examinations in Terms of Technical, Authentication, and Environmental, Where Are We?" authored by Dr. Babak Sokouti from Tabriz University of Medical Sciences, Iran and Dr. Massoud Sokouti from Mashhad University of Medical Sciences, Iran, discusses potential security aspects of conducting a robust secure e-exam and proposes a hybrid security model for satisfying most security properties.

The fifth and final chapter in this section, "A Three-Vector Approach to Blind Spots in Cybersecurity," authored by Profs. Mika Westerlund, Dan Craigen, Tony Bailetti, and Uruemu Agwae from Carleton University, Canada, examines eight cases of successful cyberattacks from economic, technological, and psychological perspectives to blind spots, termed as "the core vectors."

Section 4, "IT Security and Ethics," is comprised of 15 chapters and explores ethical and security issues relating to the latest information technologies. The first chapter in this section, "Computer Fraud Challenges and Its Legal Implications," authored by Prof. Amber A. Smith-Ditizio from Texas Woman's University, USA and Prof. Alan D. Smith from Robert Morris University, USA, provides a position-based discussion in reference to selective cyberthreats to devices and data breaches (which include malware, phishing, social engineering, data communication interception, malicious insider actions, just to name a few) and further provides information on applicable defenses and its legal implication.

The second chapter in this section, "Cost Estimation and Security Investment of Security Projects," authored by Profs. Yosra Miaoui, Boutheina Fessi, and Noureddine Boudriga from the University of Carthage, Tunisia, examines the different cost estimation models developed for security projects and discusses the technical and managerial factors affecting the cost estimation and management of projects.

The third chapter in this section, "Development of Personal Information Privacy Concerns Evaluation," authored by Profs. Anna Rohunen and Jouni Markkula from the University of Oulu, Finland, presents and analyzes the historical development of the most widely used privacy concerns evaluation instruments regarding privacy concerns' dimensions.

The fourth chapter in this section, "Digital Video Watermarking Using Diverse Watermarking Schemes," authored by Profs. Yash Gupta, Shaila Agrawal, Susmit Sengupta, and Aruna Chakraborty from Maulana Abul Kalam Azad University of Technology, India, proposes a technique that instills different watermarking schemes to different sets of frames.

The fifth chapter in this section, "Ethical Computing Continues From Problem to Solution," authored by Dr. Wanbil William Lee from The Computer Ethics Society, Hong Kong & Wanbil and Associates, Hong Kong, examines ethical computing and how it is instrumental in identifying and reaching a near-ideal solution to the problems arising from an environment that is technology-driven information-intensive.

The sixth chapter in this section, "Group Signature System Using Multivariate Asymmetric Cryptography," authored by Prof. Sattar J. Aboud from the University of Bedfordshire, UK, presents a new group signature scheme using multivariate asymmetric cryptography. Compared with the exited signature schemes, the proposed scheme is applicable to e-voting schemes and can convince the requirements of e-voting schemes because it has two important characteristics, traceability and unlinkability.

The seventh chapter in this section, "Hexa-Dimension Code of Practice for Data Privacy Protection," authored by Dr. Wanbil William Lee from Wanbil & Associates, Hong Kong, proposes a framework that comprises the newly developed hexa-dimension code of practice based on the six-dimension metric (represented by the LESTEF model) and an operationalization scheme, where the code in which the gist of the adopted policies is incorporated, promises to be a handy reference or a quick guide capable of alleviating the information security staff's burden.

The eighth chapter in this section, "Information and Communication Technology Ethics and Social Responsibility," authored by Prof. Tomas Cahlik from Charles University Prague, Czech Republic & University of Economics Prague, Czech Republic, examines what "living a good life" and "being a good person" could be in the information age and identifies some challenges and opportunities ICTs offer in this context.

The ninth chapter in this section, "Intrusion Tolerance Techniques," authored by Prof. Wenbing Zhao from Cleveland State University, USA, surveys the state-of-the-art techniques for building intrusion tolerant systems. It also points out that to build secure and dependable systems, a concerted effort in intrusion prevention, intrusion detection, and intrusion tolerance is needed.

The tenth chapter in this section, "New Perspectives of Pattern Recognition for Automatic Credit Card Fraud Detection," authored by Profs. Addisson Salazar and Gonzalo Safont from the Universitat Politècnica de València, Spain, Prof. Alberto Rodriguez from the Universidad Miguel Hernández de Elche, Spain, and Prof. Luis Vergara from the Universitat Politècnica de València, Spain, outlines a new conceptual framework for automatic credit card fraud detection considering decision fusion and surrogate data, including a case study with different proportions of real and surrogate data.

The eleventh chapter in this section, "Privacy, Algorithmic Discrimination, and the Internet of Things," authored by Prof. Jenifer Sunrise Winter from the University of Hawaii at Manoa, USA, introduces the internet of things (IoT), addressing its definition and related concepts, outlining anticipated application areas, and highlighting challenges for its development. The chapter also examines concerns about privacy, surveillance, and unjust algorithmic discrimination.

The twelfth chapter in this section, "The Protection Policy for Youth Online in Japan," authored by Prof. Nagayuki Saito from Ochanomizu University, Japan and Prof. Madoka Aragaki from Business Breakthrough University, Japan, analyzes national research data from the internet literacy assessment indicator for students to explore the relationship between students' backgrounds and online literacy. The results have revealed several political challenges, including the need for policies on educational awareness in low literacy areas, regional literacy differences, and the need to support children in learning to avoid risk.

The thirteenth chapter in this section, "Security of Identity-Based Encryption Algorithms," authored by Profs. Kannan Balasubramanian and M. Rajakani from Mepco Schlenk Engineering College, India, discusses identity-based encryption schemes based on the random oracle model identity-based encryption and compares them with the standard model identity-based encryption.

The fourteenth chapter in this section, "Steganography Using Biometrics," authored by Profs. Manashee Kalita and Swanirbhar Majumder from NERIST, India, presents an introduction to the concept of steganography with a scope. It also discusses the basics of biometrics and the different types. It also examines steganography with the idea of biometrics, such as biometric image as a cover image and biometric image as a secret image.

The fifteenth and final chapter in this section, "Usable Security," authored by Prof. Andrea Atzeni from Politecnico di Torino, Italy, Prof. Shamal Faily from Bournemouth University, UK, and Dr. Ruggero Galloni from Square Reply S.r.l., Italy, explores the increased availability of information and services that has led to the affirmation of the Internet involvement of a large segment of the population and the implied paradigm shift for computer security: users become less skilled and security-aware, requiring an easier interface to communicate with "the machine" and more specific and comprehensible security measures. It also analyzes the goals and the state of the art of usability and security to understand where and how they might be effectively "aligned" to assist users.

The comprehensive coverage this publication offers is sure to contribute to an enhanced understanding of all topics, research, and discoveries pertaining to system security, information privacy, and forensics. Furthermore, the contributions included in this publication will be instrumental to the expansion of knowledge offerings in this area. This publication will inspire its readers to further contribute to recent discoveries, progressing future innovations.

Mehdi Khosrow-Pour, D.B.A.
Information Resources Management Association, USA

Section 1
Criminal Science and Forensics

Chapter 1
Forensic Investigations in Cloud Computing

Diane Barrett
Bloomsburg University of Pennsylvania, USA

ABSTRACT

Cloud computing environments add an inherent layer of complication to a digital forensic investigation. The content of this chapter explores current forensic acquisition processes, why current processes need to be modified for cloud investigations, and how new methods can help in an investigation. A section will be included that provides recommendations for more accurate evidence acquisition in investigations. A final section will include recommendations for additional areas of research in the area of investigating cloud computing environments and acquiring cloud computing-based evidence.

INTRODUCTION

Cloud computing environments add an inherent layer of complication to a digital forensic investigation. The content of this article explores current forensic acquisition processes, why current processes need to be modified for cloud investigations, and how new methods can help in an investigation. A section will be included that provides recommendations for more accurate evidence acquisition in investigations. A final section will include recommendations for additional areas of research in the area of investigating cloud computing environments and acquiring cloud computing based evidence.

BACKGROUND

Cloud Computing Environments

Cloud computing is encompassed in the capabilities of almost all existing technologies. The concept behind cloud computing is a production environment in which resources and software services do not function locally. Instead, the Internet or the internal network of an organization seamlessly connects numerous host machines running on a virtualized platform (Budriene & Zalieckaite, 2012).

DOI: 10.4018/978-1-5225-7492-7.ch001

Pallis (2010) provides a general layered architecture of cloud infrastructures as a basic model by classifying the architecture into three abstract layers using two models: deployment and service, along with a set of characteristics. The layers from the bottom up are infrastructure, platform, and application. The infrastructure layer provides fundamental computing resources such as processing, storage, and networks. The platform layer delivers higher-level services and abstractions for integration of the ability to perform application functions in the environment. The application layer allows the capability for applications as a service (AaaS).

These three layers are further broken down into service models, deployment models, and attributes. The three well-recognized cloud service models are infrastructure as a service (IaaS), platform as a service (PaaS), and software as a service (SaaS). The four cloud deployment models are community, hybrid, public, and private. The attributes consist of measured and on-demand self-service, resource pooling, rapid elasticity, and broad network access. This is the exact layered architecture outlined by National Institute of Standards and Technology (NIST) in the final issuance of the cloud computing definition dated September 2011.

Environmental Variables

Complex and dynamic business environments such as cloud computing environments drive organizations of all sizes to respond rapidly to market changes and pursue creative resource saving solutions. In addition to being a technology solution, cloud computing is a new business model. Cloud computing environments offer unrestricted scalability and lower data-center setup costs by using multitenancy.

The multitenancy and virtualization characteristics of a cloud computing environment present difficult implementation demands in the areas of security and access control (Almutairi, Sarfraz, Basalamah, Aref, & Ghafoor, 2012). The unique security and access control challenges presented by the use of multitenancy and virtualization in cloud computing environments exist because many individual environments share the same set of hardware. The sharing of storage blocks can result in the accidental and unauthorized flow of information (Werner, 2011). The diversity of services offered in cloud computing environments requires variable levels of granularity when implementing access control mechanisms. The risk of resource exploitation by unauthorized users is significantly increased when there are insufficient or untrustworthy authorization mechanisms implemented in a cloud computing environment (Werner, 2011).

Cloud computing environments offer many organizational benefits by providing scalable but complex computing infrastructures. Every cloud deployment and service model instance is different. For example, one SaaS implementation can be completely different from the next. There are many newly emerging challenges associated with the use of cloud computing environments and existing issues are not yet addressed. Automated service provisioning, virtual machine migration, server consolidation, and the management of power and security are just beginning to garner research community attention.

Digital Evidence Seizure

Digital forensics focuses on the retrieval and analysis of data found on digital devices relative to some type of unauthorized or criminal activity (Garfinkel, 2010). Traditional digital forensics processes consist of crime scene evidence collection, evidence preservation, evidence analysis, and presentation of the analysis results (Greengard, 2012). Current traditional digital acquisition processes include maintaining chain of custody control of forensic evidence data. This chain of custody control occurs in the evidence collection phase through the imaging of a system (Decker, Kruse, Long, & Kelley, 2011).

Cloud computing technology disrupts the initial step of evidence collection in conducting a digital forensic investigation. Traditionally, the seizure of forensic evidence occurs through a search warrant or other legal request. In a cloud computing environment, the emphasis is on the cloud provider contract as opposed to a search warrant or legal request because the data can be geographically disbursed and is under the control of the service provider (Dykstra & Sherman, 2011). Cloud contracts play a very important part in forensic practitioner's ability to conduct a sound forensic investigation (Svetcov, 2011). In some cases, the forensic investigator never gets to acquire the evidence. The designated employee at the service provider performs the evidence acquisition and supplies the results to the client, who then sends the information to the investigator (James, Shosha, & Gladyshev, 2013). This is contrary to current forensic practice where legal documents provide the case investigator the ability to acquire the evidence.

In a cloud computing environment, data are spread out amongst numerous servers and other components. When a crime happens, the location of recoverable data includes the client machine, the equipment of the Internet Service Provider (ISP), and the data backups of the cloud service provider (Shin, 2013). This makes acquiring evidence from a crime committed in a cloud computing environment much more difficult since the environment is not localized like it is in a traditional digital forensic evidence acquisition (Dykstra & Sherman, 2011). Traditional imaging cannot be performed because it is not possible to take down and create a forensic image of such a large environment (James et al., 2013).

The digital forensics discipline faces new challenges where cloud computing is concerned (Berman, Kesterson-Townes, Marshall, & Srivathsa, 2012). Traditional forensic evidence acquisition processes do not fit well into cloud computing because of the way cloud computing works (Svetcov, 2011). Traditional digital forensic acquisition processes focus on individual computers and isolated environments, while cloud computing forensic acquisition processes include the intricacies of complex infrastructures including virtual servers, applications, and diverse operating platforms that may be located in foreign countries (James et al., 2013).

Common forensic procedure is to shut down the system in order to take a forensic image of the system. This procedure cannot apply to hosted cloud services due to disruption of service to a wide scope of users (Cho, Chin, & Chung, 2012). Cloud computing systems consist of multiple user environments, using a variety of services. Shutting down a cloud computing system disrupts services to all the user environments hosted on the system.

When the user or service provider shuts down the virtual machine because of inactivity, service providers reallocate the storage space originally allocated to the virtual machine to other virtual machines (Huth & Cebula, 2011). Upon deletion of the virtual machine and the overwriting of storage space, the evidence disappears (Svetcov, 2011). Although it is possible to recover forensic data from a running virtual machine, if the files associated with the virtual machine are not collected, valuable evidence is missed (Fiterman & Durick, 2010). Associated virtual machine files contain information such as configurations settings and memory content are often not collected as part of the acquisition process.

Two well-known and commonly used commercial cloud services are Amazon Elastic Compute Cloud (EC2) and Rackspace's cloud services. Hosting cloud services on geographically diverse servers using distributed file systems provides scalability and reliability (Cho et al., 2012). Current forensic methods do not exist for analyzing this type of cloud computing environment. The only way to recover evidence is through vendor provided tools that are designed for gathering metrics. Forensic analysis of distributed file systems is very difficult (Cho et al., 2012). Multi-national web-based organizations such as Facebook and Yahoo use the Hadoop file system. Hadoop is a common distributed file system used in large data environments such as cloud computing. Due to the way the Hadoop file system works, it processes petabytes of data and erasure of forensic evidence could easily go without notice (Cho et al., 2012). The development of Hadoop occurred with fast processing of data in mind and there was very little consideration given to security or forensic analysis capabilities.

Current Cloud Acquisition Approaches

Without a clear understanding of how cloud computing works and the underlying infrastructure components, law enforcement agencies cannot properly investigate cloud computing environments (James et al., 2013). Some forensic practitioners have taken the view that the acquisition of evidence from the cloud is merely an extension of existing actions used to acquire data from a network because the cloud data is stored similar to network data (Adams, 2013). Contrary to this view, there are differences between cloud computing forensics and network forensics. The primary similarities and differences between cloud computing forensics and network forensics stem from the key areas of physical access, logical access, segregation of evidence, methodology, and legal considerations.

Ruan, Carthy, and Kechadi (2012) proposed that cloud forensics is a subsection of network forensics and a cross-discipline between cloud computing and digital forensics, adopting the same definitions of cloud computing and digital forensics provided by NIST. The methodology used originates at three distinct dimensions: legal, technical, and organizational. Choosing this methodology encompasses jurisdictional issues, the lack of international cooperation, and formation of foundational standards and sound policies. Ruan et al. (2012) developed a high-level conceptual model that analyzed the forensic impact of cloud computing environments based on deployment models, service offerings, cloud actor roles, segregation of duties, and forensic artifacts obtainable from the environment.

Adams (2013) proposed the advanced data acquisition model (ADAM). The model breaks down forensic processes into three main functions derived from analysis of previous models introduced between the years 2001 and 2004. The actions in the first stage occur upon notification of the scope of work to the investigator. The activities in this stage happen prior to arriving at the incident location. In the next stage, the investigator prepares for the data acquisition upon entry of the incident scene. The final stage consists of acquiring and handling the evidentiary data.

Adams (2013) used a distinctions, systems, relationships, and perspectives (DSRP) thinking patterns in creating ADAM, tying scientific thinking to the forensic processes. Initial testing of ADAM compared ADAM to the processes used in three previous investigations. The results produced a viable model because cases in Australia and New Zealand are seeing flowcharts introduced as a manner in which to help the jury and court understand scientific forensic evidence.

Shende (2010) approached the digital investigations of cloud computing environments as the mapping of computational and storage structures falling within the investigative scope. Emphasizing the cross boundaries of responsibility and access, service level agreements play a large part in the ability to investigate a cloud computing environment. The key to data access in cloud computing investigations lies in the dialogue between the organization and cloud service vendor in establishing incident response requirements, processes, and protocols when drafting a service level agreement (SLA) (Shende, 2010).

Lu, Lin, Liang, and Shen (2010) proposed using a secure source structure based on the bilinear pairing technique to deliver reliable digital forensic evidence in cloud computing environments. Using a cloud computing architecture comprised of a cloud service provider (SP), a trusted system manager (SM), and an enterprise size user environment, the secure provenance SP method demonstrates confidentiality of information, authorized access, anonymous authentication, and ownership tracking. Extending this method for forensic use provides ownership information associated with every version of a document to the SM. The SM then uses an ownership-tracking algorithm to follow the evidence to a unique user identity. This proposed design encompasses a wide range of security features, making it ideal for use in the forensic investigation of cloud computing environments.

Wittek and Daranyi (2012) took an approach similar to Lu et al. (2010), in that the work focused on the tracking of digital assets. Using a digital preservation (DP) policy methodology ensures that digital objects remain valid over an extended time period. Cloud computing infrastructure provides a platform ad-hoc computation along with distributed digital preservation. Wittek and Daranyi (2012) proposed a middleware solution in the business services layer of the Sustaining Heritage Access through Multivalent Archiving (SHAMAN) core infrastructure. The business layer serves as the intermediary between the top presentation layer and the lower infrastructure layer. The proposed solution has promising future implications for digital preservation.

Current Theory Approaches

Bayesian theory and Dempster-Shafer theory are among the few theories that have any documented research on forensic application. There is widespread use of Dempster-Shafer theory in information security because it applies in many areas such as risk assessment, attack analysis, and forensic image analysis. In forensic analysis, combining Dempster-Shafer theory with other theories and methodologies allows a more accurate means to identify evidence. Current methods of application using Bayesian theory and Dempster-Shafer theory have limitations where cloud computing is concerned (Zhou & Mao, 2012). Bayesian and Dempster-Shafer approaches use the mathematics of probability theory and numerical measures of uncertainty. These theories are applicable in intrusion detection systems, data mining techniques, and data privacy, but cloud computing environments have too many variables to postulate correct hypotheses for successful mathematical calculation (Chou, 2011). Additionally, the objective of the research is to provide a framework for human use. Bayesian and Dempster-Shafer theories are machine-based applicable theories that are not conducive to human application (Zhou & Mao, 2012).

Although there is proven application of Dempster Shafer to forensic image analysis, this is a limited use application. Little is known about the application of current forensic evidence acquisition methods to cloud computing environments (Lallie & Pimlot, 2012).

APPLYING TRADITIONAL ACQUISITION METHODS TO CLOUD COMPUTING

Although there are theories about when traditional forensic acquisition methods are applicable in cloud forensic environments, when the methods can be modified, and when new methods are required, it is not currently known which traditional forensics methods apply to cloud computing environments, which traditional processes can be modified, and when new methods are required to be developed. Carlton (2007) used a grounded theory methodology to identify the tasks forensic examiners perform during forensic data acquisitions. Carlton's (2007) study identified distinct acquisition procedures for live or running systems that include performing a random access memory (RAM) dump, collecting volatile data, performing a live acquisition, and determining the programs currently running. Concluding tasks commonly used by examiners include preserving and sealing original acquisition media, placing original media in an evidence vault, performing an inspection to verify the acquired image is readable, and creating a restore image of the original media for return to the owner (Carlton, 2007).

The acquisition tasks of Carlton's (2007) survey were reviewed for relevance and the 20 top ranked tasks were selected. A panel of international experts then reviewed the tasks for applicability to cloud computing environments. The findings indicated that about 50% of the current digital acquisition processes applied to cloud computing environments; the rest required modification or new process development. Post-acquisition processes were most suited for application in cloud computing environments. Following post-acquisition processes in order of applicability were live acquisition processes. The main limitation in this area was access to the cloud server in order to perform the processes. The results analysis suggested this category of processes had solutions for digital evidence acquisitions in cloud computing environments because the processes were modeled after already established network forensic processes.

Ten percent of the 20 pre-selected traditional forensic processes required the development of new processes for the forensic acquisition of digital evidence in cloud computing environments. The panel experts agreed that current acquisition processes in the category of dead drive acquisitions did not fit into cloud computing environments and many of the processes should no longer be included because they were not applicable or modifiable. From the results, the contingency framework shown in Table 1 was built based on the understanding of when current traditional forensic processes apply, identifying when process modification is acceptable, and when the development of new processes is required for forensic evidence acquisitions in cloud computing environments. The categories for forensic evidence acquisition activity are summarized as pre-acquisition, acquisition, imaging, and post-acquisition processes.

The digital forensic acquisition cloud contingency model combines the key contributions from the process design contingency model proposed by Austin and Devin (2009) and the information security management contingency model demonstrated by Tassabehji (2005).

The model depicts the processes first because processes are the only constant. Once the digital forensic examiner choose the process to be performed, the cloud computing environment uncertainty is introduced which produces the contingency. Based on the contingency, the appropriate application methodology is executed. Figure 1 represents a diagrammatical illustration of the digital evidence forensic acquisition cloud contingency model.

The contingency framework in Table 1 used the panel results as the foundation to create a digital forensic acquisition cloud contingency model, concentrating on how uncertainty and contingencies affect particular processes and guide a course of research that can support and enrich the model. When the

Table 1. Contingency framework

Process Category	Recommended Application	Contingency Variable(s)
Pre-acquisition processes	Modification	Fluidity of environment
Live acquisition processes	Application with limitations	Access, tools, scope
Dead acquisition processes	Partial application, modification or develop new	Cloud implementation, access
Imaging processes	Application, modification or develop new	Cloud implementation, access, scope
Post-acquisition processes	Application with limitations	Fluidity of environment, access

Figure 1. A diagrammatical illustration of digital evidence forensic acquisition cloud contingency model

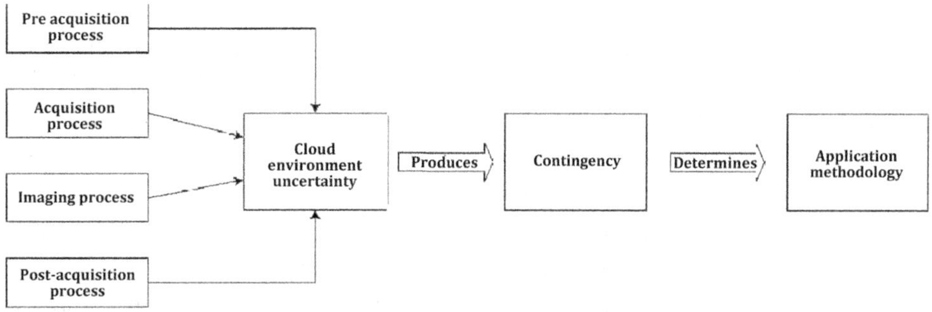

world changes in a way that requires different functionality in a process or practice currently used, flexibility allows adjustment of the process or practice to reflect the changed world (Austin & Devin, 2009).

RECOMMENDATIONS

When forensic examiners lack knowledge about the environments from which evidence is being acquired, there is a high likelihood that critical information is missed during the acquisition process (Hale, 2013). Tools will gradually become outdated and computer forensic practitioners will no longer be able to rely on forensic analysis results, unless the forensic community formulates a vibrant strategy for developing methods that build upon each other (Garfinkel, 2010). Cloud forensics is a relatively new area of digital forensic practices with few industry professionals capable of providing required training (Ruan et al., 2012).

Currently, NIST and the Scientific Working Group on Digital Evidence (SWGDE) offer policy and guidance on a federal level. The digital evidence forensic acquisition cloud contingency model does not fit into the SWDGE model because the digital evidence forensic acquisition cloud contingency model has contingent variables requiring deviation from the proven reliable processes established in the SWDGE model (SWDGE, 2014). When working groups create models on which policy is based, a broader more flexibly model and policy is required to reflect the fluid environment that is now part of every business and most digital forensic acquisitions.

The organizations and universities that build and deliver curriculum in digital forensic areas need to participate in the advancement of the digital forensics field by addressing cloud computing acquisitions. Guidance organizations must work together to provide solid direction in order to establish agreement on basic definitions and simplified models regarding cloud computing environments to help the industry move forward so practitioners accept and implement suggested guidance.

Academia and the digital forensic training community will need to create and encourage the development of new training programs so that practitioners may better respond to situations where the acquisition of cloud computing environments are required. Standards will also have to be set by legal departments where service level agreements are concerned and when other parties must be relied upon to provide evidence. In setting new standards for proper acquisition of forensic evidence in cloud computing environments, organizations must create legal requirement documentation encompassing both vendor contracts and the organization. After the legal requirements are set, digital forensic practitioners have the availably to set best practices, but those best practices will be contingent upon the existing conditions.

FUTURE RESEARCH DIRECTIONS

The opportunity for researchers to make innovative contributions and have a substantial impact on the cloud computing industry has only just begun. The findings in this panel study are a bridge to a very small body of literature, setting the stage for new and promising lines of inquiry. The results of the study produced a contingency framework and digital evidence forensic acquisition cloud contingency model to help guide a course of research that can test the model.

Using contingency frameworks to address other research questions provides a fresh perspective on the application of digital forensic acquisition methods to cloud computing environments. Additional studies could firmly establish that the choices available for the application of digital forensic methods to cloud computing environments are ingrained in contingency frameworks. One of the significant contributions of this panel study is the identification of contingency factors such as available tools, access, availability, and acquisition scope as the underlying elements when choosing the application of digital forensic methods to cloud computing environments. These contingency factors are easily ported to other evidence acquisition methods for expanding research in this area.

The digital evidence forensic acquisition cloud contingency model suggests other important directions of research. Accepting a contingency perspective on how to choose digital process application in cloud computing environments can serve as a powerful theoretical lens both in interpreting the results of prior models and in shaping rigorous research models for future inquiry. Another direction for future research would be to examine the influence of multiple contingencies on the process application within individual cloud types.

CONCLUSION

As an industry, digital forensics is lacking the tools, published processes, and guidance for proper acquisition of digital evidence in cloud computing environments. Pre-acquisition processes are most suited for modification in cloud computing environments while post-acquisition processes are most suited for application in cloud computing environments. The digital acquisition processes that applied to cloud computing environments were modeled after already established network forensic processes. The cloud computing environment uncertainty produces contingencies that affect selecting the appropriate acquisition process application.

The result of this panel study was a developed robust contingency framework for deciding when to use traditional forensic acquisition practices, when to use modified processes, and when it is necessary to develop new forensic acquisition processes through the evaluation of 20 conventionally recognized forensic acquisition processes by a panel of experts. The presented contingency framework used the study results as the foundation to create a digital forensic acquisition cloud contingency model, concentrating on how uncertainty of cloud computing environments and contingencies affect particular processes. The contingencies are easily ported to other evidence acquisition methods for expanding research in this area.

REFERENCES

Adams, R. (2013). The emergence of cloud storage and the need for a new digital forensic process model. In K. Ruan (Ed.), *Cybercrime and cloud forensics: Applications for investigation processes* (pp. 79–104)., doi:10.4018/978-1-4666-2662-1.ch004

Almutairi, A., Sarfraz, M., Basalamah, S., Aref, W., & Ghafoor, A. (2012). A distributed access control architecture for cloud computing. *IEEE Software, 29*(2), 36–44. doi:10.1109/MS.2011.153

Austin, R. D., & Devin, L. (2009). Weighing the benefits and costs of flexibility in making software: Toward a contingency theory of the determinants of development process design. *Information Systems Research, 20*(3), 462–479. doi:10.1287/isre.1090.0242

Berman, S. J., Kesterson-Townes, L., Marshall, A., & Srivathsa, R. (2012). How cloud computing enables process and business model innovation. *Strategy and Leadership, 40*(4), 27–35. doi:10.1108/10878571211242920

Budriene, D., & Zalieckaite, L. (2012). Cloud computing application in small and medium-sized enterprises. *Issues Of Business & Law, 4*(1), 99–130. doi:10.520/ibl.2012.11

Carlton, G. H. (2007). A grounded theory approach to identifying and measuring forensic data acquisition tasks. *Journal of Digital Forensics, Security and Law, 2*(1), 35-56. Retrieved from http://www.jdfsl.org/

Cho, C., Chin, S., & Chung, K. S. (2012, July). Cyber forensic for hadoop based cloud system. *International Journal of Security and Its Applications., 6*(3), 83–90. Retrieved from http://www.sersc.org/journals/IJSIA/

Chou, T. S. (2011). Cyber security threats detection using ensemble architecture. *International Journal of Security and Its Applications, 5*(2), 11–15. Retrieved from http://www.sersc.org/journals/IJSIA/

Decker, M., Kruse, W., Long, B., & Kelley, G. (2011). *Dispelling common myths of "live digital forensics".* Retrieved from http://www.dfcb.org/docs/LiveDigitalForensics-MythVersusReality.pdf

Dykstra, J., & Sherman, A. T. (2012, August). Acquiring forensic evidence from infrastructure-as-a-service cloud computing: Exploring and evaluating tools, trust, and techniques [Supplement]. *Digital Investigation, 9*, S90–S98. doi:10.1016/j.diin.2012.05.001

Fiterman, E. M., & Durick, J. D. (2010). Ghost in the machine: Forensic evidence collection in the virtual environment. *Digital Forensics Magazine, 2*, 73–77. Retrieved from http://www.digitalforensicsmagazine.com/

Garfinkel, S. L. (2010). Digital forensics research: The next 10 years. *Digital Investigation, 7*(Supplement), S64–S73. doi:10.1016/j.diin.2010.05.009

Greengard, S. (2012, November). On the digital trail. *Communications of the ACM, 55*(11), 19–21. doi:10.1145/2366316.2366323

Hale, J. S. (2013, October). Amazon cloud drive forensic analysis. *Digital Investigation*, *10*(3), 259–265. doi:10.1016/j.diin.2013.04.006

Huth, A., & Cebula, J. (2011). The basics of cloud computing. *United States Computer Emergency Readiness Team (US-CERT)*. Retrieved from http://www.us-cert.gov/reading_room/USCERT-Cloud-ComputingHuthCebula.pdf

James, J. I., Shosha, A. F., & Gladyshev, P. (2013). Digital forensic investigation and cloud computing. In K. Ruan (Ed.), *Cybercrime and cloud forensics: Applications for investigation processes* (pp. 1–41)., doi:10.4018/978-1-4666-2662-1.ch001

Lallie, H., & Pimlott, L. (2012). Challenges in applying the ACPO principles to cloud forensic investigations. *Journal of Digital Forensics Security and Law*, *7*(1), 71–86. Retrieved from http://www.jdfsl.org/

Lu, R., Lin, X., Liang, X., & Shen, X. S. (2010, April). Secure provenance: the essential of bread and butter of data forensics in cloud computing. *Proceedings of the 5th ACM Symposium on Information, Computer and Communications Security*, 282-292. 10.1145/1755688.1755723

Ruan, K., Carthy, J., & Kechadi, T. (2012, May). NIST cloud computing reference model and its forensic implications. *Journal of Digital Forensics, Security and Law, Conference Proceedings*. Retrieved from http://www.digitalforensics-conference.org/ subscriptions/proceedings_2012.htm

Shende, J. (2010). Live forensics and the cloud. *DFI News*. Retrieved from http://www.dfinews.com/article/live-forensics-and-cloud-part-1

Shin, D. H. (2013). User centric cloud service model in public sectors: Policy implications of cloud services. *Government Information Quarterly*, *30*(2), 194–203. doi:10.1016/j.giq.2012.06.012

Svetcov, E. (2011). *An introduction to cloud forensics*. Retrieved from http://blog.datacraft-asia.com/2011/01/an-introduction-to-cloud-forensics/

Tassabehji, R. (2005). Principles for managing information security. Encyclopedia of Multimedia Technology and Networking, (pp. 842-848). doi:10.4018/978-1-59140-561-0.ch119

Werner, D. (2011). *Wake-up call*. Retrieved from: http://www.defensenews.com/section/C4ISR/C4ISR-Journal C4ISR

Wittek, P., & Darányi, S. (2012). Digital preservation in grids and clouds: A middleware approach. *Journal of Grid Computing*, *10*(1), 133–149. doi:10.100710723-012-9206-7

Zhou, X., & Mao, F. (2012, August). A semantics web service composition approach based on cloud computing. *Fourth International Conference on Computational and Information Sciences (ICCIS)*, 807-810. 10.1109/ICCIS.2012.43

ADDITIONAL READING

Almulla, S. A., Iraqi, Y., & Jones, A. (2014). State-of-the-art review of cloud forensics. Journal of Digital Forensics. *Security and Law, 9*(4), 7–28.

Dalins, J., Wilson, C., & Carman, M. (2015). Monte-Carlo Filesystem Search – A crawl strategy for digital forensics. *Digital Investigation, 13*, 58–71. doi:10.1016/j.diin.2015.04.002

Daryabar, F., Dehghantanha, A., & Udzir, N. I. (2013). A review on impacts of cloud computing on digital forensics. *International Journal of Cyber-Security and Digital Forensics, 2*(2), 77–94.

Desai, P., Solanki, M., Gadhwal, A., Shah, A., Patel, B.(2015, January) Challenges and Proposed Solutions for Cloud Forensic. International Journal of engineering Research and Applications, 1(5), 37-42

Farina, J., Scanlon, M., Le-Khac, N., & Kechadi, T. (2105, August). Overview of the Forensic Investigation of Cloud Services. *International Workshop on Cloud Security and Forensics (WCSF 2015)*.

Grispos, G., Storer, T., & Glisson, W. B. (2012). Calm Before the Storm: The Challenges of Cloud Computing in Digital Forensics. *International Journal of Digital Crime and Forensics, 4*(2), 28–48. doi:10.4018/jdcf.2012040103

Pătraşcu, A., & Patriciu, V. V. (2014). Digital Forensics in Cloud Computing. Advances in Electrical and Computer Engineering, 14(2).

Pichan, A., Lazarescu, M., & Soh, S. T. (2015). Cloud forensics: Technical challenges, solutions and comparative analysis. *Digital Investigation, 13*, 38–57. doi:10.1016/j.diin.2015.03.002

Shirkhedkar, D., & Patil, S. (2014). Analysis of Various Digital Forensic Techniques for Cloud Computing. *International Journal of Advanced Research in Computer Science, 5*(4), 104–107.

Zawoad, S., & Hasan, R. (2016, March). Trustworthy Digital Forensics in the Cloud. *Computer, 49*(3), 78–81. doi:10.1109/MC.2016.89

KEY TERMS AND DEFINITIONS

Cloud Computing: Cloud computing is an environment in which the Internet or the internal network of an organization seamlessly connects numerous host machines running on a virtualized platform to provide resources and software services.

Digital Forensics: Digital forensics is the division of forensic science that focuses on investigating and analyzing information artifacts located on digital devices involved in computer crime cases.

Infrastructure as a Service (IaaS): IaaS is an Internet delivered virtual environment in which the service provider supplies cloud infrastructure services that can include software, hardware, and networking equipment.

Multitenancy: Multitenancy is a software architecture in which one server hosts a multitude of different virtual environments for unrelated organizations, or tenants.

Platform as a Service (PaaS): PaaS is an Internet delivered virtual environment in which the service provider supplies cloud platform services that include the operating system and other platform-associated services.

Service-Level Agreement (SLA): A SLA is a binding contract between service providers and purchasing organizations that specifies the service parameters and recourse if an unexpected business interruption occurs.

Software as a Service (SaaS): SaaS is an Internet delivered virtual environment in which the service provider supplies commercial applications, eliminating associated purchasing and installation costs for the organization.

Virtual or Virtualized: Virtual or virtualized is a term used to explain the process of running an environment other than the native computing environment.

This research was previously published in the Encyclopedia of Information Science and Technology, Fourth Edition edited by Mehdi Khosrow-Pour, pages 1356-1365, copyright year 2018 by Information Science Reference (an imprint of IGI Global).

Chapter 2
Internet–Facilitated Child Sexual Exploitation Crimes

Keith F. Durkin
Ohio Northern University, USA

Ronald L. DeLong
University of Dayton, USA

ABSTRACT

Internet crimes against children are a problematic yet often misunderstood phenomenon. Prominent examples of these offenses include child pornography, adults soliciting minors online, and the commercialized sexual exploitation of minors (e.g., human trafficking). Drawing upon recent research, the characteristics of offenses, offenders, and victims are examined. A multitude of issues related to the psychological assessment, classification, and treatment of the individuals who commit these offenses are also explored. Strategies for the prevention of this behavior and protection of minors online are discussed.

INTRODUCTION

The computer innovations of the late 20th Century had a transformative impact on society, revolutionizing many aspects of social life including education, commerce, and recreation. These technological developments have also impacted crime. Many types of criminal behavior have changed and new forms emerged in response to the advent of the Internet. Examples include hacking, cyberbullying, fraud, cyberstalking, and gambling. Internet crimes against children are among the most prominent manifestations of this phenomenon.

BACKGROUND

Internet crimes against are defined as those offenses that include an element of computer-facilitated sexual exploitation of minors (Alexy, Burgess, & Baker, 2005). First, the Internet is now the main mechanism for accessing and distributing child pornography. Second is the well-publicized problem of adults soliciting

DOI: 10.4018/978-1-5225-7492-7.ch002

minors for sex. Third, the Internet is used to facilitate the commercial sexual exploitation of children (e.g., sex trafficking of juveniles, commercial distribution of child pornography). Fourth, the Internet serves as a social consolidation mechanism allowing adults with a sexual interest in children to network with each other. Additionally, the Internet plays a secondary role in the victimization of children by allowing offenders who have a pre-existing relationship with a minor (e.g., family members or acquaintances) to use this medium to facilitate contact offending.

Offenses, Offenders, and Victims

The Internet is now the primary medium for accessing and distributing child pornography. These materials can now be instantaneously shared with, an anonymously accessed, by a global audience. For instance, an Interpol child abuse image data base contains more than a half a million images (Elliot & Beech, 2009). A recent study of the peer-to-peer file sharing network Gnutella found approximately 250,000 American computers shared 120,148 unique child pornography images during a one-year period (Wolak, Liberatore, & Levine, 2014). On the most fundamental level, these images represent a permanent record of the sexual exploitation of a minor (Lanning, 2010). The mere demand for this material fuels the further sexual abuse and exploitation of children (Seto, Hanson, & Babchishin, 2011). Concerns have been raised that this easy access to child pornography online might contribute to a new category of offender who succumbs to temptations that might have otherwise been held in check (Babchishin, Hanson, & VanZuylen, 2015).

Individuals who collect and/or traffic child pornography via the Internet are traditionally referred to as "traders" by law enforcement (Alexy et al., 2005). The National Juvenile Online Victimization (NJOV) studies have gathered data from a national sample of law enforcement agencies regarding arrests for child pornography (Wolak, Finkelhor, & Mitchell, 2011; 2012a; 2012b). The results revealed that offenders in these cases are overwhelmingly single white men over the age of 25. Most of the offenders arrested on child pornography charges had material depicting prepubescent children, and a substantial portion had images of children less than 5 years of age. There appears to be an association between the possession of child pornography and engaging in contact sexual offenses against minors. An examination of 2009 arrest data suggests that one-third of suspects arrested for online child pornography offenses were actively molesting minors (Wolak et al, 2012a). Moreover, a meta-analysis of published studies of online (primarily child pornography) offenders found that approximately 1 in 8 of these men had a prior criminal record for contact sexual offenses (Seto et al., 2011). However, the same analysis found that about one-half of these individuals self-reported committing contact offenses. Similarly, Bourke and Hernandez (2009), who conducted a study of 155 offenders who were serving terms for online child pornography charges, found that although 26% of these men had official criminal records for sex crimes against minors, 85% of these men admitted to having committed at least one contact offense against a minor while in treatment.

A second category of Internet crimes against children involves adults using the Internet to solicit children for sexual purposes. These offenders have been called "travelers" by law enforcement (Alexy et al., 2005), and their online behavior has been referred to a "grooming", "luring" or "predation" (Urbas, 2010). They engage in sexually orientated communications with minors, often with the intention of arranging offline encounters. They have been the subject of intense media scrutiny in the United States, and police stings aimed at catching these offenders were sensationally featured on the popular television show *Dateline NBC: To Catch a Predator*. Communication is frequently on-going, and a relationship between the offender and target can develop over the course of several weeks or months. These solicitations are sometimes aggressive, and can contain explicit sexual content. Offenders may send pornography to their target, as well as exposing their genitals and masturbating on web cams (Marcum, 2007). They may also encourage minors to send them suggestive or explicit photos (Wolak et al., 2011). The most recent research suggests these offenders are increasingly turning to social networking sites to locate and groom potential victims (Balfe et al., 2015).

It is important to understand that the online behavior of these men frequently constitutes a crime. The sexually explicit communication with a minor may constitute the offense of enticement or importuning (DeLong, Durkin, & Hundersmarck, 2010). However, the media coverage of "Internet predators" tends to give an inaccurate picture of this type of offense. Based on research this evidence, this crime often fits the model of statutory rape, inasmuch as adult men try to develop a relationship with young teens and "seduce" them into an eventual encounter (Wolak, Finkelhor, Mitchell, & Ybarra, 2008). Data form the NJOV studies indicate that over 90% of the victims in these cases are between the ages of 13-17. Most of the victims are female adolescents. Violence or force is used less than 5% of these cases. A study of online solicitation in Europe produced very similar findings (Schulz, Bergen, Schuhmann, Hoyer, & Santtila, 2015). These offenders are normally not pedophiles, rather they are antisocial adult males who are willing to purse sexual activities with minors who show signs of sexual development but who are below the age of consent (Seto, 2010).

Research has also focused on the risks factors associated with the online sexual solicitation of minors. Results of the second Youth Internet Safety Survey (YISS2), a national study of 11 to 17 year old adolescents, identified various factors that are associated with receiving aggressive online sexual solicitations (Mitchell, Ybarra, & Finkelhor, 2007). These included being female, visiting chat rooms, discussing sexual topics online, and sharing personal information with individuals they met online. According to Wolak, Evans, Nguyen and Hines (2013), there is a higher risk of victimization for troubled youths, such as those with a history of abuse or poor parental relations, as well as boys who are gay or questioning. Many of the minors who are solicited online are not stereotypical innocents. These young people may be curious and rebellious adolescents who are actively seeking sexual information or contact (Lanning, 2010).

The Internet is playing a major role in the commercial sexual exploitation of juveniles (Mitchell, Jones, Finkelhor, & Wolak, 2011). With these offenses, children are exploited a commodities in the pursuit of profit. One example that is receiving a great deal of public attention is juvenile prostitution. Classified advertisement sites such as Craigslist can be used by the purveyors of child prostitution to place advertisements complete with a physical description of available children to potential consumers online (McCabe, 2008). In a study of Internet-related juvenile prostitution cases, Wells, Mitchell, and Ji (2012) discovered more than two-thirds of the victims were age 15 or younger, and in more than one-quarter of these cases the adult exploiter was a family member or acquaintance of the victim. The Internet is also used to promote sexual tourism. This phenomenon, which involves traveling with the intent to engage in sexual behavior, often, involves child victims. For a number of years, sex tours in Southeast Asia involving juvenile workers have been promoted via the Internet (Hughes, 2000). There have been reports of pedophiles trading information about potential child victims for pedophiles traveling abroad (Holt, Blevins, & Burkert, 2010).

Moreover, the Internet can serve a networking or social consolidation function for individuals who are sexually attracted to children. There is an entire subculture online of adults with a sexual interest in minors (Holt et al., 2010). This consists of a myriad of websites, computer forums, and chat rooms. Adult-child sex advocacy groups such as NAMBLA (the North American Man/Boy Love Association) are remarkably active online. There is a vast array of literature, such as BoyWiki and The Boylove Manifesto, which supports the pedophile viewpoint (Durkin & Hundersmarck 2008). Although this networking is generally not criminal (Lanning, 2010), there are serious concerns that these networks may encourage criminal conduct. Research on this phenomenon has concluded these sites were criminogenic since they foster relationships among users and expose these users to rationalizations and justifications (e.g., this behavior does not harm children, children can freely consent to sex with an adult) conducive to sexual offending (Balfie et al., 2015; D'Ovidio, Mitnam, El-Burki, & Shumar, 2009; Durkin & Bryant, 1999; O'Halloran & Quayle, 2010). Furthermore, Schulz et al. (2015) found that among adults who solicit juveniles online, those individuals who participate in pedophilia websites and forums are much more likely to target minors age 13 and younger.

The Internet also plays a secondary (rather than primary) role in the sexual abuse of children. An offender can use computer technology to facilitate sex crimes against juveniles whom they already have a face-to-face relationship with (Wolak et al., 2012b). These offenders can be relatives, teachers, people in the ministry, coaches, or family friends. They can use chat or e-mail to seduce or "groom" the victim, as well as to arrange meetings where the abuse will occur. Data from an NJOV study reveals that nearly half of the victims in these cases are between the ages of 6 and 12 (Mitchell, Finkelhor, & Wolak, 2005). This is significant since the supra majority of victims in Internet initiated cases are older juveniles (between the ages of 13 and 17). Additionally, Internet pornography, including child pornography, can be used by sex offenders to lower the inhibitions of children they already have a face-to-face relationship with, thus facilitating their eventual victimization (Lanning, 2010).

Assessment and Classification of Internet Sex Offenders

Since this is a relatively new type of offending many different types of general sex offender assessments are currently utilized (e.g., pre-sentence, treatment planning and placement, classification, and risk assessment). Due to the unknown elements of associated with this type of offender; risk-level appears to be most requested type of assessment. Additional goals of this assessment should focus level of deviance, identification of pro-offending attitudes, accountability, level of denial and general psychosocial areas (see DeLong et al., 2010). Questions should be formulated in a manner to ascertain the degree, nature, and extent of the sexual and legal problems of the offender. Important in this process is the clinician's ability to address areas that may be uncomfortable for general practitioners such as sexual practices, fantasy, use and description of sexually explicit materials (including child pornography)(Quayle & Taylor, 2002). One should be aware of the offender's level of guardedness and defensiveness, as well as their possible high degree of shame and guilt. Asking questions in a gentle, nonjudgmental and non-confrontational manner is imperative to have an environment where the offender can discuss their offense dynamics and private areas of their life without the fear of judgment and retribution.

Quayle and Taylor (2002) developed a four factor framework that could be utilized in a semi-structured setting in order to address Internet specific issues during an assessment and to identify possible offense cycle dynamics. These four areas are: action, reflection, excitement, and arousal. In *action*, information obtained is from questions addressing length of time on the Internet, contact with others, emotional withdraw from significant others, degree of pleasure received from the activities, level of social isolation, images obtained or developed and sent. *Reflection* focuses on the offender's level of preoccupation with re-living past experiences; details of other online persons contacted; breaking promises about quitting; and difficulties in concentrating or keeping off-line. *Excitement* addresses degree and type of risks in accessing materials and persons; if the materials were obtained while others were present (especially child pornography with children present); if the offender corresponds with others with a sexual interest in children; and attempts to make contact with children. *Arousal* involves the offender's level of mastur-bation associated with online activities; changes in sexual behaviors since beginning online activities; changes in the receipt of images and text messages particularly with children; material accessed; and if arousal happens with other non-child images.

Assessing the dynamics of the Internet offending process may help to formulate an explanation of online behaviors in order to understand the motive, intent, and goal(s) of the offender. This will assist the clinician in identifying factors pertinent to establishing treatment goals for the offender. Unfortunately, *the Diagnostic and Statistical Manual of Mental Health Disorders, Fifth Edition* does not identify a specific diagnosis or diagnostic criteria for Internet sex offenders. Therefore, the utilization of offense-specific typologies could appear a logical instrument for the understanding and classification of this population. There are a variety of typologies which attempt to identify a specific set of criteria based on the behavior demonstrated by the online behaviors and processes of the offender (see Seto, 2013 for a listing). These can permit a clinician or other evaluator to simplify and organize the complexities of the behaviors in order to understand similarities and differences in these offenses and offenders. How-ever, it is imperative to note that the typology should be a tool for understanding and assimilating the behaviors, not a diagnosis.

Important in the development of the typologies is Cusson's (1993, in Taylor & Quayle, 2006) multi-stage explanation of the criminal process with Internet sex offenders which focuses on the tasks of search, pre-criminal situations, pre-criminal opportunity, and criminal tactics. This process identifies the following stages: 1) the offender searchers for a need to find a pre-criminal situation, 2) once found the pre-criminal stage is introduced with the potential to commit an offense, 3) once the perceived payoff exceed the risk for the offender, the pre-criminal opportunity is established thereby allowing the offender to seek online communications, and 4) criminal tactics are utilized in order for the offender to demonstrate a sequence of events for the act to occur. Although offenses seemingly well thought out, the offender does not take into account that the actions are restrictive due to the physical limitation of the communicative processes and technologies (Taylor & Quayle, 2006). Therefore, an important consider-ation involved in whether or not an offender will travel to engage a physical meeting with an intended victim, is the method of communication and ease of transmission regarding messages, images and other items of interests for the offender (Elliot & Beech, 2009; DeLong, et al., 2010).

Treatment of Internet Sex Offenders

Andrews and Bonta (2010) promoted the concept and use of risk, need, and responsivity (RNR), with each area identifying a specific principle in which the offender would be treated. The *"risk principle"* addresses the intensity of services for the offenders should be in line with their level of recidivism risk. Thus, this assumes that the lower risk offender would need less restrictive services versus the high risk offender. The *"need principle"* focuses on the dynamic risk factors which are consistent to the crimino-genic needs of the offender. This principle attests that dynamic risk factors which can be changed which are consistent with the offender's recidivism risk. Finally, the *"responsivity principle"* identifies that when treatment is utilized, the information provided should meet the level and skill of the offender for maximum effect. Although many other factors are important (i.e., client-counselor relationship, genuine approach by the counselor, etc.), the impact by the utilization of the RNR approach has been found to be a much more effective treatment dynamic (Hanson, Bourgen, Helmus, & Hodgson, 2009).

Since the inception of online offending, treatment options have increased but are not absolute in the consistency of treatment. In fact, the need for separating contact and Internet-only offenders has been addressed as imperative since the treatment needs of each group differs. Seto (2013) identified several treatment programs that have increased in use and awareness. For instance, sexual addiction groups and cybersex addiction programs have increased in availability. A cybersex addictions model has been developed by the Internet Behavior Consulting group, which has a combination of their own workbook, relapse prevention, cognitive therapy, and a 12-step program approach (http://www.internetbehavior. com). Because of the research suggesting some Internet-only offenders are lower in risk (Seto, 2013), such treatment would not have to be lengthy or intensive but focused on the dynamics of RNR principals. It would be of importance to assess online behaviors which are central to this behavioral pattern: length of computer time with general viewing, legal adult pornographic materials, social networking sites, and visiting/interacting with other likeminded persons regarding their sexual interests. However, increased risk (online offending which progresses or used in concert to physical sex offending) would need more intensive treatment focusing on both dynamics of online and direct contact offending.

SOLUTIONS AND RECOMENDATIONS

Law enforcement agencies in the U.S. have taken a very active role in combating Internet crimes against children, and it has been estimated that 95% of their criminal cases involving these offenses result in guilty pleas or convictions (Wolak, Finkelhor, & Mitchell, 2009). In 2009, U.S. law enforcement agencies made an estimated 8,194 arrests for technologically-facilitated child sexual exploitation offenses (Wolak et al., 2012b). The most common offenses are those related to child pornography, with approximately 5,000 arrests for child pornography possession in 2009 (Wolak et al., 2012a), Law agencies are becoming more aggressive in trying to locate child pornography offenders. This includes officers posing as fellow "traders" in proactive investigations, as well as tracking suspects through peer-to-peer file sharing services. This has resulted in a progressive increase in the number of child pornography arrests since 2000. On the other hand, arrests of offenders who solicit undercover police officers posing as minors have been decreasing in recent years (Wolak et al., 2012b). There are two possible explanations for this decline. First, resources used for proactive investigations have been shifted to child pornography offenders. Second, the extensive media coverage has raised public awareness about online solicitation of minors and has possibly deterred some adult men from engaging in this conduct.

One of the most popular theories in criminology, routine activities theory (Cohen & Felson, 1979), provides a useful framework to address strategies to prevent these offenses. According to this theory, crime is a function of everyday life, and it occurs when there factors simultaneously converge. The first factor is motivated offenders. These are individuals who are seeking a criminal opportunity. Victimization risks are considered a function of an individual's exposure to offenders (Mustaine & Tewksbury 2000). The second factor is attractive targets. These are individual targets that are appealing to offenders --- whether it is a vulnerable individual or something worth stealing. The final factor is a lack of capable guardians—people who can discourage an offense from happening (Felson, 2001). Individuals can also exercise personal guardianship to prevent their own victimization. Proactive police investigations designed to catch individuals involved with child pornography or solicitation is one way to try and curb the presence of motivated offenders. Furthermore, prevention efforts should be targeted at children and adolescents to increase their levels of personal guardianship. There is a need for developmentally appropriate prevention strategies that target high-risk behaviors (e.g., visiting chat rooms, corresponding with strangers, and discussing sexual matters online). Some examples include teaching children avoidance skills and educating adolescents about the problematic (and criminal) nature of sexual relationships with adults (Wolak et al., 2008).

CONCLUSION

As technology advanced, so did the opportunities for the exploitation of children. Internet crimes against children constitute a serious albeit misunderstood problem. Child pornography is now a worldwide problem with horrific consequences for victims. The adults who are involved with this material often represent a very serious threat to society. The online solicitation of minors is another contemporary problem. However, the majority of these cases are consistent with statutory rare. Proactive police investigations, particularly into child pornography, are an especially value asset in reducing Internet crimes against children. Moreover, realistic prevention strategies offer promise in further reducing online victimization. As technology continues to expand with handheld personal communication devices such as cellular phones, opportunities for sex offenses against minors will also expand. It is essential that society be aware of these possibilities, and be ready to act an in adaptable fashion to prevent the victimization of children and adolescents.

FUTURE RESEARCH DIRECTIONS

Since Internet crimes against children are a new phenomenon, research on this topic is in its infancy. There appear to be two especially compelling directions for future research. First, it will be important to know the relative risk of future contact offending for adults arrested for soliciting minors online. Second, research should focus on determining which specific strategies are effective in controlling these offenses and preventing victimization of minors online.

REFERENCES

Alexy, E. M., Burgess, A. W., & Baker, T. (2005). Internet offenders: Traders, travelers, and combination trader-travelers. *Journal of Interpersonal Violence*, 20(7), 804–812. doi:10.1177/0886260505276091 PMID:15914702

Andrews, D. A., & Bonta, J. (2010). The psychology of criminal conduct (5th ed.). Cincinnati, OH: Anderson.

Babchishin, K. M., Hanson, R. K., & VanZuylen, H. (2015). Online child pornography offenders are different: A meta-analysis of the characteristics of online and offline sex offenders against children. *Archives of Sexual Behavior, 44*(1), 45–66. doi:10.100710508-014-0270-x PMID:24627189

Balfe, M., Gallagher, B., Masson, H., Balfe, S., Brugha, R., & Hackett, S. (2015). Internet child sex offenders concerns about online security and their use of identity protection technologies: A review. *Child Abuse Review, 24*(6), 427–439. doi:10.1002/car.2308

Bourke, M. L., & Hernandez, A. E. (2009). The Butner Study redux: A report of the incidence of hands-on child victimization by child pornography offenders. *Journal of Family Violence, 24*(3), 183–191. doi:10.100710896-008-9219-y

Cohen, L. E., & Felson, M. (1979). Social change and crime rate trends: A routine activity approach. *American Sociological Review, 44*(4), 588–608. doi:10.2307/2094589

D'Ovidio, R., Mitnam, T., El-Burki, J., & Shumar, W. (2009). Adult-child sex advocacy websites as social learning environments. *International Journal of Cyber Criminology, 3*, 421–440.

DeLong, R., Durkin, K. F., & Hundersmarck, S. (2010). An exploratory analysis of the cognitive distortions of a sample of men arrested in Internet sex stings. *Journal of Sexual Aggression, 16*(1), 59–70. doi:10.1080/13552600903428235

Durkin, K. F., & Hundersmarck, S. F. (2008). Pedophiles and child molesters. In E. Goode & D. Angus Vail (Eds.), *Extreme Deviance* (pp. 144–150). Thousand Oaks, CA: Pine Forge Press.

Elliott, I. A., & Beech, R. (2009). Understanding online pornography use: Applying sexual offense theory to Internet offenders. *Aggression and Violent Behavior, 14*(3), 180–193. doi:10.1016/j.avb.2009.03.002

Felson, M. (2001). Routine activity theory: The theorist's perspective. In C.D. Bryant (Ed.), Encyclopedia of Criminology and Deviant Behavior, Volume I: Historical, Conceptual, and Theoretical Issues (pp. 338-339). Philadelphia: Brunner-Routledge.

Hanson, R. K., Bourgon, G., Helmus, L., & Hodgson, S. (2009). The principals of effective correctional treatment also apply to sexual offenders: A meta-analysis. *Criminal Justice and Behavior, 36*(9), 865–891. doi:10.1177/0093854809338545

Holt, T. J., Blevins, K. R., & Burkert, N. (2010). Considering the pedophile subculture online. *Sexual Abuse, 22*, 3–24. PMID:20133959

Hughes, D. (2000). Welcome to the rape camp: Sexual exploitation and the Internet in Cambodia. *Journal of Sexual Aggression, 6*(1-2), 1–23. doi:10.1080/13552600008413308

Lanning, K. V. (2010). *Child molesters: A behavioral analysis.* Washington, DC: National Center for Missing & Exploited Children.

Marcum, C. (2007). Interpreting the intentions of Internet predators: An examination of online predatory behavior. *Journal of Child Sexual Abuse, 16*(4), 99–114. doi:10.1300/J070v16n04_06 PMID:18032248

McCabe, K. A. (2008). The role of Internet service providers in cases of child pornography and child prostitution. *Social Science Computer Review, 26*(2), 247–251. doi:10.1177/0894439307301438

Mitchell, K. J., Finkelhor, D., & Wolak, J. (2005). The Internet and family and acquaintance sexual abuse. *Child Maltreatment, 10*(1), 49–60. doi:10.1177/1077559504271917 PMID:15611326

Mitchell, K. J., Jones, L. M., Finkelhor, D., & Wolak, J. (2011). Internet-facilitated commercial sexual exploitation of children: Findings from a nationally representative sample of law enforcement agencies in the United States. *Sexual Abuse, 23*, 43–71. PMID:20852011

Mitchell, K. J., Ybarra, M., & Finkelhor, D. (2007). The relative importance of online victimization in understanding depression, delinquency, and substance abuse. *Child Maltreatment, 12*(4), 314–324. doi:10.1177/1077559507305996 PMID:17954938

Mustaine, E. E., & Tewksbury, R. (2000). Comparing the lifestyles of victims, offenders, and victim-offenders: A routine activity theory assessment of similarities and differences for criminal incident participants. *Sociological Focus, 33*(3), 339–362. doi:10.1080/00380237.2000.10571174

OHalloran, E., & Quayle, E. (2010). A content analysis of a boy love support forum: Revisiting Durkin and Bryant. *Journal of Sexual Aggression, 16*(1), 71–85. doi:10.1080/13552600903395319

Quayle, E., & Taylor, M. (2002). Pedophiles, pornography, and the Internet: Assessment issues. *British Journal of Social Work, 32*(7), 863–875. doi:10.1093/bjsw/32.7.863

Schulz, A., Bergen, E., Schuhmann, P., Hoyer, J., & Santtila, P. (2015). Online Sexual Solicitation of Minors How Often and between Whom Does It Occur? *Journal of Research in Crime and Delinquency, 53*(2), 165–188. doi:10.1177/0022427815599426

Seto, M. (2010). Child pornography use and Internet solicitation in the diagnosis of pedophilia. *Archives of Sexual Behavior, 39*(3), 591–593. doi:10.100710508-010-9603-6 PMID:20182786

Seto, M. (2013). *Internet sex offenders.* Washington, DC: American Psychological Association. doi:10.1037/14191-000

Seto, M., Hanson, K. R., & Babchishin, K. M. (2011). Contact sexual offending by men with online sexual offenses. *Sexual Abuse, 23*, 124–145. PMID:21173158

Taylor, M., & Quayle, E. (2006). The Internet and abuse images of children: Search, pre-criminal situations and opportunity. In R. Wortley & S. Smallbone (Eds.), *Situational Prevention of Child Sexual Abuse* (pp. 169–195). New York: Criminal Justice Press.

Urbas, G. (2010). Protecting children from online predators: The use of covert Investigation techniques by law enforcement. *Journal of Contemporary Criminal Justice, 26*(4), 410–425. doi:10.1177/1043986210377103

Wells, M., Mitchell, K. J., & Ji, K. (2012). Exploring the role of the internet in juvenile prostitution cases coming to the attention of law enforcement. *Journal of Child Sexual Abuse, 21*(3), 327–342. doi:10.1080/10538712.2012.669823 PMID:22574847

Wolak, J., Evans, L., Nguyen, S., & Hines, D. A. (2013). Online predators: Myth versus reality. *New England Journal of Public Policy, 25*, 1–6.

Wolak, J., Finkelhor, D., & Mitchell, K. (2009). Trends in Arrests of "Online Predators". Durham, NC: Crimes Against Children Research Center.

Wolak, J., Finkelhor, D., & Mitchell, K. (2011). Child pornography possessors: Trends in offender and case characteristics. *Sexual Abuse, 23*, 22–42. PMID:21349830

Wolak, J., Finkelhor, D., Mitchell, K., & Ybarra, M. L. (2008). Online predators and their victims: Myths, realities, and implications for prevention and treatment. *The American Psychologist, 63*(2), 111–128. doi:10.1037/0003-066X.63.2.111 PMID:18284279

Wolak, J., Finkelhor, D., & Mitchell, K. J. (2012a). Trends in Arrests for Child Pornography Possession: The Third National Juvenile Online Victimization Study (NJOV-3). Durham, NC: Crimes against Children Research Center.

Wolak, J., Finkelhor, D., & Mitchell, K. J. (2012b). Trends in Law Enforcement Responses to Technology- Facilitated Child Sexual Exploitation Crimes: The Third National Juvenile Online Victimization Study (NJOV-3). Durham, NC: Crimes against Children Research Center.

Wolak, J., Liberatore, M., & Levine, B. N. (2014). Measuring a year of child pornography trafficking by US computers on a peer-to-peer network. *Child Abuse & Neglect, 38*(2), 347–356. doi:10.1016/j.chiabu.2013.10.018 PMID:24252746

ADDITIONAL READING

Bourke, M. L., & Hernandez, A. E. (2009). The Butner Study redux: A report of the incidence of hands-on child victimization by child pornography offenders. *Journal of Family Violence, 24*(3), 183–191. doi:10.100710896-008-9219-y

DeLong, R., Durkin, K. F., & Hundersmarck, S. (2010). An exploratory analysis of the cognitive distortions of a sample of men arrested in Internet sex stings. *Journal of Sexual Aggression, 16*(1), 59–70. doi:10.1080/13552600903428235

Elliott, I. A., & Beech, R. (2009). Understanding online pornography use: Applying sexual offense theory to Internet offenders. *Aggression and Violent Behavior, 14*(3), 180–193. doi:10.1016/j.avb.2009.03.002

Mitchell, K. J., Finkelhor, D., & Wolak, J. (2005). The Internet and family and acquaintance sexual abuse. *Child Maltreatment, 10*(1), 49–60. doi:10.1177/1077559504271917 PMID:15611326

Mitchell, K. J., Jones, L. M., Finkelhor, D., & Wolak, J. (2011). Internet-facilitated commercial sexual exploitation of children: Findings from a nationally representative sample of law enforcement agencies in the United States. *Sexual Abuse, 23*, 43–71. PMID:20852011

OHalloran, E., & Quayle, E. (2010). A content analysis of a boy love support forum: Revisiting Durkin and Bryant. *Journal of Sexual Aggression, 16*(1), 71–85. doi:10.1080/13552600903395319

Quayle, E., & Taylor, M. (2002). Pedophiles, pornography, and the Internet: Assessment issues. *British Journal of Social Work, 32*(7), 863–875. doi:10.1093/bjsw/32.7.863

Wolak, J., Finkelhor, D., Mitchell, K., & Ybarra, M. L. (2008). Online predators and their victims: Myths, realities, and implications for prevention and treatment. *The American Psychologist, 63*(2), 111–128. doi:10.1037/0003-066X.63.2.111 PMID:18284279

Wolak, J., Finkelhor, D., & Mitchell, K. J. (2012). Trends in Law Enforcement Responses to Technology- Facilitated Child Sexual Exploitation Crimes: The Third National Juvenile Online Victimization Study (NJOV-3). Durham, NH: Crimes against Children Research Center.

Wolak, J., Liberatore, M., & Levine, B. N. (2014). Measuring a year of child pornography trafficking by US computers on a peer-to-peer network. *Child Abuse & Neglect, 38*(2), 347–356. doi:10.1016/j.chiabu.2013.10.018 PMID:24252746

KEY TERMS AND DEFINITIONS

Child Molester: Any adult who engages in any type of sexual contact with an individual legally defined as a child.

Internet-Facilitated Child Sexual Exploitation: Offenses in which Internet technology is utilized for purposes of sexually exploiting minors.

Pedophilia: A psychiatric disorder involving an adult who experiences a primary or exclusive sexual attraction to prepubescent children (13-years-old or younger).

Traders: Individuals who traffic and/or collect child pornography.

Travelers: Individuals who use the Internet attempting to solicit minors for sexual purposes.

Chapter 3
Knowledge–Based Forensic Patterns and Engineering System

Vivek Tiwari
International Institute of Information Technology Naya Raipur, India

R. S. Thakur
Maulana Azad National Institute of Technology, India

ABSTRACT

This chapter outlines a devoted framework that can store forensic digital data patterns permanently. The issues, challenges, conceptual multilayer framework for developing forensic pattern warehouse for betterment of forensic prediction and forecasting has been discussed. A sequence of phases is involved during the design processes of forensic pattern warehouse, and initially, conceptual modeling is one of the significant and the initial phase of forensic pattern warehouse design, because it constructs the solid framework for the next level of phases. In view of high semantic nature, there is a need to take a different approach for forensic pattern warehouse design to accommodate flexibility, isolation, extensibility, and robustness. In this way, the context-oriented forensic pattern warehouse design is one of the possible ways to manage patterns in a better way. The context of underlying pattern also helps to guide the queries to give a more satisfactory result.

INTRODUCTION

The primary center behind this chapter is outline a devoted framework which can store forensic digital data patterns permanently. The issues, challenges, conceptual multilayer framework for developing forensic pattern warehouse for betterment of forensic prediction and forecasting has been discussed. A sequence of phases is involved during the design processes of forensic pattern warehouse and initially, conceptual modeling is one of the significant and the initial phase of forensic pattern warehouse design, because it constructs the solid framework for the next level of phases. In view of high semantic nature, there is a need to take a different approach for forensic pattern warehouse design to accommodate flex-

DOI: 10.4018/978-1-5225-7492-7.ch003

ibility, isolation, extensibility and robustness. In this way, the context oriented forensic pattern warehouse design is one of the possible ways to manage patterns in a better way. The context of underlying pattern also helps to guide the queries to give more satisfactory result. Moreover, the logical modeling of the pattern warehouse should incorporate a mechanism to properly hierarchized the patterns and able to make sharp isolation among patterns. Furthermore, there is a need to provide additional information in logical modeling with patterns to improve query processing by revealing the sense of the underlying domain of source data.

BACKGROUND

In the mid of the 90s, organizations have started to recognize the strategic use of databases as a new discipline which was entirely different from theme of operational database (Tiwari V. at al 2010). Traditionally, operational database has been used to full fill mission-critical, day to day needs for online transaction processing (Inmon W.H., 2005). Organizations have a variety of computer based data processing system such as financial, making, feedback, attendance, and sales etc. which generate operational data (Agrawal R. & Srikant R. 1994). These kinds of data contain detailed, non-redundant and updated values. Those organizations that have recognized the power of information timely will have huge advantages over their competitors and it leads to design an effective data warehouse strategy (Kimball R. & Ross M. 2011). A data warehouse and data mining have given a platform to recognize the role of information behind successful business and much more. Data warehousing improves the productivity of an expert's decision making though consolidation, conversion, transformation, and integration of scattered data, and represents a trusted view of the enterprise. The data warehouse should not consider as a product rather than it is an environment. The data warehousing is a layered process to construct of information system that helps with organization in their decision making by giving historical data (Romero et al, 2010)). There are some following reasons that make data warehouse is very special:

- Prompt decision need to be made correctly by analyzing available data.
- Business workers are expert in their domain, not in the computer.
- The amount of data doubles in every one and half year, which create the problem in deep data analysis.
- The required infrastructure cost of development of a data warehouse is continuing to decline.
- Organizations have to take critical decisions based on the entire data rather than using rough estimates based on incomplete data.

In the recent evolution of database technology as depicted in Figure 1, patterns are being managed and maintained by Pattern Warehouse Management System (PWMS). Pattern warehouse is a brand-new concept and little emphasis has been given till date. A pattern warehouse is as attractive as data warehouse as the main repository of an organization's historical pattern and is optimized for on-demand reporting and analysis (Mohammad R. et al (2009), Bartolini et al, (2003)). By nature, patterns are not persistent. There is a need to execute pattern generating methods when patterns are required. Pattern warehouse is a way to make the patterns persist by storing them permanently and it can be considered as a collection of persistently stored patterns.

Figure 1. Evolution of database technology

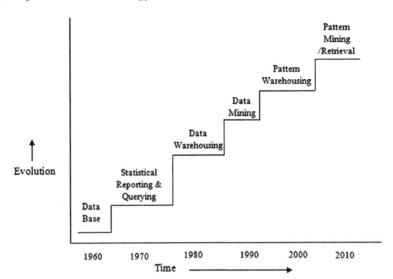

In order for someone to be able to exploit these patterns on-demand, an efficient general PWMS is required for handling (storing/processing/retrieving) the patterns. The general means, the system must be able to handle all kinds of patterns. Patterns share some characteristics that make traditional DBMSs unable to represent and manage them. Patterns thus, can be regarded as knowledge units that effectively describe entire subsets of data (in this sense, they are compact) (Tiwari V. & Thakur R.S. 2015b). Patterns can be generated from different application domain so they are very heterogeneous in structures and often, heterogeneous patterns are needed to be managed together. The structure of patterns is required to be investigated for the design of a flexible pattern warehouse management system. Pattern management is an important issue in many different contexts and domains. The most important contexts in which pattern management is required are business intelligence and data mining. Business intelligence concerns a broad category of applications and technologies for gathering, storing, analyzing, and providing access to data to help enterprises in business decisions.

Moreover, many government and private forensic databases can help to both law enforcement investigators and the scientists who support their work in the lab. Forensic Pattern Warehouse (FPW) is a centralized forensic data repository that integrates forensic data from various transactional, legacy, applications and external sources. The Forensic Pattern warehouse provides an environment that is separate from the operational systems and is completely designed for decision-support, analytical-reporting, ad-hoc queries, and data mining. This isolation and optimization enables queries to be performed without any impact on the daily transactional and operational systems (Tiwari V. & Thakur R.S., 2015c). Benefits with a successful implementation of a forensic pattern warehouse include:

- Enhanced forensic intelligence.
- Increased processing of large and complex queries.
- Forensic intelligence from multiple sources.
- Instant access to forensic pattern (Save Time).
- Enhanced forensic pattern quality and consistency.

- Provide historical forensic pattern intelligence.
- Convert forensic data into actionable form.
- Increase scope of forensic data availability.
- Generates a high ROI (return on investment).
- Provide wide variety of forensic patterns.
- Provide various kinds of trends report.
- Decrease computational cost and increase productivity.

Decision making on forensic data is very crucial. Decisions that affect the strategy and operations of organizations will be based upon credible facts and will be backed up with evidence and actual data (Geradts Z. & Bijhold J, (2002), David L.W. & Andrew J. (2013)). Insights will be gained by using forensic pattern warehouse (FPW) through improved information access. A data warehouse is designed for storing large volumes of data and being able to rapidly query the data but forensic pattern warehouse is designed and constructed with a focus on speed of knowledge retrieval and analysis. Pattern warehouse does not concentrate for creation and modification of forensic data. In contrast, the forensic pattern warehouse is built for analysis and decision making. In conventional ways, forensic data are stored around transactional database and have limited accessibility (Geradts Z. & Bijhold J, (2001), Mikkonen S. & Astikainen T., (1994)). It is almost impossible to any organization to share their transactional databases. There are large amount of forensic data in country but scattered in organization and institute wise. They hardly exchange their forensic data for analysis purpose (Sibert R.W., (1994), Catherine et al. (2016)). The result of any analysis process is directly depends on amount of quality data. Decision making process lies on credibility of analysis. Analysis on single organization's forensic data cannot bring such credibility (Tobias K. et al, 2011). For many organizations, forensic information systems are comprised of multiple subsystems, physically separated and built on different Platforms and formats. Moreover, gathering data from multiple disparate data sources is a common need when conducting forensic data analysis for decision making (John H. et al, 2011). We need to gather forensic data from various small or big organizations time to time and need to put in central repository system (Werrett D.J., 1997). We perform integration of existing disparate data sources and make them accessible in one place. This repository system consisted of same grade (forensic) of data with different formats. These technical issues can be covered in preprocessing phase. There is a separate forensic data integration system, known as ETL, within a forensic pattern warehouse environment (Tiwari V. & Thakur R.S. 2015a). This system consolidates forensic data from multiple source systems and transforms the data into a useful format. Further, user of forensic data will be able to query data directly with less information technology support. This allow to users to spend more time performing data analysis and less time gathering data.

MAIN FOCUS

A Multi-Layered Architecture

An elementary model is proposed to develop an overall integrated environment for uniformly representing (create, store and update) and querying various kinds of forensic patterns. A multi-layered architecture is introduced and considered one of the suitable solutions for forensic pattern warehouse management system. The architecture is made up of the number of interconnected layers which include Physical layer, Pattern storage layer and Application layer as depicted in Figure 2.

Physical Layer

Bottom of the architecture depicts the data store that contains the raw data. Raw data can be either managed by a DBMS (Database Management System) or can be stored in files, streams or any other external physical data source. External data sources are operational systems/flat files/ text files, etc., used to manage the data to support critical operations and relatively small number of well-defined business transactions (Golfarelli M. & Rizzi S., 2009).

Pattern Storage Layer

The middle layer contains patterns, which forms the core part of the pattern warehouse management system. The pattern stored in the pattern warehouse is uploaded by pattern interface. This layer can be further divided into Pattern-Tier and Context-Tier.

- **Pattern-Tier:** This is populated with patterns which are extracted through various techniques pushed here from the preceding layer.
- **Context-Tier:** Context gives the ability to organize patterns according the context and helps to give sense about what kind of knowledge they are carrying. It defines schema and procedure to organize patterns contextually. It holds built-in and user defined types for patterns and also it describes the syntax of the patterns.

Collectively, pattern tier and context tier form the pattern warehouse where patterns, trends, and knowledge reside. Pattern warehouse is the core of the pattern warehouse management system and it can think as a logical and compact representation of processed and mined data.

Figure 2. Layered forensic pattern warehouse framework

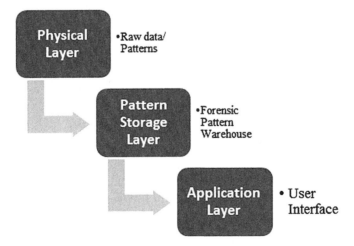

Application Layer

The top of the architecture consists application layer. This is the representation of other applications, machines, users, etc. The application layer of the pattern management architecture is the layer to the end-user deals with directly. This layer also includes the hardware and software involved in displaying and presentation of patterns.

Pattern Representation

The following section covers are various ways to define and declare the forensic patterns to keep the sematic of patterns and forensic data intact (Manolis T. & Panos V. (2003), Rizzi, S. et al (2003)).

Patterns are represented with triple (Pattern_Type, Pattern, Class).

Pattern_Type: A pattern type *'pt' is a quintuple -*

pt = (n, ss, ds, ms, f)

Where:

n is the name of pattern type.
ss (structure schema) is a definition of pattern space.
ds (source schema) define related raw data space.
ms (measure schema) quantify the quality
f is a function that describes the relationship between source space and pattern space.

Pattern: Let *pt = (n, ss, ds, ms, f) be a pattern type . A pattern 'p' instance of 'pt' is a quintuple:*

P = (pi, s, d, m, e)

Where:

pid- pattern identifier
s- is a value for type 'ss'
d- dataset
m- is a value of type ms
e- region of the source space

Example of a pattern of association type is:

pid: 001
s: (head = {'Thumb_Finger_Print'}, body = {'Knife, 'Minor_Age'})
d: 'SELECT SETOF record FROM

minor_age_prison_db GROUP BY recordID
m: (confidence = 0.75, support = 0.30)
e: { transaction: { 'Thumb_Finger_Print', 'Knife', 'Minor_Age' }

In this chapter, the attention is given on the central issues: conceptual and logical schema design only. In the view, Figure 3 depicts very abstract the conceptual view of forensic pattern warehousing including data sources, patterns, type and pattern warehouse. There is not found context based conceptual and logical schema. The conceptual modeling of pattern warehouse is with clear goals and objectives, such as completeness (all kinds of patterns), summarizability (ability to compute aggregate or derived pattern), and knowledge Independence (every pattern can be answered using the pattern warehouse only) as constraints (Tiwari V. & Thakur R.S. 2015b).

FUTURE RESEARCH DIRECTIONS

The presented work covers conceptual the forensic pattern warehouse while discussion on physical modeling is missing. Future work includes the dynamics of changing, modifying and updating of forensic patterns in warehouse. We must address the pattern's storage technology and schema toward quantity, quality and heterogeneity. There are also need to explore about duplication, compression, optimization and pattern placement. Forensic pattern warehouse refreshment problem is very important to handle carefully.

Figure 3. An abstract conceptual view of pattern warehousing

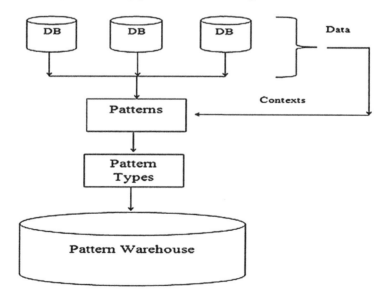

CONCLUSION

An elementary model is proposed to develop an overall integrated environment for uniformly representing (create, store and update) and querying various kinds of forensic patterns. A multi-layered architecture is introduced and considered one of the suitable solutions for pattern warehouse management system. The architecture is made up of the number of interconnected layers which include Physical layer, Pattern storage layer and Application layer. In presented model, each layer is proposed to perform concise and specific task. The model has enough flexibility and extensibility to use its own way. This allows the user to: 1) use standard pattern types or define new ones; 2) generate patterns and represented according to existing standards; 3) allow using new standards and mapping.

REFERENCES

Agrawal, R., & Srikant, R. (1994). Fast algorithms for mining association rules. *Proc. 20th Int. Conf. Very Large Data Bases*, *1215*, 487-499.

Bartolini, L., Elisa, B., Barbara, C., Paolo, C., Matteo, G., Marco, P., & Rizzi, S. (2003). Patterns for Next-generation DAtabase systems: preliminary results of the PANDA project. *Proceedings of the Eleventh Italian Symposium on Advanced Database Systems*.

Catherine, C., Aaron, K., & Robert, C. (2016). Development of a normalized extraction to further aid in fast, high-throughput processing of forensic DNA reference samples. Forensic Science International: Genetics, 25, 112-124.

David, L. W., & Andrew, J. (2013). *Digital Forensics Processing and Procedures* (1st ed.). Elsevier.

Geradts, Z., & Bijhold, J. (2001). New developments in forensic image processing and pattern recognition. *Science & Justice*, *41*(3), 159–166.

Geradts, Z., & Bijhold, J. (2002). Content Based Information Retrieval in Forensic Image Databases. *Journal of Forensic Sciences*, *47*(2), 40–47.

Golfarelli, M., & Rizzi, S. (2009). *Data warehouse design: Modern principles and methodologies*. McGraw-Hill, Inc.

Inmon, W. H. (2005). *Building the data warehouse*. New York: John Wiley & Sons, Inc.

John, H., David, J., & Lamb, M. (2011). *A Framework for the Forensic Investigation of Unstructured Email Relationship data. International Journal of Digital Crime and Forensics, 3(3)*.

Kimball, R., & Ross, M. (2011). *The data warehouse toolkit: the complete guide to dimensional modeling*. John Wiley & Sons.

Manolis, T., & Panos, V. (2003). *Architecture for Pattern Base Management Systems*. Department of Electrical and Computer Engineering. National Technical University of Athens.

Mikkonen, S., & Astikainen, T. (1994). Database classification system for shoe sole Patterns - identification of partial footwear impression found at a scene of crime. *Journal of Forensic Sciences, 39*(5), 1227–1236.

Mohammad, R., Keivan, K., Reda, A., & Mick, J. (2009). *Data modeling for effective data warehouse architecture and design. International Journal of Information and Decision Sciences, 1(3)*, 282–300.

Rizzi, S., Bertino, E., Catania, B., & Terrovitis, M. (2003). Towards a logical model for patterns. *Proceedings. ER Conference.*

Romero, Oscar, & Abelló. (2010). A framework for multidimensional design of data warehouses from ontologies. *Data & Knowledge Engineering*, 1138-1157.

Sibert, R. W. (1994). DRUGFIRE revolutionizing forensic firearms identification and providing the foundation for a national firearms identification network. *USA Crime Lab Digest, 21*(4), 63–68.

Tiwari, V., & Thakur, R. S. (2015a). *Improving Knowledge Availability of Forensic Intelligence through Forensic Pattern Warehouse (FPW). In Encyclopedia of Information Science and Technology* (3rd ed., pp. 1326–1335). IGI-Global.

Tiwari, V., & Thakur, R. S. (2015b). Contextual snowflake modelling for pattern warehouse logical design. *Sadhana, 40*(1), 15-33.

Tiwari, V., & Thakur, R. S. (2015c). P^{2}MS: a phase-wise pattern management system for pattern warehouse. *International Journal of Data Mining, Modelling and Management, 7*(4), 331-350.

Tiwari, V., Tiwari, V., Gupta, S., & Tiwari, R. (2010). Association rule mining: A graph based approach for mining frequent itemsets. *2010 International Conference on Networking and Information Technology*, 309-313. 10.1109/ICNIT.2010.5508505

Tobias, K., Claus, V., & Marcus, L. (2011). *Automated Forensic Fingerprint Analysis: A Novel Generic Process Model and Container Format. In Biometrics and ID Management* (Vol. 6583, pp. 262–273). Springer.

Werrett, D. J. (1997). The national DNA database. *Forensic Science International, 88*(1), 33–42. doi:10.1016/S0379-0738(97)00081-9

KEY TERMS AND DEFINITIONS

Business Intelligence: The process, technologies, and tools needed to turn data, patterns into information, information into knowledge, and knowledge into plans that help for forensic decisions.

Data Acquisition: It is a process used to collect information to document or analyze some phenomenon.

Data Mining: It is the practice of analyzing, examining data from different perspectives and summarizing to generate new information.

Forensic Data Analysis (FDA): It is the process of using of controlled and documented analytical and investigative techniques to identify, collect, examine, and preserve digital information.

Heterogeneous Pattern: Pattern with different structure.

Pattern: It is a compact and rich in semantic representation of raw data.

Pattern-Warehouse: It is a collection of persistently stored patterns.

Pattern Warehouse Management System (PWMS): Pattern management system used to model, store, retrieve, and manipulate patterns in an efficient and effective way.

This research was previously published in the Encyclopedia of Information Science and Technology, Fourth Edition edited by Mehdi Khosrow-Pour, pages 1376-1383, copyright year 2018 by Information Science Reference (an imprint of IGI Global).

Chapter 4
Uncovering Limitations of E01 Self–Verifying Files

Jan Krasniewicz
Birmingham City University, UK

Sharon A. Cox
Birmingham City University, UK

ABSTRACT

In computer forensics, it is important to understand the purpose of evidence file formats to maintain continuity of acquired data from storage devices. Evidence file formats such as E01 contain embedded data such as cyclic redundancy check (CRC) and hash values to allow a program to verify the integrity of the data contained within it. Students in computer forensics courses need to understand the concepts of CRC and hash values as well as their use and limitations in evidence files when verifying acquired data. That is the CRC and hash values in evidence file only verify the acquired data and not the evidence file per se. This important difference in E01 files was highlighted by showing students an anomaly in E01 files where certain bytes can be changed in E01 files without detection by computer forensic software using the embedded CRC and hash values. The benefit to students is that they can see the advantages of self-verification and limitations of what is verified giving the opportunity for a deeper understanding of evidence files and good practice.

INTRODUCTION

Teaching good practice in computer forensics is important to understand the correct operation and limitations of computer forensic hardware and software. One task is to demonstrate the self-verification feature of evidence file formats such as the EnCase E01 file format that contains an image of acquired data. The E01 file contains the data plus extra data in the form of hash values and Cyclic Redundancy Check (CRC) values used by computer forensic software to check the data contained within the file has not been tampered with. Students are taught how to carry out this task and verify the file by making a change to the generated file and observing mismatches between hash values and Cyclic Redundancy Check (CRC) values generated when the data was copied and when the file is loaded into computer forensic

DOI: 10.4018/978-1-5225-7492-7.ch004

software. Whilst creating teaching materials for students to carry out this task an anomaly was identified in one of the forensic file formats, the E01 format, commonly used by practitioners. The anomaly allows changes to be made to certain bytes within the file that are not detected by computer forensic software when verified by the associated hash and CRC values. This paper describes the anomaly in the file format, discussed the implications for relying on the self-verification feature of the E01 file format and concludes on methods to make any change to the file contents detectable.

Background

One of the first tasks before conducting a computer forensic analysis of data is to make a forensically sound copy of the data stored on, for example, a hard disk drive. This task forms the acquisition stage of an investigation. By "forensically sound" it is meant that the copying process does not alter the source data resulting in an exact copy of the data (Casey, 2007). This task involves making a bit-for-bit copy of the data and using a method that assists in determining the integrity of the resulting copy as part of the chain of custody.

It is important to be able to determine that the copy of data has not been changed before it is analysed. It is common practice and recommended by organisations such as the Association of Chief Police Officers (ACPO) and National Institute of Standards and Technology (NIST) to use a mathematical function to calculate a unique value for the data at the time of copying. Examples of mathematical functions used to check the integrity of data are Cyclic Redundancy Check (CRC) and cryptographic hash (Schneier, 1996). These functions are implemented in computer programs to compute a value from a computer file or entire contents of a storage device. The value is recorded so that whenever the digital evidence is analysed the value is recomputed and compared to the original value.

Computer programs have been developed to automate the copying process and calculate the integrity values for the acquired data. These values are stored within the resulting copy of the data. Storing the integrity values within the file allows the copy to be *self-verifying* when analysed with computer forensic software. When the copy is used by a computer forensic software application, such as Guidance Software's EnCase and AccessData's FTK, the application recalculates the unique value and then compares it with the value stored in the file. The program displays a warning message when the original and calculated values are different as this difference indicates the file has changed, the change could be as a result of corruption or it could be more sinister due to a deliberate change by an individual.

This paper considers the integrity values stored in the copy of the data, commonly known as the image file or digital evidence container file (Common Digital Evidence Storage Format Working Group, 2006). The paper describes mathematical functions used to calculate the integrity values and how the property of the function allows data to be validated. The paper then describes how a practical exercise to demonstrate self-verification features to students identified an anomaly where it was possible to change a byte within the file without the self-verification detecting that the copy had been changed. The paper explains why additional integrity values should be calculated based on the entire data, copy and integrity values combined, to further enhance confidence the copy has not been altered after it has been made.

Hash Functions in Computer Forensics

Hash functions are one approach to solving the problem in computer systems of being able to perform a fast lookup of data in a data store such as RAM or disk drive (Knuth, 1998). The hash function takes as input a characteristic or characteristics of data and computes a value based on the characteristic. This value is used to locate the data within a data store, for example. When a program needs to find data within a set of data the hash value is calculated and the value used to examine a location in the data store for the presence of that data. As a result, the hash value offers almost direct access to the data.

In comparison algorithms such as linear search are slow as it involves examining each data location for the presence of a specific data value from the first to the last. The amount of time to find data in the data store using a linear search is proportional to the number of data items in the data store and as the number of items increases so does the time to search the data store. The advantage of the hash function is it computes a hash value in constant time irrespective of the location of the data in the data store. Consider the example of searching for an individual's personal details based on some identifying data within a data store comprising of 1,000,000 individuals. A linear approach would inspect every location until a match is found where the time take to find the data is proportional to the amount of data, more data results in a longer search, potentially. A hash function would be applied to the identifying data and a value calculated that is then used to access a location directly.

Ideally hash values calculated are unique for different data but for some applications this is not entirely a requirement (Knuth 1998). Computer forensics make use of hash functions but a specific type called cryptographic hash functions that are designed to produce unique values for data. This property of calculating a unique value allows the value to be considered as a digital signature or fingerprint of the data allowing for data to be found by its hash value or verified because its value is unique (Cowen, 2013).

Cryptographic hash functions are used for the validation of arbitrary messages (the data) between individuals (Schneier, 1996). A key property of cryptographic hash algorithms is that they permit the verification of arbitrary streams of data by producing a unique value for that message exactly. In the case of cryptographic hash functions like MD5 (Rivest, 1992) and SHA1 (RFC3174), they are designed to produce a different value when there is a small change to the message such as the changing of one bit. This property of cryptographic hash functions allows an individual to check the integrity of the data before use. The MD5 function produces a 128bit value from a data stream of any length, for example an individual file or contents of an entire storage device, where this value is unique to the data theoretically. The uniqueness of MD5 is that there is a 1 in 2^{128} or 1 in $3.4028236692093846346337460743177 \times 10^{38}$ chance of two streams of data producing the same MD5 hash value even when the difference between the two streams is one bit and the stream of bits is many millions of bits. The SHA-1 function calculates a 160 bit value where the chances of two different data producing the same value is 2^{160} or 1 in 1.4615 $0163733090291820368483271163 \times 10^{48}$. However there is the issue of collisions in cryptographic hash functions where a collision occurs when two different messages produce the same hash value (Sotirov et al., 2011). Collisions present a problem as a malicious data could be constructed to generate a hash value with the same value as valid data (sKyWIper Analysis Team, 2012). Thomson (2005) discusses the implications for collisions and birthday attacks to computer forensics and concludes that whilst there are problems with MD5 collisions they can be overcome by using alternative algorithms. There have been a number of legal challenges to Encase regarding the verification process as covered in (Encase, 2014) where Encase 6 was augmented the Secure Hash Algorithm (SHA1) to provide an additional means to verify the data contained in an E01 file.

Further properties of cryptographic hash functions are that (Schneier, 1996):

- It is easy to compute the hash value for any message.
- It is difficult to compute the message from the hash value.
- It is difficult to determine another message that produces the same hash value of the message.

This latter property gives the function the property of being collision resistant where it should not be easy to compute another message that results in the same hash value. If this should happen then it would be easy to substitute one message with another without being detected. Examples of cryptographic hash functions are Message Digest (MD), Secure Hash Algorithm (SHA) and RACE Integrity Primitives Evaluation Message Digest (RIPE-MD) (Schneier, 1996). These properties of cryptographic hash functions are significant to computer forensics as they allow data to be verified after acquisition by calculating and comparing hash values.

MD5 and SHA1 functions are implemented in computer programs that are used to make the copy of the data, examples of which are AccessData's FTK Imager and EnCase. There have been some concerns with using MD5 and SHA-1 (Wang, Yin and Yu, 2005) as attacks on the algorithms have demonstrated that it is possible to generate the same value for different data. However it is acceptable and standard practice to use MD5 and SHA-1 in a legal court (Guidance Software, 2009).

As well as using cryptographic hash functions to verify the overall integrity of the data, the CRC function is used to calculate values for blocks of acquired data and stored in the digital evidence file. The CRC value's properties are that it allows data to checked for errors where CRC is used to check packets of data communicated over a network (Halsall, 1995). A CRC value is calculated for a block of data and transmitted over the network with the data. The receiver performs the CRC check only on the received data and compares with the received CRC value. If the CRC values are the same then this means no errors have been introduced into the data as a result of transmission. If the CRC values are different then this means there are errors in the data due to transmission and the receiver would request retransmission of the data. CRC function has similar properties to the hash function but it does not generate a unique value for data only a value that allows the data to be verified. CRC is used in digital evidence files to validate smaller blocks, for example 64 sectors worth of data (Bunting, 2012), within the data so should there be a hash mismatch a program can identify a location within the file.

It is important to note CRC and cryptographic hash functions cannot verify the data acquired are correct; they only assist in determining acquisition produced an exact copy of the original data. As a result any existing corruption in the data or successful attempts to wipe the data cannot be identified with cryptographic functions or CRC.

Concentrating on cryptographic hash functions, the hash value generated at acquisition and then the hash value generated when the data are verified are called the acquisition and verification hash values, respectively (Bunting, 2012). When the acquisition and verification hash values are the same then the data in the file are understood to be consistent with the original data copied from the device. Issues about the acquisition process are outside the scope of this paper. This paper assumes that the process of acquisition is correct and that a valid evidence file has been produced. When the values are different this means there has been some alteration of the evidence file contents. For example, it may be the case that the device the evidence file is stored on has some hardware fault corrupting the file. It could be that person or persons unknown have tried to tamper with the file by using a hex editor to modify key bytes in the file. In both cases the CRC and hash values help in determining that corruption has occurred and where this corruption affects the acquired data, for example corruption in the file corresponds to specific sectors. This self-verification property of the evidence file format allows it to be forensically sound.

Evidence File Formats

The inclusion of extra data to allow the digital evidence file to be validated automatically has resulted in a number of evidence file formats (Common Digital Evidence Storage Format Working Group, 2006). The primary objectives of evidence file formats are to be an accurate copy of the original data and allow for corruption and/or alteration of the contents to be detected. Unlike other file formats evidence file formats cannot be updated with new data; they are effectively sealed. Should an error in the creation of the evidence file occur for example, incorrectly selecting source devices and data were not copied, then, the entire process has to be repeated to create a new file.

Examples of evidence file formats are Access Data's Advanced Forensic Format (AFF), Guidance Software's E01 format and ASR Data's SMART format. These file formats all make a binary copy of data and use CRC and cryptographic hash values to validate the data. The evidence file format used for the exercise is the E01 evidence file format described below.

The E01 Evidence File Format

The E01 format is used by a number of computer forensic software such as Guidance Software's EnCase and AccessData's FTK. The logical structure of the E01 format is shown in Figure 1.

The evidence file is generated at acquisition time by a computer program called an imager (Casey, 2009). The Header stores details of the acquisition such as a case name, evidence number, examiner name and brief notes. The Data Blocks in Figure 1 are regions containing the binary copies of the acquired data. A CRC value calculated for the Header and Data Block is stored in the file at creation. The purpose of the CRC values is for performing an integrity check on the Data Blocks and Header separately. As a software application loads the data from the file it recalculates the CRC value based on the data in the block and compares it to the stored CRC value identifying any corruption in the data block.

At the end of the file is the MD5 cryptographic hash value. This is calculated only on the acquired data and does not include the header and CRC values stored in the file. The E01 file format now includes a SHA-1 hash value (not shown in Figure 1) that is also calculated on only the acquired data and stored at the end of the file. The purpose of this additional hash is to provide a second way to check integrity using a different function to calculate hash and therefore having two values to compare against. The inclusion of the SHA-1 value helps with mitigating claims about the reliability of the MD5 algorithm to produce unique values for different data and discussed in section 2 of this paper. In combination, CRC values determine if there has been corruption in a data block and the cryptographic hash function values determine if there is corruption in the entire acquired data. This combination addresses the smaller (in terms of number of bits) CRC value where there is a greater possibility of corruption producing the correct CRC value and, hence, the corruption not being detected.

Figure 1. The logical structure of the E01 evidence file format
(source: Bunting 2012)

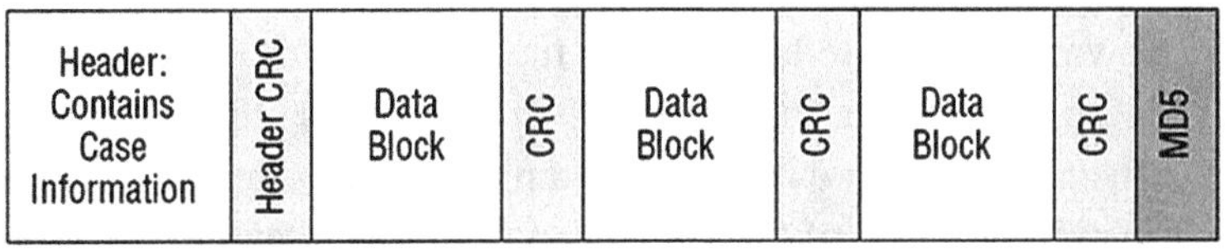

When an evidence file is loaded into computer forensic software the software begins recalculating CRC and cryptographic hashes based on the acquired data. Once the software completes recalculating the values it compares the CRC and hashes calculated with the CRC and hashes in the file. The software displays an error message indicating a mismatch when the cryptographic hash values, acquisition and verification, do not match and an examiner can find out which data blocks are in error.

It is good computer forensic practice to check these values before conducting an analysis on the data as results based on an invalid data could be called into question. Students on a BSc Forensic Computing complete a practical exercise on verifying a digital evidence file and see the value self-validating evidence file formats by making a change to the file to produce a mismatch between acquisition and verification hashes. The exercise is described in the following section.

File Verification Exercise

One of the initial exercises students on a BSc Forensic Computing course do is to validate an evidence file and gain experience to determine whether a file is valid or not. The exercise comprises of two parts. Part one requires students to load the test evidence file into computer forensic software and wait for verification to complete. They then check the acquisition and verifications hash values displayed by the program are the same or what message the program should display when the verification has been completed without mismatch.

The second part involves students using a hex editor program to load and view the binary contents of the evidence file. They are instructed to change a byte at a location within the file from its current value to a different value. The file is saved and reloaded into computer forensic software for validation where students are instructed to check the acquisition and verification hash values are different as a result of the change. The hash values themselves are not of significance to the exercise but the fact they are different is significant as it indicates a problem in the integrity of the file.

The location of the byte to be changed in the second part of the exercise was determined by obtaining the logical size of the file and dividing by two to be the approximate mid-point. The total size of the evidence file is 1,960,680 bytes and for simplicity the byte at 980340 was to be changed by students from its original value to 0xFF. The choice of the value 0xFF was arbitrary based on the assumption any change in the value whether it was a minor or major change should result in a verification error. A minor change would be to calculate the binary value for the byte value stored at the location and change one bit, for example the original value is D0 in the hexadecimal number system. The binary value for D0 is 11010000 where changing the right most bit that is the least significant in the number results in 11010001 or D1. A major change is to change many bits to result in a significantly different number such as reverse the binary value from 11010000 to 00101111. FF was chosen as this results in the binary pattern 11111111 with 5 bits changed. Figure 2 shows the location and original value stored at that location.

The value at the location D0 was overwritten with the value FF as shown in Figure 3.

RESULTS

The exercise was conducted by the tutor in order to check that the exercise would produce the mismatch for the second part of the exercise. The file was saved and loaded into the EnCase computer forensic

Figure 2. Location of byte to be changed for the exercise showing the original value

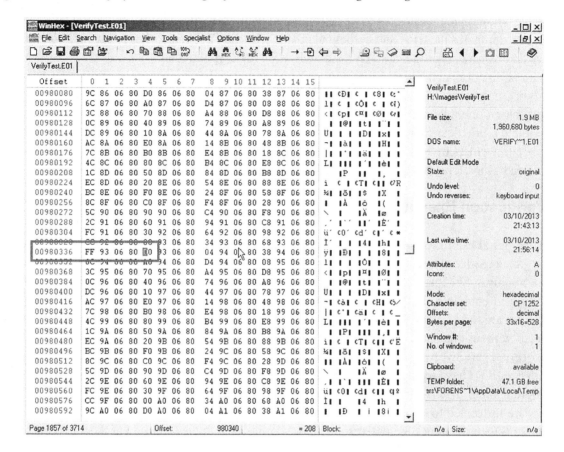

software where the expected result from the program was that there is a verification error due to the calculated hash values being different. However, the actual result was that the program completed the verification successfully with no verification errors indicated. The EnCase function to verify file integrity was invoked explicitly where the same result of no verification errors was received. Figure 4 shows the results of verifying the file's integrity.

This result was not expected and the test was repeated by loading the evidence file into another computer forensic program AccessData's FTK Imager that performs a verification check using the same MD5 and SHA-1 cryptographic hash functions. The experiment was repeated to identify if the problem was specific to EnCase. On completing verification FTK Imager also displayed no difference in the computed verification hash values and they match. Figure 5 shows the results of verifying the file's integrity using the FTK Imager program. The conclusion based on this result alone is that the values, CRC and hash, stored have not been sufficient to allow the program to detect a change in the evidence file itself. The CRC and hash values are computed solely for the acquired data not the evidence file per se. As a result changes to data outside the data blocks, CRC and hash value are susceptible to change without detection.

Figure 3. Location of byte after being changed to FF

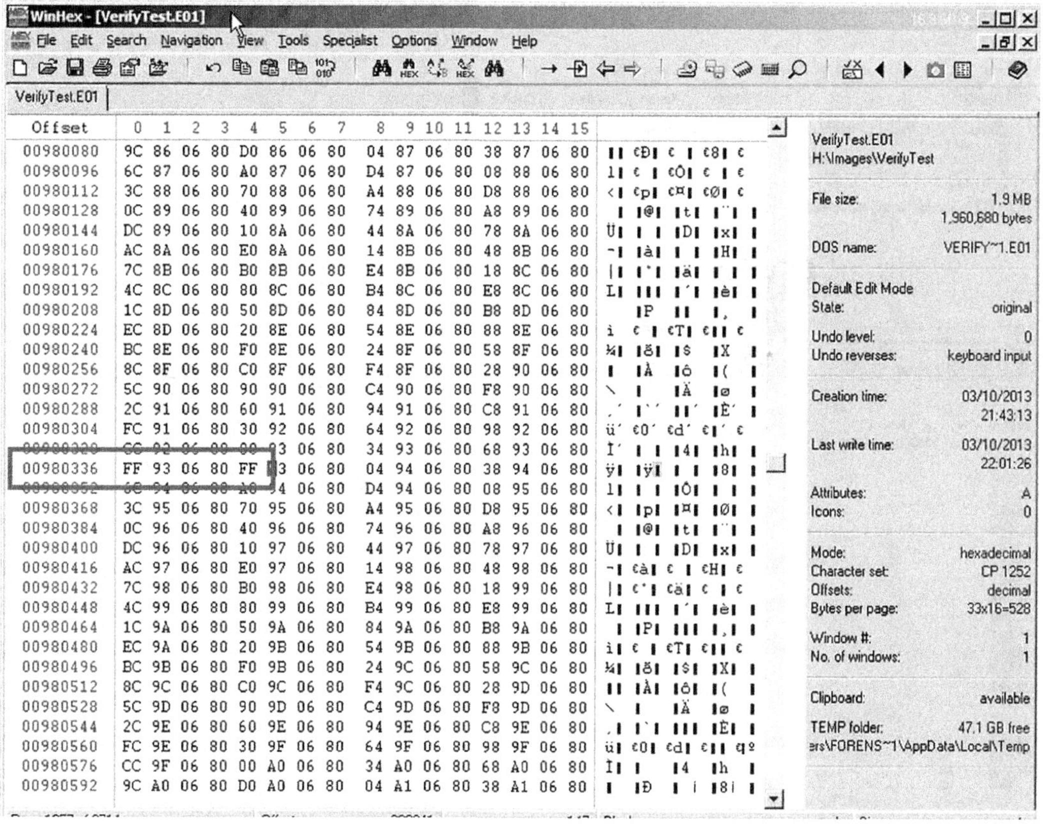

DISCUSSION OF RESULTS

The results in the previous section suggest that a byte can be changed in an E01 evidence file without resulting in an error being detected when the file is verified automatically by computer forensic software such as EnCase and FTK Imager. This result was unexpected given the claims that E01 files are self-verifying and changes to the file are detected through the use of CRC and hash values embedded in the evidence file. As a result the self-verification hash values and CRC should only be considered as validating the acquired data and not the entire file. Based on the E01's specification a mismatch should occur when a byte has changed, as that change will either be in a data block and identified by the hash value and CRC as expected. Alternatively the change should be detected because it occurred in a CRC or hash value because these data are the only other data in the file. The change results in an invalid CRC or hash value in the E01 file and results in a verification error because the CRC and hash calculated from the data block will be different. It would appear there is at least one location in the file that can be changed without being detected using the file's self-verification feature.

Confirming the integrity of the entire E01 file is achievable by calculating the hash value for the entire image file after it has been created. This would be consistent with computer forensic practices of using hashes to confirm data integrity (Kumar et al. 2012).

Figure 4. Modified file verification of modified showing no errors

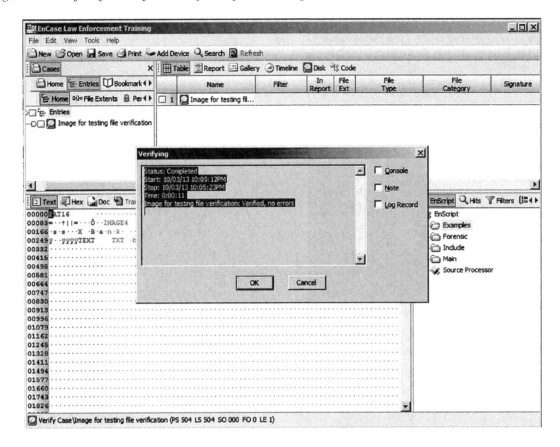

This result calls into question relying purely on the self-verification of the E01 evidence file format to verify the data. A similar problem occurred when a legal challenge to the E01 file format was made due to the use of MD5 hash function used to verify the data. The challenge was made based on academic research that demonstrated it was possible to generate the same hash value for two different data (Boer and Bosselaers, 1994). The challenge was successfully countered and where an additional hash value was used in the file to further improve data integrity (Guidance Software, 2009).

Likewise the results presented in this paper show a problem in self-verification property of the E01 file format for the whole file but significance of the result to the E01 file format may not be major. Further work is needed to confirm this assertion that the change made to a file was at a location that was not in a data block, CRC or hash value.

A solution to relying on the internal hash and CRC values is to use hash function such as the MD5 and SHA-1 to calculate the hash value for the E01 file as a whole, header, data blocks, CRC values and hash values. The E01 file hash value would be calculated immediately after acquisition was completed and a record made of the hash value. The hash value is recalculated whenever the E01 file is to be used in an analysis and the calculated hash value compared with the original hash. The result of the comparison would verify the file's integrity or indicate there has been some change to the file after acquisition. This check could be performed manually by using a program such as the one above to calculate hash values. Alternatively the E01 file can be augmented to include extra hash values for validating the file.

Figure 5. Verification results produced by the FTK Imager program on the modified file.

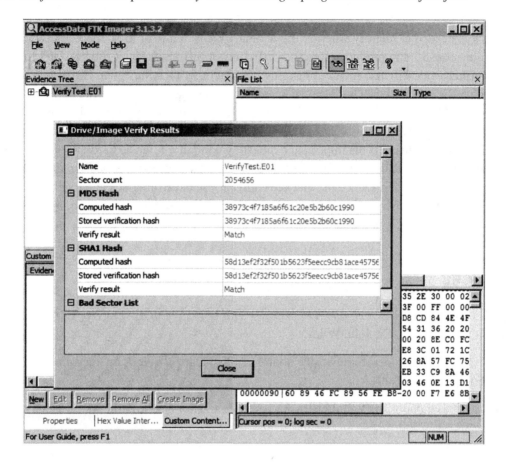

CONCLUSION

The primary conclusion of this paper is that is possible to make a change to a E01 evidence without that change being detected though the self-verification feature of the file format. This result contradicts the accepted fact that E01 files are self-verifying and can detect the changes to the file. A more correct interpretation is the verification feature of E01 files detects changes that have occurred only within data blocks acquired. As a result confidence in the E01 file format to be forensically sound with regards to verifying the data in contains is maintained. However the same is not true for verifying the E01 file in its entirety.

The recommendation of this paper is that to verify the integrity of the entire E01 file an additional hash value using an accepted hash function such as MD5 or SHA-1 or both is calculated and recorded as part of good practice. This hash value is calculated at the same time the image file is created. Whenever the E01 file is to be used the hash value is recalculated on the entire image file and compared with the original hash. When the values are the same it can be taken that the E01 file has integrity and can be used. When the values are different then there is some doubt over the integrity of the file irrespective of the CRC and hash values embedded in the E01 file.

FUTURE RESEARCH DIRECTIONS

Further work is needed to identify whether the anomaly identified in an E01 file is specific to the test file or it can be consistently produced for other E01 files of differing sizes (in bytes) and for split E01 files. This further work will also involve changing bytes at other locations in an E01 file in order to ascertain whether the acquired data has been changed but the change not detected during self-verification as described previously. In addition other evidence file formats will be tested as well as using alternative programs such as hashmyfiles.

The secondary conclusion is the importance of testing computer forensic hardware and software and associated artefacts in computer forensic teaching. Testing helps students understand using hardware and software in order to build confidence in what the hardware and software does and its correct operation. It also helps with emphasising the need for a rigorous testing in order to demonstrate procedures are correct to ensure evidence is admissible.

REFERENCES

Bunting, S. (2012). *EnCase Computer Forensics -- The Official EnCE: EnCase Certified Examiner Study Guide*. Indianapolis, IN: John Wiley.

Casey, E. (2007). What does forensically sound really mean? *Digital Investigation*, 4(2), 49–50. doi:10.1016/j.diin.2007.05.001

Casey, E. (2010). Handbook of Digital Forensics and Investigation. Burlington, MA: Elsevier Academic Press.

Common Digital Evidence Storage Format Working Group. (2006). *Survey of Disk Image Storage Formats* [PDF document]. Retrieved October 25, 2013 from http://www.dfrws.org/CDESF/survey-dfrws-cdesf-diskimg-01.pdf

Cowen, D. (2013). *Computer Forensics InfoSec Pro Guide*. New York: McGraw Hill.

Den Boer, B. (1993, May). *A. Collisions for the compression function of MD5*. Paper presented at Advances in Cryptology — EUROCRYPT '93 Workshop on the Theory and Application of Cryptographic Techniques, Lofthus, Norway.

Eastlake, D. (2001). *US Secure Hash Algorithm 1 (SHA1)*. Retrieved October 25, 2013 from https://www.ietf.org/rfc/rfc3174.txt

Encase Legal Journal. (2014). *Encase Legal Journal*. Retrieved September 22, 2016 from https://www.guidancesoftware.com/docs/default-source/document-library/publication/encase-legal-journal---5th-edition.pdf?sfvrsn=12

Guidance Software. (2009). *EnCase Legal Journal*. Retrieved October 29, 2010 (Requires registration) from https://www.guidancesoftware.com/resources/Pages/doclib/Document-Library/EnCase-Legal-Journal.aspx

Halsall, F. (1992). *Data Communications, Computer Networks and Open Systems* (3rd ed.). Wokingham, UK: Addison-Wesley.

Knuth, D. (1998). The Art of Computer Programming: Vol. 3. *Sorting and Searching* (2nd ed.). London: Addison-Wesley.

Kumar, K., Sofat, S., Jain, S. K., & Aggarwal, N. (2012). Significance of Hash Value Generation in Digital Forensic: A Case Study. *International Journal of Engineering Research and Development, 2*(5), 64–70.

Rivest, R. (1992). *The MD5 Message-Digest Algorithm.* Retrieved October 25, 2013 from https://www.ietf.org/rfc/rfc1321.txt

Schneier, B. (1996). *Applied Cryptography: Protocols, Algorithms and Source Code in C* (2nd ed.). Chichester, UK: John Wiley.

sKyWIper Analysis Team. (2012). *sKyWIper (a.k.a. Flame a.k.a. Flamer): A complex malware for targeted attacks.* Retrieved September 22, 2016 from http://www.crysys.hu/skywiper/skywiper.pdf

Sotirov, A., Stevens, M., Appelbaum, J., Lenstra, A., Molnar, D., Osvik, D. A., & de Weger, B. (2011). *MD5 considered harmful today.* Retrieved September 22, 2016 from http://www.win.tue.nl/hashclash/rogue-ca/

Wang, X., Yin, Y. L., & Yu, H. (2005, August). *Finding Collisions in the Full SHA-1. In* Advances in Cryptology – CRYPTO 2005, Paper presented at the 25th Annual International Cryptology Conference, Santa Barbara, CA.

ADDITIONAL READING

Boddington, R. (2016). *Practical Digital Forensics.* Birmingham, UK: Packt Publishing.

Encase image file format (n. d.). Retrieved from http://www.forensicswiki.org/wiki/Encase_image_file_format

Hayes, D. R. (2014). *A Practical Guide to Computer Forensics Investigations* (1st ed.). Indianapolis, IN: Pearson IT Certification.

Robinson, M. K. (2015). *Digital Forensics Workbook: Hands-on Activities in Digital Forensics.* Scotts Valley, CA: On-Demand Publishing LLC.

Sammes, A., & Jenkinson, B. (2010). *Forensic Computing: A Practitioner's Guide* (2nd ed.). London, UK: Springer.

Sammons, J. (2014). *The Primer for Getting Started in Digital Forensics* (2nd ed.). Burlington, MA: Syngress.

Sammons, J. (2014). *The Basics of Digital Forensics* (2nd ed.). Burlington, MA: Syngress.

KEY TERMS AND DEFINITIONS

Acquisition: The process by which data is acquired from a storage device and stored in an image file.

Bit-for-Bit Copy: A bit level copy of an arbitrary stream of data.

Cyclic Redundancy Check: An algorithm that computes a value for a data stream to use used for error detection and possible correction.

E01: A type of image file format that includes a bit-for-bit copy of source data plus hash values calculated from the original data.

Image File: A file containing acquired from a storage device.

MD5: A type of hashing algorithm that computes a fixed size value for an arbitrary data stream.

Verification: The process by which an image file is verified before use. Involves comparing hash values computed when the image file was made and when it is loaded into computer forensic software. Any discrepancy between the hash values suggests tampering or corrupting of the data within the image file.

This research was previously published in the Encyclopedia of Information Science and Technology, Fourth Edition edited by Mehdi Khosrow-Pour, pages 1384-1394, copyright year 2018 by Information Science Reference (an imprint of IGI Global).

Section 2
Cyber Crime, Cyber Bullying, and Digital Terrorism

Chapter 5
Cyber Security Protection for Online Gaming Applications

Wenbing Zhao
Cleveland State University, USA

ABSTRACT

In this chapter, the authors point out the threats to online gaming applications and present two strategies that can be used to build secure and dependable online gaming applications. These strategies not only seek the solution for gathering entropy to seed the PRNG used in such applications but also intend to eliminate malicious intrusions to protect the seed and to maintain replica consistency. By applying these techniques, the online gaming applications can ensure service integrity (both the service providers and the innocent players are protected) and guarantee high availability despite the presence of Byzantine faults. Finally, the authors outline some open research issues in this field.

INTRODUCTION

By online gaming applications, we mean both distributed applications that enable large number of users to play multiplayer games and those that enable people to gamble online because both types of applications could have huge financial stakes and the security and dependability challenges for both are rather similar. On the one hand, such systems must ensure continuous high availability so that users around the globe could play the games 24 by 7. This requires that the game servers be replicated to provide non-stop services. On the other hand, state-machine replication requires that the replicas be deterministic or rendered deterministic. This requirement does not work well with gaming applications because random numbers are essential to their operation. For example, in a card game, the random numbers are used to shuffle the cards. If the random numbers used are not robust, the hands in the card game may become predictable, which could damage the integrity of the game and may lead to financial losses to the game provider and/or honest game players. The nature of this type of applications poses a particular challenge to ensure cyber security because it is difficult to ensure high availability while preserving the integrity of the operation of these applications (Arkin et al., 1999; Viega & McGraw, 2002; Young & Yung, 2004; Zhao, 2007; Zhao, 2008; Zhang et al., 2011).

DOI: 10.4018/978-1-5225-7492-7.ch005

Byzantine fault tolerance (Castro & Liskov, 2002) is a well-known technique to achieve cyber security (Zhao, 2014). The technique aims to tolerate various malicious attacks to online systems by employing state machine replication (Schneider, 1990). However, as we mentioned earlier, Byzantine fault tolerance cannot be used as it is because it is not equipped with built-in solution to resolve the conflict of replication determinism requirement and the intrinsic randomness of the server operation. In this article, we elaborate how we address this dilemma using an online poker game application as a running example. In this application, a pseudo-random number generator (PRNG) is used to generate the pseudo-random numbers for shuffling the cards. We present two alternative strategies to cope with the intrinsic application nondeterminism. One depends on a Byzantine consensus algorithm and the other depends on a threshold signature scheme. Furthermore, we thoroughly discuss the strength and weaknesses of these two schemes.

BACKGROUND

In this section, we provide a brief introduction of PRNG, the entropy concept, and the methods to collect and enhance entropy.

A PRNG is a computer algorithm used to produce a sequence of pseudo-random numbers. It must be initialized by a seed number and can be reseeded prior to each run. The numbers produced by a PRNG are not truly random because computer programs are in fact deterministic machines. Given the same seed, a PRNG will generate the same sequence of numbers. Consequently, if an adversary knows the seed to a PRNG, then he/she can generate and predict the entire stream of random numbers (Young & Yung, 2004). Therefore, to make the random numbers unpredictable, it is important that the seeds to the PRNG cannot be guessed or estimated. Ideally, a highly random number that is unpredictable and infeasible to be computed is required to seed the PRNG in order to produce a sequence of random numbers.

The activity of collecting truly random numbers is referred to as "collecting entropy" by cryptographers (Young & Yung, 2004). Entropy is a measure of the degree of randomness in a piece of data. As an example, consider using the outcome of coin flipping as 1 bit of entropy. If the coin-toss is perfectly fair, then the bit should have an equal chance of being a 0 or a 1. In such a case, we have a perfect 1 bit of entropy. If the coin-toss is slightly biased toward either head or tail, then we have something less than 1 bit of entropy. Entropy is what we really want when we talk about generating numbers that cannot be guessed. In general, it is often difficult to figure out how much entropy we have, and it is usually difficult to generate a lot of it in a short amount of time.

It is a common practice to seed a PRNG with the current timestamp. Unfortunately, this is not a sound approach to preserve the integrity of the system, as described by Arkin et al (1999) in the context of how a Texas Hold'em Poker online game can be attacked. They show that with the knowledge of the first few cards, they can estimate the seed to the PRNG and subsequently predict all the remaining cards.

TECHNIQUES FOR ENHANCING THE TRUSTWORTHINESS

In this section, we describe two possible strategies for enhancing the trustworthiness of online gaming applications. One depends on a Byzantine consensus algorithm and the other depends on a threshold signature algorithm. Both algorithms ensure that all replicas adopt the same value to seed their PRNGs, while each replica is taking entropy from its respective entropy source.

Byzantine Fault Tolerance

A Byzantine fault (Lamport, Shostak, & Pease, 1982) is a fault that might bring a service down, or compromise the integrity of a service. A Byzantine faulty replica may use all kinds of methods to disrupt the normal operation of a system. In particular, it might propagate conflicting information to other replicas. To tolerate f Byzantine faulty replicas in an asynchronous environment, we need to have at least 3f+1 number of replicas (Castro & Liskov, 2002). An asynchronous environment is one that has no bound on processing times, communication delays, and clock skews. Internet applications are often modeled as asynchronous systems. Usually, one replica is designated as the primary and the remaining ones as backups.

Any robust Byzantine fault tolerance (BFT) algorithm can be modified to cope with the use of random numbers. In the following, we describe a solution based on the well-known Practical BFT (PBFT in short) algorithm developed by Castro and Liskov (2002). The PBFT algorithm has three communication phases in normal operation. During the first phase, the pre-prepare phase, upon receiving a request from the client, the primary assigns a sequence number and the current view number to the message and multicasts a Pre-Prepare message to all backups. In the second phase, referred to as the prepare phase, a backup broadcasts a Prepare message to the rest of replicas after it accepts the Pre-Prepare message. Each non-faulty replica enters into the commit phase, i.e., the third phase, only if it receives 2f Prepare messages (from other replicas) that have the same view number and sequence number as the Pre-Prepare message, then it broadcasts the Commit message to all replicas including the primary. A replica commits the corresponding request after it receives 2f matching commit messages from other replicas. To prevent a faulty primary from intentionally delaying a message, the client starts a timer after it sends out a request and waits for f+1 consistent responses from different replicas. Due to the assumption that at most f replicas can be faulty, at least one response must have come from a non-faulty replica. If the timer expires, the client broadcasts its request to all replicas. Each backup replica also maintains a timer for similar purposes. On expiration of their timers, the backups initiate a view change and a new primary is selected. In the PBFT algorithm, digital signature or an authenticator is employed to ensure the integrity of the messages exchanged.

The above PBFT algorithm is modified in the following way to cope with the replica nondeterminism caused by the use of random numbers. The modified algorithm also consists of three phases, as shown in Figure 1. In the beginning of the first phase, the primary invokes ENTROPY-EXTRACTION operation to extract its entropy and append the entropy to the Pre-Prepare message. It then multicasts the Pre-Prepare message to the backups. Each replica records the primary's entropy from the Pre-Prepare message in its log and then invokes the ENTROPY-EXTRACTION operation to obtain its own share of entropy as well. Each backup then multicasts a Pre-Prepare-Update message, including its share of entropy extracted. When the primary collects 2f Pre-Prepare-Update messages from the backups, it constructs a Pre-Prepare-Update message, including the digest of the 2f+1 entropy shares (2f received, plus its own), together with the corresponding contributor's identity, and multicasts the message.

Upon receiving the Pre-Prepare-Update message from the primary, each replica invokes the EN-TROPY-COMBINATION operation to combine the entropy from the 2f+1 shares. The outcome of the ENTROPY-COMBINATION operation ensures a highly random number, due to the contributions from the non-faulty replicas. The combined number is provable secure and will be used to seed the PRNG if the BFT algorithm terminates.

The second and third phases are similar to the corresponding phases of the PBFT algorithm, except each replica will append the digest of the entropy set determined in the first phase to the Prepare and Commit messages. These two phases are necessary to ensure all nonfaulty replicas to agree on the same message total ordering and the entropy value despite the presence of Byzantine faulty replicas.

We now highlight the details of the ENTROPY-EXTRACTION and the ENTROPY-COMBINATION operations.

Entropy-Extraction

The ENTROPY-EXTRACTION operation is based on software-based entropy collection. There are a number of techniques that can be used to extract the entropy, most of which are based on the timing of internal activities in a computer (Young & Yung, 2004). A well-known technique is called TrueRand, developed by Don Mitchell and Matt Blaze. The idea behind TrueRand is to gather the underlying randomness from idle CPUs by measuring the drift between system clock and the generation of interrupts on the processor. Other frequently used techniques include recording network traffic as it comes into the server, timing how long it takes to seek the disk, and capturing kernel state information that changes often.

Figure 1. The adapted BFT algorithm to handle entropy extraction and combination

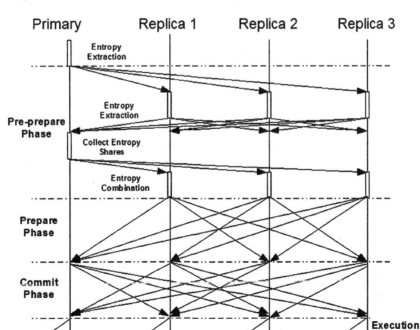

Entropy-Combination

The ENTROPY-COMBINATION operation combines the 2f+1 entropies the replica collected using the exclusive-or (XOR) operator (Young & Yung, 2004). This operation has several benefits.

First, it combines a number of weak sources of entropy to form an effective strong entropy source. Consider two entropy sources from coin flipping, and the case which source 1 results in head and source 2 results in tail, or source 1 results in tail and source 2 results in head, and the probability for source 1 to result in head is 10/16 and that for source 2 is 12/16 (i.e., both are biased). If we combine these two sources, the probability of getting a head is 7/16. This shows that the coin flipping resulting from XOR-ing the bits from the two sources is the same or better than the best flip in either of the two sources. Furthermore, the more sources we use, the higher entropy we get.

Second, the ENTROPY-COMBINATION operation eliminates any negative impact from malicious replicas. Among the 2f+1 entropy shares collected, there can be up to f of them coming from faulty replicas. The XOR operation guarantees that if at least one share coming from a good entropy source, the combined entropy is at least as good as that entropy share. This requirement is met because there are at least f+1 shares contributed by non-faulty replicas. Any low-entropy or predicable shares generated by faulty replicas are virtually ignored.

Third, the ENTROPY-COMBINATION operation results in a single high entropy share used by all non-faulty replicas, which ensures the consistency of the replicas when they are involved with intrinsically nondeterministic operations.

Threshold Signature

The other strategy to ensure consistent Byzantine fault tolerance replication for nondeterministic operations is to employ threshold cryptography (Deswarte, Blain, & Fabre, 1991; Desmedt & Frankel, 1990). Threshold cryptography is a good way to distribute trust among a group of players to protect either information or computation (Zhou, Schneider, & Renesse, 2002).

A well-known secret sharing scheme (Shamir, 1979) is the (k, n) threshold digital signature scheme. In the (k, n) secret sharing scheme, a secret is divided into n sets and distributed to the same number of players. The secret can be reconstructed if k out of n number of players could combine their shares. However, fewer than k players cannot collude to forge the secret. The (k, n) threshold digital signature scheme allows a set of servers to collectively generate a digital signature in a way similar to reconstructing a secret using the (k, n) secret sharing scheme.

In the (k, n) threshold digital signature scheme, a private key is divided into n shares, each owned by a player. To produce a valid threshold digital signature, at least k players must pool their shares together (i.e., fewer then k players would not be able to generate a valid threshold digital signature). Each player uses its private key share to generate a partial signature on a message and these partial signatures can be combined into a threshold signature on the message. The threshold signature can be verified using the public key corresponding to the divided private key.

The RSA Shoup scheme (Shoup, 2000) is one of the practical threshold digital schemes. In this scheme, a dealer generates a key pair and divides the private key into n shares at first. Each key share has a key verifier. Then the dealer distributes the message to be signed and the key shares to n players. Each player uses its key share to generate a partial signature on the message. Furthermore, each player sends the signed message with the verifier to a trusted server, which verifies the signature shares and combines the partial signatures into a threshold signature verifiable by the public key.

In the following, we show how to integrate the threshold digital signature scheme with Byzantine fault tolerance for online gaming applications, The adapted PBFT algorithm consists of three phases (under normal operation) for Byzantine agreement and an additional phase run at the beginning for key shares distribution. The Byzantine agreement algorithm works similar to the PBFT algorithm except the third phase, where each replica generates a partial signature (using its key share) to sign the client's message and piggybacks the partial signature to the Commit message. Each replica combines the partial signatures into a threshold signature. The signature is then mapped into a number to seed the PRNG.

Despite the elegancy of the threshold signature, the algorithm, however, might not be practical in the Internet environment. First of all, it depends on a trusted dealer at the beginning to generate a key pair, divide the private key into several key shares and it must also be responsible for distributing the key shares to all replicas. If the dealer is compromised, the entire system would become vulnerable to adversaries. Furthermore, the threshold signature is computationally expensive, especially when generating the threshold signature. For example, for a 1024-bit threshold signature it usually takes 73.9ms on a PC equipped with a single 1.0GHz Pentium III CPU and 1.5 GB RAM (Rhea et al., 2003). Furthermore, the validity on the use of the threshold signature as the seed to the PRNG remains to be proved secure.

FUTURE TRENDS

Not only for online gaming applications, PRNGs are widely used in nearly every field in computer and networking area. In particular, for cryptography, the access to truly random numbers is extremely important. Even though there is moderate success in implementing PRNG, it remains to be vulnerable under cryptanalytic attacks and the attacks against its internal state. Furthermore, it is easy to see that even if the PRNG is robust against many potential threats, once the seed is discovered the numbers generated by the PRNG are no longer unpredictable. In light of this observation, more efforts should be engaged in how to gather and evaluate entropy in a secure and dependable manner. The research described in this article can be regarded as the first step towards this direction.

There are many open issues to be resolved before we can confidently apply these techniques in practice. The most interesting research issue is how to maintain replica consistency. Common Byzantine fault tolerance techniques require deterministic execution of replicas despite the fact that all practical applications contain some degree of nondeterminism (Zhao, 2007), for example, clock values, CPU speed, multithreading, etc. Note that these types of nondeterminism are not considered as good entropy sources accordingly to the cryptography standard, but the presence of these types of nondeterminisms nevertheless poses a big threat to maintaining replica consistency. We recently proposed a Byzantine fault tolerance framework that is able to handle various nondeterministic applications in a systematic and efficient manner (Zhang et al., 2011).

So far we have focused on addressing the issues for the client-server based online gaming applications. Peer-to-peer (P2P) based online games have become popular in recent years. The P2P design brings additional challenges to enhancing trustworthiness of such applications because each client maintains substantial private state. There are new attacks that may be launched from clients to the systems. Various schemes have been designed to enforce the integrity of such applications (Jha, 2007; Wierzbicki, 2006).

Finally, we only addressed the high availability and the associated integrity issues for online gaming applications. Additional research is needed to address other aspects of risks faced by such applications. For example, a player could cheat by changing the rendering routines so that he/she could see scenes that are not allowed, thereby gaining an unfair advantage over honest players. These types of threats cannot be addressed by resorting to replication.

CONCLUSION

In this article, we pointed out the threats to online gaming applications and presented two strategies that can be used to build secure and dependable online gaming applications. These strategies not only seek the solution for gathering entropy to seed the PRNG used in such applications, but also intend to eliminate malicious intrusions to protect the seed and to maintain replica consistency. By applying these techniques, the online gaming applications can ensure its service integrity (both the service providers and the innocent players are protected) and guarantee high availability despite the presence of Byzantine faults. Finally, we outlined some open research issues in this field.

REFERENCES

Arkin, B., Hill, F., Marks, S., Scjmod, M., & Walls, T. (1999). *How we learned to cheat at on-line poker: A study in software security*. Available at http://www.developer.com/java/other/article.php/10936_616221

Castro, M., & Liskov, B. (2002). Practical Byzantine fault tolerance and proactive recovery. *ACM Transactions on Computer Systems*, *20*(4), 398–461. doi:10.1145/571637.571640

Desmedt, Y., & Frankel, Y. (1990). Threshold cryptosystems. *Lecture Notes in Computer Science*, *435*, 307–315. doi:10.1007/0-387-34805-0_28

Deswarte, Y., Blain, L., & Fabre, J. (1991). Intrusion tolerance in distributed computing systems. *Proceedings of the IEEE Symposium on Research in Security and Privacy*, 110–121.

Jha, S., Katzenbeisser, S., Schallhart, C., Veith, H., & Chenney, S. (2007, May). Enforcing semantic integrity on untrusted clients in networked virtual environments. In *Proceedings of the IEEE Symposium on Security and Privacy*, (pp. 179-186). IEEE.

Lamport, L., Shostak, R., & Pease, M. (1982). The Byzantine generals problem. *ACM Transactions on Programming Languages and Systems*, *4*(3), 382–401. doi:10.1145/357172.357176

Luby, M. (1996). *Pseudorandomness and Cryptographic Applications*. Princeton University Press.

Rhea, S., Eaton, P., Geels, D., Weatherspoon, H., Zhao, B., & Kubiatowicz, J. (2003). Pond: the Ocean-Store Prototype. *Proceedings of the 2nd USENIX Conference on File and Storage Technology*, 1-14.

Rivest, R., Shamir, A., & Adleman, M. (1978). A method for obtaining digital signatures and public key cryptosystems. *Communications of the ACM*, *21*(2), 120–126. doi:10.1145/359340.359342

Schneider, F. (1990). Implementing fault-tolerant services using the state machine approach: A tutorial. *ACM Computing Surveys*, *22*(4), 299–319. doi:10.1145/98163.98167

Shamir, A. (1979). How to share a secret. *Communications of the ACM*, *22*(11), 612–613. doi:10.1145/359168.359176

Shoup, V. (2000). Practical threshold signature. *Lecture Notes in Computer Science*, *1807*, 207–223. doi:10.1007/3-540-45539-6_15

Viega, J., & McGraw, G. (2002). *Building Secure Software: How to Avoid Security Problems the Right Way*. Addison-Wesley.

Wierzbicki, A. (2006). Trust enforcement in peer-to-peer massive multi-player online games. Lecture Notes in Computer Science: vol. 1180. On the Move to Meaningful Internet Systems 2006: CoopIS, DOA, GADA, and ODBASE (pp. 1163-1180). Springer Berlin Heidelberg. doi:10.1007/11914952_7

Young, A., & Yung, M. (2004). *Malicious Cryptography: Exposing Cryptovirology*. Indianapolis, IN: Wiley Publishing.

Zhang, H., Zhao, W., Moser, L. E., & Melliar-Smith, P. M. (2011). Design and implementation of a Byzantine fault tolerance framework for non-deterministic applications. *Software, IET*, *5*(3), 342–356. doi:10.1049/iet-sen.2010.0013

Zhao, W. (2007). Byzantine Fault Tolerance for Nondeterministic Applications. *Proceedings of the 3rd IEEE International Symposium on Dependable, Autonomic and Secure Computing*, 108-115. 10.1109/DASC.2007.11

Zhao, W. (2008, December). Integrity-preserving replica coordination for byzantine fault tolerant systems. In *Proceedings of the 14th IEEE International Conference on Parallel and Distributed Systems* (pp. 447-454). IEEE. 10.1109/ICPADS.2008.45

Zhao, W. (2014). *Building dependable distributed systems*. John Wiley & Sons. doi:10.1002/9781118912744

Zhou, L., Schneider, F., & Renesse, R. (2002). COCA: A secure distributed online certification authority. *ACM Transactions on Computer Systems*, *20*(4), 329–368. doi:10.1145/571637.571638

ADDITIONAL READING

Atighetchi, M., Pal, P., Webber, F., Schantz, R., Jones, C., & Loyall, J. (2004). Adaptive cyber defense for survival and intrusion tolerance. *IEEE Internet Computing*, *8*(6), 25–33. doi:10.1109/MIC.2004.54

Baughman, N. E., & Levine, B. N. (2001). Cheat-proof playout for centralized and distributed online games. In *Proceedings of the Twentieth Annual Joint Conference of the IEEE Computer and Communications Societies*. (Vol. 1, pp. 104-113). IEEE. 10.1109/INFCOM.2001.916692

Bessani, A. N., Sousa, P., Correia, M., Neves, N. F., & Verissimo, P. (2007). Intrusion-tolerant protection for critical infrastructures.

Bessani, A. N., Sousa, P., Correia, M., Neves, N. F., & Verissimo, P. (2008). The CRUTIAL way of critical infrastructure protection. *Security & Privacy, IEEE, 6*(6), 44–51. doi:10.1109/MSP.2008.158

Chen, T., Hsiao, T.-C., & Chen, T.-L. (2004). An efficient threshold group signature scheme. *Proceedings of the IEEE Region 10 Conference*, Volume B (pp. 21-24). Chiang Mai, Thailand.

Deswarte, Y., & Powell, D. (2006). Internet security: An intrusion-tolerance approach. *Proceedings of the IEEE, 94*(2), 432–441. doi:10.1109/JPROC.2005.862320

Feng, D., & Xiang, J. (2005, July). Experiences on intrusion tolerance distributed systems. In *Proceedings of the 29th Annual International Computer Software and Applications Conference* (Vol. 1, pp. 270-271). IEEE.

Garcia, M., Bessani, A., Gashi, I., Neves, N., & Obelheiro, R. (2011, June). OS diversity for intrusion tolerance: Myth or reality? In Proceedings of the IEEE/IFIP 41st International Conference on Dependable Systems & Networks (pp. 383-394). IEEE.

Hampel, T., Bopp, T., & Hinn, R. (2006, October). A peer-to-peer architecture for massive multiplayer online games. In *Proceedings of 5th ACM SIGCOMM workshop on Network and system support for games* (p. 48). ACM. 10.1145/1230040.1230058

Hoglund, G., & McGraw, G. (2007). *Exploiting online games: cheating massively distributed systems*. Addison-Wesley Professional.

Hsiao, T. Y., & Yuan, S. M. (2005). Practical middleware for massively multiplayer online games. *IEEE Internet Computing, 9*(5), 47–54. doi:10.1109/MIC.2005.106

Iimura, T., Hazeyama, H., & Kadobayashi, Y. (2004, August). Zoned federation of game servers: a peer-to-peer approach to scalable multi-player online games. In *Proceedings of 3rd ACM SIGCOMM workshop on Network and system support for games* (pp. 116-120). ACM. 10.1145/1016540.1016549

Kim, J., Bentley, P. J., Aickelin, U., Greensmith, J., Tedesco, G., & Twycross, J. (2007). Immune system approaches to intrusion detection–a review. *Natural Computing, 6*(4), 413–466. doi:10.100711047-006-9026-4

Li, S., Chen, C., & Li, L. (2007, November). Using group interaction of players to prevent in-game cheat in network games. In Proceedings of the First International Symposium on Data, Privacy, and E-Commerce, (pp. 47-49). IEEE. 10.1109/ISDPE.2007.112

Li, S., Chen, C., & Li, L. (2008, January). Prevent In-Game Cheat in Network Games. In *Proceedings of the First International Workshop on Knowledge Discovery and Data Mining*, (pp. 513-518). IEEE. 10.1109/WKDD.2008.95

Loose, T. C. (2014). U.S. Patent No. 8,632,405. Washington, DC: U.S. Patent and Trademark Office.

Mettouris, C., Maratou, V., Vuckovic, D., Papadopoulos, G. A., & Xenos, M. (2015). Information Security Awareness through a Virtual World: An end-user requirements analysis. In *Proceedings of the 5th International Conference on Information Society and Technology* (pp. 273-278).

Nae, V., Prodan, R., & Fahringer, T. (2010, January). Monitoring and fault tolerance for real-time online interactive applications. In Proceedings of the Euro-Par 2009–Parallel Processing Workshops (pp. 255-265). Springer Berlin Heidelberg. 10.1007/978-3-642-14122-5_30

Nguyen, B. T., Wolf, B. D., & Underdahl, B. (2014). U.S. Patent No. 8,708,791. Washington, DC: U.S. Patent and Trademark Office.

Yan, J. (2003, December). Security design in online games. In *Proceedings of the 19th Annual Computer Security Applications Conference*, (pp. 286-295). IEEE.

Yan, J., & Randell, B. (2005, October). A systematic classification of cheating in online games. In *Proceedings of 4th ACM SIGCOMM workshop on Network and system support for games* (pp. 1-9). ACM. 10.1145/1103599.1103606

Yan, J., & Randell, B. (2005). Security in computer games: From pong to online poker. University of Newcastle upon Tyne. *Computer Science*.

Yan, J., & Randell, B. (2009). An investigation of cheating in online games. *Security & Privacy, IEEE*, *7*(3), 37–44. doi:10.1109/MSP.2009.60

Zhao, W. (2008, May). Towards practical intrusion tolerant systems: a blueprint. In Proceedings of the 4th Annual Workshop on Cyber security and information intelligence research: developing strategies to meet the cyber security and information intelligence challenges ahead (p. 19). ACM. 10.1145/1413140.1413162

KEY TERMS AND DEFINITIONS

Byzantine Fault: It is used to model arbitrary fault. A Byzantine faulty process might send conflicting information to other processes to prevent them from reaching an agreement.

Byzantine Fault Tolerance: A replication-based technique used to ensure high availability of an application subject to Byzantine fault.

Dependable System: A dependable system is one that is trustworthy to its users. It requires that the system to be highly available (to legitimate users) while ensuring high degree of service integrity.

Digital Signature: A digital signature aims to serve as the same purposes as a real-world signature. A sound digital signature ensures that the sender of the digital signature can be authenticated, the sender cannot later repudiate that she has sent the signed message, and a receiver cannot forge a digital signature (without being detected).

Entropy Combination: The operation that combines a number of entropy shares into one. The combination is usually achieved by using the exclusive-or (XOR) operator. Entropy combination is an effective defense against adversaries that substitute a random value by a predictable one. The combined entropy is often of higher quality than each individual share.

Entropy Extraction: The operation that extracts entropy from a random variable (referred to as the entropy source). Entropy can be extracted using both software and hardware based methods.

Entropy: A metric used to evaluate and describe the amount of randomness associated with a random variable.

Pseudorandom Number Generator (PRNG): A PRNG is a computer algorithm used to produce a sequence of pseudo-random numbers. It must be initialized by a seed number and can be reseeded prior to each run. The numbers produced by a PRNG are not truly random. Given the same seed, a PRNG will generate the same sequence of numbers.

Threshold Digital Signature: In the (k, n) threshold digital signature scheme, a private key is divided into n shares, each owned by a player. A valid threshold digital signature can be produced if k players combine their shares. However, no valid signature can be generated by fewer than k players. Each player uses its private key share to generate a partial signature on a message and these partial signatures can be combined into a threshold signature on the message. The threshold signature can be verified using the public key corresponding to the divided private key.

This research was previously published in the Encyclopedia of Information Science and Technology, Fourth Edition edited by Mehdi Khosrow-Pour, pages 1647-1655, copyright year 2018 by Information Science Reference (an imprint of IGI Global).

Chapter 6
Piracy and Intellectual Property Theft in the Internet Era

Shun-Yung Kevin Wang
University of South Florida – St. Petersburg, USA

Jeremy J McDaniel
Principal Financial Group, USA

ABSTRACT

Stealing ideas is not something new, but stealing and transporting ideas in a massive amount has become possible in the era of the internet. Based on the frameworks of criminological theory/thesis, this chapter intends to elaborate intellectual property theft and piracy in cyberspace. Contemporary cases of intellectual property theft and piracy are used to illustrate the blurred line between victims and offenders. The impacts of related information technology should be carefully appraised, as more and more intellectual properties are in digital format.

INTRODUCTION

Internet has quickly become an essential part of contemporary society across country borders for its capacity to offer a wide array of functions, ranging from information distribution, communications, financial and business management, to entertainments. Also, the Internet has evidenced itself as a unique medium with the fastest speed of diffusion in human history. With hundreds of thousand miles of optical fiber that connect servers and mega-storing devices together globally, several terabytes of digital information, as huge as those stored in the U.S. Congress Library, can be easily transferred from one end of the world to the other within minutes (Britz, 2013). In conjunction with widely available Wi-Fi and telecommunication (e.g., 3G, 4G, LTE) in many areas of the world, it is never this easy for an average user to transmit valuable information in digital format via mobile devices.

The information technology advances with incremental innovation, but business is the instrument that facilitates the widespread of the technology. The mechanism of business determines when to release certain technology, and the nature of business makes it user friendly for the purpose of obtaining a larger market share and a higher level of profit (Felson and Clarke, 1997). While legitimate opportunities are

DOI: 10.4018/978-1-5225-7492-7.ch006

created in the process, some offenders may take advantage. Like many innovations that have a tendency to crime (Merton, 1968), the growing capacity of Internet probably is too good to be true, as it has created new forms of intellectual property (IP). Before further discussing IP and elaborating the victimization of piracy, background of some theoretical frameworks of crime is necessary.

BACKGROUND

Basic Elements of Crime and Socio-Technical Gap

In their theory of crime, Cohen and Felson (1979) point out three elements of a crime incident: a suitable target, a motivated offender, and the absence of capable guardians. A suitable target is something valuable to potential offenders, and the target must be easy enough to be removed. Although crime rate is the highest among young males, motivated offenders can be anybody in the population, if an adequate opportunity is present. The guardians against crime do not necessarily refer to law enforcement. Instead, the owner of the targeted property, friends and neighbors of the property owners serve better roles of capable guardians that discourage potential offenders. In the scenario of burglary, potential perpetrators probably would less likely to choose houses that the owners are present or their friends/neighbors pay attention to. In the business settings, for another example, an office suite's receptionists who watch people entering the office can serve as the role of guardian. In sum, for a crime to occur, the above three elements have to emerge.

There is little doubt that industry has incentives to make their products lighter, more portable, more convenient, and more added functions and values, but this tendency naturally leads to some unwanted consequences of the products, such as suitable targets to theft. However, the social system (e.g., laws, justice agencies) usually simply reacts to the consequences of technological advancements pushed by industry and business. That is, technology proactively runs at the front, and the social system passively chases behind and (hopefully) fixes problems and challenges. In the era of Internet, the discrepancy between fast-growing Internet and information technology and the slow-reacting social system in the virtual space has created a cybergap in which crimes emerge (Huang and Wang, 2009). Explicitly, many more new digital IP are valuable targets with little to no meaningful guardians that trigger motivation of potential offenders in the cyberspace. The following section provides a description of IP theft and piracy. The discussion of IP and piracy in the present article is focused within the arena of those using digital technology, with an intention to compare and contrast several major incidents.

IP, IP Theft, and Piracy

The discussion of IP traditionally revolves copyrights, patents, trademarks, and trade secrets. Piracy has been generally defined as "the unauthorized use or reproduction of another's work," and it encompasses any individual or corporation that utilizes intellectual property in a digital form without the authorization of the originator (Business Software Alliance, n.d.; Filby, 2007). The nature of such behaviors is perceived as illegitimate, with some noticeable variation across different levels of civilization and cultures. For example, in some Asian societies with long histories, scholarly works are traditionally viewed as public goods contributing to the advancement of the entire society, and the scholars are informally "rewarded" with socially-recognized reputations and their social status. On the other hand, in the United States and many European countries, where the right of tangible or intangible personal property are better defined and protected by laws, such kind of theft has been criminalized. Generally speaking, intellectual properties are well respected, formally and informally, in civilized societies.

Properties can be generally divided into tangible and intangible items, and the age-old theft usually involves tangible goods that perpetrators have to physically move away and turn into financial gains. IP theft is different from stealing of physical property in many ways: IP theft implies depriving people of their ideas, inventions, or creative expressions, and thereby this type of asset is intangible. Nevertheless, it is not saying that there is no overlapping between tangible and intangible properties, as IP also requires some kind of medium to load on, to store, or to distribute. For instance, the physical piracy of music – the production and/or distribution of illegally made copies of sound recordings without the consent of the rights proprietor – needs cassettes, discs, USB, hard drives, or other storing media. Within the past two decades, the significant improvement of personal computing devices equipped with large storage capacity inflamed the popularity of digital IP. In addition, in conjunction with growing Internet users, the expanding capacity of broadband and wireless technology increases the movement of digitalization. Collectively, the advancement of information technology has dramatically increased the amount of IP in digital format.

Based on the contents, there are two broad groups of highlighted IP: entertainment (music[1], movies, games, TV programming, etc.) and instrumental software. This typology is adopted for its exhaustive categories that ease the discussion, although 'Internet piracy' and 'digital piracy' are the terms used more often in varied news media and public reports. Internet piracy is a somehow broadly used term which generally means that the Internet is employed to distribute unauthorized creative content amongst users[2], and this term is used to generalize any use of creative content on the Internet that infringe on copyright laws (Higgins, 2011). It had been a common myth to some that customers who purchase a legal copy of a music CD or USB believe that they own the music because they bought it in the format of optical disc or portable storage. In fact, the ownership of the recorded music, as a form of IP protected by the copyright laws, belongs to the writers. Consequently, if the purchasers massively multiply the disc/USB or upload the content to computers and share with others via the Internet, they would be committing so-called 'Internet piracy.' In a similar vein, piracy offenders may use the Internet for advertising, offering, acquiring, or distributing of other copyright protected contents.

Naturally, IP theft and piracy are business-threatening issues to the corporations of the ownership, and they can be problems to individuals as well. Intuitively, the pirated copies, which may appear to be legitimate ones, hurt the profit of the producing industry. Counterfeits sound recordings are produced without the required permission of the proprietor and then packaged to bear a resemblance to the original. Another noticeable type of piracy, bootlegs, consist of recording live or broadcast concerts without the consent of the proprietor that are replicated and re-sold. Similar violation may include other forms of performance and artworks. These actions are taken to mislead customers into believing that they are buying an original (and legal) version and supporting the creations.

The other substantial IP subject to today's piracy is instrumental software. Software piracy is commissioned by unlawfully multiplying or distributing of copyrighted software with the intention to gain financially. Legally purchased software (only) grants buyers the licenses of usage. The consensus, as it is reflected in the laws in many developed countries, is that buyers pay for user licenses, not the ownership of the IP of software. Based on the purpose and volume of duplication, two categories of software piracy are recognized: end user piracy and reseller piracy. End user piracy is the installation of the software onto computers or terminals exceeds the user license allows. Reseller piracy occurs when an individual or an organization consciously produces multiple copies of the software for the purpose of selling for profits. Sometimes, pirate copies even come with counterfeit certificates with an obvious intent to deceive purchasers. In sum, copying, downloading, installing, sharing, or selling multiple copies of copyrighted software are behaviors subject to software piracy.

Corporations have adopted a good number of strategies to fight against software piracy. The most straight-forward method is to establish a call-free reporting hotline by the corporations. The operating system giant Microsoft, for example, utilized its anti-piracy hotline to collect information and sued 8 Toronto-area computer resellers suspected of unlawfully dispensing unlicensed software. The lawsuit was the single largest piracy sweep operation in a North American city of the time (National Post, 1999). A related strategy, similar to criminal case reporting system or campaign (e.g., "see something, say something"), is collaboration among stakeholders and offer meaningful incentives to encourage reporting. Business Software Alliance (BSA) promoted a program named "know it, report it, reward it" that provides qualified individuals who report software piracy a cash reward of up to $1 million. This program led to a lawsuit that BSA filed against a Nevada based engineering company that duplicated and distributed unauthorized copies of Autodesk software used for drafting (PR Newswire, 2009). Another developed approach is working with direct-related industries or holding them legally accountable, such as Internet platform providers. In 2008, the Software and Information Industry Association (SIIA) filed nine separate lawsuits on behalf of members of Adobe Systems and Symantec alleging that the defendants deliberately sold illicit copies of software on eBay (The Daily Record of Baltimore, MD., 2008). This largest round of lawsuits, since eBay initiated its auction website anti-piracy program, signaled the seriousness of the issue and also sent out a clear message to similar industries. Still another approach is called digital rights management (DRM) that places control over digital products. The methods of managing the digital products can be as simple as entering serial numbers to activate installed software, and the methods can be as sophisticated as requiring authentication with an online server and/or with a smart-card (Kumari, Khan, & Li, 2016). This approach has been adopted to ensure authorized access, distribution, and consumption of the products/services by software and entertainment companies. The implications of this approach can cover the entire lifecycle of the digital products.

Amplified by the global economy, the matter of IP theft and piracy can be much more complicated and worse when the majority of IP thefts initiated outside of the property owner's country territory where the right of IP are usually better protected by laws. Traditionally, stealing of ideas emerged in the developing countries where the criminal and civil laws are permissive and the enforcement of law is more likely to be compromised for economic reasons. However, Sweden has ironically been a piracy haven because of the well-known file-sharing website Pirate Bay is hosted within its territory. Although the Swedish court system convicted four major players of the website and punished them with prison sentences and a substantial amount of fines in 2009, the website is astoundingly running (Pfanner, 2009)[3]. Another extreme example is the entire counterfeit Apple store, in which the staffs even believe that they are Apple employees, found in Kunming, China (BBC, 2011), and such kind of "fake" Apple store did not seem to exist solely (Chang, 2015). It appears that some well-off Chinese appreciate real Apple products by paying double amount of the money, but they do not seem to care the sources of IP products. At the same time, surveys show that the overall rate of IP infringement in mainland China is close to the global average (Broadhurst, Bouhours, & Bouhours, 2013).

Proactive approaches to combating piracy have been spread both domestically and internationally. For example, in 2006, the United States government created an organization called Strategy Targeting Organized Piracy (STOP) in an effort to deal with piracy. Following suit was the European Union that has created a different strategy based off of the STOP ideology. The European Union began working with some developing countries through effective implementation and enforcement of existing laws of IP. This proactive approach by both the United States and the European Union has in turn influenced the Nigerian government, for example, to take similar actions. The Nigerian government worked in partnership with the private sector and other stakeholders to set up the Strategic Action Against Piracy (STRAP), and the Nigerian Copyright Commission (NCC) worked with Microsoft to combat piracy (Africa News, 2006).

VICTIMIZATION OF PIRACY AND IP THEFT AND PROTECTIVE ACTIONS

The victimization of piracy and IP theft usually involves multiple parties in different context. The advancing information technology makes it easy for pirating websites to sell illegally duplicated IP, or even portray themselves as a legitimate business to deceive inexperienced online consumers[4]. In another scenario, many people who acquire pirated software over the Internet never actually receive the software or entertainment items they paid for. In that sense, those who consciously purchase pirated IP online potentially play dual roles: law violators and victims.

There used to be a clear-cut distinction between the victim(s) and the offender(s) when a criminal act takes place. We have little to no doubt that a street thief who snatches a purse is the obvious criminal offender, and the victim is the individual whose purse was stolen. As this series of behavior occurs in the physical world, it could be witnessed by others or video recorded by devices that leave evidence for criminal investigations. However, the Internet has changed the rule, and thereby somehow changes the distinction between victims and offenders. With the advancement of information technologies, the physicality of traditional crimes has become intertwined with the creation of new types of criminal acts in the cyberspace, which are much less visible. Internet also substantially lowers the threshold of committing crimes, especially true in the violation of IP – clicking the mouse or touching on the screen and downloading a pirated copy of software, film or music from a remote server (wherever it is physically located in the world) can be a violation of criminal codes! Furthermore, the sense of borderless of many cybercrimes complicates the issue, as multiple countries, with a general disagreement about the seriousness of IP violations, are typically involved (Altbach, 1988). Collectively, it has become more challenging to define a victim in an intellectual theft incident. This has also created burdens on policy makers and police when defining and enforcing new criminal and civil statutes intended to protect truly innocent victims.

In the short history of digital piracy, the creation of Napster and its impact on music industry is one of the important milestones. In 1999, Shawn Fanning, a college student at the University of Boston, created an online music peer-to-peer file sharing service called Napster. This ground-shaking service allowed some music enthusiasts around the world to share music with each other without purchasing music CDs or tapes from physical stores. From many aspects, Napster could be a successful business, as it rapidly became the largest platform of music sharing of the time. Rather, Napster has often been blamed from the economic perspective – its existence leads to a major revenue lost of recording industry. Largely because of the erosion of industry's profit, the Recording Industry Association of America (RIAA) sued Napster on behalf of the major record labels and proprietors (musicians) that are the victims of music piracy (Richtel, 2001). RIAA won the law suit, however, the winning lawsuit that shutdown Napster did not lead to the intended consequences – regain billions of dollars in potential revenue. In contrast, the result in Napster's disappearance created a number of unregulated peer-to-peer file sharing networks such as BearShare, Grokster, Gnutella, KaZaa, Morpheus, Pirate Bay, and others (Dodge, 2005). Even in a report, IFPI (2010) claims that the revenues from recorded music reduced by 50% in a decade after the creation of Napster. In a sense, the RIAA probably ironically retain the financial damages to its party by shutting down Napster instead of working with this emerged online platform, which once had 38 million users, to rectify their strategic flaws of business. The law case symbolizes the significance of copyrighted content protection, but the music industry is still somehow suffering from this lawsuit. The advancement of related information technology has made it difficult for corporations to protect themselves from being victimized, if the fundamental changes that can be made by new technologies are not carefully appraised. It is hard to deny that "as long as Philips makes and sells CD burners, and as long as Sony makes and sells MiniDisc players/recorders, they're directly profiting from the very technology that they claim is hurting them" (Rodman & Vanderdonckt, 2006: 253). In other words, the increase of digital piracy of music and the decline of music industry revenues are largely the consequences of information technology advancement.

Piracy of music has existed for decades, but digital piracy of music significantly hit the industry because of its slower, if not unwise, response to the technologies, in addition to passive response from the social system (Huang & Wang, 2009). An interesting fact is that the successful business model of selling music online was accomplished by a computer company, not the music industry – Apple introduced iTune online music store after Napster lawsuit, and it remained its leading place in the market when this manuscript was prepared in 2016.

In addition to corporations being impacted by the emerged cyber-platforms, individual users are subjects to corporations' legal actions. In 2003, the music recording industry sued over 200 Americans for sharing songs on peer-to-peer file sharing networks, and the message cannot be clearer when a minor living under poverty was on the list. Moreover, the recording industry has filed, settled, or threatened legal actions against at least thirty thousand individuals in order to protect its potential profits. It probably is socially justified to consider these individual offenders in that they illegally shared intellectual property, regardless the media that are used. However, the proportionality of penalties (e.g., charges and retributions that these individuals have to pay) and damages might be debatable. To some, this case makes sued individuals become scapegoat when the balance and rules are greatly impacted by the introduced new applied technology. For instance, Jammie Thomas of Brainerd, MN was accused of unlawfully sharing over 1,500 songs, and the RIAA lawsuit sought damages under a federal law that allowed a fine of $750 to $30,000 for each copyright violation, which totaled a judgment of over $1.2 million (Freed, 2007). To others, "it's stupid (and reckless) to antagonize one of your principal sources of long-term income by publicly attacking them as criminals" (Rodman & Vanderdonckt, 2006: 259).

Similarly, the widespread of BitTorrent and illegal download of movie contents had significantly impacted revenues of film makers. Another important milestone of combating piracy is focusing on sites that offer free massive online storage space, which were misused by some to store and share contents of large files, such as movies. In a recent study that assesses the economic impacts of supply-side intervention of illegal downloading indicates that the shutdown of Megaupload[5] chronologically leads to a significant increase in digital sales and rentals. Countries with higher pre-shutdown usage of Megaupload experience larger increase of digital sales than their counterparts with lower pre-shutdown usage do (Danaher & Smith, 2013).

IP theft and piracy will undoubtedly continue to occur, but the approaches of solutions can be different. In the case of film and music piracy, it will be up to stakeholders, including policy makers, legal experts, and the industry to come out a balanced approach. More efforts should be taken placed in innovative ways to better educate consumers about sharing movies and music and to reduce costly legal actions. A more recent case of a Vietnam-based social media website "Zing," which includes an infringing deeplinking music portal, shows that collaborations, instead of lawsuits, may have been identified as a win-win solution between right holders and online platforms (Executive Office of the President of the United States, 2012).

FUTURE RESEARCH DIRECTIONS

From the preceding sections, the trend of working with continuously-advancing information technology and online platforms instead of fighting against it appears to be a more effective approach in IP protection with more beneficial results to stakeholders. Although the Internet is borderless, the undeniable "territory" in cyberspace is largely structured by users and administrations' nationality, culture, ideology, and language, which is somehow related to their geographical locations. Future research can systematically compare cases in the area of IP protection strategies and evaluate their outcomes across different geographical regions and industries. Instead of narrowing down to the benefits of certain stakeholders like music industry, the outcomes should include social and economic indicators that capture the impacts on the development of legal system and competitive advantage of the economy. Future research probably should investigate the impacts of cultures, including pop cultures, on how people perceive and support IP rights. Given some contradicting phenomenon between international survey findings and news reports, using dimensions like the socioeconomic development, level of civilization, and law protections seem to overly simplify global citizens by their nationality.

CONCLUSION

The main challenge of piracy and IP violations that today's societies face is the discrepancy between the fast-pace information technology, which is believed by some to lead advancement of human societies, and the slow reactions of laws, which is supposed to guide and protect citizens. The rapid progression of technology, combined with weak laws, has allowed criminals to exploit the international community and run illegal "business" of piracy. As a result, the entertainment and software industries, in particular, have been victimized of extensive pirating schemes, which have caused substantial revenue and job loss worldwide. Information technology has greatly expanded the avenues that copyright-protected works can be duplicated and distributed, while lowering the costs. After the mass investment of optical fiber in late 1990s, the Internet has facilitated the transfer of vast amounts of information among large numbers of people at little cost to law violators. But, the cost of piracy, ranging from financial, economic, safety, to health, is tremendous to the IP owners and the entire society, as the pirates require no investment in research, development, and warranties, and consumers are risked by failing counterfeiting parts and products.

The uniqueness of Internet's fastest diffusion, along with the reactive nature of social system, has created a good number of challenging social issues in the socio-technical gap. From a criminological perspective like routine activities, this information super highway does provide very fast transportation of attractive targets with some to not-meaningful guardians in the cyberspace to motivated (and somewhat skilled) offenders. The Internet and related technology might have also blurred the clear line of ownership of productive assets, as well as the products and services originate from them. These clear lines are central to the foundation of capitalism; the social system cannot continue to function without a set of understandable rules that define ownership of the properties and legitimate business models (Thurow, 2000). Rather than making progress, the system would fall apart starting from the erosion of the incentive structure that encourages the continuity of research and development, which leads to further loss of trust in business and confidence in the economy (van Dijk and Terlouw, 1996). Indeed, the Internet probably has brought another wave of significant challenges to the issues of intellectual property and piracy, since Xerox introduced its first commercial photocopy machine in 1959.

The advancement of information technology has also intentionally increased digitalized IP and "migrate" those in earlier generation formats to the cyberspace. The Internet search giant Google, for example, has implemented many ambitious projects to massively digitalize social artifacts. There is no doubt that information is so affordable to so many people in the human history because of the Internet, and Google, so far, has been the leading private provider that effectively organizes and prioritizes the online contents to the majority users of the developed countries. While some may argue against Google's project of "displaying" instead of "copying" the IP in the cyberspace, another wave of concern of IP and piracy may involve the conflicts between the profit-making nature of business and the belief of public-belonging of human heritage (Vaidhyanathan, 2011).

REFERENCES

Africa News. (2006, December 6). *Nigeria: Tackling the problem of piracy in Nigeria*. Retrieved from www.lexisnexis.com/hottopics/lnacademic

Altbach, P. G. (1988). Economic progress brings copyright to Asia. *Far Eastern Economic Review, 139*(9), 62–63.

BBC. (2011). *Fake Apple store found in China*. Retrieved July 11, 2016, from http://www.bbc.co.uk/news/technology-14258135

Britz, M. (2013). *Computer Forensics and Cyber Crimes: An Introduction* (3rd ed.). Upper Saddle River, NJ: Pearson Education Inc.

Broadhurst, R., Bouhours, B., & Bouhours, T. (2013). Business and the risk of crime in China. *The British Journal of Criminology, 53*(2), 276–296. doi:10.1093/bjc/azs059

Business Software Alliance. (n.d.). *What is software piracy*. Retrieved July 10, 2016, from http://www.bsa.org/country/Anti-Piracy/What-is-Software-Piracy.aspx

Chang, C. (2015). *The Most Phenomenal Fake Apple Store in China*. Retrieved July 20, 2016, from http://micgadget.com/14648/the-most-phenomenal-fake-apple-store-in-china/

Cohen, L. E., & Felson, M. (1979). Social change and crime rate trends: Routine activity approach. *American Sociological Review, 44*(4), 588–608. doi:10.2307/2094589

Danaher, B., & Smith, M. (2013). *Gone in 60 Seconds: The Impact of the Megaupload Shutdown on Movie Sales*. Available at SSRN # 2229349.

Dodge, D. (2005). *Perspective: Napster's learning curve*. Retrieved February 17, 2014, from http://news.cnet.com/Napsters-learning-curve/2010-1027_3-5901873.html

Executive Office of the President of the United States. (2012, December 13). *Out-of-Cycle Review of Notorious Markets*. Author.

Felson, M., & Clarke, R. V. (1997). *Business and Crime Prevention*. Monsey, NY: Criminal Justice Press.

Filby, M. (2007). Confusing the captain with the cabin boy: the dangers posed to reform of cyber piracy regulation by the misrepresented interface between society, policy makers and the entertainment industries. In *Proceedings of the British & Irish law, education and technology association conference* (pp. 1-47). Stanford, CA: Creative Commons.

Freed, J. (2007). *Brainerd woman first to go to trial for music sharing: Jammie Thomas at risk for a judgment of millions of dollars*. Retrieved February 17, 2014, from http://brainerddispatch.com/stories/100207/new_20071002025.shtml

Higgins, G. E. (2011). *Digital Piracy: An Integrated Theoretical Approach*. Durham, NC: Carolina Academic Press.

Huang, W., & Wang, S. K. (2009). Emerging Cybercrime Variants in the Socio Technical Space. In B. Whitworth, & A. de Moor (Eds.), Handbook of Research on Socio-Technical Design and Social Networking Systems. Hershey, PA: IGI.

IFPI. (2010, July). *IFPI Response to Commission Green Paper on Creative and Cultural Industries*. IFPI.

Kumari, S., Khan, M. K., & Li, X. (2016). A more secure digital rights management authentication scheme based on smart card. *Multimedia Tools and Applications, 75*(2), 1135–1158. doi:10.100711042-014-2361-z

Merton, R. K. (1968). *Social Theory and Social Structure*. Glencoe, IL: The Free Press.

National Post. (1999, August 13). *Eight computer resellers face lawsuits after latest Microsoft anti-piracy sweep: Computers allegedly loaded with unlicensed software*. Retrieved from www.lexisnexis.com/hottopics/lnacademic

Newswire, P. R. (2009, March 31). *BSA settles lawsuit against Nevada-based engineering company for $205,000*. Retrieved from www.lexisnexis.com/hottopics/lnacademic

Pfanner, E. (2009, April 18). Four convicted in Sweden in Internet piracy case. *The New York Times*, p. 2.

Richtel, M. (2001, February 13). The Napster decision: The overview; appellate judges back limitations on copying music. *The New York Times*, p. 1.

The Daily Record of Baltimore. (2008). *News Summary - 3/21*. Retrieved from www.lexisnexis.com/hottopics/lnacademic

Thurow, L. C. (2000). The product of a knowledge-based economy. *The Annals of the American Academy of Political and Social Science, 570*(1), 19–31. doi:10.1177/0002716200570001002

Vaidhyanathan, S. (2011). *The Googlization of Everything: (And Why We Should Worry)*. Berkeley, CA: University of California Press.

van Dijk, J., & Terlouw, G. (1996). An international perspective of the business community as victims of fraud and crime. *Security Journal, 7*, 157–167. doi:10.1016/0955-1662(96)00168-3

ADDITIONAL READING

Allum, F., & Siebert, R. (Eds.). (2003). *Organized crime: The challenge to democracy*. London: Routledge.

Beresford, A., Desilets, C., Haantz, S., Kane, J., & Wall, A. (2005). Intellectual property and white-collar crime: Report of issues, trends, and problems for future research. *Trends in Organized Crime, 8*(4), 62–78. doi:10.100712117-005-1014-z

Bhattacharjee, R., Gopal, R. D., Lerwachara, K., & Marsden, J. R. (2006). Impact of legal threats on online music sharing activity: An analysis of music industry legal actions. *The Journal of Law & Economics, 49*(1), 91–114. doi:10.1086/501085

Branstetter, L. G., Fisman, R., & Foley, C. F. (2006). Do stronger intellectual property rights increase international technology transfer? Empirical evidence from U.S. firm-level panel data. *The Quarterly Journal of Economics, 121*(1), 321–349. doi:10.1093/qje/121.1.321

Broadhurst, R. G. (2005). International Cooperation in Cyber-crime Research. In *Proceedings 11th UN Congress on Crime Prevention and Criminal Justice, Workshop 6: Measures to Combat Computer Related Crime*, 1-12, Bangkok, Thailand.

Chen, Y., & Puttitanum, T. (2005). Intellectual property rights and innovation in developing countries. *Journal of Development Economics, 78*(2), 474–493. doi:10.1016/j.jdeveco.2004.11.005

Choate, P. (2005). Hot Properties: The Stealing of Ideas in an Age of Globalization. New York, NY: Knopf: Distributed by Random House.

Drahos, P. (2002). Developing countries and international intellectual property standard-setting. *The Journal of World Intellectual Property, 5*(5), 765–789. doi:10.1111/j.1747-1796.2002.tb00181.x

Eaton, J., & Kortum, S. (1996). Trade in ideas: Patenting and productivity in the OECD. *Journal of International Economics, 40*(3-4), 251–278. doi:10.1016/0022-1996(95)01407-1

Friedman, T. L. (2005). *The world is flat: A brief history of the twenty-first century.* New York: Farrar, Straus, and Giroux.

Grossman, G. M., & Lai, E. L. C. (2005). International protection of intellectual property. *The American Economic Review, 95*(5), 1635–1653.

International Federation of the Phonographic Industry (IFPI). (2003). *The record industry commercial piracy report, 2003.* London: IFPI.

Keller, W. (2004). International technology diffusion. *Journal of Economic Literature, 42*(3), 752–782. doi:10.1257/0022051042177685

Lai, E. L. C. (1998). International intellectual property rights protection and the rate of product innovation. *Journal of Development Economics, 55*(1), 133–153. doi:10.1016/S0304-3878(97)00059-X

Maher, M. K., & Thompson, J. M. (2002). Intellectual property crimes. *The American Criminal Law Review, 39*(2), 763–816.

Motivans, M. (2004). *Intellectual Property Theft, 2002.* Bureau of Justice Statistics, U.S. Department of Justice. doi:10.1037/e306472005-001

Nhan, J. (2009). "It's like printing money": Piracy on the Internet. In F. Schmalleger & M. Pittaro (Eds.), *Crimes of the Internet* (pp. 356–383). Upper Saddle River, NJ: Pearson Education Inc.

Piquero, N. L., & Piquero, A. R. (2006). Democracy and intellectual property: Examining trajectories of software piracy. *The Annals of the American Academy of Political and Social Science, 605*(1), 104–127. doi:10.1177/0002716206287015

Ponte, L. M. (2009). The warez scene: Digital piracy in the online world. In F. Schmalleger & M. Pittaro (Eds.), *Crimes of the Internet* (pp. 384–407). Upper Saddle River, NJ: Pearson Education Inc.

Rodman, G. B., & Vanderdonckt, C. (2006). Music for nothing or, I want my MP3. *Cultural Studies, 20*(2-3), 245–261. doi:10.1080/09502380500495734

Ryan, M. P. (1998). *Knowledge Diplomacy: Global Competition and the Politics of Intellectual Property.* Washington, D.C.: Brookings Institution Press.

Singer, P. W., & Friedman, A. (2013). *Cybersecurity and Cyberwar: What Everyone Needs to Know.* Oxford: Oxford University Press.

Wall, D. S. (2007). *Cybercrime: The Transformation of Technology in the Networked Age.* Cambridge: Polity Press.

World Intellectual Property Organization (WIPO). (2001). *WIPO intellectual property handbook: Policy, law, and use. WIPO Publication no. 489(E).* Geneva, Switzerland: WIPO.

KEY TERMS AND DEFINITIONS

End User Piracy: The installation of the software onto computers or terminals exceeds the user license allows.

Intellectual Property (IP): Copyrights, patents, trademarks, and trade secrets. Copyrights protect literary or artistic creation, ranging from books, articles, scripts, and audio and video recordings. Patents protect registered and determined inventions or discoveries that exclude others from making, using, offering for sale, or selling, and the examples include the composition of a new medication. Trademarks protect a companies' name, products' name, logos, slogans, or package designs. Trade secrets secure formulas, production procedures, and even business lists, and Coca Cola's secret recipe is an example.

Internet Piracy: Piracy that is conducted or facilitated by the Internet where unauthorized creative contents are distributed.

IP Theft: Stealing law-protected intellectual property that reflects creators' ideas, inventions, or creative expressions, in tangible or intangible format.

Piracy: The unauthorized use or reproduction of works that belong to another individual(s) or entity for the purpose of financial gain.

Reseller Piracy: When an individual or organization consciously produces multiple copies of the software with the intent of selling for profits.

Software Piracy: Unauthorized duplicating or distributing of copyrighted software with the intention to gain financially.

ENDNOTES

[1]   According to the International Federation of the Phonographic Industry, there are four kinds of illegal activities that fall under the music piracy umbrella: physical music piracy, counterfeit, bootlegs, and Internet piracy.

[2]   Like many other oft-used terms describing Internet-related crimes, such a term that includes the medium/instrument (Internet) carrying IP in its name usually distracts the discussions and thereby confuses people.

[3]   One of the four founders was later arrested for the conviction in 2012 in Cambodia.

[4]   According to the Business Software Alliance, a software industry trade association, there are roughly 840,000 Internet sites partaking in the illegal selling of software as the real thing.

[5]   Megaupload at one point was the 13th most visit site online, according to Alexa.com. It was accounted for 4% of worldwide Internet traffic.

This research was previously published in the Encyclopedia of Information Science and Technology, Fourth Edition edited by Mehdi Khosrow-Pour, pages 1656-1666, copyright year 2018 by Information Science Reference (an imprint of IGI Global).

Chapter 7
Secure Group Key Sharing Protocols and Cloud System

Vaishali Ravindra Thakare
VIT University, India

John Singh K
VIT University, India

ABSTRACT

Cloud computing has been envisioned as the next-generation architecture of IT enterprise. Secure and reliable communications have become critical in modern computing. The centralized services like e-mail and file sharing can be changed into distributed or collaborated system through multiple systems and networks. Basic cryptographic requirements such as data confidentiality, data integrity, authentication, and access control are required to build secure collaborative systems in the broadcast channel. For several groupware applications like voice and video conferences, distributed computation over the insecure network, developing an efficient group key agreement protocol for secure communication is required in internet. According to the recent rule released by health and human services (HHS), healthcare data can be outsourced to cloud computing services for medical studies. The aim of this study is to provide the details about secure group data sharing protocols available and how it will be applicable in healthcare cloud applications to share data securely over healthcare cloud.

INTRODUCTION

Secure group communication is an important research issue in the field of cryptography and network security, because group applications like online chatting programs, video conferencing, distributed database, online games etc. is expanding rapidly. Group key agreement protocols allow that all the members agree on the same group key, for secure group communication, and the basic security criteria must be hold. Many group key agreement protocols have been established for secure group communication.

Since the group generation processes takes many modular exponentiations and long time in generation of group key. For achieving higher security, group key protocol should be dynamic, means it should change for each new join or leave member, so that new member have not any knowledge about prior

DOI: 10.4018/978-1-5225-7492-7.ch007

information. Therefore group key management protocol focusing on the group key generation efficiently. The authors have identified the research gaps in the existing protocols and these are communication, computation overhead while generating and sharing digital envelopes and security issues while sharing group key with encryption algorithms. These research problems in existing framework motivate authors to focus on security and efficiency of the system. Many practical systems have been proposed (Liu et al., 2014a, 2015; Pan et al., 2011; Sanchez-Artigas, 2013; Li et al., 2015) of which the most familiar one is the TGDH key distribution system. After analyzing the demand for sharing data with multiple users in groups by reducing computational complexity and for achieving productive benefits, an efficient solution is proposed in this paper.

Modular exponentiation is very expensive in computation of group key. The number of exponentiations for membership depends on group size as when the group size increased the number of exponents will also increase. Tree Based Group Diffie Hellman (TGDH) (Kim et. al., 2004) uses the concept of Diffie-Hellman key exchange with logical tree structure to achieve efficiency. The efficiency of TGDH is O (log2n), where n is the group size. However, some extra overhead occurred in maintaining a perfect key tree balance. Skinny tree has lower communication overhead, but it increases computation. Burmester–Desmedt (BD) distributes and minimizes computation by using more messages broadcast. All these protocols using similar security properties including group key independence. From the broad study it is found that, tree-based CGKA (Contributory Group Key Agreement) methods are more efficient since they reduce the complexity from O (n) to O (log n) while computing the new group key, where n is the group size. Consequently, this unit considers only the existing tree-based CGKA protocols.

BACKGROUND

Group key agreement protocols allow that all the members agree on the same group key, for secure group communication, and the basic security criteria must be hold. In 1994 Mike Burmester and Yvo Desmedt Proposed A Secure and Efficient Conference Key Distribution System (BD Protocol), In 2000 Group Diffie Hellman (GDH) was proposed by Steiner et.al., Skinny Tree (STR) Wong et al. 2000, ID-AGKA (Identity based authenticated group key agreement protocol) by K C Reddy and Divya Nalla in 2002, Kim et al. proposed TGDH (Tree Based Group Diffie Hellman) in 2004, In 2006 CCEGK was proposed by Szheng, Moreover in 2009 QGDH (Queue Based Group Diffie Hellman) by Hong S.

After understanding the real time issues in real time groupware applications like voice & video conferences, distributed computation over the insecure network.

(Zheng et al., 2007) Proposed a two round key agreement protocol for dynamic peer group (DPG). The protocol is proven secure against passive attack by using indistinguishable method. Moreover, both perfect forward secrecy (PFS) and key independence (KI) were achieved. Author's proposed protocol greatly reduces the computation complexity of each member, definite identification and time stamp are added to the protocol to effectively avoid replay attacks and it satisfies PFS, dynamic and it provides a session key for wireless group members due to which its messages are transmitted through broadcasting. Meanwhile, authors proved correctness, tolerance for passive attacks, secure against active adversaries in the random oracle model as the security and efficiency analysis of this protocol.

(Liu et al., 2013) Proposed a secure multi-owner data sharing scheme (Mona) for dynamic groups in cloud applications. The Mona aims to realize that a user can securely share the data with others via the un-trusted cloud servers, and efficiently support dynamic group interactions. In this scheme, a new user can directly decrypt data files without pre-contacting with data owners, and user revocation is achieved by revocation list without updating the secret keys of the remaining users.

(Xue & Hong., 2013) proposed a novel secure group sharing framework for public cloud and it can take the effective advantage of cloud help by taking care that no sensitive data should be exposed to cloud provider and an attacker. It combines proxy signature, enhanced TGDH-based binary tree, proxy re-encryption as a protocol, using which the authors have achieved the objective. In this scheme, authors used TGDH with binary tree to negotiate and update the group key pairs with the help of cloud servers

(Jaiswal & Tripathi., 2015) Proposed an alternative approach to group key agreement, i.e., a novel queue-based group key agreement protocol, which uses the concepts of elliptic curve cryptography to reduce unnecessary delays, considers member diversity with filtering out low performance members in group key generation processes. After analyzing many prior group key agreement protocols like TGDH, STR, BD, and QBDH, they provide better security. They take more computational overheads. So, authors have used elliptic curve cryptographic technique that removes exponentiation to reduce computational overheads, and hence the results are better than that of the other group key agreement protocols.

Figure 1 shows the tree structure of CGKA, the management of secure communication among groups of participants requires a set of secure and efficient operations some protocols are better in communication cost some are in computation of secure group key while some are having security issues. These all protocols fall under CGKA (Contributory Group Key Agreement) scheme. CGKA is further again Divided into two sub categories:

Tree Based-CGKA

STR (Skinny Tree)

The STR protocol is modified to provide dynamic group operations. The protocol has a relatively low communication overhead and is well suited for adding new group members. Robustness is easily provided. However, it is relatively difficult for member exclusion (O(n) modular exponentiation) The GK = $g^{Kn}g^{Kn-1}...g^{K2}g^{K1}$. The STR is communication efficient and it is more secure against attacks specific to group communication

TGDH (Tree Based Group Diffie Hellman)

The first tree based CGKA protocol called TGDH was proposed in which key tree and DH protocol are combined to generate the group key. After comparison of TGDH with STR and GDH protocol. The TGDH is comparatively efficient in join events, and it is best in leave events. The TGDH is more efficient in both computation and communication than GDH. The 'Skinny Tree' (STR) employs the key tree concept used in TGDH. TGDH provides the most efficient group key agreement protocol. The protocol has low communication overhead and low computation overhead (O(logn) modular exponentiation). In addition, TGDH provides robustness. The GK $= g^{g^{g^{K1K2gk3k4........g^{gKn-3Kn-2gKn-1Kn}}}}$

In every operation of TGDH (e.g., Join, merge, leave, and partition), every message uses thebroadcast scheme, so authors implement the initialization operation in TGDH using a broadcast scheme. TGDH key management protocol for dynamic secure group data sharing In ternary tree with TGDH all group members are initially arranged as the leaves of ternary tree and three party TGDH generates the final group key. This generation of group key is done in two stages:

Figure 1. Tree structure of CGKA (contributory group key agreement) protocols

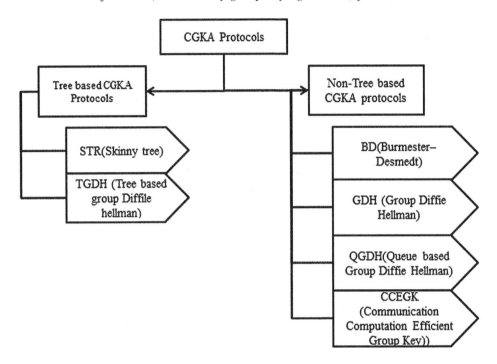

1. Up-flow stage,
2. Down-flow stage.

Consider two prime numbers p and q such that q/p-1 and size of p and q are large enough so that solving the discrete logarithm problem in G is infeasible computational, where G is a subgroup with order q of a finite field Zp* [2] g is the generator. Consider, Alice, Bob and Charlie are three users that generates a shared secret key between them.

Up-flow:

- Alice constwructs a set {g^x mod p} and send it to Bob.
- Bob constructs a set {g^{xy} mod p, g^y mod p, g^x mod p (received from Alice)}. Bob sends this set to Charlie- Similarly, Charlie also construct a set { g^{xyz} mod p, g^{yz} mod p, g^{xz} mod p }.
- Here, gxyz mod p is a cardinal value and treated as a group key K. Where, x, y and z are random numbers assumed by Alice, Bob and Charlie respectively.

Down-flow:

- Charlie broadcast the remaining set element (g^{yz} mod p, g^{xz} mod p) to other members in a group i.e. Alice and Bob.
- Now, every members assumes their random numbers for computing the same group key.
- (Alice => K: $(g^{yz})^x$ mod p and Bob => K: $(g^{xz})^y$ mod p).

Non Tree Based-CGKA

BD (Burmester-Desmedt)

The BD protocol (Burmester and Desmedt, 1994) supports dynamic group operations. The protocol has a relatively low computational overhead due to two modular exponentiations. However, it needs more message exchanges to generate GK. The GK $= g^{K1K2+K2K3+...+Kn-1Kn}$.

GDH (Group Diffie-Hellman)

It provides high security assurance (Cui et. al., 2014). However, it has a relatively high computation cost (O(n) modular exponentiation) and is relatively hard to provide robustness. The GK $= g^{K1K2K3K4...Kn-1Kn}$

QGDH (Queue Based Group Diffie Hellman)

Figure 2 shows Queue-based Group Diffie-Hellman Entity Model (Hong S., 2009, Jaiswal & Tripathi, 2015). In Figure 2, a Group Controller Server (GCS) has a member information DB containing a current login member list, MAC addresses, IDs, Passwords, and Blind Key Queues (BKQ). If each member logins to the GCS, then the GCS will validate his ID, password, and MAC (Media Access Control) address by checking his member information DB. After approving member's identification, all members start to generate a group key by sending his blind key to the GCS who collects all blind keys and store them into the Blind Key Queues (BKQ) in order of arrival. Then the GCS informs participants who will join the next level of the group key generation.

CCEGK (Communication–Computation Efficient Group Key Algorithm)

The CCEGK was developed for large and dynamic groups that combine two existing protocolssuch as EGK and TGDH (Lee et. al., 2003). It outperforms EGK, TGDH and STR protocols. CCEGK designed to provide both efficient communication and computation, addressing performance, security and authentication issues of CCEGK. An analytical comparison of all algorithms revealed eight similar methods: add, remove, merge, split, mass add, mass remove, initialize, and key refresh. Comparing the cost in terms of communication and computation, we found CCEGK to be more efficient across the board. With the

Figure 2. Queue-based group diffie-hellman entity model

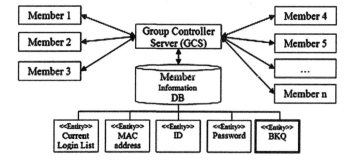

advent of new arenas such as wireless ad-hoc and low powered distributed computing and communication devices, designers of group key encryption algorithms can no longer ignore communication in favor of computation or vice versa. In some environments the power cost of communication may be sufficiently high to warrant low cost communication protocols, whereas in other environments computation cost may be the dominant feature. CCEGK is a group key management algorithm based upon two preceding group key management algorithms, EGK and TGDH By extending this previous work, CCEGK considerably improves both communication and computation costs of their related operations.

CCEGK, as do EGK and STR, always joins at the root of the tree, resulting in potentially far fewer sequential exponentiations. TGDH will join at the root only if the tree is a full tree, in an attempt to keep the tree more balanced. STR, on the other hand always has a skinny tree, where every internal node has one child that is a leaf.

CCEGK, as with EGK, merges the two roots of the trees, resulting in lower cost but a potentially more unbalanced tree. TGDH merges the shallower tree to the deeper one, or at the root, whichever creates the shallowest final tree. STR adds one tree to the bottom of the other.

SOLUTIONS AND COMPARITIVE ANALYSIS OF SECURE GROUP KEY SHARING PROTOCOLS

Group Key Management Operations

Throughout this chapter authors addressed several group key management operations used by group key systems. The operations are described as following:

- **Initialization Operation:** This is the initial creation of the group key and organization of the key management infrastructure.
- **Join:** This operation brings a new member into the existing group.
- **Leave:** This operation is used to remove a member from the group.
- **Partition:** This operation, different from mass leave, occurs when a single group is divided into two or more component groups.
- **Merge:** This operation, as opposed to mass join, is used when another group is combined with the existing group to become a new group.
- **Key Refresh:** To prevent the secret key from becoming stale, it should be changed. Moreover, to prevent an adversary from breaking in, users should refresh the original key and generate a new secret key periodically.
- **Number of Rounds:** This is a generic time unit used to compare the number of steps taken in different operations. The algorithms often require synchronization between rounds; therefore, this number becomes important when taking synchronization time into account.
- **Number of Messages:** This is the sum of all unicast messages and broadcast messages. users use this number to determine the total time of communication in an underlying broadcast network.

- **Number of Exponentiations:** During an operation there will be a series of computationally expensive cryptographic operations (such as modular exponentiation used in the DH algorithm). The algorithms in the literature often require the results of one cryptographic operation prior to the execution of another. This metric represents the worst case scenario, the longest sequence of dependencies of these costly cryptographic operations in the operation.

The authors of this article have analyzed many existing group key agreement protocols like TGDH, STR, BD, QBDH and CCEGK. They provide better security, but some take more computational overheads, some take more communication overhead. So, Following Table 1 shows communication and computation cost analysis of Tree Based-CGKA Protocols and Table 2 shows communication and computation cost analysis of Non Tree Based-CGKA Protocols.

FUTURE RESEARCH DIRECTIONS

Recently, group data sharing (GDS) has attracted significant attention for its wide applications in many different fields. A GDS can be seen as a special dynamic and distributed group, so the secure communication is essential in it. Surely, the most common method is to encrypt messages with a group key only shared by the included nodes, so that those outside the group cannot decode the encrypted messages. Thus, the protocol to achieve the group shared key is crucial, which users often name the *key agreement protocol*.

Table 1. Communication and computation cost analysis of tree based-CGKA protocols

Tree Based CGKA Protocols		Communication Cost		Computation Cost
		Rounds	**Messages**	**Exponentiation**
STR	Join	2	3	4
	Leave	1	1	$\frac{3n}{2}+2$
	Partition	1	1	$\frac{3n}{2}+2$
	Merge	2	k+1	3m+1
TGDH	Join	2	3	$\frac{3n}{2}$
	Leave	1	1	$\frac{3n}{2}$
	Partition	$\mathrm{Min}(\log_2 p, h)$	2h	3n
	Merge	$\log_2 k + 1$	2k	$\frac{3n}{2}$

Table 2. Communication and computation cost analysis of non tree based-CGKA protocols

Non Tree Based CGKA Protocols		Communication Cost		Computation Cost
		Rounds	Messages	Exponentiation
BD	Join	2	2n+2	3
	Leave	2	2n-2	3
	Partition	2	2n-2p	3
	Merge	2	2n+2m	3
GDH	Join	4	n+3	n+3
	Leave	1	1	n-1
	Partition	1	1	n-p
	Merge	m+3	n+2m+1	n+2m+1
QDGH	Join	2	2n-2	$\dfrac{3(\log_2 n)}{2}$
	Leave	1	2n-2	$\dfrac{3(\log_2 n)}{2}$
	Partition	1	2n-2	$3(\log_2 n)$
	Merge	2	2n-2	$\dfrac{3(\log_2 n)}{2}$
CCEGK	Join	1	2	1
	Leave	1	1	3h-3
	Merge	1	N	n-1

Over the years, numerous excellent key agreement protocols for dynamic peer group have been proposed, such as the GDH, TGDH and extended STR protocols. However, not all of them are communication efficient when applied to cloud networks. All of these have better security built-ins. Now a day in every fields cloud computing is used, health care, IT industries, small and medium enterprises (SMEs). So, The scope of these protocols is everywhere widely growing because of the requirements of the changing world towards cloud computing. There will be various kinds of requirements of healthcare organizations, as healthcare organizations are the primary priority in every country, Healthcare clouds must be as secure as possible. According to the organizations requirements healthcare cloud groups will be formed for the secure communication between other organizations in healthcare and these protocols will take care about security and confidential data, communication and computation overheads.

CONCLUSION

Data sharing in cloud environment by forming groups is considered as a common approach. But secure data sharing in groups is still a challenging issue for the researchers. There are many frameworks available to share data in groups in the previous researches listed in above discussion of this chapter, after analyzing the existing frameworks drawbacks; it is found the tree based CGKA protocols are more efficient than others. From Table 2, TGDH is better protocol for secure group data sharing and it can be used in healthcare cloud applications. From Table 3, CCEGK protocol is better but it is non-tree CGKA protocol but its communication and computation overhead cost is lesser than the BD, GDH and QGDH protocols.

REFERENCES

Burmester, M., & Desmedt, Y. (1994, May). A secure and efficient conference key distribution system. In *Workshop on the Theory and Application of of Cryptographic Techniques* (pp. 275-286). Springer Berlin Heidelberg.

Cui, Y., Peng, Z., Song, W., Li, X., Cheng, F., & Ding, L. (2014, September). A Time-Based Group Key Management Algorithm Based on Proxy Re-encryption for Cloud Storage. In *Asia-Pacific Web Conference* (pp. 117-128). Springer International Publishing. 10.1007/978-3-319-11116-2_11

Hong, S. (2009). Queue-based Group Key Agreement Protocol. *International Journal of Network Security*, *9*(2), 135–142.

Jaiswal, P., Kumar, A., & Tripathi, S. (2015). Design of Queue-Based Group Key Agreement Protocol Using Elliptic Curve Cryptography. In *Information Systems Design and Intelligent Applications* (pp. 167–176). Springer India. doi:10.1007/978-81-322-2250-7_17

Kim, Y., Perrig, A., & Tsudik, G. (2004). Tree-based group key agreement. *ACM Transactions on Information and System Security*, *7*(1), 60–96. doi:10.1145/984334.984337

Lee, S., Kim, Y., Kim, K., & Ryu, D. H. (2003, October). An efficient tree-based group key agreement using bilinear map. In *International Conference on Applied Cryptography and Network Security* (pp. 357-371). Springer Berlin Heidelberg. 10.1007/978-3-540-45203-4_28

Liu, X., Zhang, Y., Wang, B., & Yan, J. (2013). Mona: Secure multi-owner data sharing for dynamic groups in the cloud. *IEEE Transactions on Parallel and Distributed Systems*, *24*(6), 1182–1191. doi:10.1109/TPDS.2012.331

Renugadevi, N., & Mala, C. (2014). Tree based group key agreement–a survey for cognitive radio mobile ad hoc networks. In Advanced Computing, Networking and Informatics (vol. 2, pp. 85-94). Springer International Publishing. doi:10.1007/978-3-319-07350-7_10

Shi, H., He, M., & Qin, Z. (2006, December). Authenticated and communication efficient group key agreement for clustered ad hoc networks. In *International Conference on Cryptology and Network Security* (pp. 73-89). Springer Berlin Heidelberg. 10.1007/11935070_5

Steiner, M., Tsudik, G., & Waidner, M. (2000). Key agreement in dynamic peer groups. *IEEE Transactions on Parallel and Distributed Systems*, *11*(8), 769–780. doi:10.1109/71.877936

Wong, C. K., Gouda, M., & Lam, S. S. (2000). Secure group communications using key graphs. *IEEE/ACM Transactions on Networking*, *8*(1), 16–30. doi:10.1109/90.836475

Xue, K., & Hong, P. (2014). A dynamic secure group sharing framework in public cloud computing. *IEEE Transactions on Cloud Computing*, *2*(4), 459–470. doi:10.1109/TCC.2014.2366152

Zheng, S., Manz, D., & Alves-Foss, J. (2007). A communication–computation efficient group key algorithm for large and dynamic groups. *Computer Networks*, *51*(1), 69–93. doi:10.1016/j.comnet.2006.03.008

Zheng, S., Wang, S., & Zhang, G. (2007). A dynamic, secure, and efficient group key agreement protocol. *Frontiers of Electrical and Electronic Engineering in China*, *2*(2), 182–185. doi:10.100711460-007-0034-7

Zou, X., Ramamurthy, B., & Magliveras, S. S. (2005). Dynamic Conferencing Schemes. *Secure Group Communications over Data Networks*, 91-103.

Zou, X., Ramamurthy, B., & Magliveras, S. S. (2005). Tree Based Key Management Schemes. *Secure Group Communications over Data Networks*, 49-89.

ADDITIONAL READING

Asokan, N., & Ginzboorg, P. (2000). Key agreement in ad hoc networks. *Computer Communications*, *23*(17), 1627–1637. doi:10.1016/S0140-3664(00)00249-8

Kim, Y., Perrig, A., & Tsudik, G. (2004). Group key agreement efficient in communication. *IEEE Transactions on Computers*, *53*(7), 905–921. doi:10.1109/TC.2004.31

Kumar, A., & Tripathi, S. (2014). Ternary Tree based Group Key Agreement Protocol Over Elliptic Curve for Dynamic Group. *International Journal of Computers and Applications*, *86*(7).

Roman, A., & Szykuła, M. (2015). Forward and backward synchronizing algorithms. *Expert Systems with Applications*, *42*(24), 9512–9527. doi:10.1016/j.eswa.2015.07.071

Samanthula, B. K., Elmehdwi, Y., Howser, G., & Madria, S. (2015). A secure data sharing and query processing framework via federation of cloud computing. *Information Systems*, *48*, 196–212. doi:10.1016/j.is.2013.08.004

Sanchez-Artigas, M. (2013). Toward efficient data access privacy in the cloud. *IEEE Communications Magazine*, *51*(11), 39–45. doi:10.1109/MCOM.2013.6658650

Tripathi, S., & Biswas, G. P. (2009, January). Design of efficient ternary-tree based group key agreement protocol for dynamic groups. In *2009 First International Communication Systems and Networks and Workshops* (pp. 1-6). IEEE. doi:10.1109/COMSNETS.2009.4808834

Wang, L. L., Chen, K. F., Mao, X. P., & Wang, Y. T. (2014). Efficient and provably-secure certificateless proxy re-encryption scheme for secure cloud data sharing. *Journal of Shanghai Jiaotong University (Science), 19*(4), 398–405. doi:10.100712204-014-1514-6

KEY TERMS AND DEFINITIONS

Cloud Computing System: Cloud computing is a model for delivering information technology services in which resources are retrieved from the internet through web-based tools and applications rather than a direct connection to a server.

Computational Complexity: A mathematical characterization of the difficulty of a computing group key which describes the resources required by a computing machine to compute the group key. The mathematical study of such characterizations is called computational complexity theory and is important in many branches of theoretical computer science, especially cryptography.

Proxy Re-Encryption: Proxy re-encryption schemes are cryptosystems which allow third parties (proxies) to alter a ciphertext which has been encrypted for one party, so that it may be decrypted by another.

Proxy Signature: Proxy signature, which allows an original signer to delegate his/her signing right to another party (or proxy signer), is very useful in many applications.

Section 3
Cyber and Network Security

Chapter 8

Security of Internet-, Intranet-, and Computer-Based Examinations in Terms of Technical, Authentication, and Environmental, Where Are We?

Babak Sokouti
Tabriz University of Medical Sciences, Iran

Massoud Sokouti
Mashhad University of Medical Sciences, Iran

ABSTRACT

Worldwide, increasing trends on distance learning provided by different educational and academic organizations require robust secure environments for carrying out the distance examinations. The security of online examinations is prone to many threats including the local cheaters and outside attackers. Several studies have been carried out in terms of technical, authentication algorithms, and environmental monitoring (supervised or unsupervised). None of these categories can satisfy the required security services to stop candidate cheating during the examination. A robust secure model will be needed to include all three categories in order to provide secure environments for examinees while no manual supervision is required by proctor or professors.

INTRODUCTION

Over the past decades, the use of Internet and its various applications in several environments such as academic communities and industries has been dramatically increased. Fundamental aspects of these applications are commonly related to sending and receiving small or large amounts of data through the local or global network communications. Transferring data over the insecure tunnel of Internet requires applying security services when especially the sensitive data are involved. The main security services

DOI: 10.4018/978-1-5225-7492-7.ch008

are confidentiality, integrity, and availability namely called the CIA triad. The recent advancements in computer networking lead many technologies to be solely or partly upgraded their traditional environments into e-environments and hence, dependent on electronic-based objects such as e-mail and digitalized records and images. The security of shared or archived data or information personally or in organizations are vital and important due to the development of information science in modern society with everyday dramatically increase. Because of its rapid changing nature driven mostly by technology such as smart phones and development of new virtual communities, there are several demands for generating information systems in which security properties play vital roles. By considering these developments, the e-learning parts of academic communities (i.e., online education) at universities have been affected in order to keep up with the knowledge innovation and they also provide some of their degrees and courses in a distance-based structure by taking the advantage of web-based infrastructures such as LMS (Learning Management System) and MOODLE (Modular Object- Oriented Dynamic Learning Environment). And, this makes the research areas open for modern education era to conduct paperless examinations by providing more security and efficiency. Although, this technological transition in the educational section is to some extent valuable and time effective, however, in most cases the evaluations and examinations of examinee are carried out and monitored in a supervised manner. Precisely speaking, for taking an exam in a traditional examination environment generally examinees, proctors, professors, pen and exam papers and a secure or isolated examining hall are included. For implementing such exams in a distance- or electronic-based model, many security issues whether they are technical or environmental are raised and essential to be resolved. In this regard, an examinee may take the exam alone at home; the professor makes the exam questions and sends them to a web server; the proctors' role can be performed supervised or unsupervised; the sufficient security measurements should be in place of e-exam's environments.

As of now, providing the most of security services for unsupervised e-exams is still in its infancy and needs much of attention to be taken in to consideration, however, most of technical and communication-based security issues have been addressed in abundance.

In this chapter, the literature researches carried out on potential security aspects of conducting a robust secure e-exam are discussed, then their pros and cons with respect to their provided security services are evaluated and reviewed, and finally a hybrid security model for satisfying most of security properties will be proposed as a secure e-exam model for all conditions along with negotiating future directions.

BACKGROUND

For managing and conducting any types of e-exam systems, literature researchers have performed diverse studies considering special security aspects of them whether they are supervised or unsupervised including technical (e,g,. networking, question generation, servers, clients), examinee authentication and identification (e.g., passwords, tokens, and biometrics), environmental monitoring (e.g., webcams, microphones) for preventing possible cheatings during the examination period. Nowadays, for universities providing distance learning courses and degrees are getting epidemically widespread and educationally of much of interest over the world. To survey the current position of state of art related to online exams considering the security aspects, the SCOPUS database is searched and reviewed with the keywords "online" AND "exam" AND "security" in which 19 out of 49 were filtered out based on their relevant contents (i.e., by using title and abstract) for this study. However, one out of 19 was proposed as a web tool for teachers and did not discuss the security aspects of the online examinations (Castillo-Ramoran, 2008).

In order to prevent various types of cheatings, some of the supervised approaches are carried out by employing video and audio devices such as webcams and microphones, biometric recognition tools, manually controlling the port and IP of the connected network devices most of which are relevant case studies for their classrooms in the local area networks (LANs) (Bari, Sullivan, & Blair, 2004; Jung & Yeom, 2009; Savulescu, Polkowski, & Alexandru, 2015). However, these environments are monitored manually via instructor-student networking communications.

From technical point of view and assuming that the only security problems can be carried out by outside attackers, Ming-Ming and Yan have proposed a simple security environment by considering only the data encryption by using triple DES algorithm and secure communication channel (i.e., virtual private network (VPN)) for secure connection of students and stopping the outside attackers (Ming-Ming & Yan, 2013). Also recently, a simple secure computer based examination was also carried out using the B/S structure (Singh & Tiwari, 2016). Another two approaches were conducted as frameworks in which the security countermeasures and the access control to the database servers (e.g., SQL server) were considered (Darong & Huimin, 2010; Hai-yan, GHong, Lijun, & Jie, 2014).

For physically distance monitoring of a classroom or a room in which online exams were conducted, an environmental based secure framework was proposed by Stocco and colleagues by incorporating sets of logical and physical sensors (Stocco, Otsuka, & Beder, 2012). Employing the logical architecture of object oriented business application which has five layers including interface layer, interface control business layer, data access, and data storage and management will also bring some advantages (Basar & Haji-zada, 2014). These pros are summarized in scalability, flexibility, and security (Basar & Haji-zada, 2014). So, only the network access manages to stop all types of attacks applied on local and global networks. In other study, the authors have considered four phases (i.e., registration, examination, marking, and notification) for providing security properties (Giustolisi, Lenzini, & Bella, 2013). In these phases, eligibility, identification, authorization, authentication, authorship, integrity, anonymous marking, mark integrity and privacy are of great importance. Another type of supervised framework is the study which incorporates both teacher and manager to monitor and manage the students during the online exams by considering security properties such as authenticity, privacy, secrecy, receipt of exam answer and copy detection (Castella-Roca, Herrera-Joancomarti, & CDorca-Josa, 2006). During the technological improvements, tablets with their built-in cameras took researchers attentions to develop secure apps for their courses (Gramoll, 2015).

The remaining literature studies have discussed the security properties of the online based examinations in terms of cryptographic algorithms in order to authenticate exam candidates(Karim & Shukur, 2015).Karim and Shukur have demonstrated a review on the list of various authentication methods derived from different databases including Scopus, IEEE Xplore, Springer link, Science Direct, ACM, and Google Scolar(Karim & Shukur, 2015). Some of the samples of the review performed by Karim and Shukur took the advantages of uni or multi authentication methods using biometric properties along with/without username and password each of which have their own strengths and weaknesses. The biometric features include palm print(Al-Saleem & Ullah, 2014), keystroke dynamic, voice recognition, stylometry, face recognition, iris recognition, mouse movements, and hand writing (Karim & Shukur, 2015). Besides these, use of challenge questions (Ullah, Xiao, Barker, & Lilley, 2014) and IP addresses with timestamps (Gao, 2012) are other methods to mention a few.

A typical multimodal biometric technology embedded for authenticating the candidates was proposed to enhance the security of the users' authentication (Asha & Chellappan, 2008). This dynamic based authentication incorporates the physiological (fingerprint technology) and behavioral (mouse dynamics) properties of the user by means of a mouse device with built-in fingerprint scanner (Asha & Chellappan, 2008). An interactive and secure e-examination unit (ISEEU) was proposed by Sabbah and colleagues where its one-on–one supervised based framework makes it good for continuous authentication using webcams during the video calls in order to reduce the potential user cheatings (Sabbah, Saroit, & Kotb, 2011) by considering that for having a secure environment three user security properties including identity, authentication, and presence should be checked continuously. Moreover, checking the presence via tracking the timestamp having been spent in front of the computer have also discussed elsewhere (Agulla, Rifon, Castro, & Mateo, 2008). It has also been shown that using the keystroke recognition on long-text input under different conditions has less accuracies while different devices in terms of laptop and desktop pc are used which is not applicable for real world conditions (Villani et al., 2006).

Although, these available research papers have proposed, assessed and emphasized on different aspects of security issues related to electronic-based or online exams, however, there are no robust models or protocols to satisfy all security aspects.

MAIN FOCUS OF THE ARTICLE

Issues, Controversies, Problems

Based on the abovementioned literature articles published in the theme of online-exams in terms of security issues, it can be deduced that all of them are not proposed as a whole response for providing and considering all aspects of security. Some of them were only technical based and required information security protocols and standards for a network engineer to meet the essential security measures. On the other hand, several algorithms and approaches were proposed in order to authenticate the user by incorporating several aspects of authentication whether they were used in a uni or multi factor authentication using properties for "What you are" (i.e., it can satisfied by providing biometric features), "What you have" (i.e., it can be met by a token), and "What you know" (i.e., username and password or multiple question challenges). However, more terms also need to be considered such as "Where you are" and "What you do" that can be checked by monitoring the target environment using video calls, surveillance cams and web cams. Most of recent studies do only satisfy one, two or three out of abovementioned terms which are not a complete answer for having a secure online-examination environment.

These three categories including technical, authentication, and monitoring of the environment are studied several times but not all together in the literature by its special category. However, they have still their own threats and issues in terms of security and still need more researches on proposing new cryptographic algorithms for identification and authentication in different situations.

SOLUTIONS AND RECOMMENDATIONS

By considering the strengths and weaknesses of the approaches studied in the themes of three categories, none of the categories alone by themselves can be enough for meeting the required security properties that have been discussed before. So, for having a comprehensive security model which includes all five security services shown in Figure 1, it is required to merge all three categories to one and took the advantages of the resulted model in all online exams whether they are taken in a local or global network. By incorporating all of three categories with various combinations, one may conclude that the current model will satisfy all the security properties required for stopping the users' cheating in any types of local positions or internet based conditions.

In other words, by implementing the unsupervised online exam environments one must be assured of that all of the security services listed in Figure 1 are in place. For example, providing technical security is solely depending on the local or global administrators' opinion in order to stop any types of insider (i.., student, manager, and teacher) and outsider attacks, denial of services (DOS), distributed denial of service (DDOS), and replay attacks by setting up required security countermeasures such as securing the network communication channels (VPNs), data encryption, tracking timestamps, and etc. For the sake of user authentication depending on the situation, username and passwords, tokens, and multi biometric (e.g., fingerprint, mouse dynamics) features are required as one multi authentication package. And finally, the security needs required for an unsupervised situation, several environmental monitoring devices should be employed such as behavioral and movement sensors, webcams, and environmental microphones.

FUTURE RESEARCH DIRECTIONS

Nowadays, the shadow of security can be seen spreading its wings all over the technology ranging from the intelligent tablets to professional laptops and new car products. The improvements covering all aspects of an object which may include the hardware and technology, software and applications, and cryptographic algorithms and their assessments (i.e., encryption, decryption, digital signatures, key

Figure 1. Required security services for a secure online examination

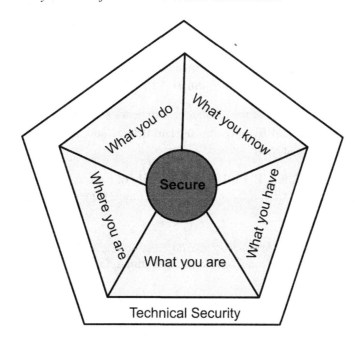

generations) (Bahar, Sokouti, & Sokouti, 2010; M. Sokouti, Sokouti, & Pashazadeh, 2009; Massoud Sokouti, Sokouti, Pashazadeh, Feizi-Derakhshi, & Haghipour, 2013; M. Sokouti, Sokouti, Pashazadeh, & Khanli, 2010; M. Sokouti, Zakerolhosseini, & Sokouti, 2014) will have extensive effects on the performance of online exams in terms of security.

Moreover, in the future studies it is essential for the authors to provide a web site or database server of their implementations as it can be seen widely in the bioinformatics and systems biology realm (B. Sokouti, Church, Morris, & Dastmalchi, 2015; B. Sokouti, Rezvan, & Dastmalchi, 2015, 2016; B Sokouti, Rezvan, Yachdav, & Dastmalchi, 2014). This will help the researchers assessing their new conducted model or algorithms with previously published approaches.

The last but not the least, it is sometimes recommended to assess and find out the shortcomings of the existing methodologies in order to improve them rather than implement an unknown method with high risks of security issues.

CONCLUSION

In this chapter, security aspects of online exams in different situations were discussed. Three categories of the research interest including technical, authentication methodologies, and environmental monitoring were also covered in terms of both supervised and unsupervised. Moreover, based on the shortcomings and weaknesses in all three categories, a new security model can be carried out considering various combinations of these categories to reach a gold standard and a secure framework for online exams without any types of cheatings.

REFERENCES

Agulla, E. G., Rifon, L. A., Castro, J. L. A., & Mateo, C. G. (2008). *Is my studnet at the other side? applying biometric web authenntication to e-learning environments*. Paper presented at the Eighth IEEE International Conference on Advanced Learning Technologies. 10.1109/ICALT.2008.184

Al-Saleem, S. M., & Ullah, H. (2014). Security considerations and recommendations in computer-based t esting. *TheScientificWorldJournal*, *2014*, 1–7. doi:10.1155/2014/562787 PMID:25254250

Asha, S., & Chellappan, C. (2008). *Authentication of E-learners using multimodal biometric technology*. Paper presented at the International Symposium on Biometrics and Security Technologies (ISBAST 2008). 10.1109/ISBAST.2008.4547640

Bahar, H. B., Sokouti, M., & Sokouti, B. (2010). A first study of improving transposition cryptosystem. *Journal of Discrete Mathematical Sciences and Cryptography*, *13*(1), 1–9. doi:10.1080/09720529.201 0.10698272

Bari, J., Sullivan, R., & Blair, J. (2004). *Security method in distance-learning*. Paper presented at the 34th ASEE/IEEE Frontiers in Education Conference, Savannah, GA.

Basar, E., & Haji-zada, T. (2014). *Object oriented business archtechture on online-exam and assignment system*. Paper presented at the 25th Annual Conference EAEEIE.

Castella-Roca, J., & Herrera-Joancomarti, J., & CDorca-Josa, A. (2006). *A secure E-exam management system*. Paper presented at the Proceedings of the 1st International Conference on Availability, Reliability and Security (ARES'06). 10.1109/ARES.2006.14

Castillo-Ramoran, V. (2008). *Web tool for teachers: Information systems on categorized teacher materials and online examination. In Innovative Techniques in Instruction Technology, E-learning, E-assessment, and Education* (pp. 570–575). Springer Science-Business Media.

Darong, H., & Huimin, H. (2010). *Realiation and research of online exam system based on S2SH framework*. Paper presented at the International Conference on Web Information Systems and Mining.

Gao, Q. (2012). Biometric Authentication to Prevent e-Cheating. *International Journal of Instructional Technology & Distance Learning, 9*(2), 3–13.

Giustolisi, R., Lenzini, G., & Bella, G. (2013). *What security for electornic exams?* Paper presented at the International Conference on Risks and Security of Intrnet and Systems (CRiSIS'13).

Gramoll, K. C. (2015). *Development and implementation of a tablet-based exam app for engineering course*. Paper presented at the 122nd ASEE Annual Conference & Exposition, Seattle, WA. 10.18260/p.23850

Hai-yan, L. V., GHong, L. V., Lijun, Z., & Jie, Z. (2014). *Research and design of the common curriculum online examination system that used in military academies*. Paper presented at the 2nd International Conference on Information Technology and Electronic Commerce (ICITEC 2014), Dalian, China. 10.1109/ICITEC.2014.7105585

Jung, I. Y., & Yeom, H. Y. (2009). Enhanced security for online exams using group cryptography. *IEEE Transactions on Education, 52*(3), 340–349. doi:10.1109/TE.2008.928909

Karim, N. A., & Shukur, Z. (2015). Review of user authentication methods in online examination. *Asian Journal of Information Technology, 14*(5), 166–175.

Ming-Ming, F., & Yan, M. (2013). The online examination system of distance education. *Applied Mechanics and Matrials, 411-414*, 2901–2905. doi:10.4028/www.scientific.net/AMM.411-414.2901

Sabbah, Y., Saroit, I., & Kotb, A. (2011). *An interactive and secure e-examination unit (ISEEU)*. Paper presented at the 10th Roedunet International Conference (RoEduNet2011). 10.1109/RoEduNet.2011.5993713

Savulescu, C., Polkowski, Z., & Alexandru, A. I. (2015). *The online and computer aided assessment*. Paper presented at the ECAI 2015-International Conference on Electronics, Computers, and Artificial Intelligence, Bucharest, Romania. 10.1109/ECAI.2015.7301226

Singh, S. K., & Tiwari, A. K. (2016). Design and implementation of secure computer based examination system based on B/S structure. *International Journal of Applied Engineering Research, 11*(1), 312–318.

Sokouti, B., Church, W. B., Morris, M. B., & Dastmalchi, S. (2015). Structural and Computational Approaches in Drug Design for G Protein-Coupled Receptors. In M. Khosrow-Pour (Ed.), *Encyclopedia of Information Science and Technology* (pp. 479–489). Hershey, PA: IGI Global. doi:10.4018/978-1-4666-5888-2.ch046

Sokouti, B., Rezvan, F., & Dastmalchi, S. (2015). Applying random forest and subtractive fuzzy c-means clustering techniques for the development of a novel G protein-coupled receptor discrimination method using pseudo amino acid compositions. *Molecular BioSystems*, *11*(8), 2364–2372. doi:10.1039/C5MB00192G PMID:26108102

Sokouti, B., Rezvan, F., & Dastmalchi, S. (2017). GPCRTOP v.1.0: One-step web server for both predicting helical transmembrane segments and identifying G protein-coupled receptors. *Current Bioinformatics*, *12*(1), 80-84. doi:10.2174/1574893611666160901122236

Sokouti, B., Rezvan, F., Yachdav, G., & Dastmalchi, S. (2014). GPCRTOP: A novel G protein-coupled receptor topology prediction method based on hidden Markov model approach using Viterbi algorithm. *Current Bioinformatics*, *9*(4), 442–451. doi:10.2174/1574893609666140516010018

Sokouti, M., Sokouti, B., & Pashazadeh, S. (2009). An Approach in Improving Transposition Cipher System. *Indian Journal of Science and Technology*, *2*(8), 9–15.

Sokouti, M., Sokouti, B., Pashazadeh, S., Feizi-Derakhshi, M.-R., & Haghipour, S. (2013). Genetic-based random key generator (GRKG): A new method for generating more-random keys for one-time pad cryptosystem. *Neural Computing & Applications*, *22*(7), 1667–1675. doi:10.100700521-011-0799-8

Sokouti, M., Sokouti, B., Pashazadeh, S., & Khanli, L. M. (2010). FPGA Implementation of Improved Version of Vigenere Cipher. *Indian Journal of Science and Technology*, *3*(4), 459–462.

Sokouti, M., Zakerolhosseini, A., & Sokouti, B. (2014). Improvements over GGH Using Commutative and Non-Commutative Algebra. In M. Khosrow-Pour (Ed.), *Encyclopedia of Information Science and Technology* (3rd ed.; pp. 3404–3418). IGI-Global.

Stocco, J. A., Otsuka, J. L., & Beder, D. M. (2012). *Logical and physical sensor-based online assessment security support.* Paper presented at the 12th IEEE International Conference on Advanced Learning Technologies.

Ullah, A., Xiao, H., Barker, T., & Lilley, M. (2014). Evaluating security and usability of profile based challenge questions authentication in online examinations. *Journal of Internet Services and Applications*, *5*(2), 1–16.

Villani, M., Tappert, C., Ngo, G., Simone, J., Fort, H. S., & Cha, S.-H. (2006). *Keystroke bimetric recognistion studies on long-text input under ideal and application-oriented conditions.* Paper presented at the IEEE Proceedings of the 2006 Conference on Computer Vision and Pattern Recognistion Workshop (CVPRW'06). 10.1109/CVPRW.2006.115

ADDITIONAL READING

Baumgart, D. C., Wende, I., & Grittner, U. (2016). Tablet computer-based multimedia enhanced medical training improves performance in gastroenterology and endoscopy board style exam compared with traditional medical education. *Gut*, *65*(3), 535–536. doi:10.1136/gutjnl-2015-309895 PMID:26123026

Blevins, A., & Besaw, M. E. (2011). Reflecting on quiz placement in online tutorials: Creating a more active learning experience. *Medical Reference Services Quarterly*, *30*(3), 316–324. doi:10.1080/02763 869.2011.590427 PMID:21800988

Emery, M. (2010). With no shelf exam available, SAEM online clerkship testing tool best option. *Academic Emergency Medicine*, *17*(9), 1028, author reply 1029. doi:10.1111/j.1553-2712.2010.00855.x PMID:20836790

Gibson, S. I. (2015). Promoting an active form of learning out-of-class via answering online study questions leads to higher than expected exam scores in General Biology. *PeerJ*, *3*, e1322. doi:10.7717/ peerj.1322 PMID:26500828

Glatz, K., Savic, S., Glatz, D., Francz, G., Barascud, A., Grilli, B., ... Bubendorf, L. (2006). An online quiz uncovers limitations of morphology in equivocal lung cytology. *Cancer*, *108*(6), 480–487. doi:10.1002/ cncr.22286 PMID:17091509

Gray, J., & Jackson, C. (2004). The development of an online quiz for drug calculations. *Nursing Times*, *100*(4), 40–41. PMID:14974263

Johnson, B. C., & Kiviniemi, M. T. (2009). The Effect of Online Chapter Quizzes on Exam Performance in an Undergraduate Social Psychology Course. *Teaching of Psychology*, *36*(1), 33–37. doi:10.1080/00986280802528972 PMID:20046908

Khan, R., Krupinski, E., Graham, J. A., Benodin, L., & Lewis, P. (2012). Assessing first year radiology resident competence pre-call: Development and implementation of a computer-based exam before and after the 12 month training requirement. *Academic Radiology*, *19*(6), 752–758. doi:10.1016/j. acra.2011.12.019 PMID:22297203

Metz, A. M. (2008). The effect of access time on online quiz performance in large biology lecture courses. *Biochemistry and Molecular Biology Education*, *36*(3), 196–202. doi:10.1002/bmb.20184 PMID:21591191

KEY TERMS AND DEFINITIONS

Authentication: A process for knowing if someone who he is declared to be.

Availability: A guarantee for an information resource being accessed all the time by authorized users.
CIA Triad: There most required ones for security services (i.e., Confidentiality, Integrity, and Availability).

Confidentiality: A security service equivalent to privacy which can be achieved by encrypting the message using a cryptographic algorithm.

Identification: It is related to the identity of a person who claims about it.

Integrity: An assurance for information not being altered or changed during the communication.

Online Exam: A type of exam which can be taken overseas or locally with or without manual supervision.

This research was previously published in the Encyclopedia of Information Science and Technology, Fourth Edition edited by Mehdi Khosrow-Pour, pages 1676-1683, copyright year 2018 by Information Science Reference (an imprint of IGI Global).

Chapter 9
A Three–Vector Approach to Blind Spots in Cybersecurity

Mika Westerlund
Carleton University, Canada

Dan Craigen
Carleton University, Canada

Tony Bailetti
Carleton University, Canada

Uruemu Agwae
Carleton University, Canada

ABSTRACT

Cyberattacks are often successful due to "blind spots": biases and preconceived information that affect human decision making. Blind spots that obstruct a person's view of malicious activity may result in massive economic losses. This chapter examines eight cases of successful cyberattacks from economic, technological, and psychological perspectives to blind spots, termed the "core vectors." While previous research has focused on these vectors in isolation, this chapter combines the vectors for an integrated view. As a result, the chapter provides a novel list of blind spots that enable cybercrime.

INTRODUCTION

With the increased use of network technologies (Clements & Kirham, 2010), cybercrime is on the rise. PricewaterhouseCoopers estimates that 120,000 cyberattacks occur daily (PwC, 2016). There is a need for cybersecurity throughout society. Cybersecurity is defined as "the organization and collection of resources, processes, and structures used to protect cyberspace and cyberspace-enabled systems from occurrences that misalign de jure from de facto property rights" (Craigen, Diakun-Thibault, & Purse, 2014). It is also the measure of preparedness including recovery, protection, and triage against the losses caused by cyberattacks (Maughan, 2010).

DOI: 10.4018/978-1-5225-7492-7.ch009

Cybersecurity is key for protecting valuable assets such as intellectual property, virtual currencies, and industrial control systems (Kritzinger & Solms, 2010; Smith & Rupp, 2002). However, cyberattacks are often successful due to "blind spots," which refer to various biases and preconceived information that affects organizational and human decision making (Heuer, 1999; Pronin, Lin, & Ross, 2002), leading to unawareness of malicious activity (Boehm & Turner, 2005). It is important to understand how to mitigate all blind spots, particularly those that can lead to massive economic losses (Flowers, Zeadally, & Murray, 2013).

The objective of this chapter is to investigate eight cyberattack cases ("attack scenarios") from the viewpoint of "the core vectors" which include economic, technological and psychological perspectives to blind spots. While previous research has viewed core vectors in isolation from each other (Baker, 2014; Garfinkel, 2012; Singer & Friedman, 2014), this chapter focuses on how to mitigate blind spots in cybersecurity by using a holistic three-vector approach. The holistic view to cybersecurity has been suggested by many authors (Emami-Taba, Amoui, & Tahvildari, 2013; Hua & Bapna 2013; Hughes & Cybenko, 2013).

Section one provides an overview of cyberattacks and blind spots that enable attacks. Section two discusses core vectors conceptualized as psychological, economic, and technical perspectives to blind spots. Sections three and four discuss research methods and eight scenario cases. Section five presents a summary table of the cases included in the sample. Finally, sections six and seven discuss future research avenues and implications to practice.

BACKGROUND

Han and Dongre (2014) list political, economic, and socio-cultural motives as primary motives for cyberattacks, and emphasize that attackers can be organizational insiders or outsiders. Political motives include cyber terrorism against foreign nations or multinationals (Hua & Bapna, 2013) and ethically fighting for justice and human rights (Gandhi et al., 2011). Other motives may be plain entertainment. Regardless, there is a propensity for harm when cyberattacks occur. Understanding what enables these attacks enables mitigation, and will contribute to the theory on blind spots in cybersecurity (Chen, Huang, Xu, & Lai, 2015; Nathan & Petrosino, 2003).

Blind spots are dangerous because they are about biases and preconceptions (Pronin et al., 2002). Humans tend to interpret new information so that prior conclusions remain intact. A 2012 survey by the National Cyber Security Alliance (NCSA) and Symantec revealed that 83% of small U.S. companies did not have a formal plan for keeping their business cyber-secure although over 70% responded that a safe and trusted Internet is critical to their day-to-day operations. A total of 76% thought that their company was safe from cyber-security breaches.

Given that blind spots are inevitable, there is a need to develop more efficient means to mitigate them. Thus, it is critical to understand how (i) the business, (ii) the psychological, and (iii) the technological perspectives might help organizations and individuals to recognize and avoid blind spots. This core vector thinking is supported by the cybersecurity assessment factors by Gavins and Hemenway (2010) and the categorization of attacker motivations by Han and Dongre (2014). Combining vectors enables a comprehensive analysis of past cyberattack scenarios in order to mitigate blind spots.

PERSPECTIVES TO CYBERSECURITY

Cybersecurity should be examined through psychological, economic, and technological vectors. Wiederhold (2014) argues that psychology in human nature is the weakest link in cyberspace. Although technology is sophisticated, humans still fall victim to social engineering (Bauer & van Eeten, 2009). Economic factors are important as computers are infested with malware to enrich attackers, and victims ponder associated costs (Hua & Bapna, 2013).

Psychological Vector

Human factors affect cybersecurity the most (Baker, 2014), and when cyber threats are not understood or are ignored, adverse consequences accrue. What people perceive of risks affects how they behave (West, 2008). The 2012 NCSA/McAfee survey showed that 64% of Americans feel their smartphone is safe from cyberattacks even though they had not installed any security software.

Sukamol and Markus (2008) argue that many individuals make security decisions from a simplistic understanding of risk. In organizations, risk has focused on technology, but firms are now expanding their technology-centered perspective to include people and processes (PwC, 2016). Heuer (1999) notes that it takes more information and more unambiguous information to recognize an unexpected phenomenon than an expected one. Moreover, Cebula and Young (2010) argue that many people use the same combination of user ID and password for different information systems because of human memory limitations thereby creating a huge risk to cybersecurity.

The psychological vector is associated to human thinking and cognitive limitations affecting decision making. Humans are especially prone to blind spots when it comes to complex systems like law, politics, or cyberspace. A typical user may not be able to identify an email phishing attack or a cloned website; whatever captures their minds as close enough is good enough. Thus, "unknown unknowns" associated with complex systems make an intellectual blind spot (Brotherton, 2015), and human understanding of risk plays a big role in fostering secure actions.

Economic Vector

Different industries are exposed to different cyber threats. The banking and finance sector is most concerned about financial fraud, and 65% of the frauds are cyberspace related (Chakrabarty, 2012). The information and communication technology sector is most concerned about illicit access to email and other electronic communications, because they offer access to trade secrets and business-sensitive information potentially harming the whole value chain (PwC, 2016). The insurance sector is primarily concerned about financial losses due to sensitive information being exposed unintentionally. Attackers clearly have financial motives and the victim normally suffers economic losses. Globally, the financial loss from cybersecurity incidents is increasing by 34% annually (PwC, 2016).

Unfortunately, individuals and organizations decide on cybersecurity investments under economic constraints such as limited budgets (Heuer, 1999). Although the increased engagement of the Board of Directors has impacted a boost in security spending (PwC, 2016), the financial cost attributed to cybersecurity investment is seen as huge by most businesses. Major issues among businesses is the inability to devise a cybersecurity investment strategy and the organizational inability to invest in the necessary personnel and processes to guard against attacks. Security risks can be mitigated through understanding one's own vulnerabilities and the motivations of cybercriminals.

Supply chain partners are also dangerous. More than two-thirds of companies in the automotive industry attribute security incidents to partners such as resellers that have trusted access to their internal networks and data (PwC, 2016). However, security checks for such partners are normally not practiced. The 2012 NCSA/Symantec survey shows that two-thirds of small companies are not protecting nor letting the partners know of their cybersecurity practices. Companies that have not suffered an attack may not know where to prioritize their cybersecurity investments, while companies that have suffered an attack are better handling security gaps and investing wisely.

Technological Vector

It is often assumed that technically inclined individuals have the knowledge to solve cybersecurity issues. However, the responsibility of handling security issues is not purely an IT department concern, but is everyone's responsibility (Kritzinger & von Solms, 2010). This raises the question of whether technology is a solution. West (2008) argues that sophisticated technology does not decrease system vulnerabilities, and that the more complex the technology the more vulnerabilities. Although organizations and individuals may use technology to avert attacks, they cannot guarantee immunity.

Many network security solutions, such as firewalls, are automated background processes (Garfinkel, 2012). However, cybersecurity requires users or operators to act appropriately; the lack of network security understanding may result in abuse of privacy and security (Singer & Friedman, 2014).

Simpler designs may help in developing technology with fewer security vulnerabilities. A system with many features and functionality is more likely to be compromised (Saltzer & Schroeder, 1975). It is important to check access and objects continually, enforce automatic security updates, and provide multiple levels of security so that if any bit is compromised, there is a safe alternative. Encryption makes it more difficult for data to be compromised, and technical alert systems can be used to prevent or mitigate unwanted occurrences (Shapiro & Cohen, 2007). However, technological risks will never be totally eliminated as attackers shift to targeting vulnerable mobile technology.

METHODS

This study analyzes eight scenarios of successful cyberattacks. These scenarios occurred between 2007 and 2013, and the information used was collected from various online news websites. Possible vulnerabilities of each cyberattack is elaborated from the perspective of psychological, technological, and business vectors. Blind spot theory recognizes that people tend to focus on their perceptions of relevance, yet there are blind spots in regard to what people consider irrelevant or "unknown unknowns" (Taleb, 2012). These vectors provide an understanding of the enablers of blind spots; had these vulnerabilities been identified and addressed before a cyberattack, threats could have been mitigated and attacks avoided.

The analysis makes use of cybersecurity operational risks by Cebula and Young (2010), according to whom actions of people can be deliberate (fraud, sabotage, theft) or accidental (mistakes, errors), or a lack of action. Increased risk can also result from technology failures (systems design, specifications, and complexity; software configuration, settings, and practices; hardware capacity and obsolescence). Moreover, failed internal processes (problems in the internal business process flow, documentation, and alerting), process controls (status monitoring), and supporting processes (staffing, training, funding) affect the ability to implement, manage, and sustain cybersecurity. Finally, external events (dependencies on service providers, economic conditions) may result in risks.

FINDINGS

This sections summarizes eight cybersecurity incidents; the findings from the perspective of the three core vectors are emphasized with brackets.

- **U. S. Banks:** In September 2012, there was a series of Distributed Denial of Service (DDoS) attacks on major U.S. financial institutions, including JPMorgan and Citigroup. Virtual private webservers were used to flood the online banking system with junk email, attacking vulnerable web applications. The high volume of Internet traffic made the websites unavailable and resulted in client disruption. Iran was suspected to be the attacker to retaliate for the economic sanctions from the U.S. and its Arab allies. The banks assumed their servers were secure but discovered otherwise when they were attacked (psychology), although the technical functionalities of the hosted servers worked according to design (technology). The attack failed to affect the core of the business (business).
- **Mat Honan:** In August 2012, Mat Honan's entire digital life was destroyed by a hacktivist group who called Applecare customer tech support to obtain a temporary password for Honan's me.com email using his billing address and last four digits of the credit card for identification. They found Honan's billing address by searching his web domain information and received the last four digits by calling Amazon.com and requesting to add an additional credit card to Honan's existing account. Although hackers failed to pass security questions, they were able to reset Honan's AppleID password. His iPhone was disconnected from the Internet and iCloud login disabled, his twitter and Gmail accounts were deleted, and all his Apple devices were remotely erased. Honan had daisy-chained his Google and iCloud accounts using the same email prefix and did not have two-factor authentication for convenience reasons (psychology). The 'Find my Mac' application, a supposedly helpful feature, turned into an attacking tool used to wipe out Honan's details (technology). Apple violated their internal security processes and Amazon.com made access to sensitive information too easy for the sake of business and customer convenience (business).
- **Dalai Lama:** In 2008, the Office of His Holiness the Dalai Lama (OHHDL) sent out a confidential email to an unnamed country who was later warned by the Chinese government not to host the Dalai Lama. Investigations revealed infiltrations into the OHHDL's system. There were several unauthorized logins into email accounts from IP addresses belonging to Chinese and Hong Kong providers. The hackers composed emails that appeared to come from the OHHDL, causing recipients to visit malicious websites. Using phishing, the hackers were able to install rootkits on computers in several embassies, foreign ministries, and organizations and download sensitive data. Obviously, human thinking assumed it was safe to open these emails and click the links (psychology). OHHDL's web service was not encrypted and the vulnerabilities in office software allowed malicious content to be downloaded (technology). Organizations affected by the attack focused on their core processes and did not evaluate the potential loss of data or information due to their unsafe practices (business).

- **Koobface:** The Koobface worm has terrorized users of social media since 2008. Infection allowed hackers to access users' sensitive banking information and passwords. They aimed at users with invitations to watch a funny or sexy video. Those who clicked the link got a message to update their computer's Flash software, which began the download of the malware. Victims' computers were drafted into a network of infected computers, and were sent advertisements of fake antivirus software. Also, their web searches were hijacked and the clicks delivered to unscrupulous marketers. The group made money from people who bought the bogus software and from unsuspecting advertisers. Koobface checks the user's Internet cookies to identify the social network the user has access to. Thus, they were able to send messages to the networking site for the user and there was no need to create a fake account on the social networking site (technology). They also capitalized on their victims' unwise click choices and the trust between the user and their social network contacts to increase the rate of malicious infection (psychology). More users, more traffic, more revenue is the pattern of thought of social media sites, and security that would prevent this kind of abuse comes later (business).

- **Cutting Sword of Justice:** Aramco is Saudi Arabia's largest oil and gas firm with affiliates all over the world. In 2012, Aramco's computer network was infested with a replicating virus Shamoon that affected its business process and caused the loss of data. Shamoon infected over 30,000 computers and caused a major disruption to the firm's business. It took almost two weeks to recover from the effect of the attack. The virus activates at a particular time, displays an image of a burning American flag and then sends reports of information to the attacker; moreover, files can be deleted from infected computers. The effects of the Shamoon can cause a firm to lose its Intellectual Property. Both an anti-oppression group and the Cutting Sword of Justice group took responsibility for the attack. The virus only affected computers used for Aramco's enterprise activities, not those used for oil production (technology). Thus, an in-house security issue may be involved (psychology). Surprisingly, there was no backup done for the drilling and production data during the period of the attack (technology). Later, Aramco invested heavily on cybersecurity and fast recovery from similar situations (business).

- **Target:** The U.S. retailing company Target was attacked in late 2013. The attack was enabled by a malware planted in their point-of-sale terminals that allowed hackers to steal customers' information from the magnetic stripe of millions of debit and credit cards. The hackers accessed Target's network through a third party that had access to the network because they were monitoring the energy and temperature in stores for fluctuations in temperature that might affect the shopping experience (psychology). The hackers accessed the third party network using an email malware. Target's information system was not upgraded to work with the EMV chip technology that would enable them to read card information in an encrypted format (technology). Target had worked with Visa for over ten years to introduce smart cards, which would limit fraud by encrypting sensitive data contained on the card. However, they discarded the project after spending tens of millions because it was cheaper to issue and accept traditional magnetic-stripe cards than credit cards with silicon chips (business).

- **Spamhaus:** In 2013, Spamhaus, an anti-phishing group, added Cyberbunker to its public black list, suspecting Cyberbunker to be an avenue of spam. Cyberbunker was a commercial Internet Service Provider with apparently undisclosed and shady activities. After Spamhaus blacklisted Cyberbunker, they experienced a severe DDoS against their email and webservers making it impossible for anyone to access their website. Soon thereafter, the spokesman of Cyberbunker, who was arrested, said "Spamhaus had too much control in determining and in deciding what spam is and what isn't". He operated within a mobile computing van from a well-equipped bunker and the attacks were generated by swarms of computers known as botnets (technology). After his arrest, there was an anonymous demand for his release, adding that if he were not released, there would be a larger attack. Since Cyberbunker felt hurt by Spamhaus, they decided to hurt and attack Spamhaus in return (psychology). Spamhaus was doing their job by listing those hosts who they felt were a spamming threat. Cyberbunker, on the other hand, was also pursuing their business interests by allowing spamming services to be hosted on their servers (business).

- **New York Times (NYT):** In 2013, hackers were able to access every employee's password. The attack was achieved through spear-phishing where the hackers emailed malicious attachments or links to employees. Once an employee clicked on the email or link containing the malicious code, the hackers were able to install a remote access tool which aided them to extract data, passwords, images, keystrokes, documents, computer webcam and microphone recordings. The hackers focused on reporters who were preparing investigative reports on how the Chinese Prime Minister's family had gained their billion-dollar fortune from questionable business dealings. The hackers, assumed to be Chinese, wanted to determine the writers' sources of information for these reports. The attackers installed malicious software for a period of three months, during which time the firewall and antivirus program only discovered one instance of the presence of malicious software and had it quarantined. Hackers no longer focus their efforts in attempting to break firewalls, rather they capitalize on the social lapses of an unassuming human who will click on suspicious links and files received by email (psychology). Hashed passwords were made available for employees to make it difficult to steal their passwords, but rainbow tables used by hackers nullify the security (technology). The NYT relied on a security provider to combat malicious threats while focusing on their own core business; however, no provider can mitigate all hacker exploits of human vulnerabilities (business).

A THREE-VECTOR APPROACH

The scenario analysis used three perspectives to blind spots in cybersecurity: (i) psychological (limitations of the human mind), (ii) technological (critical flaws and the need for secure technology), and (iii) business (commercial logic behind attacks and security investments). Table 1 provides a combined three-vector approach to attack scenarios in order to illustrate blind spots as enablers of cyberattacks.

The resulting eight blind spots explain how human cognitive limitations; technological exploitation of vulnerable information systems; and economic motives of attackers lead to cyberattacks towards under-resourced. The eight blind spots are identified in Table 1. The blind spots were derived from a multi-vector analysis, providing a more holistic view compared to traditional approaches to cybersecurity risks.

FUTURE RESEARCH DIRECTIONS

Many individuals and organizations guard themselves against cyberattacks; yet some are affected by the lack of implementing sufficient safe practices. In lieu of this, there are newly devised and sophisticated avenues of attacks that are highly dynamic. It would take substantial effort to provide guidance to respond

Table 1. Blind spots and their mechanisms identified from the eight scenario cases

Example	Blind Spot	Mechanism of Enabler
U.S. Banks	Internal focus	Emphasis on digital technology that protects core operations and systems and secures internal processes (prevents hacking aimed at fraud and theft) allows attackers to harm non-core activities by targeting the outside interface (DDoS to prevent customers from entering a bank website)
Mat Honan	Convenience first	Allowing the customer to turn off critical security features and ignoring corporate security procedures in favor of customer convenience allows attackers to exploit holes, especially when the customer links social media accounts and login credentials for convenience
Dalai Lama	Habitual aspect	Office solutions have security vulnerabilities, and the attacker can exploit the victims' habitual aspect for unauthorized access to their systems
Koobface	Hedonistic enjoyment	The attacker is able to lure victims to click malicious files while they search for funny and entertaining content; installed malware is configured to spread through the victim's online social networks arising from a human need for social interaction and social enjoyment
Cutting Sword of Justice	Insider sabotage	Sabotage is driven by political or economic motives, and may require an insider who is able to contaminate the victim's systems and hinder their ability to recover from the attack; sabotage may be based on deterrence and creates harm even when aimed at the victim's non-core activities
Target	Wrong priorities	Wrong priorities for the sake of business and smooth operations, such as customer convenience, costs savings and functionality before technical security, as well as the unnecessary technical connection between core systems and supportive systems expose organizations to cyberattacks
Spamhaus	Egotistical behavior	Egotistical behavior of actors may spark cyber warfare, where both parties feel that their actions are justified; one side's under-evaluation of the other side's narcissistic motivation (i.e. revenge) and subsequent actions exposes them to large-scale and systematic full-frontal cyberattacks
NY Times	Technology effect	Overreliance on technology is dangerous if organizations and people believe a single technology prevents all kinds of cyber threats; however, such one-stop technology does not exists, and even the most complex security solutions are useless when "the keys to the lock" are easily accessible

to all avenues. Thus, this chapter addresses 'what perspectives can be used to identify blind spots and how the perspectives can be combined to help us mitigate blind spots?'

The examined scenarios showed that attacks could be averted or mitigated, if the victims focused attention on the basic principles and limitations of their actions. Future research could analyze additional scenarios to better contribute to the theory of blind spots and to spark the building of a systematic tool that applies the results to real businesses. The tool could be enriched by a more in-depth "what happened and what did not happen" analysis of the scenarios. An evident limitation to this type of research is data availability; many attacks are not publicized because of victims' reluctance to discuss their specific scenarios.

CONCLUSION

The outcome of this study is that the theory of blind spots in the cybersecurity context can be advanced by making use of a combination of perspectives ("a three-vector approach"). Blind spots exist because there is no focus or there are unknowns, and because people tend to focus on what they think is relevant. These blind spots, illustrated by findings from the study, allow hostile parties to execute cyberattacks. Thus, the responsibility of handling security issues in organizations is not solely for the IT department; rather it is everyone's responsibility. Organizations and individuals who handle valuable assets in cyberspace will find the present study useful because they will be better able to spot cybersecurity gaps and avoid social and economic costs from successful cyberattacks.

Suggested ways of improving cybersecurity include creating defenses against immediate threats by enhancing mutual situational awareness of threats and vulnerabilities. Moreover, organizations and individuals should develop the ability to swiftly respond to vulnerabilities and prevent network intrusions. In addition, expanding cyber education, research and development efforts, and strategies will likely mitigate malicious activities in cyberspace. A number of organizations, however, are not willing to increase awareness or disclose vulnerabilities because they believe it will create a negative impression for investors and organizational image. In order to enhance cybersecurity return on investment, businesses should provide funding for shorter terms rather than the typical 3-5 years business planning.

REFERENCES

Baker, E. W. (2014). A model for the impact of cybersecurity infrastructure on economic development in emerging economies: Evaluating the contrasting cases of India and Pakistan. *Information Technology for Development*, *20*(2), 122–139. doi:10.1080/02681102.2013.832131

Bauer, J. M., & van Eeten, M. J. (2009). Cybersecurity: Stakeholder incentives, externalities, and policy options. *Telecommunications Policy*, *33*(10), 706–719. doi:10.1016/j.telpol.2009.09.001

Boehm, B., & Turner, R. (2005). Management challenges to implementing agile processes in traditional development organizations. *Software, IEEE*, *22*(5), 30–39. doi:10.1109/MS.2005.129

Brotherton, R. (2015). *Suspicious minds: Why we believe conspiracy*. Bloomsbury.

Cebula, J. J., & Young, L. R. (2010). *A taxonomy of operational cyber security risks*. Technical Note CMU/SEI-2010-TN-028. Retrieved from Carnegie Mellon University website: http://www.sei.cmu.edu/reports/10tn028.pdf

Chakrabarty, K. C. (2012). Indian Banking Sector: Towards the next orbit. In Academic Foundation (Ed.), Economic developments in India: Analysis, reports, policy documents. New Delhi: AF.

Chen, Y.-Z., Huang, Z.-G., Xu, S., & Lai, Y.-C. (2015). Spatiotemporal patterns and predictability of cyberattacks. *PLoS ONE, 10*(5), e0124472. doi:10.1371/journal.pone.0124472 PMID:25992837

Clements, S., & Kirkham, H. (2010). Cyber-security considerations for the smart grid. In *Proceedings of the IEEE Power and Energy Society General Meeting*. Minneapolis, MN: PES. 10.1109/PES.2010.5589829

Craigen, D., Diakun-Thibault, N., & Purse, R. (2014). Defining cybersecurity. *Technology Innovation Management Review, 4*(10), 13–21.

Emami-Tabla, M., Amoui, M., & Tahvildari, L. (2013, August). On the road to holistic decision making in adaptive security. *Technology Innovation Management Review*, 59-64.

Flowers, A., Zeadally, S., & Murray, A. (2013). Cybersecurity and US legislative efforts to address cybercrime. *Journal of Homeland Security and Emergency Management, 10*(1), 29–55. doi:10.1515/jhsem-2012-0007

Gandhi, R., Sharma, A., Mahoney, W., Sousan, W., Zhu, Q., & Laplante, P. (2011). Dimensions of cyber-attacks: Cultural, social, economic, and political. *Technology and Society Magazine, IEEE, 30*(1), 28–38. doi:10.1109/MTS.2011.940293

Garfinkel, S. L. (2012). The cybersecurity risk. *Communications of the ACM, 55*(6), 29–32. doi:10.1145/2184319.2184330

Gavins, W., & Hemenway, J. (2010). Cybersecurity: A joint terminal engineering office perspective. In *Proceedings of the IEEE Military Communications Conference*. San Jose, CA: MILCOM. 10.1109/MILCOM.2010.5679588

Han, C., & Dongre, R. (2014). What motivates cyber-attackers? *Technology Innovation Management Review, 4*(10), 40–42.

Heuer, R. J. (1999). *Psychology of intelligence analysis*. Washington, DC: CIA.

Hua, J., & Bapna, S. (2013). The economic impact of cyber terrorism. *The Journal of Strategic Information Systems, 22*(2), 175–186. doi:10.1016/j.jsis.2012.10.004

Hughes, J., & Cybenko, G. (2013, August). Quantitative metrics and risk assessment: The three tenets model of cybersecurity. *Technology Innovation Management Review*, 15-24.

Kritzinger, E., & von Solms, S. H. (2010). Cyber security for home users: A new way of protection through awareness enforcement. *Computers & Security, 29*(8), 840–847. doi:10.1016/j.cose.2010.08.001

Maughan, D. (2010). The need for a national cybersecurity research and development agenda. *Communications of the ACM, 53*(2), 29–31. doi:10.1145/1646353.1646365

Nathan, M. J., & Petrosino, A. (2003). Expert blind spot among preservice teachers. *American Educational Research Journal, 40*(4), 905–928. doi:10.3102/00028312040004905

Pronin, E., Lin, D. Y., & Ross, L. (2002). The bias blind spot: Perceptions of bias in self-versus others. *Personality and Social Psychology Bulletin*, *28*(3), 369–381. doi:10.1177/0146167202286008

PwC. (2016). *The global state of information security survey 2016*. Industry Report. Retrieved from PricewaterhouseCoopers website: www.pwc.com/gsiss

Saltzer, J., & Schroeder, M. (1975). The protection of information in computer systems. *Proceedings of the IEEE*, *63*(9), 1278–1308. doi:10.1109/PROC.1975.9939

Shapiro, J. N., & Cohen, D. K. (2007). Color bind: Lessons from the failed homeland security advisory system. *International Security*, *32*(2), 121–154. doi:10.1162/isec.2007.32.2.121

Singer, P. W., & Friedman, A. (2014). *Cybersecurity and cyberwar: What everyone needs to know?* Oxford University Press.

Smith, A. D., & Rupp, W. T. (2002). Issues in cybersecurity; understanding the potential risks associated with hackers/crackers. *Information Management & Computer Security*, *10*(4), 178–183. doi:10.1108/09685220210436976

Sukamol, S., & Markus, J. (2008). Using cartoons to teach internet security. *Cryptologia*, *32*(2), 137–154. doi:10.1080/01611190701743724

Taleb, N. N. (2012). *Antifragile: Things that gain from disorder*. Random House.

West, R. (2008). The psychology of security. *Communications of the ACM*, *51*(4), 34–40. doi:10.1145/1330311.1330320

Wiederhold, B. K. (2014). The role of psychology in enhancing cybersecurity. *Cyberpsychology, Behavior, and Social Networking*, *17*(3), 131–132. doi:10.1089/cyber.2014.1502 PMID:24592869

ADDITIONAL READING

Davis, A. (2015). Building cyber-resilience into supply chains. *Technology Innovation Management Review*, *5*(4), 19–27.

Kadivar, M. (2014). Cyber-attack attributes. *Technology Innovation Management Review*, *4*(11), 22–27.

Muegge, S., & Craigen, D. (2015). A design science approach to constructing critical infrastructure and communicating cybersecurity risks. *Technology Innovation Management Review*, *5*(6), 6–16.

Uma, M., & Padmavathi, G. (2013). A survey on various cyberattacks and their classification. *International Journal of Network Security*, *15*(5), 390–396.

KEY TERMS AND DEFINITIONS

Attack Scenario: A cybersecurity incident where an attacker was able to gain illegitimate access to a victim's sensitive information and/or information systems.

Blind Spots: Various biases and preconceived information that affect organizational and human decision making; enabled by unknowns or false focus on what is relevant.

Core Vectors: Economic, technological and psychological perspectives to blind spots; used in combination to obtain a better understanding of what enables cyberattacks.

Cyberattack: A deliberate exploitation of computer systems, technology-dependent enterprises and networks.

Cybersecurity: The organization and collection of resources, processes, and structures used to protect cyberspace from occurrences that misalign de jure from de facto property rights.

This research was previously published in the Encyclopedia of Information Science and Technology, Fourth Edition edited by Mehdi Khosrow-Pour, pages 1684-1693, copyright year 2018 by Information Science Reference (an imprint of IGI Global).

Chapter 10
Cyber Bullying

Jo Ann Oravec
University of Wisconsin – Whitewater, USA

ABSTRACT

"Cyberbullying" comprises a wide spectrum of behaviors that have negative and often devastating impacts upon their targets (or "victims"). This chapter is intended to analyze research trends on cyberbullying as well as related concerns involving online harassment, online reputational damage, and cyberstalking. Its focuses are as follows: (1) analyze the conceptual work and research that have emerged on the technological and social aspects of the issues, with an emphasis on social media scenarios; (2) present insights as to how cyberbullying and reputational damage can best be mitigated, given current mental health insights and technological know-how; and (3) discuss why cyberbullying is of continuing importance to business, government, non-profit, and educational audiences. The chapter includes reflections about the moral and personal dimensions of cyberbullying. Cyberbullies can often combine anonymous interactions with personally identifiable ones to make it appear that more than one individual is participating, potentially intensifying the negative social impacts involved.

INTRODUCTION

"Cyberbullying" comprises a wide spectrum of behaviors that have negative and often devastating impacts upon their targets (or "victims"). This article is intended to analyze research trends on cyberbullying as well as related concerns involving online harassment, online reputational damage, and cyberstalking. Its focuses are as follows: (1) analyze the creative and innovative conceptual work and research that have emerged on the technological as well as social and ethical aspects of these issues; (2) present insights as to how cyberbullying and reputational damage can best be mitigated, given the technological capabilities and emerging know-how of technical specialists, educators, and organizational consultants; and (3) discuss why cyberbullying is of continuing importance to a broad business, government, non-profit, and educational audience. The article also includes reflections about the moral and personal dimensions of cyberbullying.

DOI: 10.4018/978-1-5225-7492-7.ch010

Bullying incidents are intricate and frustrating phenomena from whatever contexts they emerge, face-to-face or online. Cyberbullying often involves words and pictures that are considered as protected speech under various national and local laws, often providing cover for those who are attempting to abuse or unsettle a victim (Fraser, Bond-Fraser, Buyting, Korotkov, & Noonan, 2013; Oravec, 2012). The prevalence of cyberbullying is difficult to determine, given the privacy with which many cases dealing wth juvenile offences (as well as offences in workplace settings) are handled. In their "Scoping Review on Studies of Cyberbullying Prevalence Among Adolescents," Brochado, Soares, and Fraga (2016) found the following:

Most of the studies tend to assess cybervictimization experiences. However, even considering the same perspective, the same country, and the same recall period, a high variability in the estimates was observed. As a main conclusion, the way in which the prevalence of cyberbullying is estimated is influenced by methodological research options.

Added to the difficulties in studying cyberbullying is the observation that some individuals who are victimized may not display signs of damage or even choose to respond to the bully. Other individuals may be extremely harmed by comparable words and pictures; some may choose to fight back while others become depressed or even suicidal. Generally, cyberbullying consists of repetitive behavior that has a particular focus on a victim; the bully's attacks can be shielded from video from others who could possibly intervene. As related in Bonanno and Hymel (2013), "Cyberbullying also takes place on a virtual playground that makes it possible to victimize a peer within the sanctity of one's own home, at any time of the day or night, in complete anonymity, and with maximal exposure and hence potential embarrassment for the intended target" (p. 646). Kamali (2015) adds an angle relating to the growing assortment of networked devices: "the perpetrator can employ varied means (e.g., cell-phones, texts, blogs, Internet, social media, etc.)" in conducting the bullying (p. 43). Anonymity can give some protection to bullies in shielding them from observation in whole or part of their bullying (Barlett, Gentile, & Chew, 2016). Cyberbullies can also combine anonymous interactions with personally-identifiable ones to make it appear that more than one individual is involved in the attacks, potentially intensifying the negative social impacts of the bullying.

Equipping individuals in workplace, community, and educational contexts to be aware of cyberbullying issues may enable them to become more sensitive and empathetic as well as more effective as the front line of defense against these phenomena. It will also help them to mitigate bully-related problems in their organizational and community roles and provide an "early warning system" for the new forms of bullying various technological changes may engender (such as drones and virtual reality). Emerging research efforts may also enhance understanding of cyberbullying as well as empower citizens and organizational participants in their efforts to mitigate it.

BACKGROUND

Public discourse on bullying and mobbing has increased dramatically in the past decade: in the *Journal of Psychohistory*, Dervin (2010) labelled 2010 as "The Year of the Bully" because of the number of shocking incidents involving young people, many of which incorporated some social media component. The classic novel *Lord of the Flies* (Goulding, 1960) has often been mentioned in discourse on youth-related cyberbullying; many of the young people characterized by Goulding had forms of autonomy and power within their environments but did not have the moral guidance to understand fully the consequences of their actions. Cyberbullying attracted public attention in part because of cases such as that of Rutgers University student Tyler Clementi who committed suicide after having some of his sexual activities broadcast via webcam on the Internet (Byers, 2013; Oravec, 2012). "Cyberstalking" has been distinguished as a phenomenon related to and often overlapping with cyberbullying (Adam, 2002; Kamali, 2015); it is more often associated with the conduct of adults than cyberbullying, the latter which has been more often associated with children and adolescents (Carter, 2015). Research from Milosevic (2015) shows that in US mainstream media "overall debate on cyberbullying is narrow, focused on incidents that resulted in suicides, and subsequent blaming of individuals involved. Such framing can have implications for audience's support of punitive policies, inability to comprehend complexity of the issue and moral panic around children's use of technology." (p. 492).

Computer networking is adding new and complex dimensions to bullying, providing the venue for complex cases of online reputational damage and privacy invasion via social media (Oravec, 2013; Van Royen, Poels, Daelemans, & Vandebosch, 2015). Victims, bullies, and onlookers can often interact in debilitating and confusing patterns in cyberbullying incidents, given their relatively-recent emergence in society and lack of common understandings concerning them. As new forms of cyberbullying emerge, individuals who work online and engage in networked educational and social activity can encounter harassment, belittling, damaging or doctored materials that refer to them, and related harms. Technologies such as digital video, text messaging, and social media can be combined in ways that make victims perceive that they have nowhere to hide and no real legal or social recourse. Victims often lose the ability to contribute their full efforts to their jobs, schoolwork, and social interactions, and sometimes even choose to end their lives.

Cyberbullying can affect people of all gender affiliations; it can also affect individuals of various religious heritages as well as racial and ethnic backgrounds (Cappadocia, Craig, & Pepler, 2013; Stanbrook, 2014). Individuals with disabilities can be targeted as well as become perpetrators themselves (Kowalski *et al.*, 2016). Certain patterns can be found in the way cyberbullying and online reputational damage emerge in the context of various groups and settings, which can help in detecting bullying and mitigating its consequences. For example, some varieties of cyberbullying infuse forms of hate speech (as described in Adam, 2002, Byers, 2013, and Oravec, 2000), integrating themes involving race, gender, religion, or other perceived affiliation; some of this speech, however debilitating to the victim and bystanders, may be protected by the First Amendment (Conn, 2015).

MAIN FOCUS OF THE ARTICLE

Issues, Controversies, Problems

As individuals engage in increased levels of online activity, the prospects that they will find their online interactions and reputations negatively impacted by others who have somehow targeted them increase as well. Many recent political debates have been affected by cyberbullying, often preventing individuals from engaging fully in citizenship and public forums. For example, Schwartz (2016) describes a number of circumstances in which women's blogs with some political content have been placed under attack with repetitive harassment and abuse. Gender-related and ethnic insults have been common in the online attacks perpetrated in social media as well as email, listservs, and texting venues (Slonje, Smith, & FriséN, 2013); attacks involving sexting (sex-themed technologically-mediated communications) have proliferated as well (Durham, 2016; Oravec, 2012b). In many of these incidents, cyberbullies are enabled to remain anonymous or disguise their identities in ways that only a few of their followers would be able to decipher, increasing the difficulties for law enforcement or administrators to mitigate the situations.

For its victims, cyberbullying has been shown to be linked with subsequent stress and even suicidal ideation (Kowalski et al., 2014). The impact of cyberbullying is often intensified by the ubiquitous nature of computer networking: "For the victim, cyber bullying is pervasive and persistent; once a cyberattack is launched, it is difficult, if not impossible, to eliminate… As a result, the impact of cyber victimization can be (or can be perceived to be) far more negative than that of traditional forms of bullying, and victims may have a much more difficult time coping" (Bonanno & Hymel, p. 686). Cyberbullying has also been shown to affect academic and workplace motivation, making its control and mitigation a practical as well as moral concern for institutions (Oravec, 2012a; Young-Jones, 2015). Research by Coyne *et al.* (2016) explores "the relationship between experiencing workplace cyberbullying, employee mental strain and job satisfaction," formulating a "disempowerment" approach to understanding its negative effects on the workplace. Kamali (2015) calls for increases in college-directed activity in this arena: "Cyberbullying research on college campuses lacks a unified definition of the concept. Although the states mandated most school districts to develop and enact some sort of policy, the law is silent on the college level cyberbullying" (p. 43).

The study of "serial cyberbullying" (cyberbullying behaviors that are repeated over time by one individual or group) is providing clues as to how bullying operates and who perpetrates it. From an organizational systems perspective, serial bullying is "a cycle that generates when a target is singled out, bullied, and driven from the workplace and regenerates when another target is singled out, bullied, driven from the workplace, and so on" (Lutgen-Sandvik & Tracy, 2012, p. 16). Serial bullies, simply put, can become increasingly proficient in what they do, and their negative impacts on organizations and individuals can be compounded over time as reinforcing network structures grow around them. Repetitive cyberbullying conduct on the part of particular individuals could signal deepseated psychological conditions that can be mitigated through mental health treatment. There are dangers in labeling specific individuals as "serial bullies," however; if these individuals are blocked from subsequent employment and educational opportuntities (perhaps unfairly) their life chances can be diminished and opportunities to rehabilitate reduced. However, learning about serial bullying patterns and watching for them can empower human resource specialists and educators to contain repetitive bullying behaviors before they injure more people.

SOLUTIONS AND RECOMMENDATIONS

Cyberbullying prevention and response often involves assistance with the technologies incorporated in cyberbullying for those with low levels of computer literacy. For example, victims often need guidance in documenting cyberbullying and online reputational damage so that their cases can be examined and cyberbullying mitigated. They may need updating on aspects of social media reputation protection and personal privacy guardianship. Unfortunately, many of the organizations that support online platforms (as well as obtain profits from their use) are slow to respond to cyberbullying complaints; a combined initiative among many organizational and online units needs to be maintained for cyberbullying to be mitigated (Stanbrook, 2014). It may certainly be difficult in many workplace contexts for administrators to admit that their organizations have issues with cyberbullying and seek assistance. New research findings about cyberbullying along with various social and artistic initiatives are beginning to generate insights for assistance in helping victims and concerned onlookers. For example, YouTube videos, compelling posters and artwork, and celebrity appearances along with Twitter emojis are being used in public service campaigns to signal that bystanders are becoming aware and involved and cyberbullying is not acceptable behavior (Hayman & Coleman, 2016). Doane, Kelley, and Pearson (2016) describe their research showing that "a brief cyberbullying video is capable of improving, at one-month follow-up, cyberbullying knowledge, cyberbullying perpetration behavior, and TRA constructs known to predict cyberbullying perpetration" (p. 136).

Many well-meaning individuals apparently have an impulse to disseminate widely information about particular cyberbullying cases in public venues. However, publicity about cyberbullying can backfire, despite the intentions of reducing negative outcomes (Pieschl, Kuhlmann, & Porsch, 2015). Publicity can sometimes put the victim's own personal history and personal characteristics in a problematic light as people wonder why he or she was targeted. Such publicity may have bad repercussions whether or not the victim's name was directly mentioned as rumors spread about who was involved.

Surveillance by well-meaning organizational or governmental authorities can play roles in mitigating some aspects of bullying, identifying and documenting potential bullying situations in hopes of containing their damage (Van Royen, *et al.*, 2015). However, with surveillance measures, privacy invasions can emerge as well as the real potential that whatever materials are collected will be misused or taken out-of-context. In turn, Mendola (2015) presents the case that such monitoring has the potential to displace the roles of household controls in a "Big Brother as Parent" scenario. Understanding how surveillance and monitoring can be used to document and frame bullying so as to mitigate its effects will require extensive experimentation in organizational contexts as well as the sharing of best practices.

FUTURE RESEARCH DIRECTIONS

The needs for continuing research on cyberbullying and for the proactive approaches and insights it will engender are considerable. As forms of social media expand, cyberbullying is developing new modes and inflicting new kinds of reputational and emotional devastation.Many participants, onlookers, and victims in cyberbullying and online reputational damage are young adults who may not yet understand the full gravity of harassment, misrepresentation, and related behaviors (Carter, 2015; Oravec, 2013). They are being faced with a difficult and confusing assortment of challenges as they establish their social lives as well as take on moral leadership roles in these contexts. It can be difficult to make a decision as to whether to join with a cyberbully in an online attack (and participate in "mobbing," defined in the glossary) or have a positive and effective role as an active intervener or victim supporter. Bullies can be perceived as powerful people, and joining with them may seem at first as a way to enlarge one's own presence and become more powerful in a workplace or educational context (Bussey, Fitzpatrick, & Raman, 2015). Some of the creative tactics against cyberbullying that have been examined by researchers include forms of humor levied by the victims themselves. In a study of Turkish adolescents, Sari (2016) found that "as aggressive humor decreases [on the part of victims], likelihood of cyberbullying perpetration increases. These results indicate that maladaptive humor styles (aggressive humor and self-defeating humor) may successfully address cyberbullying behavior" (p. 555). Research on perceptions of cyberbullying, and how positive associations of them can be eroded (perhaps through humor), may elicit insights as to how to deal with these phenomena.

International comparisons and cross-cultural investigations of cyberbullying will reveal a great deal not just about bullying as a phenomenon but about cultural variations in social psychology (Bayraktar, 2015). For example, in some pioneering longtudinal research on adolecents in Canada, Cappadocia, Craig, and Pepler (2013) found that "Risk factors associated with cyberbullying included higher levels of antisocial behaviors and fewer prosocial peer influences. Risk factors associated with cybervictimization included being in the transition year for high school, as well as higher levels of traditional victimization and depression." (p. 171). Scales such as the Revised Cyberbullying Inventory (RCBI) can be used to elicit results that can provide some sort baselines for what is happening with cyberbullying phenomena over time and across cultures. Using the RCBI in a study of British adolescents, Brewer and Kerslake (2015) found the following:

Empathy was a significant individual predictor of cyberbullying perpetration, such that as empathy decreases, likelihood of cyberbullying perpetration increases. These findings indicate that self-esteem and empathy oriented interventions may successfully address cyberbullying behavior. (p. 255)

Cultural and psychological insights on cyberbullying may be productively combined with cybercounseling approaches to design workplace and educational interventions (Mishna, Bogo, & Sawyer, 2015) which can be implemented and evaluated in real-life contexts.

CONCLUSION

Decades ago, many of the future projections for the uses of computer networks seemed to present bright and optimistic portraits (Natale & Balbi, 2014; Oravec, 1996); computing technology innovations would be used primarily to inform, share, and befriend others. However, many dystopian scenarios are emerging worldwide of individuals who are afraid to participate in online interaction because of the negative impact it can have on their lives, scenarios that are echoed in the real-life experiences of many students and employees (Adam, 2002; Byers, 2013). Cyberbullying research has indeed documented specific cases of cyberbullying and elicited trends, but the deeper and more difficult moral questions remain of why so many individuals use computer technology in ways that disempower and wound people. These phenomena are apparently taking on new forms as computing technologies expand their reach societally (in terms of their national and international permeation) and personally (in terms of how we live our everyday lives).

In conclusion, managers, administrators, educators, and concerned citizens need to consider how to deal with generations of individuals (from young people to older adults) who have suffered from painful and reputation-damaging personal attacks online. Workplaces have also been sites for extended and sophisticated cyberbullying efforts, which have served to decrease levels of organizational morale as well as productivity. Many students have become acquainted with cyberbullying in school contexts, in some cases learning how to be participants and in others how it feels to be a victim; educational institutions may be able to foster more positive and healthy behaviors as well. Inclusive excellence cannot be obtained if individuals live in fear. People cannot be expected to learn effectively or produce their best work if they regularly need to deal with cyberbullies or are themselves inappropriately or unfairly being construed in that light. Continuing research and public discourse on these matters is necessary for society to benefit fully from computer technology and social media.

REFERENCES

Adam, A. (2002). Cyberstalking and Internet pornography: Gender and the gaze. *Ethics and Information Technology*, *4*(2), 133–142. doi:10.1023/A:1019967504762

Barlett, C. P., Gentile, D. A., & Chew, C. (2016). Predicting cyberbullying from anonymity. *Psychology of Popular Media Culture*, *5*(2), 171–180. doi:10.1037/ppm0000055

Bayraktar, F. (2015). *Cross-national and cross-cultural variances in cyberbullying. In The Wiley Handbook of Psychology, Technology and Society* (pp. 158–175). New York: Wiley.

Bonanno, R. A., & Hymel, S. (2013). Cyber bullying and internalizing difficulties: Above and beyond the impact of traditional forms of bullying. *Journal of Youth and Adolescence*, *42*(5), 685–697. doi:10.100710964-013-9937-1 PMID:23512485

Brewer, G., & Kerslake, J. (2015). Cyberbullying, self-esteem, empathy and loneliness. *Computers in Human Behavior*, *48*, 255–260. doi:10.1016/j.chb.2015.01.073

Brochado, S., Soares, S., & Fraga, S. (2016). A scoping review on studies of cyberbullying prevalence among adolescents. *Trauma, Violence & Abuse*. doi:10.1177/1524838016641668 PMID:27053102

Bussey, K., Fitzpatrick, S., & Raman, A. (2015). The role of moral disengagement and self-efficacy in cyberbullying. *Journal of School Violence*, *14*(1), 30–46. doi:10.1080/15388220.2014.954045

Byers, D. (2013). Do they see nothing wrong with this?: Bullying, bystander complicity, and the role of homophobic bias in the Tyler Clementi case. *Families in Society*, *94*(4), 251–258. doi:10.1606/1044-3894.4325

Cappadocia, M. C., Craig, W. M., & Pepler, D. (2013). Cyberbullying prevalence, stability, and risk factors during adolescence. *Canadian Journal of School Psychology*, *28*(2), 171–192.

Carter, S. (2015). *The hostile environment: Students who bully in school*. New York: Lexington Books.

Conn, K. (2015). From Student Armbands to Cyberbullying: The First Amendment in Public Schools. Legal Frontiers in Education: Complex Law Issues for Leaders, Policymakers and Policy Implementers (Advances in Educational Administration, Volume 24). New York: Emerald Group Publishing Limited, 35-58.

Coyne, I., Farley, S., Axtell, C., Sprigg, C., Best, L., & Kwok, O. (2016). Understanding the relationship between experiencing workplace cyberbullying, employee mental strain and job satisfaction: A dysempowerment approach. *International Journal of Human Resource Management*, 1–28. doi:10.1080/09585192.2015.1116454

Dervin, D. (2011). 2010: The Year of the Bully. *The Journal of Psychohistory*, *38*(4), 337–345.

Doane, A. N., Kelley, M. L., & Pearson, M. R. (2016). Reducing cyberbullying: A theory of reasoned action-based video prevention program for college students. *Aggressive Behavior*, *42*(2), 136–146. doi:10.1002/ab.21610 PMID:26349445

Durham, M. G. (2016). *Technosex: Precarious corporealities, mediated sexualities, and the ethics of embodied technics*. New York: Springer. doi:10.1007/978-3-319-28142-1

Fraser, I., Bond-Fraser, L., Buyting, M., Korotkov, D., & Noonan, S. (2013). Cyber bullying and the law: Are we doing enough. *The American Association of Behavioral and Social Science Journal*, *17*(1), 26–39.

Goulding, W. (1960). *Lord of the flies*. London: Faber & Faber.

Hayman, S., & Coleman, J. (2016). *Parents and digital technology: How to raise the connected generation*. New York: Routledge.

Kamali, A. (2015). Assessing cyber-bullying in higher education. *Information Systems Education Journal*, *13*(6), 43.

Kowalski, R. M., Giumetti, G. W., Schroeder, A. N., & Lattanner, M. R. (2014). Bullying in the digital age: A critical review and meta-analysis of cyberbullying research among youth. *Psychological Bulletin*, *140*(4), 1073–1137. doi:10.1037/a0035618 PMID:24512111

Kowalski, R. M., Morgan, C. A., Drake-Lavelle, K., & Allison, B. (2016). Cyberbullying among college students with disabilities. *Computers in Human Behavior*, *57*, 416–427. doi:10.1016/j.chb.2015.12.044

Leymann, H. (1990). Mobbing and psychological terror at workplaces. *Violence and Victims*, *5*, 119–126. PMID:2278952

Lutgen-Sandvik, P., & Tracy, S. J. (2012). Answering five key questions about workplace bullying how communication scholarship provides thought leadership for transforming abuse at work. *Management Communication Quarterly*, *26*(1), 3–47. doi:10.1177/0893318911414400

Mendola, C. E. (2015). Big Brother as parent: Using surveillance to patrol students' Internet speech. *British Columbia Journal of Law & Social Justice*, *35*, 153.

Milosevic, T. (2015). Cyberbullying in US mainstream media. *Journal of Children and Media, 9*(4), 492-509.

Mishna, F., Bogo, M., & Sawyer, J. L. (2015). Cyber counseling: Illuminating benefits and challenges. *Clinical Social Work Journal*, *43*(2), 169–178. doi:10.100710615-013-0470-1

Natale, S., & Balbi, G. (2014). Media and the imaginary in history. *Media History, 20*(2), 203–218. do i:10.1080/13688804.2014.898904

Oravec, J. A. (1996). *Virtual individuals, virtual groups.* New York: Cambridge University Press. doi:10.1017/CBO9780511574986

Oravec, J. A. (2000). Countering violent and hate-related materials on the Internet: Strategies for classrooms and communities. *Teacher Educator, 35*(3), 34–45. doi:10.1080/08878730009555233

Oravec, J. A. (2012a). Bullying and mobbing in academe: Challenges for distance education and social media applications. *Journal of Academic Administration in Higher Education, 49,* 46–58.

Oravec, J. A. (2012b). *The ethics of sexting: Issues involving consent and the production of intimate content. In Digital Ethics: Research and Practice* (pp. 129–145). New York: Peter Lang.

Oravec, J. A. (2013). Gaming Google: Some ethical issues involving online reputation management. *Journal of Business Ethics Education, 10,* 61–81. doi:10.5840/jbee2013104

Pieschl, S., Kuhlmann, C., & Porsch, T. (2015). Beware of publicity! Perceived distress of negative cyber incidents and implications for defining cyberbullying. *Journal of School Violence, 14*(1), 111–132. doi :10.1080/15388220.2014.971363

Sari, S. V. (2016). Was it just a joke? Cyberbullying perpetrations and their styles of humor. *Computers in Human Behavior, 54,* 555–559. doi:10.1016/j.chb.2015.08.053

Schwartz, A. (2016). Critical blogging: Constructing Femmescapes online. *Ada: A Journal of Gender, New Media, and Technology,* (9).

Slonje, R., Smith, P. K., & Frisé, N. A. (2013). The nature of cyberbullying, and strategies for prevention. *Computers in Human Behavior, 29*(1), 26–32. doi:10.1016/j.chb.2012.05.024

Stanbrook, M. B. (2014). Stopping cyberbullying requires a combined societal effort. *Canadian Medical Association Journal, 186*(7), 483–483. doi:10.1503/cmaj.140299 PMID:24664656

Van Royen, K., Poels, K., Daelemans, W., & Vandebosch, H. (2015). Automatic monitoring of cyberbullying on social networking sites: From technological feasibility to desirability. *Telematics and Informatics, 32*(1), 89–97. doi:10.1016/j.tele.2014.04.002

Young-Jones, A., Fursa, S. F., Byrket, J. B., & Sly, J. S. (2015). Bullying affects more than feelings: The long-term implications of victimization on academic motivation in higher education. *Social Psychology of Education, 18*(1), 185–200. doi:10.100711218-014-9287-1

ADDITIONAL READING

Jaffe, E. M. (2016). Swatting: The new cyberbullying frontier after Elonis v United States. *Drake Law Review*, *64*, 455–553.

Maiuro, R. (Ed.). (2015). *Perspectives on bullying: Research on childhood, workplace, and cyberbullying*. New York: Springer Publishing Company.

Starcevic, V., & Aboujaoude, E. (2015). Cyberchondria, cyberbullying, cybersuicide, cybersex: New psychopathologies for the 21st century? *World Psychiatry; Official Journal of the World Psychiatric Association (WPA)*, *14*(1), 97–100. doi:10.1002/wps.20195 PMID:25655165

KEY TERMS AND DEFINITIONS

Bystanders: Individuals who have access to information about current or potential bullying or harassment incidents, whether or not they choose to respond. In online contexts, information that is received by bystanders may be fragmented and highly confusing.

Cyberstalking: Repetitive and personally invasive surveillance and monitoring of a target or victim, often with unsettling forms of unwanted contact. Cyberstalking is often associated with adult behaviors more than those of children or young adults (Kamali, 2015).

Mobbing: Group member cooperation and collaboration in bullying. From the victim's perspective, mobbing compounds the negative power of abusive behavior with the sense of exclusion from the group, producing a form of "psychological terror." From the mobbers' perspectives, mobbing may make the participants feel less guilty about their behaviors since their peers and comrades are also engaging (Leymann, 1990).

Online Reputational Damage: Injury to the online profiles and compiled reputational information about an individual. This injury can be conducted through such means as doctoring photographs and manipulating online information in a negative way (Oravec, 2013).

Serial Cyberbullying: Individuals who engage in bullying who have chosen more than one target or victim, either simultaneously or sequentially. Serial bullying has been widely documented in non-computer assisted forms of bullying as well as online varieties. It has also been observed among children and young people (Carter, 2015).

Victim: The intended target of the online abuse. The term "victim" can it itself have negative implications for those for whom it is applied, with connotations of "opportunistic victimhood" and assumptions that the target somehow is benefiting from the abuse or did something to attract it intentionally.

This research was previously published in the Encyclopedia of Information Science and Technology, Fourth Edition edited by Mehdi Khosrow-Pour, pages 1695-1703, copyright year 2018 by Information Science Reference (an imprint of IGI Global).

Chapter 11
Cyberbullying Among Malaysian Children Based on Research Evidence

Sarina Yusuf
Universiti Putra Malaysia, Malaysia

Md. Salleh Hj. Hassan
Universiti Putra Malaysia, Malaysia

Adamkolo Mohammed Mohammed Ibrahim
Universiti Putra Malaysia, Malaysia & University of Maiduguri, Nigeria

ABSTRACT

Previous studies have highlighted that the internet offers various online opportunities to users, for example, children, and that the internet possesses great potential to boost their education and provide health information. Scholars have emphasized the great utility of the internet in successfully raising awareness regarding children's online safety issues and enhancing social relationships. However, despite the positive effects of the internet, it has negative effects as well. Nowadays, children and adolescents are increasingly using the internet at younger ages, through diverse platforms and devices, and there have been rising concerns about children's safety online. The chapter investigated the level of cyberbullying among Malaysian children and discovered that the level of cyberbullying among Malaysian children is moderate. However, since the results of the study found a majority of the children surveyed had experienced cyberbullying at least once, there is a likelihood that cyberbullying could become a menace to the Malaysian child online.

DOI: 10.4018/978-1-5225-7492-7.ch011

INTRODUCTION

The Internet, a technology that cuts across geographical borders and overcomes the challenges of time is considered the most influential technological development in the 21st Century (Dholakia & Kshetri 2004). It has been described as the modern Pandora's Box that has opened a new cyberspace of threats to unwary users (Ktoridou, Eteokleous & Zachariadou 2012). Given the broad use and the rapid sophistication of the cyber technology over the years, the Internet is gradually replacing conventional (traditional) media of communication and becoming not only a new means communication but also a new means of interaction and socialization for millions of users nowadays (Ktoridou et al. 2012).

Rapid innovative advancements in the cyber technology and cyber-related technologies have exceptionally augmented the capacity and categories of users over the decades. According to Dholakia and Kshetri (2004), the Internet took only three years to reach 50 million users around the world compared to the 13 years taken by the radio and 38 years by the television. Approximately 2.9 billion people all over the world have access to the Internet, representing around 41% of the world population, and this number continues to increase (Kenda 2014).

The cyberspace is rapidly becoming a medium for people to meet their everyday needs like searching for information, communicating and entertainment (University of Southern California, [USC] Annenberg School Center for the Digital Future [ASCDF], 2008). The cyberspace has certainly provided enormous benefits and advantages to the people (Lenhart, Madden & Hitlin 2005). A meta-analysis study by Guan and Subrahmanyam (2009) has found that the cyber technology is a useful tool for promoting youth cognitive, social and physical development. In addition, scholars have emphasised the great utility of the Internet in successfully raising awareness regarding health issues, enhancing social relationships, maintaining community links among the young people and numerous other benefits (Barak & Sadovsky 2008; Subrahmanyam & Greenfield 2008; Flicker, Maley, Ridgley, Biscope, Lambardo & Skinner 2008).

Despite the positive effects of the cyberspace on users, the technology exerts some negative influences as well (e.g., cyberbullying), especially on children and the youth (Livingstone, 2012). Nowadays, Malaysian children and adolescents are increasingly using cyber technology at younger ages, with diverse devices and technologies (Balakrishnan 2015). In recent years however, there has been growing concern by the public, schools and parents about children and youth involvement in online risk behaviors such as cyberbullying and harassment (Finkelhor, Mitchell & Wolak 2000; Wolak, Mitchell & Finkelhor 2006). Many Malaysian youth and children have been exposed on daily basis to numerous Internet risks and harms (Balakrishnan 2015).

Given the ease of access and use of Internet technologies, even children learn how to use it; some children even go to the extent of protecting their online privacy from the prowling eyes of their parents (Yusuf, Osman, Hassan & Teimoury 2014). With just a click on the keyboard/keypad, children can access almost anything, including any kind of video, article and image they desire, including what they might stumble across accidentally (Balakrishnan 2015; Ktoridou et al. 2012), which often leads to incidences of cyberbullying, where children are being bullied by others while online (Yusuf et al. 2014).

This suggests that cyberbullying has been posing growing concern, especially for the online safety of the youth and children. Furthermore, there have been significant and rapid changes in children and youth's online activities in the last one decade in the country (Balakrishnan 2015; Yusuf et al. 2014). Evidently, there has been remarkable increase in the use of smartphones by the youngsters coupled with their migration from social activity to social networking sites across societies in the world (Jones, Mitchell & Finkelhor 2012) and in Malaysia (Abu Bakar 2013; Balakrishnan 2015).

Abu Bakar (2013) has empirically supported the issue that cyberbullying is a silent epidemic in the Malaysian society. The scholar indicated that online harassment and sexually based cyberbullying are the most common forms of cyberbullying in the country. Over the recent years, many incidents of cyberbullying had occurred on the Internet, which led to cases such as homicide, sexual assault, humiliation and assault. Cyberbullying incidents are increasing every in the country and becoming a potent threat to children, parents and other stakeholders (Neging, Musa, R. &Abdul Wahab 2013).

Norton Family Report (NOFR) (2010) indicates that he rising popularity of the new media and the increasing amount of time children spend online pose great challenges to parents and or guardians who want to protect their children from the threats and harms of the cyberspace. Hence, this study was prompted by the urge to understand the prevalence of cyberbullying in Malaysia by determining the level of the phenomenon among children. One major area that this chapter has contributed to is the development of a scale suitable for measuring cyberbullying in Malaysian society. Given that previous research focuses on qualitative approach such as face-to-face and telephone interviews, there has been a dearth of quantitative scale to measure cyberbullying, particularly on sexually based cyberbullying and online harassment dimensions. Therefore, this study adopted a quantitative approach.

BACKGROUND

Cyberbullying in Malaysia

According to an Interpol statistics, online harassment is growing rampantly all around the world, and Malaysia is no exception. It has been reported that one in every five children online becomes the target of cyber predators and 30% of female children have been sexually harassed in a chat room (Azizan 2012).

The cyber security unit of Malaysia have conducted a survey on the effect of cyber threats on children and adolescents and found that about 60% of the cases reported to them were about cyberbullying on social networking sites such as Facebook and MySpace (Nik Anis, Abdul Rahim, & Lim 2012). Despite the limited number of literature on cyberbullying among Malaysian youngsters, a study conducted by Balakrishnan (2015) found that cyberbullying does occur among Malaysian youth. However, Balakrishnan (2015) suggests that occurrence of the phenomenon among the respondents of the study (youth aged 17 to 30 years old) was not as prevalent as it is among children and teenagers, and that social networking sites are the most likely domains where cyberbullying incidences take place.

In addition, there are many none-empirical evidences of cyberbullying occurrences in Malaysia. In 2010, not less than 60 cases of cyberbullying were reported to the cyber security unit of Malaysia in 2007 (McKenna 2010). Surprisingly however, the number of reported cases rose to 5,181 in 2009 and 11,930 in 2010 (Cyber Security Malaysia Report [CSMR] 2011). Furthermore, various media reports in Malaysia have suggested that cyberbullying is prevalent among children and the youth. However, much of it could have been under-reported because most people are unaware that it has become a serious issue (Eek 2009).

According to Roberts and Samani (2013), the McAfee and ABA (Anti Bullying Alliance) surveys have found that cyberbullying is one of the critical online phenomena that children and youth face nowadays. Nik Anis et al. (2012) also reported that besides cyberbullying, the main online threats to Malaysian children while online are cyber-grooming, identity theft and child pornography.

The findings of a national survey conducted by Malaysian Cyber Security in 2011 indicates that more than 90% of children aged 5 to 18 in Malaysia may have been exposed to cyber threat. Findings of NOFR (2010) survey indicate that due to their excessive use of the Internet, 87% of 553 Malaysian children surveyed indicated having been bullied by cyber predators. Furthermore, the results of a national survey of school-going children in Malaysia shows that almost 30% of the children indicated that they have been bullied while online. However, only 13% of them admitted being bullied almost every day on the Internet (CSMR 2014, 2013).

LITERATURE REVIEW

Children in Digital Age

The literature stresses that social networking sites like Facebook and Twitter, search engines such as Google, MSN (Microsoft Network), Yahoo and WIKIs are an established part of Internet users' daily life events (Eteokleous & Pavlou 2010). Adolescents mainly under the age of 18 are the highest users of this digital realm. These adolescents are commonly referred to as Digital Learners (Murugesan 2009), Net Generation (Myers, McCaw & Hemphill 2011), Millennial Teens or Generation Y (Neging et al. 2013) and Digital Natives (Prensky 2001) since they were born and growing up in the Information Technology (IT) age (Ktoridou et. al 2012). This group of users is the main consumer of the Internet since the first official outbreaks of the Internet in the mid-1990s (Ward 2011).

In contrast, children that were born or growing up during the time of Internet technological evolution are classified as the digital immigrants (Prensky 2001). These users are using the cyber technology and associated technologies based on their needs for survival by adjusting to the environments as part of their daily lives (Ktoridou et al. 2012). Since new generations are the frequent users of the Internet, it follows that they are more aware of the use, the tools and the features of the Internet than the older generations (Davidson & Martellozzo 2008). Consistent with the facts, a research conducted in 21 European countries has showed that 75% of children in European countries are using the Internet and the rate continues to grow everyday (Livingstone & Haddon 2009).

Adolescents and youths are the most fervent users of the Internet, who have embraced cyber technology and digital media as a lifestyle for communicating, making connections, interacting and social networking (Ktoridou et al. 2012). The researchers further indicated that the Internet has the ability to communicate with people without limits regardless of the languages, cultural and geographical diversity, simply by using the social network (e.g. Facebook and Twitter), chat rooms (e.g. Skype and Yahoo Messengers) and various other forums. Through all the convenient tools for socializing, people from all over the world with various background and cultures can connect easily and quickly. According to Eteokleous (2011), this technology enabled children to understand, to discover new things, and to express their feelings without boundaries and limitations. In addition, a survey by the Malaysian Communication and Multimedia Commission (MCMC 2014) reports that almost 65% of Malaysian population has access to the Internet out of which 17% are children and adolescents aged 7 to 19 years old.

A recent research conducted in the United Kingdom (UK) reported that one of the main predictors of risks and harm among children as young as nine years old is indulging in risky online behaviors (Livingstone & Gorzig 2014). Furthermore, nearly 11% and 13% of adolescents within the age range of 9 to

16 years old in the UK have already seen an online pornography and seen or received hateful messages respectively (Livingstone 2012).

A study found that 95% of young adults aged 18 to 29 have easy access almost anywhere to the Internet via high-speed broadband and smartphones (Pew Internet and American Life Project [PI&ALP] 2013; Zickhur & Smith 2013). According to them, this scenario has led us to the disturbing reality of the Internet norms these days that not all of the access to the Internet is safe, particularly for adolescents and children.

A number of research surveys have suggested that majority of children aged between 12 and 14 years use the Internet intensively, spending about 15 to 20 hours per week communicating, passing pastime and entertaining themselves (Livingstone, Bober & Helsper 2005; USC ASCDF 2008, 2005; Van den Eijnden, Spijkerman, Vermulst, Van Rooij & Engels 2010; World Internet Project [WIP] 2013; Zamaria & Fletcher 2007).

The Concept of Bullying

According to Carter (2011), resolving conflicts amongst adolescence is a normal part of their maturation process, and usually will be disclosed in bullying behaviors, with bullies threatening other students who may be perceived as vulnerable or weak. This kind of behavior is identified as either traditional bullying or cyberbullying. Since bullying behaviors occurred during the process of growing up, Banks (1997) has identified that bullying might increase during elementary school, will be at uttermost frequency during middle school years and will be decreasing in high school.

In order to comprehend the phenomenon called cyberbullying, it is important to understand the concepts of traditional bullying better. Olweus (2002) formulated a systematic terminology of bullying. The researcher defines victimization or bullying as a situation when a student is exposed repeatedly and over time to negative actions on the part of one or more students. The researcher further explains that negative action is when someone intentionally inflicts, or attempts to inflict, injury or discomfort upon another (Olweus 2002). Smith, Mahdavi, Carvalho, Fisher and Russell (2008) comprehensively but concisely defined bullying as the act of verbal, physical, relational and indirectly bullying often referred to in the scholarly literature, media and Internet as traditional bullying.

This early concept of bullying has been used for decades by researchers to identify the bullying behaviors among children and adolescents. Nansel, Overpeck, Pilla, Simons-Morton and Scheidt (2001) reinforced the term bullying with an additional important characteristic, the imbalance of power that exists in which the bully or bullies are considered more powerful by attacking a victim who is less powerful. Based on this consideration, experts of bullying behaviors have shared same views that bullying is a major concern in the society as it leads to negative outcomes for the victims' physical and psychological well-being (Noordahl, Poole, Stanton, Walden & Beran 2008; Smokowski & Kopasz 2005). Many victims of bullying can vividly recall being harassed during childhood, especially victims who cannot properly defend himself or herself because of the difference in strength and size (Hinduja & Patchin 2009). According to a dissertation by Carter (2011), bullying problems often go undetected and unreported because many people view bullying as a normal part of life especially in middle and high school, as most people believe that it is normal for children to fight and they have to learn how to protect themselves the hard way.

The Concept of Cyberbullying

Cyberbullying has been defined as the act of willfully using electronic and/or cyber technologies to deliberately and repeatedly harass or threaten someone by sending or posting cruel text and/or graphic messages (Abu Bakar 2013; Berson, Berson & Ferron 2002; Finkelhor, Mitchell & Wolak 2001, 2000; Hinduja & Patchin 2009). Smith et al. (2008) defined cyberbullying as an aggressive, intentional act carried out by a group or individuals, using electronic forms of contact, repeatedly and over time against a victim who cannot easily defend him or herself.

Researchers argued that cyberbullying could occur anywhere and at any time, this empowers bullies much more than traditional bullying does because more targets could be harassed through cyberbullying with less effort on the part of the bully (Garinger 2008). This indicates that the time taken by a cyberbully to harass someone is now limited to the speed of a click of the mouse and the spread of threats is no longer limited to the cyberbully and cybervictim (Mitchell 2011). Meanwhile, surveys have reported that in Malaysia, majority of children spend as many as 19 hours per week on average using the Internet (NOFR 2010). According to the report, the rising popularity of the new media and the increasing amount of time children spend online pose great challenges to parents and or guardians who want to protect their children from the threats and harms of the cyberspace. A new form of bullying commonly referred to as cyberbullying has become a new growing problem on the Internet in nowadays (Carter 2011). Smith et al. (2008) defined cyberbullying as an aggressive, intentional act carried out by a group or individual, using electronic forms of contact, repeatedly and over time against a victim who cannot easily defend him or herself.

Generally, cyberbullying is not that much different from traditional bullying, even though it has changed overtime through the advancement of technology. Bullies nowadays have moved from the school grounds to behind-the-cellular-phone or computer screen (Hinduja & Patchin 2010). According to the researchers, the availability and use of technology by the young people is on the rise and so is the ability to become cyberbullies or cyber predators.

Similarly, Sharif (2008) indicate that rapid advancement of Internet and cellular technologies has opened up a new and infinite space that young people can explore with fewer restrictions, as the digital media offers convenient opportunities to humiliate, bully, or harass someone online. A new variation of bullying has transformed from the physical to the virtual, it becomes insidious when cyberbullying grows into a form of psychological cruelty (Sharif & Hoff 2007) and in some cases will end up with the loss of lives (Abu Bakar 2013).

Types of Cyberbullying

Cyberbullying could take place every hour, every day, throughout the week (24/7) from anywhere (Willard 2007). According to the researcher, cyberbullying can take place through the information technology that (IT) students access every day, including cell phones, text messages, e-mail, instant messaging, social networks, pictures and video clips. Garinger (2008) suggests that since cyberbullying can occur anywhere and at any time, this empowers bullies to a greater degree compared to traditional bullying. More targets can be harassed through cyberbullying with less effort on the part of the bully (Garinger 2008; Willard 2007). This implies that the time a cyberbully uses to perpetrate an attack is now limited to the speed of a mouse click and the spread of threatening attack is no longer limited to the bully and target (Mitchell 2011). There are eight distinct forms of cyberbullying, namely flaming, harassment, denigration, impersonation, outing and trickery, exclusion, cyberstalking and cyberthreats (Willard 2007). Table 1 contains eight distinct forms of online harassment, which Willard (2007) has outlined.

Trolling, happy slapping and sexually based bullying are other forms of cyberbullying (Ybarra & Mitchell 2004). Online harassment is defined as "threats or other offensive behaviors targeted directly at youth through new technology channels (e.g., Internet, text messaging) or posted online about youth for others to see" (Jones et al. 2012, p. 54). According to Willard (2007) online harassment is the act of aggressive behaviors, including insulting someone online, making nasty or threatening remarks through e-mail or instant messages, spreading unwanted images or video clips of someone and creating offensive pictures or images and posting them online in order to humiliate somebody.

Sexually based cyberbullying is also a common form of cyberbullying (Mitchell & Jones 2011) and it involves sexual solicitations and unwanted exposure to sexual materials such as pornographic pictures, pornographic video clips and sexually suggesting gestures posted online or done with the aim of arousing sexual feelings in the targeted persons or making them feel sexually abused. According to Abu Bakar (2013), online harassment and sexually based cyberbullying are the two most prevalent forms of cyberbullying in Malaysia.

Table 1. Categories of cyberbullying

Type of Bullying	Description
Flaming	• Short lived argument between protagonists • Extended, heated argument leading to threats of violence • Questionable credibility of threats
Harassment	• Repeated ongoing assault • Usually one sided • Can have multiple protagonists harassing a target • Some protagonists may not even know the target • Could be criminal especially if involving hate or bias • Target is direct recipient of material
Denigration	• Harmful, untrue, or cruel speech about a target • Posted online and/or circulated via email, texting, instant messenger • Target is not direct recipient • Included public postings and sending of digital images (which may have been digitally altered) • May include defamation or invasion of privacy
Impersonation	• Falsely identifying as the target • Posting or sending material that shows the target in a bad light or interferes with target's relationships and friendships • Often a means of the protagonist getting the target in trouble with authorities
Outing and Trickery	• Posting or otherwise circulating images and other personal communications that are embarrassing to the target • Target is not direct recipient of the attack • Images are often sexually suggestive and verge on sexual harassment
Exclusion	• Deliberate exclusion of the target from communications to which he or she was previously privy to • Often occurs when the protagonist convinces multiple people to defriend [unfriend] the target
Cyberstalking	• Including the repeated harassment threats of harm • Can be intimidating, offensive, or involve extortion • Protagonist often lulls target into sense of false security before slowly escalating harassment

Source: Willard (2007).

According to Mitchell and Jones (2011), sexual solicitations and exposure to unwanted sexual materials are a wide range of negative cyber experiences affecting children. The researchers defined sexual based cyberbullying as sexual solicitation, which involves an urge to participate in a sexual activity willingly or unwillingly, made by someone online. Sexually based cyberbullying also involves exposure to sexual materials such as pictures of naked people or people having sex while surfing the web, doing online search, opening e-mails or instant messages, or opening links in e-mails or instant messages (Abu Bakar 2013; Mitchell & Jones 2011).

Patterns of Cyberbullying

Furthermore, through commonly used channels such as blogs, chat rooms, file-sharing applications, social networking sites and mobile phone messages, children and young people can be threatened, excluded from activities or humiliated by having misleading messages or photos about them posted online (Eek 2009). According to an online survey, these aggressions among youngsters are mostly channeled through social networking sites; 54% of 10,000 participants aged 12 to 17 have reported having experienced cyberbullying on Facebook (Roberts & Samani 2013).

Impact of Cyberbullying

Over the past decade, cyberbullying has become more dangerous and more virulent form of bullying to the extent that insidious forms of victimization now lurk in online community resulting from cyber-bullying (Raskauskas & Stoltz 2007). Cyberbullying is one of the biggest threats confronted by young people and it has become a common phenomenon among youth nowadays (Abu Bakar 2013). The effect of cyberbullying is more traumatic than traditional bullying since victims can be bullied 24 hours and 7 days a week from anywhere as long as there is a working Internet connection (Willard 2007). Besides the unlimited accessibility to the victims, cyberbullying also causes psychological abuse to the victims including teasing, intimidation and exclusion in ways that do not exist in traditional bullying (Raskauskas & Stoltz 2007).

Cyberbullies usually seek to exert dominance and power over the victim and inflict psychological torture such as the feeling of low self-esteem, loneliness, poor mental health, peer rejection, depression, isolation and hopelessness in their victims (Hinduja & Patchin 2010; Pranjic & Bajraktarevic 2010). According to the Center for Disease Control and Prevention [CDC&P] (2010), these negative feelings could even influence children to consider committing a suicide.

Between 2003 and 2012, some 34 cases involving cyberbullicides (committing suicide because of being cyberbullied) were reported, while in 2013 alone, seven cases were reported (Abu Bakar 2013). In 2007, suicide was found to be the third leading cause of death among younger citizens of USA aged 15 to 24 years old (American Foundation for Suicide Prevention [AFSP] 2007). Generally, however, research directly linking cyberbullying to suicide is quite limited (Brunstein-Klomek, Sourander & Gould 2010; Pranjic & Bajraktarevic 2010).

Material and Methods

Cyberbullying dimensions were constructed based on the conceptual framework of this study and a review of extant literature. As mentioned earlier, there are many forms of cyberbullying. However, this study focuses on sexually based cyberbullying and online harassment. For the measurement of sexually based cyberbullying dimension, a scale developed by Mitchell and Jones (2011) and Livingstone et al. (2011) was adopted. While, for the measurement of online harassment dimension (which is related to acts of aggressive behavior online), a scale developed by Livingstone et al. (2011) was adopted with modifications. The original survey scale consists of four items on risk and harm towards child's safety (i.e. bullying, pornography, sexting and meeting strangers online).

This study designed a scale consisting of an inventory of 10 items measured using five-point Likert scale was developed. Two constructs (online harassment and sexually based cyberbullying) were involved, each measured by five items. However, to ensure that the scale is valid in Malaysian context and to help the respondents (children) understand the questions better, several modifications were made. Respondents were asked to answer the questions based on a 5-point Likert scale: "1 never, 2 seldom, 3 sometimes, 4 often and 5 very often. As part of the modifications, some words/phrases in the original scale that sound sensitive in Malaysian context were changed based on the advised given by Ministry of Education in the country. For example, having sex was replaced with obscene acts and pictures of naked persons was replaced with inappropriate materials in the modified scale. Table 2 shows the complete original and modified items in the scale.

Given that Malay language is the primary national language and English language is treated as a secondary national language, to ensure that the respondents understood the questions very well, the survey instrument was designed in both languages.

Stratified random sampling perspective was adopted to select 378 pupils aged 9 to 16 years old from eight primary schools in Selangor State. Only children that had experienced cyberbullying in the past 12 months were selected. Paired, coded survey forms were administered to the young participants in order to avoid non-response bias respondents (see Singer 2006).

The respondents were collected into small groups during class hours and were administered with the questionnaire, which they completed under the supervision of their researchers. Either of the children's parents was also selected to participate as a respondent. A few trained enumerators were employed who read out the questionnaire aloud for the younger respondents aged 9 to 11 years old. Although the average time to complete the questionnaire was about 15 minutes, it took the younger respondents about 30 minutes or more to complete. The questionnaires were retrieved on the same day after the pupils had finished completing them; 61 forms from the children and 49 forms from their parents were recovered.

Factor analysis was used, and the questionnaire was reduced to 378 after data cleansing. Construct reliability test was then run. The Cronbach alpha coefficient value (α) for the construct for pre-test was $\alpha = .830$ (n = 63)[1] while for actual data collection was $\alpha = .75$ (n = 375). This indicates that the scale was very reliable (see Salkind 2008). Furthermore, a committee of experts reviewed the cyberbullying items and validated it. Approval from Malaysian ministry of education and the Selangor State department of education was also obtained. Similarly, consent was obtained from authors whose works were adopted in this study.

Table 2. Original and adapted cyberbullying scales

Original Items (Qualitative Approach)	Adapted Items (Quantitative Approach)	Dimension and Source
Has anyone ever sent you nude or nearly nude photos or videos of kids who were under the age of 18 that others took?	I have been sent inappropriate messages on the Internet	Sexually-based Cyberbullying (YISS 1, 2 and 3) by Mitchell and Jones (2011)
Did you ever open a message or a link that showed actual people/naked people/people having sex that you did not want?	I have seen inappropriate materials posted where other people could see it on the Internet.	
Did you ever find yourself in a website that showed pictures of naked people/having sex when you did not want to be in it?	I have seen other people perform obscene acts.	
Did anyone on the Internet ask you for sexual information? Like, what your body looks like or sexual things you have done.	I have been asked on the Internet for a photo or video showing my private parts.	
Did anyone on the Internet ever try to get you to talk online about sex when you did not want?	I have been asked to talk about nasty acts with someone on the Internet.	
Nasty or hurtful messages were sent to me.	I have received nasty or hurtful messages.	Online Harassment (EUkidsonline) by Livingstone et al. (2011)
Nasty or hurtful messages about me were passed around or posted where others could see.	Nasty or hurtful messages about me were posted or passed around online where others could see.	
Other nasty or hurtful things on the Internet.	I have received other nasty or hurtful things on the Internet.	
I was threatened on the Internet.	No changes made	
I was left out or excluded from a group or activity on the Internet.	No changes made	

RESULTS

Respondent's Demographic Profile: Children

The respondents' demographic information shows female respondents were almost twice as many as male respondents. That is, the disparity between the proportion of the male (35.2%) and female (64.8%) pupils was very wide. The respondents were divided into two age groups for data analysis convenience. The first group was the younger group, comprising 155 pupils aged between 9 and 11 years old. The second group was the teenage group, comprising 232 respondents aged between 13 and 16 years old, with

Table 3. Descriptive statistic of respondents' demographic profile (n=375)

Variables	Frequency	Percentage
Gender		
Male	132	35.2
Female	243	64.8
Age		
9	48	12.8
10	49	13.1
11	54	14.4
13	83	22.1
14	90	24.0
16	51	13.6
Ethnicity		
Malay	275	73.3
Chinese	49	13.1
Indian	46	12.3
Others	5	1.3
Religion		
Islam	277	73.9
Buddha	41	10.9
Hindu	42	11.2
Christian	12	3.2
Others	3	.8
Living area		
Urban	216	57.6
Rural	159	42.4

exception of 15 year-old age group whose members were sitting a compulsory examination. Generally, the respondents were aged between 9 and 16 years old (M=12.51), with more than two-thirds of them (60.1%) aged between 13 and 14 years old. Many (57.6%) of them lived in urban areas (see Table 3).

Respondents' Demographic Profile: Parents

Male parents are slightly fewer than the female parents were, fathers, 44.8% and mothers, 55.2%. Many (56.8%) of them were aged between 42 and 53 years old. Quite many (40.5%) of them were aged 30 to 41 years old, with only few of them (2.4% and .3%) were aged between 54 to 65 years old and 18 to 29 years old respectively (M=43, SD=5.43) (see Table 4).

Majority of the parents were Malay (73%) by ethnic identity and Muslims (74%) by religious identity. The parents' educational qualification data indicates that 26.7% of them were Bachelor degree holders, 25.3% held SPM[2], 20.5% held Diploma and less than 10%. Only very few (1.3%, n=5) of them had never

Table 4. Descriptive statistic of parents' profile (n=375)

Variables	Frequency	Percentage
Gender		
Male	168	44.8
Female	207	55.2
Age		
18 – 29	1	.3
30 – 41	152	40.5
42 – 53	213	56.8
54 – 65	9	2.4
Mean = 42.89		
SD = 5.43		
Ethnicity		
Malay	273	72.8
Chinese	48	12.8
Indian	47	12.5
Others	7	1.9
Religion		
Islam	277	73.9
Buddha	42	11.2
Hindu	41	10.9
Christian	13	3.5
Others	2	.5
Education Level		
Never been to school	5	1.3
Standard 6	11	2.9
SRP/PMR	26	6.9
SPM	95	25.3
STPM	26	6.9
Diploma	77	20.5
Bachelor's	100	26.7
Master's	33	8.8
PhD	2	.5
Monthly Income (RM)		
< 3,000	228	60.8
3,001 – 5,000	76	20.3
>5,001	71	18.9

been to any school. The monthly disposable income data shows that majority very many (60.8%) of the parents earned RM3,000[3] or less.

Prevalence of Cyberbullying Incidences Among the Children

This study discovers that the gaps between the children's responses on 'never experienced', 'sometimes experienced' and 'often experienced' were wide. Unpredictably, nearly all (94.1%) of the respondents indicated never having experienced any online threat (M=1.11, SD=.22). Extremely few of them experienced any cyberbullying as indicated by the overall mean value (M=1.15, SD=.33) (see Table 5).

Level of Cyberbullying Incidences Among the Children

Overview

Level of cyberbullying refers to the degree of prevalence of the occurrence of cyberbullying incidences. The level is measured using 'Low', 'Moderate' and 'High' scales (see Sharma, Mukherjee, Kumar & Dillon 2005). The scores of the level are derived based on the cut-off mark method, by subtracting the minimum scores from the maximum scores of the responses and are then divided into three levels (see Sa'ari, Wong & Roslan 2005). For example, the overall mean score of cyberbullying is M=1.15, SD=.33. The level of cyberbullying (see Table 6) is determined marking off this mean score in the level scale, which was designed based on the method mentioned above.

The overall mean value of cyberbullying scale is M=1.15, SD=.33 (refer to Table 5). Based on the results in Table 6, the level of cyberbullying among Malaysian children is moderate.

Table 5. Percentage of frequency, mean and standard deviation of cyberbullying (n=375)

Items	Likert Scale (% of Frequency)					Mean	SD
	1	2	3	4	5		
I have seen an inappropriate materials posted where other people could see it on the Internet.	79.2	17.7	1.1	1.0	1.0	1.24	.44
I have received nasty or hurtful messages.	82.9	13.7	2.0	1.1	.3	1.22	.40
I have been sent an inappropriate message on the Internet.	84.0	13.5	1.0	1.0	.5	1.21	.40
I have seen other people perform obscene acts.	84.5	12.4	2.0	.5	.5	1.21	.38
I have received other nasty or hurtful things on the Internet.	87.7	10.5	1.5	.5	.3	1.14	.34
I was left out or excluded from a group or activity on the Internet.	89.9	6.2	2.1	1.0	.8	1.12	.34
I have received nasty or hurtful messages about me were passed around or posted where others could see.	90.9	7.3	1.2	.3	.2	1.11	.31
I was threatened on the Internet.	94.1	5.2	.5	.1	.1	1.11	.22
I have been asked on the Internet for a photo or video showing my private parts.	95.8	3.7	.3	.1	.1	1.05	.22
I have been asked to talk about nasty acts with someone on the Internet.	96.0	4.0	-	-	-	1.04	.20
Overall score						1.15	.33

Note: Likert scale: 1 never, 2 seldom, 3 sometimes, 4 often and 5 very often; M: Mean, SD: Standard Deviation

Table 6. Level of cyberbullying (n=375)

Level	Percentage	Overall Mean Value of the Scale	
		Mean	SD
Low (1.00 – 1.04)	10.0	1.15	.33
Moderate (1.05 – 1.23)	80.0		
High (1.24 – 5.00)	10.0		

Note: SD: Standard Deviation.

DISCUSSION

The results reveal that extremely few (3.9%) of the respondents have ever been threatened online. In addition, only quite a few of them experienced any form of sexually based cyberbullying as follows. Only a few (20.8%) of them had seen inappropriate materials at least once posted online, quite few (16.0%) of them had ever seen inappropriate materials posted online and only extremely few (14.5%) of them had seen people commit obscene acts online.

Similarly, quite few of the children have ever been harassed online as indicated by these percentages. Only 11.1% of them have ever suffered the humiliation of being expelled from an online group; and others have ever ridiculed only 10.1% of them through posting their pictures online where others could see them. Only 4.2% of them have ever been asked by someone to share the picture or video of their private parts online; and only 3.0% of them have ever been cornered by someone to talk about nasty things online. The results generally suggest that majority of the children have only mildly (moderately) experienced at least one form of cyberbullying or another at some point in time within the past one year. However, majority of them never experienced or got involved in any form of cyberbullying or its related incidence with any serious degree.

This outcome further suggests that either many of the children have been involved in cyberbullying incidences (as cybervictims or cyberbullies) more than once in the past one year but have been unaware of what it constitutes, or (fortunately) have never been exposed to any cyberbullying act. This finding is consistent with the findings of a survey conducted by the Malaysian cyber security in collaboration with a mobile telecommunication company in 2013 (CSMR 2013).

Therefore, putting the frequency distributions into perspective, this chapter suggests that mild cyberbullying incidences actually occur among Malaysian children but that majority of them have been unaware of what it constitutes. The children may have been passing it for a normal part of online social interaction, especially if the cyberbullying incidences occur on social network sites (see Balakrishnan 2015; Lenhart, Madden, Smith, Purcell, Zickhur & Rainie 2011).

Online harassment has been the most prevalent type of cyberbullying incidence in the country. Wolak et al. (2006) supports this finding empirically. Similarly, Bernama (2012) supported this finding. Although mildly, incidences of online harassment are increasingly becoming prevalent nowadays because children and youth have unprecedented access to information and communication technologies such as smartphones, tablets and Internet connection (Abu Bakar 2013; Hinduja & Patchin 2009).

FUTURE RESEARCH DIRECTIONS

This chapter identifies the absence of a standard cyberbullying measurement scale suitable for Malaysian context as a challenge and limitation. The scale adopted in this study, which were used in the United States (see Mitchell & Jones 2011) and various European countries (see Livingstone et al. 2012) have been suitably reliable in those contexts, and have produced predictable results. However, the findings of the current study have rather been unpredicted.

This study is only limited to quantitative approach. Hence, this chapter recommends that future research should focus on qualitative approach in Malaysian context. Qualitative data can be used to conduct an in-depth observation of the causal relationships between cyberbullying other social factors such as demographics or parent-child relationships. Therefore, future research should attempt to explore the relationships between cyberbullying and demographic characteristics such as gender and age, as well as parental attachments. It is expected that this approach can generate new and reliable cyberbullying scale for Malaysian society. Qualitative methodologies studies such as in-depth interviews, focus group discussion, content analysis and audio recordings can provide valuable insights and facilitate a clearer interpretation of factors affecting cyberbullying among Malaysian children (see Festl & Quandt 2013).

This study focuses on cyber victim (being a victim of cyberbullying) dimension only because most Malaysian children and adolescents that have got get involved in cyberbullying acts have been victims rather than bullies (Balakrishnan 2015). However, to get a comprehensive understanding of cyberbullying, future research should investigate the effect of cyberbullying on other parties involved in the behavior, namely the bully, the bully-victim and the by-stander (audience) (see Camacho, Hassanein & Head 2014).

CONCLUSION

This study has discovered that generally, the level of cyberbullying among Malaysian children is moderate. Specifically, however, incidences of online harassment occur more often than those of sexually based cyberbullying do. The findings also reveal that majority of the children have experienced a cyberbullying incidence at least once in a year, which gives the hints that with time, cyberbullying could become a menace to the innocent Malaysian child online (see Balakrishnan 2015). Nonetheless, the threat posed by cyberbullying to the children has been moderate, which implies that the online safety of majority of Malaysian children is guaranteed at present. Therefore, this study concludes that mild cyberbullying incidences actually do occur among Malaysian children, however, most of the children have been unaware of what it portends.

However, parents are advised to control their children's access to and usage of technologies as well as monitor their behavior. Parents should report any cyberbullying incidence case to the Police. The Malaysian cyber security should maintain the annual cyberbullying survey. Children should be pedagogically instructed about online risks and safety. Therefore, the Ministry of Education is advised to introduce subjects on cyber safety and threats in elementary and high schools. Lastly, the Malaysian Communication and Multimedia Commission (MCMC) should organize seminars on online safety and threats periodically to enlighten parents, adolescents and young adults about the dangers lurking in the online milieu and teach them ways of avoiding or managing involvement in cyberbullying.

REFERENCES

Abu Bakar, H. S. (2013). Investigating the emergence themes of Cyberbullying phenomenon: A grounded theory approach. In *Educational Media, 2013 IEEE 63rd Annual Conference International Council for Educational Media (ICEM)* (pp. 1-14). Nanyang Technological University.

AFSP. (2007). *Facts and figures: National Statistics.* Retrieved on February 4, 2014 from http://Ofea9f-b064-4092-bl-135c-3a70delfda.afsp.org/index.cfin?fuseaction_home.vievvpageandpage icl_0S

Armsden, G. C., & Greenberg, M. T. (1987). The inventory of parent and peer attachment: Individual differences and their relationship to psychological well-being in adolescence. *Journal of Youth and Adolescence, 16*(5), 427–454. doi:10.1007/BF02202939 PMID:24277469

Azizan, H. (2012). Do you know whom your kids are talking to? *The Star Online.* Retrieved on January 28, 2014 from: http://www.thestar.com.my/News/Nation/2012/04/29/Do-you-know-who-your-kids-are-talking-to/

Balakrishnan, V. (2015). Cyberbullying among young adults in Malaysia: The roles of gender, age and Internet frequency. *Computers in Human Behavior, 46*, 149–157. doi:10.1016/j.chb.2015.01.021

Banks, R. (1997). Bullying in schools. *ERIC Digest.* Retrieved on July 23, 2014 from: http://npin.org/library/pre1998/n00416/n00416.html

Barak, A., & Sadovsky, Y. (2008). Internet use and personal empowerment of hearing-impaired adolescents. *Computers in Human Behavior, 24*(5), 1802–1815. doi:10.1016/j.chb.2008.02.007

Bernama. (2012). *Early intervention on cyber security to safeguard young.* Cyber Security Malaysia. Retrieved on August 7, 2014 from http://www.cybersecurity.my/bahasa/knowledge_bank/news/2012/main/detail/2225/index.html

Berne, S., Frisén, A., Schultze-krumbholz, A., Scheithauer, H., Naruskov, K., Luik, P., ... Zukauskiene, R. (2013). Aggression and violent behavior cyberbullying assessment instruments: A systematic review. *Aggression and Violent Behavior, 18*(2), 320–334. doi:10.1016/j.avb.2012.11.022

Berson, I. R., Berson, M. J., & Ferron, J. M. (2002). Emerging risks of violence in the digital age: Lessons for educators from an online study of adolescent girls in the United States. *Journal of School Violence, 1*(2), 51–72. doi:10.1300/J202v01n02_04

Brunstein-Klomek, A., Sourander, A., & Gould, M. (2010). The association of suicide and bullying in childhood to young adulthood: A review of cross-sectional and longitudinal research findings. *Canadian Journal of Psychiatry, 55*(5), 282–288. PMID:20482954

Camacho, S., Hassanein, K., & Head, M. (2014). *Understanding the factors that influence the perceived severity of cyber-bullying.* Paper presented at Human-Computer Interaction (HCI) International, Crete, Greece. 10.1007/978-3-319-07293-7_13

Carter, J. M. (2011). *Examining the relationship among physical and psychological health, parent and peer attachment and cyberbullying in adolescents in urban and suburban environments* (PhD Thesis). Wayne State University.

CDC&P. (2010). *Suicide: Risk and protective factors*. Retrieved on March 17, 2014 from http://ViolencePrevention/youthvlolence/risk-protectivefactors.html

CSMR. (2011). Children and teenagers exposed to negative cyber culture. *Bernama News*. Retrieved on January 28, 2014 from http://www.cybersecurity.my/en/knowledge_bank/news/2011/main/detail/2087/index.html

CSMR. (2014, 2013). *A National Survey Report 2013. Safety net: Growing awareness among Malaysian schoolchildren on staying safe online*. Cyber Security of Malaysia. Retrieved on December 4, 2014 from https://digi.cybersafe.my/files/article/DiGi_Survey_Booklet_COMPLETE.pdf

Davidson, C. J., & Martellozzo, E. (2008). Protecting vulnerable young people in cyberspace from sexual abuse: Raising awareness and responding globally. *Police Practice and Research*, *9*(41), 277–289. doi:10.1080/15614260802349965

Dholakia, N., Dholakia, R. R., & Kshetri, N. (2004). Global diffusion of the Internet. In H. Bidgoli (Ed.), The Internet Encyclopedia (2nd ed.; pp. 38-51). John Wiley & Sons. doi:10.1002/047148296X.tie072

Eek, T. S. (2009). *A big sister helps students cope with bullying*. UNICEF. Retrieved October 4, 2009, from http://www.unicef.org/infobycountry/malaysia_51549.html

Eteokleous, N., & Pavlou, V. (2010). Digital natives and technology literate students: Do teachers follow? *Proceedings of the Cyprus Scientific Association of Information and Communication Technologies in Education*, 113-124.

Festl, R., & Quandt, T. (2013). Social relations and cyberbullying: The influence of individual and structural attributes on victimization and perpetration via the Internet. *Human Communication Research*, *39*(1), 101–106. doi:10.1111/j.1468-2958.2012.01442.x

Finkelhor, D., Mitchell, K., & Wolak, J. (2001). *Highlights of the youth Internet safety survey*. Juvenile Justice Fact Sheet-FS200104. Washington, DC: US Government Printing Office. Retrieved November 20, 2007 from http://www.unh.edu/ccrc/pdf/jvq/CV46.pdf

Finkelhor, D., Mitchell, K. J., & Wolak, J. (2000). *On-line victimization: A report on the nations' youth*. Alexandra, VA: National Centre for Missing and Exploited Children.

Flicker, S., Maley, O., Ridgley, A., Biscope, S., Lambardo, C., & Skinner, H. A. (2008). Using technology and participatory action research to engage youth in health promotion. *Action Research*, *6*(3), 285–303. doi:10.1177/1476750307083711

Garinger, H. M. (2008). Cyber pox: A look at female adolescent cyber bullying. *Michigan Journal of Counseling*, *35*, 24 32.

Guan, S. A., & Subrahmanyam, K. (2009). Youth Internet use: Risks and opportunities. *Current Opinion in Psychiatry*, *22*(4), 351–356. doi:10.1097/YCO.0b013e32832bd7e0 PMID:19387347

Hinduja, S., & Patchin, J. W. (2007). Offline consequences of online victimization. *Journal of School Violence*, *6*(3), 89–112. doi:10.1300/J202v06n03_06

Hinduja, S., & Patchin, J. W. (2009). *Bullying beyond the schoolyard: Preventing and responding to cyberbullying*. Thousand Oaks, CA: Corwin Press.

Hinduja, S., & Patchin, J. W. (2010). Bullying, cyberbullying and suicide. *Archives of Suicide Research*, *14*(3), 206–221. doi:10.1080/13811118.2010.494133 PMID:20658375

Jones, L. M., Mitchell, K. J., & Finkelhor, D. (2012). Online harassment in context: Trends from three youth Internet safety surveys (2000, 2005, 2010). *Psychology of Violence*, *3*(1), 53–69. doi:10.1037/a0030309

Kenda, M. (2014). *Internet Society Global Internet Report 2014: Open and sustainable access for all.* Global Internet Report. Retrieved July 2, 2014, from http://www.Internetsociety.org/map/global-Internet-report/

Kraft, E. (2006). *Cyberbullying: A worldwide trend of misusing technology to harass others*. WIT Transactions on Information and Communication Technologies. Retrieved on June 19, 2014 from http://www.witpress.com/elibrary/wit-transactions-on-information-and-communication-technologies/36/16302

Ktoridou, D., Eteokleous, N., & Zachariadou, A. (2012). Internet uses and threats for students: Investigating parents' awareness. In T. Bastiaens & M. Ebner (Eds.), *Proceedings of World Conference on Educational Multimedia, Hypermedia and Telecommunications 2011* (pp. 179-188). Chesapeake, VA: Association for the Advancement of Computing in Education (AACE). Retrieved January 25, 2015 from http://www.editlib.org/p/37862/

Lenhart, A., Madden, M., & Hitlin, P. (2005). *Teens and technology. Youth are leading the transition to a fully wired and mobile nation. 2005*. Pew Internet and American Life Project. Retrieved from: http://www.pewInternet.org/pdfs/PIP Teens_Tech_JuIy2005web.pdf

Lenhart, A., Madden, M., Smith, A., Purcell, K., Zickhur, A., & Rainie, L. (2011). *Teens, kindness and the cruelty on social network sites*. Pew Internet and American Life Project.

Livingstone, S. (2012). Critical reflections on the benefits of ICT in education. *Oxford Review of Education*, *38*(1), 9–24. doi:10.1080/03054985.2011.577938

Livingstone, S., Bober, M., & Helsper, E. (2005). *Inequalities and the digital divide in children and young people's Internet use: Findings from the UK Children Go Online project*. London, UK: The London School of Economics and Political Science.

Livingstone, S., & Gorzig, A. (2014). When adolescents receive sexual messages on the Internet: Explaining experiences of risk and harm. *Computers in Human Behavior*, *33*, 8–15. doi:10.1016/j.chb.2013.12.021

Livingstone, S., & Haddon, L. (2009). Risky experiences for children online: Charting European research on children and the Internet. *Children & Society, 22*(4), 314–323. doi:10.1111/j.1099-0860.2008.00157.x

Livingstone, S., Haddon, L., & Görzig, A. (2012). *Children, risk and safety the Internet: Research and policy challenges in comparative perspective.* Bristol: Policy Press. doi:10.1332/policy-press/9781847428837.001.0001

Livingstone, S., Haddon, L., Gorzig, A., & Olafsson, A. (2011). *Risks and safety on the Internet: The perspective of European children: Full findings.* London, UK: EU Kids Online.

McKenna, P. (2010). Rise of cyberbullying. *Reader's Digest Asia.* Retrieved on April 3, 2014 from: http://origin-www.rdasia.com/rise_of_cyber_bullying/

MCMC. (2014). *Internet users survey 2014.* Retrieved on November 13, 2014 from http://www.skmm.gov.my/Resources/Statistics/Internet-users-survey/Hand-Phone-Users-Survey-2014

Mitchell, K. J., & Jones, L. M. (2011). *Youth Internet Safety Study (YISS): Methodology Repot.* Durham, NH: Crimes against Children Research Center University of New Hampshire. Retrieved on May 2, 2014 from: http://www.unh.edu/ccrc/pdf/YISS%20Methods%20Report%20formatted%20(final).pdf

Mitchell, M. S. (2011). *Cyberbullying and academic achievement: research into the rates of incidence, knowledge of consequences, and behavioral patterns of cyberbullying* (PhD Thesis). University of Connecticut.

Murugesan, S. (2009). *Social issues and web 2.0: A closer look at culture in e-learning. Handbook of Research on Web 2.0, 3.0, and X.0: Technologies, Business, and Social Applications, Information Science.* New York, NY: Prentice Hall.

Myers, J. J., McCaw, D. S., & Hemphill, L. S. (2011). *Responding to cyber bullying. An action tool for school leader.* Corwin Press, a Sage Company. doi:10.4135/9781483350516

Nansel, T., Overpeck, M., Pilla, R., Simons-Morton, B., & Scheidt, P. (2001). Bullying behaviors among U.S. youth: Prevalence and association with psychosocial adjustment. *Journal of the American Medical Association, 285*(16), 2094–2100. doi:10.1001/jama.285.16.2094 PMID:11311098

Neging, P., Musa, R., & Abdul Wahab, R. (2013). The determinants and outcomes of pathological Internet use (PIU) among urban millennial teens: A theoretical framework. World Academy of Science, Engineering and Technology, 74, 2-21.

Nik Anis, N. M., Abdul Rahim, R., & Lim, Y. (2012). Najib: Cyberbullying a serious threat to kids. *The Star Online.* Retrieved on January 28, 2014 from http://www.thestar.com.my/News/Nation/2012/10/10/Najib-Cyber-bullying-a-serious-threat-to-kids/

NOFR. (2010). *Global insights into family life online.* Retrieved from http://us.norton.com/content/en/us/home_homeoffice/media/pdf/nofr/Norton_Family-ReportUSA_June9.pdf

Nordahl, J. K., Poole, A., Stanton, L., Walden, L. M., & Beran, T. N. (2008). A review of school-based bullying interventions. *Democracy & Education*, *8*(1), 16–20.

Olweus, D. (2002). A profile of bullying at school. *Educational Leadership*, *60*, 12–17.

Online Bullying Is a Top Concern Among Youth. (2012, June 25). *Microsoft global youth online behavior survey*. Microsoft News Center. Retrieved from http://www.microsoft.com/en-us/news/press/2012/jun12/06-25youthbehaviorpr.aspx

PI&ALP. (2013). *The Demographic of Media Social Users-2012*. Washington, DC: Pew Internet and American Life Project. Retrieved from http://pewInternet.org/Reports/2013/Social-media-users.aspx

Pranjic, N., & Bajraktarevlc, A. (2010). Depression and suicide Ideation among secondary school adolescents involved m school bullying. *Primary Health Care Research and Development*, *1*(l), 349–362. doi:10.1017/S1463423610000307

Prensky, M. (2001). Digital natives, digital immigrants part 1. *On the Horizon*, *9*(5), 1–6. doi:10.1108/10748120110424816

Raskauskas, J., & Stoltz, A. D. (2007). Involvement in traditional and electronic bullying among adolescents. *Developmental Psychology*, *43*(3), 564–575. doi:10.1037/0012-1649.43.3.564 PMID:17484571

Roberts, L., & Samani, R. (2013). *Digital deception: The online behavior of teens*. McAfee: An Intel Company. Retrieved on May 5, 2014 from http://oxfordhandbooks.com/view/10.1093/oxfordhb/9780199561803.001.0001/oxfordhb-9780199561803-e-019

Sa'ari, J. R., Wong, S. I., & Roslan, S. (2005). Attitudes and perceived information technology competency among teachers. *Malaysian Online Journal of Educational Technology*, *2*(3), 70–77.

Shariff, S. (2008). *Cyberbullying: Issues and solutions for the school, the classroom and the home*. New York: Routledge.

Shariff, S., & Hoff, D. (2007). Cyber bullying: Clarifying legal boundaries for school supervision in cyberspace. *International Journal of Cyber Criminology*, *1*(1), 76–118.

Sharma, S., Mukherjee, S., Kumar, A., & Dillon, W. R. (2005). A simulation study to investigate the use of cut-off values for assessing model fit in covariance structure models. *Journal of Business Research*, *58*(7), 935–943. doi:10.1016/j.jbusres.2003.10.007

Smith, P. K., Mahdavi, J., Carvalho, M., Fisher, S., Russell, S., & Tippett, N. (2008). Cyberbullying: Its nature and impact in secondary school students. *Journal of Child Psychology and Psychiatry, and Allied Disciplines*, *49*(4), 376–385. doi:10.1111/j.1469-7610.2007.01846.x PMID:18363945

Smokowski, P. R., & Kopasz, K. H. (2005). Bullying in school: An overview of types, effects, family characteristics and intervention strategies. *Children & Schools*, *27*(2), 101–110. doi:10.1093/cs/27.2.101

Subrahmanyam, K. & Greenfield, P. (2008). Online communication and adolescent relationships. *The Future of Children, 8*(1), 119-146.

Tokunaga, R. S. (2010). Following you home from school: A critical review and synthesis of research on cyberbullying victimization. *Computers in Human Behavior, 26*(3), 277–287. doi:10.1016/j.chb.2009.11.014

USC ASCDF. (2005). *The digital future report 2005: Surveying the digital future: Year five*. Los Angeles, CA: University of Southern California.

USC ASCDF. (2008). *2008 Digital future report*. Los Angeles, CA: University of Southern California.

Van den Eijnden, R., Spijkerman, R., Vermulst, A., Rooij, T., & Engels, R. (2010). Compulsive Internet use among adolescents: Bidirectional parent-child relationships. *Journal of Abnormal Child Psychology, 38*(1), 77–89. doi:10.100710802-009-9347-8 PMID:19728076

Vignoli, E., & Mallet, P. (2004). Validation of a brief measure of adolescents parent attachment based on Armsden and Greenbergs three-dimension model. *Revue Europeene de Psychologie Appliquee, 54*(4), 251–260. doi:10.1016/j.erap.2004.04.003

Vivolo-Kantor, A. M., Martell, B. N., Holland, K. M., & Westby, R. (2014). A systematic review and content analysis of bullying and cyber-bullying measurement strategies. *Aggression and Violent Behavior, 19*(4), 424–434. doi:10.1016/j.avb.2014.06.008 PMID:26752229

Ward, W. (2011). Technology correspondent. *BBC News*. Retrieved 24 January 2014 from http://www.how-the-web-went-worldwide

Willard, N. (2007). *Cyberbullying and cyberthreats: Responding to the challenge of online social aggression, threats and distress*. Research Press.

WIP. (2013). International Report (5th ed.). Prentice Hall.

Wolak, J., Mitchell, K., & Finkelhor, D. (2006). Online victimization of youth: 5 years later. National Center for Missing and Exploited Children, 7, 6-25.

Yusuf, S., Osman, M. N., Hassan, M. S. H., & Teimoury, M. (2014). Parents influence on childrens online usage. *Procedia: Social and Behavioral Sciences, 155*, 81–86. doi:10.1016/j.sbspro.2014.10.260

Zamaria, C., & Fletcher, F. (2007). *Canada online: Year two highlights, 2007*. Canada Internet Project.

Zickhur, A., & Smith, A. (2013). *Digital differences*. Washington, DC: Pew Internet and American Life Project. Retrieved from http://www.pewInternet.org/2012/04/13/digital-differences/

ADDITIONAL READING

Abd Jalil, S., Abd Jalil, H., & Abdul Latiff, A. (2010). Social media and our youths today: Exploring the impact of social media on Malaysian youths. International Conference on Communications and Media (ICCM), 18 - 20 June 2010, Bayview Hotel, Malacca, Malaysia.

Abdullah, A. D. A., & Chan, C. M. (2016, September). Social media use among teenagers in Brunei Darussalam. In *Conference on e-Business, e-Services and e-Society* (pp. 195-205). Berlin, Germany: Springer International Publishing. 10.1007/978-3-319-45234-0_18

Abu Bakar, H. S. (2015). The emergence themes of cyberbullying among adolescences. *International Journal of Adolescence and Youth*, *20*(4), 393–406. doi:10.1080/02673843.2014.992027

Ang, R. P. (2016). Cyberbullying: Its Prevention and Intervention Strategies. In *Child Safety, Welfare and Well-being* (pp. 25–38). New Delhi, India: Springer India. doi:10.1007/978-81-322-2425-9_3

Ang, R. P., Tan, K. A., & Mansor, A. T. (2010). Normative beliefs about aggression as a mediator of narcissistic exploitativeness and cyberbullying. *Journal of Interpersonal Violence*, *26*(13), 2619–2634. doi:10.1177/0886260510388286 PMID:21156699

Choi, L. J., Syawal, N. B. A. R. M., & Narawi, B. (2016). Bullying Cases among students: School principals' self-efficacy. *Academy of Social Science Journal*, *1*(3), 38–53.

DAntona, R., Kevorkian, M., & Russom, A. (2010). Sexting, texting, cyberbullying and keeping youth safe online. *Journal of Social Sciences*, *6*(4), 523–528. doi:10.3844/jssp.2010.523.528

Daud, A., Omar, S. Z., Hassan, M. S., Bolong, J., & Teimouri, M. (2014). Parental mediation of children's positive use of the Internet. *Life Science Journal*, *11*(8), 360–3691.

Mustaffa, N., Ibrahim, F., Mahmud, W. A. W., Ahmad, F., Kee, C. P., & Mahbob, M. H. (2011). Diffusion of innovations: The adoption of Facebook among youth in Malaysia. *The Public Sector Innovation Journal*, *16*(3), 1–15.

KEY TERMS AND DEFINITIONS

Adolescents: This term refers to growing up children, aged between 13 and 17 years old.

Children: This is an umbrella term that refers to pupils (boys and girls), usually aged between six and 16 years old.

Cyber Predator: This term refers to online bullies, i.e., individuals who bully cyber victims.

Cyber Victim: This term refers to a boy or a girl who has been affected by cyberbullying.

Cyberbullying: This refers to intentional inflicting of psychological torture and hurling of abusive words online (in text, graphics or audio-visual formats) by a person (adult or minor) targeted at a minor or a group of minors using the Internet aimed at scaring them.

Cyberspace: This term refers to the online environment where cyberbullying occurs, i.e., the Internet.

Internet: This term refers to the global, wireless networked digital technology service that connects one computer device to another and facilitates sharing of information and effective communication between users smoothly and promptly.

Online: This term is often used as a synonym of Internet. It also refers to an activity performed on Internet-enabled platform or application such as the World Wide Web (www).

Online Risk Behavior: This refers to a particular social behavior that portends threats exhibited by persons (adult or children) online targeted at other online users, usually minors.

Online Safety: This term refers to web or online condition that guarantees a bullying-free, risk-free and threat-free surfing (use) of the Internet, especially by children.

Teenagers: This term refers to growing up children between the ages of 13 and 19 years old.

Youth: This term refers to certain age-brackets of young adults, usually between the ages of 17 and 30 years old.

ENDNOTES

[1]   n: A sample size
[2]   SPM: Sijil Pelajaran Malaysia (Malaysia Education Certificate)
[3]   RM: Ringgit Malaysia (the Malaysian unit of currency)

This research was previously published in the Encyclopedia of Information Science and Technology, Fourth Edition edited by Mehdi Khosrow-Pour, pages 1704-1722, copyright year 2018 by Information Science Reference (an imprint of IGI Global).

Chapter 12
The Nature, Extent, Causes, and Consequences of Cyberbullying

Michelle F. Wright
Masaryk University, Czech Republic

ABSTRACT

Raised in a digitally connected world, children and adolescents do not remember a time in which new media and technology were not such integral parts or their lives. There are many opportunities afforded by new media and technology, such as the ability to communicate efficiently with just about anyone and having access to an assortment of information at their fingertips. There is a darker side to children's and adolescents' immersion in the digitally connected world. One such consequence is cyberbullying, which has increased over the years, due to children's and adolescents' increasing usage of new media and technology. Further attention has been given to cyberbullying because of high profile cases of victims committing suicide as a consequence of being targeted by these behaviors. The purpose of this chapter is to describe the nature, extent, causes, and consequences of cyberbullying as well as cultural differences in these behaviors and theoretical underpinnings. Concluding this chapter are recommendations for future research and public policy.

INTRODUCTION

Children and adolescents spend a great deal of time using and interacting through electronic technologies, including cell phones, gaming consoles, and the Internet. Some of their engagement with electronic technologies involves many benefits, such as the ability to engage in quick communication with just about anyone, including friends and family, and having access to a multitude of rich information. Despite the many opportunities afforded by electronic technologies, many children and adolescents are exposed to risks. One risk associated with electronic technology usage among adolescents and children is cyberbullying. Cyberbullying occurs through electronic technologies, including gaming consoles, email, instant messaging, chatrooms, social media, and text messages via mobile phones. The literature in this chapter draws on research from various disciplines, including communication, computer science, education, media studies, psychology, social work, and sociology. Furthermore, the literature involves a

DOI: 10.4018/978-1-5225-7492-7.ch012

variety of different research designs, including cross-sectional and longitudinal methodologies as well as qualitative and quantitative designs. The chapter is organized into the following eight sections:

1. The first section provides a background of the nature of cyberbullying by focusing on defining it and describing the technologies used to target others and the features of anonymity as applied to cyberbullying.
2. The second section describes the extent of cyberbullying by focusing on the prevalence rates of children's and adolescents' involvement in cyberbullying.
3. The third section describes the individual characteristics and risks associated with children's and adolescents' involvement in cyberbullying.
4. The fourth section details the role of parents and families in children's and adolescents' cyberbullying perpetration and victimization.
5. Similar to the fourth section, the fifth section explains the role of peers and school in children's and adolescents' cyberbullying involvement.
6. The purpose of the sixth section is to review literature on the psychological, behavioral, and academic consequences associated with cyberbullying involvement among children and adolescents.
7. The seventh section discusses future research directions.
8. The final section provides concluding remarks on cyberbullying.

BACKGROUND

As deliberately embarrassing or intimating, cyberbullying involves the usage of modern electronic technologies to harm others using hostile and repetitive behaviors (Wolak, Mitchell, & Finkelhor, 2007; Ybarra, West, & Leaf, 2007). Cyberbullying is described as an extension of traditional face-to-face bullying, and it also includes elements of an imbalance of power between the bully and the victim as well as the incorporation of a technological component (Olweus, 1999). These behaviors are repetitive, deliberate, and intentionally carried out by bullies with malicious intent. Similar to traditional face-to-face bullying, cyberbullying can also include behaviors with a face-to-face equivalent, such as spreading a rumor about a victim, harassment, physical threats, social exclusion, humiliation, gossiping about a victim to get others not to like the victim, and/or verbal insults. There are also physical forms of cyberbullying, like in traditional face-to-face bullying, which can include hacking. It can include making anonymous phone calls, theft of identity information by pretending to be someone else, distributing explicit videos via various websites, and harassment using instant messenger, social networking websites, and text messages through mobile phones (Wolak et al., 2007; Ybarra & Mitchell, 2004). Other forms of cyberbullying involve happy slapping and flaming (Smith et al., 2008). Furthermore, cyberbullying can involve using various electronic technologies, instant messaging tools and social networking websites.

Researchers have attempted to understand why children and adolescents engage in cyberbullying. One proposal is that new electronic technologies allow cyberbullies to hide their identities, furthering the power differential between the cyberbully and the cybervictim (Wright, 2013; Ybarra et al., 2007). Many children and adolescents who engage in cyberbullying choose to remain anonymous while perpetrating cyberbullying (Dehue, Bolman, Vollink, & Pouwelse, 2012; Wright, 2014a; Ybarra & Mitchell, 2004). Another proposal relates to new electronic technologies' ability to allow the cyberbully to perpetrate frequent, repeated, and prolonged harassment (Wright, 2014a; Ybarra & Mitchell, 2004). Wright (2013; 2014a) found that when individuals felt more confidence in their ability to remain anonymous while using electronic technologies they engaged in more cyberbullying, especially when they could perpetrate cyberbullying anonymously.

THE EXTENT OF CYBERBULLYING

When an awareness of cyberbullying was gained by researchers, there were many studies conducted to understand how frequently children and adolescents were involved in these behaviors. In 2007, Wolak and colleagues (2007) conducted one of the earliest studies on cyberbullying in the United States. They found that 50% of children and adolescents in their sample were victimized by cyberbullying. Lower prevalence rates have been found in other studies conducted on cyberbullying involvement in the United States. For instance, Kowalski and Limber (2007) found that 11% of their 3,767 sample from middle school (aged 11-14) were victimized by cyberbullying, 4% had cyberbullied others, and 7% were classified as cyberbullies-cybervictims. Similar estimates were found in a study of cyberbullying by Patchin and Hinduja (2006). Among their sample, 29% of participants reported that they were cybervictims, while 47% reported to have witnessed cyberbullying at least once. More recent research revealed that 4.9% of children and adolescents in their sample ($N = 4,441$, 6-12th grade) were cybervictims within the past 30 days (Hinduja & Patchin, 2013).

Increasing evidence indicates that cyberbullying is not localized to one country. Instead, research has revealed that cyberbullying is a global concern. In one study, Cappadocia et al. (2013) found that out of their 1,972 sample of Canadian 10th graders, 2.1% perpetrated cyberbullying, 1.9% were cybervictims, and 0.6% were cyberbullies-cybervictims. Rates of cyberbullying involvement have also been examined in Australia as well. In this research, Campbell and colleagues (2012) found that 4.5% of their sample ($N = 3,112$; grades 6-12th) were victims of cyberbullying. Research has also documented cyberbullying involvement among European children and adolescents. Using a large sample of Swedish adolescents ($N = 22,544$; ages 15-18), Laftman et al. (2013) found that 5% of their sample were classified as cybervictims, 4% as cyberbullies, and 2% as cyberbullies-cybervictims. Rates were similar for cyber victimization in Ireland and Belgium such that 6% of Irish adolescents ($N = 876$; ages 12-17; Corcoran, Connolly, & O'Moore, 2012) and 6.3% of Belgian adolescents ($N = 1,042$, M age = 15.47; Heirman & Walrave, 2012) were classified as cybervictims. Prevalence rates of cyber victimization were much higher among Italian adolescents. For instance, Brighi and colleagues (2012) found that 12.5% of the 2,326 Italian adolescents in their sample were cybervictims.

Although slower to develop, some research has focused on cyberbullying involvement rates among children and adolescents in Asia. In one study, Huang and Chou (2010) found that 63.4% of their sample ($N = 545$) witnessed cyberbullying, 34.9% were cybervictims, and 20.4% were cyberbullies. Jang and colleagues (2014) examined rates of cyberbullying involvement among Korean adolescents, with findings revealing that 43% of adolescents in their sample ($N = 3,238$) were cybervictims or perpetrators of cyberbullying. Among a sample of Chinese adolescents ($N = 1,438$), Zhou et al. (2013) found that 34.8% were cyberbullies and 56.9% were cybervictims. Rates were similar among a sample of 1,676 13 through 17 year olds in Singapore such that 59.4% were cybervictims through Facebook and 56.9% were cyberbullies through Facebook (Kwan & Skoric, 2013).

Comparisons of prevalence rates are difficult as the researchers relied on different samples and measurement of cyberbullying. Regardless of the shortcomings associated with studies on prevalence rates of cyberbullying involvement, it is clear that cyberbullying is a concern for children and adolescents around the world. Such a consideration highlights the importance of studying cyberbullying by attempting to understand the risk factors related to children's and adolescents' involvement in cyberbullying as victims, perpetrators, and bystanders.

CHARACTERISTICS AND RISK FACTORS ASSOCIATED WITH CYBERBULLYING INVOLVEMENT

After much of the research on the prevalence rates of cyberbullying involvement, many researchers directed their attention to understanding the characteristics and risk factors related to children's and adolescents' involvement in cyberbullying. Most of these earlier investigations focused on the role of demographic variables in cyberbullying perpetration and victimization. Age has been examined as a factor related to cyberbullying among children and adolescents. One study revealed that younger adolescents were at a greater risk of cyber victimization, while older adolescents were most frequently classified as cyberbullies (Ayas & Horzum, 2012). On the other hand, Wade and Beran (2011) found that 9th graders in their sample experienced the greatest risk of cyberbullying involvement when compared to adolescents in middle school. Such conflicting findings from studies focused on age indicated that this variable might be an inconsistent predictor of cyberbullying involvement. Gender is also another inconsistent predictor of cyberbullying involvement among children and adolescents. In particular, some researchers (Ybarra et al., 2007) have found that boys self-reported more cyberbullying perpetration when compared to girls, with some research revealing that girls experienced more cyber victimization in comparison to boys (Hinduja & Patchin, 2013; Kowalski & Limber, 2007). In contrast, some researchers (e.g., Dehue et al., 2012) have found that girls were more often the perpetrations of cyberbullying in comparison to boys, while boys were much more likely to be victims of cyberbullying (e.g., Huang & Chou, 2010). On the other hand, some researchers have found no gender differences in children's and adolescents' cyberbullying involvement (e.g., Wright & Li, 2013).

Some research has been conducted on other characteristics and risk factors associated with cyberbullying involvement among children and adolescents. One risk factor for cyberbullying involvement is internet usage. In this research, cybervictims and cyberbullies typically report higher rates of chatting, emailing, blogging, gaming, and sending instant messages when compared to uninvolved children and adolescents (Smith et al., 2008; Ybarra & Mitchell, 2004). To explain the association between greater internet usage and cyberbullying involvement, Ybarra and colleagues (2007) proposed that cybervictims and cyberbullies are more likely to disclose personal information online, which worsens their exposure to online risks, such as cyberbullying. Thus, frequent internet usage increases children's and adolescents' willingness to disclose private information through electronic technologies. Higher normative beliefs concerning both traditional face-to-face bullying and cyberbullying were also related to cyberbullying perpetration among adolescents (Burton, Florell, & Wygant, 2013). Such findings indicate that cyberbullies view bullying behaviors as normal, which contributes to their perpetration of these behaviors. Defined as children's and adolescents' beliefs that bullying is unacceptable and that defending victims is valued, provictims attitudes are also related to cyberbullying perpetration. In particular, Elledge and colleagues (2013) found that holding lower levels of provictim attitudes were associated with greater cyberbullying perpetration. Other research has revealed that low self-control, less empathy, and moral disengagement are also contributors to cyberbullying perpetration (Jang et al., 2014; Robson & Witenberg, 2013).

Few studies have focused on the longitudinal risk factors related to cyberbullying involvement. Utilizing a longitudinal design, Fanti and colleagues' (2012) study revealed that media violence exposure, along with callous and unemotional traits, predicted cyberbullying perpetration one year later. Media violence exposure was also a risk factor associated with cyber victimization. Current research has indicated that perceived stress from parents, peers, and academics also increases cyberbullying perpetration one year later among adolescents (Wright, in press). Considering each of the studies examined in this section, it is clear that there are a variety of individual characteristics and risk factors which make children and adolescents vulnerable to cyberbullying involvement. Other research has focused on the role of other individuals in children's and adolescents' involvement in cyberbullying. Parents and families have also been examined as having a role in children's and adolescents' cyberbullying perpetration and victimization.

THE ROLE OF PARENTS AND FAMILIES

Parental monitoring and parenting styles have been examined in relation to children's and adolescents' involvement in cyberbullying. Mason (2008) found that 30% of adolescents in his sample utilized the Internet for three hours or more daily, with 50% of these adolescents reporting that their parents monitored their activities. Even when parents do monitor their children's online activities, they are usually not effective because some parents lack technological skills and many do not follow-up on the strategies that they have implemented. In addition, many parents in one sample reported that they were not certain of what their children did online and they were less certain on how to discuss the topic of online activities with their children. Because parents are not able to engage in an active and ongoing dialogue with their children about online activities, and considering that experiencing online risks is almost inevitable for children, it is not likely that some children have the skills necessary to effectively deal with problematic situations that arise online.

Another line of research focuses on the associations between family characteristics and children's and adolescents' cyberbullying involvement. In this research, Ybarra and Mitchell (2004) revealed that lower caregiver monitoring and poor emotional bonds with caregivers were risk factors associated with cyberbullying. They did not find evidence that family income, parental education, and caregiver status (single or married) were related to cyberbullying perpetration or cyber victimization. On the other hand, Aricak and colleagues' (2012) study revealed that parental unemployed increased children's and adolescents' risk of being involved in cyberbullying. Neglectful parenting is also a risk factor associated with cyberbullying perpetration and cyber victimization. In particular, Dehue and colleagues (2012) found that victims and perpetrators of cyberbullying were more likely to report that their parents engaged in neglectful parenting styles when compared to uninvolved children and adolescents. Similarly, their study also indicated that authoritarian parenting style increased children's and adolescents' risk of cyber victimization. More attention should be given to the role of parents and families in children's and adolescents' cyberbullying involvement.

THE ROLE OF SCHOOLS AND PEERS

Once children enter formal schooling, they spend most of their time in such settings until they graduate from high school or college. Consequently, some researchers have directed their attention to the linkages of peers and schools to children and adolescents' bullying involvement. Although schools' role in cyberbullying involvement is a bit complicated, some research has focused on how schools, particularly teachers and school climate, impact children's and adolescents' cyberbullying involvement. In one study, many teachers perceived the impact of overt forms of traditional face-to-face bullying as much worse than covert forms of bullying, like relational aggression and some forms of cyberbullying (Sahin, 2010). Cyberbullying and schools' involvement in these incidences is further complicated because many situations involving cyberbullying occur outside of school through electronic technologies. This makes it difficult for teachers to know about such incidences and for them to intervene or provide support to the victim. Additionally, many teachers have not been properly trained on how to deal with and recognize cyberbully behaviors as well as the risk factors associated with these behaviors, furthering hindering schools' ability to deal with these behaviors. Cassidy and colleagues (2012a) found that some of the Canadian teachers in their sample were unfamiliar with some of the newer electronic technologies. Their lack of knowledge made it difficult for them to deal with cyberbullying, even if a victim came to them for help.

A negative school climate and lower school commitment increase cyberbullying perpetration at schools (Ybarra & Mitchell, 2004). Another problem inhibiting schools' ability to deal with cyberbullying is that there are few implemented policies and programs, even when teachers were concerned with these behaviors. It is important that teachers are concerned about cyberbullying and understand how to prevent it. Teachers' motivations for learning about cyberbullying and their self-efficacy for believing in their ability to deal with these behaviors decreased from elementary school to middle school.

Another feature of the school environment are children's and adolescents' peers. Festl and colleagues (2013) examined the role of peers in adolescents' cyberbullying involvement. Their findings revealed that one of the best predictors of cyberbullying involvement were classrooms in which the highest incidences of cyberbullying occurred. In addition, adolescents who believed that their friends perpetrated cyberbullying were more likely to perpetrate these behaviors as well (Hinduja & Patchin, 2013). Some research has focused on the quality of peer relationships to understand children's and adolescents' involvement in cyberbullying. In particular, Burton and colleagues (2013) found that higher levels of peer attachment were related negatively to cyberbullying perpetration and cyber victimization. In addition, being rejected by one's peers was also related to cyberbullying, even after controlling for face-to-face victimization (Wright & Li, 2013). Research has also revealed that cyberbullying perpetration might be used to boost adolescents' social status among their peer group. For example, Wright's (2014b) study suggested that higher levels of perceived popularity, a reputational type of popularity usually linked to traditional face-to-face bullying perpetration, increased adolescents' cyberbullying perpetration six months later.

PSYCHOLOGICAL, BEHAVIORAL, AND ACADEMIC DIFFICULTIES

Researchers, educators, and parents are particularly concerned about the psychological, behavioral, and academic difficulties associated with adolescents experiencing and/or perpetrating cyberbullying. Perpetrators and victims of cyberbullying reported internalizing difficulties, such as depression and anxiety, and externalizing difficulties, including drug and alcohol use as well as violence (Patchin &

Hinduja, 2006; Ybarra et al., 2007). Cyberbullying involvement is also linked to problems in school. In one study, Wright (2015) examined the longitudinal associations between school functioning and cyberbullying involvement. She found that cyberbullying perpetration and cyber victimization were each associated with poor academic performance, absenteeism, and school behavioral problems (e.g., classroom disruptions) one year later.

The bulk of the research on the psychological, academic, and behavioral difficulties associated with children's and adolescents' cyberbullying involvement do not control for traditional face-to-face bullying involvement. Controlling for these variables is important as there are strong correlations between cyberbullying involvement and traditional face-to-face bullying involvement. To this end, Bonanno and colleagues (2013) examined cyberbullying perpetration and cyber victimization in relation to depressive symptoms and suicidal ideation. After including face-to-face bullying and victimization in the same model, they still found associations between these variables. However, Brighi and colleagues (2012) did not find a relationship between cyber victimization and loneliness or self-esteem, after accounting for traditional face-to-face bullying victimization.

FURTHER RESEARCH DIRECTIONS

There are a variety of gaps in the cyberbullying literature, which need to be investigated through future research. One recommendation is that follow-up research needs to focus on understanding more about the concept of anonymity as applied to cyberbullying. Anonymity is not only a component of cyberbullying, but anonymous forms of traditional face-to-face bullying can occur as well. For example, a nasty note can be slipped into a peer's locker anonymously. Thus, research should be conducted to understand differences in children's and adolescents' conceptualizations of anonymous acts in the cyber context and the offline world. There are few longitudinal studies conducted on cyberbullying involvement. In future research, longitudinal designs should be utilized to examine both traditional face-to-face bullying and cyberbullying involvement from childhood into late adolescence or even emerging adulthood. Investigations focused on the developmental trajectory of bullying involvement in both social contexts are important as much of the research on cyberbullying does not take into account previous levels of traditional face-to-face bullying, although these variables are strongly correlated (Wright & Li, 2013; Ybarra et al., 2007).

CONCLUSION

This chapter reviewed the nature, extent, causes, and consequences associated with cyberbullying. Researchers are beginning to understand that attacks which occur in cyberspace might be just as powerful as face-to-face attacks. Our communities need to recognize this threat and devote time to dealing with it, as it affects everyone. Cyberbullying will probably not disappear anytime soon, due to our increasing reliance of electronic technologies. Therefore, we all must stand united in our efforts to reduce or prevent cyberbullying.

REFERENCES

Aricak, T., Siyahhan, S., Uzunhasanoglu, A., Saribeyoglu, S., Ciplak, S., Yilmaz, N., & Memmedov, C. (2008). Cyberbullying among Turkish adolescents. *Cyberpsychology & Behavior*, *11*(3), 253–261. doi:10.1089/cpb.2007.0016 PMID:18537493

Ayas, T., & Horzum, M. B. (2010). *Cyberbully / victim scale development study*. Retrieved from: http://www.akademikbakis.org

Bonanno, R. A., & Hymel, S. (2013). Cyber bullying and internalizing difficulties: Above and beyond the impact of traditional forms of bullying. *Journal of Youth and Adolescence*, *42*(5), 685–697. doi:10.100710964-013-9937-1 PMID:23512485

Brighi, A., Guarini, A., Melotti, G., Galli, S., & Genta, M. L. (2012). Predictors of victimisation across direct bullying, indirect bullying and cyberbullying. *Emotional & Behavioural Difficulties*, *17*(3-4), 375–388. doi:10.1080/13632752.2012.704684

Burton, K. A., Florell, D., & Wygant, D. B. (2013). The role of peer attachment and normative beliefs about aggression on traditional bullying and cyberbullying. *Psychology in the Schools*, *50*(2), 103–114. doi:10.1002/pits.21663

Campbell, M., Spears, B., Slee, P. H., Butler, D., & Kift, S. (2012). Victims perceptions of traditional and cyberbullying, and the psychosocial correlates of their victimisation. *Emotional & Behavioural Difficulties*, *17*(3-4), 389–401. doi:10.1080/13632752.2012.704316

Cappadocia, M. C., Craig, W. M., & Pepler, D. (2013). Cyberbullying: Prevalence, stability and risk factors during adolescence. *Canadian Journal of School Psychology*, *28*, 171–192.

Cassidy, W., Brown, K., & Jackson, M. (2012a). Making kind cool: Parents suggestions for preventing cyber bullying and fostering cyber kindness. *Journal of Educational Computing Research*, *46*(4), 415–436. doi:10.2190/EC.46.4.f

Corcoran, L., Connolly, I., & OMoore, M. (2012). Cyberbullying in Irish schools: An investigation of personality and self-concept. *The Irish Journal of Psychology*, *33*(4), 153–165. doi:10.1080/03033910.2012.677995

Dehue, F., Bolman, C., Vollink, T., & Pouwelse, M. (2012). Cyberbullying and traditional bullying in relation to adolescents' perceptions of parenting. *Journal of Cyber Therapy and Rehabilitation*, *5*, 25–34.

Elledge, L. C., Williford, A., Boulton, A. J., DePaolis, K. J., Little, T. D., & Salmivalli, C. (2013). Individual and contextual predictors of cyberbullying: The influence of childrens provictim attitudes and teachers ability to intervene. *Journal of Youth and Adolescence*, *42*(5), 698–710. doi:10.100710964-013-9920-x PMID:23371005

Fanti, K. A., Demetriou, A. G., & Hawa, V. V. (2012). A longitudinal study of cyberbullying: Examining risk and protective factors. *European Journal of Developmental Psychology*, *8*(2), 168–181. doi:10.1080/17405629.2011.643169

Festl, R., Schwarkow, M., & Quandt, T. (2013). Peer influence, internet use and cyberbullying: A comparison of different context effects among German adolescents. *Journal of Children and Media*, 7(4), 446–462. doi:10.1080/17482798.2013.781514

Heirman, W., & Walrave, M. (2012). Predicting adolescent perpetration in cyberbullying: An application of the theory of planned behavior. *Psicothema*, 24, 614–620. PMID:23079360

Hinduja, S., & Patchin, J. W. (2013). Social influences on cyberbullying behaviors among middle and high school students. *Journal of Youth and Adolescence*, 42(5), 711–722. doi:10.100710964-012-9902-4 PMID:23296318

Huang, Y., & Chou, C. (2010). An analysis of multiple factors of cyberbullying among junior high school students in Taiwan. *Computers in Human Behavior*, 26(6), 1581–1590. doi:10.1016/j.chb.2010.06.005

Jang, H., Song, J., & Kim, R. (2014). Does the offline bully-victimization influence cyberbullying behavior among youths? Application of general strain theory. *Computers in Human Behavior*, 31, 85–93. doi:10.1016/j.chb.2013.10.007

Kowalski, R. M., & Limber, S. P. (2007). Electronic bullying among middle school students. *The Journal of Adolescent Health*, 41(6), 22–30. doi:10.1016/j.jadohealth.2007.08.017 PMID:18047942

Laftman, S. B., Modin, B., & Ostberg, V. (2013). Cyberbullying and subjective health: A large-scale study of students in Stockholm, Sweden. *Children and Youth Services Review*, 35(1), 112–119. doi:10.1016/j.childyouth.2012.10.020

Mason, K. (2008). Cyberbullying: A preliminary assessment for school personnel. *Psychology in the Schools*, 45(4), 323–348. doi:10.1002/pits.20301

Olweus, D. (1999). Sweden. In K. Smith, Y. Morita, J. Junger-Tas, D. Olweus, R. Catalano, & P. Slee (Eds.), *The nature of school bullying: A cross-national perspective* (pp. 7–27). New York, NY: Routledge.

Patchin, J. W., & Hinduja, S. (2006). Bullies move beyond the schoolyard: A preliminary look at cyberbullying. *Youth Violence and Juvenile Justice*, 4(2), 148–169. doi:10.1177/1541204006286288

Robson, C., & Witenberg, R. T. (2013). The influence of moral disengagement, morally based self-esteem, age, and gender on traditional bullying and cyberbullying. *Journal of School Violence*, 12(2), 211–231. doi:10.1080/15388220.2012.762921

Sahin, M. (2010). Teachers perceptions of bullying in high schools: A Turkish study. *Social Behavior and Personality*, 38(1), 127–142. doi:10.2224bp.2010.38.1.127

Smith, P. K., Mahdavi, J., Carvalho, M., Fisher, S., Russell, S., & Tippett, N. (2008). Cyberbullying: Its nature and impact in secondary school pupils. *Journal of Child Psychology and Psychiatry, and Allied Disciplines*, 49(4), 376–385. doi:10.1111/j.1469-7610.2007.01846.x PMID:18363945

Wade, A., & Beran, T. (2011). Cyberbullying: The new era of bullying. *Canadian Journal of School Psychology*, 26(1), 44–61. doi:10.1177/0829573510396318

Wolak, J., Mitchell, K., & Finkelhor, D. (2007). Does online harassment constitute bullying? An exploration of online harassment by known peers and online-only contacts. *The Journal of Adolescent Health, 41*(6), 51–58. doi:10.1016/j.jadohealth.2007.08.019 PMID:18047945

Wright, M. F. (2013). The relationship between young adults beliefs about anonymity and subsequent cyber aggression. *Cyberpsychology, Behavior, and Social Networking, 16*(12), 858–862. doi:10.1089/cyber.2013.0009 PMID:23849002

Wright, M. F. (2014a). Predictors of anonymous cyber aggression: The role of adolescents beliefs about anonymity, aggression, and the permanency of digital content. *Cyberpsychology, Behavior, and Social Networking, 17*(7), 431–438. doi:10.1089/cyber.2013.0457 PMID:24724731

Wright, M. F. (2014b). Longitudinal investigation of the associations between adolescents popularity and cyber social behaviors. *Journal of School Violence, 13*(3), 291–314. doi:10.1080/15388220.2013.849201

Wright, M. F. (2015). Adolescents cyber aggression perpetration and cyber victimization: The longitudinal associations with school functioning. *Social Psychology of Education, 18*(4), 653–666. doi:10.100711218-015-9318-6

Wright, M. F. (in press). Cyber victimization and perceived stress: Linkages to late adolescents' cyber aggression and psychological functioning. *Youth & Society.*

Wright, M. F., & Li, Y. (2013). The association between cyber victimization and subsequent cyber aggression: The moderating effect of peer rejection. *Journal of Youth and Adolescence, 42*(5), 662–674. doi:10.100710964-012-9903-3 PMID:23299177

Ybarra, M. L., Diener-West, M., & Leaf, P. (2007). Examining the overlap in internet harassment and school bullying: Implications for school intervention. *The Journal of Adolescent Health, 1*(6), 42–50. doi:10.1016/j.jadohealth.2007.09.004 PMID:18047944

Ybarra, M. L., & Mitchell, K. J. (2004). Online aggressor/targets, aggressors, and targets: A comparison of associated youth characteristics. *Journal of Child Psychology and Psychiatry, and Allied Disciplines, 45*(7), 1308–1316. doi:10.1111/j.1469-7610.2004.00328.x PMID:15335350

Zhou, Z., Tang, H., Tian, Y., Wei, H., Zhang, F., & Morrison, C. M. (2013). Cyberbullying and its risk factors among Chinese high school students. *School Psychology International, 34*(6), 630–647. doi:10.1177/0143034313479692

ADDITIONAL READING

Antoniadou, N., & Kokkinos, C. M. (2015). A review of research on cyber-bullying in Greece. *International Journal of Adolescence and Youth, 20*(2), 185–201. doi:10.1080/02673843.2013.778207

Barlett, C., & Coyne, S. M. (2014). A meta-analysis of sex differences in cyber-bullying behaviour: The moderating role of age. *Aggressive Behavior, 40*(5), 474–488. doi:10.1002/ab.21555 PMID:25098968

Bauman, S. (2011). *Cyberbullying: What counsellors need to know*. Alexandria, VA: American Counseling Association.

Bauman, S., Cross, D., & Walker, J. (2013). *Principles of cyberbullying research: Definitions, measures, and methodology*. New York, NY: Routledge.

Boyd, D. (2014). *It's complicated: The social lives of networked teens*. New Haven, CT: Yale University Press.

Cassidy, W., Faucher, C., & Jackson, M. (2013). Cyberbullying among youth: A comprehensive review of current international research and its implications and application to policy and practice. *School Psychology International, 34*(6), 575–612. doi:10.1177/0143034313479697

Chisholm, J. F. (2014). Review of the status of cyberbullying and cyberbullying prevention. *Journal of Information Systems Education, 25*(1), 1–14.

Cowie, H. (2013). Cyberbullying and its impact on young peoples emotional health and well-being. *The Psychiatrist, 37*(5), 167–170. doi:10.1192/pb.bp.112.040840

Ey, L.-A., Taddeo, C., & Spears, B. (2015). Cyberbullying and primary-school aged children: The psychological literature and the challenge for sociology. *Societies, 5*(2), 492–514. doi:10.3390oc5020492

Gorzig, A., & Frumkin, L. A. (2013). Cyberbullying experiences on-the-go: When social media can become distressing. *Cyberpsychology: Journal of Psychosocial Research on Cyberspace, 7(1),* article 4. Retrieved from: http://www.cyberpsychology.eu/view.php?cisloclanku=2013022801&article=4

Hamm, M. P., Newton, A. S., Chisholm, A., Shulhan, J., Milne, A., Sundar, P., ... Hartling, L. (2015). Prevalence and effect of cyberbullying on children and young people: A scoping review of social media studies. *JAMA Pediatrics, 169*(8), 770–777. doi:10.1001/jamapediatrics.2015.0944 PMID:26098362

Hinduja, S. K., & Patchin, J. W. (2014). *Bullying beyond the schoolyard: Preventing and responding to cyberbullying*. Thousand Oaks, CA: Corwin.

Kiriakidis, S. P., & Kavoura, A. (2010). Cyberbullying: A review of the literature on harassment through the Internet and other electronic means. *Family & Community Health, 33*(2), 82–93. doi:10.1097/FCH.0b013e3181d593e4 PMID:20216351

Kowalski, R. M., Guimetti, G. W., Schroeder, A. N., & Lattanner, M. R. (2014). Bullying in the digital age: A critical review and meta-analysis of cyberbullying research among youth. *Psychological Bulletin, 140*(4), 107–137. doi:10.1037/a0035618 PMID:24512111

Kowalski, R. M., Limber, S. P., & Agatston, P. W. (2012). *Cyberbullying: Bullying in the digital age*. Indianapolis, IN: Wiley Publishing.

Li, Q. (2015). When cyberbullying and bullying meet gaming: A systematic review of the literature. *Jahrbuch für Psychologie und Psychotherapie, 5,* 1–11.

Li, Q., Cross, D., & Smith, P. K. (2012). *Cyberbullying in the global playground: Research from international perspectives*. West Sussex, UK: Blackwell Publishing. doi:10.1002/9781119954484

Modecki, K. L., Minchin, J., Harbaugh, A. G., Guerra, N. G., & Runions, K. C. (2014). Bullying prevalence across contexts: A meta-analysis measuring cyber and traditional bullying. *The Journal of Adolescent Health*, *55*(5), 602–611. doi:10.1016/j.jadohealth.2014.06.007 PMID:25168105

Navarro, R., Yubero, S., & Larranaga, E. (2016). *Cyberbullying across the globe: Gender, family, and mental health*. Switzerland: Springer International Publishing. doi:10.1007/978-3-319-25552-1

Nixon, C. L. (2014). Current perspectives: The impact of cyberbullying on adolescent health. *Adolescent Health. Medicine and Therapeutics*, *5*, 143–158. PMID:25177157

Notar, C. E., Padgett, S., & Roden, J. (2013). Cyberbullying: A review of the literature. *Universal Journal of Educational Research*, *1*(1), 1–9.

Patchin, J. W., & Hinduja, S. (2013). *Cyberbullying prevention and response: Expert perspectives*. New York, NY: Routledge.

Perren, S., Corcoran, L., Cowie, H., Dehue, F., Garcia, D., Mc Guckin, C., ... Vollink, T. (2012). Tackling cyberbullying: Review of empirical evidence regarding successful responses by students, parents, and schools. *International Journal of Conflict and Violence*, *6*(2), 283–293.

Schneider, S. K., ODonnell, L., Stueve, A., & Coutler, R. W. S. (2012). Cyberbullying, school bullying, and psychological distress: A regional census of high school students. *American Journal of Public Health*, *102*(1), 171–177. doi:10.2105/AJPH.2011.300308 PMID:22095343

Shariff, S. (2015). *Sexting and cyberbullying: Defining the line for digitally empowered kids*. New York, NY: Cambridge University Press. doi:10.1017/CBO9781139095891

Smith, P. K., & Steffgen, G. (2013). *Cyberbullying through the new media: Findings from an international network*. New York, NY: Psychology Press.

Van Geel, M., Vedder, P., & Tanilon, J. (2014). Relationship between peer victimization, cyberbullying, and suicide in children and adolescents. *JAMA Pediatrics*, *168*(5), 435–442. doi:10.1001/jamapediatrics.2013.4143 PMID:24615300

Wright, M. F. (2016). *A social-ecological approach to cyberbullying*. Hauppauge, NY: NOVA Science Publishers.

KEY TERMS AND DEFINITIONS

Cyberbullying: When young people harass, humiliate, embarrass, intimidate, and/or threaten another young person via information and communication technologies.

Cyber Victimization: When young people experience harassment, humiliation, embarrassment, intimidation, and/or are threaten via information and communication technologies by another young person.

Face-to-Face Bullying: When young people harass, humiliate, embarrass, intimidate, and/or threaten another young person offline.

Face-to-Face Victimization: When young people experience harassment, humiliation, embarrassment, intimidation, and/or are threaten offline by another young person.

Information and Communication Technologies: This board term encompasses communication device or applications, such as computers and cellular phones.

Parental Involvement: Involves the participation of parents in their children's activities.

Parental Mediation of Technology Use: The strategies parents use to control, supervise, or interpret information and communication technology content for their children.

Peer Attachment: The feelings and beliefs that one's peers will be there when needed.

School Climate: The quality and character of school life, which includes norms, values, interpersonal relationships, social interactions, and organizational processes and structures.

This research was previously published in the Encyclopedia of Information Science and Technology, Fourth Edition edited by Mehdi Khosrow-Pour, pages 1723-1733, copyright year 2018 by Information Science Reference (an imprint of IGI Global).

Section 4
IT Security and Ethics

Chapter 13
Computer Fraud Challenges and Its Legal Implications

Amber A. Smith-Ditizio
Texas Woman's University, USA

Alan D. Smith
Robert Morris University, USA

ABSTRACT

In this chapter, the authors provide a position-based discussion in reference to selective cyberthreats to devices and data breaches (which include malware, phishing, social engineering, data communication interception, malicious insider actions, just to name a few), and further provide information on applicable defenses and their legal implications. Although the authors do not assess the different threats and defenses in order to help prevent future vulnerability towards hacking for consumers, they do provide a conceptual understanding of the growing threats of such attacks and the inability of current legal safeguards to counter such threats. Particularly vulnerable are mobile systems, which are more prone to loss and theft once intercepted.

INTRODUCTION

Computer Fraud

Computer fraud and hacking attempts have been publicized for more than a century. Although customers only think of computers and smartphones being hacked, there are examples in the early 19th century where phone lines were hacked. Cybercrime is a fast growing area and has drastically increased over the years. Its business model is evolving and the market is profitable for criminals. New activities have emerged as technology advances. Traditionally, consumers and businesses were lax with security as hackers could easily encrypt and infect any technological device. Hence, cybercriminal activities grew rampant in the global economy. Security protection, government involvement, and leading software companies have become strategic partners in combating cybercriminal activities. However, despite all these efforts, cybercrime is still growing. There are many strategic solutions to this growing epidemic,

DOI: 10.4018/978-1-5225-7492-7.ch013

such as investing in anti-virus software and commonsense approaches to password protection. In order to reduce the amount of cybercriminal activity occurring globally, action needs to be taken immediately.

The targets are computers or anything device connected to the Internet, such as tablets or smartphones (Sundarambal, Dhivya, & Anbalagan, 2010). Hackers affect the cybersecurity of large companies, government agencies and regular customers, especially if competitive or personal information is stolen for ransom or extortion purposes. In the majority of incidents, it is relatively simple to trace back to the hacker, as many are nonprofessionals with little experience. However, it has become increasing difficult to catch more sophisticated hackers. Although, if and when they are caught, there are significant penalties that come with hacking and computer fraud, many have argued that these penalties are not severe enough to deter such activities (Beldona & Tsatsoulis, 2010; Mohanty, et al., 2010; Smith, 2007). Some have suggested that such crimes as inevitable as IT systems become increasing complex and globally interconnected (Dharni, 2014; Latha & Suganthi, 2015; Chand, et al., 2015; Han, et al., 2015; Soon, et al., 2015).

Exploring Types of Computer Fraud

To illustrate these trends, Stewart and Shear of SecureWorks™ have examined many hacker markets and found that cybercriminals are increasing their activity of stealing information (Clarke, 2013). Stewart is Dell's SecureWorks™' Director of Malware Research for the Counter Threat Unit (CTU) and independent researcher Shear have done much research into the dark marketplace that is frequented by cybercriminals. There are online tutorials for novice hackers to learn the trade for under US$1. For example, one can access Social Security card numbers, name and address of customers for US$250. Cybercriminals can gain control of computers for US$20 to 50. Customers can also hire someone to hack a website for US$100 to 200. However, not everything is cheaper. The price of botnets, spam and malicious software, has increased from US$90 to US$600-1,000. Multiple sellers advertise "satisfaction guaranteed" on the data, which is designed to capture the attention of a potential or practicing hacker. It seems the traditional business model of value-added activities works well in the more hidden and illegal markets as well. However, organizations' drives to understand and anticipate their customers' needs ultimately forces management to connect valuable and vulnerable corporate systems to the general public and, thus, cyberthieves (Daim, Basoglu, & Tanoglu, 2010; Daramola, Oladipupo, & Musa, 2010; Dominic, Goh, Wong, & Chen, 2010; Kapur, Gupta, Jha, & Goyal, 2010; Keramati & Behmanesh, 2010).

Dell and its software SecureWorks™ are well-known and highly respected IT-security providers. Software and management at Dell has been investigating this illegal market for some time. Dell, as a provider of security systems, has in place this particular security software in over 61 countries with 4100 clients and has been providing top of the line service for the past 16 years. Dell SecureWorks™ provides a relatively quick warning to its clients when a cyber-attack is happening. It also provides a prediction of where the cyberattack is coming from and what it is trying to get from the computer. After the security system finds a cyberattack the system then works to get rid of it and tries to prevent the cyberattack from happening again. Counter Threat Platform (CTP) powers Dell SecureWorks™. CTP analyzes a total of 150 billion networks to find any possible threats, generate information, and find any information that could lead to a cyberattack (Alderete & Gutiérrez, 2014). Overall, CTP allows Dell's SecureWorks™ to prevent, detect, respond, and predict.

Cybercrime an industry that has shown double digit growth year after year within the current struggling global economy. Cybercriminal activities have been on the rise and are becoming more profit driven as its business model is evolving and new cybercriminal activities are emerging. Out of dozens of underground markets surveyed by SecureWorks™ researchers, a subsidiary that specializes in cybersecurity and data protection, it was found that business is booming. Not only have prices gone down on many of the services offered, but offerings have expanded as well. From basic hacking offerings to infecting networks of computers with the use of botnets, "underground hackers are monetizing every piece of data they can steal or buy and are continually adding services so other scammers can successfully carry out online and in-person fraud" (Lawrence, 2014). Cybercriminal activity has become a major global problem.

China, for example, tops the list for online crime hotspots with 83% of respondents residing there having been victimized (Bertolucci, 2016). According to the Norton Cybercrime Report ("Cybercrime Report," 2011), 41% do not have an updated security software suite to protect their personal and online data in the U.S. Within this study, more than 65% have claimed that they have fallen victim to viruses and malware attacks, online scams, phishing, social network hacking, credit card fraud, and sexual predation. Many people are uneasy about the safety of online commerce, as they feel that the majority of online criminals operate within countries where prosecution is unlikely. Illegal downloads, digital piracy, and digital harassment are some of the other more common cybercriminal activities committed on a daily basis (Shinder, 2011).

Cybercrime is up 10.4% over the previous year as stated by Kassner (2016). In general, cybercrime has risen over US$1.13 million domestically in the 2014 alone. Web-based attacks, denial of services, malicious insiders, viruses, worms, Trojans, malicious code, phishing and social engineering, malware, stolen devices, and botnets are among the top cybercriminal activities have cost the U.S. and other countries the most money it terms of lost productivity, cybertheft, and counterintelligence efforts. The actual price of cybercriminal activities paid by hacker has decreased over the years. For example, the cost for a Remote Access Trojan (RAT) has dropped considerably in recent years, on part to the increased availability of free ones now available online (Lawrence, 2014). However, the price of botnets has increased from US$600 to 1,000 for 5,000 of botnets within the U.S. With activities expanding and services more readily available, cybercrime is an ever-expanding industry and is on the rise.

Security protection, government involvement, and leading software companies have become competitive forces for cybercriminal activities. More security protection is being added towards platforms, PCs, mobile devices, and tablets. Security product vendors are also on the rise when it comes to cloud computing. As mentioned by Kassner (2016), cloud computing affords cybercriminals perfect opportunities. However, the use of cloud-based fraud detection can be used against cybercriminals. In general, applications of cloud services can pick up on patterns of criminal activity that would not otherwise be obvious with the collection and sharing of information from the millions of devices across the global economy.

Governments have also become a competitive force towards cybercrime. The U.S., as well as the U.K., has been investing heavily in their security infrastructures. The Department of Homeland Security within the U.S. is combating cybercrime by investigating a wide range of cybercrimes and conducting high-impact investigations to disrupt and defeat cybercriminals. The U.S. Secret Service maintains many electronic crimes task forces that are known to concentrate on identifying/locating global crime connected to cybercrime, bank fraud, data breaches, to name a few ("Combating cybercrime," 2016).

The U.S. Immigration and Customs Enforcement, Homeland Security Investigations, and Cyber Crimes Center, are involved in cybercrime investigations by providing computer based technical services to support both domestic and international investigations in cross-border crime. The U.K. has recently spent over 63 million pounds in building up its resources for fighting cybercrime. Large companies, such as Microsoft, have invested their resources in efforts aimed at tracking down and prosecuting cybercriminals. Microsoft, as well as other leading companies, has teamed up with NASA and the U.S. Department of Defense to develop international standards of making IT equipment far more secure than it is today. Despite the challenges presented towards cybercriminals as many cybercriminals having been prosecuted and their illicit organizations shut down, cybercrime is still on the rise and has soared 107% percent in 2015 (Watson, 2016).

Even though Dell is a leading IT-security service provider, there are several other companies that are close behind in terms of competitive offers ("SecureWorks competitors - CB insights," 2016). FireEye™ and Intellitactics™ are the two main competitors. FireEye™ provides its users with firewall, IPS, anti-virus, and gateway protections. These different types of security protocols are designed to protect the user's computer from many threats that may appear using day-to-day systems, such as e-mail and customer-service operations and normal e-commerce offerings. FireEye™ is a public service company that originated from and initial public ordering (IPO). As an IPO, initial sales to the public after being released from a private company to a public company, specifically, FireEye™ is a provider that specializes in preventing cyberattacks, such as zero-day and advanced persistent threat (APT) attacks that bypass traditional defenses and compromise over many networks. Many zero-day attacks are purposefully designed to expose computer applications' vulnerabilities; hence there has been no time to develop a proper defense against such attacks. Unfortunately, many zero-day exploits are totally unexpected and frequently used cybercriminals malicious purposes. FireEye™ attempts to provide solutions that supplements signature-based firewalls, IPS, anti-virus, and gateways, and provides cross-enterprise, signature-less protection against cyberattacks and malware problems on clients' files.

To add to this misery, APTs utilizes many different phases and methods to compromise a computer network in order to avoid detection by anti-cyberthreat software in order to gain access to important information through thefts of information leaked out have relatively long time periods. Both FireEye™ and Intellitactics™ have specific safeguards against such attacks, but technology advancements always work to undermine such solutions.

Intellitactics™, such provides information security software for comprehensive enterprise security management, is a competitor in a different way than FireEye™. Intellitactics™ is part of the Trustwave® corporate initiative, which is a larger security business. Intellitactics™ is more of a pinpointed security solution. Intellitactics™ is more of a security information and event management system solution. This essentially means that the security system is more used by a business that stores important information on a computer or a business that stores planned events on a computer.

BACKGROUND

Businesses Affected by Hackers

Virtually every modern and web-connected business uses computer systems to keep track of its records and keep in contact with customers in order to make transactions smooth and relatively seamless. Unfortunately, these same systems also put a company at risk; not just the company that is affected it is also their clients (Aeron, Kumar, & Janakiraman, 2010; Barra, Savage, & Tsay, 2010). Firewalls and encryptions can be put into place and properly maintained, but if a determined hacker knows what he/she is targeting; undoubtedly, it is only a matter of time before these systems are eventually compromised unless significant steps and constant monitoring processes are implemented. Some of the major companies have been hacked recently (e.g., Sony, Home Depot, and Target) know this scenario too well. For example, Sony Pictures Entertainment was made aware of the hack on November 24, 2014, but there is a possibility that the hacker had been in the system for almost a year (Fitz-Gerald, 2014). Names, addresses and social security numbers were exposed of over 47,000 current and former employees. Of course, as conspiracy theories develop, there was a theory that it was a current or former employee that was responsible for the hack and not terrorists' organizations as it had been originally speculated. Hence, as suggested by Barrett and Yadron (2016), companies and governmental agencies must be trusting partners in the war on cyberattacks and fighting computer hackers if such security breaches that was experienced by Sony in 2014 will become commonplace as warned by U.S. President Barack Obama stated in February 2016.

The industry position for individuals or companies that are illegally selling data on the Internet, unfortunately, still practices a number of traditionally practiced business models. These underground hacking markets are constantly changing with the new technology that is allowing for cheaper options, which makes it easier for hackers to access customers' computers. For an example, one year the black market price for a RAT could be up to US$250, and then the next year it could be down to US$20 ("Underground Hacking Markets Report," 2014). Such inconsistent markets puts pressure on the hackers not knowing if this data will be high or low on black market, which forces hackers to innovate and more dangerous ways to infect computers on a global scale. Unfortunately, what may be at risk can be both intellectual property and personally identifiable information (PII) that ties information directly to an individual company and/or customer (Shukai, Chaudhari, & Dash, 2010).

In terms of state-sponsored cyberterrorism, North Korea is typically blamed for many widespread cyberattacks, regardless of proof of their true degree of involvement. This is part to its suspected involvement in preventing a movie, *The Interview*, from being formally released. The film, about assassination of the President of North Korea, the hackers, identifying as "The Guardians of Peace," tried to prevent its release through public discourse. The hackers did not leak everything at once but slowly and information is still being released to this day. The hackers promised they would stop the leaks if Sony cancelled *The Interview's* theatrical release. Personal e-mails between company employees and actors were released, as well as confidential salaries of celebrities and top employees. Despite this pledge, significant and personally damaging information was getting released daily. Management at Sony went ahead with the movie's release, but instead in theaters, customers could buy the movie at home because movie theaters were getting threatened if they aired the movie. It was in December, 2014, that the FBI stated that North Korea appear to be involved although the government of North Korea officially denies it and threatened the White House and pentagon if the U.S. government levies any punishments. Following the Sony hack, other studio companies took precautions and cancelled their own North Korea-themed movies. Currently, Russia is accused of interfering with the 2016 U.S. presidential elections.

Another well-publicized major incident of a company that was targeted by hackers was Target. A few days before Thanksgiving, 2014 a malware was installed on Target's security and payment systems at POS, so that every time a customer's card was swiped it would take the card number and store it in a separate system for the hacker to retrieve at a later date, possibly suggesting insider involvement (Riley, Elgin, Lawrence, & Matlack, 2014). On "Black Friday," when many customers do their Christmas shopping, over 40 million customer accounts were breached. In the aftermath, over 90 lawsuits have been filed against Target from customers and bank for negligence. In March 2015, a federal judge approved an offer of 10 million from Target to settle a class action lawsuit if the customers affected can actually prove they were affected since banks usually reimburse 100% for card fraud (Riley & Pagliery, 2015).

These documented breaches on global companies that traditionally make significant profits have spent considerable financial and human resources cybersecurity on their data and networks that support them. Obviously, such investments do not guarantee protection (Kim & Tadisina, 2010; Marthandan & Tang, 2010). But how do the small businesses successfully protect their customers' information? Based on prior studies, over 90% of small businesses in the U.S. do not use data protection for their business or their customer's information and, hence, this is costing business and their customers' considerable financial and other resources (Warren, 2015). A small business can start off by making sure their employees are not visiting the wrong kind of websites and getting cybersecurity insurance. Retail and finance business are at higher risk than restaurants but they are still considered a target.

From a strategic perspective on the nature of cybercrime, the competitive forces for a company illegally selling data on the Internet are unique (Smith, 2007). The availability of automatic identification and data capture technologies (AIDC) and its relatively low cost have helped to develop the underground cybercrime industry. The cybercrime industry varies widely on the enforcement of government regulations and legality of the information exchanged (Jarrett, 2016). The barriers-to-entry are low, as anyone with enough knowledge to gain the valued information can become a seller; therefore, the threat of new entrants is high (Elysee, 2015). Buyers have a high degree of bargaining power, as there are nearly endless sources of this information available on the Web and in person. Since customer service is important in the industry, as there are many sellers and there is a need to differentiate their services. Sellers have a relatively high degree of bargaining power as well, since there is little enforcement of laws around the sale. For example, if a seller sells a "bad" ID that does not work, the buyer has little means of getting its money back and will likely not use the law to enforce a botched sale or contract.

A number of authors (Aeron, et al., 2010; Barra, et al., 2010; Shukai, et al., 2010) have discussed the available and effective security defenses that have been developed and continue to grow in effectiveness for all of the security threats mentioned. No security defense can be completely effective, but many of these can be used to help avoid major breaches, known threats, ordinary hackers, and security ignorance. Perhaps the most obvious defense is the personal firewall, which provides antivirus and antispyware. Firewalls help devices by blocking or limiting the use of Bluetooth and Wi-Fi unless asked to connect. This is difficult to ensure that every device follow because many devices encourage the user to allow connection to Bluetooth for all types of traffic. Antivirus and antispyware scan network traffic for signatures of known malware. These types of mobile security are not widely used on mobile devices but will become more available due to the target malware has on the devices as technology progresses. As suggested by Friedman and Hoffman (2008), there are limitations of firewalls, antivirus and antispyware, that are based on their inability to block malware that goes through the port that is in use. Also, virus writers and cyber criminals have found ways to evade signature based antivirus and antispyware by using short-span attacks and designer malware. Because of this additional defenses are available as a sort of back up to the backup protection. Intrusion prevention systems examine network traffic into and out of the computers and identify sketchy behavior. This form of protection establishes a baseline of normal online behavior and is alerted when there is a significant change.

For the defense against phishing and social engineering, education may be the best defense. This includes being informed on what accurate looking e-mail appears from their banks or institutions, what phishing messages, what unknown websites may appear based on URL observing and just the knowledge that giving out personal information to someone online. Content and spam filtering are known best for maintaining a large list of known websites that are known for spamming or housing malware and it in many ways blacklists them and blocks them from incoming. Other ways of preventing communication interception and spoofing can be accomplished by disabling unneeded communication, password encryption, virtual private networks, and to restrict access to hot spots. A user can disable these unneeded communication methods and ports by changing configuration settings on the system being used and avoid hackers from unknowingly obtaining information without the device users consent. Good password encryption will help the device carrier to use algorithms in order to protect the device and applications the user may have important information on as well.

Defense against loss and theft of devices are better known as many users already use locks on their devices to keep only them from accessing their device. Some devices have "time-bomb" capability, so if the device is lost or stolen and someone tries to obtain information from it, it will wipe it and destroy data on the device. Many devices also have back up or a recovery mode, which replaces lost or stolen files. Device control can be used to prevent files from being written to USB and requires that files be encrypted. By encrypting files, regardless of a loss or theft, files can remain confidential and are less likely to be leaked to outside sources.

CONCLUSION

Legal Solutions Are Inadequate

In conclusion, fraud is a crime that will always be relevant and present, even as the technology to protect against it grows and strengthens. Laws and regulations put in place to prohibit such actions can only do so much in combating against such threats. Many cases arise from fraudulent activities and will vary in degree of damage, but with each case is the degree of the crime, unique to the case. For every business that uses computer systems, managers must become beware of threats with the hope of a better functioning system and a rise in profit. Strategic recommendations for security providers vary depending on the type of security you provide. For companies, like Intellitactics™, it is to provide reassurance that their customer's information will be kept safe from the unauthorized public. To do this properly, they market protective measures to ensure that hackers cannot get into stored information. For companies, like SecureWorks™ and FireEye™, where customers are working more with individuals than other businesses, it is equally important to gain their trust by providing successful documentation and cases. It is important to keep customers in constant contact and insure that if a problem is detected that they will be alerted immediately. Keeping customers updated on the innovative hacker technologies would gain customer trust by keeping them in the information loop and alert.

It is important to raise the awareness of the potential punishment for those who may think of illegally purchasing a product or service from hackers and look for a strategic alliance where they can work with another company or companies to raise the defenses against hackers. Specifically, in the late 2015,

Lifetime, Netflix, Pandora, and Hulu accounts were being hacked and sold online for as low as US$1. For the average consumer with little technical background information, it seems like a great purchase bargain, but since these accounts are stolen, there are consequences to the consumer if they are found with such account. With the proper investment into the awareness by Internet users, hackers would have no market or interest to sell stolen accounts. If such companies as SecureWorks™ were to partner with each other to raise account security standards, these accounts would be much more challenging to hackers, as they typically go after soft targets. Ultimately, as evident from the researchers cited in this chapter, a major threat to the global economy is the general lack of Internet security. With advocates for stronger defense systems like those, there should be a stronger movement towards more secure networks and acts at tracking down sites used to sell hacked goods. In essence, there was a variety of information presented in this chapter regarding how the reader could arm himself/herself in the probability of an attack by a hacker through better education of the nature of cyberattacks.

Strategic Implications

In order to attempt to catch up to this growing epidemic, fast and decisive actions are required. Even though mobile phones and smart devices have remained relatively safe, users are vulnerable targets, as presented in the 2011 Norton Cybercrime Report. Consumers have to become more protected by installing security programs not only on their PCs, but on their mobile devices and tablets as well. Every year it is getting easier to hack computers and counterfeit items such as passports. It is also becoming more "mainstream" in the e-marketplace. The cost to hack websites, for example, has fallen 33% in the last year alone. It has become easier to be a hacker or hire a hacker than it would be to invest in advanced security protection software. In a matter of years hacking will become as easy as going to a drug-store if it is not stopped soon.

The continuous demand and growth of cybercrime has led to the development of a new industry to offset its negative impact; cybersecurity. Corporations and individuals can protect their electronic gadgets by installing anti-virus programs and file restrictions that blocks access as well as detecting and eliminating malicious ware before it expands. Anti-virus software is the most common solution to combat lower degree of cybercrime activity such as Trojans and worms. Another strategic measure that can be taken is to pay close attention to the source of e-mails and their content; if the information seems unfamiliar or the sender is unknown, the receiver should eliminate the e-mail without opening any attachment or providing any information.

Besides computer infiltration, spam and phishing, another common form of cybercrime is identity theft. This criminal activity is possible due to the amount of information that is stored in computers, social media, employment forms and e-mails. The easiest way for criminals to obtain personal information is through social media, therefore it is better if accounts on websites such as Facebook or MySpace are accessible by friends only, and all pictures that contain addresses or telephone numbers are blurred or removed. While it might seem innocent to fill out personality tests and surveys, it is better to investigate the source of these; Facebook, for example, allows independent developers to create customized applications without verifying their identity and intentions. In many cases, identity theft can be extremely difficult to detect in the beginning since criminals tend to keep a low profile. An obvious way to fight this can be by monitoring accounts and financial information on a constant basis and to report all suspicious activity to the law enforcement activities. Companies such as Discover notify customers of transactions that takes place a specified distance from a set location, and Chase Bank, for example, asks for verification codes every time a new smartphone or computer is used for a balance inquiry.

Commonsense approaches include never use the same password for more than one account as well as the use of common information for security questions. Much of cybercrime can be stopped in the effective use of passwords and 2-step verification methods, using access codes that are texted or sent via voice mail. Social media and acquaintances may provide enough information to third parties unintentionally and might allow access to bank accounts, retirement funds, e-mails and other accounts. It is highly suggested to elaborate passwords that contain numbers, different characters and unrelated dates and names. These measures can help fight cybercrime since there is no better solution than restricting the amount of information to which someone has access.

In conclusion, to fight cybercrime it is necessary to constantly monitor accounts that involve trading or savings for any suspicious activity, observe the sources of suspicious e-mails and avoid opening files or filling formats that seem illegitimate. Restrict privacy settings in social media networks and destroy physical evidence of important information, such as old utility bills or any addresses from envelopes, birthday dates, etc. If completing purchases online, using trusted sources like PayPal®; if that option is not available, use prepaid gift cards to keep bank or credit card account information safe. Installing and maintaining an anti-virus program can help prevent possible malware from infecting the user's computer. The use of different passwords and security questions for each account can also aide in the protection of being hacked. Companies and countries that have gone beyond the current standard security protocol have achieved great results in the prevention of cybercriminal activities.

FUTURE RESEARCH DIRECTIONS

Much of the information presented in this chapter typically applies to many daily business situations. They are particularly relevant in the era of big data analytics and the growth of identity theft, evident to the widespread nature of malicious attacks. The increasing likelihood of being a victim of cyberhacking is well documented by academics and practitioners alike. Fortunately, essentially every cyberthreat has a potential solution that is attainable by consumers seeking prevention, but the legal professional and governmental action leaves much to be desired in dealing with these threats.

Ultimately, perhaps the best advice when customers and organizations are confronted with these threats is the need to promote education and commonsense prevention. Cybercriminals will always seek soft targets, generally caused by lack of easy prevention techniques that could easily be prevented if proper education is made more universal. Further research needs to deals with this problem of making such educational opportunities more available and easy-to-use. The particular needs of each individual in regards to defense in dealing with the various ways they could be attacked must be addressed. If organizations can use big data analytics to e-personalize their products and services; why not apply the same technologies to customize defense and safeguards against cyberattacks? For example, when it comes to phishing, of which there are countless victims, with the proper education they can learn to detect what is fraudulent and withhold their information from getting out to these cybercriminals. Hence, essentially every attack is preventable regardless of whether it is a phishing scheme, malware attack, data communication interception, loss or theft of device internal breach, and/or a virus attack. Future research that is aimed at educating potential victims would provide much relief in these ever increasing cybercriminal problems. The authors of this chapter suggest that further research should continue on all levels of cyberattacks. Society, in general, is becoming more vulnerable to such attacks and educating customers and managers about different threats and opportunities made available to counter hackers that are becoming more intelligent on ways to undermine the various precautions put in place, makes the needs to make potential victims more intelligent about cyberthreats even more pressing.

REFERENCES

Aeron, H., Kumar, A., & Janakiraman, M. (2010). Application of data mining techniques for customer lifetime value parameters: A review. *International Journal of Business Information Systems*, 6(4), 530–546. doi:10.1504/IJBIS.2010.035744

Alderete, M. V., & Gutiérrez, L. H. (2014). Drivers of information and communication technologies adoption in Colombian services firms. *International Journal of Business Information Systems*, 17(4), 373–397. doi:10.1504/IJBIS.2014.065553

Barra, R. A., Savage, A., & Tsay, J. J. (2010). Equational zero vector databases, non-equational databases, and inherent internal control. *International Journal of Business Information Systems*, 6(3), 354–377. doi:10.1504/IJBIS.2010.035050

Barrett, D., & Yadron, D. (2016). Sony, U.S. Agencies fumbled after cyberattack: Lack of information and consultation led to flip-flops, confusion. *The Wall Street Journal*. Retrieved February 26, 2016 from http://www.wsj.com/articles/sony-u-s-agencies-fumbled-after-cyberattack-1424641424

Beldona, S., & Tsatsoulis, C. (2010). Identifying buyers with similar seller rating models and using their opinions to choose sellers in electronic markets. *International Journal of Information and Decision Sciences*, 2(1), 1–16. doi:10.1504/IJIDS.2010.029901

Bertolucci, J. (2016). Cybercrime is rampant around the world, says study. *PCWorld*. Retrieved March 7, 2016 from http://www.pcworld.com/article/205051/Norton_Study_Says_Cybercrime_is_Rampant.html

Chand, M., Raj, T., & Shankar, R. (2015). A comparative study of multi criteria decision making approaches for risks assessment in supply chain. *International Journal of Business Information Systems*, 18(1), 67–84. doi:10.1504/IJBIS.2015.066128

Clarke, E. (2013). *The underground hacking economy is alive and well*. Dell SecureWorks™. Retrieved February 26, 2016 from https://www.secureworks.com/blog/the-underground-hacking-economy-is-alive-and-well

Combating cybercrime. (2016). *Cybersecurity*. Homeland Security. Retrieved March 7, 2016 from https://www.dhs.gov/topic/combating-cyber-crime

Daim, T., Basoglu, N., & Tanoglu, I. (2010). A critical assessment of information technology adoption: Technical, organisational and personal perspectives. *International Journal of Business Information Systems*, *6*(3), 315–335. doi:10.1504/IJBIS.2010.035048

Daramola, J. O., Oladipupo, O. O., & Musa, A. G. (2010). A fuzzy expert system (FES) tool for on-line personnel recruitments. *International Journal of Business Information Systems*, *6*(4), 444–462. doi:10.1504/IJBIS.2010.035741

Dharni, K. (2014). Exploring information system evaluation in Indian manufacturing sector. *International Journal of Business Information Systems*, *17*(4), 453–468. doi:10.1504/IJBIS.2014.065564

Dominic, P. D. D., Goh, K. N., Wong, D., & Chen, Y. Y. (2010). The importance of service quality for competitive advantage – with special reference to industrial product. *International Journal of Business Information Systems*, *6*(3), 378–397. doi:10.1504/IJBIS.2010.035051

Elysee, G. (2015). An empirical examination of a mediated model of strategic information systems planning success. *International Journal of Business Information Systems*, *18*(1), 44–66. doi:10.1504/IJBIS.2015.066126

Fitz-Gerald, S. (2014). Everything that's happened in the Sony leak scandal. *Vulture*. Retrieved February 26, 2016 from http://www.vulture.com/2014/12/everything-sony-leaks-scandal.html

Friedman, J., & Hoffman, D. (2008). Protecting data on mobile devices: A taxonomy of security threats to mobile computing and review of applicable defenses. *Information, Knowledge, Systems Management*, *7*(1-2), 159–180.

Jarrett, M. H. (2016). *Prosecuting computer crimes*. Office of Legal Education Executive Office for United States Attorneys. Retrieved February 26, 2016 from http://www.justice.gov/criminal/cybercrime/docs/ccmanual.pdf

Kapur, P. K., Gupta, A., Jha, P. C., & Goyal, S. K. (2010). Software quality assurance using software reliability growth modelling: State of the art. *International Journal of Business Information Systems*, *6*(4), 463–496. doi:10.1504/IJBIS.2010.035742

Kassner, M. (2014). The New Phenomenon report shows cybercrime is on the rise. *TechRepublic*. Retrieved March 7, 2016 from http://www.techrepublic.com/article/new-ponemon-report-shows-cybercrime-is-on-the-rise/

Keramati, A., & Behmanesh, I. (2010). Assessing the impact of information technology on firm performance using canonical correlation analysis. *International Journal of Business Information Systems*, *6*(4), 497–513. doi:10.1504/IJBIS.2010.035743

Kerr, O. S. (2010). Vagueness challenges to the Computer Fraud and Abuse Act. *Minnesota Law Review, 1561*. Available at SSRN: http://ssrn.com/abstract=1527187

Kim, E., & Tadisina, S. (2010). A model of customers initial trust in unknown online retailers: An empirical study. *International Journal of Business Information Systems*, *6*(4), 419–443. doi:10.1504/IJBIS.2010.035740

Latha, T. J., & Suganthi, L. (2015). An empirical study on creating software product value in India - an analytic hierarchy process approach. *International Journal of Business Information Systems*, *18*(1), 26–43. doi:10.1504/IJBIS.2015.066125

Lawrence, D. (2014). Christmas Shopping for Cybercriminals. *BloomsbergBusiness*. Retrieved March 7, 2016 from http://www.bloomberg.com/bw/articles/2014-12-15/current-hacker-underground-markets-are-booming

Marthandan, G., & Tang, C. M. (2010). Information systems evaluation: An ongoing measure. *International Journal of Business Information Systems*, *6*(3), 336–353. doi:10.1504/IJBIS.2010.035049

Mohanty, R., Ravi, V., & Patra, M. R. (2010). The application of intelligent and soft-computing techniques to software engineering problems: A review. *International Journal of Information and Decision Sciences*, *2*(3), 233–272. doi:10.1504/IJIDS.2010.033450

Report, C. (2011). *Norton*. Retrieved March 7, 2016 from http://www.symantec.com/content/en/us/home_homeoffice/html/cybercrimereport/

Riley, C., & Pagliery, J. (2015). Target will pay hack victims $10 million. *CNN Money*. Retrieved March 2, 2016 from http://money.cnn.com/2015/03/19/technology/security/target-data-hack-settlement/

Riley, M., Elgin, B., Lawrence, D., & Matlack, C. (2014). Missed alarms and 40 million stolen credit card numbers: How Target blew it. *Bloomberg Business*. Retrieved February 26, 2016 from http://www.bloomberg.com/bw/articles/2014-03-13/target-missed-alarms-in-epic-hack-of-credit-card-data

SecureWorks competitors - CB insights. (2016). Retrieved February 23, 2016, from http://www.cbinsights.com/company/secureworks-competitors

Shinder, D. (2011). Cybercrime: Why it's the new growth industry. *IT Security*. Retrieved March 7, 2016 from http://www.techrepublic.com/blog/it-security/cybercrime-why-its-the-new-growth-industry/

Shukai, L., Chaudhari, N. S., & Dash, M. (2010). Selecting useful features for personal credit risk analysis. *International Journal of Business Information Systems*, *6*(4), 419–443. doi:10.1504/IJBIS.2010.035745

Smith, A. D. (2007). Identity theft and e-fraud driving CRM information exchanges. In A. Gunasekaran (Ed.), *Modeling and Analysis of Enterprise Information Systems* (pp. 110–133). Hershey, PA: IGI Publishing. doi:10.4018/978-1-59904-477-4.ch005

Soon, J. N. P., Mahmood, A. K., Yin, C.-P., Wan, W.-S., Yuen, P.-K., & Heng, L.-E. (2015). Barebone cloud IaaS: Revitalisation disruptive technology. *International Journal of Business Information Systems*, *18*(1), 26–43. doi:10.1504/IJBIS.2015.066130

Sundarambal, M., Dhivya, M., & Anbalagan, P. (2010). Performance evaluation of bandwidth allocation in ATM networks. *International Journal of Business Information Systems*, *6*(3), 398-417.

Underground, H. M. R. (2014). *SecureWorks*. Retrieved February 27, 2016 from https://www.secureworks.com/assets/pdf-store/white-papers/wp-underground-hacking-report.pdf

Warren, J. (2015). Why US small businesses should worry about cybersecurity and how to act. *IT Governance*. Retrieved March 2, 2016 from http://www.itgovernanceusa.com/blog/why-us-small-businesses-should-worry-about-cybersecurity-and-how-to-act/

Watson, L. (2015). Crime soars 107% as cyber offences included for the first time – as it happened. *Crime*. Retrieved March 7, 2016 from http://www.telegraph.co.uk/news/uknews/crime/11932670/Cyber-crime-fuels-70-jump-in-crime-levels.html

ADDITIONAL READING

Code, U. S. 12. (2016). Legal Information Institute, Cornell University. [Online]. Retrieved February 26, 2016 from http://www.law.cornell.edu/uscode/html/uscode18/usc_sec_18_00001030----000-.html

Computer and information technology occupations. (2016). *Occupational Handbook*. U.S. Bureau of Labor Statistics. [Online]. Retrieved March 4, 2016 from http://www.bls.gov/ooh/computer-and-information-technology/home.htm

Han, W., Ada, S., Sharman, R., Gray, R. H., & Simha, A. (2015). Factors impacting the adoption of social network sites for emergency notification purposes in universities. *International Journal of Business Information Systems*, *18*(1), 85–106. doi:10.1504/IJBIS.2015.066129

Kapitanyan, M. (2009). Beyond wargames: How the Computer Fraud and Abuse Act should be interpreted in the employment context. [Online]. Retrieved February 26, 2016 from https://www.researchgate.net/publication/265939376_Beyond_WarGames_How_the_Computer_Fraud_and_Abuse_Act_Should_Be_Interpreted_in_the_Employment_Context

More than a decade of data tracking the evolution of cyber threats. (2015). *Verizon Data Breach Investigations Reports*. [Online]. Retrieved February 23, 2016, from http://www.verizonenterprise.com/DBIR/

Ponemon study shows the cost of a data breach continues to increase. (2016). [Online]. Retrieved March 4, 2016 from https://www.ponemon.org/news-2/23

Skibell, R. (2003). Cybercrimes & misdemeanors: A reevaluation of the Computer Fraud and Abuse Act. *Berkeley Technology Law Journal*, *18*(3), 909–944.

Smith, A. D. (2004). Cybercriminal and cyberterrorism activities and its affects on online consumer confidence. *Online Information Review*, *28*(3), 224–234. doi:10.1108/14684520410543670

Smith, A. D., & Lias, A. R. (2005). Identity theft and e-fraud as critical CRM concerns. *International Journal of Enterprise Information Systems*, *1*(2), 17–36. doi:10.4018/jeis.2005040102

Theohairs, M. (2016). Computer and Internet crime laws. [Online]. Retrieved February 26, 2016 from http://www.criminaldefenselawyer.com/crime-penalties/federal/computer-crimes.htm

KEY TERMS AND DEFINITIONS

Advanced Persistent Threats (APT): Advanced Persistent Threats typically employs a number of phases and techniques to break into a network, avoid detection, and gather customers' or companies' information over an extended time period. Unfortunately, such well-planned and extensive strategy is difficult to detect, as it many techniques and phases may be extremely complex and expensive to develop a counteroffensive that is successful.

Direct Cyberattack: Direct cyberattack causes data communications interception at the hands of a specific hacker who may have located a specific person or Wi-Fi area in order to perform such cybercrime. A type of direct attach is direct access, where the criminal gains physical access to either the computer or its network in order to compromise security by loading worms, Trojans, compromising data, etc.

Personally Identifiable Information (PII): Personally identifiable information (PII) refers to all information, including personal financial and healthcare information that can be traced to an individual customer or patient.

Remote Access Trojan (RAT): In basic terms, Remote Access Trojans (RATs) are essential tools available to cyberthieves with unrestricted limited access to computers. By using stolen access privileges through properly submitted passwords, all important business and personal data, the entire customer's or company's information can be readily accessed and retrieved.

Zero-Day Attack: This term has been used in various forms and meaning. It terms of this chapter, this term refers to exploitable software or hardware vulnerabilities that have been attacked when there has been no previous information of a system flaw by the general information security community. In such a situation, unfortunately, there is no vendor fix or software security patch that have been developed or made available to the public to correct or protect against such an attack.

This research was previously published in the Encyclopedia of Information Science and Technology, Fourth Edition edited by Mehdi Khosrow-Pour, pages 4837-4848, copyright year 2018 by Information Science Reference (an imprint of IGI Global).

Chapter 14
Cost Estimation and Security Investment of Security Projects

Yosra Miaoui
University of Carthage, Tunisia

Boutheina Fessi
University of Carthage, Tunisia

Noureddine Boudriga
University of Carthage, Tunisia

ABSTRACT

This chapter aims at examining two main aspects in security: cost estimation and investment assessment. The characteristics of security projects are stressed and the importance of adopting management task is determined. In addition, the chapter examines the different cost-estimation models developed for security project and discusses the technical and managerial factors affecting the cost estimation and the management of projects. In addition, a review of research works directed toward security investment models is determined. In fact, most models have focused on determining the optimal security investment allocation based on budgetary, economic, and financial constraints. Recent models are interested to examine more specific security features when assessing the required investment (e.g., system vulnerabilities, attack types, risk factors, data privacy, and insurance). Finally, the chapter discusses future directions that could be investigated to make available useful models for cost estimation and investment on security projects.

INTRODUCTION

Project management is an important task that should be performed when dealing with security project, since it allows avoiding different project failures. This task is an effective methical approach of planning, organizing, leading, and controlling resources to achieve organization's goals. It involves, thus, identifying requirements, determining clear objectives, and balancing the triple constraints scope, time, and cost (Institute, 2013).

DOI: 10.4018/978-1-5225-7492-7.ch014

It is noted that the management of software and security projects are not performed in the same way, due to several reasons, related mainly to the software intangibility, complexity, conformity, and flexibility. It is also shown that the parameters involved in the security cost estimation differ from those of software cost estimation. Therefore, the developed methods should be adapted to consider security specificities.

In this context, organization's project managers should estimate the cost associated to a security project during its design. This estimation should include the computation of the optimal security level and residual risk accepted by the organization. Moreover, it should consider managerial aspects regarding, for example, the effort required for security monitoring of the new assets to be acquired or updated, the security training of the technical staff, the update of the managerial decisional system, and the development of policy and procedures related to the use of information processing facilities, instead of only considering the industrial source coding of the security packages.

Another significant aspect, which should be carefully examined when dealing with security, is related to security investment. The financial budget allocated to security should be well established and managed to avoid under or over expenses. Different security investment models are developed in the literature using various techniques and examining several features. Most of them have focused on determining the optimal security investment allocation based on budgetary aspect, economic, and financial constraints. Recent works are interested to examine more specific security features when assessing the required investment, such as the system vulnerabilities, attacks type, risk factors, data privacy, and insurance.

This chapter aims at examining two aspects related to security project: cost estimation and investment assessment. First, the characteristics of security projects are stressed on and the importance of adopting management is determined. Then, the chapter presents the different cost estimation models dedicated to security project and discusses the technical and managerial factors affecting the cost estimation and the management of project. In addition, a sample review of research works directed toward security investment models is determined. These models are organized according to the type of issues and aspects handled to compute the optimal amount of security investment. Finally, the chapter discusses future directions that could be investigated to make available useful models for cost estimation and investment on security projects.

SECURITY PROJECTS MANAGEMENT FRAMEWORKS

In this section, we examine the objective and features of security project and show the importance of the management task when dealing with these projects.

Definition and Characteristics

Security project is a specific type of project that implements a set of tasks to protect and secure a considered information system from attacks and potential threats. It lies usually outside the core functions of the business and aims to protect critical involved resources.

Security project is different from a software project for at least five features which characterize it:

- First, the security project requires a better knowledge of the security threats and vulnerabilities surrounding the activity of the enterprise, their future severity, and the evolving techniques they will implement. In addition, managing efficiently a security project assumes that the remaining risk related to damaging attacks, unobserved during project design, will be confined in the future. Moreover, the necessity to provide a response to significant attacks supposes that an efficient monitoring of activity and risk assessment are guaranteed.

- Second, the output of security projects is complicated and may include: (1) a security policy customized to the enterprise, its activity, and its environment describing the rules to be enforced, the security Procedures to observed, the detection to perform, and the security invariants to comply with. While a security policy acts as a specification of the security project, it differs from a specification in the way it involves the activity of an incident response team and the procedures it triggers on the occurrence of attacks; (2) a set of preventive, detective, and responsive systems to be deployed in a way that allows flexible configuration and real time connectivity to other information and decision systems in the enterprise; and (3) a set of countermeasures to introduce on preventive and monitoring tools to thwart future attacks along with security procedures and guidelines to be followed by people when immediate reactivity on the managerial procedures is needed.

- Third, estimating security project complexity is influenced by different factors, such as the size of the information system to secure in terms of number and size of interconnected sub-networks; the number of users exploiting the information system resources including customer users connecting remotely and administrators; and the complexity of the security policy defining the measures to implement and rules to enforce.

- Fourth, a great part of the work in a security project is added on the customer network in order to: (i) interview the users, security administrators, and managers, especially during the risk analysis phase to identify the managerial issues that can affect the project; (ii) integrate and configure the developed solution and update the existing networking solutions to guarantee an adequate interoperation; and (iii) assess the robustness of the resulting security system through auditing and penetration testing.

- Fifth, a security project has to keep under control the variation of the security robustness of the project over time. This need is difficult to achieve since vulnerability models cannot handle a good perception of the vulnerability evolution.

Management Role in Security Project

Security project, as all types of projects, needs a project management activity in order to better pursue its objective. Indeed, this latter is considered as a process that helps producing successful projects by ensuring that the key elements of the projects are included in the right order at the right time.

A successful security project requires a good management of ten key elements (Stahl, 2008): (1) project scope, (2) project time and schedule, (3) project cost and budget, (4) project resources (internal and external), (5) contract management, (6) procurement management, (7) project communications, (8) quality management, (9) project risk, and (10) cross-organizational coordination.

The project management activity consists in organizing, planning, and scheduling tasks. These later represent the most time-consuming project management activities. Therefore, elaborating and following a security project plan is a useful way before implementing security solutions. The developed security plan will be customized to fit the type and the needs of the organization to protect. The major steps include identifying threats, analyzing and prioritizing threats, developing plans and strategies to reduce the occurrence likelihood of the identified threats, and elaborating contingency plans.

It is noted that various benefits are determined when adopting project management to security project. In fact, the core advantage of performing the management is to avoid some projects failures, related for example to over estimation of the budget allocated to security project, unrealistic timelines for the different security tasks achievement, and large definition of the project scope. Moreover, adopting project management provides a strong framework for roles and responsibilities. This is crucial since the role of security is often misunderstood by many within an organization. A highly defined role for security can help alleviate friction between the security program and the rest of the organization (Gentil, 2015). In addition, the management allows defining for each process group of the project (i.e. initiation, planning, execution, controlling, and closing) the set of issues to be solved as it is specific for each group.

COST ESTIMATION MODELS FOR SECURITY PROJECTS

This section provides a brief survey of the developed cost estimation models for security projects. It also highlights the importance of integrating technical and managerial factors in these cost estimation models.

Review of Existing Cost Estimation Models

The developed cost estimation models for security projects are not as popular as those dedicated to software projects (Boehm, 2000). The ones described in the literature are cited in the following.

Labor Time Estimation Model (LTEM)

The model is described in (Satoh, 2009) to estimate the labor time of information security audit projects through the estimation of the labor time of its four phases, i.e., planning, implementation, reporting, and improvement. The estimation is based on factors related mainly to the type of the audit form, the operation mode, the enterprise size, and the penetration degree of information security management. These parameters are measured through performing quantitative and regression analysis of data collected from past audit projects.

Despite the suitability of the LTEM model to assess security audit projects, it is noted that it is not appropriate to estimate the cost of security projects due to a number of limitations. In fact, the model considers few parameters which affect the effort and the cost of conducting security projects. Factors related to the information system to be audited or reporting on the auditing team skills could be considered. In addition, the applied size estimation technique is only based on the number of employees involved in the audit process, and does not consider the information system components that could affect it. Another important limitation of this model lies in its lack of consideration of the security policy, which could be used as a baseline for auditing, analysis, compliance checking of the information system, and the correctness of the configuration of the security solutions to the security rules. Therefore, the security policy could introduce additional labor time on the audit activity, especially, when inconsistency is noticed. Furthermore, a security policy can be used in size estimation as it provides more constraints than a specification.

A Security Cost Model (SECOMO)

This model aims at estimating the effort required to conduct a security project (Krichene, 2003). It provides a basis for determining how much time, cost, and personnel are required for security projects. It is founded similarly to the Constructive Cost Model (COCOMO), which is a hybrid cost estimation model based on regression and expertise based techniques.

SECOMO defines three security cost models, classified into basic, intermediate, and advanced. These models differ according to their complexity, size, and the strength of the security policy they implement. In addition, they are based on the size of the network to be secured and use a set of cost drivers, decomposed in effort multipliers and scale factors, that give a measure of the security task complexity and where their effects are different. Effort multipliers have linear effect on the estimation, whereas, scale factors have an exponential impact.

Despite the contribution of this model to the management of security projects, some limitations could be identified. First, SECOMO is tailored to enterprises developing security software. It cannot be used, as it is, by any enterprise assessing the total cost of a security project it wants to acquire for itself. Different used parameters could not be estimated accurately, such as developing team capability and tool experience since they are intrinsic to a software development company. The second limit is related to the inability of SECOMO to consider the managerial effort related to the integration of the solutions to systems dealing with strategic intelligence and the organizational security documents. In fact, a large set of managerial and organizational tasks within the enterprise should be accounted during the cost estimation as they are included in the enterprise's security policy. In particular, the awareness activity following the deployment of a security solution is not considered in SECOMO.

A Managerial Issues-Aware Cost Estimation of Enterprise Security Projects (MCE)

The MCE cost estimation model is an extension of SECOMO and COCOMO models. It is developed to conduct a security project and integrates the impact of managerial and technical aspects related to five types of tasks, namely monitoring, awareness, decision making, re-engineering, and integration and compliance (Fessi, 2013). The developed model allows managers predicting the cost associated to a security solution according to the enterprise's needs, and thus they (i.e. managers) could define and manage efficiently their project budget.

The developed cost model depends on the size of the information system, the size of the existing security policy (SP), the enterprise size, in addition to a set of cost drivers. It allows estimating numerically the managerial impact on the cost associated to a security project, compared with the other existing models. Moreover, it gives an important role to the security policy supporting the security project, as it represents a key element for estimating the required effort and the expected cost.

It is noted that behind the provided benefits, the developed model is closely tied to the content of security policy (SP), which is considered as a static document during the project estimation time. In reality, SP must be adapted to the environment where the enterprises operate. This latter is characterized by its complexity and uncertainty where threats and vulnerabilities increase continuously, attackers change their behavior over time, and resources may show dynamic features. Moreover, MCE lacks of tools for the estimation of the financial cost associated to the residual risk which is not addressed by security project. In fact, by considering the risk value, the enterprise could take the appropriate decisions to invest or not in the security project. We notice that this limitation is shared with the other developed cost estimation models.

Technical and Managerial Factors Support

The presented security project cost estimation models (Krichene, 2003; Fessi, 2013; Satoh, 2009) show the involvement of two types of factors: technical and managerial. The first set of factors are those related to the enterprise assets and to the security solution, whereas the second set is associated to the enterprise management features, such as organizational, human, and risk management. This integration of managerial factors besides technical ones into the estimation of the cost of the security project allows more accuracy to determine security budget allocation.

As it is mentioned beforehand, several factors are identified in the presented models. For the LTEM model, factors that influence the labor times include the type of business, the audit form, the operation mode, the penetration degree of information security management, and the enterprise size. For the SECOMO model, 23 parameters are defined and referred to as effort multipliers factors (i.e., product, personal, project, and information system) and scale factors (i.e., precedentedness, team cohesion, project maturity, and security strategy). And for the MCE model, 19 parameters are identified and are allocated according to their relation to information system size, security policy, enterprise size and the defined five tasks (monitoring, awareness, decision making, re-engineering, and integration and compliance). Despite this variation of parameters between the presented models, it is noticed that some parameters are considered in two or all models, but have different designations such as audit form parameter in LTEM and audit frequency parameter in SECOMO; the enterprise size parameter presented in LTEM model corresponds to multi-site information system parameter in SECOMO model and it is also used as a key measure in the MCE model.

The different cost drivers could be assessed either quantitatively or qualitatively. Quantitative measures are determined on the basis of historical data, defined functions, statistical measures, or even experts opinion. Qualitative measures, in the other hand, require the intervention of experts to define the scale level of each parameter, and then approximate measure could be affected to it. For example, in SECOMO, the whole majority of parameters related to personal, are qualitative parameters, while in MCE model, strategic intelligence and awareness factors are qualitative and should be determined by experts.

SECURITY INVESTMENT MODELS FOR SECURITY PROJECTS

Several research works are developed to compute the optimal amount of security investment from the financial and economic perspectives. Recent works are directed toward integrating new aspects related mainly to cyber-insurance, security vulnerabilities patching, and game theory in cyber-security investment. These models are described in the following paragraphs.

Economics of Security Investment Models

Determining the optimal amount of security investment which minimizes the risk of security attack is still an open issue for decision-makers, due to several factors such as the limited financial budget allocated to security information systems, the near-impossibility of eliminating security residual risk, and the dynamic and evolutionary aspect of different types of vulnerabilities and threats facing the firm's information systems.

Several works have been developed to handle security investment problem using a multitude of economic and financial approaches and techniques, such as risk-return analysis (Hausken, 2014; Gordon, 2002), utility theory (Huang, 2013; Miaoui, 2015a), game theory (Cavusoglu, 2008; Hua, 2011) and real options theory (Li, 2007; Tatsumi, 2009; Ullrich, 2013). The security optimal investment model based on the maximization of expected net benefits was first proposed in (Gordon, 2002). In this model, the decision-makers, which are assumed to be risk-neutral, maximize their expected incomes from security investment by comparing the marginal financial benefits and the marginal financial costs of information security. The model analyzes the impact of several parameters, such as system's vulnerabilities and potential financial loss on the amount of optimal security investment considering two classes of security breaches, namely targeted attacks and distributed attacks.

In (Huang, 2008), utility based model is used to determine the optimal security investment with the assumption of risk averse decision-makers. Considering each class of security breach probability, as assumed in (Gordon, 2002), different scenarios are conducted to analyze the relationships between optimal security investment levels and the potential loss, the extent of the decision maker's risk aversion, and the investment effectiveness. In an extension work, the authors developed an analytic model that optimizes the allocation of security investment to defend against concurrent heterogeneous attacks on a firm's information systems (Huang, 2013). The model considers the budget constraint that all firms face and is based on the concept of scale-free networks to obtain breach probabilities for different classes of attacks.

Another context of security investment is examined in (Miaoui, 2015b), where the firms outsource or offshore their business operations. In this case, particular aspects related to bilateral security risk and data privacy are considered when computing their security investments. The developed model considers the involvement and interdependency of several stakeholders (e.g., attackers, the privacy protection firms, data sellers, and outsourcing companies) in conducting and protecting against privacy attacks in the context of an outsourced business activity. Moreover, the authors designed different models related to security threats on data privacy and consider the particular aspects of privacy attacks when determining the expected monetary loss and benefits. They also conducted a numerical analysis to assess the impact of the quality of detection and reaction to privacy breaches on the amount of optimal investment and residual risk.

Cyber-Insurance Investment

Several investments can be adopted by companies to protect their information systems against damaging security incidents, such as self-protection, self-insurance and cyber-insurance. The self-protection investment includes the development of security policy, the design of architectures and the deployment of security solutions (including, but not limited to anti-virus, firewalls or intrusion detection mechanisms) to mitigate the occurrence of security breaches, while the self-insurance investment is an internal investment made by an enterprise to cover himself from a financial potential loss. To reduce the large amount of potential losses induced by cyber-attackers, an investment in cyber-insurance can be undertaken by an enterprise (insured) to transfer the financial risk of security breaches to a third party partner (insurer). An insurance contract is, thus, established between the two parties (insurer and insured) including in particular, the insurance premium to be paid by the insured firm and the reimbursement rate at which the insurance company will cover the amount of potential loss.

While the transfer of risk through an insurance company was suggested, by practitioners and academics, to cover the expenses and losses induced by security breaches (cost of notification and response to security incidents, loss or corruption of data), complete the existing set of security countermeasures and manage the security residual risk (after investments in cyber-security have already been made), the growing evolution of cyber risk and the interdependency of information security risks (due to interconnections of computers across different firms) have made the cyber insurance investment particularly complex, unclear, and more challenging (Zhao, 2013).

Indeed, as a classic insurance, the cyber-insurance raises several issues related to: a) pricing which is the amount of premium to charge to the insured firm in turn of potential loss coverage. To determine the appropriate price, insurance company should accurately estimate the cyber risk incurred by the insured firm. However, some estimation bias can be introduced when the applicant firms have high risk interdependencies due to their high information systems openness to external environment and/or their degree of information sharing through outsourcing operations; b) adverse selection which is a hidden action problem arises when the insured firm does not communicate its real security risk in order to benefit from lower risk premium. To deal with this problem, the insurance company can estimate the security risk of the applicant's resources, the systems vulnerabilities and the threats through security audit. As the security vulnerabilities and threats severity, frequency and evolution with respect to time are increasing, security incidents occurrence probability as well as the potential loss to be reimbursed by insurer are also increasing; and c) moral hazard which is an asymmetric information problem arising from the non-ability of the insurance company to observe the behavior of insured firm after purchasing cyber-insurance. The latter may behave recklessly in order to increase the likelihood of insurance claims.

In fact, although an insurance contract does not prevent security breaches from occurring, some firms may find it cost sensitive to invest in cyber insurance than in self-protection. In the worst case, untrusted insured firms could create fictive self-attacks and ripe benefits from the insurance company. Therefore, a high premium or a low coverage (e.g., use of deductibles) should be given to firms that do not take the appropriate measures to reduce the probability of loss, or that are unable to prove that the incident is not self-generated.

In this context, several models were developed to cope with these issues (Gordon, 2003; Herath, 2011; Böhme, 2010). In particular, cyber insurance has been proposed as a promising solution to manage security risks and to optimize security investment. In (Ogut, 2005) and (Bolot, 2008), the impact of cyber-insurance investment is studied, when firms face correlated risk on the cost and efficiency of security investments, and on the increase of incentives to invest in self-protection. In (Grossklags, 2008), a model of security investments interactions using game theory was proposed. The authors show how the players decide strategically to shift between investment in self-protection and investment in cyber insurance. Recent work proposed by (Miaoui, 2015a) is focused on the importance of security investment in forensic investigation to collect digital evidence and generate provable insurance claims to ensure a better reimbursement of loss in case of security breaches occurrence. The developed investment model is based on three interdependent investment types: investment in self-defense, investment in insurance, and investment in forensic readiness.

Security Vulnerabilities Patching Investment

The detection and the patching of vulnerabilities represent important tasks that keep an information system secure. Security administrators should typically proceed as soon as possible with the application of patches or the modification of security policy rules (e.g., deactivation of vulnerable services, ports filtering) to prevent potential exploitation of the identified vulnerabilities. In practice, different reasons may delay or prevent a firm from the immediate application of security patches, such as: (1) the number of patches to be deployed is important and their implications on security vary accordingly so that it is necessary to sort and prioritize vulnerabilities, which is a labour-intensive task; (2) there may be many available fixes for an identified vulnerability (i.e., official ones released by the vendor, and other ones released by the security community experts), so a test of compliance with existing software should be performed; and (3) a maintenance period, where the production system needs to be rebooted or temporary disconnected, could introduce an economic loss if it is required.

This delayed application of patches could lead to serious economic losses and could have severe security consequences. Therefore, a firm should design a patch management strategy to determine the time and the appropriate patch to deploy for the detected vulnerability. This strategy will keep the safety of the system, reduce the operational cost, and reduce the security risk of loss to an acceptable level. In this context, some research works are directed toward this issue and propose economic models based on game theoretic approaches to derive the optimal strategy and frequency of patches update. This strategy depends on the operation cost model, the required downtime period, the patch release policy of the software provider, and the stochastic vulnerability release. The developed model in (Cavusoglu, 2006) defines an objective function to minimize the damage cost of exploiting an unpatched vulnerability and the update patch to shield vulnerability at the client company. This latter is assumed to incur attacks either because it is waiting for the release of a patch or because the patch is released but it is waiting the end of the update cycle. For the customer firm, the software vendor firm is assumed to release vulnerability fixes every predefined period of time, incurring consequently two different losses: patch development and release losses, and reputation cost.

Game Theory in Security Investments

Regarding the previous approaches, where the security investment is considered as an optimization problem that determines the best compromise between the security budget to spend and the residual risk to accept, several recent works are interested to use the game theory as a security tool to model the cyber environment under which defenders and offenders interact together. Such a theory will capture the behaviour of the attacker which varies depending on the strategy of the enterprise in defending and responding to security attacks. In most real scenarios of cyber protection, several actors interact together, including insurance companies, privacy protection firms, defender, third party companies, network and security providers, and even security authorities. All of these actors try to improve their expected benefits and therefore they adapt their behaviour to the visible or hidden properties of the cyber environment (available resources, loss of incur, identification ability, etc.).

In the context of security economics, several applications of game theory were proposed during the last years. In (Nagurney, 2015), information asymmetry between sellers and buyers is introduced to determine the optimal security investment at the seller side. In fact, contrarily to sellers which have a good knowledge of their security investment and the residual security risk they incur, and want to maximize their expected benefit from selling their products on the Internet market space (and therefore execute secure transactions); buyers set their preference regarding the product prices based on the average provided security level of the seller (this security level is imprecise due to information asymmetry and is not related to individual sellers, but simply reflects the average security level in the industry). The used game theory determines the Nash equilibrium by which sellers can assess the cyber security investment, the expected damages in case of attacks, and the attacks probabilities.

In (Panaousis, 2014), the game theory is used as a tool to model the cyber security environment of a firm, as well as a non cooperative control game between a defender and an attacker. The former abstracts decision makers in security to protect the firm's assets and the latter abstracts all untrusted parties that aim to compromise the firm's assets. In this work, a security control is defined by the firm with respect to the direct and indirect damages that it can avoid on all targets. The game is modelled based on a two player minimax game, to allow defining one security control to implement, by which the more the attacker gains, the higher will be the firm's loss. Moreover, the proposed model implements a multi-objective optimization problem to derive the optimal allocation of the security budget, since different security controls are required by the firm to defend against the different security vulnerabilities.

Another model is developed based on the game theory approach (Fielder, 2014) to support making decisions regarding the allocation of security resources, including the time consumed by administrators in security their systems. The proposed model assumes that an attacker could harm many targets, and each target is threatened using a single vulnerability. Therefore, to defend against attacks, two security levels are considered, namely baseline and best practice. The former describes the probability of an attack, while the latter denotes the percentages of attacks being defended.

FUTURE RESEARCH DIRECTIONS

This section presents a number of future research directions related to unsolved challenging issues by the current cost estimation models of security projects. It also examines new research trends expected to determine an optimal security investment model.

Cost Estimation Models

To enhance the cost estimation of security projects, a set of consideration should be involved in the computation task. The first concern is related to the management of uncertainty and dynamicity related to the environment where the solution will be deployed. In fact, the cost estimation model should be extended to include additional factors that manage this uncertainty and cope with the variation of the protected environment by the security solution. It is, therefore, important to develop proactive cost models that tolerate modifications on the security policy during the achievement of the security projects to consider new threats and vulnerabilities.

The risk factors are other important features that should be considered when estimating the cost of security projects. They are related to the risk associated to future security breaches in the operational period of the developed security solution and to the remaining residual risk after deploying the security solution. For the first type, it is necessary to develop a model that anticipates the evolution of risk, associated to the unpredictable evolution of vulnerabilities and threats over time, and integrates their variable severities in order to enhance the cost-effectiveness of the developed security projects. The second type of risk allows the improvement of the efficiency of security solution in the future, since providing a complete security solution is impossible due to the constraints of the allocated budget to the security managers.

Security Investment Models

Different aspects might be considered to improve the developed security investment models. First, it is noted that when designing an investment model, the main aim is set on the efficiency of the security solution to protect the information system regardless its usefulness and its added value for the company' shareholders. It is, thus, more useful to develop a model that allows the achievement of its primary objective and to yield profit through including new parameters related to creation of value for the shareholder (such as dividends, profitability of funds, governance and financial transparency), in addition to parameters associated to the evolution and dynamicity of vulnerabilities and threats.

The second point to deal with concerns the security investment when private data are protected by outsourcing firms. In this case, the type of the subcontracting firms has an impact on the investment computation. This type is related to the degree and the nature of control (i.e. partial, global) over the outsourced resources (e.g., data, applications, services). In addition, related parameters to private business data should be taken into account as they could have significant impacts on determining the investment model, such as the value of the information to be protected, the degrees of sensitivity of this information to security attacks, the degrees of attractiveness of business data to attackers, etc.

CONCLUSION

The project management is an important task to be performed when dealing with security project to avoid project failures. Different researches assume that security and software projects are managed in the same way using the same tools and techniques. Nevertheless, it is noted that there are differences between the two projects and additional issues should be considered when managing security project.

A number of study were conducted around different aspects of security projects but remaining issues related specifically to the dynamicity and evolution of the environment, attacks, and system resources are needed to be resolved in order to develop an efficient cost estimation model and to better assess the budget allocated to security task. Therefore, additional efforts still needed.

This chapter focuses on the security project management and the existing cost estimation models. It also presents a review of the security investment models and describes the latest developed works. In addition, the chapter underlines the relationships between cost estimation and security investment when designing security projects and examines the future directions for the development of efficient models.

REFERENCES

Boehm, B., Abts, C., & Chulani, S. (2000, November). Software development cost estimation approaches - a survey. *Annals of Software Engineering, 10*(1), 177–205. doi:10.1023/A:1018991717352

Böhme, R., & Schwartz, S. (2010, June 7-8). Modeling Cyber-Insurance: Towards a Unifying Framework. *9th Annual Workshop on the Economics of Information Security (WEIS 2010)*. Harvard University.

Bolot, J. C., & Lelarge, M. (2008, April 13-18). A New Perspective on Internet Security using Insurance. *Proceedings of the 27th Conference on Computer Communications (INFOCOM 2008)*. IEEE. 10.1109/INFOCOM.2008.259

Cavusoglu, H., Raghunathan, S., & Yue, W. (2008). Decision-theoretical and game-theoretical approaches to it security investment. *Journal of Management Information Systems, 25*(2), 281–304. doi:10.2753/MIS0742-1222250211

Cavusoglu, H., & Zhang, J. (2006). Economics of security patch management. *The fifth Workshop on the Economics of Information Security (WEIS 2006)*.

Fessi, B. A., Miaoui, Y., & Boudriga, N. (2013, June). A managerial issues-aware cost estimation of enterprise security projects. *Journal of Information Security Research, 4*(2), 81–89.

Fielder, A., Panaousis, E., Malacaria, P., Hankin, C., & Smeraldi, F. (2014, June 2-4). Game Theory Meets Information Security Management. *Proceedings of the 29th IFIP TC 11 International Conference (SEC 2014)*, 15-29.

Gentile, M., Collette, R., & CISOHandbook.com Team. (2015). Project Management As A Security Touch-Point. In *Project Management and Security*. CISOHandbook.com.

Gordon, L. A., & Loeb, M. P. (2002, November). The economics of information security investment. *ACM Transactions on Information and System Security, 5*(4), 438–457. doi:10.1145/581271.581274

Gordon, L. A., Loeb, M. P., & Lucyshyn W. (2003, May 31). Information security expenditures and real options: A wait-and-see approach. *Computer Security Journal, 19*(2).

Grossklags, J., Christin, N., & Chuang, J. (2008, April 21-25). Secure or Insure? A Game-Theoretic Analysis of Information Security Games. *Proceedings of the 17th International Conference on World Wide Web*, 209-218.

Hausken, K. (2014, April). Returns to information security investment: Endogenizing the expected loss. *Information Systems Frontiers, 16*(2), 329–336. doi:10.100710796-012-9390-9

Herath, H., & Herath, T. (2011, February 27). Copula Based Actuarial Model for Pricing Cyber-Insurance Policies. *Insurance Markets and Companies: Analyses and Actuarial Computations, 2*(1), 7–20.

Hua, J., & Bapna, S. (2011). Optimal IS Security Investment: Cyber Terrorism vs. Common Hacking. In D. F. Galletta & T.-P. Liang (Eds.), *ICIS. Association for Information Systems*.

Huang, C. D., & Behara, R. S. (2013, January). Economics of Information Security Investment in the Case of Concurrent Heterogeneous Attacks with Budget Constraints. *International Journal of Production Economics, 141*(1), 255–268. doi:10.1016/j.ijpe.2012.06.022

Huang, C. D., Hu, Q., & Behara, R. S. (2008, August). An economic analysis of the optimal information security investment in the case of a risk-averse firm. *International Journal of Production Economics, 114*(2), 793–804. doi:10.1016/j.ijpe.2008.04.002

Krichene, J., Boudriga, N., & Guemara, S. (2003). SECOMO: An estimation cost model for risk management. *Proceedings of international conference on Telecom (ConTel'03)*. 10.1109/CONTEL.2003.176966

Li, J., & Su, X. (2007), Making Cost Effective Security Decision with Real Option Thinking. *International Conference on Software Engineering Advances (ICSEA)* (p. 14). IEEE Computer Society. 10.1109/ICSEA.2007.50

Miaoui, Y., Boudriga, N., & Abaoub, E. (2015a). Insurance Versus Investigation Driven Approach for the Computation of Optimal Security Investment. *Proceedings of the 19th Pacific Asia Conference on Information Systems (PACIS 2015) on IT and Open Innovation.*

Miaoui, Y., Boudriga, N., & Abaoub, E. (2015b). Economics of Privacy: A Model for Protecting Against Cyber Data Disclosure Attacks. *Proceedings of the 3rd Information Systems International Conference (ISICO 2015)* (pp. 1-15). Surabaya, Indonesia: Procedia Computer Science, Elsevier (Scopus Indexed). 10.1016/j.procs.2015.12.165

Nagurney, A., & Nagurney, L. S. (2015, August). A game theory model of cybersecurity investments with information asymmetry. *NETNOMICS: Economic Research and Electronic Networking, 16*(1-2), 127–148. doi:10.100711066-015-9094-7

Ogut, H., Menon, N., & Raghunathan, S. (2005). Cyber Insurance and IT Security Investment: Impact of Interdependence Risk. *Proceedings of Fourth Workshop on the Economics of Information Security (WEIS 2005).*

Panaousis, E. A., Fielder, A., Malacaria, P., Hankin, C., & Smeraldi, F. (2014, November 6-7). Cyber-security Games and Investments: A Decision Support Approach. Lecture Notes in Computer Science: *Vol. 8840. Proceedings of the 5th International Conference (GameSec 2014)* (pp. 266-286). Springer. 10.1007/978-3-319-12601-2_15

Project Management Institute. (2013). *A guide to the project management body of knowledge (PMBOK' Guide)* (5th ed.). Author.

Satoh, N., & Kumamoto, H. (2009). Estimation model of labor time at the information security audit and standardization of audit work by probabilistic risk assessment. *International Journal of Computers, 3*(3), 311-320.

Stahl, S., & Pease, K. A. (2008). *A Success Strategy for Information Security Planning and Implementation.* Los Angeles, CA: Citadel Information Group, Inc.

Tatsumi, K. I., & Goto, M. (2009). Optimal Timing of Information Security Investment: Real Options Approach. In *The 8th Annual Workshop on the Economics of Information Security (WEIS 2009).* University College London.

Ullrich, C. (2013). Valuation of IT Investments Using Real Options Theory. *Business & Information Systems Engineering, 5*(5), 331–341. doi:10.100712599-013-0286-0

Zhao, X., Xue, L., & Whinston, A. B. (2013, March 11). Managing Interdependent Information Security Risks: Cyberinsurance, Managed Security Services, and Risk Pooling Arrangements. *Journal of Management Information Systems, 30*(1), 123–152. doi:10.2753/MIS0742-1222300104

KEY TERMS AND DEFINITIONS

Awareness: Is the extent to which an individual who has access to the information system assets is aware of. It is related to the importance of security and dangerousness of attacks, the enterprise's security requirements, and its responsibilities regarding the enforcement of security inside the information system.

Cost Estimation: Is an approximation of the probable cost of a project computed on the basis of the cost of all resources that will be charged to complete project activities.

Economic of Information Security: Is the discipline that applies different economic theories to resolve information security problems.

Information Security: Is the protection of the information system' resources from unauthorized access, use, disclosure, disruption, modification, perusal, inspection, recording or destruction.

Information System: Is a set of interconnected components (technology, process and people) that collect, process, store, and distribute information to sustain decision making and control in an enterprise.

Optimal Security Investment: Is the amount of investment which maximizes the Esperance of the gained loss and minimizes the risks of security attacks.

Project Management: Is a common framework providing managers with principles, techniques, and tools needed to manage project team effort efficiently and to meet successfully the enterprise's project objectives.

Residual Risk: Is a quantification of the risk or the degree of exposure that the protected information system will incur, after deciding to counter or eliminate known risk.

Security Attack: Is any form of malicious actions taken to harm the security of information system components. An action is classified as malicious with respect to the enterprise security policy.

Security Policy: Is a document that lays the framework for information system security of the enterprise. Through this framework, a security project team can draw intelligible objectives, plans, rules and formal procedures required to manage and protect the sensitive enterprise information system from different attacks.

Security Project: Is a set of activities that aim to protect and secure an information system from attacks and potential threats.

Security Risk: Is the likelihood that enterprise assets (i.e. information, systems and network infrastructures, data, programs and applications) be targeted by a successful attack.

Threat: Is an indication about a potential event that can harm the security of the protected resource. A threat can turn to a security attack once a vulnerability that can be exploited is found.

Vulnerability: Is a defect or weakness in information system's assets or mechanisms, which could lead to a security breach when exploited by malicious entities.

This research was previously published in the Encyclopedia of Information Science and Technology, Fourth Edition edited by Mehdi Khosrow-Pour, pages 4849-4861, copyright year 2018 by Information Science Reference (an imprint of IGI Global).

Chapter 15
Development of Personal Information Privacy Concerns Evaluation

Anna Rohunen
University of Oulu, Finland

Jouni Markkula
University of Oulu, Finland

ABSTRACT

Personal data is increasingly collected with the support of rapidly advancing information and communication technology, which raises privacy concerns among data subjects. In order to address these concerns and offer the full benefits of personal data-intensive services to the public, service providers need to understand how to evaluate privacy concerns in evolving service contexts. By analyzing the earlier privacy concerns evaluation instruments, we can learn how to adapt them to new contexts. In this chapter, the historical development of the most widely used privacy concerns evaluation instruments is presented and analyzed regarding privacy concerns' dimensions. Privacy concerns' core dimensions and the types of context dependent dimensions to be incorporated into evaluation instruments are identified. Following this, recommendations on how to utilize the existing evaluation instruments are given, as well as suggestions for future research dealing with validation and standardization of the instruments.

INTRODUCTION

Personal data collection and utilization are increasingly taking place today as a part of the application of personal data intensive systems and services. Both individuals and data collecting organizations benefit from this. Personal data are collected and processed by private companies and public organizations for various purposes, for example, for delivery of more personalized services and for marketing. Despite its usefulness, extensive personal data collection raises privacy concerns among data subjects, and these concerns are also discussed in public very often. For example, vehicle GPS tracking-based kilometer taxation has been recently under debate. This debate has shown that vehicle tracking data can also be

DOI: 10.4018/978-1-5225-7492-7.ch015

used for purposes other than taxation, and that it can be combined with other data, for example, for producing traffic information services by private or public organizations. Information privacy concerns derive from data subjects' desire to not be monitored, and their worries about the consequences of the use of their data. Privacy concerns often decrease data subjects' willingness to disclose their personal data or to use services that require personal data disclosure. For this reason, privacy concerns may lead to non-adoption of new services and technologies, dropping out of them, or a decline in data disclosure (i.e., omitting data or providing false information). To address these issues, we need to understand how to evaluate privacy concerns in current and future evolving service development contexts. We need insights into how privacy concerns have been evaluated in earlier contexts in order to adapt evaluations to new contexts.

In many countries, legislation sets the foundation for protecting personal data privacy and provides a framework for implementing privacy protection methods and technologies. However, it does not really suppress privacy concerns of the data intensive services' users. People's privacy concerns need to be understood to apply legislation in present-day data collection contexts, characterized by rapid technological change, expanded data collection, diverse uses for collected data, and possibilities to monitor individuals' behavior and combine data from different sources. This understanding can be gained with well-designed *privacy concerns evaluation instruments*. When privacy concerns are evaluated and analyzed, their negative effects on personal data disclosure can be mitigated. In this way, more efficient promotion of personal data intensive services and realization of their benefits for both service users and providers can be reached. In practice, privacy concerns can be addressed by various means based on their evaluation. First, the means of privacy protection and the real risks of data disclosure can be communicated to the data subjects and the general public. Second, data subjects can be given control over their information, and benefits can be offered to them for disclosing information. Third, privacy-preserving systems and service design can be facilitated by taking service users' privacy concerns into account.

Several researchers have contributed to development of information privacy concerns evaluation instruments since the beginning of the 1990s. Due to evolving technologies and new data collection contexts, the existing instruments do not necessarily match data subjects' privacy concerns anymore. Therefore, the validity of these instruments should be examined for their subsequent development and use. We have addressed this challenge by carrying out an analysis of the most widely used privacy concerns evaluation instruments. Through this analysis, we have gathered information specifically on different aspects of individuals' privacy concerns (referred to as privacy concerns' *dimensions* in the instruments) and how they should be taken into account in the instruments' development. We have identified both privacy concerns' core dimensions that have remained unchanged in the evaluations with time and the types of context dependent dimensions to be incorporated into evaluation instruments. When summarizing the results of our analysis, we pay attention to the fact that in addition to being valid and up-to-date, evaluation instruments should also be made easy-to-use enough. In this way, they can be applied to the practical development of personal data intensive services.

In this article, an overview of the existing privacy concerns evaluation instruments will be given and complemented with an outline of their future development. At first, the historical development of privacy concerns evaluation instruments is described, and the most widely used key evaluation instruments from different decades are introduced. Next, an analysis of these key evaluation instruments is presented, focusing on the privacy concerns' dimensions and their changes with technological development and evolving data collection contexts. After this, recommendations on how to utilize the existing evaluation instruments are given, as well as suggestions for future research dealing with validation and standardization of the instruments.

BACKGROUND

Opportunities for automatic processing of personal data for business purposes have evolved from the first electronic records in the 1950s to present-day comprehensive data collection and processing systems with different data sources and diverse uses. With technological development enabling this change, companies are showing increasing interest in personal data use for developing their products and services and making their operations more effective.

The rapid progress of information technology in the 1960s enabled big enterprises to, for the first time, establish extensive databanks for their customers' personal data. Later on, data warehousing type systems made it possible to easily combine, process, and analyze the collected data for corporate decision making. Along with these changes, discussion on information privacy was evoked, bringing out the need for personal data protection (cf. Westin, 1967). With the launch of e-commerce and other Internet-based services in the mid-1990s, again, new and expanded opportunities for collecting and utilizing personal data of these systems' users appeared. For example, compared to traditional customer records, customers could now be profiled and their preferences could be identified in more detail based on their clickstream. A few years later—specifically, after the introduction of smart phones—development of location and mobility data-based services gained momentum, creating possibilities for gathering even more detailed and extensive data on individuals and their behavior. As a whole, nowadays, the current technology makes possible large-scale personal data collection, integration of data sources of different types, and combination of separate data pools for diverse uses of the collected data. This enables the production of big data that is highly valuable to society, as it has the potential to boost both economic growth and utility for individuals. Increased efficiency, quality, and productivity can be reached, and customers' needs can be better met through big data use. On the other hand, it is clear that there are substantive privacy issues associated with the present-day personal data collection. These issues are being regulated by legislation which needs to be adapted to individuals' privacy behavior and personal data collection technologies and contexts. The need for regulation of automatic data processing with ongoing technological development is reflected, for example, by the General Data Protection Regulation reform in the EU (European Commission, 2012).

Evaluation of individuals' information privacy concerns is not necessarily a straightforward task, as people may be concerned about different aspects of privacy (which are usually referred to as privacy concerns *dimensions*). There has been a tendency to learn to understand and take into account privacy concerns for decades, and these concerns have been measured in opinion polls and as a part of research studies as well. However, privacy concerns evaluation instruments and their dimensionality have been developed in a methodical way only since the beginning of the 1990s. Prior to this, information privacy concerns evaluations were relatively fragmented in nature, in that they considered privacy concerns to be either a unidimensional construct or varying in their dimensions. Culnan (1993) presented some burning questions related to secondary use and publishing of personal data for direct marketing purposes in the off-line context. She stated that companies collecting consumers' personal data may find it difficult to pursue the opportunities provided by data collection technologies if they do not comply with information practices responding to consumers' privacy concerns. This challenge has been extensively studied in the literature on information privacy concerns and privacy behavior, indicating that individuals' privacy concerns often lead them to decline to disclose personal data if not being informed of appropriate privacy practices. For this reason, it is crucial to have well-designed, validated evaluation instruments for information privacy concerns evaluation. The development of these instruments initially focused on collection of off-line personal data such as customers' demographic and purchase data (e.g., Culnan, 1993; Smith et al., 1996; Stewart & Segars, 2002). With the development of e-commerce and Internet-based services, evaluation instruments specific to the Internet context started to become popular (e.g., Malhotra et al., 2004; Dinev & Hart, 2004; Castaneda et al., 2007). These instruments' items were adapted from the existing instruments, taking into account online threats and unforeseen uses of information. As for individuals' location and mobility data collection through smart mobile devices with GPS tracking, questionnaire items on continuous, large-scale mobility data collection were further developed in some studies on privacy behavior in this context (e.g., Junglas et al., 2008; Xu & Gupta, 2009, Raschke et al., 2014). People are exposed all the time to the possibility of increasingly severe privacy losses due to present-day production of big data together with mobile devices' and body sensors' collection of personal data. As data collection of this kind enables continuous monitoring of individuals and their health and physical condition, data that are often considered highly sensitive information, the need for checking the validity of the existing privacy concerns evaluation instruments is increasing.

Information privacy concerns are changing along with evolving personal data collection contexts and the trend towards increasingly comprehensive data collection and modeling of data subjects' behavior. People's attitudes towards data use may change as it becomes a part of our everyday life and we accommodate to the present-day inclusive data collection culture (cf. Nosko et al., 2010). On the other hand, people are continuously exposed to privacy related news and public discussions and hence are increasingly aware of possible privacy issues regarding personal data use. All these aspects should be taken into account when developing privacy concerns evaluation instruments for new personal data intensive services; in other words, evaluation instruments should be adapted to changes in evaluation contexts and the data disclosure culture.

PRIVACY CONCERNS EVALUATION IN EVOLVING PERSONAL DATA INTENSIVE SERVICES

Present-day and future personal data intensive services are challenging privacy concerns evaluation due to evolving technologies and new data collection contexts. We need to understand existing evaluation instruments' historical evolution to further develop and validate them. Therefore, we present a historical description and analysis of key evaluation instruments and their dimensions in the literature. Our description and analysis covers the most widely used evaluation instruments that date back to different decades and represent different data collection contexts.

Evolution of Privacy Concerns Evaluation Instruments

In the times of electronic records and data warehousing systems, the data collected from customers typically consisted of their contact information and demographic and purchase data. These data were not only used for customer service and companies' operational and strategic aims, they were also often sold for secondary purposes, specifically to direct marketing companies. At the beginning of the 1990s,

Culnan (1993) conducted a survey on data subjects' attitudes towards secondary use of their personal data for direct marketing. She identified two dimensions of privacy concerns: *loss of control* over information and *unauthorized secondary use* of information. Culnan's work was followed by an instrument developed by Smith et al. (1996) for evaluating data subjects' concerns about data collecting companies' organizational information practices for personal data use. Smith et al. identified four dimensions of information privacy concerns, one of them similar to Culnan's dimension of *unauthorized secondary use*. The other three dimensions were *data collection* (i.e., whether excessive data are collected on a data subject), *improper access* to personal information (i.e., within an organization, whether a person without the "need to know" is able to access personal information stored in the files), and *errors* in personal data (e.g., accidental errors or obsolete data). Stewart and Segars (2002) further developed the instrument by Smith et al. Their results suggested that data subjects are concerned about all of the dimensions of organizational information practices simultaneously, rather than any one dimension in particular. Stewart and Segars also found that separate dimensions are interrelated and that the *control* over the information dimension possibly accounts for these interrelationships.

At the beginning of the 2000s, new information privacy concerns evaluation instruments, intended for the Internet context, were introduced. An instrument by Dinev and Hart (2004) for Internet users' privacy concerns evaluation was based on the instruments by Smith et al. and Culnan and Armstrong (1999), and these existing instruments were modified to reflect the nature of the online context. The results by Dinev and Hart suggested an instrument with only two privacy concerns' dimensions: information *finding* on the Internet (i.e., possibilities to track data subjects' activities and their personal information) and information *abuse*. Dinev and Hart also measured *perceived ability to control* information disclosure, recognizing it a separate construct from privacy concerns. However, they pointed out that different results could have been obtained if *need for control* was measured instead of *perceived ability to control*, and that need to control information disclosure may already have been captured by privacy concerns. Almost at the same time as Dinev and Hart, Malhotra et al. (2004) presented their instrument for evaluating Internet users' information privacy concerns related specifically to data disclosure in e-commerce. They proposed three privacy concerns' dimensions by drawing on social contract theory: *collection* of personal information, *control* over the collected information, and *awareness* of information use. The items incorporated into the collection dimension were based on Smith et al. and adapted to the Internet context by slightly changing their wording. Castaneda et al. (2007) further developed privacy concerns' measurements in the Internet context. They aimed to distinguish between general Internet privacy concerns and e-commerce web site-specific privacy concerns. Two dimensions were identified for these concerns, namely concern for personal information *collection* and concern for personal information *use*, the latter one corresponding to *unauthorized secondary use*. Castaneda et al.'s instrument items in the *collection* dimension include the aspects of *loss of control* and *improper access*, reflecting the intrusive side of the Internet context.

The recent development of information privacy concerns evaluation comprises themes such as identification of different conceptualizations of privacy concerns (Hong and Thong, 2013), revisiting of existing privacy concerns evaluation (Sipior et al., 2014), privacy concerns' dependency on the types of digital applications for which data are disclosed (Bergström, 2015), and comparison of different privacy concerns evaluation instruments as a part of a privacy behavior model (Fodor and Brem, 2015). All this research reflects the nature of present-day personal data collection, characterized by high volume and continuity of data collection, digital traces, and possibilities of data mining.

It is worth noting that aspects corresponding to privacy concerns' dimensions are defined in data privacy legislation, but from the data controller's (the body collecting data and legally responsible for its processing) viewpoint instead of the viewpoints of individuals whose data are collected. The aforementioned EU privacy regulation aims to minimize personal data collection by requiring specified, predetermined, and legitimate purposes of use (cf. *collection, finding,* and *abuse*). It also sets conditions on data disclosure to third parties (cf. *unauthorized secondary use*), imposes data subjects' right of access to their data and right to demand its rectification or removal (cf. *control*), and sets right to obtain rectification of incorrect data (cf. *errors*). Further, the regulation requires implementation of appropriate technical and organizational data protection measures (cf. *improper access*), informed consent for data processing (cf. *awareness*), and provision of data subjects with specified information on processing of their data (cf. *awareness*). It should be borne in mind, however, that not all individuals' information privacy concerns are covered by legislation. This applies specifically to concerns brought up by the new data collection contexts.

A comparison of the described key information privacy concerns evaluation instruments, as regards their dimensions, is presented in Table 1.

Information privacy concerns evaluation instruments by Smith et al. (1996) and Malhotra et al. (2004) have served as standard evaluation instruments in both offline and Internet contexts. Subsequent studies have often used them as a starting point or reference for their instrument development. The instruments by Smith et al. and Malhotra et al. have been adapted into the evolving data collection contexts by modifying the wording of their items and adding new items relevant to the context. When moving to the Internet context, items originally dealing with companies' data collection and privacy practices in the offline context have been reworded to reflect online data collection. New items on Internet threats incorporated into the instruments deal with stealing or misuse of submitted information, uncertainty about its subsequent use, and continuous tracking of individuals' actions on the Internet. Furthermore, a tendency to adapt instruments better to increasing personal data collection and monitoring of individuals' behavior can be identified in some recent studies (cf. Mao & Zhang 2013, Raschke et al. 2014).

Analysis of Privacy Concerns' Dimensions

Three privacy concerns' dimensions are incorporated into most evaluation instruments regardless of their application contexts: extent of *data collection, unauthorized secondary use* of information, and *control* over personal information. Specifically, *collection* is relevant to different kinds of data collection

Table 1. Comparison of the key information privacy concerns evaluation instruments

Dimensions Incorporated Into the Instruments	Unauthorized Secondary Use	Control	Collection	Errors	Improper Access	Awareness	Finding	Abuse
Culnan (1993)	x	x						
Smith et al. (1996)	x		x	x	x			
Stewart & Segars (2002)	x	x	x	x	x			
Dinev & Hart (2004)		(x)					x	x
Malhotra et al. (2004)		x	x			x		
Castaneda et al. (2007)	x		x					

contexts, and it possibly captures the tendency toward increasingly intrusive data collection. It is worth noting that when adapting the instruments to the new contexts, the *collection* dimension has specifically been modified. In the instrument by Smith et al., developed for off-line contexts, the *collection* dimension's items reflect data subjects' views on and reactions to personal data collection by companies, that is, whether data collection and its extent bothers them, and whether they hesitate to disclose their data. Malhotra et al. adapted these items to their online context study. Castaneda et al., instead, based their items on the possibilities of non-transparent and unauthorized data collection in online contexts. *Unauthorized secondary use*, which mainly refers to direct marketing purposes in early evaluation instruments, is a relevant dimension in present-day data collection contexts as well due to the diverse uses and possibilities of combining the data. This dimension has remained relatively unchanged despite the transition in data collection contexts. It deals with data use and sharing without the data subject's permission and using of it for other purposes that it was collected for. *Control* over personal information is a key concept related to the definition of information privacy and has hence been a part of privacy concerns evaluations since their inception. It can be said that its role in privacy protection is becoming even more important with the evolution of data collection contexts and individuals' will to decide the types and uses of their data they should disclose. The *control* dimension reflects data subjects' need for control, their perceptions of loss of privacy, and their opinions on the importance of being able to make decisions about their data collection and use.

Unlike the three dimensions described above, some privacy concerns' dimensions seem to be context dependent. *Awareness* about the use and processing of collected data is an aspect closely related to *control* because the ability to control information requires knowledge and understanding about its uses. This dimension likely becomes more important with increasing, more diverse data collection. It is noteworthy that the instruments intended for online contexts do not incorporate dimensions of *improper access* or *errors* that reflect data subjects' demand for procedures to protect personal data and to ensure its accuracy. These dimensions have been highly relevant to earlier offline contexts' data collection with electronic records accessible to companies' employees and prone to errors with regard to data input. In present-day contexts, *improper access* to data can be considered included in concerns about tracking. This idea may support the exclusion of the *improper access* dimension from the instruments when more parsimonious and simple instruments are needed.

In conclusion, it seems that there are some core dimensions to be incorporated even in present and future privacy concerns evaluation instruments. On the other hand, the relevant dimensions may be dependent on the characteristics of the data collection context. Interrelationships between dimensions and their overlapping should also be taken into account when developing evaluation instruments.

SOLUTIONS AND RECOMMENDATIONS

Information privacy concerns evaluation instruments can be used to gain an understanding of users' privacy concerns regarding personal data intensive services. The existing instruments provide a solid, validated base for the development of privacy concerns evaluation. For this reason, they should be used as a starting point for evaluations and then adapted to the context in question. Our analysis showed that information privacy concerns' core dimensions are incorporated into privacy concerns evaluation instruments independently of the data collection context. These core dimensions are extent of *data collection, unauthorized secondary use* of information, and *control* over personal information. Adaptation of evaluation instruments to the data collection context can be done by varying the rest of the instruments' dimensions. Privacy concerns' dimensions specific to different data collection contexts typically reflect the extent of data collection, the level of data collection's continuity (i.e., its potential for tracking users' behavior either online or in a physical environment), and diversity of subsequent uses of the collected data. It is worth noting that in continuously evolving data collection contexts, new privacy concerns' dimensions may emerge regarding the context's nature and, for example, perceived sensitivity of data. In our research, we have identified the studies presented in this article as the key studies involving evaluation instruments that should be taken into account in privacy concerns evaluation.

FUTURE RESEARCH DIRECTIONS

This article has presented an analysis of key privacy concerns evaluation instruments and their dimensions. Due to technological changes and new data collection contexts, privacy concerns' dimensions should be investigated even in future research, specifically to identify the context-specific dimensions to be applied in the evaluations. As the literature contains a large number of studies on information privacy concerns evaluation, the present analysis should be advanced by analyzing these studies systematically. In addition to the scientific literature, it would be reasonable to extend the analysis to the privacy aspects present in legislation. Similarly, people's changing attitudes towards personal data collection as a part of cultural change should be taken into account in future research. In this way, a validated, standardized, and easy-to-use evaluation framework could be constructed for facilitating application of knowledge to different and new data collection contexts. Relations between separate privacy concerns' dimensions could be another relevant topic of research in order to determine whether different dimensions of privacy concerns always need to be incorporated into the evaluation instruments or whether there are situations in which simplified instruments could be used.

CONCLUSION

This article explored how existing information privacy concerns evaluation instruments could be adapted to match data subjects' privacy concerns in evolving data collection contexts. An overview was presented of the historical development of the information privacy concerns evaluation instruments, spanning a period from the beginning of the 1990s, with its data warehousing systems, to the 2000s, with its continuous monitoring of individuals' actions on the Internet. This overview was followed by an analysis of the key evaluation instruments, which provided insight into their validity for present-day personal data collection contexts. The analysis focused on the dimensions incorporated into privacy concerns evaluation instruments. It showed that these dimensions have changed with evolving data collection contexts and the tendency toward extensive, continuous personal data collection. However, there are core dimensions that seem to be valid even for current data collection contexts. These dimensions, namely extent of *data collection*, *unauthorized secondary use* of information, and *control* over personal information, can be used as a starting point for privacy concerns evaluation. Evaluation should then be adapted to the data collection context in question by varying the instrument's dimensions. Regarding future research, it is suggested to start construction of a validated, standardized, and easy-to-use evaluation framework for facilitating privacy concerns evaluations in different contexts.

REFERENCES

Bergström, A. (2015). Online privacy concerns: A broad approach to understanding the concerns of different groups for different uses. *Computers in Human Behavior*, *53*, 419–426. doi:10.1016/j.chb.2015.07.025

Castaneda, J. A., Montoso, F. J., & Luque, T. (2007). The dimensionality of customer privacy concern on the Internet. *Online Information Review*, *31*(4), 420–439. doi:10.1108/14684520710780395

Culnan, M. J. (1993). How did they get my name? An exploratory investigation of consumer attitudes toward secondary information use. *Management Information Systems Quarterly*, *17*(3), 341–363. doi:10.2307/249775

Culnan, M. J., & Armstrong, P. K. (1999). Information privacy concerns, procedural fairness, and impersonal trust: An empirical investigation. *Organization Science*, *10*(1), 104–115. doi:10.1287/orsc.10.1.104

Dinev, T., & Hart, P. (2004). Internet privacy concerns and their antecedents—Measurement validity and a regression model. *Behaviour & Information Technology*, *23*(6), 413–422. doi:10.1080/0144929 0410001715723

European Commission. (2012). *Proposal for a regulation of the European Parliament and of the Council on the Protection of Individuals with regard to the processing of personal data and on the free movement of such data (General Data Protection Regulation), COM (2012) 11 final*. Brussels: European Commission.

Hong, W., & Thong, J. Y. L. (2013). Internet privacy concerns: An integrated conceptualization and four empirical studies. *Management Information Systems Quarterly*, *37*(1), 275–298.

Malhotra, N. K., Kim, S. S., & Agarwal, J. (2004). Internet users information privacy concerns (IUIPC): The construct, the scale, and a causal model. *Information Systems Research*, *15*(4), 336–355. doi:10.1287/isre.1040.0032

Mao, E., & Zhang, J. (2013). The role of privacy in the adoption of location-based services. *Journal of Information Privacy and Security*, *9*(2), 40–59. doi:10.1080/15536548.2013.10845678

Nosko, S., Wood, E., & Molema, S. (2010). All about me: Disclosure in online social networking profiles: The case of FACEBOOK. *Computers in Human Behavior*, *26*(3), 406–418. doi:10.1016/j.chb.2009.11.012

Raschke, R. L., Krishen, A. S., & Kachroo, P. (2014). Understanding the components of information privacy threats for location-based services. *Journal of Information Systems*, *28*(1), 227–242. doi:10.2308/isys-50696

Sipior, J. C., Ward, B. T., & Connolly, R. (2013). Empirically assessing the continued applicability of the IUIPC construct. *Journal of Enterprise Information Management*, *26*(6), 661–178. doi:10.1108/JEIM-07-2013-0043

Smith, H. J., Milberg, J. S., & Burke, J. S. (1996). Information privacy: Measuring individuals concerns about organizational practices. *Management Information Systems Quarterly*, *20*(2), 167–196. doi:10.2307/249477

Stewart, K. A., & Segars, A. H. (2002). An empirical examination of the concern for information privacy instrument. *Information Systems Research*, *13*(1), 36–49. doi:10.1287/isre.13.1.36.97

Westin, A. F. (1967). *Privacy and freedom*. New York: Atheneum.

ADDITIONAL READING

Acquisti, A. (2009). Nudging privacy: The behavioral economics of personal information. *IEEE Security and Privacy*, *7*(6), 82–85. doi:10.1109/MSP.2009.163

Chellappa, R. K., & Sin, R. G. (2005). Personalization versus privacy: An empirical examination of the online consumers dilemma. *Information Technology Management*, *6*(2-3), 181–202. doi:10.100710799-005-5879-y

Chen, K., & Rea, A. I. (2004). Protecting personal information online: A survey of user privacy concerns and control techniques. *Journal of Computer Information Systems*, *44*(4), 85–92.

Eastlick, M. A., Lotz, S. L., & Warrington, P. (2006). Understanding online B-to-C relationships: An integrated model of privacy concerns, trust, and commitment. *Journal of Business Research*, *59*(8), 877–886. doi:10.1016/j.jbusres.2006.02.006

European Commission (1995). Directive 95/46/EC. Official Journal of the European Communities (No L 281/31).

Li, Y. (2011). Empirical studies on online information privacy concerns: Literature review and integrative framework. *Communications of the Association for Information Systems*, *28*, 453–496.

Li, Y. (2012). Theories in online information-privacy research: A critical review and an integrated framework. *Decision Support Systems*, *54*(1), 471–481. doi:10.1016/j.dss.2012.06.010

Liu, C., Marchewka, J. T., Lu, J., & Yu, C.-S. (2005). Beyond concern—A privacy-trust-behavioral intention model of electronic commerce. *Information & Management*, *42*(2), 289–304. doi:10.1016/j.im.2004.01.003

Liu, Z., Bonazzi, R., Fritscher, B., & Pigneur, Y. (2011). Privacy-friendly business models for location-based mobile services. *Journal of Theoretical and Applied Electronic Commerce Research*, *6*(2), 90–107. doi:10.4067/S0718-18762011000200009

Lwin, M., Wirtz, J., & Williams, J. D. (2007). Consumer online privacy concerns and responses: A power-responsibility equilibrium perspective. *Journal of the Academy of Marketing Science*, *35*(4), 572–585. doi:10.100711747-006-0003-3

Son, J. Y., & Kim, S. S. (2008). Internet users' information privacy-protective responses: A taxonomy and a nomological model. *Management Information Systems Quarterly*, *32*(3), 503–529.

The Privacy Act of 1974, 5 U.S.C. § 552a (1974).

U.S. Department of Health. Education & Welfare (1973). Records, computers and the rights of citizens. Report of the Secretary's Advisory Committee on automated personal data systems. Chapter IV: Recommended safeguards for administrative personal data systems. Washington, DC: U.S. Government Printing Office.

Van Slyke, C., Shim, J. T., Johnson, R., & Jiang, J. J. (2006). Concern for information privacy and online consumer purchasing. *Journal of the Association for Information Systems*, *7*(6), 415–444.

Zhou, T. (2011). The impact of privacy concerns on user adoption of location-based services. *Industrial Management & Data Systems*, *111*(2), 212–226. doi:10.1108/02635571111115146

KEY TERMS AND DEFINITIONS

Information Privacy: An individual's capability to control disclosure of information about him/her to others by determining the type, extent, uses, and users of the data to be disclosed.

Information Privacy Concerns: An individual's concerns about collection, processing, and use of information about him/her, and about the related consequences.

Personal Data: Any information relating to an identified or identifiable natural person ("data subject"); an identifiable person is one who can be identified, directly or indirectly, in particular by reference to an identification number or to one or more factors specific to his physical, physiological, mental, economic, cultural, or social identity (EC Directive 95/46/EC).

Personal Data Intensive Services: Services substantially based on collection, processing, and utilization of users' personal data for service provision. These services can be produced by private companies, public sector organizations, or non-governmental parties.

Privacy Concerns Evaluation Instrument: A way or method to measure individuals' privacy concerns, for example, a survey.

This research was previously published in the Encyclopedia of Information Science and Technology, Fourth Edition edited by Mehdi Khosrow-Pour, pages 4862-4871, copyright year 2018 by Information Science Reference (an imprint of IGI Global).

Chapter 16
Digital Video Watermarking Using Diverse Watermarking Schemes

Yash Gupta
Maulana Abul Kalam Azad University of Technology, India

Shaila Agrawal
Maulana Abul Kalam Azad University of Technology, India

Susmit Sengupta
Maulana Abul Kalam Azad University of Technology, India

Aruna Chakraborty
Maulana Abul Kalam Azad University of Technology, India

ABSTRACT

As the significance of the internet is increasing day by day so is the need of protecting the media over the internet. In order to protect the copyright information of the media over the internet, the authors use the technique of watermarking. Watermarking is the process of embedding a watermark in the media and then extracting it for ownership verification. Different types of watermarking schemes exist in the world, but we always look for techniques which are highly imperceptible and do not lead to loss of fidelity. Here the researchers have put forward a technique that instills different watermarking schemes to different sets of frames.

INTRODUCTION

With the advent of internet in 1967, it has revolutionized the fields of communication and computer unlike anything before (Maity & Kundu, 2002). Since then it has grown exponentially and has become a vast information reserve. Nowadays people prefer to search the internet than looking into any book, to gain knowledge on the subject that intrigues them.

DOI: 10.4018/978-1-5225-7492-7.ch016

Internet has now become the easiest way of sharing information and with the growth of social networking sites, doing the latter with the masses has become even easier and it can be done quite briskly. People now buy storage spaces over the internet so that they can have access to their works from anywhere in the world. With the increase of information and digital content over the internet the need and necessity of multimedia security and copyright protection arises (Agrawal, Gupta, & Chakraborty, 2015; Natarajan & Makhdumi, 2009). So in order to stop theft and lose of fidelity of digital content we need to develop techniques to safeguard the digital contents (Lai, & Tsai, 2010). Digital Watermarking is one such technique that is used for copyright protection of digital media.

BACKGROUND

What Is Digital Watermarking?

Copyright Protection incorporates a logo or some ownership information into the digital media without affecting its perceptibility (Agrawal, Gupta, & Chakraborty, 2015; Yeo, & Yeung, 1997). Hence, in case of a conflict, the logo can effectively be extracted from the digital media in order to claim the ownership rights. Watermarking is a process of embedding some data called the watermark or the digital signature into the digital media (Sinha, Bardhan, Pramanick, Jagatramka, Kole, & Chakraborty, 2011). Here the researchers will primarily focus on Digital Video Watermarking.

What Is Digital Video Watermarking?

Digital Video Watermarking is a method of copyright protection of videos in which a watermark is added to the original video without affecting its perceivable quality (Yeo, & Yeung, 1997; Doerr, & Dugelay, 2003). For a watermarking scheme to be used for copyright protection, it should fulfill two criterions i.e. it must be robust against attacks like signal processing and lossy compression and it should not lead to loss of fidelity (Al-Khatib, Al-Haj & Lama-Rajab, 2008). Some watermarking techniques require the original video for the detection of the watermark. This is called a non-blind watermark detection method while there are some watermarking techniques which do not require the original video for watermark detection (Maity & Kundu, 2002). This is called blind watermark detection method and is usually preferred.

Types of Watermarks

As per human perception the watermark can be of three types, visible, invisible and dual. (Potkar, & Ansari, 2014).As the name suggests, a visible watermark is perceivable but an invisible watermark is not. For e.g. a watermark is to be added to an image or a video then in case of a visible watermark, the watermark can be seen on the image or on the video frames but in case of invisible watermarks, a layman would not be able to differentiate whether a watermark has been added to the digital media or not. A Dual watermark incorporates both visible and invisible watermarks to the video. Here the invisible watermark is kept as a backup for the visible watermark. The researchers' can choose anyone of them as per our requirements and necessities.

Factors to Be Considered While Embedding a Watermark on a Video

While embedding a digital image watermark on the video the following things should be kept in mind:

1. **Imperceptibility:** The watermark should not be visible in the copyrighted video (Maity, & Kundu, 2011).
2. **Robustness:** It should be impossible for the attacker to detect or extract or manipulate the watermark (Maity, & Kundu, 2011).
3. **Fidelity:** The perceivable quality of video should not degrade.
4. **Security:** It should be impossible to generate a duplicate of the authentic watermark to claim false ownership. The watermark should also be non-invertible.
5. **Verification:** The watermark can be extracted from the watermarked video to prove ownership.
6. **Constant Bit Rate:** As the transmission channel bandwidth has to be obeyed so the watermarked video should also have the same bit rate.

Classification of Video Watermarking

Many Video watermarking schemes have been proposed till date, while some are deployed on uncompressed videos, the others are deployed on the compressed versions (Hartung, & Girod, 1998; Meng, & Chang, 1998). Video Watermarking is classified into two categories based on the methods of embedding the watermark bits in the host video. The two categories are:

1. **Spatial Domain Technique:** In this method the watermark can be embedded and detected by directly manipulating the pixel intensity values of the video frame (Sinha, Bardhan, Pramanick, Jagatramka, Kole, & Chakraborty, 2011).
2. **Transform Domain Technique:** Here the spatial pixel values of the host video are altered according to some predefined algorithm. The watermark is dispersed throughout the host video and this makes the technique robust against malicious geometric attacks (Sinha, Bardhan, Pramanick, Jagatramka, Kole, & Chakraborty, 2011).

Thus, transform domain watermarking schemes ensures more imperceptibility, randomness in the distribution of the watermark and have also proven to enhance robustness against geometric attacks. Hence, it is better to use the transform domain technique rather than the spatial domain technique (Sinha, Bardhan, Pramanick, Jagatramka, Kole, & Chakraborty, 2011).

Types of Attacks on Video Watermarks

A successful attack is one in which the watermark has been modified in a manner to prevent its successful extraction without affecting the quality of the video significantly. A successful attack does not mean that the digital media cannot be restored to its original state but it means that watermark detection and extraction techniques are no longer useful for claiming ownership rights as the watermark has been modified (Potkar & Ansari, 2014). The attacks are of two types (Singh & Chadha, 2013):

1. **Intentional Attacks:** These attacks are done deliberately to prevent successful extraction of the watermark. Types of Intentional attacks are:
    a. **Geometric Attacks:** Here minor geometric distortions are made to the video frames to de-synchronize the extraction procedure. The changes induced in the video frame can be negligibly perceived but it prevents successful extraction of the watermark (Potkar & Ansari, 2014). It instills attacks like rotation, scaling, etc. to the video frames. This type of attacks usually affects each frame of the video (Voloshynovskiy, Pereira & Pun, 1999; Husain, 2012).
    b. **Statistical Attacks:** Videos are susceptible to attacks which are not applicable in the case of images. These attacks take advantage of this inherent redundancy between the frames to remove the watermark. Attacks like frame averaging, frame swapping and statistical analysis comes under this head (Potkar & Ansari, 2014).
    c. **Protocol Attacks:** This type of attacks try to destroy the digital content itself rather than trying to remove or destroy the watermark. Examples are Copy attack and watermark inversion. In copy attack the watermark is copied from one frame to another without any knowledge of the watermarking technique used. A watermarking scheme is not resistant to copy attack then the watermark used for verification cannot be trusted as it might have been copied from somewhere else (Potkar & Ansari, 2014).
    d. **Removal Attacks:** This type of attacks usually employ filtering techniques to remove the embedded watermark. Its examples are spatial averaging filter, Wiener de-noising filter (Potkar & Ansari, 2014).
2. **Unintentional Attacks:** These attacks are introduced into the system by normal signal processing and compression but are not done intentionally. Types of Unintentional attacks are (Potkar & Ansari, 2014):
    a. Analog to Digital and Digital to Analog Conversion.
    b. Scaling and Cropping Operations.
    c. Frame Rate Conversion.
    d. Aspect Ratio Conversion.
    e. Quantization,
    f. Compression, and
    g. Noise Addition.

Applications of Video Watermarking

According to Van Huyssteen's thesis the applications of video watermarking are numerous but they can be brought down under six heads, they are:

1. **Transaction Tracking:** It is used to track the manner in which the content was distributed in the system or through multiple points. In situations where illegal distribution of data occurs then it should be ideally possible for us to track the source from where the distribution has occurred in order to identify the misappropriating party. This is done by embedding a unique identifier into the media at the time of playback which can be extracted at a later time (Potkar & Ansari, 2014; Singh, Jain & Jain, 2013).

2. **Broadcast Monitoring:** It is used by the broadcasters or content owners to check if their content had been completely broadcasted or just a part of the material had been used. The watermark is automatically extracted to verify the latter. The watermark is usually embedded by the content owner itself while it is extracted either by monitoring sites in the broadcast chain or by a third party at the receiving end (Potkar & Ansari, 2014; Singh & Chadha, 2013).

3. **Content Authentication:** The content is watermarked with a semi-fragile watermark, which is designed to be affected by signal transformations. So on tampering with the content the watermark gets either destroyed or modified and can be used to prove that the content is not authentic. It is used for detecting tampering of the content (Potkar & Ansari, 2014; Singh, Jain & Jain, 2013).

4. **Ownership Identification:** The watermark is extracted from the digital content and verified to prove or claim ownership rights in case of any conflicts. The pirates may also embed their own watermark to the digital content and in such a situation it becomes quite difficult to tell that which one is the original watermark. This is phenomenon is also termed as ownership deadlock problem (Potkar & Ansari, 2014; Singh, Jain & Jain, 2013).

Video Watermarking Schemes Currently in Use

The transform domain techniques which are commonly being used today are Discrete Wavelet Transform (DWT), Discrete Cosine Transform (DCT), Discrete Fourier Transform (DFT) (Jiansheng, Sukang & Xiaomei, 2009; Chaturvedi & Basha, 2012; Rahman, 2013). There are other techniques as well like Discrete Walsh Transform, Discrete Hartley Transform (DHT), Discrete Kekre Transform (DKT), Singular Value Decomposition, Principal Component Analysis, etc.

These techniques are often combined to form new video watermarking schemes so as to produce better results. For example DCT along with DWT (Jiansheng, Sukang & Xiaomei, 2009), or DWT along with SVD and PCA (Sinha, Bardhan, Pramanick, Jagatramka, Kole, & Chakraborty, 2011) forms different watermarking schemes and the list continues. The basis of comparison of these techniques is by calculating the Peak Signal to Noise Ratio (PSNR) values and Normalization Coefficient (NC) value. PSNR gives us a measure about the imperceptibility of the watermark in an attacked video frame. The higher the PSNR values higher is the imperceptibility (Sinha, Bardhan, Pramanick, Jagatramka, Kole, & Chakraborty, 2011). NC is used to find the similarity between the extracted and original watermark. Its peak value is 1. It is used to make judgments on extraction fidelity (Sinha, Bardhan, Pramanick, Jagatramka, Kole, & Chakraborty, 2011). So the higher the PSNR and NC values, better is the watermarking scheme.

Discrete Wavelet Transform

Discrete Wavelet Transform or (DWT) is used widely in the field of signal processing. A two-dimensional DWT is a combination of two single 1-D DWT's applied to both the horizontal and vertical directions. 2-D DWT is used to decompose the image into lower resolution approximation sub-band (LL) as well as horizontal (HL), vertical (LH) and diagonal (HH) detail components, (Figure 1). The embedding process is carried out in the LL sub-band to make the watermarked image withstand lossy compression (Shaikh, Khan & Kelkar, 2012).

Figure 1. DWT sub-bands

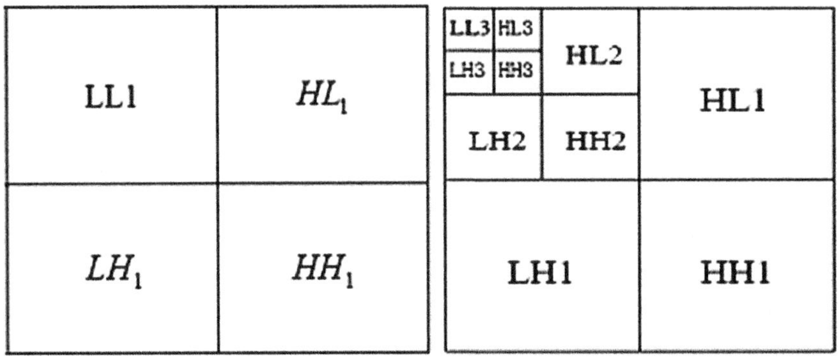

Discrete Fourier Transform

Discrete Fourier Transform or DFT is one of the oldest techniques of image compression. A Fourier Transform converts a signal into sinusoids. It takes as input a time-continuous signal and its output is a signal in frequency-domain. However, DFT takes as input samples of the signal in time-domain and converts them into samples in frequency-domain. DFT is easily calculated in computers using Fast Fourier Transform or FFT algorithms. The time complexity in this calculation is O *(N log N)*.

Discrete Cosine Transform

Discrete Cosine Transform (DCT) is another commonly used transform technique in signal processing. It aims at converting an image from its spatial domain to frequency domain in order to make it robust against different attacks like contrast adjustment, low pass filtering, etc. (Chaturvedi & Basha, 2012). Discrete Cosine transform is defined by the equations, (1) and (2).

$$f\left(mn\right) = a\left(j\right)a\left(k\right)\sum_{m=0}^{N-1}\sum_{n=0}^{N-1}f\left(mn\right)\cos\left[\frac{\left(2m+1\right)j\pi}{2N}\right]\cos\left[\frac{\left(2n+1\right)k\pi}{2N}\right] \tag{1}$$

and the Inverse Discrete Cosine transform is given as:

$$f\left(mn\right) = \sum_{m=0}^{N-1}\sum_{n=0}^{N-1}a\left(j\right)a\left(k\right)f\left(mn\right)\cos\left[\frac{\left(2m+1\right)j\pi}{2N}\right]\cos\left[\frac{\left(2n+1\right)k\pi}{2N}\right] \tag{2}$$

Singular Value Decomposition

Singular Value Decomposition is a technique for expressing a matrix as a product of a diagonal matrix and two orthogonal matrices (Seema, 2012). The SVD of a given image A in the form of a matrix is defined by equation (3).

$$A = USV^T \qquad\qquad (3)$$

where U and $V \in$ R and are N x N unitary matrices and $S \in$ R with dimensions N x N is a diagonal matrix.

COMPARISON BETWEEN DIFFERENT SCHEMES

1. **DFT and DWT:** DFT is helpful in determining the frequency components present in a signal. It can even be used on a signal of variable frequency components. However, it does not show the temporal localization of these frequency components. This can be achieved by using DWT which illustrates which frequency component of the signal is present at a given time. DWT can, thus, also be applied on non-stationary signals. Hence, DWT has replaced DFT in most of the applications because of its extended usability. The PSNR value from a watermarking scheme using DWT is better than that of a scheme using DFT.
2. **DWT and SVD:** DWT is the outcome of the electrical treatment being given to an image. SVD is a procedure applied to a matrix to approximate some values in the final SVD matrix with a view of minimizing the useful data part of the original matrix. Here, an image is treated on the basis of its storage in a system, i.e., in the form of a matrix. It is to be noted that the original data is subject to manual alterations and the SVD procedure may not always yield the desired results. The same is not true for DWT where the user cannot meddle with the electrical signal directly.

Conventional Watermarking Methodology

The original watermarking methodology involved the application of a single decomposition technique with the algorithm to embed the watermark. Eventually, a combination of two or more techniques began being used to yield better results in terms of the PSNR. The combinations included DFT-DCT, DWT-DCT, DWT-SVD, etc. (Podilchuk, & Delp, 2001). Here, one decomposition algorithm followed the other. However, in video watermarking applications, the same watermarking scheme(s) were used for all video

Figure 2. Representation of singular value decomposition

$$SVD(A) = \begin{bmatrix} U_{1,1} & . & . & U_{1,n} \\ U_{2,1} & . & . & U_{2,n} \\ . & . & . & . \\ U_{n,1} & . & . & U_{n,n} \end{bmatrix} \begin{bmatrix} \sigma_{11} & 0 & 0. & 0 \\ 0 & \sigma_{22} & 0 & 0 \\ . & . & . & . \\ 0 & 0 & 0 & \sigma_{nn} \end{bmatrix} \begin{bmatrix} V_{1,1} & . & . & V_{1,n} \\ V_{2,1} & . & . & V_{2,n} \\ . & . & . & . \\ V_{n,1} & . & . & V_{n,n} \end{bmatrix}^T$$

frames, with the fidelity of the scheme being same for all the video frames. Thus, the researchers have developed a new idea to watermark digital videos with great diversity in the schemes.

Method Used

The researchers realized that the inherent property of videos being composed of frames could be used to improve the efficiency of watermarking algorithm in terms of its PSNR and NC values (Agrawal, Gupta, & Chakraborty, 2015). Thus, a Composite Watermarking Technique had been proposed where different watermarking scheme(s) could be applied to different sets of video frames. Then, the watermark could be extracted from each set of frames for all of them to be superimposed to give the final extracted watermark. The number of different sets of frames in which the video is divided and the manner in which the sets are formed depends on whatever seems suitable.

Suppose a video contains 'N' frames and it is to be divided into 'n' number of sets. There is a variable 'i' whose value ranges from 1 to N and a variable 'k' whose value is given by (i mod n) and its value ranges from 0 to n-1. Thus, on performing modular function on every ith frame, we obtain a value of k by the equation, k= i mod n and allot i to the kth set. This gives us n distinct sets (0 – (n-1)). Then for each different set, a different watermarking scheme(s) would be applied to all frames in it.

The researchers have implemented this watermarking technique by dividing the video into two sets of frames, to obtain two values of k as 0 and 1. The set corresponding to $k = 0$ is the set of even numbered frames and that corresponding to $k = 1$ is the set of odd numbered frames. Here, DWT has been applied to the odd numbered frames with a DCT transformed watermark while another scheme of SVD is applied to the even numbered frames. The extraction process again follows the same approach for dividing the frames and each set has its own extraction procedure. The final extracted watermark is obtained by superimposing the individual watermarks obtained from the different sets (Agrawal, Gupta, & Chakraborty, 2015). The algorithms for the aforesaid scheme are given in the next section.

Watermarking Algorithms

The algorithms proposed for embedding and extracting the watermark are given below (Agrawal, Gupta, & Chakraborty, 2015).

Step 1: Watermark Embedding

Step 1: Input the original video and extract the individual frames.
Step 2: For odd,-numbered frames follow algorithm 1, cited by Chaturvedi, N., & Basha, D. S. (2012). Comparison of Digital Image watermarking Methods DWT & DWT-DCT on the Basis of PSNR. *International Journal of Innovative Research in Science, Engineering and Technology*, *1*(2).
Step 3: For even-numbered frames follow algorithm 2, based on SVD (Rahman, 2013; Seema, 2012).
Step 4: Combine the outputs obtained from step 5 of algorithm 1 and from step 6 of algorithm 2 to obtain the watermarked video.

Figure 3. The flow chart for the proposed method with n=2

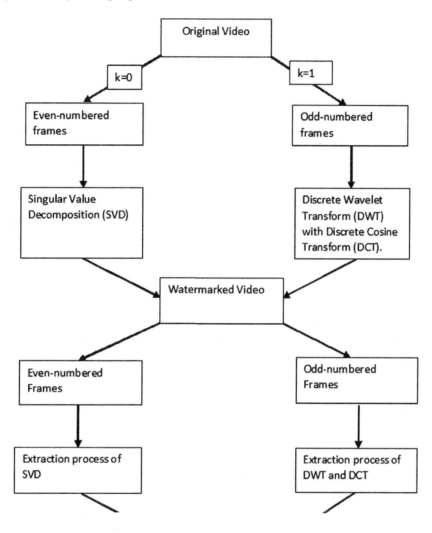

Algorithm 1

Step 1: Input the watermark, change it to YUV form (Y component– stands for luminance, i.e. brightness of the color, U and V components determines the color) (gray scale) from RGB (Red - Green – Blue color model) form and extract the luminance or the Y component of it.

Step 2: Apply 2-D DCT to the extracted Y component.

Step 3: For every odd numbered frame, change it from RGB form to YUV form and apply 2-D DWT to the Y component of it.

Step 4: Resize the 2-D DCT transformed watermark according to the LL part of the image and embed it into the LL part with a strength alpha by equation (4).

$$LL1 = LL + alpha * WM \tag{4}$$

Here, LL is the approximation image obtained from 2-D DWT, WM is the resized watermark matrix and LL1 is the watermarked approximation image.

Step 5: Reconstruct the original frame from LL1 by applying inverse 2-D DWT to the Y component and changing it back to RGB form.

Algorithm 2

Step 1: Input the watermark, change it from RGB to YUV form and apply SVD on the Y component of it.
Step 2: To the even numbered frames extracted from step 1 of algorithm 1, change the color format from RGB to YUV and extract the Y component of it.
Step 3: Apply SVD on the Y component of the frames.
Step 4: Embed the watermark into the frames with strength alpha (same as that in algorithm 1), using equation (5).

$$Sf1 = Sf + alpha * Sw \tag{5}$$

Here, *Sf* is the singular matrix obtained from single value decomposition of the video frame, Sw is the singular matrix obtained through single value decomposition of the watermark and Sf1 is the final singular matrix.

Step 5: Reconstruct the Y component of the watermarked frame by applying equation (6).

$$Y1 = Uf * Sf1 * Vf' \tag{6}$$

where, Uf and Vf are the matrices obtained by SVD of the video frame.

Step 6: Change the watermarked frame obtained from YUV to RGB format.

Step 2: Watermark Extraction

Step 1: Input the watermarked video, together with the matrices, Uw and Vw obtained by performing SVD on the watermark image.
Step 2: Extract the individual frames. For odd-numbered frames, follow algorithm 1 for extraction, cited by Chaturvedi & Basha 2012.
Step 3: For the even-numbered frames, follow algorithm 2, cited in (Shaikh, Khan & Kelkar, 2012; Lai & Tsai, 2010).
Step 4: Resize the image matrices obtained from step 5 of algorithm 1 and from *Step 5* of algorithm 2 to match their dimensions.
Step 5: Add the two images to obtain the final watermark image.

Algorithm 1

Step 1: Convert the frames from RGB TO YUV color format and separate the Y component.
Step 2: Perform 2-D DWT on the Y component.
Step 3: From the LL1 component obtained from step 3, obtain the watermark by the following equation.

$$WM = \left(LL1 - LL\right) / alpha \tag{7}$$

Here, WM is the embedded watermark component and LL is the Y component of the original video frame.

Step 4: Perform inverse 2-D DCT on the output of step 4 to obtain the Y component of the watermark.
Step 5: Convert the YUV watermark image to RGB format.

Algorithm 2

Step 1: From the extracted even-numbered frames, convert the color format of the image from RGB to YUV.
Step 2: Obtain the Y component and perform SVD on it to get Uf1, Sf1 and Vf1.
Step 3: From SF1, obtain Sw using the equation,

$$Sw = \left(Sf1 - Sf\right) / alpha \tag{8}$$

Step 4: From Sw obtained from the previous step, reconstruct the Y component using the following equation,

$$Y = Uw * Sw * Vw' \tag{9}$$

where, Uw and the Vw are the matrices obtained from the SVD of the original watermark in the embedding process.

Step 5: Convert the image from YUV to RGB color format.

ALGORITHM RESULTS

The performance of the method mentioned above is measured in terms of the imperceptibility and robustness against possible attacks like filtering, noise addition, geometric attacks. The results are given in Table 1.

Peak Signal to Noise Ratio

The Peak Signal to Noise Ratio (PSNR) is a measure of the imperceptibility of the watermark. A high value of PSNR indicates more imperceptibility. The PSNR is calculated by (10).

$$PSNR = 10\log10\left(MAXi2\,/\,MSE\right) \tag{10}$$

where MAX_i is the maximum possible value of a pixel in an image, MSE is the mean squared error which is calculated by (11).

$$MSE = \left(\frac{1}{mn}\right)\sum_{i=0}^{m}\sum_{j=0}^{n}\left[I\left(i,j\right)-I'\left(i,j\right)\right]^2 \tag{11}$$

where I and I' are pixel values at location (i, j) of the original and the extracted frames respectively.

Normalized Correlation Coefficient

The normalized coefficient (NC) is used to determine the robustness of the watermarking and has a peak value of 1 (Sinha, Bardhan, Pramanick, Jagatramka, Kole, & Chakraborty, 2011). The formula for calculating NC is given in (12).

$$NC = \frac{\sum_i\sum_j W\left(i,j\right)W'\left(i,j\right)}{\sqrt{\left(\sum_i\sum_j W\left(i,j\right)\right)}\sqrt{\left(\sum_i\sum_j W'\left(i,j\right)\right)}} \tag{12}$$

Where W and W' represents the original and extracted watermarks respectively.

Algorithm 1 and 2 are applied on a video, with the watermark and the extracted watermark is obtained.

The value of PSNR and NC for the proposed method is found to be 65.073dB and 0.547 respectively. These are the values without noise or any other attack. The values of both PSNR and NC under some of the attacks are given in Table 1.

Table 1. Values of PSNR and NC under different attacks

Attacks	PSNR (dB)	NC
Gaussian Noise	53.397	0.509
Median Filtering	61.356	0.530
Poisson Noise	65.097	0.547
Salt & Pepper Noise	47.749	0.349
Sharpening Filter	45.532	0.968

FUTURE RESEARCH DIRECTIONS

The method used by the researchers holds immense potential in furthering researches related to the field of digital video watermarking. The use of composite methodology is highly promising. Many different schemes can be combined based on their productivity and also their compatibility with each other. The value of n can be varied to accommodate as many such combinations as required. When n=1, the same scheme can be applied to all the frames. Thereafter, combinations can be used.

CONCLUSION

The method used is potent of diversifying the use of the same set of schemes by applying them in the same or different sets of frames. The values of PSNR and NC are different for such diversification. For example, DWT and SVD can be applied to one set of frames in the given algorithm followed by DCT in another set of algorithms. The result is not the same as that for the demonstrative algorithm. The whole idea behind the use of such technology is in the improvement of the quality of the extracted watermark. Most of the attacks are more destructive for a set of schemes and cause negligible changes in the other. The choice of schemes should be such that the effects of different attacks cause different degrees of modification, so that the extracted watermarks from different sets could together yield a more resilient watermark.

REFERENCES

Agrawal, S., Gupta, Y., & Chakraborty, A. (2015, October). A Composite Approach to Digital Video Watermarking. In *International Congress on Information and Communication Technology*. ICICT.

Al-Khatib, T., Al-Haj, A., & Lama Rajab, H. M. (2008). *A Robust Video Watermarking Algorithm 1*. Academic Press.

Chaturvedi, N., & Basha, D. S. (2012). Comparison of Digital Image watermarking Methods DWT & DWT-DCT on the Basis of PSNR. *International Journal of Innovative Research in Science, Engineering and Technology, 1*(2). Retrieved from ece.mits.ac.in

Doerr, G., & Dugelay, J. L. (2003). A guide tour of video watermarking. *Signal Processing Image Communication, 18*(4), 263–282. doi:10.1016/S0923-5965(02)00144-3

Doërr, G., & Dugelay, J. L. (2004). Security pitfalls of frame-by-frame approaches to video watermarking. *Signal Processing. IEEE Transactions on, 52*(10), 2955–2964. doi:10.1109/TSP.2004.833867

Hartung, F., & Girod, B. (1998). Watermarking of uncompressed and compressed video. *Signal Processing, 66*(3), 283–301. doi:10.1016/S0165-1684(98)00011-5

Husain, F. (2012). A survey of digital watermarking techniques for multimedia data. *Int'l Journal of Electronics and Communication Engineering, 2*(1), 37–43.

Jiansheng, M., Sukang, L., & Xiaomei, T. (2009, May). A digital watermarking algorithm based on DCT and DWT. In *International Symposium on Web Information Systems and Applications (WISA'09)* (pp. 104-107). Academic Press.

Lai, C. C., & Tsai, C. C. (2010). Digital image watermarking using discrete wavelet transform and singular value decomposition. *Instrumentation and Measurement. IEEE Transactions on, 59*(11), 3060–3063.

Langelaar, G. C., Setyawan, I., & Lagendijk, R. L. (2000). Watermarking digital image and video data. A state-of-the-art overview. *IEEE Signal Processing Magazine, 17*(5), 20–46. doi:10.1109/79.879337

Lin, Y. R., Huang, H. Y., & Hsu, W. H. (2006, August). An embedded watermark technique in video for copyright protection. In *Pattern Recognition, 2006. ICPR 2006. 18th International Conference on* (Vol. 4, pp. 795-798). IEEE.

Maity, S. P., & Kundu, M. K. (2002, December). Robust and Blind Spatial Watermarking. In *Digital Image*. ICVGIP.

Maity, S. P., & Kundu, M. K. (2011). Performance improvement in spread spectrum image watermarking using wavelets. *International Journal of Wavelets, Multresolution, and Information Processing, 9*(01), 1–33. doi:10.1142/S0219691311003931

Meng, J., & Chang, S. F. (1998, October). Embedding visible video watermarks in the compressed domain. In *Image Processing, 1998. ICIP 98. Proceedings. 1998 International Conference on* (Vol. 1, pp. 474-477). IEEE.

Natarajan, M., & Makhdumi, G. (2009). Safeguarding the digital contents: Digital watermarking. *DESIDOC Journal of Library & Information Technology, 29*(3), 29–35. doi:10.14429/djlit.29.249

Podilchuk, C., & Delp, E. J. (2001). Digital watermarking: Algorithms and applications. *Signal Processing Magazine, IEEE, 18*(4), 33–46. doi:10.1109/79.939835

Potkar, A. N., & Ansari, S. M. (2014). Review on Digital Video Watermarking Techniques. *International Journal of Computers and Applications, 106*(11).

Rahman, M. (2013). *A dwt, dct and svd based watermarking technique to protect the image piracy*. arXiv preprint arXiv:1307.3294

Seema, S. S. (2012). DWT-SVD based efficient image watermarking Algorithm to achieve high robustness and perceptual quality. *International Journal of Advanced Research in Computer Science and Software Engineering, 2*(4), 75–78.

Shaikh, H., Khan, M. I., & Kelkar, Y. (2012). A Robust DWT Digital Image Watermarking Technique Basis On Scaling Factor. *International Journal of Computer Science. Engineering and Applications, 2*(4), 63.

Singh, A., Jain, S., & Jain, A. (2013). A Survey: Digital Video Watermarking. *International Journal of Scientific & Engineering Research, 4*(7), 1261–1265.

Singh, P., & Chadha, R. S. (2013). A survey of digital watermarking techniques, applications and attacks. *International Journal of Engineering and Innovative Technology, 2*(9), 165–175.

Sinha, S., Bardhan, P., Pramanick, S., Jagatramka, A., Kole, D. K., & Chakraborty, A. (2011). Digital video watermarking using discrete wavelet transform and principal component analysis. *International Journal of Wisdom Based Computing, 1*(2), 7–12.

Thakur, M. K., Saxena, V., & Gupta, J. P. (2010, July). A Performance analysis of objective video quality metrics for digital video watermarking. In *Computer Science and Information Technology (ICCSIT), 2010 3rd IEEE International Conference on* (Vol. 4, pp. 12-17). IEEE. 10.1109/ICCSIT.2010.5564962

Voloshynovskiy, S., Pereira, S., & Pun, T. (1999). Watermark attacks. *Erlangen Watermarking Workshop 99.*

Yeo, B. L., & Yeung, M. M. (1997, October). Analysis and synthesis for new digital video applications. In *Image Processing, 1997. Proceedings, International Conference on* (Vol. 1, pp. 1-4). IEEE.

KEY TERMS AND DEFINITIONS

Fidelity: The quality of the media (image, video and other) should not degrade on addition of the watermark to it.

Imperceptibility: The watermark should not be visible in the copyrighted video.

Robustness: The watermark should be robust against a wide range of attacks, so that the attacker cannot extract or manipulate the watermark.

Security: It should be impossible to create a duplicate watermark as this will lead to ambiguity during ownership verification.

Verification: The watermark can be extracted from the media and compared with the original watermark to prove ownership.

Watermark: It is a logo or digital signature which is used in watermarking.

Watermarking: It is the process of embedding a logo or digital signature in a media (image, video and other) for Copyright protection.

This research was previously published in the Encyclopedia of Information Science and Technology, Fourth Edition edited by Mehdi Khosrow-Pour, pages 4872-4883, copyright year 2018 by Information Science Reference (an imprint of IGI Global).

Chapter 17
Ethical Computing Continues From Problem to Solution

Wanbil William Lee
The Computer Ethics Society, Hong Kong & Wanbil & Associates, Hong Kong

ABSTRACT

Ethical computing is instrumental in identifying and reaching a near-ideal solution to the problems arising from an environment that is technology-driven and information-intensive. Many of these problems that could have been avoided occur because we are either insensitive to or ignorant of their ethical implications. As a result, we could reach only a partial, compromised solution at best. An ideal solution is expected to be technically efficient, financially viable, legally admissible, ethically acceptable, socially desirable, and in many situations environmentally friendly (the so-called hexa-dimension criteria), and balanced in terms the six criteria or five criteria (in case the problem does not involve ecological concerns). An exposition of an ideal solution in terms of the requisite competence and the additive is presented.

INTRODUCTION

Ethical Computing (Lee, 2015a) is instrumental in identifying and reaching a near-ideal solution to the problems arising from an environment that is *technology-driven information-intensive*. These problems raise techno-ethical issues, particularly information security concerns. *Post-implementation* and *post-contract* problems are cases in point. Many of these problems could have been avoided, occur; because we are either insensitive to or ignorant of their ethical implications. As a result, we could reach only a partial, compromised solution at best.

Ideally, the solution is not only technically efficient, financially viable and legal admissible, but also ethically acceptable, socially desirable, and in many situations environmental-friendly (the so-called *hexa-dimension criteria*) (Lee, 2015b & 2015d). In addition, the solutions sought must be capable of balancing the potential inter-conflicts among these demands or satisfying the five or six criteria. Given the conditions, a deep understanding of the basic ethical principles and the requisite technical know-how (the *requisite competence*) are necessary, and shifting our view on risk culminating in a new type of risk called techno-ethical risk or simply *ethical risk* and adopting a new tool of analysis to cater for the new risk (the *additive*) are also required (Lee, 2015c).

DOI: 10.4018/978-1-5225-7492-7.ch017

BACKGROUND

The Problem

Symptoms

Contemporary business organizations rely increasingly on information technology to accumulate and process the data needed to advertise their services and products, aiming at, for example, capturing market share and attracting customers. As a result, the marketplace becomes more transparent, and the consumers are better-informed thus more demanding. Consequently, more information is required, technology is increasingly relied upon to handle the increased amount of information generated and demanded, and new technological facilities such as call center and weblining (for marketing), and Big Data, Internet of Things, Cloud Computing (for communication and data management) are developed to aid business, to provide the processing power and contain the information explosion. This forms a vicious circle: *increase in demand for information leads to increase in reliance on technology, and increase in use of technology consumes and generates more information*, culminating in the so-called technology-driven information-intensive phenomenon (Lee, 2015d), raises ethical issues, and creates techno-ethical problems. Of these problems, many are commonly found in post-implementation and post-contract situations.

The one described below is typical of techno-ethical problems in post-implementation situations:

An online monitoring system was implemented successfully to replace an existing offline help-desk platform a high-tech facilities distributor. The new system enables help-desk staff to see exactly what is on the users' screens and to respond to users' requests for assistance quickly. Impressed by the fast response time and the increased user satisfaction, the executive vice president (EVP) asks the chief information officer (CIO) to have a copy of the system installed in her office for she wants to use this surveillance function to track down drug dealing allegedly occurring on company premises. The EVP's request raises indeed ethical dilemma for the Chief Information Officer (CIO).

Described in the following is another example of techno-ethical problems in post-contract situations:

The system specification (spec) was approved by the provider and client, and a contract duly signed. A senior project consultant assigned to the project discovered a fault in the inventory control function in the spec. The client is a fashion boutique so the fault is critical. The fault was confirmed after the consultant's site visit. Keep quiet or tell the boss or the client or both is a dilemma the consultant faces.

Causes

What causes this kind of problem is not the technology because the technology per se is neutral. What creates techno-ethical risks is the use of the technology. Two major reasons are cited here to make the point. First, we are insensitive to or ignorant of the ethical aspect of the problems and its ramifications because mainly of our lack of deep appreciation of the ethical principles. Second, we have hitherto treated risk as a technical, corporate/personal matter when it is in fact a managerial, social concern under the influence of the so-called *flawed education across science and technology* and *misinterpretation of risk*. Three cases are described in the following to exemplify situations where techno-ethical risks arise:

First: Planning to replace a corporate legacy system by a web-based facility but concentrating on potential economic efficiency such as improved speed, elimination of redundancy or even reduced head-counts only, will miss such adverse consequences as deterioration in morale and end-user dissatisfaction (due to the disturbance to inertia).

Second: Evaluating information governance of a computer-based system but failing to include an audit of or a check for ethical issues will run the risk of a deficient information security management review.

Third: Assessing softlifting (the software equivalent of shoplifting) by focusing on the economic and legal impact such as infringement of copyright law and leaving out the social impact such as personal use of sensitive proprietary information will result in a risk of an incomplete assessment.

An Ideal Solution

As alluded earlier, an ideal solution is required to satisfy the hexa-dimension criteria, and is structured around, requisite competence and additive to supplement the requisite competence which alone is not sufficient.

REQUISITE COMPETENCE

Technical Know-How

Professional practitioners and layman users of IT presumably possess the basic rudiments. So this primary competence can be safely assumed.

The Basic Ethical Principles

IT professionals of various ranks, including CIOs, tend to offer support when asked for an opinion on the importance of computer ethics, but when pressed for elaboration as to what computer ethics is or why it is important, many may respond in silence. In order to proceed, we need a real appreciation of the basic ethical principles. To know what these theories are and how they can be used to explain the dilemmas, let us illustrate using the Edward Snowden episode. Was he a whistle-blower or simply a rumor-monger? Some respect him, calling him a hero; others disapprove of his actions, calling him a traitor. Is he defensible on ethical grounds? One might have heard of these arguments: "Snowden is not the only one. There are plenty other whistle-blowers," or "If Tom, Dick and Harry can do it, why not Edward Snowden?" These arguments are based on the concept of relativism.

Relativism:

Right or wrong is not absolute, that is, what is right for you may not be right for me or I can decide to do what I think is right for me, but you can decide what is right for you.

Hence, if one person thinks it is right to say Snowden is a hero, but another individual does not think so, the argument is pointless, as it allows two people to decide right and wrong for themselves. In the end, no moral distinction between the opinions of the two individuals can be made. Certainly, the debate does not tell us whether Snowden's actions are morally right or wrong.

Snowden is no ordinary worker; he is a professional, one who engages in a job that handles a highly sophisticated commodity—confidential information. He was an employee of the US National Security Agency (NSA). In this capacity, Snowden appears to be wrong, disloyal to his employer in stealing and disclosing confidential information without authority. However, while in the role of a professional, Snowden is expected to respect professionalism and to observe his professional code of conduct, he has, as a person, a duty to himself and to his moral convictions. This duty-based argument is based on the theory of deontology.

Deontology:

An act is morally right if it is done out of a sense of duty.

So, as an employee, Snowden failed as he was disloyal and leaked confidential information. But, as a professional, he was right in exposing the stealth act because he was acting in accordance with professional conduct. While helpful in defending duty-bound actions, this principle is inherently troublesome because the actor owes responsibility to a multitude of stakeholders, and each of the stakeholders has its own aims that may be conflicting with one another.

Next, let us think of the impact or the consequences of Snowden's actions. The consequences may be beneficial or harmful. Snowden might have done something "good" for the victims in particular and the world at large, and "bad" for NSA and the US government. This result-based argument, which is influenced by the concept known as consequentialism.

Consequentialism:

An action is morally right if its consequences are beneficial, and an action is morally wrong if its consequences of are harmful.

The consequentialist argument is not sufficient and raises such questions as for whom or for how many is the result good, how good or how bad. This argument needs to be supplemented with a utilitarian view.

Utilitarianism:

An action is morally wrong if its harmful results are greater than its beneficial results, and all persons should pursue the greatest good for the greatest number of people.

A utilitarian argument may be useful to suggest the issue: for whom or what purpose the good result is beneficial or the bad result is harmful, but it raises further questions that include, among others, quantifying and comparing the results.

Besides these, others which are noteworthy are the Categorical Imperative and Social Contract Theory, and the so-called Golden/Silver Rule.

Kantian Categorical Imperative:

Never treat human beings merely as means to an end; always treat them as ends in themselves.

Social Contract Theory:

An action is morally wrong if someone's rights are being violated.

Golden Rule:

"Do unto others as you would have them do unto you" or "we should do to others what we would want others to do to us"; this is derived from "Do not do unto others what you would not have them do unto you" (sometimes referred as Silver Rule).

ADDITIVE

As can be seen, none of these principles alone can help to arrive at the ideal solution. To meet this end, a mix of some or all of these principles is necessary. Obvious, having the requisite knowledge is not enough, and something in addition is needed. That something, it is argued, comprises a new concept of risk, Ethical Risk, and a new tool for analysis of the dilemmas, Ethical Matrix (Lee, 2015a). This new view of Computer Ethics forms the core of the Ethical Movement in Cyberspace (Ethical Movement) (Lee, 2015b) advocated by the Computer Ethics Society (iEthics) (The Computer Ethics Society, 2012).

A New Concept of Risk

Connecting Security/Risk and Ethics

The human users of technology who create the risks, take them as *techno-economic risks* (due to *misinterpretation of risk* and the *flawed education*) (Lee, 2015a). It has been argued that abusing or not abusing the technology depends on the users' sense of morality which is influenced by many factors, amongst which is their understanding of the ethical principles. Using the technology in contradiction to ethical principles constitutes a different type of risk called *ethical risk vis-à-vis* risk of a technical, legal or financial nature, because it is a technical and managerial concern and should be measured in financial, legal and moral terms with equal priority.

For example, taking home from work a USB containing corporate data for personal convenience runs the risk of breaching the security for privacy or confidentiality. This is a situation where threat (t) exploits vulnerability (v), thus causing loss, damage or destruction to an asset (a), or $R = f(t, v, a)$. In this case, the person who takes home an un-encrypted USB in which confidential data are stored is a Threat, taking home an USB is a Vulnerability, and this action is a violation of data privacy, thus a risk.

This new risk is related partly to technology (the USB) and partly to people (both the perpetrator and the victims); it is therefore a risk of technological cum social nature in cyberspace, a new risk that can be called a *techno-ethical risk,* simply *ethical risk*. Figure 1 below depicts this phenomenon.

Figure 1. Techno-ethical risk (connecting philosophy/technology)
Source: Lee, 2015d.

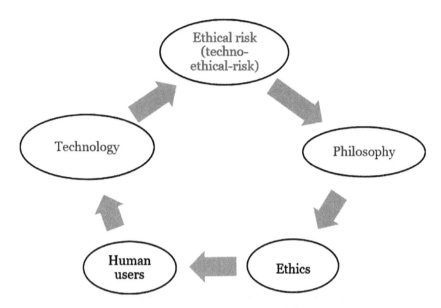

In cyberspace, as in the physical world, security relies on trust; trust depends on privacy; privacy is breached if law is not observed and if ethical principles are not followed. So, you would trust or disclose anything confidential to only those who respect privacy; you would trust your security in the protecting agent who would act according to ethical principles. Hence, trust will be lost or damaged, and undesirable consequences will follow if there is no privacy. Figure 2 is a sketch of the interrelationship of these entities.

Figure 3 combines the figures 1 and 2, and also shows the influence of law on privacy, and the link of techno-ethic risk to cybersecurity.

Shifting Our View of Risk

Security problems, be they of a technical or non-technical nature, is rooted in human mistakes to which none of us is immune. Wherever and whenever is there vulnerability, there is threat ready to exploit. Risk will result whenever a threat is actually carried out. To mitigate *risk* (that is, the damage, loss or destruction of we what we want to protect), we must identify *threat* and deal with *vulnerability*. Obviously, risk is a function of vulnerability and threat, or $r = f (v, t)$, and exposure of risk is a function of probability (the likelihood that risk occurs) and damage (of technical, financial and ethical nature) or $R = f (p, d)$.

Computer Ethics, as advocated by the Computer Ethics Society, can be viewed as a double duality representing a dual mission: computer ethics as a practice and a discipline, and as a dual function: computer ethics playing the role of a different type of risk and an alternative category of (Lee, 2015a). The impact of knowledge of Computer Ethics on students' behaviour, as hypothesized by in a classroom study, empirically supports the anti-risk mechanism role of Computer Ethics (Lee and Chan, 2008). The double duality (Lee, 2014-15) is reproduced below, shown as Figure 4.

Figure 2. Connecting security/risk and ethics
Source: Lee, 2015d.

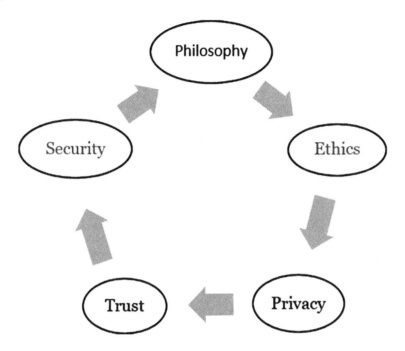

Figure 3. Connecting philosophy/technology and ethics/(security/risk)
Source: Lee, 2015d.

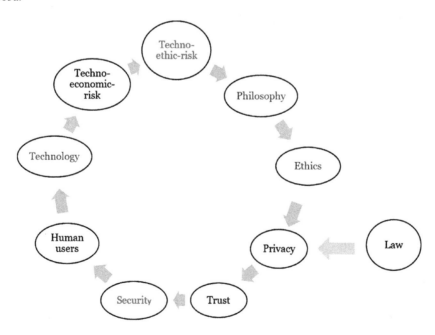

Figure 4. Conceptual graph: double duality
Source: Lee, 2014-2015.

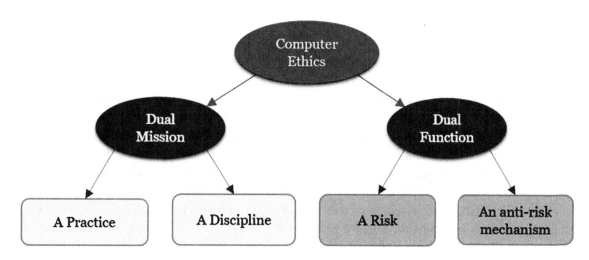

The support of the Lee-Chan hypothesis, which was deduced from the empirical data of investigating the effect of Computer Ethics in a Computer Science syllabus (Lee & Chan 2008), showing i) 62% of the students claimed that they never heard nor aware of Computer Ethics and were not sure if they used the computer ethically before taking the course (Question ii response) and 72% understood Computer Ethics and would use the computer according to ethical principles after finishing the course (Question iv response), ii) a small percentage (4.5% - Question viii responses) of the students claimed that they were indifferent to or did not care about Computer Ethics (Question viii response), and iii) 2.5% (the union of Question vi and Question vii response) claimed that they would not change their view (Lee, 2015a). It should be of interest to note that the number of participants in the annual survey averages about 100 over the six years (2006 to 2012). It is also worthy of further investigation to ascertain of the 2.5% of students who claimed not to change their view, 1% is clearly anti-ethics, what view the 1.5% of the students (Question vi response) would adopt. On account of a typo discovered in the response rate (Question viii), which should be 4.5% and not 5.5%, the corrected Table 1 (Lee, 2015a) is reproduced.

Table 1. Average response rates

Questions before Attending the Course	Rate
I heard or was aware of computer ethics, but I did not know if I used my computer ethically.	8%
I never heard of, nor was I aware of, computer ethics and I was not sure if I used my computer ethically.	62%
I never heard of, nor was I aware of, computer ethics and I thought I used my computer ethically.	30%
Questions after Attending the Course	**Rate**
I understand computer ethics and I will use my computer according to ethical principles.	72%
I understand computer ethics and I will not use my computer according to ethical principles.	21%
I will not change my view because I do not fully understand the subject of computer ethics.	1.5%
I will not change my view because I do not subscribe to the subject of computer ethics.	1%
I am indifferent because I do not care much about computer ethics.	4.5%

Source: Lee & Chan (2008).

A New Tool for Ethical Analysis

Ethical Matrix

Ethical Matrix, newly adopted by Ethical Computing as an additional approach to its tools and methods for performing ethical analyses (Lee, 2015a), poises to supplement the requisite competence. Checking for potential ethical and social impact (in addition to technical and economic efficiency) adds a step or steps to the other established anti-risk countermeasures. For example, going through the process of applying the Ethical Matrix method will force decision makers to consider adverse consequences. This may reveal such risks as user morale and satisfaction or potentially undesirable consequences of a social or moral nature that would otherwise be missed in the typical anti-risk checks and audits, in addition to technical and economic efficiency issues such as improved speed, elimination of redundancy or reduced head counts. This makes computer ethics a different kind of anti-risk mechanism *vis-à-vis* the extant risk countermeasures including the following.

- Technical access control comprises physical and logical access controls such as passwords, firewalls, intrusion prevention systems (IPS), secure web, email gateways, cryptographic algorithms and Anti-Virus Systems or Software (AVS). However, these mechanisms can handle only the physical, tangible errors or risks, but not risks of a sociotechnical nature.
- Computer law is useful as a reference framework for remedy and can be a forceful deterrent to prevent abusive acts by virtue of its power to punish. However, it is not as effective as expected: It is too slow to combat rapidly developed cybercrimes, and the process of creating new laws when needed is too complex and time consuming. Furthermore, people are, in general, reluctant to proceed with legal action or they opt for legal action only as a last resort.
- Risk analysis relies on the probability of occurrence and the associated damage or loss that the analyst estimates based on the threats identified and the related vulnerabilities in a risk assessment exercise. It is helpful in detecting risks but not very useful in preventing or powering them.
- Computer audit is useful for detecting deviation from set policies of performance and checking and verifying that compliance is properly enforced and results are consistent with the set standards, but in physical, cost-benefit terms only. The audit-based mechanism is, therefore, limited as a deterrent.

These extant countermeasures are being rendered impotent by such emerging applications and technologies as the Internet of Things (IoT), big data and cloud computing, all of which are complex and sophisticated, and by the ever-lurking perpetrators who are always ready to crack any new countermeasures soon after they are developed and released. Anti-risk is becoming more difficult. New anti-risk mechanisms are, therefore, called for in order to strengthen the weakened existing mechanisms.

Illustration of Ethical Matrix

The Story

The story about an online monitoring system implemented by Libnaw, a high-tech facilities distributor, and the dilemmas that CIO faced thereof, is that descried earlier in this article to exemplify a post-implementation problem. The dilemmas created and needed to be addressed include 'deviation from the firm's policy for acquisition approval (company policy), privacy invasion, staff being treated as a means, and staff morale (staff), corporate image damage (HRM), professionalism (CIO), duty (EVP). (Lee, 2014)

The Dilemma

The EVP's request worries the CIO.

First, managerial-technical functional conflict: The online surveillance capability in the hands of the EVP will become a *managerial control function*. This deviates from the originally approved purpose: to provide the help-desk staff with an online diagnosis and problem solving aid (*a technical support function*).

Second, management-staff interest conflict: Watching (by the EVP or someone from her office) over the users' screens without the users knowing it has the potential of breaching personal privacy in the work place. This certainly alarms both the staff (for fear of privacy invasion) and the firm (for concern over corporate image and personnel welfare).

Third, professional interest-contractual obligation conflict: Entertaining the EVP's request implies using the surveillance function for spying on the staff. This affects not only the CIO (with respect to professionalism and deontological obligations) but also the EVP (on her duty to protect the corporate image from possible damage), the staff (about being exploited by one or more rotten apples) and the firm (about staff morale and company policy).

Analysis

The stakeholders identified are the firm, staff, EVP, and CIO, and the categories of ethical values considered relevant to the identified stakeholders' concern are well-being, autonomy and justice/fairness. The results of a first-cut analysis is shown in Table 2.

The next steps including modifying, deleting or adding, stakeholders and/or category of ethical values and the final steps including quantifying and comparing the concerns, and concluding are left for the interested readers to contemplate.

Table 2. The first-cut results

Respect for Stakeholders	Well Being	Autonomy	Justice/Fairness
Firm	Personnel welfare, corporate image	Personnel protection	Staff morale
Staff	Personal privacy	Freedom of personal movement	Exploitation by minority
EVP	Job security	Firm's welfare	Entitlement of support resources
CIO	System utility	Professionalism	Distribution of computer resources

Source: Lee (2014).

REMEDIAL ACTION: FROM CONCEPT TO PRACTICE

Scenario 1: Chuck's Dilemma: Contract Spec Fulfilled but Problem Unsolved

The Story

Alluded to earlier in the description of a post-contract problem, the story goes like this: Chuck is a senior project consultant working for A1 ASP, an application software provider. A1 signed a contract with Alwaays21, a fashion boutique in town, for the provision of a total system, and Chuck was assigned to take full charge of the project. Reading through the system specification, Chuck was hit by a couple of loopholes which could cause intermittent logic errors in the update routine of the inventory control function. These errors, though rarely occur, could, if triggered, be vital to the time-critical fashion business. Chuck has to decide: Keep quiet or tell (the boss and/or the client).

Keep Quiet

Chuck is very tempted keep quiet about his finding since it is probably the most popular option. Also, relativism allows him to go the way he thinks is right. Keeping quiet can save him the trouble of confronting the boss and/or the client and avoid suffering a highly likely unpleasant reaction. But taking this option may be against his sense of duty, and worries him when thinking of the potential, unpleasant consequences.

Tell the Boss or the Client or Both

As an employee, Chuck knows that he is obliged to protect company property, to uphold company welfare, and to be loyal to the boss. As a professional, he should look after the client's welfare as well as that of the employer and other stakeholders. The Golden Rule tells Chuck to treat Alwaays21 as he would treat A1; Categorical Imperative advises Chuck to be fair to both parties. Chuck begins to incline to telling both the boss and the client. However, he hesitates as the issue of extra cost pops up. The extra cost might incur as a result of increase in labour cost and resource for implementing the amended version. Who is to bear that extra cost? Has he got a case? It occurs to Chuck that a consequentialist argument would help.

Tell the Boss

When told, as Chuck expects, the boss is upset about the oversight (the flaw in the inventory control function design), and furious when the issue of extra cost is raised. The boss appears unwilling to bear the full cost.

Chuck makes these points on utilitarian grounds that the value associated with the potential damage to A1's reputation plus the cost of potential law suit and the ruin to the relationship with Alwaays21 or loss of its business will far exceed the extra cost, and this may also lead to serious morale issues, loss of customer trust including that of Alwaays21, damage to brand name, among others. In deontological terms, implementing a project knowingly with inherent weakness is an act of dishonesty, a violation of the company's code of conduct and a deviation from fair trade practice.

The boss's attitude seemed softened.

Tell the Client

Dolly appeared shocked upon learning the problem. She demanded to have the vulnerabilities dealt with thoroughly before implementation, or to withdraw the contract.

In response, Chuck argued that Alwaays21 should bear some or even equal responsibility: the contract was signed by both parties as a result of a mutually agreed feasibility study and a fully validated spec (on deontological grounds).

A1 doesn't have to reveal the problem voluntarily in the first place and just went on to implement according to the contract (in relativistic terms).

Further, the extra cost is negligible compared to the potential loss of business and the interruption to operation, etc. if the hidden errors pop up and the cost for amending and repairing in future if the system is implemented now according to the original design (a similar argument with the boss in consequentialist terms).

Now A1 has run the altruistic extra mile. This honest and ethical practice should be encouraged and praised, not rebuked and punished.

Closure

In the end, both A1 and Alwaays21 agree to amend the design and the contract, and to contribute equally to the extra cost.

Scenario 2: Taking Home a USB From Work

Taking home something like a biro from work is so common that it happens all the time, and probably nobody really cares about it. But taking home a USB is a different kettle of fish, and should not be taken lightly. People who do that unconsciously or for a purpose should realize that it is company property; it may contain proprietary data which may or may not have been encrypted; leaving where it belongs may be vulnerable to leaking (the content), physical damage to or loss of the device; and the potential liability to breach of privacy policy, thus incurring cost for law suit, and resulting in bad publicity, diminished trust, and so on.

The Story

One day in the early afternoon, Alex took with him a USB when he left office his (in Causeway Bay) in a hurry because he was trying to get to an evening seminar in Central in time and intended to continue working on his assigned project at home after the seminar. Alice accidentally spotted the act when passing Alex's office on her way to the staff pantry.

Complication

- Alex and Alice had been dating for almost two years and are getting steady.
- Betty (the boss) recommended to promote Alex only last week.
- The USB contains classified information, forbidden by company rules to leave company premises.
- The USB is not encrypted.

Dilemmas

- For Alice: report the case or not.
- For Alex: pretend to be ignorant of the rules or confess and defend on ground that though deviating from the rule, the intent of taking the USB away from office was to work at home, a contribution to increase in productivity.
- For Betty, the boss, when Alice reported Alex's act: to reprimand, to dismiss the report, or what?

Concerns

- Loyalty (Alex and Alice have for each other due to their intimate relationship, and for the company)
- Professionalism (Both Alex and Alice regard themselves as IT professionals)
- Alex's pending promotion (a concern shared by Betty, Alex, Alice and the team)
- Upholding company welfare, protecting company property
- Observing data privacy policy

Analysis

Obviously, there are four stakeholders: Alice, Alex, Betty and the team. The ethical values considered relevant to the identified stakeholders' concern are deontology, utilitarianism and consequentialism. The results of a first-cut analysis is shown in Table 3.

FUTURE RESEARCH DIRECTIONS

Ethical Matrix is a viable tool for ethical analysis of cyber-security issues. Application of this tool should be further developed and the first to develop is a quantification scheme for prioritizing remedial actions on the concerns, for only after a metric is developed and well validated can the concerns be compared and remedial actions taken. Interest in Computer Ethics is growing, though not as fast as expected; it must grow as cybercrimes grow; it needs time to accelerate as we take time to shift our view of risk (Lee, 2015c). Ethical Computing is to grow in importance in combating the constantly increase of ethical issues due to the alleged increase in hacking instances, insider perpetrators, security and privacy concerns associated with the emerging technology such as Big Data, Cloud Computing, and Internet of Things.

Table 3. The first-cut results: the USB case

Respect for Stakeholders	Deontology	Utilitarianism	Consequentialism
Alice	loyalty to Alex, company, professionalism	Alex's promotion	violation of data privacy policy
Alex	productivity	promotion	data protection
Betty	firm's welfare & property	her recommendation of Alex's promotion	data leaking
The team	team spirit & morale	promotion opportunity, fairness of treatment	data privacy

Source: Lee (2015d).

CONCLUSION

Many of the problems in the technology-driven information-intensive environment that could have been avoided or mitigated, occur because the ethical aspect of these problems is ignored or not recognized. It has been argued that solutions for these cyber-problems need to meet the six criteria: technical efficiency, financial viability, legal admissibility, social desirability, environmental sustainability, and ethical acceptability. It has been further argued that a deep understanding of the basic ethical principles, a shift in our view of ethics to include Ethical Risk, and a new tool for analysis of Ethical Risk (Ethical Matrix) are required. A completely ideal solution may not be readily and easily achieved. Some remedial action has been illustrated by means a few cases.

Computer Ethics that connects Technology (security and risk) and Philosophy (ethics and privacy). Ethical Computing as a practice that aims at establishing the ethical standards for guiding specialists and laymen alike through the ethical dilemmas are getting more important as a weapon against cyber-abuses that cause damage in excess of billions of US dollars. Further development is necessary and worthwhile.

REFERENCES

Lee, W. W. (2014). Why Computer Ethics Matters to Computer Auditing. *ISACA Journal, 2*, 48–52.

Lee, W.W. (2014-15). *Ethical, Legal & Social Issues*. Postgraduate Diploma in eHealth Informatics, The University of Hong Kong.

Lee, W. W. (2015a). Ethical Computing. In M. Khosrow-Pour (Ed.), *Encyclopedia of Information Science and Technology* (3rd ed.; pp. 2991–2999). doi:10.4018/978-1-4666-5888-2.ch292

Lee, W. W. (2015b). Ethical Movement: An alternative anti-crime mechanism in cyberspace. *Trusted Computing – A Security Oxymoron or The Future? 16th Info-Security Conference*.

Lee, W.W. (2015c). *e-Crime & understanding Risk & Ethics in cyberspace*. Inaugural e-Crime Congress, Hong Kong.

Lee, W.W. (2015d, September 11). *Ignorant of ethical pitfalls can hurt information security – Implications for IT users & Information Security Professionals*. The Hong Kong Jockey Club.

Lee, W. W., & Chan, K. C. C. (2008). Computer Ethics: A Potent Weapon for Information Security Management. *Information Systems Audit & Control Journal*. Retrieved from www.isaca.org/jonline

ADDITIONAL READING

Johnson, D. G. (2009). Computer Ethics (4th Ed.). Upper Saddle River, NJ: Prentice Hall Josephson Institute of Ethics. (1999). Five Steps of Principled Reasoning. Retrieved from http://www.ethicsscoreboard.com/rb_5step.html

Josephson Institute of Ethics. (2002). Making Ethical Decisions: A 7-Step Path. Retrieved from http://blink.ucsd.edu/finance/accountability/ethics/path.html

Kallman, E. A., & Grillo, J. P. (1996). *Ethical Decision Making and Information Technology*. Watersonville, CA: McGraw-Hill.

Lee, W. W. (2010). *Information Security Management: Semi-intelligent Risk-analytic Audit*. VDM Verlag.

Mepham, B., Kaiser, M., Thorstensen, E., Tomkins, S., & Millar, K. (2006). Ethical Matrix Manual. The Hague: LEI http://www.ethicaltools.info/content/ ET2 Manual EM (Binnenwerk 45p).pdf

Moor, J. H. (1985). What is Computer Ethics? *Metaphilosophy*, *16*(4), 266–275. doi:10.1111/j.1467-9973.1985.tb00173.x

KEY TERMS AND DEFINITIONS

Additive: This is a supplement to the requisite competence which alone is not sufficient, and a requirement of a change in viewing risk as having not only technical, physical, financial and legal but also ethical and social implications, and a tool or method to cater for this type of risk.

Computer Ethics: Applied Ethics referring ethical issues arising out of using the computer and its peripherals.

Ethical Computing: The practice of Computer Ethics and can be regarded as a branch of Computing, somewhat akin to Green Computing, Mobile Computing, and Cloud Computing. Whereas the others deal with tangible aspects of Computing, Ethical Computing handles techno-ethical aspects.

Ethical Risk (Short for Techno-Ethical Risk): Abusing technology or technology-based systems constitutes a risk called techno-ethical risk or ethical risk. Using the computer or developing computer-based systems or software inconsistent with ethical principles results in computer-ethical risk or simply ethical risk.

Hexa-Dimension Criteria: This refers to an ideal state expected of a solution that is technically efficient, financially viable, legally admissible, socially desirable, and ethically acceptable. Another dimension "environmentally sustainable" was added making a hexa-dimension model was developed and presented for consideration as a metric for the design of a code of conduct corporate-wide or functional unit based (Lee, 2015d).

Ideal Solution: To solve the problem which is required to satisfy the penta-dimensional criteria, the proposed solution is structured around the two major components, *requisite competence* and *additive* (to supplement the requisite competence which alone is not sufficient).

Requisite Competence: This comprises the technical-know (the rudimentary skills and knowledge to use the computer) and a deep understanding of the basic ethical principles.

Technology-Driven Information-Intensive: This is a phenomenon that characterized the contemporary society and attributes to the vicious circle: increase in demand for information leads to increase in reliance on technology, and increase in use of technology consumes and generates more information. One the one hand, to capture market share and attract customers, contemporary business organizations rely increasingly on information technology to accumulate and process data needed to advertise services and products. Hence, the marketplace becomes more transparent, and the consumers are better-informed thus more demanding. More information is required and technology is more heavily relied upon. On the other hand, to aid business, to increase the processing power, and to handle the increase in data volume, new technological facilities such as call center and weblining (for marketing), and Big Data, Internet of

Things, Cloud Computing (for communication and data management) are developed and used by business but these facilities consume and generate more data. In turn, reliance on technology increases to handle the information explosion.

The Basic Ethical Principles: For the purpose of this exposition, included are relativism, deontology, consequentialism and utilitarianism, categorical imperative, Social Contract Theory, and Golden Rule.

The Computer Ethics Society: Was established in 2012, aiming to promote professional and ethical standards, and to foster an open platform for sharing and interchanging experience and knowledge of moral issues associated with the use and development of ICT-based systems (www.iEthicsSoc.org).

The Problem: Referred to in this article: Its symptom is the phenomenon called technology-driven information-intensive. Its cause is techno-ethical risk or *ethical risk*. This type of risk created because the user not only is insensitive to or ignorant of the ethical aspect of the problems and its ramifications, attributing to a lack of deep appreciation of the ethical principles, but also treats risk as a technical, corporate/personal matter when it is in fact a managerial, social concern under the influence of the so-called *flawed education across science and technology* and *misinterpretation of risk*. Post-contract problems and post-implementation problems are typical examples.

This research was previously published in the Encyclopedia of Information Science and Technology, Fourth Edition edited by Mehdi Khosrow-Pour, pages 4884-4897, copyright year 2018 by Information Science Reference (an imprint of IGI Global).

Chapter 18
Group Signature System Using Multivariate Asymmetric Cryptography

Sattar J. Aboud
University of Bedfordshire, UK

ABSTRACT

This chapter presents a new group signature scheme using multivariate asymmetric cryptography. Compared with the exited signature schemes, the proposed scheme is applicable to e-voting schemes and can convince the requirements of e-voting schemes because it has two important characteristics, traceability and unlinkability. Traceability denotes that a group director cannot open the signature alone. He has to collaborate with a verifier to disclose an identity of the signer. Unlinkability denotes that the group signature can be split accordance to time durations. Then signatures are linkable in the same time range but un-linkable between dissimilar time periods. Therefore, the count authority can notice the double votes prior to opening them. Thus, there are two features in the proposed signature for count and supervision authority. Also, the size of signatures and the calculation overhead are private from the group members in the proposed scheme. So, it is efficient for large groups.

INTRODUCTION

The group signature lets the group of people to sign document anonymously on behalf of other group. In the case of the dispute, the designated director can open the signature to disclose the identity of its generator. To the degree that we know the majority of the group signatures are relied on the known schemes, such as RSA and ElGamal. However, these schemes could be broken when quantum computers appear. The problem typed multivariate asymmetric key cryptography is the notable option to common asymmetric schemes for its possible to withstand future attacks of quantum computers. The initial group signature scheme relied on the multivariate asymmetric cryptography that is introduced in this chapter.

DOI: 10.4018/978-1-5225-7492-7.ch018

The proposed scheme have two extraordinary attributes. In the first one, the group signatures are divided to dissimilar time intervals. The signatures are linkable in the same time interval, but un-linkable among dissimilar time intervals. In the second one, the duties of the group director is restricted. The group director does not allow him to open the signature without the assist from the verifier. These attributes are vital in selected uses such as e-voting schemes. The concept of the proposed scheme is straightforward and its security bases on both an arbitrary hash function and an isomorphism of polynomial problem.

In 1991, Chaum-Heyst presented the first idea of group signature. The group signature scheme give permission to the group of people to sign the documents on behalf of the group. The verifier can only inform that the signature is signed by the person from the group, but cannot determine the identity of the signer. In addition, the verifier cannot differentiate if the two signatures are published by the same person of the group. But, in special case such as official dispute, the designated group director can open the signature to disclose the identity of its generator. At the same time, no one even the group director can forge the signature of other group people.

The characteristics of group signature construct it smart for many specific applications, like e-voting, e-cash and e-games. For instance, in e-voting systems, the electorate are not allowable to vote many times. Thus the count authority should be capable to differentiate the reduplicate votes without opening an election. Furthermore, there is a rule exist supervision authority to constraint the duties of the count authority and promise the fairness of the voting in the voting system. Thus, the group signature schemes cannot be employed the e-voting systems straight. Most of the group signatures are using known cryptography schemes, such as RSA and ElGamal. However, the algorithm proposed by Shor illustrates that solving the factoring integers and the discrete logarithms can be achieved in polynomial time on the quantum computer. If the quantum computers become a reality, the common asymmetric key cryptography under these problem, such as RSA and Elliptic curve will be broken. multivariate asymmetric key cryptography is studied to be one of the best option. The security basis of multivariate asymmetric key cryptography is the information that solving the set of multivariate polynomial formulas over the finite field is the NP-hard problem. Quantum computers do not seem to have any benefit if managing this NP-hard problems, and it appears that we cannot recover the solution to the set of polynomial formulas efficiently even in the future. Furthermore, multivariate asymmetric key cryptography schemes are more efficient than common asymmetric key cryptography. It makes them appropriate for restricted computing tools, for example smart cards. Different multivariate asymmetric key cryptography schemes have been presented.

QUANTUN COMPUTING THREATENS

Quantum computing threatens definite techniques and does not threaten others. Public key encryption, is being used considerably for securing the internet payments, banking transactions, and also emails and webs. The majority of today cryptography schemes are using public-key cryptography, that is in fact secure anti-attacks from contemporary computers.

Suppose that quantum cryptography can easily break many schemes by inverse the computing private-keys and quicker than the classical computer. While quantum cryptography are still in their early stages and non- equipped, with publicly known new quantum computers, small to attack traditional cryptography algorithms, many public authorities have begun to know the risk included if this technology becomes the practical applications. Since quantum computers is to process huge amounts of information in the quite short of time.

Traditional cryptography schemes provide computational security but is not ensure perfect or resistant security. The power of the existing cryptography algorithms based on composite mathematical problems, for example integer factoring, elliptic curve and discrete logarithm problem. Such difficulties can deciphered by applying large-scale quantum cryptography and thus can simply break traditional schemes. Consequently, experts have started planning new encryption schemes that are considered quantum-resistant that cannot be broken as fast as traditional algorithms.

The National Security Agency recognized the quantum processing threat by publicly announcing their strategies for changing to quantum unbreakable methods. However, the quantum processing threat has increased over public key infrastructure that is applied greatly in protecting the webs.

Quantum cryptography can be attack both symmetric schemes such as block ciphers, and asymmetric schemes such as RSA and DSA. Such cryptography can break each single public key algorithm in the small amounts of time. Quantum methods, for example Shor scheme, can be applied to retrieve the RSA key in polynomial time, but quantum cryptography with sufficient power at present is not existed.

Post-quantum encryption is being utilized for designing cryptography methods that are believed to be secure anti-attack by quantum processors. It is expected that 2048-bit RSA keys can be defeated on the quantum computer containing 4000 qubits and 100 million gates. Even if there are some public-key methods that are believed resistant, they are not utilized currently, since Quantum algorithms is based on difficult and complicated mathematical problems to give security that is stronger than conventional cryptography. If quantum cryptography becomes the truth, it will product in re-engineering and improvements in existing encryption schemes.

BACKGROUND

Due to its significant attributes, group signature draw many authors attentions. However, in addition to the first scheme proposed by Chaum-Heyst, there are many other schemes appear. For example, Chen-Pedersen in 1994 presented the new group signature scheme which conceal an identity of the signer categorically and permitted new persons to associate the group. Also, in 1997 Camenish-Stadler introduced an efficient group signature scheme for large groups, with the size of public keys and the size of signatures are free of the group persons. In 2000, Ateniese *et al.* presented the group signature scheme relied on other number theory topics with good efficiency and robust security. In 2003 Chen-Yang proposed another digital signature scheme called TTS/4. It is from the family of multivariate cryptography schemes. They claim that TTS/4 is competitive and better compare with other schemes. In 2004, Ding introduced the new variant scheme from the concept of perturbation. This scheme employs the set of small number linearly independent functions. The difference between the proposed thought and the similar concept of the concealed field equation and Oil-Vinegar scheme is that perturbation is internal, while other schemes are external perturbation. In 2010, Petzoldt, *et al.* they extend the thought of the Rainbow signature scheme. They claim that the construction of their scheme able to decrease the length of the public-key up to 62%. In 2011, Jintai Ding published a patent contains three schemes to construct new multivariate public-key schemes that are better in security and efficiency. The three schemes are entitled the internal perturbation plus, the enhanced internal perturbation and the multi-layer Oil-Vinegar construction. In 2012, Noaki Ogura, proposed scheme concerning the multivariate public-key scheme. In 2014, Ning Huang analyzed and solved the errors of the medium field multivariate public-key encryption scheme.

In the multivariate asymmetric-key cryptography schemes, the asymmetric-key is the set of polynomials $p = (p_1, ..., p_m)$ in integers $x = (x_1, ..., x_n)$, with all parameters and coefficients are in $K = GF(k)$. This is typically achieved by:

$$P = S \circ Q \circ T : K^n \to K^m$$

or

$$P : w = (w_1, ..., w_n) \in K^n \overset{T}{\mapsto} x = M_T w + c_T$$
$$\overset{Q}{\mapsto} y \overset{S}{\mapsto} z = Msy + c_S = (z_1, ..., z_m) \in K^m$$

The central map Q be owned by the certain class of quadratic maps whose inverse does calculated straightforwardly. The maps S and T are affine and bijective. The private-key contain the central map Q and affine maps S, T.

MAIN FOCUS OF THE CHAPTER

In this section, we are going to describe the contribution, then the traditional schemes, the solution scheme, then the discussions and finally the conclusions and remarks.

The Contribution

This Chapter presents a new group signature scheme using multivariate asymmetric cryptography. Compared with the exited signature schemes, The proposed scheme is applicable to e-voting schemes and can convince the requirements of e-voting schemes because it has two important characteristics, Traceability and Unlinkability. Traceability denotes that a group director cannot open the signature alone. He has to collaborate with a verifier to disclose an identity of the signer. Unlinkability denotes that the group signature can be split accordance to time durations. Then signatures are linkable in the same time range, but un-linkable between dissimilar time periods. Therefore, the count authority can notice the double-votes prior to open them. Thus, there are two features in the proposed signature, for count and supervision authority. Also, the size of signatures and the calculation overhead are private from the group members in the proposed scheme. So, it is efficient for large groups.

The Proposed Group Signature Scheme

The customary group signature schemes permit the user to sign documents anonymously on the behalf of his group. The verifier can check that the signature was signed by the user of the group, nevertheless cannot determine which user of the group signed it. Also, the signatures are un-linkable, which means that provided two group signatures, the verifier cannot distinguish if they are published by the same group user or not. However, the unlinkability pears not modified to some uses for example the e-voting schemes. The verifier must be capable to differentiate the over-votes, in the meantime the anonymity must be certain. In addition, in customary group signatures the group director can open any group signature randomly.

Although in the e-voting schemes, there is typically the supervision organization to assurance the fairness of the voting. Thus we want to constraint the duties of the group director. Thus, the customary group signatures cannot be useful with e-voting schemes straight. In order to solve these difficulties, we introduce the new group signature scheme fitted with e-voting schemes. The proposed scheme is described as follows.

1. **Unlinkability:** The group signature is divided into time duration. The signatures in the same time range are linkable. The verifier can check if two signatures are published by a same group member. But the signatures between dissimilar time period are un-linkable. They are entirely anonymous. This property is useful in the e-voting schemes. For instance, in the voting there are numerous positions require to be chosen. Every duration for one position. As the votes in the same period are linkable, the verifier is capable to differentiate the over-votes without opening them. All at once, the ballots between dissimilar ranges are un-linkable, thus ballots for diverse position are anonymous.
2. **Traceability:** The group director and the verifier cannot disclose an identity of the signature individually, but they can do it jointly.
3. **Correctness:** The group signature published by a valid group entity and should be accepted by a verifier.
4. **Unforgeability:** Only the legitimate group entities are capable to sign documents on behalf of the group.
5. **Undeniable:** Both the group entity and the group director is capable to sign documents on behalf of other group entities. This also causes the group signature undeniable.
6. **Anonymity:** Provided the legitimate group signature, no entity can disclose the identity of a real signer, unless the group director opens the signature with an assist of the verifier.

In the proposed scheme, the group director cannot open the signature randomly. His duties is restricted. This characteristic is significant in some application such as the e-voting schemes. The management usually contains the count authority and the supervision authority. Neither of them can disclose an identity of the vote alone. They have to act jointly to open the vote to disclose a real identity. This characteristic lets the voting more open.

Signature of Knowledge

In this section, we present the signature of knowledge using multivariate asymmetric key cryptography, which is the construction block of the proposed scheme.

Isomorphism of Polynomials Problem

The isomorphism of polynomials problem was first presented by Patarin in 1996. It is the basic problem of multivariate encryption because it is connected with the difficulty of the key recovery of the schemes. The idea of Isomorphism of Polynomials is illustrated as follows.

Suppose that $K = GF(k)$ is the finite field. All parameters are over the field K. Assume that A are the set of u quadratic formulas with n parameters $x_1, ..., x_n$ that provide y values from x values:

$$y_k = \sum_i \sum Y_{ijk} x_i x_j + \sum_i u_{ik} x_i + \delta_k \text{ where } k = 1, ..., u$$

Given B is the set of u quadratic formulas with n parameters $x_1', ..., x_n'$ that provide y' values from x' values:

$$y_k' = \sum_i \sum Y_{ijk}' x_i' x_j' + \sum_i u_{ik}' x_i' + \delta_k' \text{ where } k = 1, ..., u$$

Suppose that T is the bijective affine transformation of the parameters x_i' where $1 \leq i \leq n$ with S is the bijective affine transformation of the parameters y_k, such that $1 \leq k \leq u$. Then

$$T(x_1', ..., x_n') = (x_1, ..., x_n)$$
$$S(y_1, ..., y_u) = (y_1', ..., y_u')$$

When there is the transformation pair (S, T) to convince $B = S \; o \; A \; o \; T$, we said to be A and B are isomorphic, and the bijective affine transformation pair (S, T) is the isomorphism from $(A$ to $B)$. When A and B are two public sets of u quadratic formulas, and A and B are isomorphic, get isomorphism (S, T) from $(A$ to $B)$.

Signature of Knowledge Protocol

Zero-knowledge proofs permit the prover to show the knowledge of the secret, without disclose any important information. Patarin introduced the non-interactive zero-knowledge proofs of knowledge scheme using a isomorphism of polynomial problem [13]. In this Chapter, we will use the simplicity but practical scheme we entitled it signature of knowledge which is as follows.

Assume K is the finite field. Given n, u, q are three variables, and H is the secure hash function $H : (0,1)^* \rightarrow (0,1)^q$ that maps the binary bits of random size to q-bit hash value. Assume A and B are two sets of u quadratic formulas with n parameters as follows:

$$A : y_k = \sum_i \sum Y_{ijk} x_i x_j + \sum_i u_{ik} x_i + \delta_k$$

where $k = 1, ..., u$

$$B : y_k' = \sum_i \sum Y_{ijk}' x_i' x_j' + \sum_i u_{ik}' x_i' + \delta_k'$$

where $k = 1, ..., u$

Suppose m is a document to be signed. Request $q+1$ parameters $V = h, (S_1, T_1), ..., (S_q, T_q)$ the signature of knowledge involved (A, B) and document m, when the following conditions are convinced: $C_i = S_i \circ A \circ T_i$, if $h(i) = 0$ or $C_i = S_i \circ B \circ T_i$, if $h(i) = 1$ with $1 \leq i \leq q$, and $h = H(m \parallel C_1 \parallel C_2 \parallel ... \parallel C_q)$.

When a prover identifies the isomorphism (S, T) from $(A$ to $B)$ means $B = S \circ A \circ T$, then a signature of knowledge can be created as follows.

The prover chooses q arbitrary bijective affine transformation pairs $(S_1', T_1'), ..., (S_q', T_q')$ which appear like:

$$T_1'(x_1^{(1)}, ..., x_n^{(1)}) = (x_1, ..., x_n), \; S_1'(y_1, ..., y_u) = (y_1^{(1)}, ..., y_u^{(1)})$$
$$T_q'(x_1^{(q)}, ..., x_n^{(q)}) = (x_1, ..., x_n), \; S_q'(y_1, ..., y_u) = (y_1^{(q)}, ..., y_u^{(q)})$$

The prover finds:

$$C_1 = S_1' \circ A \circ T_1'$$
$$C_2 = S_2' \circ A \circ T_2'$$
$$\vdots$$
$$C_q = S_q' \circ A \circ T_q'$$

Then, gets q sets of u quadratic formulas with n parameters as follows:

$$y_k^{(1)} = \sum_i \sum_j Y_{ijk}^{(1)} x_i^{(1)} x_j^{(1)} + \sum_i u_{ik}^{(1)} x_i^{(1)} + \delta_k^{(1)}$$

where $k = 1, ..., u$

$$y_k^{(q)} = \sum_i \sum_j Y_{ijk}^{(q)} x_i^{(q)} x_j^{(q)} + \sum_i u_{ik}^{(q)} x_i^{(q)} + \delta_k^{(q)}$$

where $k = 1, ..., u$

The prover finds a hash outcome $h = H(m \parallel C_1 \parallel C_2 \parallel ... C_q)$. Assume that the binary format of result h is introduced as $h(q)...h(2)h(1) \in (0, 1)^q$. The prover finds $(S_i, T_i) = (S_i', T_i'$, if $h(i) = 0$, or $(S_i' \circ S^{-1}, T^{-1} \circ T_i')$ if $h(i) = 1$ where $1 \leq i \leq q$. Therefore, the signature of knowledge V is built.

If the verifier receives the public key (A, B), the document m, and the signature of knowledge V, the steps of the signature verification is as follows.

The verifier finds q sets of u quadratic formula by

$$C_i = S_i \circ A \circ T_i, \; if \; h(i) = 0 \; or \; C_i = S_i \circ B \circ T_i, \; if \; h(i) = 1 \; where \; 1 \leq i \leq q$$

The verifier finds the hash value $h = H(m \parallel C_1 \parallel C_2 \parallel ... \parallel C_q)$, and verifies if the new hash value h' is equal to h.

The Description of the Proposed Scheme

In this section, we introduce the new group signature scheme using multivariate asymmetric key cryptography, deal with the e-voting schemes.

Scheme Initialization

The group director setup the scheme parameters as follows:

1. Suppose that n, u, q are three integers. Also, let $K = GF(k)$ is the finite field.
2. H is the secure hash function $H : (0,1)^* \rightarrow (0,1)^q$ that maps the binary bits of random size to q - bit hash value.
3. Q is the central map chosen by a group director.
4. Every entity i has a secret key $(L_{1,i}, L_{2,i})$, and a public key $A_i = L_{1,i} \circ Q \circ L_{2,i}$.

Joining Group

Each user wants to join the group to get the ability of signing on behalf of the group. Assume that the user i needs to join the group.

1. User i chooses arbitrary bijective affine transformation pair (S_i, T_i) and maps A_i to B_i by $B_i = S_i \circ A_i \circ T_i$. The, A_i and B_i are isomorphic and affine transformation (S_i, T_i) is an isomorphism from (A_i to B_i). This pair (A_i, B_i) is the public key of user i in the group, while (S_i, T_i) is the secret key of user i in the group.
2. User i makes the signature of knowledge of (A_i, B_i), represented by V_i, and passes the knowledge V_i and (A_i, B_i) to the group director. In this case, the interaction between a user i and a group director must be secure.
3. The group director checks the signature of knowledge. If it is true, he stores the knowledge V_i and (A_i, B_i). if not, he erases the knowledge V_i and (A_i, B_i), and reject the user i request.

Signing Documents

The group director can split the group signature to a number of time periods. The amendment of the period is ruled by the group director. So as to alter the period, the group director should do the following two phases.

First Phase: Change Period

The steps of this phase are as follows:

1. The group director chooses the public keys of various group users. These users form the sign group.
2. 2. For each public key (A_i, B_i) in a sign group, the director makes the arbitrary bijective affine transformation pair $(S_{1,i}, T_{1,i})$, and finds

$$A_i^{(1)} = S_{1,i} \circ A_i \circ T_{1,i}$$
$$B_i^{(1)} = S_{1,i} \circ B_i \circ T_{1,i}$$

The group director issued $(A_i^{(1)}, B_i^{(1)})$ to the bill-board. Then he posts each affine transformation pair $(S_{1,i}, T_{1,i})$ to the related user i in the sign group by a secure communication.

Second Phase: Signing

Inside every period, group users in the sign group can sign any documents on the behalf of the group, where the signatures are linkable. Assume that group user i needs to sign the document m, entity should perform the second phase as follows. The steps of this phase are as follows:

1. The user i passes $(A_i^{(1)}, B_i^{(1)})$ to verifier v.
2. The verifier v verifies that if $(A_i^{(1)}, B_i^{(1)})$ is in the bill-board. If yes, he chooses the arbitrary bijectiveaffinetransformationpair $(S_{2,i}, T_{2,i})$ andpostsittouser i.Thenhefinds $A_i^{(2)} = (S_{2,i} \circ A_i^{(1)} \circ T_{2,i}, B_i^{(2)} = S_{2,i} \circ B_i^{(1)} \circ T_{2,i}$ and stores $(A_i^{(2)}, B_i^{(2)})$ and $(S_{2,i}, T_{2,i})$ in the database.
3. The user i finds $(A_i^{(2)}, B_i^{(2)})$. Then, he calculates the isomorphism (A_i', B_i') from $A_i^{(2)}$ to $B_i^{(2)}$ by:

$$S_i' = (S_{2,i} \circ S_{1,i}) \circ S_i \circ (S_{2,i} \circ S_{1,i})^{-1}$$
$$T_i' = (T_{1,i} \circ T_{2,i})^{-1} \circ T_i \circ (T_{1,i}$$

With (S_i', T_i') user i can produce the signature of knowledge of document m and $(A_i^{(2)}, B_i^{(2)})$ indicated by $V_i^{(2)}$. Therefore $[V_i^{(2)}, (A_i^{(2)}, B_i^{(2)})]$ is the group signature published by user i.

Verifying Signatures

Upon receiving the group signature $[V_i^{(2)}, (A_i^{(2)}, B_i^{(2)})]$, a verifier v verifies the validity of the signature by two steps.

1. The verifier v decrypts the $(A_i^{(1)}, B_i^{(1)})$ by

$$A_i^{(1)} = S_{2,i}^{-1} \circ A_i^{(2)} \circ T_{2,i}^{-1}$$
$$B_i^{(1)} = S_{2,i}^{-1} \circ B_i^{(2)} \circ T_{2,i}^{-1}$$

Then he verifies $(A_i^{(1)}, B_i^{(1)})$ if it is in the bill-board. If yes, he moves to the next step. If not the signature is invalid.

2. The verifier v verifies if $V_i^{(2)}$ is the valid signature of knowledge of document m and $(A_i^{(2)}, B_i^{(2)})$. If yes, he accepts the signature. If not the signature is invalid.

Linking Signatures

Suppose that the two group signatures $[V_i^{(2)}, (A_i^{(2)}, B_i^{(2)})]$ and $[V_j^{(2)}, (A_j^{(2)}, B_j^{(2)})]$. So, to check the double-signature is easy.

1. The verifier verifies if $(A_i^{(2)}, B_i^{(2)}) = (A_j^{(2)}, B_j^{(2)})$ then the two signatures are published by the same user. If not move to the next step.
2. The verifier decrypts the $(A_i^{(1)}, B_i^{(1)})$ and the $(A_j^{(1)}, B_j^{(1)})$ as follows:

$$(A_i^{(1)}, B_i^{(1)}) = (S_{2,i}^{-1} \circ A_i^{(2)} \circ T_{2,i}^{-1}, S_{2,i}^{-1} \circ B_i^{(2)} \circ T_{2,i}^{-1})$$
$$(A_j^{(1)}, B_j^{(1)}) = (S_{2,j}^{-1} \circ A_j^{(2)} \circ T_{2,j}^{-1}, S_{2,j}^{-1} \circ B_j^{(2)} \circ T_{2,j}^{-1})$$

If $(A_i^{(1)}, B_i^{(1)})$ and $(A_j^{(2)}, B_j^{(2)})$ are still dissimilar then the two signatures are published by unlike group users. If not, they are published by the same user.

-   **Remark:** When the two signatures are from dissimilar periods, they are un-linkable. It means that the outcome of the Link operation is published by dissimilar group users.

Opening Signatures

To open the group signature to disclose the real identity of the signer, the group director has to assist with a verifier. For instance, $[V_i^{(2)}, (A_i^{(2)}, B_i^{(2)})]$ the group director receives the affine transformation pair $(S_{2,i}, T_{2,i})$ from the verifier. Then the group director finds (A_i, B_i) using $(S_{2,i}, T_{2,i})$.

$$A_i = (S_{2,i} \circ S_{1,i})^{-1} \circ A_i^{(2)} \circ (T_{i,1} \circ T_{2,i})^{-1}$$
$$B_i = (S_{2,i} \circ S_{1,i})^{-1} \circ B_i^{(2)} \circ (T_{i,1} \circ T_{2,i})^{-1}$$

The isomorphism from $(A_i^{(2)}, B_i^{(2)})$ to (A_i, B_i) is $((S_{2,i} \circ S_{1,i})^{-1}, (T_{1,i} \circ T_{2,i})^{-1})$. Therefore the group director obtains an identity of the real signer.

Security of the Proposed Scheme

The proposed scheme properties are as follows.

- **Unlinkability:** The signatures are linkable in the same time period, but un-linkable in dissimilar time periods.

Proof: In one period, group user j can obtain only one license (S_1, T_1) from the group director. Therefore he can only generate one $A_j^{(1)}, B_j^{(1)}$. He can inquire a verifier twice for (S_2, T_2) and (S_2', T_2') then generates $(A_j^{(2)}, B_j^{(2)})$ and $(A_j'^{(2)}, B_j'^{(2)})$ but a verifier will decrypt the same $(A_j^{(1)}, B_j^{(1)})$ using (S_2, T_2) and (S_2', T_2') respectively. Thus the signatures in the same time period are linkable. Whereas in dissimilar periods, the user j will obtain dissimilar licenses (S_1, T_1) and (S_1', T_1') from group director, and he generates $(A_j^{(1)}, B_j^{(1)})$. The verifier can decrypt them using (S_2, T_2) and (S_2', T_2') but he cannot decrypt the origin (A_j, B_j). Thus, the signatures between dissimilar time periods are unlikable.

- **Traceability:** Both the group director and the verifier cannot disclose an identity of the signature alone, but they can disclose it jointly.

Proof: In the proposed scheme, after the computing of $(A_i^{(1)}, B_i^{(1)})$ the signer i maps the $((A_i^{(1)}, B_i^{(1)})$ to $(A_i^{(2)}, B_i^{(2)}))$ by using an affine transformation pair $(S_{2,i}, T_{2,i})$ provided by a verifier. So, the group director cannot sets up the relationship between $(A_i^{(2)}, B_i^{(2)})$ and $(A_i^{(1)}, B_i^{(1)})$ without $(S_{2,i}, T_{2,i})$. Thus, the group director cannot disclose an identity of the signature. Also, a verifier cannot sets up the relationship between $(A_i^{(1)}, B_i^{(1)})$ and original (A_1, B_1). Thus, the verifier cannot open the signature alone, unless otherwise there is a cooperation between the group director and the verifier to decrypt the identity of the signature.

- **Correctness:** The group signature published by a valid group user should be accepted by a verifier. where u is the polynomial numbers in Q, n is the parameter numbers.
- **Unforgeability:** The group user is capable to sign documents on behalf of the group.

Proof: The verifier can verify the public keys in the bill-board. Thus, to obtain the transformation pair $(S_{2,i}, T_{2,i})$ from verifier and produce the signature, the user i has to obtain the qualification from the group director.

- **Undeniable:** Both the group user and the group director are not capable to sign the documents on behalf of other group users.

Table 1. The best algorithms for isomorphism of polynomials

Problem	Sub-Case	Complexity
Isomorphism of Polynomials	degree $= 2$, $u = n$, inhomogeneous	$O(n^3) / O(n^6)$
	degree $= 2$, $u = n$, homogeneous	$O(n^{3.5} \cdot q^{n/2})$

Proof: Assume that the group user j needs to sign documents on the behalf of a group user i. The user j can inquire the group director for the affine transformation pair (S_1, T_1) and inquire a verifier for an affine transformation pair (S_2, T_2). Then he finds $(A_i^{(2)}, B_i^{(2)})$:

$$A_i^{(2)} = S_2 \circ S_1 \circ A_i \circ T_1 \circ T_2$$
$$B_i^{(2)} = S_2 \circ S_1 \circ B_i \circ T_1 \circ T_2.$$

To produce the signature of knowledge $(A_i^{(2)}, B_i^{(2)})$ he must discover the isomorphism from ($A_i^{(2)}$ to $B_i^{(2)}$). It means that he must resolve the isomorphism of polynomial problem. It is arithmetically difficult without the secret key (S_i, T_i) of user i.

- **Anonymity:** Provided the valid group signature, no one can disclose an identity of the real signer, unless the group director opens the signature with an assist of the verifier.

Proof: Provided the group signature $[V_i^{(2)}, (A_i^{(2)}, B_i^{(2)})]$, to disclose an identity of the signer, a hacker has to discover the affine transformation pair (S_i', T_i') that maps (A_i, B_i) to $(A_i^{(2)}, B_i^{(2)})$. This means that he has to resolve an isomorphism of polynomial problem. It is arithmetically difficult without $(S_{1,i}, T_{1,i})$, and $(S_{2,i}, T_{2,i})$ which hold by the group director and the verifier respectively.

COMPARISONS

We compare the proposed scheme with some other group signature schemes. The proposed scheme is the group signature scheme using multivariate asymmetric key cryptography, and is possible the first group signature scheme that withstands the future attacks of quantum computers. Thus, we can only compare the proposed scheme with the schemes using conventional cryptography. The early proposed group signature schemes are impractical for large groups, as the size of signatures. In the proposed scheme, the calculation of the operations are based on the number of group users. The size of signatures and the size of user keys are determined. But the size of keys of group director are linear in the number of group users, thus decreasing the storage space of the scheme can be part of the future work. But, this scheme is efficient for large groups. Also, compared with other schemes, the proposed scheme can be used in e-voting schemes directly because of two unique characteristics, the linkability and the traceability. Table 2 shows the comparisons between dissimilar group signatures.

FUTURE RESEARCH DIRECTIONS

In the future work, we will consider conditions that undertaking an attack of Faugere and Spaenlehaner versus Akiyama *et al.* to make it works better. Also, we can produce keys that are more arbitrary than the keys of Faugere and Spaenlehaner applied then we can proved the effectiveness of their attack by our tests. In their attack we can infer data of the divisor polynomial f by finding the resulting of se-

Table 2. The comparisons between dissimilar group signatures

Characteristic	Chaum [1]	Petersen [25]	Ateniese [5]	Proposed Scheme
Cryptography Assumption	Discrete Log	Discrete Log	RSA and Diffie-Hellman	Isomorphism of Polynomial
Quantum Attack	Yes	Yes	Yes	No
Sign	$O(n)$	$O(n)$	Constant	Constant
Verify	$O(n)$	$O(n)$	Constant	Constant
Open	$O(n)$	$O(n)$	Constant	Constant
Size of Signature	$O(n)$	$O(n)$	Constant	Constant
Size of Key	$O(n)$	Constant	Constant	Director: $O(n)$ User: Constant

lected polynomials according to the encrypted document. Then, we can examine the scheme by using the theory of Gröbner basis computation.

However, we can introduced another multivariate public-key system by applying wild automorphisms, which are deeply examines in affine algebraic geometry. However, we create the private key as selected polynomial functions created by $\rho -$ derivations, and announce the composition of such functions. As, we employ polynomial functions which ranges are high, the length of keys and the time complexity of scheme tend to be considerable. Thus, we have to decrease the key length and the time complexity.

CONCLUSION

This Chapter presents the group signature scheme under multivariate asymmetric key cryptography. Its security based on the isomorphism of polynomial problem and the secure hash function. Compared with other group signature schemes, the proposed scheme is design to e-voting schemes. Because of two characteristics, the unlinkability and the traceability, the proposed scheme can convince the additional requirements of the e-voting schemes. Also, the size of signatures and a calculation overhead are regardless of the number of group users. It is efficient for large groups.

REFERENCES

Akiyama, K., Goto, Y., & Miyake, H. (2009). An Algebraic Surface Cryptosystem, public-key cryptography-PKC09. *Lecture Notes in Computer Science*, 5443, 425-442.

Ateniese G., Camenisch J., Joye M., and Tsudik G., (2000). A practical and provably secure coalition-resistant group signature scheme. In *Advances in Cryptology-CRYPTO 2000*. Springer.

Camenisch, J., & Stadler, M. (1997). Efficient group signatures schemes for large groups. In *Advances in Cryptology-CRYPTO 1997*. Springer.

Chaum, D., & Heijst van. (1991). Group signatures. In *Advances in Cryptology-EUROCRYPT 1991*. Springer.

Chen, L., & Pedersen, T. (1994). New group signature schemes. In *Advances in Cryptology-EUROCRYPT 1994*. Springer.

Ding, J. (2004). A new variant of the Matsumoto-Imai cryptosystem through perturbation. In *Public-key cryptography-PKC 2004*. Springer.

Ding, J. (2011). *Method to produce new multivariate public key cryptosystems*. Patents US 7961876 B2.

Fangere, J., & Spaenlehaner, P. (2010). Algebraic Cryptanalysis of the PKC2010 Algebaic Surface Cryptosystem. Public-Key Cryptography PK- 2010. Springer.

Huang, N. (2014). Analysis of a multivariate public-key cryptosystem and Its application in software copy protection. *Journal of Software*, 9(8), 8. doi:10.4304/jsw.9.8.2010-2017

Li. (2011). *Gröbner Bases in Ring Theory*. World Scientific Publishing.

Ogura, N. (2012). *On multivariate public-key cryptosystem* (PhD Dissertation). Tokyo Metropolitan University.

Patarin, J. (1996). Hidden fields equations and isomorphism of polynomials: Two new families of asymmetric algorithms. In *Advances in Cryptology-EUROCRYPT 1996*. Springer.

Petersen, H. (1998). How to convert any digital signature scheme into a group signature scheme. In Security Protocols. Springer.

Petzoldt, A., Bulygin, S., & Buchmann, J. (2010). A multivariate signature scheme with a partially cyclic public-key. *Proceedings of the 2nd international conference on symbolic computation and cryptography (SCC 2010)*, 229-235. 10.1007/978-3-642-17401-8_4

Shor, P. (1994). Algorithms for quantum computation: Discrete logarithms and factoring. *Proceeding 35nd Annual Symposium on Foundations of Computer Science*, 124-134. 10.1109/SFCS.1994.365700

Yang, B., & Chen, J. (2003). A more secure and efficacious TTS signature scheme. In *Information Security and Cryptology-ICISC 2003*. Springer.

KEY TERMS AND DEFINTIONS

Cryptography: Is the science and study of secret writing.

Group Signature Scheme: Is a method for allowing a member of a group to anonymously sign a message on behalf of the group.

Hacker: Is a term used by some to mean a clever programmer and by other, especially those in popular media to mean someone who tries to break into computer systems.

Isomorphism of Polynomials Problem: Is a well-known problem studied in multivariate cryptography. It is related to the hardness of the key recovery of some cryptosystems.

Multivariate Cryptography: Is the generic term for asymmetric cryptography based on multivariate polynomials over finite fields. Solving systems of multivariate polynomial equations is proven to be NP-hard. Today multivariate quadratics can be used only to build signatures.

NP-Hard Problems: Is a class of problems that are, at least as hard as the hardest problems in NP. More precisely, a problem H is NP-hard when every problem L in NP can be reduced in polynomial time.

Quantum Computers: Is the direct use of quantum-mechanical phenomena, to perform operations on data. Quantum computers are different from digital computers based on transistors. Whereas digital computers require data to be encoded into binary digits (bits), quantum computation uses quantum bits which can be in super positions of states.

This research was previously published in the Encyclopedia of Information Science and Technology, Fourth Edition edited by Mehdi Khosrow-Pour, pages 4898-4908, copyright year 2018 by Information Science Reference (an imprint of IGI Global).

Chapter 19
Hexa–Dimension Code of Practice for Data Privacy Protection

Wanbil William Lee
Wanbil & Associates, Hong Kong

ABSTRACT

Cyberspace inhabitants live under threat of a complex data privacy protection problem in a technology-dependent and information-intensive phenomenon grown out of a vicious circle. The frontline information security professionals are among the first to bear the brunt and are in dire need of guidance for enforcing effectively the policies and standards and mitigating the adverse consequences of data privacy breaches since the policy statements are invariably dated due to the rapid advances of the technology, limited to cope with techno-socio threats, inadequate to deal with the well-equipped and cunning cybercriminals, and vague and less than user-friendly, or simply difficult to absorb and follow. A framework that comprises the newly developed hexa-dimension code of practice based on the six-dimension metric (represented by the LESTEF model) and an operationalization scheme are proposed, where the code in which the gist of the adopted policies is incorporated promises to be a handy reference or a quick guide capable of alleviating the information security staff's burden.

INTRODUCTION

Contemporary cyberspace inhabitants live and work in a *technology-driven information-intensive* era, a *phenomenon* born out of a *vicious circle*. The consequence is a mixture of blessing and nightmare. Data protection emerges as a critical concern and data privacy protection an urgent and vital problem for information security management. Given the situation, the front-line information security personnel is among the first to bear the brunt and in dire need of a pragmatic guidance.

A recently developed set of International Data Privacy Principles as a reference can be considered for tackling the *first need* (Zankl, 2016). Hong Kong's Personal Data (Personal) Privacy Ordinance (PDPO, 1966), a data protection principle-based law like many others legislated in western jurisdic-

DOI: 10.4018/978-1-5225-7492-7.ch019

tions, which has been in force for a number of years (Chang, 2016), can make a contribution the *second need*. To address the *third need*, a framework that comprises a 6-d code based on the 6-d metric and an operationalization scheme is recommended.

A first-cut version of the framework, which was recently presented to an audience of Information Security Management specialists (Lee, 2015a), together with the rationale of the metric, the definition of the code and its worthiness for recommendation, and an indicative guideline to operationalize the code, are described in this article.

BACKGROUND

The Vicious Circle and Technology-Driven Information-Intensive Phenomenon

Netizens are provided with such technologies as *Customer Relationship Management*, *Web-lining* and *Call Centre*, and so on; they can by means of these facilities conduct their daily activities more efficiently and effectively, and optimize the outcome of these activities, because they are better-informed and able to innovate marketing, to accelerate business promotion, to enlarge data storage capacity and communication coverage, to increase retrieval facilities, and to improve transaction speed in a more transparent and open environment. But then they will need to rely increasingly heavily on the technologies. While transparency and communication keep on improving, more and more data are consumed and correspondingly generated. This is akin to a vicious circle that "the happier the consumers of information and the higher the demand for more information leading to heavier reliance on the technology". Or in other words, as the suppliers of goods or providers of services generate more and more data in order to sustain transparency and maintain the market share thus gained, the consumers demand more and more information after having enjoyed good bargains, and consequently, the technology expands storage capacity to process the increase in volume of the data generated, and upgrades processing power to handle the increase in complexity of the applications required. This can be called a technology-driven information-intensive phenomenon. (See Figure 1).

The consequence of the technology-driven information-intensive phenomenon is good and bad. The good is the accelerated arrival of such technologies as Big Data, Cloud Computing, Internet of Things and social engineering tools. These technologies enable integration of massive, scattered datasets, efficient interpretation of the integrated data, and speedier communication of the information. An obvious benefit is that with a huge amount of information being made available, the cyber-world becomes more transparent and netizens are better informed. And the bad is that there emerges numerous additional security threats bred in the loopholes in the new technologies, in the use of them or in the facilities enabled by the massive volume of data they generate, which the cyber-miscreants are ever lurking around to exploit when detected. However, it is noteworthy that some clandestine activities which are brought to light, for example, the Snowden episode (*South China Morning Post*, 2013) and the Panama Papers leak (Wilson, 2016), can be beneficial to some people/organizations and adversary to others.

Data Privacy Protection Problem

The problem is rooted in the *way* the data are collected about and are used adversely against data subjects, and in the *right* of the data subjects to that data. It has to deal the *techno-ethical-risk* which is originated

Figure 1. A conceptual graph of the circle and the phenomenon

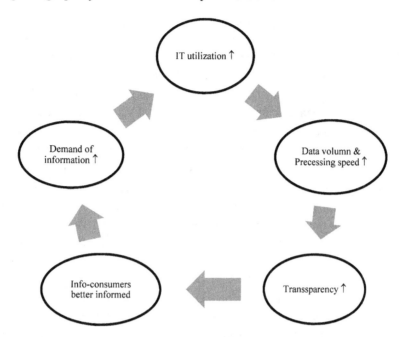

in the way the technology is applied and the human users of the technology and the data, though the technology per se is neutral, yet the use of the technology is not (Parker, 1986; Neumann, 1995; and Williams, 1997). The protection of data privacy means to ensure that data privacy is not breached, that is, the data content is securely stored and accessed only with proper authority, and that the right of the data subjects not abused. Solving the problem means developing, reviewing, and implementing information protection and data privacy policies, standards, guidelines and processes (the policies), and mitigation measures; it also means identifying new technology risk and ensuring that the policies are appropriately enhanced, communicated and complied with, and that mitigation measures are properly implemented.

The issue of data privacy invasion and the harmful impacts thereof have extended beyond the individuals and corporations to the regional/national governments, instanced by the UK House of Commons' advocating a data ethics council and more urgency on data privacy, and sometime later the UK Government accepting the data ethics council proposal (*Computer Weekly*, 2016). These are strong reasons to suggest that data privacy security is no longer a personal and corporate concern but also a concern of governments, and international organizations, much more so than ever before.

Data Privacy and Concept of Data Privacy Category

Data privacy, which is basically about collecting and using the data about individuals and organizations, also about the right of the data subjects to that data, is hitherto taken as a personal (individual) as well as an impersonal (corporate) issue. It is *personal data privacy* if the data subjects refer to individuals; it is *corporate data privacy* if the data subjects refer to organizations including government agencies. For example, the secret formula that a corporation adopts in determining the special fringe benefits in addition the total annual remuneration (which is normally published in the annual report) as a means to retain the service of their top-ranked staff is not trade secret but corporate privacy, and accessing or revealing it without authority is an act of breaching corporate data privacy.

This categorization is necessary. There are two supporting reasons for this view. The first reason is that an individual makes a decision differently depending on his/her role: "as a member of an organization, the individual makes decisions not in relationship to personal needs and results, but in an impersonal sense as part of the organizational intent" (Barnard, 1938). The second reason is that the consequences of data privacy breach might mean differently to the individual vis-à-vis a group (organization) due to four considerations. The first consideration is the data owner's right to control over the access to and use of the information. The second consideration is the owner's integrity and provision of confidential data that include such personal data as biometric measurement (in the case of individuals) or corporate data as the formula adopted by a company to determine the hidden portion of benefits in each senior executive's total annual remuneration (hidden because such information is usually withheld from a company's annual report) (in the case of business concerns) (bodily privacy). The third consideration is the data being observed by surveillance and the like (behavioural privacy). The last consideration is freedom of communication that includes speech or expression and dialogue with third parties (communicational privacy).

The dichotomy is recognized in the International Data Privacy Principles (Zankl, 2016), but generally missed in the extant data for example, the Personal Data (Privacy) Ordinance of Hong Kong (DPDO, 1966). It pays, it is argued, all stakeholders, particularly those involved in law making and enforcement, and the information security scholars and practitioners to be clear about the hitherto muddled concept.

Data Privacy Protection and Changes in Demand and Status

Data protection has long been regarded as a technical and economic matter and requires technical actions to ensure accuracy, completeness, integrity and availability of the data content, and to admit only authorized access. However, the impact on the scope and level of data privacy breach has changed, extending from personal/corporate to governmental and the UK government pronouncement alluded earlier proves a case in point. Also, the nature data privacy breach has changed because the problem and the consequences thereof are found to be of techno-economic as well as legal, ethical, social and ecological.

Limitations of the Extant Policies and Code of Conduct/Practice

The policies and standards in current use are invariably *dated* due to the rapid advances of the technologies, *limited* to cope with techno-socio threats as a result of the technology-driven information phenomenon, and *inadequate* to deal with the well-equipped and cunning cyber-miscreants. This is an obvious shortcoming.

Further, the policy statements tend to be vague and less than user-friendly or simply difficult to absorb and follow, easily forgotten and probably ignored in the end. For example, a 70-page Code of Professional Conduct for the Registered Medical Practitioners (Hong Kong Medical Council, 2009) is certainly unpalatable for the busy doctors. Another case in point is that when asked, the Deputy Commissioner of a police force could not tell what the code was, though he admitted being aware of one in existence and posted on the force's web-site. Alluded to earlier, the text of the policy and the code tend to be difficult to comprehend, wordy, and lengthy. This is another limitation.

On the one hand, the extant policies usually focus on the quantitative/tangible/technical efficiency, aiming at achieving targets against such indicators as *return on investment* (ROI), *net present value* (NPV) and *payback period* based on cost-benefit (Portney, 2008) and risk considerations (Wharton, 1992; Moore, et al, 1976), and satisfying the minimum requirements of the law. In some cases, ethical acceptability is embedded in professionalism but hardly touches or misses the qualitative/intangible social desirability (despite the rhetoric by some organizations in response to *corporate social responsibility* CSR), and ecological sustainability is hardly into consideration (despite Green Computing which advocates environment-friendly and paper-free design and application). On the other hand, professionals (in the field of Science and Technology, like others) grow up under the influence of the *misinterpretation of risk* and the *flawed curricula* across science and technology (Lee, 2015b), and their decision-making mentality developed along the Simon doctrine which is essentially to "select the alternative, among those available, which will lead to the most complete achievement of your goals" (Simon, 1976b). The goals are not necessarily personal despite the personal possessive adjective, according to Barnard (1938) who asserted that "the decisions that an individual makes are quite distinct from his personal choice" so as a member of an organization, the individual makes decisions not in relationship to personal needs and results, but in an impersonal sense as part of the organizational intent. This is why the policy, a product of our decision, and the code of practice/conduct are inherently technical and financial, and evaluated in terms of financial performance/economic value, and found short when dealing with many a problem commonly found in *post-implementation* and *post-contract* situations. It is noteworthy what IT professionals face frequently daily is of an ethical and/or a social nature. This is an inherent weakness, a hidden reason.

Many organizations have a code of conduct in place but just as many lack effective to encourage staff to familiarize and comply with their code. So, it is not uncommon to find that the code exists in name and not in substance. This is arguably a limitation, definitely an operational issue.

RECOMMENDED SOLUTION

Information security policy is propelled to centre-stage by the protection problem, and the front-line functional group is among the first to bear the brunt. To alleviate some burdens on the front-line information security staff who are always working against a tight schedule, a handy reference or a quick guide in the form of a code of conduct or practice, into which the gist of the adopted policies is incorporated, as an aid, was conceived. This document will contribute to cultivate a corporate culture of ethics conducive to the compliance with the data privacy protection policy organization-wide. A framework that comprises a 6-d code based on the 6-d metric and an operationalization scheme to make the code work, is proposed.

The Hexa-Dimension Metric and Its Rationale

The hexa-dimension LESTEF (pronounced "*lest ye forget*"), which was initially conceived as a checklist for decision making in technology-driven and information-intensive organizations, is proposed for developing a code of practice or corporate charter as an aid for ensuring and enhancing information security policies including data privacy preservation. By implication, hefty amount of money is invested in the expensive technologies, thus it is a matter of course to expect a justifiable return on that the investment (*financial viability*) and an optimized utilization of the technologies (*technical effectiveness*). In the same vein, huge amount of information that is generated can be abused, thus *legal validity*, *ethical acceptance*, and *social acceptability*. Running the technologies consumes a lot of natural resources (electricity, water, paper, etc.), and generates air and noise pollution, thus *ecological sustainability* – the six attributes representing efficiency (requirements) of the hexa-dimension model.

The Hexa-Dimension Code of Practice/Conduct

Code of Conduct

In general, a code of conduct or practice comprises a set of rules and regulations that encapsulate the gist of the policies and standards adopted by the organization. It has arguably the capability to provide a guide, a handy reference, and a reminder to the stakeholders, especially the constantly busy front-line operational staff.

If properly and appropriately formulated and articulated, the code would be useful in permeating the policies and standards throughout the organization and around, thus cultivating a corporate-wide ethical, professional conduct. While such codes may serve to deter potential offensive actions, they are limited in driving home those rules or standards as they can rely only and purely on the moral obligation of the stakeholders concerned primarily because violation of the code by itself does not in general attract any criminal charges. Auxiliary measures must put in force to arrive at desirable results, such as executive actions that empower to grant rewards and to impose punishment (for example, annual performance appraisal).

The Hexa-Dimension Code

Organizations of various varieties might have some kind of code of practice in place. However, the extant codes invariably tend to focus on technical, financial and probably legal issues; they are insufficient when considering also social, ethical and probably ecological issues. The hexa-dimension code based on the hexa-dimension model poises to make up for the deficiency.

Operationalization Schedule

Prerequisite

To operationalize, it is mandatory to secure the support of the Board of Directors with respect to corporate policy aspects and to aquire the supporting infrastructures that include the organization's human resources management (HRM), legal, finance, and ICT functional units with respect to technical support and reference, and have an appraisal of ethical consistency in conduct included in an annual performance review (by the HRM Department). In addition, and ideally, GCF Computing (Patrignani & Whitehouse, 2014) be adopted. The characteristic features of GCF Computing are provided in Table 1.

Procedure

There are three major preparatory steps (summarized in Table 2):

Table 1. GCF computing

GCF	Target	Enabler	Contribute to
Good Computing	Workable & technically efficient deliverables	Internet technologies, Big Data, Cloud Computing, Ubiquitous computing (Evasive Computing), etc.	Legal, Technical & Financial efficiencies
Clean Computing	Energy & materials saving	Green Computing	Environmental efficiency
Fair Computing	Corporate social responsibility	Ethical Computing (Lee, 2015b)	Social & Ethical efficiencies

Table 2. Schedule of operationalization

Generic				User specific	
Attributes/ Factors	Remarks	Control	Targets	Drivers (*)	Supported by
Legal validity	Abiding the law, rule & regulations currently in force	External	Local law and convention	Corporate counsel /legal dept.	Good Computing
Social desirability	Beneficial to all stakeholders including the general public	External	Local culture and habit; standards for perceivable benefits to primary stakeholders and the public		Fair Computing
Ecological sustainability	Friendly to natural and industrial/business environment	External	Policy/guidelines for energy/ materials saving; ecology related law (if any)		Clean Computing
Ethical acceptability	Consistent with ethical principles	Internal	Corporate social responsibility; corporate culture	PR, HRM	Fair Computing
Technical effectiveness	Use up-to-date technology to meet targets effectively and efficiently	Internal	Sufficient & necessary human & technological resources to support infrastructural support	ICT, HRM	Good Computing
Financial viability	financially sound and viable	Internal	Corporate policy (performance metrics: operational goal, risk absorption standards & limits, etc.)	Finance, Operations	Good Computing

- Identify the relevant critical factors depending on the target end-users (nature of operation corporate-wide or of a functional unit – for example, environmental impact is critical for a mining company or a factory, but may probably be skipped for an Information Security Unit)
- Secure the support of the Board of Directors and the supporting infrastructures including in an annual performance review to assess awareness and compliance of the code in carrying out assignments/duties (by the HRM Department).
- Determine a schedule for quantifying the elements of each factor for measuring, prioritizing and balancing the factors and the steps to be taken to measure the effectiveness.

Briefly,

- Legal validity is to ensure that the laws current in force and the organization's rules and conventions are abided at the advice of the corporate counsel or the Legal Department, and is measured by the extent and degree the law is obeyed.
- Social desirability is to make sure that the benefit of all stakeholders including that the public has been considered and deliberated consistent with local culture and custom and can be measured by survey results of the extent of public benefited based on the ethical principles of utility and consequence.
- Ecological sustainability means the actions taken must be friendly (not harmful) to the environment and is measured by indication of energy/materials saving, noise and air pollution, radiation emission rate and so on using EIA (environmental impact assessment) (Hong Kong Government).
- Ethical acceptability demands that the actions taken must be consistent with ethical principles with the help of the corporation's Public Relations Unit and Human Resource Management Department, and can be measured using the Ethical Matrix method to assess the consistency with the relevant ethical principles of duty and reciprocity (Lee, 2015b).
- Technical effectiveness means using up-to-date technology to meet targets effectively and efficiently.
- Financial viability is to ensure that the actions taken are financially sound and viable, consistent with the corporation's performance metric on operational goal, risk absorption standards and limits, etc. as advised by the Finance and Operations experts, and is measured by ROI and NPV.

FUTURE RESEARCH DIRECTIONS

The concept that a decision should meet the six criteria is new, but the individual criterion itself in the hexa-dimension metric model is not new. The metric has the potential to serve others purposes, for example, Management Science, in enhancing identification and evaluation of the relevant factors of the traditional and popularly adopted decision model like the rationality and logic based Simon model (1976) which is no longer sufficient because decision makers are not always rational and sometimes non-rational, or judgmental decision making based on procedural or bounded rationality (Gigerenzer, 2001) and escalation of commitment decision making that "under certain conditions, decision makers who make an initial decision become overly committed to the original choice and then subsequently make decisions biased by psychological commitment" (McCarthy, Schoorman and Cooper (1993, p. 9). Also, that the decision variables are formulated and measured mainly in economic terms must be updated as they are also legal, ethical, social, and more recently, ecological in nature. This raises many questions that seek an answer, to name a few:

- The hexa-dimension code can be a prototype for designing a code of practice for an IT organization, as proposed in this article. At this exploratory stage, its efficiency needs to be demonstrated, field-tested and validated against actual results. An on-site study of its effectiveness as a handy reference at the different levels of the corporate is also a worthwhile exercise.
- Supporting infrastructures including human resources management action such annual performance appraisal and so on, must be in place and work in concert since the code would not by itself brings about the results desired as it is only a handy reference for the stakeholders, particularly employees. This raises two research questions: How the mechanisms concerned are coordinated

and cooperated? Can corporations or functional units expect an effective enforcement of the code of practice and an ethical atmosphere be cultivated corporate-wide or within a functional unit after a compulsory annual appraisal scheme that includes an assessment of ethical/social elements in the assigned duty is in force?

- An empirical study of applicability and acceptability of the hexa-dimension metric to enhance the chance and scope of finding factors likely to bring about ethical, social and ecological repercussion on decision making warrants serious consideration.

CONCLUSION

The information security professionals are in urgent need of effective and pragmatic guidance as the information security function in a technology-driven information-intensive environment becomes more complicated and the problems involved harder to handle due to the new socio-techno risks, and data privacy protection becomes a primary concern as privacy infringement occurs more frequently and leads to potentially devastating consequences to the individuals, corporations and governments. The newly developed framework, though at this embryonic stage of growth still awaiting empirical evidence and popular acceptance in the IT arena, coupled with the Personal Data (Privacy) Ordinance (Hong Kong's privacy law) (Chang, 2016) and the International Data Privacy Principles (Zankl, 2016), poises to play a useful role in releasing some burden on the extant policies and standards. It noteworthy that

- An international standard is useful and necessary when regular (hard) law often fails to handle issues such as those arising from inter-border data transfer or cross-border trading, and when formulating corporate policies that meet not only legal but also ethical demands.
- Privacy laws of many jurisdictions are based on the principle-based OECD Privacy Guidelines. Many of these principles have been implemented by jurisdictions across the globe including Australia, Canada, Hong Kong and the UK, and the ethical dimensions of these principles have been realized and expressed in legal terms. Many organizations have found themselves insufficient to follow just the letters and they must also follow the spirit of the law to satisfy a more knowledgeable public who know and expect their privacy rights.
- The hexa-dimension Code of Conduct/Practice aims at alerting stakeholders to exercise their duties so that they do not breaking the law in force; do not harm to the individuals and society at large; are not wasteful of the resources available (the computer facilities, the workforce, the budget, etc.); and are environmentally-friendly. Since different organizations have their own unique policies, thus code of conduct, there can be no universal receipt but a general guideline. Since the code by itself is limited in enforcing compliance with the policies and standards, a framework was developed and a 3-step procedure are recommended.
- Decision makers may face unavoidable competing circumstances when considering the various issues including those of ethical and social nature, balancing the competing issues is necessary in resolving them. Apart from the linear menus, the Ethical Matrix (Lee, 2015b) is worthy of consideration.
- The hexa-dimension code of practice will be of interest not only to the information security personnel but also to the practitioners and scholars in Information Science and Technology and perhaps other fields such as Information Systems Audit, Management, and Public Policy.

REFERENCES

Association for Computing Machinery. (1992). *Code of Ethics and Professional Conduct*. Retrieved February 13, 2016, from http://www.acm.org/about-acm/acm-code-of-ethics-and-professional-conduct

Barnard, C. I. (1938). *The Functions of the Executive*. Cambridge, MA: Harvard University Press. Retrieved April 13, 2016, from https://en.wikipedia.org/wiki/Herbert_A_Simon#CITEREFBarnard1938

House of Commons Science and Technology Committee calls for Data Ethics Council. (n.d.). Retrieved February 13, 2016, from http://www.computerweekly.com/news/4500272963/House-of-Commons-Science-and-Technology-Committee-calls-for-Data-Ethics-Council

Government accepts data ethics council proposal. (n.d.). Retrieved on 28 April 2016, from http://www.computerweekly.com/news/450294474/Government-accepts-data-ethics-council-proposal

Donaldson, J. (1992). The Ethics of Risk Management. In J. Ansell & F. Wharton (Eds.), *Risk Analysis, Assessment and Management*. Chichester, UK: John Wiley & Sons.

Gigerenzer, G. (2001). *Decision Making: Nonrational Theories. In International Encyclopedia of the Social and Behavioral Sciences* (Vol. 5, pp. 3304–3309). Oxford, UK: Elsevier. doi:10.1016/B0-08-043076-7/01612-0

Hong Kong Government. (n.d.). *A guide to the EIA (Environmental Impact Assessment) Ordinance*. Retrieved on April 25, 2016, from http://www.epd.gov.hk/eia/english/guid/index1.html

Lee, W. W. (2015a). Ignorant of ethical pitfalls can hurt information security: Implications for IT users & Information Security Professionals. Special Seminar on Information Security, the Hong Kong Jockey Club.

Lee, W. W. (2015b). Ethical Computing. In M. Khosrow-Pour (Ed.), *Encyclopedia of Information Science and Technology* (3rd ed.; pp. 2991–2999). doi:10.4018/978-1-4666-5888-2.ch292

McCarthy, A. M., Schoorman, F. D., & Cooper, A. C. (1993). Reinvestment decision by entrepreneurs: Rational Decision-making or escalation of commitment? *Journal of Business Venturing*, 8(1), 9–24. doi:10.1016/0883-9026(93)90008-S

Moore, P. G., Thomas, H., Bunn, D. W., & Hampton, J. M. (1976). *Case Studies in Decision Analysis*. Penguin Books.

Neumann, P. G. (1995). *Computer Related Risk*. New York, NY: ACM Press /Addison-Wesley.

Parker, D. B. (1986). Computer Crime. *Financial Executive*, 2(12), 31–33.

PDPO (1966). *The Personal Data (Privacy) Ordinance*, Chapter 486 (amended 2012 and 2013). Retrieved February 13, 2016, from https://www.pcpd.org.hk/english/files/pdpo.pdf

Patrignani, N., & Whitehouse, D. (2014). Slow Tech: A quest for good, clean and fair ICT. *Journal of Information, Communication and Ethics in Society*, 78-9.

Portney, P. R. (2008). Benefit-Cost Analysis. In D. R. Henderson (Ed.), *Concise Encyclopedia of Economics* (2nd ed.). Indianapolis, IN: Library of Economics and Liberty.

Simon, H. A. (1976a). From Substantive to Procedural Rationality. In S. J. Latsis (Ed.), *Method and Appraisal in Economics*. Cambridge, UK: Cambridge University Press. doi:10.1017/CBO9780511572203.006

Simon, H. A. (1976b). *Administrative Behaviour* (3rd ed.). New York: The Free Press.

South China Morning Post. (2013). Retrieved April 17, 2016, from http://www.scmp.com/news/hong-kong/article/1259422/edward-snowden-let-hong-kong-people-decide-my-fate

Wharton, F. (1992). Risk Management: Basic Concepts and General Principles. In J. Ansell & F. Wharton (Eds.), *Risk Analysis, Assessment and Management*. Chichester, UK: John Wiley.

Williams, K. (1997). Safeguarding Companies from Computer/Software Fraud. *Management Accounting*, *78*(8), 18.

Wilson, S. (2016). The Panama Papers scandal. *MoneyWeek*. Retrieved April 17, 2016, from http://moneyweek.com/the-panama-papers-scandal

ADDITIONAL READING

Berthold, M. (1994). Hong Kong's data privacy proposals, *Privacy Law and Policy Reporter*, 124. Retrieved February 13, 2016, from http://www.austlii.edu.au/au/journals/PrivLawPRpr/1994/124.html

International Journal of Green Computing (IJGC). Retrieved February 13, 2016, from www.igi-global.com/journal/international-journal-green-computing.../1175

Lee, W. W. (2014). Why Computer Ethics Matters to Computer Auditing. *ISACA Journal*, *2*, 48–52.

Lee, W. W., & Chan, K. C. C. (2008). Computer Ethics: a Potent Weapon for Information Security Management. *Information Systems Audit & Control Journal*, December (www.isaca.org/jonline)

Moore, P. G., & Thomas, H. (1976). *The Anatomy of Decisions*. Marmonsworth: Penguin Books. *OECD Guidelines on the Protection of Privacy and Transborder Flows of Personal Data*. Retrieved February 13, 2016, from http://www.oecd.org/sti/ieconomy/oecdguidelinesontheprotectionofprivacyandtransborderflowsofpersonaldata.htm

Pazowski, P. (2015). *Green computing: latest practices and technologies for ICT sustainability*. Retrieved February 13, 2016, from www.toknowpress.net/ISBN/978-961-6914-13-0/papers/ML15-377.pdf

KEY TERMS AND DEFINITIONS

Data Privacy: Can be personal data privacy if the data subjects refer to individuals or corporate data privacy if the data subjects refer to organizations including government agencies.

GCF Computing: Slow Tech is not a technology that is slow but a movement that parallels with the same concept of the Slow Food movement. Slow Food International claimed in 1989 that the Slow Food Movement was set up to "counter the rises of fast food and fast life": to strive for good food (food that tastes good, is a pleasure to eat and selected according to its quality), clean food (food that is produced by such a process that respects the environment and should promote biodiversity and sustainability), and fair food (food that is cultivated and produced by ways that must respect the farmers). GCF Computing (Good Computing, Clean Computing, Fair Computing) was proposed and defined following the Slow Tech concept (Patrignani & Whitehouse, 2014).

International Data Privacy Principles: Comprise 13 principles (Zankl, 2016).

Operationalization Scheme: Acquire Board's endorsement and infrastructural support from other relevant departments, and determine the relevant criteria/factors according to the nature of the problem and the target users and a quantification system for measuring against and balancing the criteria.

PDPO Data Protection Principles (DPP): (1) Data Collection and Purpose; (2) Accuracy and Retention; (3) Data Use; (4) Data Security; (5) Openness; and (6) Data Access and Correction (https://www.pcpd.org.hk/english/data_privacy_law/ordinance_at_a_Glance/ordinance.html).

PDPO: Personal Data (Privacy) Ordinance (Hong Kong's privacy law), enacted in 1995 (https://www.pcpd.org.hk/english/files/pdpo.pdf).

Post-Contract Problem (an example): The specification was approved by provider and client, and contract duly signed. A senior project consultant who was assigned to the project discovered a fault in the specification, a fault in the inventory control function. Inventory control is a critical function for the business of the client, a fashion boutique, because supply and demand of the goods for sale is time –critical and zero error-tolerance is expected according to the specification. The fault was confirmed after the consultant's site visit. The consultant faces the dilemma: Keep quiet or tell the boss or the client or both.

Post-Implementation Problem (An Example): An online monitoring system was implemented to replace an existing offline help-desk platform. The Executive Vice President (EVP) is impressed by the performance, particularly the online monitoring capability provided by the system, and asks the Chief Information Officer (CIO) to have a copy of the system installed in her office to track drug dealing allegedly taken place on company premises. Dilemmas that need to be addressed include deviation of approval of acquisition, privacy invasion, corporate image damage, professionalism (CIO), duty (EVP); treated as a means (staff); staff morale & corporate policy (Firm).

Technology-Driven Information-Intensive Phenomenon: A state that characterizes the modus operandi in cyberspace and attributes to the vicious circle: More and more information is needed to sustain more transparent business operations, thus satisfying the more demanding consumers of information; higher utilization of more technologies is needed to generate more information to handle the enlarged data volume, and to further increase the processing speed.

The Data Privacy Protection Problem: To develop and implement data privacy policies, standards, guidelines and processes (the policies), to ensure that the policies are appropriately enhanced, communicated and complied with, and to devise a set of effective mitigation measures.

The Solution: A *hexa-dimension code of practice*, a list of rules and regulations that encapsulates the gist of the policies and standards adopted by the organization, and embraces the six criteria.

This research was previously published in the Encyclopedia of Information Science and Technology, Fourth Edition edited by Mehdi Khosrow-Pour, pages 4909-4919, copyright year 2018 by Information Science Reference (an imprint of IGI Global).

Chapter 20

Information and Communication Technology Ethics and Social Responsibility

Tomas Cahlik
Charles University Prague, Czech Republic & University of Economics Prague, Czech Republic

ABSTRACT

Information and communication technologies (ICTs) have penetrated during the last 20 years all human activities everywhere on the Earth. Humanity has entered into the information age, virtual reality and even virtual worlds have been crated. The basic ethical questions stay as they have always been: How are we to live? What are we to be? Of course, we ought to live good lives and be good persons. The aim of this chapter is to specify what "living a good life" and "being a good person" could be in the information age and to identify challenges and opportunities ICTs offer in this context. It is impossible to predict if the positive impacts outweigh the negative ones. Anyway, it is impossible to stop the development of ICTs. The open question is if the society ought to try to increase the costs of ICTs activities that are negative from the ethical point of view and to increase benefits of activities that are positive from the ethical point of view, who ought to do it and how. All members of society have responsibility to participate in discourse of this question.

INTRODUCTION

Information and Communication Technologies (ICTs) have penetrated during the last 20 years all human activities everywhere on the Earth. Humanity has entered into the information age, virtual reality and even virtual worlds have been crated.

The basic ethical questions stay as they have always been: How are we to live? What are we to be? Basic answers are, of course, that we ought to live good lives and be good persons.

The aim of this article is:

DOI: 10.4018/978-1-5225-7492-7.ch020

- To specify what "living a good life" and "being a good person" could be in the information age;
- To identify some challenges and opportunities ICTs offer in this context.

Having absolutely stabilized basic questions and basic answers makes the methodology of ethics quite different from the methodology in sciences. In sciences, one starts with a thorough review of previous research, specifies some new and interesting research question, makes hypotheses about possible answers and bases argumentation on data. In ethics, one reflects problems of the current age in a mirror that was created centuries ago and has been polished by many ethical reflections ever since. Forms of ethical texts are rich: dialogs, even poems, but the most used form is an essay.

BACKGROUND

Literature review in research articles is used for showing that the research described in the article fits into research themes that are interesting for contemporary research community. Literature review in ethical reflections is used differently, just for illustration of ideas that have been published in the area of interest and for "opening the scene".

Looking into the Web of Science database in September 2015 and using keywords "information technology", "ethics" and "social responsibility" 60 entries are obtained (from that 55 articles or conference proceedings), 31 entries being published since 2010. This reveals not high but steady and increasing activity on the interdisciplinary border between ICTs and that part of ethics that is linked to social responsibility.

Looking closer into the content of those articles, following themes can be identified in the last decade:

- Ethical questions linked with the creation and use of "big data", including creation of agreed standards of good practice - e.g. (Rizk&Choueiri, 2006), (Light,& McGrath, 2010), (Celen, & Seferoglu, 2013);
- Development of sustainable information society - e.g. (Tsai&Chen, 2013), (Busch, 2011), (Nieme la&Ikonen&Leikas&Kantola&Kulju&Tammela&Ylikauppila, 2014) in the sense of an inclusive and environmentally friendly society; application of precautionary principle in the development of ICTs (Som&Hilty& Kohler, 2009);
- Corporate social responsibility of both ICT suppliers and users – e.g. (Tsai&Chen, 2013), (Busch, 2011), (Vaccaro&Madsen, 2009), including suggestions for standards of good practice (Patrignani&Whitehouse, 2014) and how to enable consumers to push companies to behave ethically with the use of ICTs (Watts& Wyner, 2011);
- University social responsibility (Arntzen, 2010); new teaching and learning culture based on ICTs (Stepien, 2010).

This indicates research activity that is driven by applications and can be contrasted with the research activity from the years before, that was pushed by theoretical considerations. (Lianos, 2000) e.g. starts with sociological concepts and identifies the threat that ICTs can atomize society through making development of personal trust obsolete. Lianos uses credit card as an example: one does not need to be trusted by the provider of money, the only thing that is relevant is the validity of the card. Technical norms replace moral and social norms.

Research fields may have different dynamics. It is quite usual that after the theoretical development some themes or even the whole field dissolve in applications. Nevertheless, after some time, both practitioners and applied researchers may find it useful to return to more generalizing theoretical reflection. In this article, the most general level of ethical reflection is being considered.

Ethics as practical philosophy offers a lot of valuable ideas that have been generalized from the real life problems of the whole human history. In this article, especially ideas developed by utilitarian philosophers, existential philosophers and the proponents of the "virtue ethics" can be identified. Two more areas of ethics linked with this article are "ethics of norms" and "casuistry". Readers are advised to find more detailed summaries of those three schools and two areas on web.

"LIVING GOOD LIFE" AND "BEING A GOOD PERSON" IN THE INFORMATION AGE

Issues, Controversies, Problems

Let us identify three challenges and three opportunities ICTs directly offer in the context of ethics. This gives a framework to this article from which the discussion of economic costs and benefits stays mostly out, even if economic costs and benefits surely have ethical impacts.

Specification of the first challenge builds upon the above described conclusion in (Lianos, 2000) that technical norms replace moral and social norms. Problem is that the network of moral and social norms has always been considered as something absolutely necessary for the identity of specific society and that the dissolution of this network means atomization and threatens the whole society.

The second challenge is linked with the current research frontier of ICTs, with virtual reality. Economic and social thinking is strongly based on utilitarianism and its basic persuasion that for having a good life pleasures must be maximized and pains minimized. ICTs allow creating a virtual reality in which the choice of pleasures is almost unlimited and in which we are able to avoid pain. The basic question here is the authenticity of such a life. It can be easy and pleasant but it loses any sense.

Above the basic utilitarian life level, another level ought to be built in which we ask if our activities are right. What is the right activity has been discussed in Western thinking for centuries since Plato and two basic outcomes are as follows:

- In a right activity, humans are used not as tools only. E.g. authors of new software ought to take into consideration not only how much they earn but if the software allows better self-realization of users, too;
- Real circumstances must be taken into consideration in following the basic target of "being better humans". E.g. software firms must follow the profit motive as well as the moral one to stay in the business.

ICTs have not changed these basic outcomes but have surely changed the real circumstances and this opens the stage for discussion of what the right activities are in these changed circumstances. All new technologies have always done this, but what makes ICTs specific is the scale and speed of change.

One lives a good life if one realizes his or her potential in right activities. A person can develop its potential and become a virtuous person through cultivating its virtues and fighting its vices. Good people are virtuous people and there exists a positive correlation between being good people and doing right activities. So there exists a strong link between being a good person and living a good life.

The second challenge of ICTs lies in the possibility that people could be sucked too much into the virtual reality, enjoy pleasures there and try to avoid reality. Their lives would lose authenticity and they would not leave the basic utilitarian life level. Impacts on both the individual and society would be analogic to impacts of drugs addiction.

There exists a positive feedback between the first and second challenge: instead of being identified with a real society existing at some geographical place, people are identified with the usually anonymous social group sharing the same virtual reality. In the process of atomization of real society, the motivation for its members to find substitutes of social ties in virtual reality increases. This closes the loop.

In this context, we could ask about the geo-political impact of having socially atomized countries in which a lot of citizens avoid reality together with socially homogenous countries where people live more in reality. Let us imagine a possibly violent conflict and ask who would probably win in such a conflict? Or let us imagine mass immigration of people from the second type of countries to a country of the first type. What would happen? It is surely not socially responsible to ignore these scenarios.

The first opportunity of the virtual reality ICTs have created lies in quick detection of suspect economic, political and other social activities in a real society and in facilitating the discourse about such activities. By definition, discourse is discussion in which participants are free in the sense that they are not influenced by exogenous incentives or constraints in the expression of their opinions. Virtual reality, if it is free - without censorship - and anonymous offers an optimal environment for discourses on any topic. Discourses on suspect social activities help to create socially accepted moral norms and push firms and politicians to social responsibility.

The second opportunity lies in the enormous educational potential of the virtual world. For Aristotle, being educated was considered to be a virtue by itself, even if not being a moral virtue. For Plato, if people just knew what were right they would behave in that way. It may be too optimistic but we know that there exists a negative correlation between educational level in a country and e.g. crime.

Instead of discussing this intuitively clear opportunity on general level let us illustrate how ICTs can be used for benchmarking and looking for best practices in ethical issues. In (Codes of Ethics Collection), there are thousands of different ethical codes. Each of them presents norms that have been accepted by some organization (firm, association, university etc.). Ethical Codes are classified according to professional categories, one of them being "Computer and Information Science". In September 2015, 56 organizations are found in this category, some of them with ethical codes for specific activities, some of them with different versions of the same code showing how it has been developed in time.

Any organization interested in development of its ethical norms can use this enormous source to compare the norms it already has with norms of its peers in the Codes of Ethics Collection. In an internal discourse, it can then formulate and accept the best for itself.

We can see another positive feedback, now between both opportunities: educational material easily accessible through ICTs can be used in discourses and additional knowledge created in discourses becomes easily accessible through ICTs.

The third opportunity lies in using ICTs for supporting the creation of virtues and the third challenge in supporting the creation of vices. The lists of moral virtues and vices have been changing during the centuries since Aristotle and there is not full consent about what ought to be on the lists. The most of virtues and vices get stronger with the repetition of either good or bad activities.

Let us take the (List of virtues) and (List of vices) from the webpage http://www.virtuescience.com/, choose some of them and analyze how they can be strengthened by ICTs. (We could surely take any other list, but the advantage of these two lists is that the list of virtues has 120 items and the list of vices 17 only. This supports the optimistic attitude towards human nature.)

"Compassion" and "Charity": ICTs allow watching repeatedly and with high frequency poor people around the World what develops compassion among the most of watchers; psychologically especially among young people who are in the same time the most knowledgeable users of ICTs. This positive correlation can make this effect quite strong. ICTs offer a very easy way (e.g. donation through SMS) to do charitable activities what makes compassioned people to do such activities repeatedly. This strengthens the virtue charity.

"Curiosity", "Commitment" and "Creativity": Anderson in (Anderson, 2010) describes a nice example how web video powers global innovation. A slum boy watches video with street dance. Watching wakes up his curiosity and he makes commitment to master street dance himself. He surely has to be highly creative in transferring the knowledge from video into reality. There are millions of different activities and millions of web users, many of them behaving similarly as the slum boy, so ICTs have a very strong effect on these three virtues.

"Enthusiasm" and "Cooperation": For economists, it is really difficult to explain the very existence of the open source software or Wikipedia because of non-existence of material incentives. Possible explanation is following: Knowledgeable users of ICTs are usually quite enthusiastic about the possibilities ICTs offer. They form a global community and identify strongly with this community. This has created the situation in which they like to cooperate not for material benefit but for achieving a shared goal. This works if individual costs of cooperation are negligible, what they with the use of ICTs can really be. Social benefits are enormous.

"Chastity" as a virtue or "Lack of Chastity" as a vice: In this context, pornographic content of web sites ought to be discussed. Watching pornography repeatedly creates habit - sometimes addiction – and weakens chastity. This discussion is not relevant for all World societies, e.g. in Japan people do not consider chastity as having sexual context. Watching pornography is clearly linked with the second challenge of ICTs discussed above; real sexual activity can shift to virtual reality what could have demographic impacts.

"Sloth": Let us understand laziness as aversion to be active in the real world. Being active in that part of virtual reality that overlaps with reality perhaps weakens sloth; ICTs can increase the efficiency of our real activity what increases our motivation for doing it. Problem is that ICTs have created an enormous potential for procrastination – for doing less urgent but pleasurable tasks in preference to more urgent but less pleasurable ones. The seductive power can be strong and yielding to temptation is surely positively correlated with sloth.

Solutions and Recommendations

The positive impact of above discussed opportunities can neutralize or outweigh the negative impact of above discussed challenges - threats. We cannot say for sure what happens because we know that all systems with positive feedbacks can considerably and dis-continually change very quickly their behavior and that it is impossible to predict when the change comes and what the behavior of the system would be after the change. Similar situation has occurred with the spread of each new technology and some recommendations can be done based on historical experiences.

It would not have any sense to try to stop the development of ICTs, it is simply impossible. What is possible is to try to increase the costs of ICTs activities that are negative from the ethical point of view and to increase benefits of activities that are positive from the ethical point of view. If it ought to be done, how to do it and who ought to do it opens a lot of questions. Let us take as an example the possibility of censorship.

Censorship can decrease negative impact through forbidding access to pages that could create addiction. Problem is that it constrains freedom in the virtual reality that is the basic condition for using up the opportunities of ICTs. In each society, some equilibrium level of censorship has been created that reflexes different opinions on this issue. Both opinions and the equilibrium shift in time, we can imagine that in Western societies more www pages than child pornography could be blocked and in China some of the currently blocked www pages could be unblocked.

Previous example shows that discourse of ethical issues linked with ICTs can never stop and that all members of society have responsibility to take part in it.

FUTURE RESEARCH DIRECTIONS

Following research questions would deserve more attention:

- What is the impact of ICTs on social identity? Could possible changes in social identity have a geo-political impact?
- What other virtues and vices are influenced by ICTs and how?
- Is it possible to increase the costs of ICTs activities that are negative from the ethical point of view, ought it to be done and by whom?
- Is it possible to increase the benefits of ICTs activities that are positive from the ethical point of view, ought it to be done and by whom?

CONCLUSION

ICTs offer a lot of possibilities and present some challenges – threats - for living a good life in the ethical sense and being a good person. It is impossible to predict if the positive impacts outweigh the negative ones. Anyway, it is impossible to stop the development of ICTs. The question is if the society ought to try to increase the costs of ICTs activities that are negative from the ethical point of view and to increase benefits of activities that are positive from the ethical point of view, who ought to do it and how. All members of society have responsibility to participate in discourse of this question.

REFERENCES

Anderson, C. (2010). *How web video powers global innovation*. Retrieved September 30, 2015 from https://www.ted.com/

Arntzen, A. A. B. (2010). Knowledge, Technology and University Social Responsibility (USR): A Conceptual Framework. *Proceedings of the 11th European Conference on Knowledge Management, 1-2*, 74-81.

Busch, T. (2011). Capabilities in, capabilities out: Overcoming digital divides by promoting corporate citizenship and fair ICT. *Ethics and Information Technology, 13*(4), 339–353. doi:10.100710676-010-9261-3

Celen, F. K., & Seferoglu, S. S. (2013). Investigation of Elementary School Students' Opinions Related to Unethical Behavior in the use of Information and Communication Technologies. *2nd World Conference on Educational Technology Research, 83*, 417-421. doi:10.1016/j.sbspro.2013.06.082

Codes of Ethics Collection. (n.d.). Retrieved September 30, 2015 from http://ethics.iit.edu/ecodes/introduction

Lianos, M. (2000). Dangerization and the end of deviance - The institutional environment. *The British Journal of Criminology, 40*(2), 261–278. doi:10.1093/bjc/40.2.261

Light, B., & McGrath, K. (2010). Ethics and social networking sites: A disclosive analysis of Facebook. *Information Technology & People, 23*(4), 290–311. doi:10.1108/09593841011087770

List of Virtues and List of Vices. (n.d.). Retrieved September 30, 2015 from http://www.virtuescience.com/vicelist.html

Niemela, M., Ikonen, V., Leikas, J., Kantola, K., Kulju, M., Tammela, A., & Ylikauppila, M. (2014). Human-Driven Design: A Human-Driven Approach to the Design of Technology. *ICT and Society, 431*, 78–91.

Patrignani, N., & Whitehouse, D. (2014). Slow Tech: The Bridge between Computer Ethics and Business Ethics. In K. Kimppa, D. Whitehouse, T. Kuusela, & J. Phahlamohlaka (Eds.), *ICT and Society* (Vol. 431, pp. 92–106). doi:10.1007/978-3-662-44208-1_9

Rizk, N. J., & Choueiri, E. M., & Insticc. (2006). The concept of ethics in electronic qualitative research. *ICEIS 2006: Proceedings of the Eighth International Conference on Enterprise Information Systems: Information Systems Analysis and Specification*, 126-134.

Som, C., Hilty, L. M., & Kohler, A. R. (2009). The Precautionary Principle as a Framework for a Sustainable Information Society. *Journal of Business Ethics, 85*(S3), 493–505. doi:10.100710551-009-0214-x

Stepien, T. (2010). Transcultural and transdisciplinar competences. Technological transformations of society and education. *3rd International Conference of Education, Research and Innovation (Iceri2010)*, 4815-4824.

Tsai, H. Y., & Chen, W. C. (2013). Exploring Intelligent Information Communication Services: A Case of Corporate Social Responsibility. In X. H. Liu, K. F. Zhang, & M. Z. Li (Eds.), Manufacturing Process and Equipment, Pts 1-4 (Vol. 694-697, pp. 3636-3641). doi:10.4028/www.scientific.net/AMR.694-697.3636

Vaccaro, A., & Madsen, P. (2009). Corporate dynamic transparency: The new ICT-driven ethics? *Ethics and Information Technology*, *11*(2), 113–122. doi:10.100710676-009-9190-1

Watts, S., & Wyner, G. (2011). Designing and theorizing the adoption of mobile technology-mediated ethical consumption tools. *Information Technology & People*, *24*(3), 257–280. doi:10.1108/09593841111158374

KEY TERMS AND DEFINITIONS

Casuistry: Branch of ethics that uses case studies to make clear moral principles and norms in typical situations. All ethical codes specify some norms of conduct. These norms are usually explained with the use of different case studies.

Existential Philosophy: Branch of Philosophy that starts with individual existence and the problem of its being in the World. Important predecessor was Søren Kierkegaard (19th century), among main representatives we can find Martin Heidegger and Jean-Paul Sartre (both 20th century). They looked for authentic existence and have found different solutions depending especially on the religiosity of the specific philosopher.

Ethics: Practical philosophy, scientific analysis of moral contents.

Ethics of Norms: Branch of ethics that analyses the structure of norms and what they are based on.

Norms: Norms are the shared and sanctioned rules. Sanctions can be both formal (e.g. law) and informal (e.g. pressure of social group).

Utilitarianism: Branch of ethics that bases moral reasoning on consequences of actions. Actions are good if they maximize pleasure and minimize pain. Among grounders are Jeremy Bentham and John Stuart Mill (18th -19th century). It has penetrated the mainstream economics. It can be shown that total utility of consumers can be increased by redistribution.

Virtue Ethics: Branch of Ethics that considers humans as being bearers of given or developed virtues. Humans have to develop virtues and fight with vices for becoming good. Basic concepts go back as far as to Plato and Aristotle (5th, 4th century BCE).

Virtual Reality: Created and accessed by ICTs. It usually overlaps with "reality" but the overlapping is changing and fuzzy. Extremes of Virtual Reality are Virtual Worlds, in which "avatars" of humans can live parallel lives.

This research was previously published in the Encyclopedia of Information Science and Technology, Fourth Edition edited by Mehdi Khosrow-Pour, pages 4920-4926, copyright year 2018 by Information Science Reference (an imprint of IGI Global).

Chapter 21
Intrusion Tolerance Techniques

Wenbing Zhao
Cleveland State University, USA

ABSTRACT

The authors believe that the research and development of intrusion tolerant systems will gain more momentum as more and more services are offered online. The expectation of such services is high, considering their essential roles in everyday operations of businesses and individuals as well. The impact of service unavailability and security breaches will only grow more serious. In this chapter, the authors survey the state-of-the-art techniques for building intrusion-tolerant systems. They also illustrate a few of the most urgent open issues for future research. Finally, they point out that to build secure and dependable systems we need a concerted effort in intrusion prevention, intrusion detection, and intrusion tolerance.

INTRODUCTION

Intrusion tolerance refers to the capability of maintaining the system availability and integrity despite malicious attacks. Intrusion tolerance has been a hot research area for more than a decade and various techniques have been introduced to achieve various degrees of intrusion tolerance (Castro & Liskov, 2002; Chai & Zhao, 2014 June; Chai & Zhao, 2014 August; Deswarte et al., 1991; Verissimo et al., 2003, Yin et al., 2003; Zhao, 2013; Zhao, 2014). Such techniques can tolerate intrusion attacks in two respects: (1) a system continues providing correct services (may be with reduced performance) and (2) no confidential information is revealed to an adversary. The former can be achieved by using the replication techniques, as long as the adversary can only compromise a small number of replicas. The later is often built on top of secrete sharing and threshold cryptography techniques. Plain replication is often perceived to reduce the confidentiality of a system, because there are more identical copies available for penetration. However, if replication is integrated properly with secrete sharing and threshold cryptography, both availability and confidentiality can be enhanced.

DOI: 10.4018/978-1-5225-7492-7.ch021

BACKGROUND

In this section, we introduce some basic security and dependability concepts and techniques related to intrusion tolerance. A secure information system is one that exhibits the following properties (Pfleeger & Pfleeger, 2002):

- **Confidentiality:** Only authorized users have access to the information.
- **Integrity:** The information can be modified only by authenticated users in authorized ways. Any unauthorized modification can be detected.
- **Availability:** The information is available whenever a legitimate user wants to access it.

Confidentiality is often achieved by using encryption, authentication, and access control. Encryption is a reversible process that scrambles a piece of plaintext into something uninterpretable. Encryption is often parameterized with a security key. To decrypt, the same or a different security key is needed. Authentication is the procedure to verify the identity of a user that wants to access confidential data. Access control is used to restrict what an authenticated user can access.

Integrity can be protected by using secure hash functions, message authentication code (MAC) and digital signatures. For data stored locally, including the application binary files, a checksum is often used as a way to verify data integrity. The checksum can be generated by applying an oneway secure hash transformation on the data. Before the data is accessed, one can verify its integrity by recomputing the checksum and comparing it with the original one. The integrity of a message transmitted over the network can be guarded by a MAC. A MAC is generated by hashing on both the original message and a shared secret key (and often with a sequence number as well). If it is tampered with, the message can be detected in a way similar to that for checksum. For stronger protection, a message can be signed by the sender. A digital signature is produced by first hashing the message using a secure hash function, and then encrypting the hash using the sender's private key.

High availability is achieved by using replication, checkpointing and recovery techniques. Replication is a technique that relying on running redundant copies of an application so that if one copy fails, the services can be provided by the remaining copies. Checkpointing means to take a snapshot of the state of a replica. The saved state can be used to bring a new or a restarted replica up to date. Checkpointing is also useful to avoid log buildup (when a checkpoint is taken, all previously logs can be garbage collected). Recovery techniques concern the tasks of removing faulty replicas, repairing them, and reintegrating them back to the system.

INTRUSION TOLERANCE TECHNIQUES

Intrusion tolerance is built on top of two fundamental techniques: replication and secret sharing/threshold cryptography (Deswarte et al., 1991). In the context of intrusion tolerance, a very general fault model must be used because a compromised replica might exhibit arbitrary faulty behaviors. Such a fault model is often termed as Byzantine fault (Lamport et al., 1982).

Byzantine Fault Tolerance

An intrusion attack might bring a service down, or compromise the integrity of a service. An effective defense is to introduce redundancy into the system, i.e., to replicate critical components in the system. Assuming that an intrusion attack can only penetrate a small fraction of the replicas, the service availability and integrity can be preserved by the remaining correct replicas. However, achieving this goal is not trivial – we must ensure consistent execution of all correct replicas despite the attacks launched by faulty replicas.

A Byzantine faulty replica may use all kinds of strategies to prevent the normal operations of a replica. In particular, it might propagate conflicting information to other replicas or components that it interacts with. To tolerate f Byzantine faulty replicas in an asynchronous environment, we need to have at least 3f+1 number of replicas (Castro & Liskov, 2002). An asynchronous environment is one that has no bound on processing times, communication delays, and clock skews. Internet applications are often modeled as asynchronous systems. Usually, one replica is designated as the primary and the rest are backups.

There are two different approaches to Byzantine fault tolerance. In a Byzantine quorum system (Malkhi & Reiter, 1997), read and write operations issued by some clients are applied on a set of data items (which consists of the state of a service). It is assumed that the read and write operations are synchronized. A read operation retrieves information from a quorum of correct replicas and a write operation applies the update to a quorum of correct replicas. In a system with 3f+1 replicas, a quorum can be formed by 2f+1 replicas so that any two quorums overlap by at least f+1 replica, among which at least one is not faulty. This guarantees the correct operations of the quorum-based system.

A more general method is the state-machine based approach (Schneider, 1990). In the state-machine based approach, a replica is modeled as a state machine. The state change is triggered by remote invocations on the methods offered by the replica. This approach is applicable to a much wider range of applications. Consider a client server application where the server is replicated using the state-machine based approach (Castro & liskov, 2002). The client first sends its request to the primary replica. The primary then broadcasts the request message to the backups and also determines the execution order of the message. To prevent a faulty primary from intentionally delaying a message, the client starts a timer after it sends out a request. It waits for f+1 identical replies from different replicas. Because at most f replicas are faulty, at least one reply must come from a correct replica. If the timer expires before it receives a correct reply, the client broadcasts the request to all server replicas. This enables the correct replicas to detect the primary failure so that a new primary can be elected (this is often called a view change).

All correct replicas must agree on the same set of input messages with the same execution order. In other words, the request messages must be delivered to the replicas reliably in the same total order. To understand this better, consider the scenario illustrated in Figure 1. There are four server replicas R_1, R_2, R_3, and R_4, and two clients C_1 and C_2. Client C_1 multicasts a request m_1 to all the replicas, and concurrently, the other client C2 multicasts another request m_2 to all the replicas. Without controlling the ordering of the messages, it might happen that R_1 and R_2 deliver m_1 ahead of m_2, and R_3 and R_4 deliver m_1 after m_2. Assume that the initial state at each replica can be represented as an integer with a value of 10, the request m_1 asks for the addition of 5 to the state, and the request m2 asks for the doubling of the state value. With the different ordering, state at R_1 and R_2 after processing m_1 and m_2 would be 30 while the state at R_3 and R_4 after processing m_2 and m_1 would be 25. Hence, the states of the replicas diverge due to inconsistent request delivery ordering.

Figure 1. An example scenario showing the importance of totally ordering incoming requests

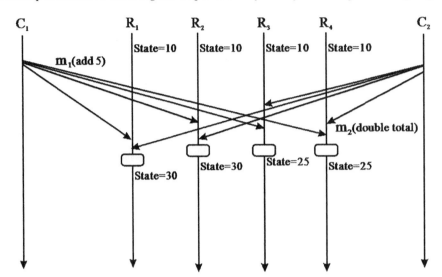

Furthermore, replicas may not process the same request deterministically, i.e., given the same request (delivered in the same order to all replicas), they may not produce identical reply. There are many factors that can cause non-deterministic execution of a request, e.g., differences in local clocks, process identifiers, and many other local resources that might be referenced by the replicas, and multithreading. These factors must be controlled properly so that the replicas appear to execute deterministically. This is a rather difficult task in the face of Byzantine fault. Until recently, the issue was addressed in a very limited manner, for example, by assuming that the replicas are single-threaded and all non-deterministic operations are known a priori. The primary replica determines the values to be used for all replicas and disseminates them to the backups. The backups subsequently verify the proposed values. If the primary is detected to be faulty, a view change is initiated. Recently, we introduced a framework that systematically handles variously types of replica nondeterminism (Zhang et al., 2011).

Byzantine fault tolerance mechanisms tend to suffer from scalability problems. Amir et al. (2006) have tackled the size scalability problem by using a hierarchical replication architecture so that Byzantine fault tolerance can be achieved in large scale application running over wide area networks. Aiyer et al. (2005) considered the challenges faced by ensuring Byzantine fault tolerance over multi-administrative domains (administration scalability problems) and invented mechanisms to cope with selfish members, in addition to arbitrary faulty members.

Secret Sharing and Threshold Cryptography

Another aspect of intrusion tolerance is to protect confidential information (e.g., security keys) even if some replicas have been penetrated (Deswarte et al., 1991). If all the secrets are maintained by a single process, an adversary may obtain these secrets by compromising the process. To defend against such an attack, each secret is divided into multiple shares and each share is stored in a separate process. To obtain the secret, an adversary must now break into a significant number of processes. This is the basic objective of secret sharing.

A popular secret sharing scheme is the (k, n) threshold scheme, where n is the total number of shares and k is the minimum number of shares needed to reconstruct the secret. No useful information can be obtained as long as the number of shares collected is less than k, the threshold. This scheme is first proposed by Shamir (1979) and implemented using polynomial interpolation. In this scheme, each share is of similar size to the original secret and shares can be dynamically added or deleted.

The (k, n) threshold scheme is quite expensive computationally and space-wise. Therefore, they are used only to protect the most crucial secret such as security keys. It might not be practical to apply them to file systems or databases. Consequently, a more cost effective scheme, called Fragmentation-Replication-Scattering (FRS), is proposed (Deswarte et al., 1991). It was initially designed to provide intrusion tolerance for file systems and was later extended to object-based systems (Fabre & Randell, 1992). The FRS scheme involves three steps. First, a file is partitioned into many smaller pieces. (To enhance the confidentiality, the file can be encrypted prior to the fragmentation step.) Second, each piece is replicated. Finally, the pieces are distributed pseudo-randomly according to some algorithm to the storage sites. The fragmentation and scattering protect data confidentiality against intrusion attacks because to obtain the file, an adversary must first find out the locations of the fragments belonging to the file and then penetrate all the sites that store the fragments. The replication protects the availability of the file so that even if some pieces are destroyed by an adversary, there are enough copies left to reconstruct the original file.

Despite the elegancy of the secret sharing schemes, the secret must be reconstructed before it can be used. This poses a security threat because if the process that performs this task is compromised, the secret may be exposed. This prompted the development of threshold cryptography (Desmedt & Frankel, 1989). In threshold cryptography, security operations such as encryption, decryption, signature generation and verification can be performed by a group of processes without reconstructing the shared secret. Threshold cryptography has been applied primarily to public key based security services by sharing the private key among a group of processes (Zhou et al., 2002). The shares can be proactively updated to further enhance the security. By sharing the private key, each process can produce a partial signature. If a client obtains enough number of partial signatures, it can compute the complete signature. During this process, the private key is never reconstructed.

Protecting Both Availability and Confidentiality

Byzantine fault tolerance ensures service high availability, but it does not protect data confidentiality against intrusions. Threshold cryptography guarantees both confidentiality and high availability of some security operations, but not general services one might use. All secret sharing schemes require the reconstruction of the secret at a trusted site, which may be vulnerable to intrusion attacks.

COCA (Zhou et al., 2002) is the first attempt to integrate a Byzantine quorum system with threshold cryptography in the context of a certificate authority (CA) service. In COCA, the most critical state, i.e., the service private key (used to generate signatures for the certificates issued to clients) is shared among the replicas to prevent an adversary from stealing it. There are other states in a CA service, such as the certificate issued to the clients. A client can query and update the certificate information through the CA services. The high availability of the CA services is provided by the group of CA replicas. To enhance failure resiliency, the replicas are periodically restarted proactively with a correct binary image and the latest state collected from other correct replicas. The server keys (used to communicate securely among the replicas) are also periodically refreshed.

FUTURE TRENDS

Even though there is moderate success in applying intrusion tolerance techniques to a few specific applications, it remains to be seen how to introduce intrusion tolerance to other types of information systems, such as credit card processing systems, online banking systems, and e-commerce systems. The lack of effective solutions has left many mission critical systems vulnerable. This is evidenced by the increasingly frequent reports of high impact security breaches that resulted in massive disclosure of confidential information (Baker et al., 2011), such as the break-in of CardSystems Solutions, which exposed the confidential data of more than 40 million credit card holders (Dash & Zelle, 2005), the Veteran Affairs incident, which has caused the potential loss of personal data of more than 26.5 million veterans to the hands of adversaries (Dunham, 2006), and recently the Sony PlayStation online network break, which led to exposure of personal data of over 77 million user accounts (Baker & Finkle, 2011).

There are many open issues to be resolved before we see widespread adoption of intrusion tolerance techniques. The most interesting research problem seems to be the design of a systematic methodology that allows direct operation on the shared secret that is dispersed among a number of processes. This will eliminate the vulnerability introduced by relying on a trusted process to reconstruct the secret. Another urgent issue is how to address replica non-determinism problem, especially that caused by multithreading. Practical information systems are very complicated and contain extensive non-deterministic operations. Unfortunately, all Byzantine fault tolerance strategies require deterministic execution of replicas. Even though the non-determinism resulted from a replica's accessing of some local resources (such as clock values and file descriptors) can be easily controlled if the access pattern is known in advance (Yin et al., 2003), there is no straightforward solution to render a multithreaded application deterministic without significantly impacting the application's performance and correctness (Zhao, 2005). Recently, we proposed a drastically different architecture to avoid replicating execution, which would eliminate the need for controlling the replica nondeterminism (Zhao, 2008).

Furthermore, intrusion tolerance favors design diversity to avoid common vulnerabilities among the replicas. N-version programming was proposed as a potential solution by Chen and Avizienis (1978). However, it might not be an economically viable solution due to its heavy software development cost. Alternative, less costly solutions are needed to diversify the replica implementations. Code randomization appears to be a good approach to achieve replica diversity (Forrest, 1997).

Intrusion tolerance design does not conflict with the effort of intrusion prevention and intrusion detection (Verissimo et al., 2003). In fact, they are all indispensable techniques for building secure and dependable systems. Without applying good intrusion prevention techniques, the application would contain too many vulnerabilities for the replication strategy to take effect. Similarly, intrusion detection plays an essential role in intrusion tolerant systems. To remove a faulty replica and to recover it subsequently, the fault must be detected as quickly as possible. Intrusion detection also helps deter future intrusion attacks if there is enough information logged that can be used to prosecute the intruders (Dunlap et al., 2002).

CONCLUSION

We believe that the research and development of intrusion tolerant systems will gain more momentum as more and more services are offered online. The expectation of such services is high, considering their essential roles in everyday operations of businesses and individuals as well. The impact of service unavailability and security breaches will only be more serious. In this chapter, we have surveyed the state of the art techniques for building intrusion tolerant systems. We also illustrated a few most urgent open issues for future research. Finally, we pointed out that to build secure and dependable systems, we need a concerted effort in intrusion prevention, intrusion detection, and intrusion tolerance.

REFERENCES

Aiyer, A., Alvisi, L., Clement, A., Dahlin, M., Martin, J., & Parth, C. (2005). BAR fault tolerance for cooperative services. *ACM Symposium on Operating Systems Principles*. Brighton, UK: ACM Press.

Amir, A., Danilov, C., Dolev, D., Kirsch, J., Lane, J., Nita-Rotaru, C., ... Zage, D. (2006). Scaling Byzantine fault-tolerant replication to wide area networks. *Proceedings of International Conference on Dependable Systems and Networks*. Philadelphia, PA: IEEE Computer Society Press. 10.1109/DSN.2006.63

Baker, L. B., & Finkle, J. (2011). *Sony PlayStation suffers massive data breach*. Reuters.

Baker, W., Hutton, A., Hylender, C. D., Pamula, J., Porter, C., & Spitler, M. (2011). *2011 data breach investigations report*. Verizon RISK Team. Available: www. verizonbusiness. com/resources/reports/rp_databreach-investigations-report-2011_en_xg. pdf

Castro, M., & Liskov, B. (2002). Practical Byzantine fault tolerance and proactive recovery. *ACM Transactions on Computer Systems*, *20*(4), 398–461. doi:10.1145/571637.571640

Chai, H., & Zhao, W. (2014, June). Towards trustworthy complex event processing. In *Proceedings of the 5th IEEE International Conference on Software Engineering and Service Science* (pp. 758-761). IEEE.

Chai, H., & Zhao, W. (2014, August). Byzantine Fault Tolerant Event Stream Processing for Autonomic Computing. In *Proceedings of the 12th IEEE International Conference on Dependable, Autonomic and Secure Computing* (pp. 109-114). IEEE. 10.1109/DASC.2014.28

Chen, L., & Avizienis, A. (1978). N-version programming: A fault-tolerance approach to reliability of software operation. *Proceedings of International Symposium on Fault Tolerant Computing*. Toulouse, France: IEEE Computer Society Press.

Dash, E., & Zeller, T. (2005, June 18). MasterCard says 40 million files are put at risk. *New York Times*.

Desmedt, Y., & Frankel, Y. (1990). Threshold cryptosystems. *Lecture Notes in Computer Science*, *435*, 307–315. doi:10.1007/0-387-34805-0_28

Deswarte, Y., Blain, L., & Fabre, J. (1991). Intrusion tolerance in distributed computing systems. *Proceedings of the IEEE Symposium on Research in Security and Privacy*. Oakland, CA: IEEE Computer Society Press.

Dunhm, W. (2006, May 22). Personal data on millions of U.S. veterans stolen. *Computerworld*.

Dunlap, W., King, S., Cinar, S., Barsai, M., & Chen, P. (2002). ReVirt: Enabling intrusion analysis through virtual-machine logging and replay. *Proceedings of the Symposium on Operating Systems Design and Implementation*, 211-224. 10.1145/1060289.1060309

Fabre, J., & Randell, B. (1992). An object-oriented view of fragmented data processing for fault and intrusion tolerance in distributed systems. *Lecture Notes in Computer Science, 648*, 193–208. doi:10.1007/BFb0013899

Forrest, S., Somayaji, A., & Ackley, D. (1997). Building diverse computer systems. *Proceedings of the Workshop on Hot Topics in Operating Systems*. Cape Cod, MA: IEEE Computer Society Press.

Lamport, L., Shostak, R., & Pease, M. (1982). The Byzantine generals problem. *ACM Transactions on Programming Languages and Systems, 4*(3), 382–401. doi:10.1145/357172.357176

Malkhi, D., & Reiter, M. (1997). Byzantine quorum systems. *Proceedings of the ACM Symposium on Theory of Computing*. El Paso, TX: ACM Press.

Pfleeger, C., & Pfleeger, S. (2002). *Security in Computing* (3rd ed.). Prentice Hall.

Schneider, F. (1990). Implementing fault-tolerant services using the state machine approach: A tutorial. *ACM Computing Surveys, 22*(4), 299–319. doi:10.1145/98163.98167

Shamir, A. (1979). How to share a secret. *Communications of the ACM, 22*(11), 612–613. doi:10.1145/359168.359176

Verissimo, P., Neves, N., & Correia, M. (2003). Intrusion-tolerant architectures: Concepts and design. *Lecture Notes in Computer Science, 2677*, 90–109. doi:10.1007/3-540-45177-3_1

Yin, J., Martin, J., Venkataramani, A., Alvisi, L., & Dahlin, M. (2003). Separating agreement from execution for Byzantine fault tolerant services. *Proceedings of the ACM Symposium on Operating Systems Principles*. Bolton Landing, NY: ACM Press. 10.1145/945445.945470

Zhang, H., Zhao, W., Moser, L. E., & Melliar-Smith, P. M. (2011). Design and implementation of a Byzantine fault tolerance framework for non-deterministic applications. *Software, IET, 5*(3), 342–356. doi:10.1049/iet-sen.2010.0013

Zhao, W. (2008, May). Towards practical intrusion tolerant systems: a blueprint. In *Proceedings of the 4th Annual Workshop on Cyber security and information intelligence research: developing strategies to meet the cyber security and information intelligence challenges ahead* (p. 19). ACM. 10.1145/1413140.1413162

Zhao, W. (2013, April). Towards practical intrusion tolerant systems. In *Proceedings of the IET International Conference on Information and Communications Technologies* (pp. 280-287). IET.

Zhao, W. (2014, August). Application-Aware Byzantine Fault Tolerance. In *Proceedings of the 12th IEEE International Conference on Dependable, Autonomic and Secure Computing* (pp. 45-50). IEEE. 10.1109/DASC.2014.17

Zhao, W., Moser, L., & Melliar-Smith, P. (2005). Deterministic scheduling for multithreaded replicas. *Proceedings of the IEEE International Workshop on Object-oriented Real-time Dependable Systems*. Sedona, AZ: IEEE Computer Society Press. 10.1109/WORDS.2005.26

Zhou, L., Schneider, F., & van Renesse, R. (2002). COCA: A secure distributed online certification authority. *ACM Transactions on Computer Systems*, *20*(4), 329–368. doi:10.1145/571637.571638

ADDITIONAL READING

Atighetchi, M., Pal, P., Webber, F., Schantz, R., Jones, C., & Loyall, J. (2004). Adaptive cyberdefense for survival and intrusion tolerance. *IEEE Internet Computing*, *8*(6), 25–33. doi:10.1109/MIC.2004.54

Bessani, A. N., Sousa, P., Correia, M., Neves, N. F., & Verissimo, P. (2007). Intrusion-tolerant protection for critical infrastructures.

Bessani, A. N., Sousa, P., Correia, M., Neves, N. F., & Verissimo, P. (2008). The CRUTIAL way of critical infrastructure protection. *Security & Privacy, IEEE*, *6*(6), 44–51. doi:10.1109/MSP.2008.158

Chai, H., & Zhao, W. (2012). Byzantine Fault Tolerance as a Service. In Computer Applications for Web, Human Computer Interaction, Signal and Image Processing, and Pattern Recognition (pp. 173-179). Springer Berlin Heidelberg. doi:10.1007/978-3-642-35270-6_24

Deswarte, Y., & Powell, D. (2006). Internet security: An intrusion-tolerance approach. *Proceedings of the IEEE*, *94*(2), 432–441. doi:10.1109/JPROC.2005.862320

Feng, D., & Xiang, J. (2005, July). Experiences on intrusion tolerance distributed systems. In *Proceedings of the 29th Annual International Computer Software and Applications Conference* (Vol. 1, pp. 270-271). IEEE.

Garcia, M., Bessani, A., Gashi, I., Neves, N., & Obelheiro, R. (2011, June). OS diversity for intrusion tolerance: Myth or reality? In Proceedings of the IEEE/IFIP 41st International Conference on Dependable Systems & Networks (pp. 383-394). IEEE.

Kim, J., Bentley, P. J., Aickelin, U., Greensmith, J., Tedesco, G., & Twycross, J. (2007). Immune system approaches to intrusion detection–a review. *Natural Computing*, *6*(4), 413–466. doi:10.100711047-006-9026-4

Liu, P. (2002). Architectures for intrusion tolerant database systems. In *Proceedings of the 18th Annual Computer Security Applications Conference* (pp. 311-320). IEEE.

Min, B. J., & Choi, J. S. (2004). An approach to intrusion tolerance for mission-critical services using adaptability and diverse replication. *Future Generation Computer Systems*, *20*(2), 303–313. doi:10.1016/S0167-739X(03)00146-8

Pal, P., Webber, F., Schantz, R. E., & Loyall, J. P. (2000, October). Intrusion tolerant systems. In *Proceedings of the IEEE Information Survivability Workshop* (pp. 24-26).

Ramasamy, H. V., Pandey, P., Cukier, M., & Sanders, W. H. (2008). Experiences with building an intrusion-tolerant group communication system. *Software, Practice & Experience*, *38*(6), 639–666. doi:10.1002pe.848

Sousa, P., Bessani, A. N., Correia, M., Neves, N. F., & Verissimo, P. (2007, December). Resilient intrusion tolerance through proactive and reactive recovery. In Dependable Computing, 2007. PRDC 2007. 13th Pacific Rim International Symposium on (pp. 373-380). IEEE. 10.1109/PRDC.2007.52

Sousa, P., Bessani, A. N., Dantas, W. S., Souto, F., Correia, M., & Neves, N. F. (2009, June). Intrusion-tolerant self-healing devices for critical infrastructure protection. In Dependable Systems & Networks, 2009. DSN'09. IEEE/IFIP International Conference on (pp. 217-222). IEEE. 10.1109/DSN.2009.5270333

Verissimo, P., Correia, M., Neves, N. F., & Sousa, P. (2009). Intrusion-resilient middleware design and validation. Information Assurance. *Security and Privacy Services*, *4*, 615–678.

Wang, F., Uppalli, R., & Killian, C. (2003, October). Analysis of techniques for building intrusion tolerant server systems. In *Proceedings of the IEEE Military Communications Conference* (Vol. 2, pp. 729-734). IEEE.

Ye, N. (2001). Robust intrusion tolerance in information systems. *Information Management & Computer Security*, *9*(1), 38–43. doi:10.1108/09685220110366786

Young, M., Kate, A., Goldberg, I., & Karsten, M. (2010, June). Practical robust communication in DHTs tolerating a byzantine adversary. In *Proceedings of the 2010 IEEE 30th International Conference on Distributed Computing Systems* (pp. 263-272). IEEE. 10.1109/ICDCS.2010.31

Young, M., Kate, A., Goldberg, I., & Karsten, M. (2013). Towards Practical Communication in Byzantine-Resistant DHTs. *IEEE/ACM Transactions on Networking*, *21*(1), 190–203. doi:10.1109/TNET.2012.2195729

Zhao, W. (2007, October). BFT-WS: A Byzantine fault tolerance framework for web services. In *Proceedings of the Eleventh International IEEE EDOC Conference Workshop* (pp. 89-96). IEEE. 10.1109/EDOCW.2007.6

Zhao, W. (2007) A Byzantine fault tolerant coordination for Web services atomic transactions. In *Proceedings of the 3rd IEEE International Symposium on Dependable, Autonomic and Secure Computing* (pp. 37-44). Columbia, MD. 10.1109/DASC.2007.10

Zhao, W. (2009). Design and implementation of a Byzantine fault tolerance framework for Web services. *Journal of Systems and Software*, *82*(6), 1004–1015. doi:10.1016/j.jss.2008.12.037

Zhao, W. (2014). *Building dependable distributed systems*. John Wiley & Sons. doi:10.1002/9781118912744

Zhao, W. (2015). Optimistic Byzantine fault tolerance. *International Journal of Parallel, Emergent and Distributed Systems*, 1-14 (preprint).

KEY TERMS AND DEFINITIONS

Byzantine Fault: It is used to model arbitrary fault. A Byzantine faulty process might send conflicting information to other processes to prevent them from reaching an agreement.

Byzantine Fault Tolerance: A replication-based technique used to ensure high availability of an application subject to Byzantine fault.

Byzantine Quorum System: The system offers read and write services to its clients on a set of replicated data items. A read operation retrieves data from a quorum of correct replicas and a write operation applies the update to a quorum of correct replicas. Any two quorums must overlap by at least one correct replica.

Fragmentation Redundancy Scattering: A secret sharing scheme that involves the following three steps: fragmenting a file, replicating each fragment, and distributing the replicated fragments to different storage sites.

Intrusion Tolerance: It refers to the capability of maintaining the system availability and integrity despite malicious attacks.

(k, n) Thread Scheme: A secret is divided into n shares. To reconstruct the secret, at least k shares are needed. No useful information can be obtained from k-1 shares.

Replica Consistency: The states of the replicas of an application should remain to be identical at the end of the processing of each request. Replica consistency is necessary to mask a fault in some replicas.

Threshold Cryptography: Security operations such as encryption, decryption, signature generation and verification can be performed by a group of processes without reconstructing the shared secret. Threshold cryptography utilizes (k, n) threshold schemes internally.

This research was previously published in the Encyclopedia of Information Science and Technology, Fourth Edition edited by Mehdi Khosrow-Pour, pages 4927-4936, copyright year 2018 by Information Science Reference (an imprint of IGI Global).

268

Chapter 22
New Perspectives of Pattern Recognition for Automatic Credit Card Fraud Detection

Addisson Salazar
Universitat Politècnica de València, Spain

Gonzalo Safont
Universitat Politècnica de València, Spain

Alberto Rodriguez
Universidad Miguel Hernández de Elche, Spain

Luis Vergara
Universitat Politècnica de València, Spain

ABSTRACT

Automatic credit card fraud detection (ACCFD) is a challenge issue that has been increasingly studied considering the expanded potential of new technologies to emulate legitimate operations. Solution has to handle changing fraud behavior, detection in data with very small fraud/legitimate operations ratio, and accomplish operation requirements of very low false alarm in real-time processing. In this chapter, main issues related with the problem of ACCFD and proposed solutions are discussed from theoretical and practical standpoints. The perspective of detection analyses from receiving operating characteristic curves and business key performance indicators are jointly analyzed. A new conceptual framework for ACCFD considering decision fusion and surrogate data is outlined including a case of study with different proportions of real and surrogate data. In addition, the sensitivity of the methods to different proportions of fraud/legitimate ratios is tested. Finally, theoretical and practical conclusions are provided, and several open lines of research are proposed.

DOI: 10.4018/978-1-5225-7492-7.ch022

INTRODUCTION

The automatic detection of frauds in financial operations using credit cards is a challenge issue that has been increasingly studied. The rapid expansion of information and communication technologies has expanded the potential to emulate legitimate operations by fraudsters. The solution to that problem has to be able to be adaptive since the behavior of frauds is changing constantly in time; to handle the detection in data with a very small ratio of fraud amount to legitimate operations, e.g., 5e-5; and accomplish operation requirements of very low false alarm ratios in real-time processing. Thus, several approaches have been proposed from pattern recognition and machine learning areas.

Main issues related with the problem of automatic credit card fraud detection (ACCFD) and proposed solutions are discussed from theoretical and practical standpoints. The perspective of detection analyses from receiving operating characteristic (ROC) curves and business key performance indicators (KPI) are jointly analyzed (Girgenti & Hedley, 2011) (Wells, 2011) (Montague, 2010). Therefore, a new conceptual framework for ACCFD considering modern techniques such as decision fusion and surrogate data is outlined. There are only a few references from the research field of signal processing for ACCFD, see for instance (Salazar, Safont, Soriano, & Vergara, 2012).

A case of study that combines different proportions of real and surrogate data is included. Several scenarios considering different single and combined methods are considered. ROC and KPI curves are analyzed bearing in mind numeric and operational requirements. The sensitivity of the methods to different proportions of fraud/legitimate ratios is tested. Thus, limitations and advantages of the studied methods are demonstrated.

BACKGROUND

Cyber-security and privacy have become very important subjects of research in recent years. This research spans many different fields, such as: security in the physical layer of wireless communications (Poor, 2012)); database security (Sankar, Rajagopalan, & Poor, 2013); distributed systems (Pawar, El Rouayheb, & Ramchandran, 2011); and biometrics (Lifeng, Ho, & Poor, 2011). One activity where the security and privacy mechanisms are critical is the e-commerce by using credit cards. This application features a massive volume of on-line transactions that are continuously exposed to frauds. Fraud detection in credit card transactions is a critical problem affecting large financial companies and involving annually loss of billions of dollars (Bhattacharyya, Jha, Tharakunnel, & Westland, 2011).

Basically two strategies can be raised. The first consists of defining the problem as one-class classification, and thus, characterizing the largest data population (the legitimate transactions) and considering all the data with different characteristics as outliers (Hodge & Austin, 2004) (Tax & Duin, 2001). The second strategy is to define the problem as a two-class classification characterizing legitimate and fraudulent transaction data. We have concentrated in this later detection approach which takes full advantage of the available labeled data.

There is extensive literature that reviews and provides taxonomies and comparisons about the large number of ACCFD methods that have been developed during the last two decades (e.g., (Danenas, 2015)). However, only few of these references are from the research field of signal processing. The particular characteristics of ACCFD make this a challenging problem for signal processing algorithms (Salazar,

Safont, Soriano, & Vergara, 2012). Optimum design of the algorithms depends on the detection models employed to estimate the multidimensional joint distribution of the random variables underlying the data.

Figure 1 shows an outline of the proposed signal processing procedure. The multivariate surrogate data is obtained following the methods explained in (Salazar, Safont, & Vergara, Surrogate techniques for testing fraud detection algorithms in credit card operations, 2014). The pre-processing step consists of applying principal component analysis (PCA) to reduce dimensionality of the data preserving 95% of data variance.

SURROGATE DATA

Bank enterprises collect large amount of historical records corresponding to millions of credit cards operations, but, unfortunately, only a small portion, if any, is open access. This is because, e.g., the records include confidential customer data and banks are afraid of public quantitative evidence of existing fraud operations (Bhattacharyya, Jha, Tharakunnel, & Westland, 2011). A solution is to generate synthetic records which replicate as much as possible the behavior of the real data. Surrogate techniques give an approach to this problem. Surrogates algorithms have been extensively used to detect the possible presence of non-linearities in a given time series realization. Basically, surrogate replicas of the original data are generated trying to preserve the correlation (second-order statistic) and amplitude distribution (first-order statistic). These replicas are generated in such a form that linearity applies. Then some statistics for detecting possible presence of non linearities are computed from both the surrogate replicas and the original data. If significant differences are given, then existence of non-linearity is decided (Prichard & Theiler, 1994).

The main idea of surrogate techniques is to synthesize new stationary data by randomization in the Fourier domain. For multivariate series, cross-correlation among the variables should be conserved. The randomization in the Fourier domain is chosen so that the differences of phase between components stay the same. Let $X(n)$ be a multivariate series with M components ($x_j(n)$ with $n=0,\ldots,N-1$ being its j-th component). For initialization, the Fourier transform of each component can be computed:

$$\left(Fx_j\right)(f) = \sum_{n=0}^{N-1} x_j(n)e^{-i2\pi\frac{nf}{N}} = Ax_j(f)e^{i\Psi x_j(f)} \tag{1}$$

Figure 1. Outline of the signal processing procedure

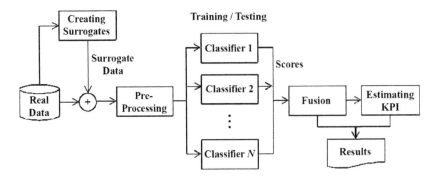

A classical multivariate surrogate can be computed using the following expression:

$$S(n) = \left[s_1(n), \ldots, s_M(n) \right]^t ,$$

$$s_j(n) = \frac{1}{N} \sum_{f=0}^{N-1} A x_j(f) e^{i\left(\Psi x_j(f) + \Theta(f) \right)} e^{-i2\pi nf/N} , \tag{2}$$

where $\Theta(f)$ is a random phase i.i.d. uniform in $[0, 2\pi]$.

However the algorithm of (1) does not impose any constraint to the surrogates that should be restricted to have the same marginal distributions and covariance as the original series (variables). The iterative IAAFT (Iteratively Amplitude Adjusted Fourier Transform) algorithm that projects on the two constraints (the covariance function expressed in the Fourier domain and the prescribed marginal distributions was proposed in (Schreiber & Schmitz, 2000). We applied a new extension of IAAFT algorithm considered in (Borgnat, Abry, & Flandrin, 2012) using a reduced set of real credit card data to generate surrogate multivariate series of credit card data transactions.

SCORES AND LIKELIHOOD RATIO: A SIGNAL PROCESSING PERSPECTIVE FOR ACCFD

Detection of credit card frauds may be approached from a signal processing perspective. It is comparable to the classical problem of detecting signals in a noise background. The "signal presence" hypothesis (H_1) would be equivalent to "fraud presence", meanwhile "absence of signal" hypothesis (H_0) would correspond to "absence of fraud". In both cases hypothesis H_1 has much lower a priori probability than hypothesis H_0, hence Neyman-Pearson criterion is the most appropriate. Implementation of a Neyman-Pearson detector is made by the test $\Lambda(\mathbf{x}) = \dfrac{f(\mathbf{x}/H_1)}{f(\mathbf{x}/H_0)} \underset{H_0}{\overset{H_1}{\underset{<}{>}}} \lambda$, where $f(\mathbf{x}/H_i)$ is the probability density of the observation vector $\mathbf{x}$ conditioned to hypothesis H_i, and λ is a threshold selected to fit an acceptable probability of false alarm (PFA). $\Lambda(\mathbf{x})$ is the likelihood ratio (LR) and its computation is the essential signal processing required to implement the optimum detector. Determination of LR mainly depends on the assumed models about the signal and noise. Different optimum detectors may be designed assuming multivariate Gaussian noise and different amount of knowledge about the signal, e.g., matched filter, subspace matched filter, and energy detector.

Similarly, the usual test in fraud detection is of the form $s(\mathbf{x}) \underset{H_0}{\overset{H_1}{\underset{<}{>}}} t$, where $s(\mathbf{x})$ is a score or qualification between 0 and 1, assigned to the transaction under analysis. The higher the value $s(\mathbf{x})$, the higher the probability of a fraudulent transaction. The threshold t filters the transactions that would be passed to the human operator. Actually, the daily number of false positive frauds which the human operators can manage imposes a limit in the PFA in much the same manner that it happens in other areas like radar signal detection. For those filtered transaction, the score $s(\mathbf{x})$ is part of the information taken into account by the operator to arrive to a final decision about authorization.

A natural candidate for $s(\mathbf{x})$ is $P(H_1/\mathbf{x})$, the "a posteriori" probability of having a fraud conditioned to the observation. It is straightforward to show the relation between $s(\mathbf{x})$ and $\Lambda(\mathbf{x})$ by using the Bayes theorem:

$$s(\mathbf{x}) = P(H_1/\mathbf{x}) = \frac{f(\mathbf{x}/H_1)P(H_1)}{f(\mathbf{x})} =$$

$$= \frac{f(\mathbf{x}/H_1)P(H_1)}{f(\mathbf{x}/H_1)P(H_1) + f(\mathbf{x}/H_0)P(H_0)} =$$

$$= \frac{\Lambda(\mathbf{x})}{\Lambda(\mathbf{x}) + \dfrac{P(H_0)}{P(H_1)}} \Leftrightarrow \Lambda(\mathbf{x}) = \frac{s(\mathbf{x})\dfrac{P(H_0)}{P(H_1)}}{1 - s(\mathbf{x})} \tag{3}$$

So we see the LR is implicitly considered given a scoring function, and, vice versa, a score value may be computed from the LR. In consequence, a test based in comparing the score (computed as the a posteriori probability of H_1) with a threshold is an LR test:

$$s(\mathbf{x}) \underset{H_0}{\overset{H_1}{\underset{<}{>}}} t \quad \Leftrightarrow \quad \Lambda(\mathbf{x}) \underset{H_0}{\overset{H_1}{\underset{<}{>}}} \frac{t}{1-t}\frac{P(H_0)}{P(H_1)} \tag{4}$$

Notice that the observation vector $\mathbf{x}$ will be formed by a set of heterogeneous features such as money amount, commerce code, country code, operation date and so on, that are extracted directly from the records. Besides, taking into account that the behavior of fraudsters normally emulates regular customer behavior in directly measured features; additional indirect features can be estimated to highlight differences (e.g., transaction velocity, transaction acceleration, and country commuting). Thus, it is not easy to find parametric models for the statistical distributions of the observations under fraud and no fraud conditions. Hence, deriving optimum sufficient statistics or implementing generalized likelihood ratio tests (GLRT) are not practical options. However, it is usual that sets of training observations for both hypotheses are available, so that supervised learning of the LR or of a score function is possible. This is an advantage in comparison with signal detection, where sets of the expected signals are difficult to measure or to generate: it is difficult to learn $f(\mathbf{x}/H_1)$ from observation samples.

Other differences between these conceptually equivalent problems are in the type of performance measures. In signal detection the Receiving Operating Characteristic (ROC) curves (probability of detection, PD, as function of probability of false alarm, PFA) are the most usual. In addition, the dependence of PD on the signal-to-noise-ratio (SNR) for a given PFA, is very familiar. SNR is not a practical concept in fraud detection, as the presence of a fraud modifies the distribution of $\mathbf{x}$ in an arbitrary an unpredictable form rather than a simple change in energy. Moreover, PD is a relative measure of good performance as the final goal is to save money, i.e., it is better to detect one fraud involving a lot of money that many frauds of small amounts of money. Thus the Value Detection Rate (VDR) defined as the percentage of saved money is usually preferred. In addition, the Account False to Positive Rate (AFPR) defined in (5) is considered as a sample estimate of the average number of useless interventions in non-fraudulent operations produced for every detected fraud.

$$AFPR = \frac{True\ positives + False\ positives}{True\ positives} =$$

$$= 1 + \frac{False\ positives}{True\ positives} \tag{5}$$

In conclusion, there are clear similarities between signal and fraud detection, but some differences exist, positioning the fraud problem somewhere in between signal processing and patter recognition areas.

FUSION OF SCORES

Fraud detection is a difficult problem due to the arbitrary and variant nature of the statistical models under both hypotheses. This imposes the need of adaptive supervised learning of reasonable (probably non-optimum) detectors from datasets of millions of labeled transactions. The extremely large amount of available legitimate operations in comparison with the moderate number of confirmed frauds introduces an additional difficult for a balanced learning of the models under both hypotheses. All this suggests that approaches based on deriving one "sophisticated" detector, having many degrees of freedom and/ or parameters to be dynamically and continuously learned, will not be an appropriate approach. Instead, the idea of combining or fusing complementary robust detectors is tempting (some formal ideas about this intuitive concept emanates from the so-called evidence theory (Shafer, 1976)). Fusion of detectors has been considered since long time ago in different areas and under different terminologies: multimodal fusion (Atrey, Hossain, El Saddik, & Kankanhalli, 2010), mixture of experts (Yuksel, Wilson, & Gader, 2012) and classifier combiners (Kittler, Hatef, Duin, & Matas, 1998), to mention a few, but there is convenient to focus into the fraud detection context.

Let us assume that N different detectors are designed to detect possible frauds. Different designs may be the result of using different training sets on the same detector structure, of using different detector structures or both. In any case, every detector i produces a score s_i and we must find a fusion function to compute a final score s_f. Then, finding the optimum fusion function is a design objective. This can be approached in a similar manner to the original problem of determining one score from the observation vector $\mathbf{x}$. We may consider that the vector of individual scores $\mathbf{s} = [s_1 ... s_N]^T$ is a new observation vector, and then s_f may be computed from the LR of scores

$$s_f(\mathbf{s}) = \frac{\Lambda(\mathbf{s})}{\Lambda(\mathbf{s}) + \frac{P(H_0)}{P(H_1)}} \qquad \Lambda(\mathbf{s}) = \frac{f(\mathbf{s}/H_1)}{f(\mathbf{s}/H_0)} \tag{6}$$

So, ultimately, the optimum fusion function depends on the joint probability densities functions of the scores under both hypotheses, $f(\mathbf{s}/H_1)$ and $f(\mathbf{s}/H_0)$. If we assume that the scores are independent and identically distributed random variables then (6) can be expressed as

$$s_f(\mathbf{s}) = \frac{\dfrac{f(s_1/H_1)....f(s_N/H_1)}{f(s_1/H_0)....f(s_N/H_0)}}{\dfrac{f(s_1/H_1)....f(s_N/H_1)}{f(s_1/H_0)....f(s_N/H_0)} + \dfrac{P(H_0)}{P(H_1)}} \tag{7}$$

In that case non-parametric estimates of the marginals can be obtained from training set of scores and introduced in the computation of the final score (plug-in methods, (Jain A. K., 2000)). But the fusion problem becomes more complicated if statistical independence among the individual scores cannot be assumed (Vergara, Soriano, Safont, & Salazar, 2016). Actually, presence of dependence can be expected if all the detectors share the same input **x**. Unless Gaussianity could be assumed, capturing the dependence of multivariate random variables is not an easy problem. Gaussian and Non-Gaussian Mixtures Models are possible options (Tzikas & Likas, 2008) (Salazar, Vergara, Serrano, & Igual, 2010), they require the estimation of many parameters and the determination of the best number of mixture components. Another alternative is based on the use of copulas. Copula methodology has been used during years in econometrics, although it is only recently considered in the signal processing community (Iyengar, Varshney, & Damarla, 2011). The multivariate probability density function is factorized in the marginals and a copula function which captures dependence. The copula function is the multidimensional probability density function of uniform variables derived from the original dependent variables. A family of parametric functions exists having the required copula properties, so that a variety of dependence models are possible. Another option is α-integration (Soriano, Vergara, Ahmed, & Salazar, 2015), which is expressed as

$$s_f(\mathbf{s}) = \begin{cases} \left(\displaystyle\sum_{i=1}^{N} w_i \cdot s_i^{\frac{1-\alpha}{2}}\right)^{\frac{2}{1-\alpha}}, & \alpha \neq 1 \\[2ex] \exp\left(\displaystyle\sum_{i=1}^{N} w_i \cdot \log(s_i)\right), & \alpha = 1 \end{cases} \tag{8}$$

First, every score is modified by a nonlinear function controlled by the α parameter. Then, a weighted mean of the modified scores is computed, and the nonlinear inverse function is finally applied to the weighted mean. The α parameter and the weights w_i $i = 1,...,N$ can be estimated so that a predefined cost function is minimized. One interesting aspect of α-integration is that some simple cases are included for particular values of α and w_i. Thus, assuming that $w_i = \frac{1}{N}$, we see that $\alpha = -1,1,3$ respectively renders the arithmetic mean, the geometric mean and the harmonic mean. Similarly, $\alpha = \infty / -\infty$ is equivalent to compute the minimum/maximum.

The proposed signal processing procedure was applied using a set of real data provided by a large financial company. These data were combined with surrogate data following the methods described in (Salazar, Safont, & Vergara, Surrogate techniques for testing fraud detection algorithms in credit card operations, 2014). Thus, a total dataset of 37.000.000 transactions were available (90% surrogate). These dataset correspond to about 3 million credit cards with a total of 2005 fraudulent transactions from 682 credit cards. The proportion between fraudulent and legitimate transactions is different from the real proportion, but it is small enough for evaluating the methods. This dataset was divided 5% for training stage and 95% for testing stage. Figure 2 shows the distribution of the data in the first two components space estimated by PCA. It can be seen that the fraud data are crowded together the genuine data making difficult the separation of the two kinds of data. Although the genuine data have been sub-sampled 100 times, it can be seen the high disproportion between the two kinds of data.

Seven different representative detectors were selected. Three of them are individual detectors selected from generally applied methods: Linear Discriminant Analysis (LDA), Quadratic Discriminant Analysis (QDA) and NonGaussian Mixture Models (NGM) (Salazar, On Statistical Pattern Recognition in Independent Component Analysis Mixture Modelling, 2013). Two more were considered because they have been previously used in the ACCFD problem: Random Forest (RF) and Support Vector Machines (SVM). Finally two fusion methods were applied. The first is α-integration (α-INT). The second fusion method was based on the use of a Gaussian copula (COP). Several experiments show that SVM and RF did not contribute to improve fused results, so the final methods included in the fusion step were LDA, QDA and NGM.

Figure 3 shows the ROC curves corresponding to transactions summarized by cards for the seven methods. Actually, the detectors are applied to every transaction, but once a transaction is detected as fraudulent the associated card is considered fraudulent in the observed period of analysis. Thus ROC curves of transactions may differ from ROC curves of cards, being these latter more significant in the ACCFD context. In Figure 3 we only represent the acceptable margins for the PFA [0, 0.04]. We can see that PDs under 0.5 are obtained; this can be unacceptable in other applications but are very significant in ACCFD as this can potentially lead to saving big amount of money. Finally, we deduce from Figure 3 the following main conclusions. First, LDA is clearly below the rest of methods, thus suggesting that Gaussian models are not appropriate in this case. Second, fusion methods improve the individual detectors, especially for the lowest values of PFA.

Figure 2. Scatter plot of the data in two component space. Localization of fraud data is highlighted.

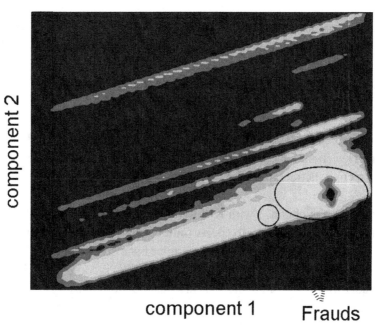

For a more accurate representation see the electronic version.

Figure 3. ROC estimated from the results of detection methods

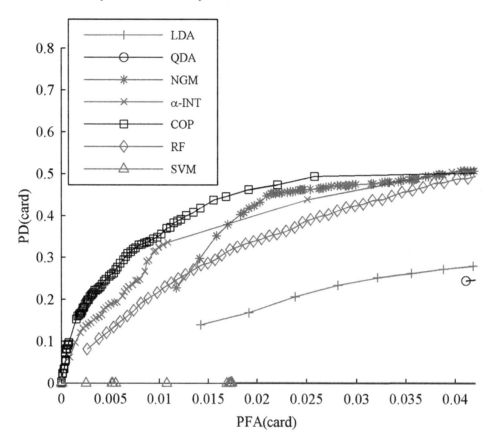

KPI CURVES

KPI are estimated after processing in order to evaluate the results from the business operational perspective. They provide different information than the ROC curves because they take into account not only the transactions themselves, but also variables such as grouping of transactions using card number; the amount of each transaction; and the period of time until the fraud is detected (VDR and AFPR were defined above):

- **ADR:** Account Detection Rate, the percentage of detected fraudulent cards.
- **ADT:** Average Detection Time, the average amount of fraudulent transactions on the same card required for detecting its fraudulent use.

Figure 4 shows the results obtained with KPI to be compared with Figure 3. It represents VDR as function of the normalized number of daily alerts (number of daily alerts divided by the total number of processed cards in a day). In general, results are similar but a significant difference is present, in this case, α-INT performs better than COP when VDR instead of PD is computed. There are several discussions that can be made from KPI results, but they are outside the scope of this work.

Figure 4. VDR with respect to normalized alerts per day estimated from detection methods

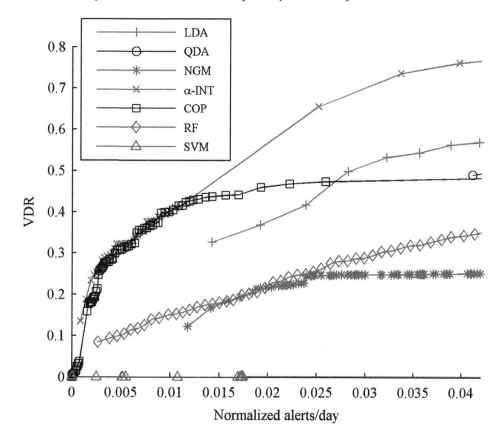

SURROGATE AND FRAUD/LEGITIMATE RATIOS

Figures 2 and 3 show results of the surrogate algorithm for legitimate and fraud operations, respectively. Figure 1a shows 500 samples of the surrogate data for the first eight components. Figure 1b shows the histogram of the eight components in surrogate data, in black bars, with the histogram of the legitimate operations superimposed in red. Note, that those distributions are non-Gaussians. Figure 1c compares the autocorrelations of each surrogate component (in blue) with the corresponding autocorrelation of the legitimate data (in red). Finally, Figure 1d shows the cross-correlations of the first component with the other components (first seven rows) and the cross-correlation of the second component with the third component (eighth row). The cross-correlations of the surrogate data are shown in blue, and the cross-correlations of the legitimate data are shown in red. It can be seen that surrogate legitimate operations were very close to the real legitimate operations from standpoints of marginal distributions of the components and autocorrelation and cross-correlations between variables.

Figure 7a shows the joint probability density functions (pdf) of real (blue) and surrogate (red) legitimate operations. Similarly, joint pdfs for fraud operations are shown in Figure 7b. Although the joint pdfs are calculated for all 8 components at once, they are shown in slices of two components to make the result more readable. The results in Figure 7 show that the surrogate data had very similar joint pdf to that of real legitimate data. The peaks of the pdf for the surrogates were located at the same positions

Figure 5. Results of surrogate data from legitimate operations

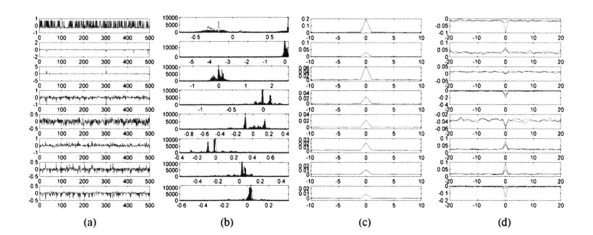

(a)   (b)   (c)   (d)

Figure 6. Results of surrogate data from fraud operations

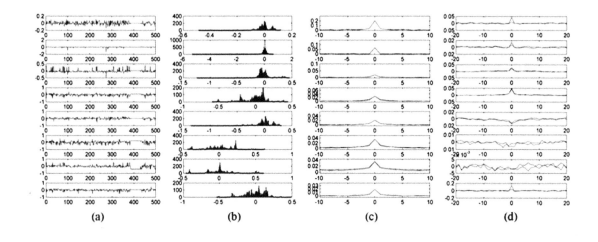

(a)   (b)   (c)   (d)

as the peaks of the pdf for the true data, and the shapes of both pdfs were very close in all cases. The pdf of the surrogates were more diffuse (i.e. less discrete), which might be caused by the amount of non-stationarity in the legitimate operations.

Similarity of the surrogates and the real operations was also tested by performing ACCFD using the method $\alpha - \text{INT}$ explained above. A certain amount of randomly-selected operations were replaced with surrogate operations and the detection was repeated. The amount of replaced operations was changed from 0% (only true operations) to 50%, 75%, and 100% (only surrogate operations). The obtained ROC curves are shown in Figure 8 showing that the curves are similar in all cases even for low false alarm values (Figure 8b). There are some differences in value for very low amounts of FPR. In all cases, the lower the amount of surrogate operations, the closer the ROC became to that of the real operations (all the curves were very close for FPR above 0.06).

Figure 7. Joint distribution of a) legitimate and b) fraud operations

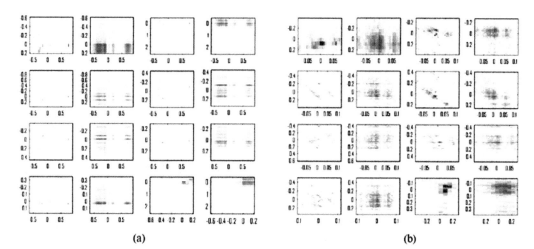

Figure 8. ROC curves for different percentages of surrogate data: a) complete curves; b) zoom in a zoom of interest

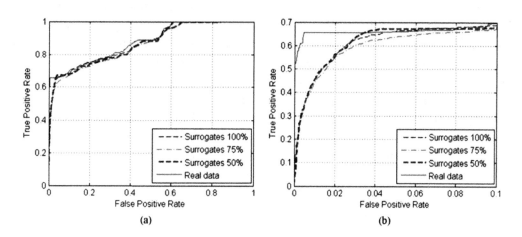

Figure 9 shows the results of applying different algorithms for ACCFD changing the fraud/legitimate ratio. It can be seen that the performance decreases the ratio decreases with $\alpha - \text{INT}$ method obtaining best results for all ratios. Furthermore, $\alpha - \text{INT}$ performance shows robustness at very-low false alarm values. Thus, exploiting complementarities of basic detectors seems to be immune for the fusion method.

FUTURE RESEARCH DIRECTIONS

Improvement of fusion techniques to take full advantage of complementarities among detectors is still required. A challenging issue is to consider in the fusion method that the behavior of the detectors for

Figure 9. ROC curves for different proportions of fraud/legitimate operations obtained by different methods

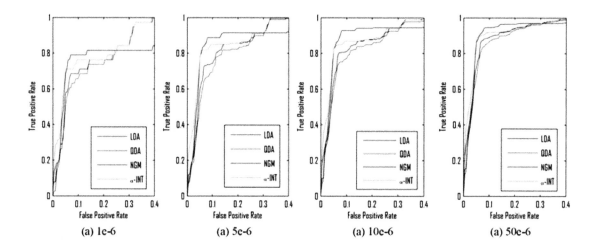

(a) 1e-6   (a) 5e-6   (a) 10e-6   (a) 50e-6

transaction scoring is not regular for the whole dataset. Also changing fraud dynamics might continuously distorts the complementarities among the detectors making tighter the design of an optimum fusion method. Methods that incorporate prediction and temporal dependence should be devised for ACCFD.

Besides, the combination of different kinds of general detectors presented here, there are other alternatives that can be explored. Several versions of a kind of detector that are trained in different ways can be combined, for instance, using different versions of the data, searching specialized decision tress for each of the features, etc. Some examples of that kind of methods are boosting, bagging, and mixtures of experts. One of the critical issues for these ensemble approaches is to adequately handle with the so-called bias-variance tradeoff. Small bias indicates that training data has been learned well (small error of prediction) and small variance indicates capability of generalization, i.e., unobserved data might be predicted with small error. The problem consists of a low variance causes a low bias and vice-versa.

Technological constraints and prospective arising from big data context including data storage, privacy and security, and time processing issues are also subjects for future research.

CONCLUSION

We have presented a new application having unquestionable interest for the signal processing community. Some similarities and differences with classical detection problems in the signal processing area have been emphasized. Then it has been considered the use of fusion as a powerful technique to derive algorithms having reasonable performance to solve this very complex problem. Experimental results using large real and surrogate datasets have been showed, where the improvements of using fusion of scores have been illustrated. Different well-known methods were compared with the new approaches. The detection results obtained for different mixtures of real and surrogate data were comparable under real requirements of very low false alarm.

An important aspect to have in mind is the context. Thus, arriving to probabilities of detection of 40% (to give a number) may be useless in other areas like radar detection, but can be extremely significant in credit card fraud detection, as it could imply a big amount of money saving. Also the usual figures of merit should be replaced by the KPI. In this sense, much work remains to arrive to methods suited to "modified cost functions", which better reflect the actual optimization to be reached, or to practical methods that can select the best detectors for a simultaneous fitting of the KPI.

ACKNOWLEDGMENT

This work was supported by Spanish Administration and European Union under grant TEC2014-58438-R and Generalitat Valenciana under grant PROMETEO II/2014/032.

REFERENCES

Atrey, P., Hossain, M., El Saddik, A., & Kankanhalli, M. (2010). Multimodal fusion for multimedia analysis: A survey. *Multimedia Systems*, *16*(6), 345–379. doi:10.100700530-010-0182-0

Bhattacharyya, S., Jha, S., Tharakunnel, K., & Westland, J. C. (2011). Data mining for credit card fraud: A comparative study. *Decision Support Systems*, *50*(3), 602–613. doi:10.1016/j.dss.2010.08.008

Borgnat, P., Abry, P., & Flandrin, P. (2012). Using surrogates and optimal transport for synthesis of stationary multivariate series with prescribed covariance function and non-Gaussian joint distribution. *Proceedings of ICASSP* (págs. 3729-3732). Kyoto, Japan: IEEE. 10.1109/ICASSP.2012.6288727

Danenas, P. (2015). Intelligent financial fraud detection and analysis: A survey of recent patents. *Recent Patents on Computer Science*, *8*(1), 13–23. doi:10.2174/2213275907666141101001436

Girgenti, R. H., & Hedley, T. P. (2011). *Managing the risk of fraud and misconduct: meeting the challenges of a global, regulated and digital environment*. McGraw-Hill.

Hodge, V., & Austin, J. (2004). A survey of outlier detection methodologies. *J. of Art. Intell.*, *22*(2), 85–126.

Iyengar, S. G., Varshney, P. K., & Damarla, T. (2011). A Parametric Copula-Based Framework for Hypothesis Testing Using Heterogeneous Data. *IEEE Transactions on Signal Processing*, *59*(5), 2308–2319. doi:10.1109/TSP.2011.2105483

Jain, A. K., Duin, P. W., & Jianchang Mao. (2000). Statistical pattern recognition: A review. *IEEE Transactions on Pattern Analysis and Machine Intelligence*, *22*(1), 4–37. doi:10.1109/34.824819

Kittler, J., Hatef, M., Duin, R. P., & Matas, J. (1998). On combining classifiers. *IEEE Transactions on Pattern Analysis and Machine Intelligence*, *20*(3), 226–23. doi:10.1109/34.667881

Lifeng, L., Ho, S. W., & Poor, H. V. (2011). Privacy-Security Trade-Offs in Biometric Security Systems - Part I: Single Use Case. *IEEE Trans. Inf. Forensics Security*, *6*(1), 122–139. doi:10.1109/TIFS.2010.2098872

Montague, D. A. (2010). Essentials of online payment security and fraud prevention. Wiley.

Pawar, S., El Rouayheb, S., & Ramchandran, K. (2011). Securing Dynamic Distributed Storage Systems Against Eavesdropping and Adversarial Attacks. *IEEE Transactions on Information Theory*, *57*(10), 6734–6753. doi:10.1109/TIT.2011.2162191

Poor, H. V. (2012). Information and inference in the wireless physical layer. *Wireless Communications*, *19*(1), 40–47. doi:10.1109/MWC.2012.6155875

Prichard, D., & Theiler, J. (1994). Generating surrogate data for time series with several simultaneously measured variables. *Physical Review Letters*, *73*(7), 951–954. doi:10.1103/PhysRevLett.73.951 PMID:10057582

Salazar, A. (2013). *On Statistical Pattern Recognition in Independent Component Analysis Mixture Modelling*. Berlin, Germany: Springer. doi:10.1007/978-3-642-30752-2

Salazar, A., Safont, G., Soriano, A., & Vergara, L. (2012). Automatic credit card fraud detection based on non-linear signal processing. *46th Annual IEEE International Carnahan Conference (ICCST)* (pp. 207-212). Boston, MA: IEEE. 10.1109/CCST.2012.6393560

Salazar, A., Safont, G., & Vergara, L. (2014). Surrogate techniques for testing fraud detection algorithms in credit card operations. *48th International Carnahan Conference on Security Technology (ICCST2014)* (pp. 1-7). Rome, Italy: IEEE. 10.1109/CCST.2014.6986987

Salazar, A., Vergara, L., Serrano, A., & Igual, J. (2010). A General Procedure for Learning Mixtures of Independent Component Analyzers. *Pattern Recognition*, *43*(1), 69–85. doi:10.1016/j.patcog.2009.05.013

Sankar, L., Rajagopalan, S. R., & Poor, H. V. (2013). Utility-Privacy Tradeoff in Databases: An Information-theoretic Approach. *IEEE Trans. Inf. Forens. Sec.*, *8*(6), 838–852. doi:10.1109/TIFS.2013.2253320

Schreiber, T., & Schmitz, A. (2000). Surrogate time series. *Physica D. Nonlinear Phenomena*, *142*(3-4), 346–382. doi:10.1016/S0167-2789(00)00043-9

Shafer, G. (1976). *A Mathematical Theory of Evidence*. Princeton University Press.

Soriano, A., Vergara, L., Ahmed, B., & Salazar, A. (2015). Fusion of Scores in a Detection Context Based on Alpha Integration. *Neural Computation*, *27*(9), 1983–2010. doi:10.1162/NECO_a_00766 PMID:26161815

Tax, D., & Duin, R. (2001). Uniform object generation for optimizing one-class classifiers. *Journal of Machine Learning Research*, *2*, 155–173.

Tzikas, D. G., Likas, A. C., & Galatsanos, N. (2008). The variational approximation for Bayesian inference. *IEEE Signal Processing Magazine*, *25*(6), 131–146. doi:10.1109/MSP.2008.929620

Vergara, L., Soriano, A., Safont, G., & Salazar, A. (2016). On the fusion of non-independent detectors. *Digital Signal Processing*, *50*, 24–33. doi:10.1016/j.dsp.2015.11.009

Wells, J. T. (2011). *Corporate fraud handbook: prevention and detection* (3rd ed.). Wiley.

Yuksel, S. E., Wilson, J. N., & Gader, P. D. (2012). Twenty Years of Mixture of Experts. *IEEE Trans. On Neural Networks and Learning Systems*, *23*(4), 1177–1193. doi:10.1109/TNNLS.2012.2200299 PMID:24807516

ADDITIONAL READING

Safont, G., Salazar, A., Rodriguez, A., & Vergara, L. (2014). On Recovering Missing Ground Penetrating Radar Traces by Statistical Interpolation Methods. *Remote Sensing*, *6*(8), 7546–7565. doi:10.3390/rs6087546

Safont, G., Salazar, A., Soriano, A., & Vergara, L. (2012). Combination of multiple detectors for EEG based biometric identification/authentication. *Proceedings of 46th Annual 2012 International Carnahan Conference on Security Technology (ICCST)* (págs. 230-236). Boston: IEEE. 10.1109/CCST.2012.6393564

Salazar, A., Vergara, L., & Miralles, R. (2010). On including sequential dependence in ICA mixture models. *Signal Processing*, *90*(7), 2314–2318. doi:10.1016/j.sigpro.2010.02.010

Slavakis, K., Giannakis, G. B., & Mateos, G. (2014). Modeling optimization for big data analytics. *IEEE Signal Processing Magazine*, *31*(5), 18–31. doi:10.1109/MSP.2014.2327238

Zhai, Y., Ong, Y. S., & Tsang, I. W. (2014). The emerging big dimensionality. *IEEE Computational Intelligence Magazine*, *9*(3), 14–26. doi:10.1109/MCI.2014.2326099

KEY TERMS AND DEFINITIONS

Classifier: A computational method that can be trained using known labeled data for predicting the label of unlabeled data. If there's only two labels (also called classes), the method is called "detector".

Fusion of Scores: A process for efficient combination of a set of scores or probabilistic grades granted by a set of detectors/classifiers. Evaluation of combination performance depends on the application objectives.

KPI: Key performance indicator is an index that defines the performance of a process. In the case of ACCFD, roughly, the set of KPIs serves to translate ROC results into business terms.

Pattern Recognition: Automatic process of extracting, representing, and splitting conspicuous characteristics from a dataset to produce several subsets that can be associated with concepts normally accepted by humans.

Receiving Operating Characteristic (ROC) Curve: A numeric tool for the evaluation of a detection process that implements comparison in a coordinate plane of probability of detection and probability of false alarm at different operating points from 0 to 1.

Surrogate Data: Data that are computationally generated that behave with statistical features similar to that of real data.

This research was previously published in the Encyclopedia of Information Science and Technology, Fourth Edition edited by Mehdi Khosrow-Pour, pages 4937-4950, copyright year 2018 by Information Science Reference (an imprint of IGI Global).

Chapter 23

Privacy, Algorithmic Discrimination, and the Internet of Things

Jenifer Sunrise Winter
University of Hawaii at Manoa, USA

ABSTRACT

The internet of things (IoT) is a paradigm encompassing a wide range of developments that enable everyday objects to be tagged and uniquely identified over the internet. The IoT ecosystem is comprised of networks of physical objects embedded with the ability to sense, and sometimes act upon, their environment, as well as related communication, applications, and data analytics. This chapter introduces the internet of things, addresses its definition and related concepts, outlines anticipated application areas, and highlights challenges for its development. Concerns about privacy, surveillance, and unjust algorithmic discrimination are discussed.

INTRODUCTION

The Internet of Things (IoT) is a paradigm encompassing a wide range of developments that enable everyday objects to be tagged and uniquely identified over the Internet. Although there is no single definition for the Internet of Things, competing visions agree that it relates to the integration of the physical world with the virtual world, with any object having the potential to be connected to the Internet via short-range wireless technologies, such as radio frequency identification (RFID), near field communication (NFC), or Wireless Sensor Networks (WSNs). This merging of the physical and virtual worlds will "enable the Internet to reach out into the real world of physical objects" (Internet of Things Conference Organizing Committee, 2010). Further, it will allow increased instrumentation, tracking and measurement of the natural world, enabling analytic tools to enhance business management processes and offer citizens increased convenience and safety (Uckelmann, Harrison, & Michahelles, 2010).

DOI: 10.4018/978-1-5225-7492-7.ch023

The IoT is imagined as a "backbone for ubiquitous computing, enabling smart environments to recognize and identify objects, and retrieve information from the Internet to facilitate their adaptive functionality" (Weber & Weber, 2010, p. 1). In this regard, the IoT is an emerging global architecture that will enable enhanced machine intelligence to automate the exchange of goods and services. In addition to improving supply chain management, this integration of tags and sensor networks will also be employed in diverse application scenarios, including smart appliances and smart homes, disaster warning, structural engineering, farming, and in-vivo health applications (Atzori, Iera, & Morabito, 2010). This chapter will introduce the Internet of Things, address its definition and related concepts, outline anticipated application areas, highlight challenges, and discuss privacy and surveillance concerns.

BACKGROUND

Related Areas

Current research agendas focus on the IoT ecosystem – networks of physical objects embedded with the ability to sense, and sometimes act upon, their environment, as well as related communication, applications, and data analytics (Gartner, 2014). The IoT is often mentioned in relation to other, overlapping research paradigms, particularly Ubiquitous Computing, Pervasive Computing, and Ambient Intelligence, research agendas that address the integration of myriad, heterogeneous objects into the everyday environment. Weiser's (1991) vision of Ubiquitous Computing emerged in the late 1980s and emphasized the potential of multiple computers per person, in a variety of forms, to activate the physical environment and make computational intelligence an extension of human activity. Ubiquitous Computing research is distinguished by its human-centered focus and has increasingly addressed interaction contexts (Abowd, Ebling, Hunt, Lei, & Gellersen, 2002). The related concept of Pervasive Computing (Hoffnagle, 1999) emerged as a corporate vision at IBM during the late 1990s. This agenda has focused on the technical systems required to embed numerous, networked devices throughout the environment. Over time, the two research communities have overlapped, and the two leading conferences, ACM's Pervasive and UbiComp, merged in 2013. Ambient Intelligence research has been guided by the European Union's Fifth Framework Programme (Information Society Technologies, 1998-2002) and focuses on embedded devices, particularly those in smart homes, which are context-sensitive and tailored towards personal needs. While the IoT overlaps technical developments in these related areas, it is distinguished by several concepts. These include 1) goals for an architecture that provides billions, or trillions, of heterogeneous objects with unique identifiers that allow them to interact over a global network; and 2) an emphasis on machine-to-machine (M2M) communication. Although all of these paradigms tend to focus on near-term visions of potential future environments (Dourish & Bell, 2011), the IoT is already manifest in various ways today.

Origin and Evolution of the Concept

Kevin Ashton is credited with the first use of the phrase "Internet of Things" in 1999. He focuses on the potential of M2M intelligence to capture real-time data about the physical world and use it without direct human oversight (Ashton, 2009), stating that the goals of IoT research and development focus on endowing computers *with their own means of gathering information, so they can see, hear and smell the world for themselves, in all its random glory. RFID and sensor technology enable computers to observe, identify and understand the world—without the limitations of human-entered data. (Ashton, 2009, para. 5)*

Although the concept arose in the context of supply chain management, he emphasizes that the IoT now applies to nearly any aspect of the physical world.

Since Ashton's first use of the phrase, the IoT has been associated with a wide variety of academic, government, and corporate research projects. An early and substantial influence was the Massachusetts Institute of Technology's Auto-ID Center, which was formed in 1999 to create an RFID-based IoT architecture for global supply-chain management. In 2003, the Auto-ID Center closed, and EPCglobal took over its commercial work. This effort spun off into the Auto-ID Labs, seven academic research labs that focus on building a global infrastructure using RFID or other short-range, wireless technologies. The Auto-ID Labs developed the Electronic Product Code (EPC), an RFID tag that uniquely identifies a product, and the EPCglobal stack is the de facto standard for retail and consumer goods industries.

Other large-scale efforts include IBM's Smarter Planet strategy initiated in 2008 (IBM, 2008), which has focused on the potential of instrumenting the physical world with tens of billions (perhaps trillions) of interconnected sensors. Here, the IoT is envisioned as a way to fuel economic growth, business and government efficiency, improve physical security, and enhance scientific knowledge. Similarly, HP's Central Nervous System for the Earth (CeNSE) initiative relies on billions of nanoscale sensors to detect vibration and motion (HP, n.d.)

The IoT has also figured prominently in national and international technology policy strategies. Following the International Telecommunication Union's special report on the IoT (International Telecommunication Union, 2005a), the European Union's Directorate, General Information Society and Media shifted concern to the IoT (European Commission, Community Research and Development Information Service, 2012) with its i2010 policy framework for the information society and media (2005-2010). Under its Seventh Framework Programme (FP7), the EU funded the CASAGRAS (Coordination and support action for global RFID-related activities and standardization) program, which has provided a framework for research to aid the European Commission in navigating international issues related to RFID, in particular the IoT (CASAGRAS, 2009). This project defines the IoT as

A global network infrastructure, linking physical and virtual objects through the exploitation of data capture and communication capabilities. This infrastructure includes existing and evolving Internet and network developments. It will offer specific object-identification, sensor and connection capability as the basis for the development of independent cooperative services and applications. These will be characterised by a high degree of autonomous data capture, event transfer, network connectivity and interoperability. (CASAGRAS, 2009, p.10)

Simultaneously, the industry-driven policy initiative EPoSS (European Technology Platform on Smart Systems Integration) has sought to direct research and innovation needs related the IoT (European Technology Platform on Smart Systems Integration, n.d.).

China is also taking a lead role in IoT research and development. In 2009, Chinese Premier Wen Jiabao announced that IoT will be central to China's coordinated, national strategic development (GSMA, 2015). The IoT appears in China's 12th Five Year Plan, which guides policy from 2011–2015 (Hvistendahl,

2012). This has led to a number of IoT research parks throughout China, including an Internet of Things Center established in Shanghai and the City of Wuxi redesigned as a research and development center.

Components of the Internet of Things

Atzori et al. (2010) argue that the IoT arises from three different, overlapping visions: 1) things-oriented visions focusing on real-world objects embedded with RFID or sensor technologies; 2) Internet-oriented visions; and 3) semantic-oriented visions. The components of each of these are addressed next.

'Things' are objects in the natural world that we wish to instrument. Each thing must be connected to a communication device, such as an RFID chip, a sensor, or an actuator. These can be embedded in a variety of objects, including mobile phones, automobiles, home appliances, clothing, or even the human body. In addition to RFID-tagged objects or NFC-embedded smartphones, things may include nanoelectronics, sensors, or other embedded systems that detect, measure, compute, and communicate (Vermesan et al., 2011). Data about these objects can include location-based information, data from the environment that the object is sensing, or other, stored data. According to Vermesan et al. (2011), things are

expected to become active participants in business, information, and social processes where they are enabled to interact and communicate among themselves and with the environment by exchanging data and information "sensed" about the environment, while reacting autonomously to the "real/physical" world events and influencing it by running processes that trigger actions and create services with or without direct human intervention. (p. 10)

These developments will be supported by the emergence of linked data, standards and practices for connecting structured data via the World Wide Web, creating a massive, global data space that can be navigated and processed by machine intelligence (Heath & Bizer, 2011). This will enable the Semantic Web (Berners-Lee, 2000), a web of data that can be processed by machines without human intervention.

Networks are a second area of research concern. The maturity of RFID, NFC, and wireless sensor networks (based on IEEE 802.15.4) is poised to allow the interconnection of various smaller networks to the Internet. However, whereas the Internet relies on the TCP/IP protocol stack for end-to-end transmission, there is no single standard to connect these intranets of objects to the Internet. A variety of communication standards operating at various layers are in development. To reach a global scale and maximize the interoperability of heterogeneous systems, there is a need for development of flexible, open standards.

Semantic specifications, the third area of interest, are concerned with how to represent, store, organize, and query objects and data. Here, research focuses on the developments of autonomous software agents and semantic standards for machine communication. Vermesan et al. (2011) highlight the need for "ontology-based semantic standards [that] will enable mapping and cross-referencing between them, in order to enable information exchange" (p. 42).

Application Areas

Applications for the IoT are numerous and diverse, addressing tasks such as measuring location, temperature, acceleration, pollution, or chemical components. Data collected from these sensors is expected to enhance resource management in virtually every sector. The following is a list of potential uses:

- **Logistics/Supply Chain Management:** e.g., item tracking (Ashton, 2009); restocking; payment systems (Uckelmann & Harrison, 2010; Atzori et al., 2010).
- **Scientific Research:** e.g., remote or small scale experiment monitoring.
- **Health Care/Biomedical:** e.g., ambient sensors for independent living; implantable or edible medical devices (CERP-IoT, 2010).
- **Environment:** e.g., natural disaster prediction, such as flood, fire, earthquake, tsunami warning systems (CERP-IoT, 2010); chemical, and gas leak identification; pollution and temperature monitoring (Hvistendahl, 2012); water potability testing.
- **Security:** e.g., motion-sensitive camera activation; access control; radiation monitoring (Ishigaki, Matsumoto, Ichimiya, & Tanaka, 2013); intrusion detection (Khan, Khan, Zaheer, & Khan, 2012).
- **Structural Engineering:** e.g., monitoring and identifying faults in buildings, roads, or bridges (Agrawal & Lal Das, 2011).
- **Food Safety:** e.g., testing (Hvistendahl, 2012) and recall of tainted food (CERP-IoT, 2010).
- **Agriculture:** e.g., monitoring hydration, chemical composition, or soil quality; livestock tracking (CERP-IoT, 2010).
- **Smart Cities:** Infrastructure monitoring; management of smart grids to govern cost- and resource-efficient use of energy (Khan et al., 2012; Atzori et al., 2010); "Green ICT" to lower environmental impact (Vermesan et al., 2011).
- **Smart Homes:** e.g., automatic lighting and power allocation (CERP-IoT, 2010).
- **Transportation:** Aerospace part authentication (CERP-IoT, 2010); sensor-enabled roads; assisted driving (Atzori et al., 2010).
- **Augmented Reality Maps:** e.g., maps equipped with tags enabling NFC-equipped phones to automatically interact with Web services (Atzori et al., 2010).
- **Social Networking:** e.g., automated updates of information on social networks (Atzori et al., 2010).
- **Transparency of Government Data:** Anti-corruption (Bertot, Jaeger, & Grimes, 2010).

PRIVACY AND THE INTERNET OF THINGS

An estimated Zettabyte (1,000,000,000,000,000,000,000 bytes) of data will flow over the Internet in 2016 (Cisco, 2014), as much data as in the entire history of the Internet since its creation in 1969. However, threats to privacy introduced by the IoT are not merely related to the increased magnitude of data collection. The following are unique challenges to privacy in the context of the IoT (Winter, 2013):

1. **Lack of Transparency:** Small components are not necessarily visible. One may not be aware when and where data is being collected (Langheinrich, 2001).
2. **Sheer Number of Objects Monitoring the Environment:** Even under a scheme where one could "opt out" of data sharing, the interface to accomplish this would be unmanageably complex. Similarly, if an individual wishes to deactivate, or temporarily halt, an object's communication potential, the number of objects might make this difficult.
3. **Novel Data Types:** Billions, or trillions, of everyday objects, even the human body itself, may be equipped with networked sensors. Many novel data types can be collected. For example, a variety of biometric data in aggregate form.

4. **Increased Aggregation of User Data:** As data analytics is increasingly embedded into the core of business and operational functions (Davenport, Barth, & Bean, 2012), there is a strong economic incentive to model user data. Thus, data may be collected indiscriminately for future use.

5. **De-Anonymization of Personal Data:** Data that has been anonymized in order to meet legal requirements can be "re-personalized" via data mining techniques (Schwartz & Solove, 2011; Winter, 2016).

6. **M2M Processing and Communication:** Machine intelligence will be used both to collect and to analyze these data, increasing both the scope and analytic potential of big data analytics.

Unjust Algorithmic Discrimination

Unjust discrimination based on big data analytics is a growing concern (e.g., Custers, 2013, boyd, Levy, & Marwick, 2014). Various data about our daily lives are being mined to reveal associations or behaviors, leading to potential political or economic discrimination by governments and corporations in the form of offering different services, products, or prices to individuals based on their data profile (Turow, 2012; Winter, 2015). Examples include:

- Insurers are beginning to allocate risk differently (Upturn, 2014). As new forms of price differentiation emerge, risk calculations by insurers will no longer be spread across a large pool of people, leading to higher burdens (e.g., denial of coverage or higher costs) for some.

- In the criminal justice system, data-based risk assessment is now being considered for use at sentencing. The State of Pennsylvania may allow "some offenders considered low risk to get shorter prison sentences than they would otherwise or avoid incarceration entirely. Those deemed high-risk could spend more time behind bars" (Barry-Jester, Casselman, & Goldstein, 2015, para. 4).

- Data gathered via the smart grid might be used to collect personal information. The National Institute of Standards and Technology observed that smart grid data might reveal specific lifestyle information that could be used by insurers or commercial service providers (National Institute of Standards and Technology, 2010).

- Researchers were able to uniquely identify males who had shared personal DNA sequences on Internet genealogy forums based on publicly available data (Gymrek, McGuire, Golan, Halperin, & Erlich, 2013).While in the United States the *Genetic Information Nondiscrimination Act* is intended to prevent abuse of genetic data, the financial incentives for mining these data are immense, and big data analytics may enable non-protected "proxy" fields (i.e., other patterns or data-based evidence that is not explicitly protected) to be used instead (Barocas & Selbst, 2016).

In 2013, news coverage about the existence of Internet surveillance programs by the United States' National Security Agency and its partners in other countries was credited for growing public awareness and concern about government surveillance (Pew Research Center for the People and the Press, 2013). This growing concern may cause additional resistance to IoT developments. Further, self-censorship due to privacy concerns may limit citizens' freedom of access to information or discussion of issues relevant to democratic decision-making.

Challenges for the Internet of Things

The IoT research community is addressing a wide variety of technical and social issues. Overall, key challenges for development of the IoT include:

- Development of a universal architecture based on open, layered standards (Vermesan et al., 2011).
- Network scalability (Uckelmann et al., 2011).
- Integration of non-IP-based things into the network (Uckelmann et al., 2011).
- Design of energy-efficient objects (Atzori et al., 2010).
- Addressing schemes (Vermesan et al., 2011).
- Autonomous agent design (Vermesan et al., 2011).
- Data storage, representation, and querying standards (Vermesan et al., 2011).
- Mobility management (Atzori et al., 2010).
- Creation of large-scale testbeds for real-world experimentation (Gluhak, Krco, Nati, Pfisterer, Mitton, & Razafindralambo, 2011).
- Spectrum efficiency (Khan, Khan, Zaheer, & Khan, 2012).
- Object and network security (Weber, 2010).

Each of these areas presents a set of robust challenges, and *privacy* should be considered throughout the design process and product lifecycle, rather than as an afterthought. Below, solutions and recommendations for this complex problem are outlined.

SOLUTIONS AND RECOMMENDATIONS

There is no single solution to address privacy concerns related to the Internet of Things. A complex and ongoing approach addressing three domains – sociological, technical, and regulatory – is required (International Telecommunication Union, 2005b).

The sociological domain includes public education and ongoing negotiation about acceptable uses in various contexts. Fostering discussion with a broad range of stakeholders at an early stage of IoT development is necessary to ensure that these developments align with community values and goals (Winter, 2008).

The technological domain includes an array of privacy enhancing technologies (PETs). PETs can include software that allows users to set privacy preferences, "hide" from others on the network, or erase traces of activity. Other means include encryption tools, peer-to-peer systems (P2P), or the ability to switch off tags or sensors (Weber & Weber, 2010). All of these approaches have limitations and, due to the scale and heterogeneity of the IoT, do not provide a satisfactory solution to privacy concerns. Cavoukian and Kursawe (2012) argue that privacy must be introduced during the earliest stages of system development. Privacy by design is a design framework with principles that protect personal privacy while enabling high-quality data collection and analysis. Using the principles in the framework, a variety of systems with diverse goals and contexts can be designed with privacy at the core, rather than as an afterthought.

Because the IoT is a global system, the regulatory domain is particularly complex. Weber and Weber (2010) argue that the time to create legal protections is before major problems arise. Weber (2010) argues that a new privacy approach is required. "The nature of the IoT asks for a heterogeneous and differentiated legal framework that adequately takes into account the globality, verticality, ubiquity and technicity of the IoT" (p. 30). He acknowledges that neither industry self-regulation nor national laws will be sufficient. As Hildner (2006) observes, "Experience demonstrates that legally unenforceable self-regulation will not be a sufficient limitation on RFID's threat to privacy" (p. 159). On the other hand, omnibus laws (such as those in the European Union) may be difficult to enforce outside of their jurisdiction. Weber (2010) argues for the development of key principles to be set by a transparent, international organization complemented with more detailed regulation originating in the private sector. However, the feasibility of this approach is uncertain. In December, 2013, the United Nations General Assembly adopted a consensus resolution strongly supporting a right to privacy (United Nations News Centre, 2013). The IoT is a complex sociotechnical system comprised of a plurality of actors, networks, institutions, and contexts, and efforts to regulate privacy at an international level may not be sufficient. Instead, we may see global privacy regulations continue at a variety of levels and contexts rather than as a global, coordinated approach.

FUTURE RESEARCH DIRECTIONS

As outlined above, there are a number of critical technical challenges for the Internet of Things, including issues of network scalability, integration of non-IP-based objects into the network (Uckelmann et al., 2011), standards for data storage, representation, and querying (Vermesan et al., 2011), and spectrum efficiency (Khan, Khan, Zaheer, & Khan, 2012). Further, there is a need for increased focus on security and privacy (Weber, 2010). Focusing on privacy, each of the three domains outlined by the International Telecommunication Union (2005b) – sociological, technical, and regulatory – present fertile areas for research related to privacy and the emerging Internet of Things. Within the sociological domain, research is needed to better understand users' behaviors and attitudes related to IoT use, particularly in specific contexts of use. Within the technological domain, many aspects of IoT network and object design will benefit from robust security- and privacy-enhancing technologies, especially those that are built into overall system design. Within the regulatory domain, there is a need for development of an internationally-recognized set of key principles related to privacy rights. Research is also required to map and assess the distributions of social benefits and harms related to the IoT in order to determine whether the resulting distributions serve the public good. Further, there is a need for studies that promote a clearer understanding and assessment of privacy regulation at national, regional, and international levels.

CONCLUSION

This chapter introduced the IoT and provided an overview of its main components and various research initiatives that guide its development. The IoT is likely to have many beneficial applications that impact nearly every sector, and a number of these noted in the literature were addressed. Further, key challenges were outlined, including the issues of privacy and unjust algorithmic discrimination. Foresight activities involving a broad range of stakeholders are necessary both for the formulation of legislation and to inform system design. IoT systems should be designed with privacy in mind from the start.

REFERENCES

Abowd, G. D., Ebling, M., Hunt, G., Lei, H., & Gellersen, H.-W. (2002). Context-aware computing. *IEEE Pervasive Computing / IEEE Computer Society [and] IEEE Communications Society, 1*(3), 22–23. doi:10.1109/MPRV.2002.1037718

Agrawal, S., & Lal Das, M. (2011, December). *Internet of Things – a paradigm shift of future Internet applications.* Paper presented at the Second International Conference on Current Trends in Technology (NUiCONE 2011), Ahmedabad. 10.1109/NUiConE.2011.6153246

Ashton, K. (2009). That 'Internet of Things' thing. *RFID Journal.* Retrieved May 11, 2010, from http://www.rfidjournal.com/article/view/4986

Atzori, L., Iera, A., & Morabito, G. (2010). The Internet of Things: A survey. *Computer Networks, 54*(15), 2787–2805. doi:10.1016/j.comnet.2010.05.010

Barocas, S., & Selbst, A. D. (2016). Big data's disparate impact. *California Law Review, 104.*

Barry-Jester, A. M., Casselman, B., & Goldstein, C. (2015, August 4). *Should prison sentences be based on crimes that haven't been committed yet?* Retrieved from http://fivethirtyeight.com/ features/prison-reform-risk-assessment/

Berners-Lee, T. (2000). *Weaving the Web: The past, present and future of the World Wide Web by its inventor.* London: Texere.

Bertot, J. C., Jaeger, P. T., & Grimes, J. M. (2010). Using ICTs to create a culture of transparency: E-government and social media as openness and anti-corruption tools for societies. *Government Information Quarterly, 27*(3), 264–271. doi:10.1016/j.giq.2010.03.001

boyd, d., Levy, K., & Marwick, A. (2014). The networked nature of algorithmic discrimination. In S. Gangadharan (Ed.), *Data and discrimination: Collected essays* (pp. 53-57). Washington, DC: Open Technology Institute – New America Foundation.

CASAGRAS. (2009). *RFID and the inclusive model for the Internet of Things: Final report.* EU Framework 7. Retrieved from http://www.grifs-project.eu/data/File/CASAGRAS%20FinalReport%20(2).pdf

Cavoukian, A., & Kursawe, K. (2012). Implementing privacy by design: The smart meter case. *Proceedings of the 2012 IEEE International Conference on Smart Grid Engineering* (pp. 1-8). Piscataway, NJ: IEEE. 10.1109/SGE.2012.6463977

CERP-IoT. European Union, Cluster of European Research Projects on the Internet of Things. (2010). *Vision and challenges for realising the Internet of Things.* Brussels: European Commission – Information Society and Media.

Cisco. (2014, June 10). *The Zettabyte era: Trends and analysis.* Cisco White Paper. San Jose, CA: Cisco Systems. Retrieved from http://www.cisco.com/c/en/us/ solutions/collateral/service-provider/visual-networking-index-vni/VNI_Hyperconnectivity_WP.pdf

Custers, B. (2013). Data dilemmas in the information society: Introduction and overview. In B. Custers, T. Calders, B. Schermer, & T. Zarsky (Eds.), *Discrimination and privacy in the information society: Data mining and profiling in large databases* (pp. 3–26). New York: Springer. doi:10.1007/978-3-642-30487-3_1

Davenport, T. H., Barth, P., & Bean, R. (2012). *How 'big data' is different.* Retrieved from http://sloan-review.mit.edu/article/how-big-data-is-different/

Dourish, P., & Bell, G. (2011). *Divining a digital future: Mess and mythology in ubiquitous computing.* Cambridge, MA: The MIT Press. doi:10.7551/mitpress/9780262015554.001.0001

European Commission, Information Society and Media. (2008). *Internet of Things in 2020: Roadmap for the future. European Technology Platform on Smart Systems Integration.* Version 1.1. Author.

European Technology Platform on Smart Systems Integration (EPoSS). (n.d.). *Objectives and mission.* Retrieved from http://www.smart-systems-integration.org/public/about/objectives-mission

Gartner. (2014, November 11). *Gartner says 4.9 billion collected 'Things' will be in use in 2015.* Retrieved from https://www.gartner.com/newsroom/id/2905717

Gluhak, A., Krco, S., Nati, M., Pfisterer, D., Mitton, N., & Razafindralambo, T. (2011). A survey of facilities for experimental Internet of Things research. *IEEE Communications Magazine, 49*(11), 58–67. doi:10.1109/MCOM.2011.6069710

GSMA. (2015). *How China is scaling the Internet of Things.* Retrieved from http://www.gsma.com/newsroom/wp-content/uploads/16531-China-IoT-Report-LR.pdf

Gymrek, M., McGuire, A. L., Golan, D., Halperin, E., & Erlich, Y. (2013). Identifying personal genomes by surname inference. *Science, 339*(6117), 321–324. doi:10.1126cience.1229566 PMID:23329047

Haggerty, K. D., & Ericson, R. V. (2006). The new politics of surveillance and visibility. In K. D. Haggerty & R. V. Ericson (Eds.), *The new politics of surveillance and visibility* (pp. 3–25). Toronto: University of Toronto Press.

Heath, T., & Bizer, C. (2011). Linked data: Evolving the Web into a global data space. *Synthesis Lectures on the Semantic Web: Theory and Technology, 1*(1), 1-136.

Hildner, L. (2006). Defusing the threat of RFID: Protecting consumer privacy through technology-specific legislation at the state level. *Harvard Civil Rights-Civil Liberties Law Review, 41*, 133–176.

Hoffnagle, G. F. (1999). Preface. *IBM Systems Journal, 38*(4), 502–503. doi:10.1147j.384.0502

HP. (n.d.). *CeNSE.* Retrieved from http://www8.hp.com/us/en/hp-information/environment/cense.html#.Uo1MKMQQZhE

Hvistendahl, M. (2012). China pushes the Internet of Things. *Science, 336*(6086), 1223–1223. doi:10.1126cience.336.6086.1223 PMID:22679075

IBM. (2008, November). *A mandate for change is a mandate for smart.* Conversations for a smarter planet series, 1. Retrieved from http://www.ibm.com/ smarterplanet/ global/files/us__en_us__general__smarterplanet_overview.pdf

International Telecommunication Union. (2005a). *The Internet of Things.* Geneva: International Telecommunication Union.

International Telecommunication Union. (2005b). Privacy and Ubiquitous Network Societies: Background paper. *ITU Workshop on Ubiquitous Network Societies.* Geneva: International Telecommunication Union.

Internet of Things Conference Organizing Committee. (2010). *Internet of Things.* Retrieved from http://www.iot2010.org/outline/

Ishigaki, Y., Matsumoto, Y., Ichimiya, R., & Tanaka, K. (2013). Development of mobile radiation monitoring system utilizing smartphone and its field tests in Fukushima. *IEEE Sensors Journal, 13*(10), 3520–3526. doi:10.1109/JSEN.2013.2272734

Khan, R., Khan, S. U., Zaheer, R., & Khan, S. (2010). Future Internet: The Internet of Things architecture, possible applications and key challenges. *10th International Conference on Frontiers of Information Technology,* 257-260. DOI: 10.1109/FIT.2012.53

Langheinrich, M. (2001). Privacy by design: Principles of privacy-aware ubiquitous systems. In *Proceedings of the 3rd International Conference on Ubiquitous Computing* (pp. 273-291). London: Springer-Verlag. 10.1007/3-540-45427-6_23

National Institute of Standards and Technology. (2010). *Introduction to NISTIR 7628: Guidelines for smart grid cyber security.* Gaithersburg, MD: NIST.

Neumann, P. G., & Weinstein, L. (2006). Risks of RFID. *Communications of the ACM, 49*(5), 136. doi:10.1145/1125944.1125971

Pew Research Center for the People and the Press. (2013). *Few see adequate limits on NSA surveillance program.* Retrieved from http://www.people-press.org/ files/legacy-pdf/7-26-2013%20NSA%20release.pdf

Schwartz, P. M., & Solove, D. (2011). The PII problem: Privacy and a new concept of personally identifiable information. *New York University Law Review, 86,* 1814–1894.

Turow, J. (2012). The daily you: How the new advertising industry is defining your identity and worth. New Haven, CT: Yale University Press.

Uckelmann, D., & Harrison, M. (2010). Integrated billing mechanisms in the Internet of Things to support information sharing and enable new business opportunities. *International Journal of RF Technologies: Research and Applications, 2*(2), 73–90.

Uckelmann, D., Harrison, M., & Michahelles, F. (2010). An architectural approach towards the future Internet of Things. In D. Uckelmann & ... (Eds.), *Architecting the Internet of Things.* Berlin: Springer-Verlag Berlin Heidelberg.

United Nations News Centre. (2013). *General Assembly backs right to privacy in digital age*. Retrieved from http://www.un.org/apps/ news/story.asp? NewsID=46780&Cr=privacy&Cr1=#.UuW_5hB6dD8

Upturn. (2014). *Civil rights, big data, and our algorithmic future*. Retrieved from https://bigdata.fairness.io/

Vermesan, O., Friess, P., Guillemin, P., Gusmeroli, S., Sundmaeker, H., Bassi, A., ... Doody, P. (2011). Internet of Things strategic research roadmap. In O. Vermesan & P. Freiss (Eds.), *Global technological and societal trends from smart environments and spaces to green ICT* (pp. 9–52). Aalborg: River Publishers.

Weber, R. H. (2010). Internet of Things: New security and privacy challenges. *Computer Law & Security Report*, *26*(1), 23–30. doi:10.1016/j.clsr.2009.11.008

Weber, R. H., & Weber, R. (2010). *Internet of Things: Legal perspectives*. Berlin: Springer-Verlag Berlin Heidelberg. doi:10.1007/978-3-642-11710-7

Weiser, M. (1991). The computer for the twenty-first century. *Scientific American*, *265*(3), 94–101. doi:10.1038cientificamerican0991-94

Winter, J. S. (2008). Emerging policy problems related to ubiquitous computing: Negotiating stakeholders visions of the future. *Knowledge, Technology & Policy*, *21*(4), 191–203. doi:10.100712130-008-9058-4

Winter, J. S. (2013). Surveillance in ubiquitous network societies: Normative conflicts related to the consumer in-store supermarket experience in the context of the Internet of Things. *Ethics and Information Technology*. doi:10.100710676-013-9332-3

Winter, J. S. (2015). Algorithmic discrimination: Big data analytics and the future of the Internet. In J. S. Winter & R. Ono (Eds.), *The future Internet: Alternative visions*. New York: Springer. doi:10.1007/978-3-319-22994-2_8

KEY TERMS AND DEFINITIONS

Ambient Intelligence (AmI): Describes an environment in which many embedded, networked devices exist throughout the environment. Typically, these are tailored towards personal needs and aware of context. This research program is often associated with smart homes. Ambient Intelligence research has been guided by the European Union's Fifth Framework Programme (Information Society Technologies, 1998-2002).

Electronic Product Code (EPC): Is a standard that seeks to provide unique identification for RFID tags. It was originally created by MIT's Auto-ID Center and is currently directed by EPCglobal, an organization dedicated to the global standardization of EPC. The EPCglobal stack is the de facto standard for retail and consumer goods industries.

NFC (Near Field Communication): Is a collection of standards that enable the wireless exchange of data between mobile communication devices in close proximity. NFC is currently being used to exchange personal data and as in electronic payment systems.

RFID (Radio-Frequency Identification): Is the use of an object (typically referred to as an RFID tag) incorporated into a product for the purpose of identification and tracking using short-range wireless communication. RFID tags store information and can be read at short range with an RFID reader.

Ubiquitous Computing: Is a research paradigm that emerged from anthropological studies at Xerox Parc in the late 1980s. Marc Weiser proposed a human-centric vision of a many-to-one relationship between computers and humans.

Chapter 24
The Protection Policy for Youth Online in Japan

Nagayuki Saito
Ochanomizu University, Japan

Madoka Aragaki
Business Breakthrough University, Japan

ABSTRACT

The OECD committee adopted the Recommendation on the Protection of Children Online in February 2012. It recommended establishing an appropriate online environmental policy for children based on actual data. Arising from the international movement, the Internet Literacy Assessment Indicator for Students (ILAS) and its tests were developed; this tool aims to ensure safe and secure internet use among 15-year-old students. This chapter analyzes national research data from ILAS to explore the relationship between students' backgrounds and online literacy. The results have revealed several political challenges, including the need for policies on educational awareness in low literacy areas, regional literacy differences, and the need to support children in learning to avoid risk.

INTRODUCTION

In recent years, Internet use among young people has been associated to various social problems in many different countries. Examples include miscommunication by text, billing fraud, access to illegal content, and contact with ill-intentioned people. Especially in Japan, the use of smartphones has spread very rapidly among teenagers and young adults since 2012, generating tremendous changes in their online environment. These changes have triggered the abovementioned problems.

To tackle these problems, "the Act on the Development of an Environment that Provides Safe and Secure Internet Use for Young People" (Act No. 79 of 2008) was enforced in April 2009 in Japan. Because Article 3 defines the skills needed to use the Internet efficiently, it is important to empower teenagers and young people to develop risk management skills by using Internet effectively.

DOI: 10.4018/978-1-5225-7492-7.ch024

For this reason, it is crucial to optimize educational policy to meet the needs of young people. Doing so will require criteria on which to review the current policy. It is also important to evaluate the Internet literacy of teenagers and young people, and to reform educational policy and its implementation to reflect the results of this assessment.

This study aims to develop ILAS, the Internet Literacy Assessment Indicator for Students, making it a more effective and visible tool for developing young people's coping skills, reducing their online risks, and enabling them to use the Internet more safely. This indicator will be evidence based and designed to optimize educational policy; it can play an important role as a decision-making system for designing effective educational policy.

BACKGROUND

Review of Evidence Based Policy Making

OECD (2012a) advised all stakeholders to reduce online risks and provide a safer Internet environment. This recommendation obliges every stakeholder to provide a safer online environment for teenagers and young people. To provide effective protection, it is important to implement a youth protection policy at every level of government, as well as in the private sector and educational organizations. Without clear role definitions, it will be difficult to implement a concrete protection policy.

The most effective way to solve these problems is to think about each problem separately, clarifying the political tasks each sector should deal with. One tactic that can help to achieve this is to adopt an Evidence Based Policy (EBP).

An EBP is an approach derived from Evidence Based Medicine; it was proposed by Gordon Guyatt at Manchester University in Canada (Tsutani 2000). EBP is used in areas such as social policy, educational policy, and welfare policy (Sowaki 2010). The OECD (2007) has argued that EBP-based policy making enables people and organizations to choose clear and simple evidence from among many options. EBP has been widely adopted in various policy areas for evidence based policy making.

Nishimura (2005) pointed out that evidence should be based on "objective and politically neutral statistical indicators." Such evidence would gain public understanding and help to establish trust between government and society (OECD 2004). In addition, the OECD (2012) has emphasized the need to set indicators as metrics of the evidence, allowing people to visualize the actual condition of each political area.

From these discussions, it seems clear that EBM can be effective in supporting rational decision making for effective educational policy implementation. One key measure to promote the policy will involve establishing an indicator to evaluate the evidence.

Review of the Indicators Adopted in Each Educational Policy Area

In reviewing previous studies related to EBP, this section will focus on studies carried out at the level of government. Examples include the "Flash Eurobarometer" implemented for EU member countries and the "Fact-finding Survey on Young People's Online Usage Environment" carried out by the Japanese Cabinet Office. In addition, this study will clarify the differences between these earlier studies and ILAS, touching on the social and academic impact of this study.

1. Review of the International Situation

The EU has been a pioneer in conducting research on this problem, launching the "Safer Internet Program," which conducted actual condition surveys on Internet use in member countries. The EU also carried out quantitative research on children in 2003 and 2004. In 2005, the European Commission conducted a face-to-face questionnaire survey of children from member countries (European Commission 2005); in 2007, the group interview method was used (European Commission 2007). In the following year, the EC conducted an actual condition survey of children's Internet use and guardian control policies (European Commission 2008).

These studies focused on children's actual usage of the Internet, geographic features, psychological conditions, parental controls, and educational policies at home. Their results offered insight into the Safer Internet Program and provided basic data to both InSafe, an international organization that advocates information literacy and morals, and INHOPE, an international hotline against harmful content (European Commission 2009).

In the UK, former Prime Minister Tony Blair appointed Dr. Tanya Byron (2008) to study children's Internet use and address the emerging related social problems. Her results produced detailed policy proposals aimed at clarifying the different roles of the government and private sector. Following Byron's review, the Office of Communications released "Ofcom's Response to the Byron Review" in March 2008, highlighting the need to enhance the media literacy of children and their guardians as well as to implement self-regulation by industry groups. This report also identified the regulation of content delivery and user access as crucial methods for the self-regulation of industry groups (Office of Communications 2008).

In the United States, additional surveys were conducted by private and non-political organizations and think tanks. For example, the Family Online Safety Institute (2013), which advocates online safety for children and their families, conducted qualitative and quantitative studies on 558 children between the ages of 13–17, living in the US. Their results showed that the number of children connecting online through mobile phones increased from 43% in 2012 to 64% in 2013. The Pew Research Center (2012) researched the experience of parental control, surveying 802 guardians of children aged 12–17. Their results revealed that women (51% vs. 49% of men) under 40 years old (54% vs. 48% over 40), who were white (59% vs. 31% African American) and had higher household incomes were the main users of parental control methods. In addition, the Cyberbullying Research Center (2015) reported the results of a survey on the impact of cyberbullying on the lives of 15,000 American children since 2002. The Center's results suggested that the number of children exposed to cyberbullying had increased from 18.8% in 2007 to 36.6% in 2014.

The Organization for Economic Cooperation and Development (OECD) has emphasized the importance of evidence based policymaking. The OECD Council adopted a "Recommendation on the Protection of Children Online" in February 2012, aiming to establish a foundation to promote co-regulation by each stakeholder for efficient policy implementation to address the identified problems (OECD 2012). This recommendation focused on the need for an evidence based policymaking approach for managing complex policy through enhanced policy coordination. For example, it suggested that enhanced Internet literacy among children and their guardians would be a viable solution, to be determined by evaluating actual usage situations.

Saito (2015) reported the results of an Internet Literacy Assessment Indicator for Students (ILAS), developed through a collaborative effort by the OECD Science, Technology and Industry Directorate and the Japanese Ministry of Internal Affairs and Communications; this project targeted adolescents, measuring their capacity to use the Internet safely and securely. This report investigated the differences in the ILAS test score of students who had bad experiences online and those who had not. It found that the percentage of questions answered correctly by students who had bad experiences online was higher than that of those who had no bad experiences (71% vs. 65%). Thus, adolescents can develop online literacy by coping with bad experiences through Internet usage. These reports recommended that the policy to be implemented not be too strict (e.g., an online ban). It recommended that policies worldwide should support adolescents in developing online literacy through online experiences, while promoting filtering measures, to be implemented through a step-by-step approach.

2. Review of the Japanese Situation

In Japan, the Cabinet Office has conducted an annual "fact-finding survey on young people's online usage environment" to assess the online usage of teenagers and young adults, and their guardians' approach to protection since 2009. The main data gathered reveal hours of online use, geographical locations, and aspects of youth behavior. Guardians were asked about filtering and rules at home.

Article 3 of the "Act on Establishment of Enhanced Environment for Youth's Safe and Secure Internet Use" Appendix defines the role of the government in terms of conducting reviews: three years after implementation, appropriate measures will be summarized and undertaken. Following Article 3, a survey has been conducted to evaluate the improvement of the young people's online environment. Its main purpose was to gather basic data to evaluate the online use and behavior of teenagers and young adults, as well as filtering recognition, filtering usage, and the drawbacks of filtering.

The Importance of the Internet Literacy Assessment Indicator

As mentioned above, every governmental organization is constantly evaluating children's online usage. These results reveal the actual situation, in regard to children's online usage, education, parental education, and views of parental control. By reflecting these results for educational policy making, it will be possible to establish a protection policy for children and their parents. Political costs will be kept to a minimum by appropriately implementing effective policies.

To enhance the effectiveness of EBP, "children's ability to avoid online risks" should be evaluated, even though this factor was not included in the EU's, "Flash Eurobarometer" or the Japanese Cabinet Office research. In this section, it will be argued that problems can be tackled by evaluating "children's ability to avoid online risks."

1. Adjusting the Strength of Child Protection Measures

By evaluating children's ability to avoid risks, it is possible to adjust the strength of technical measures for child protection, such as filtering. When filtering became obligatory, the Ministry of Internal Affairs and Communications working team focusing on illegal and harmful online content argued that there were three major problems.

The first is the uniformity problem: the question of whether uniform filtering is appropriate, given the wide range of risk competency among children of elementary school to high school age. The second problem involved filtering technology. Under the white list algorithm, many harmless websites are excluded; only official websites can be accessed. On the other hand, a black list algorithm blocks all websites in certain categories, regardless of whether these websites are harmful or not. The last problem involves convenience: whether controlling access to community websites that are essential to children's social life is appropriate or not (Ministry of Internal Affairs and Communications 2008).

By evaluating children's ability to avoid risks, it will be possible to adjust the strength of technical measures for child protection to reflect a child's developmental status and computer literacy level. This adjustment will not only optimize the level of online protection, but will also ensure that children have as much freedom in their online activities as possible.

2. Optimization of the Awareness Educational Policy

By evaluating the children's ability to avoid risk, it will be possible to optimize the content of awareness education. Awareness education has depended on the discretion of educators and a limited discussion about whether to include or make it a priority to teach children about online risks.

The indicator will make visible every risk avoidance ability that children should acquire; as a result, educational content will be optimized. The optimization of educational content can and should also be customized to reflect children's skills.

Previous research results were not able to offer enough adjustment for child protection. For example, earlier research evaluated the number and type of educational experiences, but failed to assess how much online risk avoidance ability was acquired. It was difficult to assess child protection policies, because it was impossible to evaluate which types of ability were inadequate.

If online risk avoidance ability is evaluated, it will be possible for education to focus on building the abilities that children lack. Moreover, by knowing which ability is insufficient, it will be possible to change the specifications of online services for children, and to review several policies based on current lows, such as the "Act for the Establishment of an Enhanced Environment for Young People's Safe and Secure Internet Use."

3. Policy Making That Reflects Personal and Regional Backgrounds Will Be Possible Through This Analysis

Although this study has aimed to establish indicators that can evaluate the online risk avoidance ability of children, it will also help to design protection policy that reflects personal and regional backgrounds; it can achieve this by analyzing the relationship between children's test scores and background information. For example, by analyzing the relationship between risk avoidance ability test scores and regional data, it will be possible to show children's average risk avoidance ability in each region. This will make it possible to establish child protection policies that reflect regional differences. Implementing customized awareness education in each region will enhance children's risk avoidance ability and lead to both a regional and national enhancement of skills.

SOLUTIONS AND RECOMMENDATIONS

The Development and Implementation of ILAS by the Japanese Government

These discussions show that evaluating young people's online literacy and reforming and implementing educational policy that reflects these results will optimize the educational policies of all stakeholders for each childhood developmental phase. It is therefore important to develop Internet literacy indicators based on previous EBP to evaluate children's risk avoidance ability. By using risk avoidance ability as evidence, it will enable to offer appropriate protection to children, while ensuring their online freedom.

In Japan, the Ministry of Internal Affairs and Communications has developed the Internet Literacy Assessment Indicator for Students (ILAS) in 2012 in order to implement the OECD recommendations at governmental level; ILAS aims to measure children's online literacy skills and to evaluate their ability to cope with typical online risks.

ILAS systematically defined "the ability all children should acquire against online risks" (see Table 1). It is the indicator used to evaluate these abilities by means of a test (the National Institute for Information and Communications Policy 2012a). It is similar to the OECD's PISA test, which evaluates the academic skills of 15-year-old students; however, ILAS evaluates online risk coping skills. Like the PISA test, ILAS evaluates children's ability to cope with online risks and visually represents its results by area. It also provides "criteria for judgement" for governmental and regional decision-making, online companies' social responsibility, the activities of child protection organizations, and school decision-making.

Figure 1. Overview of the Internet Literacy Assessment Indicator for Students
Source: National Institute for Information and Communications Policy (2012a)

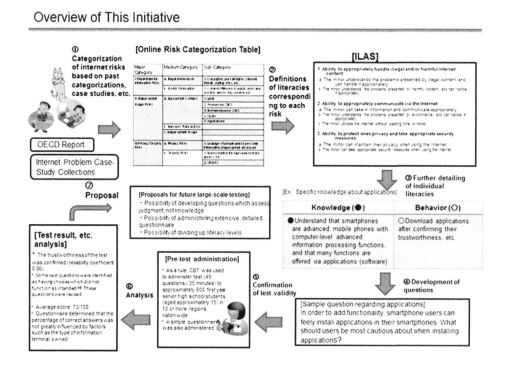

Table 1. Classification table of online risks

Main Category	Significant Category	Sub-Category
I Illegal & Harmful Information Risks	A Illegal Information	1 Copyright, portrait rights, criminal threats, dating sites, etc.
	B Harmful Information	1 Content offensive to public order and morality, adults-only content, etc.
II Inappropriate Usage Risks	A Inappropriate Contact	1 Libel
		2 Anonymous SNS
		3 Non-anonymous SNS
		4 Spam
		5 Applications
	B Improper Transactions	1 Fraud, sale of improper products, etc.
	C Inappropriate Usage	1 Excess Internet consumption
		2 Dependence
III Privacy & Security Risks	A Privacy Risks	1 Leakage of private and/or personal information, inappropriate disclosure
	B Security Risks	1 Impersonation through unauthorized access, etc.
		2 Viruses

Source: National Institute for Information and Communications Policy (2012a)

In 2012, a pre-test was given to 2,464 10th grade students from 23 high schools to evaluate online literacy in Japan. ILAS was used to evaluate online risk avoidance ability and another questionnaires used to assess awareness of cell phone risks. By analyzing these indicators, researchers tried to evaluate the relationship between risk avoidance ability and cellphone use (see Table 2).

Visualization of Children's Online Literacy by ILAS

In this section, the data collected from 2,464 students through the ILAS pre-test will be discussed.

Table 2. Overview of the pre-test

Time Required	50 Minutes
Number of questions	49 items (multiple-choice)
Contents	Description of the CBT: 10 minutes Pre-questionnaire: 5 minutes Implementation of the Pre-Test: 35 minutes Post questionnaire: 5 minutes
Investigation period	May 30, 2012 to July 30, 2012
Subjects	2,464 first year high school students
Number of schools	23 Schools

Source: National Institute for Information and Communications Policy (2012b)

1. Literacy in Each Risk Category

When analyzing online literacy as an ILAS risk category, the percentages of questions answered correctly in the sections on "irregular trading risks (55.09%)" and "security risks (59.48%)" were lower than other categories of risk (see Figure 2).

When asked about "irregular trading risks," it is likely that 15-year-old students will have had limited experience of online trading. Although it is possible to enhance their literacy through online trading, it is important to teach them the risks of online trading before they engage in it, to enhance their risk competency and avoid actual risk.

Next, "security risks" may be a challenge for students who are not familiar with technical subjects because they involve technology. It is important to ensure that students have a chance to learn about security, and teaching them in small steps to avoid learning failure. These things are important for developing the awareness education plan.

Figure 2. Average percentages of questions answered correctly in each risk category (n=2,464)
Source: Saito (2015)

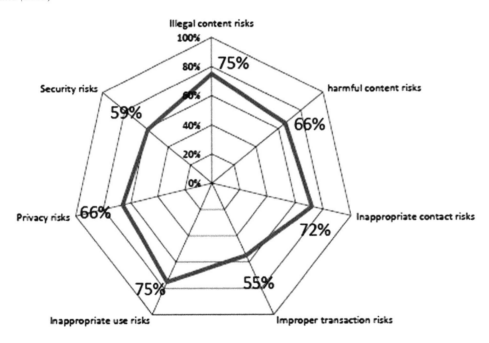

Table 3. Political challenges of awareness education at each layer

Stakeholder	Political Challenge
Governmental and regional organizations	Enhancement of awareness education relating to "irregular trading risks" and "security risks"
Educators and parent-teacher associations	Establish systematic teaching bodies and enhance their ability to teach students about "irregular trading risks" and "security risks."
Parents	Learn about "irregular trading risks" and "security risks" and enhance their ability to protect and control their children.

When thinking about the policy-making strategy of each stakeholder, governmental and regional organizations with an obligation to provide social education and online companies with social responsibility obligations must review their educational programs to make sure that they include opportunities to learn about "irregular trading risks" and "security risks."

Educators and parent-teacher associations should establish systematic teaching bodies and enhance their teaching ability. Parents should learn about these risk areas and should enhance their ability to protect and control their children (see Table 3).

2. Literacy and the Population of Cities

Next are the results about the relationship between children's online literacy and the population of their cities. These showed that the percentage of questions answered correctly by students from cities with populations of less than 300,000 were low in 3 risk category areas. In addition, the total percentage of questions answered correctly was 74% in cities of than 500,000; 73% in cities of more than 300,000 people; and 59% in cities of less than 300,000 people (F (2,461) = 192.06, p<0.001). Thus, as population declined, the percentage of questions answered correctly also declined (see Figure 3).

These results may reflect the fact that larger cities offer more access to communication services, promoting frequent communication between students in daily life enhancing their online literacy.

Results suggest that online literacy differs, depending on the city population, and that smaller cities needs to be aware of the potential for lower levels of literacy. The lower literacy rates in small cities may reflect several factors, including the real world communication divide, and a lack of social capital when acquiring online information.

When thinking about the implementation of awareness education, small cities tend to have more limited social educational networks than larger cities. For example, larger cities have organized bodies, which host social education events, such as workshops and symposiums—regularly providing aware-

Figure 3. The relationship between the percentage of questions answered correctly by students and the population size of their cities (n=2,464)
Source: Saito (2015)

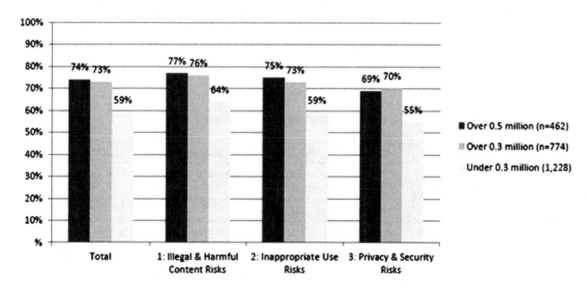

ness education. Smaller cities have fewer such organizations and face difficulties in providing awareness education. Although online networks reach every city, regardless of offline networks, the same set of online risks exists for all children in all cities, regardless of size. It is therefore important to provide awareness education throughout the country.

To tackle this problem, government should collaborate with local authorities and regional branches to provide nation-wide awareness education. The private sector should communicate with its regional branches and provide awareness education activities as an aspect of corporate social responsibility.

In addition, educational committees and parent-teacher associations need to hold workshops to enhance their teaching ability in a systematic way. Parents should actively attend local workshops and enhance their protection and control ability (see Table 4).

3. Bad Online Experiences and Online Literacy

Next, the percentage of questions answered correctly by students with bad online experiences, and students without such experiences were compared. Results showed that the percentage of questions answered correctly by students with bad online experiences was higher than that of students without such experiences (71% vs 65%, t(2,235.53) = 8.07, p<0.001) (see Figure 4). There was a particularly large difference in three areas of privacy security risks (67% vs 61%). The results suggested that students gained online literacy skills by dealing with bad online experiences.

Results showed that students who had had bad online experiences had higher levels of online literacy than students who had not had such experiences. This suggests that too much regulation of Internet use could have a negative effect on students' ability to learn online literacy. Thus, children's online freedom and protection should be balanced in any child protection initiative (OECD 2012b).

To deal with such problems, government should support appropriate technical regulation and private activities that aim to establish social systems. It should also provide many opportunities for awareness education so that children can gain risk avoidance ability. To promote effective policy implementation, the government should also continual research on children's online literacy.

The private sector should work on appropriate self-regulation through cooperation with government, and should promote awareness education so that children themselves can gain risk avoidance ability.

In addition, schools and parent-teacher associations should avoid banning online activities for children. Instead, they should communicate with homes and advocate continuously for awareness raising. Parents need to enhance their protection and control ability at home, and help their children can gain online literacy (see Table 5).

Table 4. Challenges related to regional differences in online literacy

Stakeholder	Political Challenge
Governmental and regional organizations	• Government should collaborate with local authorities to provide nation-wide awareness education • Private sector should communicate with its regional branches and provide awareness education locally
Educators and parent-teacher associations	Hold local workshops to enhance their teaching ability in a systematic way
Parents	Attend local workshops actively and enhance their protection and control ability

Figure 4. Cross analysis of the percentage of questions answered correctly by students with bad online experiences and students without such experiences (n=2,403)
Source: Saito (2015)

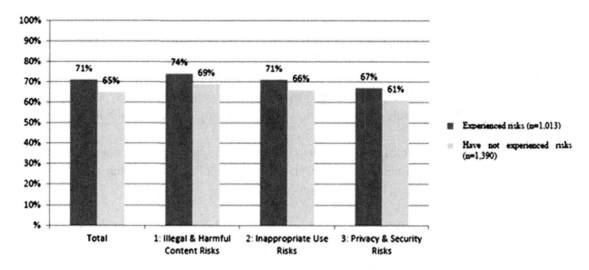

Table 5. Challenges resulting from too much online regulation

Stakeholder	Political Challenge
Governmental and regional organizations	• Government should support appropriate technical regulation and private activities aiming to establish social systems. Also, government should provide wide opportunities for awareness education to children, so that they can acquire risk avoidance ability. In addition, the government should conduct continual research on children's online literacy. • The private sector should work on appropriate self-regulation and promote awareness education so that children themselves can gain risk avoidance ability.
Educators and parent-teacher associations	Communicate with homes and advocate continuously for awareness raising.
Parents	Enhance their own protection and control ability at home, and help their children gain online literacy.

FUTURE RESEARCH DIRECTIONS

This study showed the future direction of policymaking for each layer of stakeholders working for youth protection based on ILAS analysis. The government, local authorities, and private companies form the macro-layer; schools and parental organizations constitute the meso-layer; and parents form the micro-layer.

Further research is needed on the problem, including study of "irregular trading risk" and "security risk," which were pointed out by this study. In addition, the problem of reaching out to small cities to provide awareness education has room for further inquiry, such as (1) evaluation of the implementation of child protection policy by each stakeholder and (2) analysis of the cooperation and synergy between each stakeholder.

CONCLUSION

This study developed an appropriate test to evaluate children's ability to use the Internet safely and securely. It discussed the problems involved in promoting awareness education in weaker areas, such as "irregular trading risk" and "security risk." It also discussed regional differences in online literacy and the importance of helping children to acquire risk avoidance ability through their own efforts. To tackle these problems, this study has proposed political strategies that each stakeholder (including government, local authorities, companies, schools, and parents) should use to promote child safety at each childhood developmental stage. Our proposals can support the decision-making of every stakeholder enhance the effectiveness of this policy.

The next step, following on from this study, is to implement the recommended political strategy for other stakeholders. This study provides basic evidence to support policy making, thus contributing to a safe and secure online environment for children and young people.

This research was previously published in the Encyclopedia of Information Science and Technology, Fourth Edition edited by Mehdi Khosrow-Pour, pages 4962-4974, copyright year 2018 by Information Science Reference (an imprint of IGI Global).

ACKNOWLEDGMENT

This study could not have been completed without the cooperation of the members of the Committee on the Internet Literacy Assessment Indicator for Students, Japan and the Ministry of Internal Affairs and Communications, Japan.

This research was partially supported by the Ministry of Education, Science, Sports and Culture, through a Grant-in-Aid for Scientific Research (C), 2014-2016 (26330389, Nagayuki Saito).

REFERENCES

Byron, T. (2008). *Safer children in a digital world: The report of the Byron Review*. DCSF Publications. Retrieved September 10, 2016, from http://webarchive.nationalarchives.gov.uk/20130401151715/http://www.education.gov.uk/publications/eOrderingDownload/DCSF-00334-2008.pdf

Cabinet Office. (2014). *Survey report on youth Internet environment*. Retrieved September 10, 2016, from the Cabinet Office homepage: http://www8.cao.go.jp/youth/youth-harm/chousa/h24/net-rating/pdf-index.html

Cyberbullying Research Center. (2015). *Summary of Our Cyberbullying Research (2004-2015)*. Retrieved September 10, 2016, from http://cyberbullying.org/summary-of-our-cyberbullying-research/

European Commission. (2005). *Special Eurobarometer: Safer Internet*. Retrieved September 10, 2016 from http://polis.osce.org/library/f/3652/2821/EU-EU-RPT-3652-EN-2821

European Commission. (2007). *Qualitative Study: Safer Internet for Children.* Retrieved September 10, 2016, from http://ec.europa.eu/public_opinion/archives/quali/ql_safer_Internet_summary.pdf

European Commission. (2008). *Flash Eurobarometer: Towards a Safer Use of the Internet for Children in the EU—A Parents' Perspective Analytical Report.* Retrieved September 10, 2016 from http://ec.europa.eu/public_opinion/flash/fl_248_en.pdf

European Commission. (2009). *Safer Internet Programme 2005–2008. (Safer Internet Plus).* Retrieved September 10, 2016, from http://europa.eu/legislation_summaries/information_society/Internet/l24190b_en.htm

Family Online Safety Institute. (2013). *Teen Identity Theft, Fraud, Security, and Steps Teens are Taking to Protect Themselves Online.* Retrieved September 10, 2016 from file:///C:/Users/na-saito/Downloads/Teen_Identity_Theft_Full_Report_Nov_13.pdf

National Institute for Information and Communications Policy. (2012a). 「青少年のインターネット・リテラシー指標（指標開発編）」 [Internet Literacy Indicator for Youth—Development of Indicators]. NICT. Retrieved September 10, 2016 from www.soumu.go.jp/iicp/chousakenkyu/data/research/survey/telecom/2012/ilas2012-report-build.pdf

National Institute for Information and Communications Policy. (2012b). 「青少年のインターネット・リテラシー指標（実態調査編) [Internet Literacy Indicator for Youth—Investigation of actual conditions]. NICT. Retrieved September 10, 2016, from www.soumu.go.jp/iicp/chousakenkyu/data/research/survey/telecom/2012/ilas2012-report-survey.pdf

Nishimura, K. (2005). The Need for Evidence-Based Policy . *Economic Review (Federal Reserve Bank of Atlanta), 1*, 4–7.

OECD. (2004). *Statics, Knowledge and Policy: OECD World Forum on Key Indicators.* Retrieved September 10, 2016 from http://www.oecd.org/site/worldforum06/36422528.pdf

OECD. (2007). *Knowledge Management: Evidence in Education—Linking Research and Policy.* Paris: OECD Publishing.

OECD. (2012). *The Protection of Children Online: Risks Faced by Children Online and Policies to Protect Them.* Paris: OECD Publishing.

Pew Research Center. (2012). Parents, Teens, and Online Privacy. The Berkman Center for Internet & Society at Harvard University.

Saito, N. (2015). *Internet Literacy in Japan.* Paris: OECD Publishing. doi:10.1787/18151965

Saito, N., & Aragaki, M. (2012). *Analysis on political direction of non-formal parental education to develop a safer Internet environment for adolescents* (Vol. 23). Tokyo: Japan Society of Research and Information on Public and Co-operative Economy.

Sowaki, H. (2010). The Development of an Evidence-Based Education Policy in England. *National Institute for Educational Policy Research, 139,* 153–168.

Tsutani, K. (2000). The Cochrane Collaboration and Systematic Review—Its Role in the EBM Movement. *Journal of the National Institute of Public Health, 49*(4), 313–319.

ADDITIONAL READING

Byron, T. (2010). *Do We Have Safer Children in a Digital World?—A Review of Progress Since the 2008 Byron Review.* Available at http://media.education.gov.uk/assets/files/pdf/d/do%20we%20have%20 safer%20children%20in%20a%20digital%20world%202010%20byron%20review.pdf

Japan Internet Safety Promotion Association. (2015). *ILAS2015 Final Report.* Tokyo: Japan Internet Safety Promotion Association.

Livingstone, S., Haddon, L. G. A., & Ólafsson, K. (2011). Risks and safety on the Internet: the perspective of European children: full findings and policy implications from the EU Kids Online survey of 9–16 year olds and their parents in 25 countries, EU Kids Online, Deliverable D4, EU Kids Online Network, London, UK.

Ministry of Internal Affairs and Communications. (2009). *Final report of Study Group on Measures to Illegal and Harmful Information on the Internet: Internet Safety Promotion Program.* Tokyo: Ministry of Internal Affairs and Communications.

Ofcom (2008). *Ofcom's Response to the Byron Review*, Office of Communications, http://stakeholders. ofcom.org.uk/binaries/research/telecoms-research/Byron_exec_summary.pdf

Saito, N., & Aragaki, M. (2011). An experiment in collaborative education to enhance adolescents' respect for social norms in Internet use. *Journal of the Japan Information-Culture Society, 18*(2), 60–67.

Saito, N., Tanaka, E., & Yatuzuka, E. (2014). Evolving Challenges to the Development and Assessment of Information Literacy Education for Online Safety in Japan. *Journal of Cases on Information Technology, 16*, 21–44.

Saito, N., Yoshida, T., & Akahori, K. (2012). Development and Evaluation of the Internet Literacy Assessment Indicator for Students, *Research Report of JSET Conferences,* 2012 (3), pp. 4–50, Tokyo.

Tanaka, E., Saito, N., & Yatuzuka, E. (2011). *A Usage Analysis of the Mobile Literacy e-Learning Program "Mobami" Regarding Access to Content and Rulemaking Tendencies,* World Conference on e-Learning in Corporate, Government, Healthcare, and Higher Education 2011, Honolulu, Hawaii: AACE, pp. 436–441, USA.

Tapscott, D. (2008). *Grown up digital: How the net generation is changing your world.* New York, NY. USA: McGraw-Hill.

KEY TERMS AND DEFINITIONS

Awareness Education: Education designed to enhance knowledge/attitudes that can help to avoid various online risks ensure appropriate Internet use.

Evidence Based Policy: A policy making method based on actual proof. It was first advocated as Evidence Based Medicine by Gordon Guyatt, University of Manchester, Canada in 1991. It has subsequently been used widely in social policy, educational policy, and social welfare policy.

Internet Literacy Assessment Indicator for Students (ILAS): An indicator developed to evaluate online literacy, especially the effectiveness of coping skills/morals in reducing online risks/threats. It was released by the Ministry of Internal Affairs and Communications in September, 2012.

Online Risks: Inclusive term covering various online risks, including cyberbullying, online addiction, cyber grooming, security problems, and the leakage of personal information.

Risk Categories: Classification of online risks defined by ILAS. ILAS classifies 3 major online risks as Illegal & Harmful Information Risks, Inappropriate Usage Risks, and Privacy & Security Risks. It also defines 7 significant categories and 13 sub-categories. In addition, it defines 186 coping skills, which can be used to protect against online risks.

This research was previously published in the Encyclopedia of Information Science and Technology, Fourth Edition edited by Mehdi Khosrow-Pour, pages 4951-4961, copyright year 2018 by Information Science Reference (an imprint of IGI Global).

Chapter 25
Security of Identity–Based Encryption Algorithms

Kannan Balasubramanian
Mepco Schlenk Engineering College, India

M. Rajakani
Mepco Schlenk Engineering College, India

ABSTRACT

The concept of identity-based cryptography introduced the idea of using arbitrary strings such as e-mail addresses and IP addresses to form public keys with the corresponding private keys being created by the trusted authority (TA) who is in possession of a systemwide master secret. Then a party, Alice, who wants to send encrypted communication to Bob need only Bob's identifier and the systemwide public parameters. Thus, the receiver is able to choose and manipulate the public key of the intended recipient which has a number of advantages. While IBC removes the problem of trust in the public key, it introduces trust in the TA. As the TA uses the systemwide master secret to compute private keys for users in the system, it can effectively recompute a private key for any arbitrary string without having to archive private keys. This greatly simplifies key management as the TA simply needs to protect its master secret.

INTRODUCTION

The concept of Identity Based Cryptography was proposed in (Shamir,A., 1984) which introduced the idea of using arbitrary strings such as e-mail addresses and IP Addresses to form public keys with the corresponding private keys being created by the Trusted Authority(TA) who is in possession of a system-wide master secret (Srinivasan,S.,2010). Then a party, Alice who wants to send encrypted communication to Bob need only Bob's identifier and the system-wide public parameters. Thus the receiver is able to choose and manipulate the public key of the intended recipient which has a number of advantages. While Identity Based Cryptography (IBC) removes the problem of trust in the public key, it introduces trust in the TA. As the TA uses the system-wide master secret to compute private keys for users in the system, it can effectively recompute a private key for any arbitrary string without having to archive private keys. This greatly simplifies key management as the TA simply needs to protect its master secret.

DOI: 10.4018/978-1-5225-7492-7.ch025

Some of the earlier Identity Based Cryptosystems proposed such as the one by Cocks (Cocks, C., 2010) and Boneh (Boneh, et.al.,2007) were not based on mathematics of pairings. The Identity based cryptosystem (the term Identity Based Cryptography refers to this set of algorithms whereas the term Identity Based Cryptosystem refers to a specific algorithm) was introduced by Boneh and Franklin (Boneh, et.al.,2001). An Identity Based Encryption or IBE (the term IBE is used to denote a specific Identity Based Cryptosystem) scheme has the following four algorithms: Setup, KeyDer, Enc and Dec. This chapter discusses the algorithms of the IBE schemes and compares them based on the implementation efficiency. An extention to the basic IBE scheme is the Hierarchical IBE proposed by Horwitz and Lynn(Horwitz, et.al., 2001).

In contrast to the basic standard model of IBE, a Random Oracle Model (Bellare, et.al.,1993) may be used where proofs of security are obtained by replacing hash functions with "Random Oracles" that output truly random values for every distinct output. This chapter discusses IBE schemes based on the Random Oracle Model IBEs and compares them with the standard model IBE.

An extension of the above schemes with multiple Trusted Authorities(TAs) instead of a single TA is also possible. An architecture for the implementation of the IBE is discussed along with the security of the various schemes.

BACKGROUND

The public key encryption is a cryptographic system that uses two keys -- a *public key* known to everyone and a *private* or *secret key* known only to the recipient of the message. When user Alice wants to send a secure message to user Bob, she uses Bob's public key to encrypt the message, Bob then uses his private key to decrypt it. An important element to the public key system is that the public and private keys are related in such a way that only the public key can be used to encrypt messages and only the corresponding private key can be used to decrypt them. Moreover, it is virtually impossible to deduce the private key if you know the public key. Users will exchange public keys; this transaction does not need to be done in a secure manner because the release of public keys does not threaten the security of any private information. After this swap, someone who wishes to send private information to another user will encrypt the data with the intended recipient's public key and then pass along the encrypted message. The recipient, who will keep his or her private key secure under any circumstance, can use the private key to decrypt the encoded message.

Keys in public-key cryptography, due to their unique nature, are more computationally costly than their counterparts in secret-key cryptography. Asymmetric keys must be many times longer than keys in secret-cryptography in order to boast equivalent security. Keys in asymmetric cryptography are also more vulnerable to brute force attacks than in secret-key cryptography (Halevi,S. et.al., 1987). Public-key cryptography also has vulnerabilities to attacks such as the man in the middle attack. In this situation, a malicious third party intercepts a public key on its way to one of the parties involved. The third party can then instead pass along his or her own public key with a message claiming to be from the original sender. An attacker can use this process at every step of an exchange in order to successfully impersonate each member of the conversation without any other parties having knowledge of this deception. In order to tackle the issues surrounding the generation, distribution and safekeeping of the private and public keys and also simplify the process of obtaining the public keys, the identity based Encryption was invented.

Many different Identity Based Cryptosystems have been proposed. Some of them use the concept of a Random Oracle. A popular methodology for designing cryptographic protocols consists of the following two steps. One first designs an ideal system in which all parties (including the adversary) have oracle access to a truly random function, and proves the security of this ideal system. Next, one replaces the random oracle by a "good cryptographic hashing function" (such as MD5 or SHA), providing all parties (including the adversary) with a succinct description of this function. Thus, one obtains an implementation of the ideal system in a "real-world" where random oracles do not exist. This methodology was formulated by Bellare and Rogaway (Bellare, M., et.al, 1993) and has been used in many works.

AN IBE SCHEME

An IBE scheme is defined in terms of four algorithms *Setup*, *KeyDer*, *Enc* and *Dec*:

- **Setup:** On input 1^k outputs a master public key *mpk* which includes system parameters *params*, and a master secret key *msk*. We assume that *params* contains descriptions of the message and ciphertext spaces, *MsgSp* and *CtSp*. This algorithm is randomized.
- **KeyDer:** A Key derivation algorithm that on input *mpk* and *msk* and identifier *id*, returns a private key usk_{id}. This algorithm may or may not be randomized.
- **Enc:** An encryption algorithm that on input *mpk*, identifier *id* and a message $m \in MsgSp$, returns a ciphertext $c \in CtSp$ and is written as $c = \text{Enc}(mpk,id,m)$. This algorithm is usually randomized and if randomness is emphazised it is written as $c = \text{Enc}(mpk,id,m:r)$.
- **Dec:** A decryption algorithm that on input *mpk*, a private key usk_{id} and a ciphertext $c \in CtSp$ returns either a message $m \in MsgSp$ or a failure symbol $\bot$.

PAIRINGS IN ELLIPTIC CURVE CRYPTOGRAPHY

Pairing based Cryptography which builds on the foundation of Elliptic Curve Cryptography has become an active area of research since the work of Boneh and Franklin(Boneh,D., et.al.,). Pairing based cryptography is introduced here to show how Identity based Cryptosystems can be constructed.

Let q be a large prime and m an integer with $m \geq 1$. Let F_{q^m} be a finite field with q^m elements. Here q denotes the characteristic of the field and m the extension degree. $F_{q^m}^*$ denotes the multiplicative group of F_{q^m}. The Elliptic curve E over F_{q^m} is denoted by E/F_{q^m} and is defined to be the set of elements $(x,y) \in F_{q^m} \times F_{q^m}$ satisfying an equation of the form

$$y^2 + a_1 xy + a_3 y = x^3 + a_2 x^2 + a_4 x + a_5 ,$$

where $a_i \in F_{q^m}$ for $i=1,2,3,4,5$.

A point $P = (x,y) \in F_{q^m} \times F_{q^m}$ is said to be on the curve if it satisfies the above equation. $E(F_{q^m})$ represents the set of points on the curve and together with the point at infinity forms an additive Abelian Group.

Suppose that $E(F_{q^m})$ has cyclic subgroups G_1 and G_2 of prime order p. Let G_T be the cyclic subgroup of $F_{q^m}^*$ of prime order p. Then an admissible bilinear pairing is a function e which maps a pair of elliptic curve points in G to an element G_T,

$$e : G_1 \times G_2 \rightarrow G_T,$$

having the following properties:

- **Bilinearity:** Let $P \in G_1, Q \in G_2$ and $a,b \in Z_p^*$, $e(aP,bQ) = e(P,Q)^{ab}$
- **Non-Degenerate:** $e(P,Q) \neq 1$
- **Efficiently Computable:** There must be an efficient algorithm that computes the map e for any pair of inputs.

A survey of applications of pairings in cryptography can be found in (Okamoto,T., 2006).

The mathematics behind pairing is quite involved and is usually treated as a black-box which can be used in the implementation of the security protocols.

THE BONEH-FRANKLIN SCHEME

The steps of the Boneh-Franklin scheme are as follows:

Setup

On input 1^k the algorithm works as follows:

- Runs a Pairing Generation algorithm to obtain (G, G_T, e, p, g) where $e: G \times G \rightarrow G_T$ is a bilinear map
- Sets $params = (G, G_T, e, p, g, H_1, H_2, l)$.
- Sets $h = g^s$ where s is selected from Z_p^*
- Sets $mpk = (params, h)$ and $msk = s$.

Here, $H_1: \{0,1\}^* \rightarrow G$, $H_2: G_T \rightarrow \{0,1\}^l$ for some $l = l(k)$, $MsgSp = \{0,1\}^l$, $CtSp = G \times \{0,1\}^l$.

KeyDer

On input mpk, msk and $id \in \{0,1\}^*$, sets the private key corresponding to $usk_{id} = H_1(id)^{msk}$

Enc

On input *mpk*, to encrypt a message $m \in MsgSp$, under the identifier $id = \{0,1\}^*$,

- Parses *mpk* as (*params*, *h*).
- Sets $T = e(H_1(id), h)^r$ where r is selected from Z_p^*.
- Outputs $c = (u,v) = (g^r, m \oplus H_2(T))$.

Dec

On input *mpk*, ciphertext c and the private key usk_{id} corresponding to identifier $id \in \{0,1\}^*$,

- Parses c as $(u,v) \in G \times \{0,1\}^l$,
- Sets $T = e(usk_{id}, u)$.
- Outputs $m = v \oplus H_2(T)$.

COCKS SCHEME

The Cocks Scheme (Cocks, C., 2001) of Identity Based Encryption is as follows:

Setup

The Trusted Authority gets the following inputs to generate a private key:

- An RSA modulus $n = pq$, where p,q are two private prime numbers which satisfy $p \equiv q \equiv 3 \pmod{4}$.
- A message space $MsgSp = \{-1,1\}$ and a ciphertext space $CtSp = Z_n$.
- A secure common hash function $f : \{0,1\}^* \rightarrow Z_n$

KeyDer

Input: Parameters generated by Setup and an arbitrary ID
Output: The private key *r*.

- Generate *a* which satisfies $\left(\dfrac{a}{p}\right) = 1$ with a deterministic procedure ID.

- Let $r = a^{\frac{n-5-p-q}{8}}$ which satisfies $r^2 = \pm a \bmod n$.

Encrypt

Input: Parameters generated by Setup, ID of the sender and message M.
Output: Corresponding ciphertext C.

- Select a random t which satisfies $m = \left(\dfrac{t}{p}\right)$, where m is an arbitrary bit of M.
- Let $c_1 = t + at^{-1} \bmod n$ and $c_2 = t - at^{-1}$
- Send $s = (c_1, c_2)$ to the recipient.

Decrypt

Input: Ciphertext C and the private key and parameters generated by the Trusted Authority.
Output: Original message M.

- Let $\alpha = c^1 + 2r$ if $r^2 = a$, otherwise $\alpha = c_2 + 2r$.
- Return $m = \left(\dfrac{\alpha}{n}\right)$.

AUTHENTICATED IBE

Here we discuss he authenticated IBE encryption.

Setup

1. Get a security parameter k and then generate a prime number q and Groups G_1 and G_2 of order q, and an admissible bilinear map $e: G_1 \times G_2 \rightarrow G_2$. Select a random generator $P \in G_1$.
2. Generate a random number $s \in Z_q^*$. Let $P_{pub} = sP$.
3. The Trusted Authority selects a random generator $g \in G_1$ and hash functions $H_1: F_q \times G_2 \rightarrow \{0,1\}^n$, $H_2: \{0,1\}^* \rightarrow G_1$, $H_3: \{0,1\}^* \times \{0,1\}^* \rightarrow F_q$, $H_4: \{0,1\}^n \rightarrow \{0,1\}^n$
4. Return params $= <q, G_1, G_2, g, g^s, e, n, P, P_{pub}, H_1, H_2, H_3, H_4>$ and master key $= s$.

KeyDer

1. The Trusted Authority extracts the private key of user $ID_A : d_A = H_2(ID_A)^s$

Authenticated Encrypt

User A (ID_A) uses private key d_A and another user's id to encrypt a message $M \in \{0,1\}^*$

1. Select a random number $r \in \{0,1\}^n$
2. Let $c_1 = H_3(r, M)$ and $c_2 = e(d_A, H_2(ID_B))$.
3. Return the ciphertext $C = <r \otimes H_1(c_1, c_2), E_{H_4(r)}(M)>$.

Authenticated Decrypt

User B uses A's ID ID_A, his private key d_B and params to decipher the ciphertext $<U, V, W>$

1. Let $c_2 = e(H_2(ID_A), d_B)$.
2. Let $r = V \oplus H_1(U, c_2)$
3. Let $M = D_{H_4(r)}(W)$.
4. Compare U and $H_3(r, M)$.
5. If $U \neq H_3(r, M)$, discard the ciphertext, otherwise return the message M.

THE HIERARCHICAL IBE SCHEME

In this scheme, every user has an n-tuple ID in the hierarchy tree. The n-tuple ID is composed by the IDs of the user and his ancestors. All users in the i-th level are denoted by $Level_i$. The root of the hierarchy tree $Level_0$ is the trusted Authority.

The following five algorithms form the Hierarchical IBE scheme(Cheng, P., et al.,2012):

Root Setup

1. Based on the security parameter k, generate a big prime q.
2. Use q to generate two fields G_1 and G_2 which satisfy the bilinear map e: $G_1 \times G_1 \rightarrow G_2$
3. Pick an arbitrary element P_0 in G_1 and a random number S_0 in Z_q (q is non zero) as the master-key. Calculate the system parameter $Q_0 = S_0 P_0$.
4. Generate two hash functions H_1: $\{0,1\} \rightarrow G_1$, H_2:$G_2 \rightarrow \{0,1\}^n$.

Lower-Level Setup

For each user $E_t \in Level_t$, Specify a random number $s_t \in Z_q$

Extract

1. For each user E_t with $ID=(ID_1, ID_2, \ldots ID_t)$, its parent calculates $P_t = H_1(ID_1, ID_2, \ldots . ID_t) \in G_1$, where s_0 is the identity of G_1.

2. Return the private key $S_t = S_{t-1} P_t = \sum_{i=1}^{t} s_{i-1} P_i$ of Et and parameter $Q_t = s_t P_0$

Encrypt

1. For a message M and $ID = <ID_1, ID_2, \ldots ID_t>$, calculate
   a. $P_i = H_1(ID_1, ID_2, \ldots ID_i) \in G_1$
2. For any $r \in Z_n$, return the ciphertext:
   $C = <rP_0, rP_2, \ldots rP_t, M \oplus H_2(g_r)>$, $g = e(Q_0, P_1) \in G_2$

Decrypt

For ciphertext $C = <U_0, U_2, \ldots U_t, V)$ and $ID = <ID_1, ID_2, \ldots ID_t>$, return the message:

$$M = V \oplus H_2 \left(\frac{e(U_0, S_t)}{\prod\limits_{i=2}^{t} e(Q_{i-1}, U_i)} \right)$$

THE ARCHITECTURE OF AN IBE SYSTEM

The RFC5408 document (https://tools.ietf.org/html/rfc5408) describes an architecture for the Identity Based Encryption system. A brief description is provided below:

Identity-based encryption (IBE) is a public-key encryption technology that allows a public key to be calculated from an identity and a set of public mathematical parameters and that allows for the corresponding private key to be calculated from an identity, a set of public mathematical parameters, and a domain-wide secret value. An IBE public key can be calculated by anyone who has the necessary public parameters; a cryptographic secret is needed to calculate an IBE private key, and the calculation can only be performed by a trusted server that has this secret.

The calculation of both the public and private keys in an IBE system can occur as needed, resulting in just-in-time creation of both public and private keys. The ability to calculate a recipient's public key, in particular, eliminates the need for the sender and receiver to interact with each other, either directly or through a proxy such as a directory server, before sending secure messages. A characteristic of IBE systems that differentiates them from other server-based cryptographic systems is that once a set of public parameters is fetched, encryption is possible with no further communication with a server during the validity period of the public parameters.

The server components required for an IBE system are the following:

- **A Public Parameter Server (PPS):** IBE public parameters include publicly-sharable cryptographic material, known as IBE public parameters, and policy information for an associated PKG. A PPS provides a well-known location for secure distribution of IBE public parameters and policy information that describe the operation of a PKG.
- **A Private-Key Generator (PKG):** The PKG stores and uses cryptographic material, known as a master secret, which is used for generating a user's IBE private key. A PKG accepts an IBE user's private key request, and after successfully authenticating them in some way, returns their IBE private key.

Sending a message that is IBE encrypted: In order to send an encrypted message, an IBE user must perform the following steps:

1. Obtain the recipient's public parameters

The public parameters of the recipient's system are needed to perform IBE operations. Once a user obtains these public parameters, he can perform IBE encryption operations. These public parameters may be available at a PPS that is operated by the user's organization, one that is operated by the sender's organization, or by a different organization entirely.

2.   Construct and send an IBE-encrypted message

In addition to the IBE public parameters, all that is needed to construct an IBE-encrypted message is the recipient's identity,the form of which is defined by the public parameters. When this identity is the same as the identity that a message would be addressed to, then no more information is needed from a user to send them an encrypted message than is needed to send them an unencrypted message. This is one of the major benefits of an IBE-based secure messaging system. Examples of identities are individual, group, or role identifiers.

Receiving and Viewing an IBE-Encrypted Message

In order to read an IBE-encrypted message, a recipient of such a message parses it to find the URI (Uniform Resource Identifier) or IRI (Internationalized Resource Identifier) he needs in order to obtain the IBE public parameters that are required to perform IBE calculations as well as to obtain a component of the identity that was used to encrypt the message. Next, the recipient carries out the following steps:

1.   Obtain the IBE public parameters

An IBE system's public parameters allow it to uniquely create public and private keys. The recipient of an IBE-encrypted message can decrypt an IBE-encrypted message if he has both the IBE public parameters and the necessary IBE private key. The public parameters also provide the URI or IRI of the PKG where the recipient of an IBE-encrypted message can obtain the IBE private keys.

2.   Obtain the IBE private key from the PKG

To decrypt an IBE-encrypted message, in addition to the IBE public parameters, the recipient needs to obtain the private key that corresponds to the public key that the sender used. The IBE private key is obtained after successfully authenticating to a private key generator (PKG), a trusted third party that calculates private keys for users. The recipient then receives the IBE private key over a secure connection.

3.   Decrypt the IBE-encrypted Message

The IBE private key decrypts the CEK (Content-Encryption Key). The CEK is then used to decrypt the encrypted message.

It may be useful for a PKG to allow users other than the intended recipient to receive some IBE private keys. Giving a mail-filtering appliance permission to obtain IBE private keys on behalf of users, for example, can allow the appliance to decrypt and scan encrypted messages for viruses or other malicious features.

When requesting a private key, a client has to transmit three parameters:

1.   The IBE algorithm for which the key is being requested
2.   The identity for which it is requesting a key
3.   Authentication credentials for the individual requesting the key

The identity for which a client requests a key may not necessarily be the same as the identity that the authentication credentials validate. This may happen, for example, when a single user has access to multiple aliases.

When following the above protocol, attacks may be possible on the system. The following attacks have been identified:

- Passively monitor information transmitted between users of an IBE system and the PPS and PKG
- Masquerade as a PPS or PKG
- Perform a denial-of-service (DoS) attack on a PPS or PKG
- Easily guess an IBE users authentication credential

Additional Information on the structure of the identity and the format of the request protocols can be obtained from RFC5408 ((https://tools.ietf.org/html/rfc5408)

SECURITY NOTIONS AMONG IBE SCHEMES

Let $A = (A_1, A_2)$ be an adversary and A_1 and A_2 are both Probabilistic Polynomial time algorithms. At the first stage, given the system parameters, the adversary computes and outputs a challenge template τ. A_1 can output some state information s which can be transferred to A_2. At the second stage the adversary is issued a challenge ciphertext $y*$ generated from τ by a probabilistic function in a manner depending on the goal. We say the adversary successfully breaks the scheme if she achives her goal (https://eprint.iacr.org/2005/253.pdf).

Four security goals are considered: One-wayness, Indistinguishability, Semantic Security and non-Malleability.

- **One-Wayness:** Here one-wayness is defined using a two-stage experiment: A_1 is run on the system parameters param as input. At the end of A_1's execution the adversary outputs $(s; id)$, such that s is state information (possibly including *param*) which she wants to preserve, and id is the public key which she wants to attack. One plaintext x is randomly selected from the message space **M** beyond adversary's view. A challenge y is computed by encrypting x with the public key id. A_2 tries to computer what x was.
- **Indistinguishability:** In this scenario A_1 is run on param, and outputs $(x_0 ; x_1; s; id)$, such that x_0 and x_1 are plaintexts with the same length. One of x_0 and x_1 is randomly selected, say x_b, beyond adversary's view. A challenge $y*$ is computed by encrypting x_b with id. A_2 tries to distinguish whether $y*$ was the encryption of x_0 or x_1.
- **Semantic Security:** In this scenario, A_1 is given *param* and outputs (M', h, f, s, id). Here the distribution of M' is designated by A_1 and (M', h, f) is the challenge template τ. A2 receives an encryption $y*$ of a random message $x*$ drawn from M'. The adversary then outputs a value v. The adversary hopes that $v = f(x*)$. The adversary is successful if this can be done with a probability significantly more than any simulator does. The simulator tries to do as well as the adversary without knowing the challenge ciphertext $y*$ nor accessing any oracle.

- **Non-Malleability:** In this scenario, A_1 is given *param*, and outputs a triple (M',*s*,*id*). A2 receives an encryption of $y*$ of a random message x_1. The adversary then outputs a description of a relation R and a vector $\vec{y}$ of ciphertexts. It is assumed that $y \notin \vec{y}$. The adversary hopes that R(x_1, $\vec{x}$) holds. We say the adversary is successful if this can be done with a probability significantly more than that which R(x_0, $\vec{x}$) holds. Here x_0 is also a plaintext chosen uniformly from M' independently of x_1.

The attack models for Public Key Encryption (PKE) are Chosen Plaintext attack (CPA)(Goldwasser, S., et.al.,1984), non-adaptive chosen ciphertext attack(CCA1)(Rackoff, C.,et.al., 1991), and adaptive chosen ciphertext attack(CCA2)(Dolev, D., et.al., 1991). Semantic Security is widely accepted as the natural goal of encryption scheme it formalizes an adversary's inability to obtain any information about the plaintext from a given ciphertext. IND-CCA2 is considered to be the "right" standard security notion for PKE.

For a public key encryption, the adversary has access, as anybody to the encryption key. It can encrypt any plaintext of its choice. Hence, the basic attack is called "Chosen Plaintext Attack" or CPA in short. But the adversary may have access to more information and namely some decryptions. This is modeled by an access to the decryption oracle.

An adversary is called non-adaptive chosen-ciphertext adversary (or a lunchtime adversary denoted by CCA1 adversary) if it can access the oracle before the challenge ciphertext is known only. An adversary is called an adaptive chosen-ciphertext adversary (or CCA2 adversary if it can access the oracle whenever it wants, that is before and after the challenge ciphertext is known with the sole restriction not to use it on the challenge itself. Due to the particular mechanism, the adversaries are given more power in IBE than in PKE. Essentially the adversaries have access to the *key extraction oracle*, which answers the private key of any queried public key (identity). The IND-CCA2 security for PKE can be extended to IND-ID-CCA2 security for IBE.

Among the four IBE schemes presented, the Boneh-Franklin scheme is semantically secure under the random oracle model under the Bilinear Diffie Hellman Assumption.

FUTURE RESEARCH DIRECTIONS

In almost all the existing schemes on IBE with a small number of exceptions, there is a single global TA issuing keys to all users in the system and all ciphertexts are created using the public parameters of the that single global TA. In practice there will be more than TA each issuing private keys to a set of users. In addition, some users may have keys issued by more than one TA. In such scenarios, it is not unreasonable to assume that the different TAs may share some common system parameters. This will necessitate that the system parameters may have to be reused. This and other issues in the multi TA setting have not been explored fully (Srinivasan, S., 2010a).

CONCLUSION

The Identity based encryption scheme has been put forward by the cryptographic Community to solve some the issues in obtaining the private and public keys in the Public key encryption. By using an id such as an e-mail address, the user can easily generate a public key. The receiver can obtain the corresponding private key from a Trusted Authority. We can also assume more than one Trusted Authority for providing private keys for the users. This chapter presented a number of Identity Based Encryption schemes such as the Cock's Scheme, Boneh-Franklin Scheme, Authenticated IBE and Hierarchical IBE. It also presented an architecture of the IBE scheme describing how the users will interact with the Trusted Authority and perform encryption and decryption.

REFERENCES

Bellare, M., & Rogaway, P. (1993). Random Oracles are practical: a paradigm for designing efficient protocols. *ACM Conference on Computer Communications Security*, 62-73. 10.1145/168588.168596

Boneh, D., Craig, G., & Michael, H. (2007). *Space-Efficient Identity based Cryptosystem without pairings*. IEEE Computer Society.

Boneh, D., & Franklin, M. K. (2001). Lecture Notes in Computer Science: Vol. 2139. *Identity-Based Encryption from the Weil Pairing*. Springer.

Chatterjee, S., & Sarkar, P. (2011). *Identity Based Encryption*. Springer. doi:10.1007/978-1-4419-9383-0

Cheng, P., Gu, Y., Lv, Z., Wang, J., Zhu, W., Chen, Z., & Huang, J. (2012). A Performance Analysis of Identity Based Encryption Schemes. *Lecture Notes in Computer Science, 7222*, 289–303. doi:10.1007/978-3-642-32298-3_19

Cocks, C. (2001). Lecture Notes in Computer Science: Vol. 2260. *An Identity Based Cryptosystem based on Quadratic Residues*. Springer.

Dolev, D., Dwork, C., & Naor, M. (1991). *Non-malleable Cryptography. STOC, 91*, 542–552.

Goldwasser, S., & Micali, S. (1984). Probabilistic Encryption. *Journal of Computer and System Sciences, 28*(2), 270–299. doi:10.1016/0022-0000(84)90070-9

Halevi, S., & Krawczyk, H. (1999). Public-key cryptography and password protocols. *ACM Transactions on Information and System Security, 2*(3), 230–268. doi:10.1145/322510.322514

Horwitz, J., & Lynn, B. (2002). Lecture Notes in Computer Science: Vol. 2332. *Toward hierarchical identity-based encryption*. Springer.

Joye, M., & Neven, G. (Eds.). (2009). *Identity-Based Cryptography*. IOS Press.

Martin, L. (2008). *Introduction to Identity-Based Encryption*. Artech House.

Okamoto, T. (2006). On Pairing Based Cryptosystems. *Lecture Notes in Computer Science*, *4341*, 50–66. doi:10.1007/11958239_4

Phan, D. H., & Pointcheval, D. (2004). On the Security Notions of Public Key Encryption Schemes. *LNCS*, *3352*, 33–47.

Rackoff, C., & Simon, D. R. (1991). Non-interactive zero-knowedge proof of knowledge and chosen ciphertext attack. LNCS, 576, 433-444.

Shamir, A. (1984). *Identity-Based Cryptosystems and Signature Schemes*. CRYPTO.

Srinivasan, S. (2010). *Identity-Based Encryption: Progress and Challenges. Information Security Technical Report*. Elsevier.

Srinivasan, S. (2010a). *New Security Notions for Identity Based Encryption* (Ph.D thesis). Royal Holloway, University of London.

ADDITIONAL READING

Hansen, D. M. (2009). Pairing Based Cryptography A Short Signature Scheme using Weil Pairing, M.Sc. Thesis, http://www.sagemath.org/files/thesis/hansen-thesis-2009.pdf

Küchlin, W. (1987). Public key encryption. *ACM SIGSAM Bulletin*, *21*(3), 69–73. doi:10.1145/29309.29320

Menezes, A. (1991). An Introduction to Pairing Based Cryptography http://cacr.uwaterloo.ca/~ajmeneze/publications/pairings.pdf

KEY TERMS AND DEFINITIONS

Adversary: An attacker who may try to guess the secret key or the plaintext from a given ciphertext.

Authentication: refers to verifying the identity of a particular user.

Ciphertext: The term ciphertext refers to the output message from an encryption algorithm.

Hash Algorithm: This produces a fixed size output given a message as input. This output can be used to verify message contents.

Identity Based Cryptography: The algorithms that generate the public key using an id of the user. The private key should be obtained from a Trusted Authority.

Identity: Refers to a string that is used to identify an individual. For example, an e-mail address.

Pairing Based Cryptography: The cryptographic algorithms that use the Mathematics of pairings. The most commonly used pairings include Tate Pairing, Weil Pairing etc.

Plaintext: The term plaintext refers to the input message to an encryption algorithm.

Private Key: The secret key in the public key encryption algorithms. This key is kept secret.

Public Key: The Public key is one of the keys used in public key encryption algorithms. This key is made available publicly.

Random Oracle Model: This model assumes the presence of oracle which returns answers to queries similar to Hash functions. It is suggested that the Oracle be implemented through Hash functions.

Signatures: Signing of a message by one's private key. The hash of a message is encrypted with the private key.

Trusted Authority: The Trusted Authority is a third party trusted to distribute keys. In the Identity Based Encryption Schemes, the Trusted Authority provide secret keys.

This research was previously published in the Encyclopedia of Information Science and Technology, Fourth Edition edited by Mehdi Khosrow-Pour, pages 4975-4984, copyright year 2018 by Information Science Reference (an imprint of IGI Global).

Chapter 26
Steganography Using Biometrics

Manashee Kalita
NERIST, India

Swanirbhar Majumder
NERIST, India

ABSTRACT

In this smart age, smart gadgets with internet connectivity have become a necessity. While enjoying these facilities, one must count the security of their private or confidential information. With due time, a lot of cryptographic methods have been developed for enforcing security. On the other hand, with the advancement of technologies, the intruders and hackers have also developed their skills and tools. Therefore, many times we fail to protect our information. To get rid of this situation, the developers have to focus on some other method besides cryptography. Steganography can be considered as the solution to overcome this problem, as it is the technique which conceals the existence of any secret information in a usual media file. Moreover, inclusion of biometric with steganography enhances the security level, as biometric systems are dominating the field of authentication. Here, various techniques of steganography, biometrics, and steganography using biometrics will be discussed. Finally, the present scenario of steganography using biometrics will be demonstrated.

INTRODUCTION

Steganography is one of the techniques which is used to provide security to the information. There are many other techniques available to do so. Those are cryptography, steganography and watermarking. Cryptography scrambles the message using some encryption algorithm with some secret key. When the receiver receives the scrambled message (cipher), he/she decrypt the message using the proper key (same or different). Last two methods, steganography and watermarking are very much similar to both the methods come from the set of data hiding techniques, but with a different objective. Watermarking is a technique where the cover image is digitally marked using some data hiding technique. The method has some way to logically extract the mark without destroying or harming the cover image. On the other hand, for steganography, the matter of concern is the hidden message only, not the cover image. Steganography pay attention to the degree of imperceptibility where watermarking concentrates on the

DOI: 10.4018/978-1-5225-7492-7.ch026

number robustness of the method. Application of watermarking are copy control, authentication, device control, proof of ownership, etc. Steganography mainly aims to provide the security to the information.

The word steganography is derived from Greek. The Greek word "stego" means cover and "grafia" means writing. The goal of steganography is to conceal the very existence of any secret information in the cover media file. The cover media is any media which usually doesn't come under suspicion. Selection of cover media has being changed with the change of technology. In the ancient time, the cover was different, such as messenger's body part, some natural picture, usual greeting letter, etc.

BACKGROUND

Steganography is a prehistorical practice. From the ancient times, steganography has been using to provide security to the confidential information. Italian mathematician Jerome Cardan reinvented Chinese ancient secret writing method. In that method two parties share a paper mask with holes and after that fill up the blank spaces. The final message appears as an innocuous text. Many secret writing techniques were invented during World War II, such as null cipher, microdot, invisible ink, etc. In the 5th century, BC Hiatus wanted to send some message to his friend secretly. He shaved one of the trusted slave's head and tattooed a message on it. The slave was sent after his hair grew back. During World War II, Morse codes were encoded in pictures, like long Blades of grass indicate dashes and dots were indicated by short blade.

The word biometrics is also originated from Greek word "Bio" which means life and "metric" means measure. Biometric define the measurement of statistical analysis of people's physical and behavioral characteristics. This is mainly used for authentication, access control, identification. Nowadays, authentication tool/machine developers start to prefer biometrics characteristics as identification or authentication measure rather than passwords, smart card, etc. Because biometrics is a property which can defines or identify "who are you." Various biometric characteristics are being used by different authentication machine such as palm geometry, fingerprints, iris, face, skin, etc.

Physical characteristics are related to the feature of the body, such as palm veins, retina, face recognition, DNA, fingerprint, hand geometry, etc. On the other hand, the behavioral characteristic is related to the behavior of a person. It includes signature, voice, gait, typing speed, handwriting, etc. Biometric gets the preference to be a reliable authentication measure than a password, smart card, etc. because biometric characteristics are virtually impossible to steal. Therefore, biometric starts dominating the field of authentication. We can observe the large application of biometric in regular life, e.g. Bank employees use Thumbprint to login into their system, in many universities, offices use biometric punching machine where the biometric feature of employees is used to keep the attendance.

Now, if we focus on the steganography using biometrics, it can be done in two ways, one hides your biometric information in some cover file, and another is the reserve one, i.e., biometric information will carry some secret information. Here a brief discussion related to these two mentioned types are presented.

LITERATURE SURVEY

Anil K. Jain et al. (2003) proposes another method to hide biometric information using steganography. They discuss two scenarios. In the first one, the authors embed the fingerprint information (minutiae) into another fingerprint image, so that attackers do not suspect that the visible fingerprint image is not the actual one. The stego fingerprint image is again encrypted using a secret key to increase the security level. In the second scenario, the minutiae and facial information (Eigen—face coefficient) are hidden in the fingerprint image. Again this stego image embedded in the smart card for authentication.

Hussain Ud-Din et al. (2006) proposes a system for providing better security to the online shopping customers. In this system, there are three main phases. The first phase extract the feature of the biometric information (fingerprint). In the 2ndphase the sensitive information of the electronic shopping card is encrypted and in the final phase extraction biometric feature and encrypted information are embedded in cover image (the image of the shopping card).

The author Yinghuua Lu et al. (2008) proposes a method to improve the security of biometric authentication using lossless and content- based hidden watermarking algorithm. Chaos is employed by the method to encrypt the watermark and the initial condition for chaos are generated by the biometric image of the user. Watermark includes like ID, Palmprint no. etc. which are embedded in the palm print image. Again, the stego palm print image is embedded in the cover image to provide the security to the biometric information as well as authenticate by watermarking the palm print image.

A paper by Abbas Chaddad and Joan Condell (2008), discusses the efficiency of embedding information in the skin tone color space. Anjali A. Shejul and Prof. U.L Kulkarni (2010) proposed a method where secret information is embedded by finding the location to embed using the biometric concept. A DWT based steganography algorithm is used for embedding the information in the skin tone of the human body.

A combination of cryptography, biometric and steganography approach is made by authors Hisham Al-Assam et al. (2013). In the method, the biometric feature is used for remote authentication. On the other, to protect biometric feature of individual, steganography is used. To embed the biometric feature vector, Random LSB scheme is used. Another similar approach is made by Indradip Banarjee et al. (2014) where they integrate the face extraction geometry into the cover image using DWT. Another method combines this three concept again which is suggested by Ashsa Ali, Liyamol (2010). This method uses RC5 encryption algorithm to encrypt the user's data and embeds the encrypted information into the fingerprint image using some LSB based steganography algorithm.

The author Shivendra Katiyar along with the co-authors (2011) suggests an online voting system where steganography and cryptography have been used to provide added security. The biometric feature, thump impression is used for authentication. The proposed system also uses the system generated a secret key and SSN no. to log into the voter's account. The system concentrates on the authentication of the voter's identity, but not the confidentiality of the voter's biometric features.

For secure transmission of medical information, a method is proposed by S. Barkathunisha et al. (2013) I this method, they provide a technique to enforce security to the medical information where patient need to send their report to the expert in remote station.

The method proposed by Rasher D. Rashid (2013) hides the feature of a face biometric into a cover image. The authors calculated the PSNR value for the invisibility of the system and recognition rate is calculated using Euclidian Distance. To extract the feature of the face, the method divides the face into multiple frequency bands and each band is divided into non-overlapping blocks. From the blocks, local binary pattern histogram is extracted.

WLodzimerz Kasprzak et al. (2015) suggests a method which uses a printed steganography to authenticate the photo in identity card. This method proposes a steganography technique for authentication of a printed face image.

A. Kapezynski (2011) proposed a hybrid method using biometric and steganography. This approach considers physical and behavioral biometric characteristics. The physical characteristics, the fingerprint is used to hide the behavioral biometric keystroke. Embedding is done by LSB substitution.

D. Goyal proposed Steganography authentication concept using face and voice recognition for secure banking system through mobile. The author uses multiple biometric features for identification. In the proposed system, the face is used to login into the banking server. After successful logged in, the voice of the user is used to provide better security to the transmission phase. The voice is transmitted using steganography algorithm.

P. Kamble proposed a method for ATM security using multimodal biometrics system with steganography technique. The system embeds the code in the image of the palm print of the user and image is sent to the authentication server with an iris image of the same user.

Many researchers work on steganography using DWT and biometric feature. Sarthi k, in 2013, proposed a biometric based steganography method using circular folding in DWT domain. The method hides the secret message in the skin tone region. To detect skin and non-skin, HSV color space is used. The cover image is cropped after detection of skin tone. DWT is performed on the cropped image. The third plane of the cropped cover images is rotated by 180° using circular folding technique. Next DWT is performed on the folded image and the high-frequency sub-band is used to hide the secret information. Anjali A Shejwal, S. Barve, N. Lavanya (2012) also proposed similar methods where skin tone and DWT have been used.

It has been observed that researchers are constantly searching for a solution for secure online voting system. But, very less work have done in this field. An online voting concept has proposed by N. Gandhi (2014), where the concept of steganography, cryptography using biometrics are used. Similarly, G.M. Kamau (2013) proposed a hybrid steganography method using biometrics (fingerprints) for casting a vote remotely. Using enhanced least significant bit steganography method, the fingerprint template with the voter details are embedded in the voter face image with a Stego key. S. Lokhande (2012) also presented a method using biometrics, cryptography, and steganography with the conjunction of GSM module. The method uses cryptography algorithm (MD5) to generate a unique key using users ID card, users key and time factor. Theunique key is embedded in the thumbprint image and send to the authentication server. Few more similar approaches are proposed by N. Malwade (2013), V. J Lakshmi (2014), S Bhattacharyya (2014), Shanthini (2012). S.A.Tambe (2014) approached a method where the fingerprint is used as acover image to embed the ID of the voter. Embedding process is done in the transform domain using DWT.

STEGANOGRAPHY

A basic steganography system is mainly composed of embedding process and extracting process. Figure.1 illustrates basic block diagram of a steganography system.

The sender selects an unsuspected cover image to embed the secret message. Sometimes, some "key" is used in the embedding procedure, which is optional. The embedding process produces the stego-image and then it is transmitted over the network. The receiver has to run the extracting algorithm with the proper key (if any) to get the message back accurately.

Steganography is a very broad area of application. With the digital revolution, not only mankind gets benefited, but also terrorists and criminals take the advantage to fulfill their suspicious act. Here, we are focusing only on the positive side of the development. Steganography has many useful applications such

Figure 1. Basic block diagram of steganography

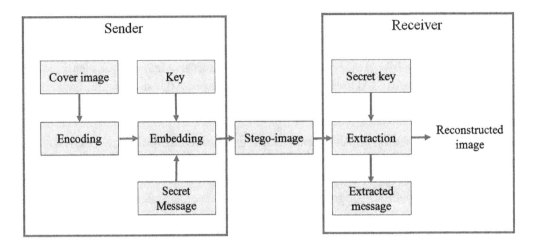

as copyright control, smart ID where details of the individual are embedded in the photos, synchronization of video audio secret information circulation etc. While designing steganography method to use in the different field, we always have to consider the main three properties of it. These are-

1. **Imperceptibility:** It is the first property one needs to keep in mind. The basic motive of steganography is to conceal the existing of any message. Higher perceptibility indicates better steganography method.
2. **Capacity:** With good imperceptibility of the stego file, the designer must look after the capacity of the method also. Application of steganography is not limited. So, as per the requirement steganography method should be capable of providing good embedding capacity.
3. **Robustness:** This is also an important property. It is the capacity of the method to withstand the message after some attack or some manipulation operation, such as cropping, rotating, etc.

Some other properties, such as security of the key used in the method, various cost such as computational cost, time cost, are also required to consider.

With the development of steganography, the counter measures of it have also developed in parallel, i.e., stegan alysis. Stegan alysis is the art of detecting hidden message in the cover file without having any knowledge of the steganography method. There are various stegan alysis methods, such as histogram analysis, statistical analysis, etc.

Steganography algorithm can be implemented in various domains. Mainly there are two domains, but further, these are subdivided into many domains. Different researchers visualize the type of steganography methods in various categories. Some of them have divided into six categories depending on the hiding technologies: Statistical method, Distortion techniques, Substitution, Cover generation techniques, Spread spectrum techniques and Transform domain techniques. On the other hand, some researchers have divided depending on the domain, where most of bits are hidden. Those are mainly spatial domain steganography, transform domain steganography, Spread spectrum steganography and model based steganography. To discuss the type steganography methods briefly, we consider the second type division case.

Spatial Domain Steganography

In Spatial domain steganography method, the embedding process is done by directly manipulating the pixel values of the cover image. These type of methods are less complex and less robust. Various approaches in spatial domain are discussed below:

1. **LSB Substitution:** This is the simplest spatial domain technique where the message is embedded in the least significant bit (rightmost). This method can provide good embedding capacity but vulnerable to even minor manipulation, such as rotation, scaling, cropping and addition of noise, lossy compression, etc. Also, it is not robust against stego attacks.
2. **Gray Level Modification:** This technique doesn't embed or hide the data. It uses a mathematical function to map data by modifying their gray level. To map data within the cover image, this technique uses some odd even mapping. For example, odd values map 1 and even maps 0. This method can provide high embedding capacity with low complexity.
3. **Pixel Value Differencing:** This method uses the difference between adjacent pixels. A larger difference indicates the presence of an edge, and according to human visual properties, the human eyes can tolerate more changes in edge areas than that of flat areas. This property leads to high embedding capacity without noticeable perceptibility. Some methods have been developed using this concept and gain good results. These methods are also vulnerable to stegan alysis method and stego attacks.
4. **Quantization Index Modulation (QIM):** Brain Chen (2001), proposed QIM algorithm which has higher embedding capacity. It also allows to control robustness and distortion. To embed the information in the cover file using QIM, it first modulates an index or sequence of indices with the embedded information and then quantized the host signal with associated quantizer or sequence of the quantizer. There are some other techniques come under this category, such as vector quantization, singular value decomposition, side-match vector quantization, search order code (SOC).
5. **Multiple Base Notational System (MBNS):** In this method, secret information is converted into symbols (e.g. integer numbers). The pixels of a cover image are modified in such a way that the remainders are equal to symbols after dividing the pixel values by the bases. The degree of the local variation of pixel values in a cover image determines the specific bases. This method achieves high payload capacity and performs better in terms of PSNR quality factor and Watson's metric.
6. **Prediction Based Steganography:** Direct manipulation or alteration of pixel value leads to the significant distortion. Predictive-based steganography is suggested to overcome this issue where pixel values are predicted using predictor. Here, prediction error values are modified to embed data instead of modifying the pixel values. The gradient adjusted prediction and median edge are mainly used in prediction based image coding.

Transform Domain

All digital images are composed of low and high-frequency component. Low frequency is represented by flat and plain areas whereas sharp transition and edges contribute in high-frequency component. Changes in the low frequency are easily visible to the human visual system. Therefore, embedding an equal number of information in both frequencies is not feasible. It embeds the message bits in optimally chosen coefficients. Coefficients are calculated from the cover image using some transformation function. There are a number of transformation functions available, such as DCT, DWT, Integer transform, Haar transform, Hadamard transform, contourlet transform, ribgelet transform, ripplet transform, DD DT DWT etc. These methods are computationally complex than spatial domain and robust against attacks and image manipulation operations. Some popular transform functions are:

1. **Discrete Cosine Transformation:** In 1974, researcher community working on an image compression has suggested DCT, which turns like a great achievement in this field. The DCT can be considered as a discrete time version of the Fourier cosine series. The computational complexity of DCT is O(nlogn), like FFT, DFT. DCT is a real-valued with fewer coefficient and better approximation of a signal. The 2D DCT compression c(u,v) of a NxN image signal f(x,y) can be defined as:

$$c\left(u,v\right) = \alpha\left(u\right)\alpha\left(v\right)\sum_{x=0}^{N-1}\sum_{y=0}^{N-1}f\left(x,y\right)\cos\left[\frac{\left(2x+1\right)u\pi}{2N}\right]\times\cos\left[\frac{\left(2y+1\right)v\pi}{2N}\right]$$

where,

$$\alpha\left(u\right) = \begin{cases} \sqrt{\dfrac{1}{N}}, & for\ u = 0; \\ \sqrt{\dfrac{2}{N}}, & for\ u = 1,2\dots N-1 \end{cases}$$

In 2016, Fengyong Li uses DCT to steganalyze over large scale social network with high order joint features and clustering ensembles.

2. **Discrete Wavelet Transformation:** The word wavelet has been used for decades in digital signal processing and exploration geophysics. First wavelet transformation is Haar wavelet proposed by Alfred haarin 1909. This is a multiresolution transform method. The wavelet transform for a square integration function f(t) is defined by-

$$w_f\left(a,b\right) = \int_{-\infty}^{\infty}f\left(t\right)\varphi_{a,b}^{*}\left(t\right)dt$$

where * denotes complex conjugate, $\varphi_{a,b}^{*}\left(t\right) = \dfrac{1}{a}\varphi\left(\dfrac{t-b}{a}\right)$, a basis (mother) wavelet $\varphi\left(t\right)$ by dilations and transition. Here, a and b are scale factor and transition factor respectively. $\dfrac{1}{a}$ is the normalization factor for energy normalization. For different application different basis function are available. A basis can be modified according to the requirement. Some popular basis are – Haar Basis, Gaussian wavelets, Gabor wavelets, Daurbechies basis.

3. **Walsh Transformation:** In 1923, Walsh defined transform, but in 1823 Hadmard had also achieved a similar result by the application of certain orthogonal matrices which called Hadamard matrices. Hadmard matrices contain only ± 1. It is equivalent to multidimensional DFT of size 2x2x2...2x2 and can be considered as being built out of size two discrete transformation.

4. **Curvelet Transform:** This technique was proposed by Candes and Donoho in 1999. It can be viewed as an extension of wavelet transformation and it became more popular in the same field. This transformation is multi-scale directional transform technique which is an almost optimal non adaptive sparse representation of object with edge.

5. **Contourlet Transformation:** It is also a multiresolution directional tight frame which design to efficiently approximate image. This transformation was proposed by Do and Vetterli in 2002. They construct a discrete domain multiresolution and multidirectional expansion. Non separable filter banks are used to do so in the same manner as wavelet filter bank. This technique represents at 2D image with smooth corners. Contourlet has the properties of multiresolution, localization, directionality, critical Sampling and anisotropy. Method proposed a filter Bank structure to obtain sparse expansion of 2D image having a smooth contour. To implement this double filter bank, the Laplacian pyramid is used for capturing point of discontinuities and to link point of discontinuities into linear structure, a direction filter bank is used.

Spread Spectrum

A well-known concept in digital communication, spread spectrum was proposed by Harvel et al. (1999). The method involves in spreading the bandwidth of a narrowband signal across a wide band of frequencies like white noise. At the decoder side, during extraction process image restoration and error control techniques can be used. It is difficult to detect because the energy of the narrow band signal is low in any frequency band after spreading. The resulting signal is embedded in the cover image to get the stego image. Due to the difference in power of signals (embedded and cover image), the SNR of stego image is very low which result in low detectability. This method provides good embedding capacity and also maintain the robustness against statistical attacks. Statistical properties are preserved because the secret message is spread throughout the cover image.

Model Based Steganography

In 2003, P Shallee proposed a spatial domain technique called Model-based steganography which based on the statistical properties of a cover medium. In this method, the cover image is divided into two parts, and one part is selected for embedding message without altering the statistical properties. A popular adaptive method is proposed by Hoki which it is known as "A block Complexity based Data Embedding (ABCDE). Here noisy block is replaced by the block obtained by embedding the message.

BIOMETRICS

We all are aware of unauthorized access to information. There are a number of methods to prevent unauthorized access. The most common way is to use username and password combination. However, mainly there are three ways to authenticate a user-

1.   Something you know. For example, password.
2.   Something you have. For example, token.
3.   Something you are. For example, measurable physical features.

These three pillars of authentication can be used separately or combinedly for stronger authentication. In some situations, only one way is not sufficient to provide stronger authentication. For example, it would be better if some biometric information is required while withdrawing money using ATM card because ATM card can be stolen, pin code can be guessed.

Biometric assures individual's unique physical and behavioral characteristics to authenticate or recognize their identity. Physical biometric features include fingerprints, facial, Iris, hand palm geometry, retina, etc. Behavioral characteristics are handwriting, signature, voice, keystroke pattern, gait, etc.

The biometric system works by scanning the fingerprint or iris to get the pattern of it, capturing a digital color/grayscale image for face recognition, etc. The feature of the imageis transformed into the template using mathematical functions. These biometric templates are added to the database for further identification. A biometric system works for two different purposes; one for adding the template to the database for further reference and another is to find a match with the existing template.

Biometric has occupied the field of authentication because of its special characteristics. Among all characteristics, biometric feature has chosen for authentication based on the following characteristic.

1.   **Uniqueness:** It is the most desirable and primary characteristic so that chances of occurring same characteristic of two people is minimum.
2.   **Stability:** Chosen feature should not change over time.
3.   **Ease of Capturing:** Capturing of the biometric template should be convenient to the user with preventing misrepresentation of the feature.

Because of the special characteristic of biometric, it occupies the place of most secure and convenient authentication tool. This section discusses some of the popular biometric features.

Physical and Behavioral Characteristics

Physical biometric comprises some of the shape or composition of the body like a fingerprint, hand geometry, face, ear, retina, etc. Most of the physical biometrics are time invariant and also satisfy the character of the uniqueness with stability.

1.   **Fingerprint:** It is the unique physical characteristic which features can be recorded as arches, loop, wholes pattern with the ridges, minutiae, and furrows. Matching Fingerprint can be done in three ways:
     a.   Minutiae based,
     b.   Correlation based,
     c.   Ridge features.
2.   **Hand Geometry:** An optical camera is used by hand geometry based system to capture two orthogonal two-dimensional image of palm and sides of hand. A number of dimensional measures are collected including height, length, width, distance between joints, etc. The system does not consider the fingerprint or Palm print.

3. **Palm Print:** Palm print system takes the image of palm. It is different from hand geometry.
4. **Face:** A quality digital camera is required to capture the facial images of the user. Characteristic of face are analyzed. Many software applications have developed which have facial image authentication, due to the ease of capturing the facial image.
5. **Facial Thermography:** It is similar to the face recognition, except an infrared camera, which is used to capture the image. It detects heat patterns emitted from the skin and created by the branching of blood vessels. Thermograms patterns are highly distinctive.
6. **Vein Recognition:** The vein pattern structure of a user is image processed and stored. It is believed by many researchers that vein biometric recognition can produce high accuracy rate than fingerprint recognition.
7. **Blood Pulse:** It is not as strong authentication measure as it has a high false matching rate. It can be measured on a finger with an infrared sensor.
8. **Retina:** This biometric analyses the layer of blood vessel situated in the back of the eye. The network of a blood vessel in the retina is not genetically determined, and therefore even identical twin do not share the same pattern. Some retina based biometric system used a low-intensity light source through an optical coupler to scan the unique pattern of retina. This kind of system has low false, positive, high reliability, high cost. It is not user convenient because it requires close contact with the reading device.
9. **Iris:** This type of biometric system analyses features of the colored ring of tissue that surrounds the pupil. Iris recognition systems apply mathematical pattern recognition technique to the images of irises of an individual's eye. There are many advantages of iris matching, besides its speed of matching, they are extreme resistant to false matches, stability, and extremely visible organ of the eyes. It also works with contact lenses, eye glasses and non-mirror sunglasses.

Apart from these, there are many more features, such as tongue print, dental scan, ear, nail bed, etc. Here, only the popular ones have been discussed. Biometrics, such as, DNA matching, ear, odor are also used but because of many issues, these characteristics are not so popular than others. Now, let us give a brief overview of some behavioral characteristic.

1. **Signature:** Signature has been widely used for authentication, and it is also a very old practice. Signature authentication may be either static or dynamic. Static authentication uses only the geometric feature whereas dynamic includes some more features such as velocity, acceleration, pressure, the trajectory of the signature, etc.
2. **Voice:** It is a combination of physical in behavioral characteristics. Physical characteristics, vocal tracts, mouth, nasal cavities, and lips are included and under behavioral, emotional and physical state are considered. Traditionally voice-based authentication divided into text dependent and text independent categories. Text independent authentication is more complex than text dependent because in text dependent, the speaker speaks a predetermined phrase and in text independent, no constraint exists. Regardless of their classification, voice based authentication faces a lot of challenges because of the variability like emotional state of the speaker, misspoken phrases, environmental noise, etc.

3. **Keystroke:** This kind of authentication systems aim to capture the latency period between keystroke and hold time of the user's keyboard interaction to provide a unique representation of each user. The main advantage of this technique is that it allows continuous authenticate since the user can be analyzed over a large period.

4. **Gait:** This type of system authenticate people by the way they walk. To create gait signature, some models are built, based on the temporal and spatial matrices of the human motion. However, gait is not supposed to be very distinctive across individuals. Therefore, it is not suitable for high security scenario. It also involves video sequence analysis, which may be comparatively expensive.

Behavioral characteristic is less stable than physiological. As time passes, changes come in handwriting, voice and gait. These characteristics are also influenced by one's emotional state, physical state, environment, etc. Therefore, the most common biometrics used for authentication is Fingerprint and Iris. These biometric features satisfy the main required properties for authentication. The properties make them popular are:

1. **Stability:** Both the characteristics remain constant in an entire lifetime.
2. **Uniqueness:** Finding two identical fingerprint or Iris is nearly impossible.
3. **Flexibility:** Fingerprint or iris recognition system can be integrated easily into the existing system. It can also be operated as standalone.

Other biometrics are also used, but all biometric features are not equally efficient, secure and user-friendly. For example, facial recognition system fails in case of identical twins and for many other factors like the beard, facial hairs, glasses, scars, etc. Voice, signature, gait also have many issues, like voice, signature is prone to forgers and are affected by environment, time variant, etc. On the other hand, some biometric analysis is costly to use for public authentication, such as DNA matching.

Fingerprint is the most common user-friendly and distinctive biometric. Same is applicable for iris biometric. In spite of all points, people prefer to use fingerprint by fingerprint scanner than placing an eye in IR scanner camera.

STEGANOGRAPHY USING BIOMETRICS

When this biometric information is used to provide security, authentication, then simultaneously they also need security, since biometrics represent a person physiologically and behaviorally. This information is itself very confidential to a person. For providing security, steganography can employ in this situation. While transferring biometric information over network we have to take care of its confidentiality. Here we have two type of use of biometrics in steganography. In one type, we can use steganography to provide security to the biometric information. In a different kind, we can use biometric information to provide security to secret information.

Security to Biometrics

To prevent the misuse or leaking of any biometric information of a person, one can take advantage of steganography method. We have already discussed that how steganography works and how does it efficient in providing security. Figure 2 shows that the biometric information, the fingerprint is embedded in the cover image 'baboon'. For embedding, any steganography method can be used as the requirement. There are various techniques with different methods in different domains which are already discussed in the former section.

Security by Biometrics

Biometrics image could be a very good/unsuspicious cover image. When a sender sends a biometric image over the network, then generally it is not suspected by the intruder, as because the confidential data biometrics is sent as it is. In that case, we can use the biometric image to hide some secret information. There are some other cases also, where biometric require to hold some information secretly. For example, in some medical report, where the patient's personal information (e.g. name, age, sex etc.) should be kept hidden to others except the receiver, the information is embedded in the medical image secretly. Figure 3 shows the use of biometric information as cover image in steganography. Figure 3(a) shows hiding of secret information in iris biometrics and Figure 3(b), the information of the patient is concealed in the MRI report.

Biometrics characteristics of an individual are very confidential since it defines the person physically and behaviorally. Security of these always should be a matter of concern for researchers. We know that many encryption algorithms being used to assist the security enhancement of biometric system, but there are still some issues to resolve. In 2001, Ratha addressed eight primary sources of attacks in biometrics system.

Figure 2. Security to biometric data

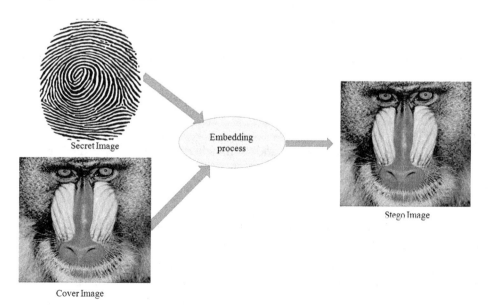

Figure 3. Biometrics image as cover image

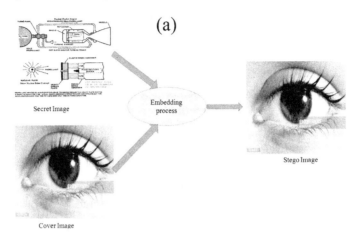

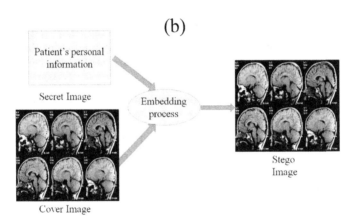

1. Fake biometric at the sensor;
2. Resubmission of old digitally stored biometrics signal (typical replay attack in voice recognition);
3. Override feature extraction;
4. Tampering with the feature representation in network environment;
5. Override matcher;
6. Tampering with stored templates in database;
7. Channel attack between stored templates and the matcher during biometric data or feature template transmission;
8. Decision level override.

We know that the cryptography algorithm scrambles the message, which attracts the intruder to decode the message. To avoid this situation, steganography is used. For example, a person needs to send his fingerprint for some normal online authentication. If that person's activities are being tracked by some intruder without his knowledge, then his fingerprint will also be leaked. That fingerprint may be misused (e.g. online fund transfer, personal account access, etc.) by the intruder further.

SOLUTIONS AND RECOMMENDATIONS

From the literature survey, it is found that biometrics has extensively been used by the developer to provide security and authenticity. Many researchers and developers use a biometric feature such as skin, iris, etc. to hide the secret information. But, the security of biometric information is not much been focused. D. Goyal proposed a steganography authentication system. In that method, the face and voice of the user are embedded in the cover image and is sent to the bank server. Bank server contacts authentication server to verify and then the transaction takes place.

Here, will present a hypothetical secure voting system for casting a vote remotely. As a responsible citizen, we all wanted to establish the voting right. But due to our busy scheduled life, we may not able to cast our vote each time. It would be beneficial if we could cast our vote through a secure trusty online system. The basic working of an example system is prototype below:

1. Login to the user account through user name and password. The username could be any unique ID, such as SSN no, Adhar no, Voter ID, etc.
2. The system will ask to provide the thump print through some fingerprint scanner which will be integrated part of the system.
3. Without user's knowledge, the system will select a cover image randomly from its database and embeds this information onto the selected cover image using some robust steganography algorithm.
4. The stego image is sent to the authentication server.
   a. If biometric verification fails, then an error message will be sent to the user.
   b. If user has already cast a vote, then also an error message will be sent.
   c. First, the server will check whether the user has already cast a vote or not. If not, then it will send the extracted data to the authentication server database. After verification, a verification number will be generated. The confirmation number will be sent to the user as well as to the voting server as shown in Figure 4 (via sms or email).
5. If the verification number match between the user and voting server, then a secure channel will be established between the two parties otherwise communication link will be disconnected with a message. The connection will be for a limited period only.
6. Now the user can cast their vote before the session expires.

Here multimodal biometric authentication can also be applied. With fingerprint, we can use iris also for stronger authentication. For scanning fingerprint, any standard fingerprint scanner can be used. Many technologies have been used including optical, capacitive, RF, thermal, piezoresistive, ultrasonic, piezoelectric.

Biometric Steganography

Fingerprint as the biometric feature is a very good choice for authentication. It holds the important properties of good biometrics: stability, uniqueness, user-friendly, etc. In steganography, the primary goal is to achieve high imperceptibility and it happens when the size the image or message to be embedded is as small as possible. In case of a fingerprint, we can represent it as a binary image without losing any important information. Converting a grayscale image to binary image saves eight times bit. Therefore using this concept we can achieve a very high-quality stego image.

Figure 4. Block diagram of secure e-voting system

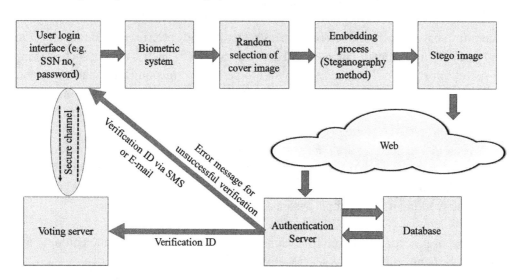

Now, for steganography method, considering the robustness property of transform domain, any one of the feasible methods can be adopted among transform domain methods. Again for the secret biometric image, we can compress the secret image to reduce the size, so that we can achieve better quality stego image. Figure 5 shows the block diagram with a compression method. Compression can be lossless or lossy. Both the methods are useable here. With lossy compression (e.g. DCT, DWT compression) fingerprint can successfully authenticate a user.

Figure 5. Transform domain steganography using compression method

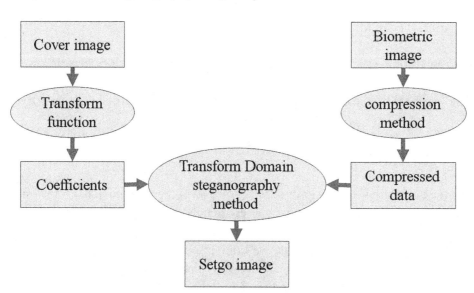

FUTURE RESEARCH DIRECTIONS

Information security has been increased here by the amalgamation of steganography and biometrics to a next level. But being a new area very less joint literature and research is available in this mixed area. The necessity of protection of intellectual property rights is increasing day by day due to most of the information and data being stored in cloud space and being readily available on the internet. Thus the inclusion of both physical and behavioral biometrics in all possible permutations and combinations with transform domain variants of steganography both on software and realization on hardware is to be addressed in future. Then based on computational complexity as well as response time and robustness best possible techniques need to be analyzed and optimized to obtain the best possible ways of enhancing security. Thereby, the future research in this area must target these areas.

CONCLUSION

In this chapter presents an introduction to the concept of steganography with a scope. It also discussed the basics of biometrics and different type of it. Steganography with the idea of biometrics such as biometric image as a cover image, biometric image as secret image have been presented. Application of these entire concepts is shown in an online voting system which is now on demand.

REFERENCES

Ahmed, N., Natarajan, T., & Rao, K. R. (1974, January). Discrete Cosine Transform. *IEEE Transactions on Computers*, C-23(1), 90–93. doi:10.1109/T-C.1974.223784

Al-Assam, H., Rashid, R., & Jassim, S. (2013). Combining steganography and biometric cryptosystems for secure mutual authentication and key exchange. *8th International Conference for Internet Technology and Secured Transactions (ICITST)*, 369-374. doi: 10.1109/ICITST.2013.6750224

Ali, A., Aliyar, L., & Nisha, V. K. (2010). RC5 encryption using key derived from fingerprint image, Computational Intelligence and Computing Research (ICCIC). *2010 IEEE International Conference on, Coimbatore*, 1-4. doi: 10.1109/ICCIC.2010.5705778

Banerjee, I., Bhattacharyya, S., Mukherjee, S., & Sanyal, G. (2014). Biometric steganography using face geometry. TENCON 2014 - 2014 IEEE Region 10 Conference, 1-6. doi:10.1109/TENCON.2014.7022450

Barkathunisha, S., & Meenakumari, R. (2013). Secure transmission of medical information using IRIS recognition and steganography. *International Conference on Computation of Power, Energy, Information and Communication (ICCPEIC)*, 89-92. 10.1109/ICCPEIC.2013.6778504

Barve, S., Nagaraj, U., & Gulabani, R. (2011). Efficient and Secure Biometric Image Stegnography using Discrete Wavelet Transform. *International Journal of Computer Science & Communication Networks, 1*(1).

Bhattacharyya, S., Banerjee, I., Chakraborty, A., & Sanyal, G. (2014). Biometric Steganography Using Variable Length Embedding. *International Journal of Computer, Electrical, Automation, Control and Information Engineering, 8*(4).

Cheddad, A., Condell, J., Curran, K., & Kevitt, P. (2010). Digital image steganography: Survey and analysis of current methods. *Signal Processing, 90*(3), 727–752. doi:10.1016/j.sigpro.2009.08.010

Cheddad, A., Condell, J., Curran, K., & Kevitt, P. M. (2008). Biometric Inspired Digital Image Steganography. Engineering of Computer Based Systems, 2008. ECBS 2008. *15th Annual IEEE International Conference and Workshop on the*, 159-168. doi: 10.1109/ECBS.2008.11

Chen, B., & Wornell, G. W. (2001). Quantization index modulation: A class of provably good methods for digital watermarking and information embedding. *IEEE Transactions on Information Theory, 47*(4), 1423–1443. doi:10.1109/18.923725

Chen, B., & Wornell, G.W. (2011). Quantization index modulation: A class of provably good methods for digital watermarking and information embedding. *IEEE Trans. Inform. Theory, 47*, 1423–1443.

Gandhi, N. (2014). Study on Security of Online Voting System Using Biometrics and Steganography. IJCSC, 5(1), 29-32.

Gonzalez & Woods. (n.d.). *Digital Image Processing*. Pearson.

Goyal, D., & Wang, S. (n.d.). *Steganographic Authentications in conjunction with Face and Voice Recognition for Mobile Systems*. Academic Press.

Hioki, H. (2010). *A data embedding method using BPCS principle with new complexity measures*. Proc. of Pacific Rim Workshop on Digital Steganography.

Hussam, U.-D., Ihmaidi, A., Al-Jaber, A., & Hudaib, A. (2006). Securing Online Shopping Using BiometricPersonal Authentication and Steganography. *Proceedings of 2nd International Conference on Information & Communication Technologies*, 233-238. doi: 10.1109/ICTTA.2006.1684376

Inthavisas, K., & Lopresti, D. (2012, March). Secure speech biometric templates for user authentication. *IET Biometrics, 1*(1), 46–54. doi:10.1049/iet-bmt.2011.0008

Itkis, G., Chandar, V., Fuller, B. W., Campbell, J. P., & Cunningham, R. K. (2015, September). Iris Biometric Security Challenges and Possible Solutions: For your eyes only?Using the iris as a key. *IEEE Signal Processing Magazine, 32*(5), 42–53. doi:10.1109/MSP.2015.2439717

Jain, A. K., & Uludag, U. (2003). Hiding Biometric Data. IEEE Transactions on Pattern Analysis and Machine Intelligence, 25(11).

Kahn, D. (2005). The History of steganography. Chapter Information Hiding. *Lecture Notes in Computer Science*, 1174, 1–5.

Kalita, M., & Tuithung, T. (2016). A comparative study of steganography algorithms of spatial and transform domain. In *National Conference on Recent Trends in Information Technology NCIT2015* (pp. 9-14). IJCA Press.

Kamau, G.M., Kimani, S., & Mwangi, W. (2013). A general Purpose Image-Based Electors Smart Card Using an Enhanced Least Significant Bit Steganographic Method for Information Hiding: A case study of the Kenyan Electoral Process. *International Journal of Computer Science Issues, 10*(2).

Kapezynski, A., & Banasik, A. (2011). Biometric Logical Access Control Enhanced by Use of Steganography Over Secured Transmission Channel. *The 6th IEEE International Conference on Intelligent Data Acquisition and Advanced Computing Systems: Technology and Applications.* 10.1109/IDAACS.2011.6072859

Kasprzak, W., Stefańczyk, M., & Wilkowski, A. (2015). Printed steganography applied for the authentication of identity photos in face verification. *2nd International Conference on Cybernetics (CYBCONF),* 512-517. 10.1109/CYBConf.2015.7175987

Katiyar, S., Meka, K. R., Barbhuiya, F. A., & Nandi, S. (2011) Online Voting System Powered By Biometric Security Using Steganography. *2011 Second International Conference on Emerging Applications of Information Technology,* 288-291. 10.1109/EAIT.2011.70

Lai, L., Ho, S. W., & Poor, H. V. (2011, March). Privacy–Security Trade-Offs in Biometric Security Systems—Part I: Single Use Case. *IEEE Transactions on Information Forensics and Security, 6*(1), 122–139. doi:10.1109/TIFS.2010.2098872

Lakshmi, V. J., Vineka, P., & Anbarasu, V. (2014). Biometrics and Steganography based Secure Online Voting System. *International Journal of Research in Engineering & Advanced Technology, 2*(2).

Lavanya, N., Manjula, V., & Rao, N. V. K. (2012). Robust and Secure Data Hiding in Image Using Biometric Technique. *International Journal of Computer Science and Information Technologies, 3*(5), 5133–5136.

Li, F., Wu, K., Lei, J., Wen, M., Bi, Z., & Gu, C. (2016, February). Steganalysis Over Large-Scale Social Networks With High-Order Joint Features and Clustering Ensembles. *IEEE Transactions on Information Forensics and Security, 11*(2), 344–357. doi:10.1109/TIFS.2015.2496910

Lokhande, S., Sawant, D., Sayyad, N., & Yengul, M. (2012). YE-Voting through Biometrics and Cryptography- Steganography Technique with conjunction of GSM Modem. *International Journal of Computer Applications.*

Lu, Y., Li, X., Qi, M., Li, J., Fu, Y., & Kong, J. (2008). Lossless and Content-Based Hidden Transmission for Biometric Verificaion. *Intelligent Information Technology Application, 2008. IITA '08. Second International Symposium on,* 462-466. 10.1109/IITA.2008.351

Majumder, S., & Das, T. S. (2013). *Watermarking of Data Using Biometrics, Handbook of Research on Computational Intelligence for Engineering, Science, and Business.* IGI Global.

Malwade, N., Patil, C. Chavan, S., & Raut, S. Y. (2013). Secure Online Voting System Proposed By Biometrics And Steganography. *International Journal of Emerging Technology and Advanced Engineering, 3*(5).

Odelu, V., Das, A. K., & Goswami, A. (2015, September). A Secure Biometrics-Based Multi-Server Authentication Protocol Using Smart Cards. *IEEE Transactions on Information Forensics and Security, 10*(9), 1953–1966. doi:10.1109/TIFS.2015.2439964

Potdar, V. M., & Chang, E. (2004). Gray level modification steganography for secret communication. *Proc. of 2nd IEEE International Conference on Industrial Informatics,* 223–228.

Prabakaran, G., Bhavani, R., & Kanimozhi, K. (2013). Dual transform based steganography using wavelet families and statistical methods. *Proc. of the 2013 International Conference on Pattern Recognition, Informatics and Mobile Engineering*, 287–293. 10.1109/ICPRIME.2013.6496488

Rane, S., Wang, Y., Draper, S. C., & Ishwar, P. (2013, September). Secure Biometrics: Concepts, Authentication Architectures, and Challenges. *IEEE Signal Processing Magazine*, *30*(5), 51–64. doi:10.1109/MSP.2013.2261691

Rashid, R. D., Jassim, S. A., & Sellahewa, H. (2013). Covert exchange of face biometric data using steganography. *5th Computer Science and Electronic Engineering Conference (CEEC)*, 134-139. 10.1109/CEEC.2013.6659460

Sajedi, H., & Jamzad, M. (2009). Contsteg: Contourlet-based steganographymethod. *Wireless Sensor Network*, *1*(03), 163–170. doi:10.4236/wsn.2009.13022

Sallee, P. (2003). Model-based steganography. Proc. of the 2nd International Workshop on Digital Watermarking, 2939, 154–167.

Santhi, K., & Kumar, A. M. N. (2013). Biometrics based Steganography using Circular Folding in DWT Domain. *International Journal of Computer Applications, 61*(10).

Shanthini, B., & Swamynathan, S. (2012). Multimodal Biometric-based Secured Authentication System using Steganography. *Journal of Computer Science*, *8*(7), 1012–1021. doi:10.3844/jcssp.2012.1012.1021

Shejul, A. A., & Kulkarni, U. L. (2010). A DWT Based Approach for Steganography Using Biometrics, Data Storage and Data Engineering (DSDE). *2010 International Conference on*, 39-43. doi: 10.1109/DSDE.2010.10

Shejul, A. A., & Kulkarni, U. L. (2011). A Secure Skin Tone based Steganography Using Wavelet Transform. *International Journal of Computer Theory and Engineering, 3*(1).

Stallings. (n.d.). *Cryptography and network security*. Pearson.

Subhedara & Mankarb. (2014). Current status and key issues in image steganography: A survey. *Computer Science Review, 13–14*, 95–113.

Tambe, S.A., Joshi, N.P., & Topannavar, P.S. (2014). Steganography & Biometric Security Based Online Voting System. *International Journal of Engineering Research and General Science, 2*(3).

Woodward, J. D. (1997, September). Biometrics: Privacys foe or privacys friend? *Proceedings of the IEEE, 85*(9), 1480–1492. doi:10.1109/5.628723

Wu, D., & Tsai, W. H. (2003). A steganographic method for images by pixel value differencing. *Pattern Recognition Letters*, *24*(9-10), 1613–1626. doi:10.1016/S0167-8655(02)00402-6

Zhang, X., & Wang, S. (2004). Vulnerability of pixel-value differencing steganography to histogram analysis and modification for enhanced security. *Pattern Recognition Letters*, *25*(3), 331–339. doi:10.1016/j.patrec.2003.10.014

ADDITIONAL READING

Bertillon, A. (1985). La couleur de l'iris. *TheReview of Scientific Instruments, 36*(3), 65–73.

Bodade, R. M., Talbar, S. N., & Ojha, S. K. (2008).Iris recognition using rotational complex wavelet filters: A novel approach.*IEEE International Conference on Innovations in Information Technology,IIT2008*,pp.658-662).AlAin. 10.1109/INNOVATIONS.2008.4781770

Boles, W., & Boashash, B. (1998). A humanidentification technique using images of the iris and wavelet transform. *IEEE Transactions on Signal Processing, 46*(4), 1185–1188. doi:10.1109/78.668573

Chicago, Illinois.Xie, L., & Arce, G. (1998).Joint wavelet compression and authentication watermarking. Proceedings of the IEEE International Conferenceon Image Processing, Vol. 2, (pp. 427-431).

Chicago, Illinois.Yao, P., Li, J., Ye, X., Zhang, Z., & Li, B. (2006).Iris recognition algorithm using-modified logGabor filters. IEEE 18th International Conference on Pattern Recognition, ICPR 2006, (pp.461-464). China.

Daugman, J. (1992). High confidence personalidentification by rapid video analysis of iristexture. Proceedings of the IEEE InternationalCarnahan Conference on Security Technology,Crime Counter-measures, (pp. 50-60).

Daugman, J. (1993). High confidence visualrecognition of persons by a test of statistical independence.*IEEE Transactions on Pattern Analysis and Machine Intelligence, 15*(11), 1148–1161. doi:10.1109/34.244676

Daugman, J. (2004). How iris recognition works. *IEEE Transactions on Circuits and Systems for Video Technology, 14*(1), 21–30. doi:10.1109/TCSVT.2003.818350

Jain, A., Bolle, R., & Pankanti, S. (2002). *Biometrics: Personal identification in networked society*. Kluwer Academic Publishers.

Kundur, D., & Hatzinakos, D. (1999). Digitalwatermarking for telltale tamper proofing andauthentica-tion. *Proceedings of the IEEE, 87*(7), 1167–1180. doi:10.1109/5.771070

Lin, E. T., & Delp, E. J. (1999). A review of fragileimage watermarks.*Proceedings of the Multimedia and Security Workshop*, (pp. 25-29).

Liu, R., & Tan, T. (2002). A SVD-based watermarking scheme for protecting rightful ownership. *IEEE Transactions on Multimedia, 4*(1), 121–128. doi:10.1109/6046.985560

Ma, L., Tan, T., Wang, Y., & Zhang, D. (2004). Efficient iris recognition by characterizing keylocal variations. *IEEE Transactions on Image Processing, 13*(6), 739–750. doi:10.1109/TIP.2004.827237 PMID:15648865

Memon, N., Shende, S., & Wong, P. (1999). Onthe security of the Yueng-Mintzer authenticationwater-mark.Final Program and Proceedings of theIS&T PICS 99, (pp. 301- 306).

Rao, R. M., & Bopardikar, A. S. (2001). *Wavelet transforms: Introduction to Theoryand applications.* Pearson Education Asia; doi:10.1117/1.482718

Ross, A. A., Nandakumar, K., & Jain, A. K. (2006). *Handbook ofmultibiometrics. Springer.Seitz, J. (2005). Digital watermarking ofdigital media.* Information Science Publishing; doi:10.4018/978-1-59140-18-4

San Jose. California.Wu, M., & Liu, B. (1998). Watermarking forimage authentication. Proceedings ofthe IEEEInternational Conference on Image Processing,Vol. 2, (pp. 437-441).

Savanna, G. Nixon, M. S., & Aguado, A. S. (2002). Featureextraction and image processing. Oxford,UK:Newness Publishers.

Shnayderman, A., Gusev, A., & Eskicioglu, A. M. (2004). *A multidimensional image quality measureusing singular value decomposition.* Bellingham, WA: Society of Photo-Optical InstrumentationEngineers; doi:10.1117/12.530554

Stinson, D. (1995). *Cryptography theory andpractice* (3rd ed.). Boca Raton, FL: CRC Press.

Sun, Z., Wang, Y., Tan, T., & Cui, J. (2004). Robust direction estimation of gradient vector fieldfor irisrecognition. International Conference onPattern Recognition, (pp. 783-786).

Swanson, M., Kobayashi, M., & Tewfik, A. (1998). Multimedia data embedding and watermarkingtechnologies. *Proceedings of the IEEE, 86*(6), 1064–1087. doi:10.1109/5.687830

Wayman, J., Jain, A., Maltoni, D., & Maio, D. (2005). *Biometric systems: Technology, designand performance evaluation.* Springer. doi:10.1007/b138151

Wildes, R. P., Asmuth, J. C., Green, G. L., & Hsu, S. C. (1994). A system for automated irisrecognition. *Proceedings of 2nd IEEE Workshopon Application of Computer Vision*, (pp. 121-128). 10.1109/ACV.1994.341298

Wolfgang, R., & Delp, E. (1996). A watermarkfor digital images. *Proceedings of the IEEE InternationalConference on Image Processing, 3*, 219–222. doi:10.1109/ICIP.1996.560423

Wolfgang, R., & Delp, E. (1999). Fragile watermarking using the VW2D watermark. Proceedings of theIS&T/SPIE Conference on Securityand Watermarking of Multimedia Contents, (pp. 204-213).

Zhang, D., Jing, X., & Yang, J. (2006). *Biometric image discrimination technologies.* Hershey, PA: IdeaGroup Publishing; doi:10.4018/978-1-59140-830-7

Zhu, X., Zhao, J., & Xu, H. (2006). A digital watermarking algorithm and implementation basedon improved SVD. *Proceedings of the 18th IEEEComputer Society International Conference onPattern Recognition (ICPR'06).*

KEY TERMS AND DEFINITIONS

Biometrics: It refers to the technology to measure physical and behavioral characteristics of an individual, such as fingerprint, palm print, iris, DNA, retina, signature, keystroke etc. Biometric characteristic are extensively used in authentication and verification process as most of the characteristics are unique.

Cover Media: In steganography, a carrier media is selected to hide the message or to carry the message in it, that carrier media is called cover media. A cover media can be any unsuspicious file, such as natural picture, family photo, video, audio clip, etc.

Cryptography: Cryptography is a technique to secure a communication. It converts the message into some meaning text (cipher) using encryption algorithm, so that no one can read that massage without knowing the decryption algorithm. Depending on the secret key used in the algorithm it is divided into two categories: symmetric - if one key is used for encryption as well as decryption and asymmetric- if two different keys are used for encryption and decryption.

Steganography: It is a technique to provide security to the secret information using data hiding technique. In steganography, a cover media is selected to hide the information. Depending on the place of data hiding it is mainly divided into two categories: Spatial domain- if information is embedded directly in the pixel values and Transform domain- if information is embedded in the coefficient values which are calculated from the pixel values of the cover image.

Stego Image: Stego image is the output of the embedding process. Stego image contain the hidden message either in pixel values or in optimally selected coefficients.

Watermarking: It is a data hiding technique which primary motive is to authenticate. Watermarking can be visible or invisible. Here the cover image is also important along with the embedded message. Robustness is the main criteria for selection of embedding algorithm.

This research was previously published in the Encyclopedia of Information Science and Technology, Fourth Edition edited by Mehdi Khosrow-Pour, pages 4985-5003, copyright year 2018 by Information Science Reference (an imprint of IGI Global).

Chapter 27
Usable Security

Andrea Atzeni
Politecnico di Torino, Italy

Shamal Faily
Bournemouth University, UK

Ruggero Galloni
Square Reply S.r.l., Italy

ABSTRACT

The increased availability of information and services has led to the affirmation of the internet involvement for a large segment of the population. This implies a paradigm shift for computer security: users become less skilled and security aware, requiring easier interface to communicate with "the machine" and more specific and comprehensible security measures. These two aspects, which are complex and challenging, have significant reciprocal influence. In practice, it has proven very intriguing to study and propose effective trade-offs among them. This chapter focus on these aspects by analyzing the goals and state of the art of usability and security to understand where and how they might be effectively "aligned."

INTRODUCTION

Recent decades have been characterized by the growth of information technologies in the private and public sectors. The positive impact that ICT has on job performance, as well as the expansion and creation of business opportunities for companies, count as the main drivers for this growth. This growth led to the proliferation of distributed applications and physical devices, and the diffusion of technologies that facilitate social participation and social interaction. All these applications, devices and interactions may contain important information, or give access to sensitive data, putting them at risk.

The rapid diffusion of technology has led to the reduction of active security monitoring, as well as the lack of technically competent people in control of applications and devices. Moreover, the increment in social interaction increases the damage other people can directly or indirectly cause.

DOI: 10.4018/978-1-5225-7492-7.ch027

Traditionally, security is only considered as strong as its weakest link, and people were considered as the weak links (Schneier, 2003). This thinking triggers a vicious circle. (Adam & Sasse, 1999) stated that users are informed as little as possible on security mechanisms took by IT departments, precisely because they are seen as inherently untrustworthy. Their work has shown that users were not sufficiently aware of security issues and tend to build their own (often inaccurate) models of possible security threats. Users have a low perception of threats because they lack the necessary information to understand their importance. According to (Sasse & al., 2001) blaming users for a security breach is like blaming human error rather than bad design. Security has, therefore, a human dimension that must be neither ignored nor neglected. The increase in the number of breaches may be attributed to designers who fail to sufficiently consider the human factor in their design techniques. Thus, to undo the Gordian knot of security, we must provide a human dimension to security.

BACKGROUND

Human-Computer Interaction (HCI) is a field concerned with the interaction between people and technology, and how this supports humans in completing tasks to achieve one of more specific goals. Traditionally, it has been involved in analyzing and improving usability.

HCI has been an active area of research since the 1980s. It has focused on improving the design of user interfaces, and helping users transforming their goals into productive actions for the computers. Improving user interfaces and usability is important because poorly designed interfaces increase the potential for human error. In particular, human behavior is largely goal-driven, therefore the execution of activities which help the users to achieve their goals is the main key to create a usable system. So, when a user "engages with a complex system of rules that change as the problem changes" (e.g. an interface does not present information clearly and coherently with a user mental model), it leads to "Cognitive Friction" (Cooper, 2004).

The "Cognitive Friction" is a by-product of the information age, and it is more evident in all the computing devices lacking a natural cause-effect relation between user input and device output, e.g. when similar inputs result in different outputs.

When a person is dealing with the cognitive friction, ancestral mechanisms of the human being come into play. As result, in this case, users cannot be modeled as purely rational beings. Thus, to understand users' behavior, and to appreciate how systems can be made usable, we need to consider the following factors:

- Users are driven by goals. People are naturally prone to pursuing goals. In achieving this, according to Krug "every question mark adds to our cognitive workload, distracting our attention from the task at hand" (Krug, 2005). This, according to Norman (Norman, 2002), creates usability issues, because it introduces the cognitive friction into play and leads users to make mistakes, which sometimes can also result into security flaws;
- Users do not read the instructions. Users proceed by trial and are not interested in reading manuals, instructions or documentation. For most of the users, it is not important to know how to do something, until the moment in which it is not necessary to use it (Krug, 2005);

- Users follow the path of least resistance. Several studies in the field of HCI have shown how users, in their task to accomplish a goal, tend to seek the path requiring them less effort (e.g. (Norman, 2002)). Once they find the first reasonable option allowing them to perform the desired action, it becomes irrelevant to them if it is not the most efficient and safe option. Furthermore, users have no incentive to improve. When users "find something that works - no matter how badly – they tend not to look for a better way" (Krug, 2005). Some operations can be inconvenient from the point of view of performance, others, in the long run, can cause damage to the system: users may be unaware of it until problems show up for the first time.

While many research studies in HCI has been focused in defining what usability is and, consequently, intervene in improving user interfaces, several studies have shown that the "ease of use" cannot be limited to those aspects alone (Whitten & Tygar, 1999) (Balfanz & al., 2004).

To increase the acceptance of the security mechanisms, conventional wisdom suggests it is sufficient to make them easier through a more usable user interface. In practice, however, it is not enough to provide a proper user interface, even in the case it is supported by specific configuration guidelines. This is what Whitten and Tygar argue, in their study "Why Johnny cannot encrypt" (Whitten & Tygar, 1999), which is a seminar paper in the usable security literature. This study focuses on analyzing data and email encryption of the security software Pretty Good Privacy 5.0 (PGP). They showed that user errors have not decreased, despite years of improvements to the graphical interface. This has led to additional studies looking beyond the interfaces.

This field of study, which deals with analyzing the usability issues related to security, is called HCI-Sec and was founded in 2000 by Whitten as a mailing list on Yahoo! Groups. It has been said that HCI-Sec "only rarely received significant attention as a primary subject for study" (Balfanz & al., 2004), this despite the fact that "usability remains one of the most pressing and challenging problems for computer security" (Whitten & Tygar, 1999).

Although HCI-Sec has only recently gained momentum, initial studies have their roots in 1975, when (Saltzer & Schroeder, 1975) argued that the usability was an essential component of a secure system. In their seminar "The protection of Information in Computer System" they presented eight basic principles that serve as guidelines for the design of systems aimed at protecting information. The principle of the "Psychological Acceptability" is one of them, and states: "it is essential that the human interface is designed for ease of use so that users routinely and automatically apply the protection mechanisms correctly".

Since then, little work has been focused on HCI-Sec and, as a result, the security systems are sometimes poorly designed, leading to cases where users seek alternative interactions with the system or completely avoid the security mechanisms. Given the difficulty in making IT systems usable, it is unsurprising that the problem of "aligning usability and security" has been almost neglected until the beginning of the early 90s of the last century.

According to Fléchais, it is wrong to justify such a dearth of research as a tension between usability and security. Until that decade, the research community was more focused on technical trade-offs, such as for example the realization of robust encryption on low energy consumption microprocessors (Flechais & Sasse, 2005). This is reasonable, because, before the growth of the Internet, security was mainly a physical concern, and physical thinking was based on a military mindset.

The problem of usability in security, however, was not limited to this, and already existed during the 80s and 90s. For example, it was already possible to improve usability and possibly weaken security by automating common tasks. Brad Reid (Reid, 1987), argued that programmer convenience is the antithesis of security because it becomes intruder convenience if the programmer's account is compromised. Reid mentioned a "programmer" because at that time the main users of the computer systems were mostly researchers or computer science specialists who possessed some programming aptitude. These individuals possessed technical skills, received specific training and were, therefore, prone to ignore usability, and failing to identify the security implications this might have.

In the 1990s, with the diffusion of personal computers and the mass adoption of the Internet, the problem of usable security has remained virtually unexplored and did not leverage pre-existing HCI research. The initial solution to the problem addressed the symptoms rather than the root cause, by updating the anti-virus software, or the patching software in known problems. Therefore, research has been focused more on short-term practical gains, rather than long-term design changes that attend to both usability and security. A further problem is that few developers are trained in usability, or have significant software security experience.

The advent of HCI-Sec introduced the idea of security as an important consideration for usability, while usability is an important aspect of security (Cranor & Garfinkel, 2005). Therefore, if the purpose of HCI was to ensure that users would reach their goals by the use of better interfaces, HCI-Sec aims to ensure that users are able to achieve these goals also in the most secure way.

MAIN FOCUS OF THE CHAPTER

The aim of this chapter is to analyze the goals and state of the art of usability and security to determine where and how they can be effectively "aligned".

ISSUES, CONTROVERSIES, PROBLEMS

Usability has become a key factor in the quality of the software and has a determining role in productivity and acceptance (Cranor & Garfinkel, 2005). This term has more than one meaning, though; it refers multiple concepts that may or may not be taken together. Some are based on *execution time, performance, user satisfaction* and *ease of learning* (also known as *learnability*). Thus, it remains something that is not unequivocally defined, and is subject to interpretation based on the stake one has in usability (Hertzum, 2010).

Over the years, the International Organization for Standardization (ISO) itself produced various, and sometimes conflicting, definitions of usability (Figure 1). These definitions can be classified into two main categories: *product-oriented* and *process-oriented*. The former category provides definitions of the qualities that belong to the final product. This appears to be a reasonable approach, because software usability is essential for end-users, as crucial for achieving particular tasks quickly and effectively. The latter category focuses on the methodological aspects of obtaining usability: for a software developer, usability describes the internal attributes of a system, including concerns such as quality of design, documentation, and maintenance.

Figure 1. Usability definitions according to ISO/IEC 9241-11, ISO/IEC 9126 and ISO/IEC 25010

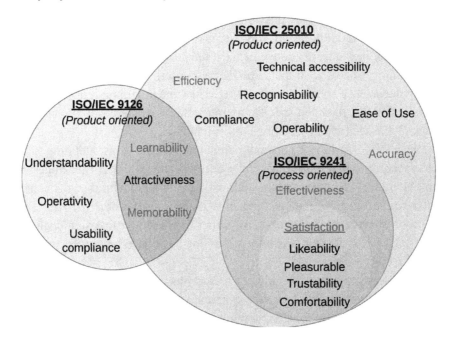

These various points of view and the different requirements have resulted in contrasting perspectives on usability, carried out by several groups of experts in a non-uniform and inconsistent way. For example, some terms have different meanings and labels. In document ISO/IEC 9241-11 (ISO, 1998) *learnability,* as a quality of a software, is designed as the "time of learning", while in ISO/IEC 9126 (ISO, 2012) is defined as "comprehensible input and output, instruction readiness, messages readiness".

Discrepancies among the standard can be even more significant: in the standard ISO/IEC 9126, usability is defined in a product-oriented way as a set of attributes that bear on the effort needed for use and on the individual assessment of such use, by a stated or implied set of users. The qualitative properties to be achieved are Understandability, Learnability, Operability, Attractiveness and Usability compliance (Abran & al, 2003). The standard that replaced it, ISO/IEC 25010, focuses on the user's goals and on how fast they are achieved, in addition to user satisfaction with the system. In this document, usability replaces learnability property in favour of o*perability* (Lew & Olsina, 2010), which is described as the degree to which the product has attributes that enable it to be understood, to be learned, to be used, and to be attractive to the user, when used under specific conditions.

With this definition of operability, the properties to be achieved are *appropriateness, recognisability, ease of use, learnability, attractiveness, technical accessibility* and *compliance*. The same standard describes however also a different model, *Quality in Use*, in which the usability appears described as the extent to which a product can be used by specific users to achieve specified goals with effectiveness, efficiency and satisfaction without adverse consequences in a specified context of use.

The process-oriented point of view was defined in the document ISO/IEC 9241, which is a suite of international standards on *"Ergonomics of Human System Interaction"*. In Part 11, the definitions of usability from different perspectives are grouped together. The key components are effectiveness and satisfaction. The former describes the interactions from the point of view of process efficiency and puts the focus on the results and valuable assets. The latter requires carefulness on the user's needs. The standard attempts to explain how to identify the information that has to be taken into account when evaluating usability in terms of measures of user performance and user satisfaction.

The criterion of satisfaction is very difficult to be measured and, for this reason, additional usability factors have been proposed in Part 2 of ISO/IEC 25010. They are *likeability, pleasurable, comfort and trust*.

Given the subjectivity and the different contexts in which the term "usability" can be used, Kainda and Flechais (Kainda et al., 2010) proposed to consolidate it in six key factors which are defined as:

- **Effectiveness:** A system is only usable if its users can achieve intended goals, and effectiveness is measured by whether users are able to complete a particular task or not;
- **Satisfaction:** A system must be accepted by users, otherwise it is bound to fail, even if is usable;
- **Accuracy:** A system demands may have an impact on the user's tasks. For example, a system may require 100% accuracy in an providing information, such as a pin code or a password. However, this accuracy, is not always achievable by the user, making the system unusable;
- **Efficiency:** To guarantee usability, a system must ensure that each user's goals are achievable within an acceptable amount of time and effort;
- **Memorability:** A system may require users to memorize secrets, namely passwords. This may be problematic since the users are cognitively burdened with credentials, and other secrets;
- **Knowledge:** This corresponds to the Learnability property. However, the user may not attempt to learn or understand the system, as users tend to care only about the parts of the system of interest to them. Therefore, knowledge of the security mechanisms or policies is required by the user;

These characteristics can be measured in different ways. Effectiveness, satisfaction, efficiency and memorability can be measured directly, while accuracy and knowledge are measured indirectly, i.e. the first set of characteristics can be measured directly by quite simple empirical indicators, while the latter are typically derived by combining more indicators.

Another HCI-sec problem is that adequate usability is essential in specific security mechanism (e.g. authentication process), but the requirements for achieving it and a high level of security may collide (Braz & Robert, 2006). For example, in the case of password-based authentication, many usability principles (e.g. use shortcuts in case of frequent use, provide informative feedback) contrast with best practices (e.g. password must not be showed during typing, and only success or failure must be reported, to mitigate social engineering and guessing).

SOLUTIONS AND RECOMMENDATIONS

From the perspective of HCI, there are several principles for building a system that is "quick to use and relatively error-free" (Johnson, 2007). One of the most important of these is ensuring the system "does what the user wants" without "complicating the user's task". Another important aspect is to evaluate the usability of a system. In this regard, the System Usability Scale (SUS) (Brooke, 1996) is a widely accepted base. The SUS is designed to give a quick impression of the overall usability of a product. It consists of ten questions (e.g. "I found this system unnecessarily complex", I found the various functions in this system were well integrated") rated on a Likert scale, resulting in an overall 0-100 value, where 100 represents excellent levels of usability. SUS has been adopted in many contexts, also in HCI-sec (De Witt, J. Kuljis, 2006) since quick to complete, thus avoiding user frustration and ensure answer accuracy.

From the perspective of methods and procedures used in HCI, many of them have been adapted to the HCI-Sec. The main difference is the focus on a balanced trade-off between usability and security.

The methodologies between HCI and HCI-Sec differ for at least five key aspects that are analyzed in the following paragraphs, detailing related recommendation as well.

THE SECONDARY GOAL

People do not generally sit at their computers wanting to manage their security; rather they want to send mail, browse web pages or download software.

Traditionally, security definitions have been defined around attackers. Unfortunately, doing so ignores the legitimate and non-malicious use, and also may adversely affect the system (Kainda & al, 2010). Users may not have the perception of damaging the system or, through making certain actions or inactions, bypassing security systems, putting their assets risk. Users must be constantly made aware of the operations involving security and the system must ensure that it is hard to make catastrophic errors. Furthermore, if such events occur, user actions should be reversible. To illustrate how this can be achieved, consider the implementation of dialog boxes requiring confirmation of a particular action. The implementation of the "Empty Trash" feature in desktop operating systems typically allows accidentally deleted files to be recovered, or the "Undo" button, now present in many desktop applications, allows for an action to be reverted. In a business setting, backup and redundancy of servers are amongst the systems used to avoid potential damages even from non-malicious users. Unfortunately, as Garfinkel has demonstrated, even "Empty Trash" functionality can behave in a manner inconsistent with a corresponding interface design (Garfinkel, 2005).

ABSTRACTION

Security policies are usually phrased as abstract rules that are easily understood by programmers but "alien" and unintuitive to many members of the wider user population.

(Johnson, 2007) proposes a focus on learnability and memorability, properties which, as we have discussed, belong to Usability. Facilitating the learning process is possible, by creating a consistent lexicon transmitted through the user interface. This is convenient since it was discovered that a particular trend also applies to IT users: they prefer not to invest time in training or reading manuals, but in learning the functionality of the system through the exploration of the user interface (Krug, 2005).

THE HIDDEN FAILURE

It is difficult to provide good feedback for security management and configuration because configurations are complex and not easy to summarize.

Making a secure system does not guarantee its security because the system must also be installed and used in a secure way. (Bishop, 2005) noted that the configuration is a key component of security because it is during the configuration of a system that it is defined who will interact with the system and how. Practitioners and security staff often make mistakes in applying default software configurations, ignoring the fact that different configurations lead to different security contexts. For example, a computer configured to be secure in a university research environment could be considered insecure in a military installation. In the former, information might be made accessible to the whole class or research group while, in the latter, they might be accessible only on a need to know basis.

One method used to counteract and minimize the adverse effects of an incorrect configuration is the "fail-safe default" principle (Saltzer & Schroeder, 1975). This states that the safest solution is a default configuration without any permission granted. During the configuration phase, a security responsible task selects the correct permissions for each system function and group of users. When configuring a firewall, this principle corresponds to the whitelist configuration: everything that is not explicitly allowed is forbidden by default. This policy contrasts with the blacklist, which grants any permission by default and chooses specifically the ones to forbid. The former one, despite being more difficult to handle, forces discussion on any permission to be enabled, thereby making the system more secure.

THE BARN DOOR

Once a secret has been left accidentally unprotected, even for a short time, there's no way to be sure it has not already been read by an attacker.

Once sensitive data or vital assets for the company are compromised and made public by mistake, it is possible that attackers will use it for their own advantage. There are several ways to approach this problem. You might try to avoid social engineering attacks, where even expert users fall victim to if channels of communication they trust and use regularly are compromised. This risk can be prevented using anti-fraud mechanisms, aimed at preventing phishing through e-mail or other channels. Should an attacker successfully obtain sensitive information such as passwords, private keys or credit card numbers, it should also be possible to erase and getting new information. In the case of commercially sensitive intellectual property, DRM can also be implemented, which can control access to resources, and revoke permissions in the event of a successful attack. DRM technology is, however, complex to maintain and not without its own usability issues (Favale & al., 2016)

THE WEAKEST LINK

The security of a networked computer is like a chain: it is only as strong as its weakest component.

It is generally recognized that the user is often the weak point of a computer system from a security perspective. However, as discussed, this creates a vicious circle in which users are kept unaware of what the security mechanisms are. Therefore, users are driven to the creation of their own security views, which fail to align with reality. To avoid this issue, security mechanisms should be complemented by specific guidelines that take into account the specific constraints of security mechanisms, minimizing discrepancies introduced by users with different backgrounds and skills.

FUTURE RESEARCH DIRECTIONS

Future research direction will address the problem of measuring usable security in a more systematic and practical way, or, as a first milestone toward the goal, understand if there are real advantages and tangible benefits resulting from formative and summative usability assessment processes. Such an assessment is not easy because of the previously discussed complex variables into play. Moreover, there are several aspects that are influenced by contextual conditions, such as economic resources, time, and other economic or innovation drivers.

To address these evaluation issues, we need to understand what it means to precisely evaluate usable security. Only then will it be possible to identify what methods can be effectively used in the analysis processes.

Also, all these facets activate different levels of sub-choices that depend on several variables and the context of use. One of these could, for example, be advancing the project in time: do you want to evaluate a system in its initial stage of development, or at a different iteration of the same application? It has already been noted that, while considering security at an early stage of a software product's design is virtuous, design techniques may be needed that specifically consider security at a later stage (Faily, 2015).

For any improvements, development should be scientifically measurable. As Lord Kevin said over 200 years ago "if you cannot measure it, you cannot improve it", meaning that without a scientifically sound evaluation methodology, would be difficult to draw any objective conclusions and take any proper improving actions (Atzeni & Lioy, 2005).

Measurement should not be an end in itself, but lead to something analogous to a benchmark, which is a result or a group of results that can become a point of reference and standard; this enables comparison and judgment on how good or bad things are.

CONCLUSION

Human behavior is goal-driven, therefore each aspect of a system interacting with users, security included, should be organized to help users to achieve their goals. In particular, security must be embedded paying attention to usability aspects, to avoid "cognitive friction".

Since usable security principles can be applied both to final product and to the production process, from one hand it is necessary to adopt methodologies to understand and measure the usability of the final artifact, from the other, all production line components should be considered in light of usability effectiveness, starting from the earliest steps in building software. This ensures that the quality of usable security is `built into' the final product, and diagnose the feedback that allows the project to be changed before its final release.

The ability to diagnose and correct an error in the usability of a software before entering the market is in itself a significant benefit, as are methods that can also be used to determine quality variations between two iterations of a given software. It is, therefore, necessary to describe and scientifically evaluate the properties of usability and security as two correlated factors, even if they are both difficult to quantify and even define. To facilitate quantification and definition, past literature split up usability and usable security in more atomic pieces (e.g. effectiveness, satisfaction, accuracy, efficiency, memorability) to make them more identifiable and comparable.

Finally, a scientifically sound usability assessment is a target of great interest. Further research is welcome because it is a complex problem (even when decomposed in sub-parts like satisfaction or memorability) and because the context of a product under evaluation can introduce influencing variables, enlarging the problem complexity.

REFERENCES

Abran, A., Khelifi, A., Suryn, W., & Seffah, A. (2003). Usability Meanings and Interpretations in ISO Standards. *Software Quality Journal, 11*(4). DOI . doi:10.1023/A:1025869312943

Adams, A. Sasse, M.A. (1999). Users are not the enemy. *Communications of the ACM, 42*(12). DOI . doi:10.1145/322796.322806

Atzeni, A., & Lioy, A. (2005). Why to adopt a security metrics? A little survey, *Proc. of QoP'05 - Quality of Protection, 1*(12).

Balfanz, D., Durfee, G., Grinter, R. E., & Smetters, D. K. (2004). In Search of Usable Security: Five Lessons from the Field. IEEE Security & Privacy, 2(5). DOI doi:10.1109/MSP.2004.71

Bishop, M. (2005). Psychological Acceptability Revisited. Security and Usability: Designing Secure Systems that People Can Use, 1(12).

Braz, C., & Robert, J. M. (2006). Security and usability: the case of the user authentication methods. *18th Conference on l'Interaction Homme-Machine*, 199-203. 10.1145/1132736.1132768

Brooke, J. (1996). SUS-A quick and dirty usability scale. *Usability Evaluation in Industry, 189*(194), 4-7.

Cooper, A. (2004). *The Inmates Are Running the Asylum: Why High Tech Products Drive Us Crazy and How to Restore the Sanity* (2nd ed.). Sams Publishing.

Cranor, L. F., & Garfinkel, S. (2005). Security and Usability: Designing Secure Systems that People Can Use. O'Reilly.

De Witt, A. J., & Kuljis, J. (2006). Aligning Usability and Security-A Usability Study Of Polaris. *Proc. of the Symp. On Usable Privacy and Security.* 10.1145/1143120.1143122

Faily, S. (2015). Engaging Stakeholders during Late Stage Security Design with Assumption Personas. *Information and Computer Security, 435*(446).

Favale, M., McDonald, N., Faily, S., & Gatzidis, C. (2016), Human Aspects in Digital Rights Management: The Perspective of Content Developers. *Fourth International Workshop on Artificial Intelligence and Law.*

Flechais, I., & Sasse, M.A. (2005). Developing Secure and usable software. *OT2003.* DOI doi:10.1234/12345678

Garfinkel, S. (2005). Sanitization and Usability. *Security and Usability: Designing Secure Systems that People Can Use, 293*(317).

Hertzum, M. (2010). Images of Usability. *International Journal of Human-Computer Interaction, 567*(600).

ISO/IEC. (1998). *ISO/IEC 9241-11 - Guidance on Usability management*. ISO.

ISO/IEC. (2012). *ISO/IEC 27002:2007 - Product quality*. ISO.

Johnson, J. (2007). *Common User Interface Design Don'ts and Dos*. Interactive Technologies.

Kainda, R., Flechais, I., & Roscoe, A. W. (2010). Security and Usability: Analysis and Evaluation. *ARES '10 International Conference on Availability, Reliability, and Security, 275*(282). DOI: 10.1109/ARES.2010.77

Krug, S. (2005). *Don't Make Me Think: A Common Sense Approach To The Web Usability*. New Riders Pub.

Lew, P., Li, Z., & Olsina, L. (2010). Usability and user experience as key drivers for evaluating GIS application quality. *International Conference on Geoinformatics, 1*(6). 10.1109/GEOINFORMAT-ICS.2010.5567803

Norman, D. A. (2002). *The Design of Everyday Things*. Basic Books.

Reid, B. (1987). Reflections on some recent widespread computer break-ins. *Communications of the ACM, 103*(105). doi:0.1145/12527.315716

Saltzer, J. H., & Schroeder, M. D. (1975). The protection of information in computer systems. *Proceedings of the IEEE, 1278*(1308). 10.1109/PROC.1975.9939

Sasse, M. A., Brostoff, S., & Weirich, D. (2001). Transforming the 'Weakest Link' - a Human/Computer Interaction Approach to Usable and Effective Security. *BT Technology Journal, 122*(131). doi:10.1023/A:1011902718709

Schneier, B. (2003). *Beyond fear: Thinking sensibly about security in an uncertain world*. Copernicus Books. doi:10.1057/palgrave.sj.8340200

Whitten, A., & Tygar, J. D. (1999). Why Johnny can't encrypt: a usability evaluation of PGP 5.0. *USENIX Security Symposium*. Retrieved from http://dl.acm.org/citation.cfm?id=1251421.1251435

ADDITIONAL READING

Nielsen, J. (1993). *Usability Engineering*. Academic Press.

KEY TERMS AND DEFINITIONS

Cognitive Friction: The affinity friction between the user and the software that originates in the user mind when a product does not behave the way the user expects (e.g. a button on the screen that does not trigger any action when the user press it). (https://www.linkedin.com/pulse/20140801230851-205508682-what-the-heck-is-cognitive-friction).

Comfort (ISO/IEC 25010): The extent to which the user is satisfied with physical comfort.

Effectiveness: The properties which measures to what extent interactions achieve objective process efficiency indicators (i.e. concrete results of user actions while using the addressed product).

Likeability (ISO/IEC 25010): The extent to which the user perceives achievement of pragmatic goals, including successful subjective results of use and consequences of use.

Memorability: A factor which measures how much a product require users to memorize secrets (e.g. passwords or passphrases).

Operability: The degree to which the product has attributes that enable it to be understood, be learned, be used and be attractive to the user, when used under specific conditions.

Pleasurable (ISO/IEC 25010): The extent to which the user is satisfied with his perceived achievement of hedonistic goals of stimulation, identification and evocation and associated emotion responses.

Psychological Acceptability: A founding principle of usable security stating that *"it is essential that the human interface is designed for ease of use so that users routinely and automatically apply the protection mechanisms correctly".*

Process-Oriented Usability: The categorization of usability aiming to achieve it addressing the characteristics of the process to obtain the final product (e.g. documentation and design effort).

Product-Oriented Usability: The categorization of usability aiming to achieve it addressing the final products characteristics (e.g. learning curve to use the product).

Satisfaction: The property which measures to what extent the user's needs are subjectively satisfied by the product.

Trust (ISO/IEC 25010): The extent to which the user is persuaded that the product will behave as intended.

This research was previously published in the Encyclopedia of Information Science and Technology, Fourth Edition edited by Mehdi Khosrow-Pour, pages 5004-5013, copyright year 2018 by Information Science Reference (an imprint of IGI Global).

Compilation of References

Abowd, G. D., Ebling, M., Hunt, G., Lei, H., & Gellersen, H.-W. (2002). Context-aware computing. *IEEE Pervasive Computing / IEEE Computer Society [and] IEEE Communications Society*, *1*(3), 22–23. doi:10.1109/MPRV.2002.1037718

Abran, A., Khelifi, A., Suryn, W., & Seffah, A. (2003). Usability Meanings and Interpretations in ISO Standards. *Software Quality Journal*, *11*(4). DOI . doi:10.1023/A:1025869312943

Abu Bakar, H. S. (2013). Investigating the emergence themes of Cyberbullying phenomenon: A grounded theory approach. In *Educational Media, 2013 IEEE 63rd Annual Conference International Council for Educational Media (ICEM)* (pp. 1-14). Nanyang Technological University.

Adam, A. (2002). Cyberstalking and Internet pornography: Gender and the gaze. *Ethics and Information Technology*, *4*(2), 133–142. doi:10.1023/A:1019967504762

Adams, A. Sasse, M.A. (1999). Users are not the enemy. *Communications of the ACM*, *42*(12). DOI . doi:10.1145/322796.322806

Adams, R. (2013). The emergence of cloud storage and the need for a new digital forensic process model. In K. Ruan (Ed.), *Cybercrime and cloud forensics: Applications for investigation processes* (pp. 79–104)., doi:10.4018/978-1-4666-2662-1.ch004

Aeron, H., Kumar, A., & Janakiraman, M. (2010). Application of data mining techniques for customer lifetime value parameters: A review. *International Journal of Business Information Systems*, *6*(4), 530–546. doi:10.1504/IJBIS.2010.035744

Africa News. (2006, December 6). *Nigeria: Tackling the problem of piracy in Nigeria*. Retrieved from www.lexisnexis.com/hottopics/lnacademic

AFSP. (2007). *Facts and figures: National Statistics*. Retrieved on February 4, 2014 from http://0fea9f-b064-4092-bl-135c-3a70delfda.afsp.org/index.cfin?fuseaction_home.vievvpageandpage icl_0S

Agrawal, R., & Srikant, R. (1994). Fast algorithms for mining association rules. *Proc. 20th Int. Conf. Very Large Data Bases*, *1215*, 487-499.

Agrawal, S., & Lal Das, M. (2011, December). *Internet of Things – a paradigm shift of future Internet applications*. Paper presented at the Second International Conference on Current Trends in Technology (NUiCONE 2011), Ahmedabad. 10.1109/NUiConE.2011.6153246

Agrawal, S., Gupta, Y., & Chakraborty, A. (2015, October). A Composite Approach to Digital Video Watermarking. In *International Congress on Information and Communication Technology*. ICICT.

Agulla, E. G., Rifon, L. A., Castro, J. L. A., & Mateo, C. G. (2008). *Is my studnet at the other side? applying biometric web authenntication to e-learning environments.* Paper presented at the Eighth IEEE International Conference on Advanced Learning Technologies. 10.1109/ICALT.2008.184

Ahmed, N., Natarajan, T., & Rao, K. R. (1974, January). Discrete Cosine Transform. *IEEE Transactions on Computers,* *C-23*(1), 90–93. doi:10.1109/T-C.1974.223784

Aiyer, A., Alvisi, L., Clement, A., Dahlin, M., Martin, J., & Parth, C. (2005). BAR fault tolerance for cooperative services. *ACM Symposium on Operating Systems Principles.* Brighton, UK: ACM Press.

Akiyama, K., Goto, Y., & Miyake, H. (2009). An Algebraic Surface Cryptosystem, public-key cryptography-PKC09. *Lecture Notes in Computer Science, 5443,* 425-442.

Al-Assam, H., Rashid, R., & Jassim, S. (2013). Combining steganography and biometric cryptosystems for secure mutual authentication and key exchange. *8th International Conference for Internet Technology and Secured Transactions (ICITST),* 369-374. doi: 10.1109/ICITST.2013.6750224

Alderete, M. V., & Gutiérrez, L. H. (2014). Drivers of information and communication technologies adoption in Colombian services firms. *International Journal of Business Information Systems, 17*(4), 373–397. doi:10.1504/IJBIS.2014.065553

Alexy, E. M., Burgess, A. W., & Baker, T. (2005). Internet offenders: Traders, travelers, and combination trader-travelers. *Journal of Interpersonal Violence, 20*(7), 804–812. doi:10.1177/0886260505276091 PMID:15914702

Ali, A., Aliyar, L., & Nisha, V. K. (2010). RC5 encryption using key derived from fingerprint image, Computational Intelligence and Computing Research (ICCIC). *2010 IEEE International Conference on, Coimbatore,* 1-4. doi: 10.1109/ICCIC.2010.5705778

Al-Khatib, T., Al-Haj, A., & Lama Rajab, H. M. (2008). *A Robust Video Watermarking Algorithm 1.* Academic Press.

Almutairi, A., Sarfraz, M., Basalamah, S., Aref, W., & Ghafoor, A. (2012). A distributed access control architecture for cloud computing. *IEEE Software, 29*(2), 36–44. doi:10.1109/MS.2011.153

Al-Saleem, S. M., & Ullah, H. (2014). Security considerations and recommendations in computer-based t esting. *TheScientificWorldJournal, 2014,* 1–7. doi:10.1155/2014/562787 PMID:25254250

Altbach, P. G. (1988). Economic progress brings copyright to Asia. *Far Eastern Economic Review, 139*(9), 62–63.

Amir, A., Danilov, C., Dolev, D., Kirsch, J., Lane, J., Nita-Rotaru, C., ... Zage, D. (2006). Scaling Byzantine fault-tolerant replication to wide area networks. *Proceedings of International Conference on Dependable Systems and Networks.* Philadelphia, PA: IEEE Computer Society Press. 10.1109/DSN.2006.63

Anderson, C. (2010). *How web video powers global innovation.* Retrieved September 30, 2015 from https://www.ted.com/

Andrews, D. A., & Bonta, J. (2010). The psychology of criminal conduct (5th ed.). Cincinnati, OH: Anderson.

Aricak, T., Siyahhan, S., Uzunhasanoglu, A., Saribeyoglu, S., Ciplak, S., Yilmaz, N., & Memmedov, C. (2008). Cyberbullying among Turkish adolescents. *Cyberpsychology & Behavior, 11*(3), 253–261. doi:10.1089/cpb.2007.0016 PMID:18537493

Arkin, B., Hill, F., Marks, S., Scjmod, M., & Walls, T. (1999). *How we learned to cheat at on line poker: A study in software security.* Available at http://www.developer.com/java/other/article.php/10936_616221

Armsden, G. C., & Greenberg, M. T. (1987). The inventory of parent and peer attachment: Individual differences and their relationship to psychological well-being in adolescence. *Journal of Youth and Adolescence, 16*(5), 427–454. doi:10.1007/BF02202939 PMID:24277469

Arntzen, A. A. B. (2010). Knowledge, Technology and University Social Responsibility (USR): A Conceptual Framework. *Proceedings of the 11th European Conference on Knowledge Management,* 1-2, 74-81.

Asha, S., & Chellappan, C. (2008). *Authentication of E-learners using multimodal biometric technology.* Paper presented at the International Symposium on Biometrics and Security Technologies (ISBAST 2008). 10.1109/ISBAST.2008.4547640

Ashton, K. (2009). That 'Internet of Things' thing. *RFID Journal.* Retrieved May 11, 2010, from http://www.rfidjournal.com/article/view/4986

Association for Computing Machinery. (1992). *Code of Ethics and Professional Conduct.* Retrieved February 13, 2016, from http://www.acm.org/about-acm/acm-code-of-ethics-and-professional-conduct

Ateniese G., Camenisch J., Joye M., and Tsudik G., (2000). A practical and provably secure coalition-resistant group signature scheme. In *Advances in Cryptology-CRYPTO 2000.* Springer.

Atrey, P., Hossain, M., El Saddik, A., & Kankanhalli, M. (2010). Multimodal fusion for multimedia analysis: A survey. *Multimedia Systems,* 16(6), 345–379. doi:10.100700530-010-0182-0

Atzeni, A., & Lioy, A. (2005). Why to adopt a security metrics? A little survey, *Proc. of QoP'05 - Quality of Protection,* 1(12).

Atzori, L., Iera, A., & Morabito, G. (2010). The Internet of Things: A survey. *Computer Networks,* 54(15), 2787–2805. doi:10.1016/j.comnet.2010.05.010

Austin, R. D., & Devin, L. (2009). Weighing the benefits and costs of flexibility in making software: Toward a contingency theory of the determinants of development process design. *Information Systems Research,* 20(3), 462–479. doi:10.1287/isre.1090.0242

Ayas, T., & Horzum, M. B. (2010). *Cyberbully / victim scale development study.* Retrieved from: http://www.akademik-bakis.org

Azizan, H. (2012). Do you know whom your kids are talking to? *The Star Online.* Retrieved on January 28, 2014 from: http://www.thestar.com.my/News/Nation/2012/04/29/Do-you-know-who-your-kids-are-talking-to/

Babchishin, K. M., Hanson, R. K., & VanZuylen, H. (2015). Online child pornography offenders are different: A meta-analysis of the characteristics of online and offline sex offenders against children. *Archives of Sexual Behavior,* 44(1), 45–66. doi:10.100710508-014-0270-x PMID:24627189

Bahar, H. B., Sokouti, M., & Sokouti, B. (2010). A first study of improving transposition cryptosystem. *Journal of Discrete Mathematical Sciences and Cryptography,* 13(1), 1–9. doi:10.1080/09720529.2010.10698272

Baker, L. B., & Finkle, J. (2011). *Sony PlayStation suffers massive data breach.* Reuters.

Baker, W., Hutton, A., Hylender, C. D., Pamula, J., Porter, C., & Spitler, M. (2011). *2011 data breach investigations report.* Verizon RISK Team. Available: www. verizonbusiness. com/resources/reports/rp_databreach-investigations-report-2011_en_xg. pdf

Baker, E. W. (2014). A model for the impact of cybersecurity infrastructure on economic development in emerging economies: Evaluating the contrasting cases of India and Pakistan. *Information Technology for Development,* 20(2), 122–139. doi:10.1080/02681102.2013.832131

Balakrishnan, V. (2015). Cyberbullying among young adults in Malaysia: The roles of gender, age and Internet frequency. *Computers in Human Behavior,* 46, 149–157. doi:10.1016/j.chb.2015.01.021

Balfanz, D., Durfee, G., Grinter, R. E., & Smetters, D. K. (2004). In Search of Usable Security: Five Lessons from the Field. IEEE Security & Privacy, 2(5). DOI doi:10.1109/MSP.2004.71

Balfe, M., Gallagher, B., Masson, H., Balfe, S., Brugha, R., & Hackett, S. (2015). Internet child sex offenders concerns about online security and their use of identity protection technologies: A review. *Child Abuse Review*, 24(6), 427–439. doi:10.1002/car.2308

Banerjee, I., Bhattacharyya, S., Mukherjee, S., & Sanyal, G. (2014). Biometric steganography using face geometry. TENCON 2014 - 2014 IEEE Region 10 Conference, 1-6. doi:10.1109/TENCON.2014.7022450

Banks, R. (1997). Bullying in schools. *ERIC Digest*. Retrieved on July 23, 2014 from: http://npin.org/library/pre1998/n00416/n00416.html

Barak, A., & Sadovsky, Y. (2008). Internet use and personal empowerment of hearing-impaired adolescents. *Computers in Human Behavior*, 24(5), 1802–1815. doi:10.1016/j.chb.2008.02.007

Bari, J., Sullivan, R., & Blair, J. (2004). *Security method in distance-learning*. Paper presented at the 34th ASEE/IEEE Frontiers in Education Conference, Savannah, GA.

Barkathunisha, S., & Meenakumari, R. (2013). Secure transmission of medical information using IRIS recognition and steganography. *International Conference on Computation of Power, Energy, Information and Communication (ICCPEIC)*, 89-92. 10.1109/ICCPEIC.2013.6778504

Barlett, C. P., Gentile, D. A., & Chew, C. (2016). Predicting cyberbullying from anonymity. *Psychology of Popular Media Culture*, 5(2), 171–180. doi:10.1037/ppm0000055

Barnard, C. I. (1938). *The Functions of the Executive*. Cambridge, MA: Harvard University Press. Retrieved April 13, 2016, from https://en.wikipedia.org/wiki/Herbert_A_Simon#CITEREFBarnard1938

Barocas, S., & Selbst, A. D. (2016). Big data's disparate impact. *California Law Review*, 104.

Barra, R. A., Savage, A., & Tsay, J. J. (2010). Equational zero vector databases, non-equational databases, and inherent internal control. *International Journal of Business Information Systems*, 6(3), 354–377. doi:10.1504/IJBIS.2010.035050

Barrett, D., & Yadron, D. (2016). Sony, U.S. Agencies fumbled after cyberattack: Lack of information and consultation led to flip-flops, confusion. *The Wall Street Journal*. Retrieved February 26, 2016 from http://www.wsj.com/articles/sony-u-s-agencies-fumbled-after-cyberattack-1424641424

Barry-Jester, A. M., Casselman, B., & Goldstein, C. (2015, August 4). *Should prison sentences be based on crimes that haven't been committed yet?* Retrieved from http://fivethirtyeight.com/ features/prison-reform-risk-assessment/

Bartolini, L., Elisa, B., Barbara, C., Paolo, C., Matteo, G., Marco, P., & Rizzi, S. (2003). Patterns for Next-generation DAtabase systems: preliminary results of the PANDA project. *Proceedings of the Eleventh Italian Symposium on Advanced Database Systems*.

Barve, S., Nagaraj, U., & Gulabani, R. (2011). Efficient and Secure Biometric Image Stegnography using Discrete Wavelet Transform. *International Journal of Computer Science & Communication Networks, 1*(1).

Basar, E., & Haji-zada, T. (2014). *Object oriented business archtechture on online-exam and assignment system*. Paper presented at the 25th Annual Conference EAEEIE.

Bauer, J. M., & van Eeten, M. J. (2009). Cybersecurity: Stakeholder incentives, externalities, and policy options. *Telecommunications Policy*, 33(10), 706–719. doi:10.1016/j.telpol.2009.09.001

Bayraktar, F. (2015). *Cross-national and cross-cultural variances in cyberbullying. In The Wiley Handbook of Psychology, Technology and Society* (pp. 158–175). New York: Wiley.

BBC. (2011). *Fake Apple store found in China.* Retrieved July 11, 2016, from http://www.bbc.co.uk/news/technology-14258135

Beldona, S., & Tsatsoulis, C. (2010). Identifying buyers with similar seller rating models and using their opinions to choose sellers in electronic markets. *International Journal of Information and Decision Sciences, 2*(1), 1–16. doi:10.1504/IJIDS.2010.029901

Bellare, M., & Rogaway, P. (1993). Random Oracles are practical: a paradigm for designing efficient protocols. *ACM Conference on Computer Communications Security,* 62-73. 10.1145/168588.168596

Bergström, A. (2015). Online privacy concerns: A broad approach to understanding the concerns of different groups for different uses. *Computers in Human Behavior, 53,* 419–426. doi:10.1016/j.chb.2015.07.025

Berman, S. J., Kesterson-Townes, L., Marshall, A., & Srivathsa, R. (2012). How cloud computing enables process and business model innovation. *Strategy and Leadership, 40*(4), 27–35. doi:10.1108/10878571211242920

Bernama. (2012). *Early intervention on cyber security to safeguard young.* Cyber Security Malaysia. Retrieved on August 7, 2014 from http://www.cybersecurity.my/bahasa/knowledge_bank/news/2012/main/detail/2225/index.html

Berners-Lee, T. (2000). *Weaving the Web: The past, present and future of the World Wide Web by its inventor.* London: Texere.

Berne, S., Frisén, A., Schultze-krumbholz, A., Scheithauer, H., Naruskov, K., Luik, P., ... Zukauskiene, R. (2013). Aggression and violent behavior cyberbullying assessment instruments: A systematic review. *Aggression and Violent Behavior, 18*(2), 320–334. doi:10.1016/j.avb.2012.11.022

Berson, I. R., Berson, M. J., & Ferron, J. M. (2002). Emerging risks of violence in the digital age: Lessons for educators from an online study of adolescent girls in the United States. *Journal of School Violence, 1*(2), 51–72. doi:10.1300/J202v01n02_04

Bertolucci, J. (2016). Cybercrime is rampant around the world, says study. *PCWorld.* Retrieved March 7, 2016 from http://www.pcworld.com/article/205051/Norton_Study_Says_Cybercrime_is_Rampant.html

Bertot, J. C., Jaeger, P. T., & Grimes, J. M. (2010). Using ICTs to create a culture of transparency: E-government and social media as openness and anti-corruption tools for societies. *Government Information Quarterly, 27*(3), 264–271. doi:10.1016/j.giq.2010.03.001

Bhattacharyya, S., Banerjee, I., Chakraborty, A., & Sanyal, G. (2014). Biometric Steganography Using Variable Length Embedding. *International Journal of Computer, Electrical, Automation, Control and Information Engineering, 8*(4).

Bhattacharyya, S., Jha, S., Tharakunnel, K., & Westland, J. C. (2011). Data mining for credit card fraud: A comparative study. *Decision Support Systems, 50*(3), 602–613. doi:10.1016/j.dss.2010.08.008

Bishop, M. (2005). Psychological Acceptability Revisited. Security and Usability: Designing Secure Systems that People Can Use, 1(12).

Boehm, B., Abts, C., & Chulani, S. (2000, November). Software development cost estimation approaches - a survey. *Annals of Software Engineering, 10*(1), 177–205. doi:10.1023/A:1018991717352

Boehm, B., & Turner, R. (2005). Management challenges to implementing agile processes in traditional development organizations. *Software, IEEE, 22*(5), 30–39. doi:10.1109/MS.2005.129

Böhme, R., & Schwartz, S. (2010, June 7-8). Modeling Cyber-Insurance: Towards a Unifying Framework. *9th Annual Workshop on the Economics of Information Security (WEIS 2010)*. Harvard University.

Bolot, J. C., & Lelarge, M. (2008, April 13-18). A New Perspective on Internet Security using Insurance. *Proceedings of the 27th Conference on Computer Communications (INFOCOM 2008)*. IEEE. 10.1109/INFOCOM.2008.259

Bonanno, R. A., & Hymel, S. (2013). Cyber bullying and internalizing difficulties: Above and beyond the impact of traditional forms of bullying. *Journal of Youth and Adolescence*, *42*(5), 685–697. doi:10.100710964-013-9937-1 PMID:23512485

Boneh, D., Craig, G., & Michael, H. (2007). *Space-Efficient Identity based Cryptosystem without pairings*. IEEE Computer Society.

Boneh, D., & Franklin, M. K. (2001). Lecture Notes in Computer Science: Vol. 2139. *Identity-Based Encryption from the Weil Pairing*. Springer.

Borgnat, P., Abry, P., & Flandrin, P. (2012). Using surrogates and optimal transport for synthesis of stationary multivariate series with prescribed covariance function and non-Gaussian joint distribution. *Proceedings of ICASSP* (págs. 3729-3732). Kyoto, Japan: IEEE. 10.1109/ICASSP.2012.6288727

Bourke, M. L., & Hernandez, A. E. (2009). The Butner Study redux: A report of the incidence of hands-on child victimization by child pornography offenders. *Journal of Family Violence*, *24*(3), 183–191. doi:10.100710896-008-9219-y

boyd, d., Levy, K., & Marwick, A. (2014). The networked nature of algorithmic discrimination. In S. Gangadharan (Ed.), *Data and discrimination: Collected essays* (pp. 53-57). Washington, DC: Open Technology Institute – New America Foundation.

Braz, C., & Robert, J. M. (2006). Security and usability: the case of the user authentication methods. *18th Conference on l'Interaction Homme-Machine*, 199-203. 10.1145/1132736.1132768

Brewer, G., & Kerslake, J. (2015). Cyberbullying, self-esteem, empathy and loneliness. *Computers in Human Behavior*, *48*, 255–260. doi:10.1016/j.chb.2015.01.073

Brighi, A., Guarini, A., Melotti, G., Galli, S., & Genta, M. L. (2012). Predictors of victimisation across direct bullying, indirect bullying and cyberbullying. *Emotional & Behavioural Difficulties*, *17*(3-4), 375–388. doi:10.1080/13632752.2012.704684

Britz, M. (2013). *Computer Forensics and Cyber Crimes: An Introduction* (3rd ed.). Upper Saddle River, NJ: Pearson Education Inc.

Broadhurst, R., Bouhours, B., & Bouhours, T. (2013). Business and the risk of crime in China. *The British Journal of Criminology*, *53*(2), 276–296. doi:10.1093/bjc/azs059

Brochado, S., Soares, S., & Fraga, S. (2016). A scoping review on studies of cyberbullying prevalence among adolescents. *Trauma, Violence & Abuse*. doi:10.1177/1524838016641668 PMID:27053102

Brooke, J. (1996). SUS-A quick and dirty usability scale. *Usability Evaluation in Industry*, *189*(194), 4-7.

Brotherton, R. (2015). *Suspicious minds: Why we believe conspiracy*. Bloomsbury.

Brunstein-Klomek, A., Sourander, A., & Gould, M. (2010). The association of suicide and bullying in childhood to young adulthood: A review of cross-sectional and longitudinal research findings. *Canadian Journal of Psychiatry*, *55*(5), 282–288. PMID:20482954

Budriene, D., & Zalieckaite, L. (2012). Cloud computing application in small and medium-sized enterprises. *Issues Of Business & Law*, *4*(1), 99–130. doi:10.520/ibl.2012.11

Bunting, S. (2012). *EnCase Computer Forensics -- The Official EnCE: EnCase Certified Examiner Study Guide*. Indianapolis, IN: John Wiley.

Burmester, M., & Desmedt, Y. (1994, May). A secure and efficient conference key distribution system. In *Workshop on the Theory and Application of of Cryptographic Techniques* (pp. 275-286). Springer Berlin Heidelberg.

Burton, K. A., Florell, D., & Wygant, D. B. (2013). The role of peer attachment and normative beliefs about aggression on traditional bullying and cyberbullying. *Psychology in the Schools*, *50*(2), 103–114. doi:10.1002/pits.21663

Busch, T. (2011). Capabilities in, capabilities out: Overcoming digital divides by promoting corporate citizenship and fair ICT. *Ethics and Information Technology*, *13*(4), 339–353. doi:10.100710676-010-9261-3

Business Software Alliance. (n.d.). *What is software piracy*. Retrieved July 10, 2016, from http://www.bsa.org/country/Anti-Piracy/What-is-Software-Piracy.aspx

Bussey, K., Fitzpatrick, S., & Raman, A. (2015). The role of moral disengagement and self-efficacy in cyberbullying. *Journal of School Violence*, *14*(1), 30–46. doi:10.1080/15388220.2014.954045

Byers, D. (2013). Do they see nothing wrong with this?: Bullying, bystander complicity, and the role of homophobic bias in the Tyler Clementi case. *Families in Society*, *94*(4), 251–258. doi:10.1606/1044-3894.4325

Byron, T. (2008). *Safer children in a digital world: The report of the Byron Review*. DCSF Publications. Retrieved September 10, 2016, from http://webarchive.nationalarchives.gov.uk/20130401151715/http://www.education.gov.uk/publications/eOrderingDownload/DCSF-00334-2008.pdf

Cabinet Office. (2014). *Survey report on youth Internet environment*. Retrieved September 10, 2016, from the Cabinet Office homepage: http://www8.cao.go.jp/youth/youth-harm/chousa/h24/net-rating/pdf-index.html

Camacho, S., Hassanein, K., & Head, M. (2014). *Understanding the factors that influence the perceived severity of cyber-bullying*. Paper presented at Human-Computer Interaction (HCI) International, Crete, Greece. 10.1007/978-3-319-07293-7_13

Camenisch, J., & Stadler, M. (1997). Efficient group signatures schemes for large groups. In *Advances in Cryptology-CRYPTO 1997*. Springer.

Campbell, M., Spears, B., Slee, P. H., Butler, D., & Kift, S. (2012). Victims perceptions of traditional and cyberbullying, and the psychosocial correlates of their victimisation. *Emotional & Behavioural Difficulties*, *17*(3-4), 389–401. doi:10.1080/13632752.2012.704316

Cappadocia, M. C., Craig, W. M., & Pepler, D. (2013). Cyberbullying prevalence, stability, and risk factors during adolescence. *Canadian Journal of School Psychology*, *28*(2), 171–192.

Cappadocia, M. C., Craig, W. M., & Pepler, D. (2013). Cyberbullying: Prevalence, stability and risk factors during adolescence. *Canadian Journal of School Psychology*, *28*, 171–192.

Carlton, G. H. (2007). A grounded theory approach to identifying and measuring forensic data acquisition tasks. *Journal of Digital Forensics, Security and Law, 2*(1), 35-56. Retrieved from http://www.jdfsl.org/

Carter, J. M. (2011). *Examining the relationship among physical and psychological health, parent and peer attachment and cyberbullying in adolescents in urban and suburban environments* (PhD Thesis). Wayne State University.

Carter, S. (2015). *The hostile environment: Students who bully in school*. New York: Lexington Books.

CASAGRAS. (2009). *RFID and the inclusive model for the Internet of Things: Final report.* EU Framework 7. Retrieved from http://www.grifs-project.eu/data/File/CASAGRAS%20FinalReport%20(2).pdf

Casey, E. (2010). Handbook of Digital Forensics and Investigation. Burlington, MA: Elsevier Academic Press.

Casey, E. (2007). What does forensically sound really mean? *Digital Investigation, 4*(2), 49–50. doi:10.1016/j.diin.2007.05.001

Cassidy, W., Brown, K., & Jackson, M. (2012a). Making kind cool: Parents suggestions for preventing cyber bullying and fostering cyber kindness. *Journal of Educational Computing Research, 46*(4), 415–436. doi:10.2190/EC.46.4.f

Castaneda, J. A., Montoso, F. J., & Luque, T. (2007). The dimensionality of customer privacy concern on the Internet. *Online Information Review, 31*(4), 420–439. doi:10.1108/14684520710780395

Castella-Roca, J., & Herrera-Joancomarti, J., & CDorca-Josa, A. (2006). *A secure E-exam management system.* Paper presented at the Proceedings of the 1st International Conference on Availability, Reliability and Security (ARES'06). 10.1109/ARES.2006.14

Castillo-Ramoran, V. (2008). *Web tool for teachers: Information systems on categorized teacher materials and online examination. In Innovative Techniques in Instruction Technology, E-learning, E-assessment, and Education* (pp. 570–575). Springer Science-Business Media.

Castro, M., & Liskov, B. (2002). Practical Byzantine fault tolerance and proactive recovery. *ACM Transactions on Computer Systems, 20*(4), 398–461. doi:10.1145/571637.571640

Catherine, C., Aaron, K., & Robert, C. (2016). Development of a normalized extraction to further aid in fast, high-throughput processing of forensic DNA reference samples. Forensic Science International: Genetics, 25, 112-124.

Cavoukian, A., & Kursawe, K. (2012). Implementing privacy by design: The smart meter case. *Proceedings of the 2012 IEEE International Conference on Smart Grid Engineering* (pp. 1-8). Piscataway, NJ: IEEE. 10.1109/SGE.2012.6463977

Cavusoglu, H., & Zhang, J. (2006). Economics of security patch management. *The fifth Workshop on the Economics of Information Security (WEIS 2006).*

Cavusoglu, H., Raghunathan, S., & Yue, W. (2008). Decision-theoretical and game-theoretical approaches to it security investment. *Journal of Management Information Systems, 25*(2), 281–304. doi:10.2753/MIS0742-1222250211

CDC&P. (2010). *Suicide: Risk and protective factors.* Retrieved on March 17, 2014 from http://ViolencePrevention/youthvlolence/risk-protectivefactors.html

Cebula, J. J., & Young, L. R. (2010). *A taxonomy of operational cyber security risks.* Technical Note CMU/SEI-2010-TN-028. Retrieved from Carnegie Mellon University website: http://www.sei.cmu.edu/reports/10tn028.pdf

Celen, F. K., & Seferoglu, S. S. (2013). Investigation of Elementary School Students' Opinions Related to Unethical Behavior in the use of Information and Communication Technologies. *2nd World Conference on Educational Technology Research, 83*, 417-421. doi:10.1016/j.sbspro.2013.06.082

CERP-IoT. European Union, Cluster of European Research Projects on the Internet of Things. (2010). *Vision and challenges for realising the Internet of Things.* Brussels: European Commission – Information Society and Media.

Chai, H., & Zhao, W. (2014, August). Byzantine Fault Tolerant Event Stream Processing for Autonomic Computing. In *Proceedings of the 12th IEEE International Conference on Dependable, Autonomic and Secure Computing* (pp. 109-114). IEEE. 10.1109/DASC.2014.28

Chai, H., & Zhao, W. (2014, June). Towards trustworthy complex event processing. In *Proceedings of the 5th IEEE International Conference on Software Engineering and Service Science* (pp. 758-761). IEEE.

Chakrabarty, K. C. (2012). Indian Banking Sector: Towards the next orbit. In Academic Foundation (Ed.), Economic developments in India: Analysis, reports, policy documents. New Delhi: AF.

Chand, M., Raj, T., & Shankar, R. (2015). A comparative study of multi criteria decision making approaches for risks assessment in supply chain. *International Journal of Business Information Systems, 18*(1), 67–84. doi:10.1504/IJBIS.2015.066128

Chang, C. (2015). *The Most Phenomenal Fake Apple Store in China.* Retrieved July 20, 2016, from http://micgadget.com/14648/the-most-phenomenal-fake-apple-store-in-china/

Chatterjee, S., & Sarkar, P. (2011). *Identity Based Encryption.* Springer. doi:10.1007/978-1-4419-9383-0

Chaturvedi, N., & Basha, D. S. (2012). Comparison of Digital Image watermarking Methods DWT & DWT-DCT on the Basis of PSNR. *International Journal of Innovative Research in Science, Engineering and Technology, 1*(2). Retrieved from ece.mits.ac.in

Chaum, D., & Heijst van. (1991). Group signatures. In *Advances in Cryptology-EUROCRYPT 1991.* Springer.

Cheddad, A., Condell, J., Curran, K., & Kevitt, P. M. (2008). Biometric Inspired Digital Image Steganography. Engineering of Computer Based Systems, 2008. ECBS 2008. *15th Annual IEEE International Conference and Workshop on the,* 159-168. doi: 10.1109/ECBS.2008.11

Cheddad, A., Condell, J., Curran, K., & Kevitt, P. (2010). Digital image steganography: Survey and analysis of current methods. *Signal Processing, 90*(3), 727–752. doi:10.1016/j.sigpro.2009.08.010

Chen, B., & Wornell, G.W. (2011). Quantization index modulation: A class of provably good methods for digital watermarking and information embedding. *IEEE Trans. Inform. Theory, 47,* 1423–1443.

Chen, L., & Pedersen, T. (1994). New group signature schemes. In *Advances in Cryptology-EUROCRYPT 1994.* Springer.

Chen, B., & Wornell, G. W. (2001). Quantization index modulation: A class of provably good methods for digital watermarking and information embedding. *IEEE Transactions on Information Theory, 47*(4), 1423–1443. doi:10.1109/18.923725

Cheng, P., Gu, Y., Lv, Z., Wang, J., Zhu, W., Chen, Z., & Huang, J. (2012). A Performance Analysis of Identity Based Encryption Schemes. *Lecture Notes in Computer Science, 7222,* 289–303. doi:10.1007/978-3-642-32298-3_19

Chen, L., & Avizienis, A. (1978). N-version programming: A fault-tolerance approach to reliability of software operation. *Proceedings of International Symposium on Fault Tolerant Computing.* Toulouse, France: IEEE Computer Society Press.

Chen, Y.-Z., Huang, Z.-G., Xu, S., & Lai, Y.-C. (2015). Spatiotemporal patterns and predictability of cyberattacks. *PLoS ONE, 10*(5), e0124472. doi:10.1371/journal.pone.0124472 PMID:25992837

Cho, C., Chin, S., & Chung, K. S. (2012, July). Cyber forensic for hadoop based cloud system. *International Journal of Security and Its Applications., 6*(3), 83–90. Retrieved from http://www.sersc.org/journals/IJSIA/

Chou, T. S. (2011). Cyber security threats detection using ensemble architecture. *International Journal of Security and Its Applications, 5*(2), 11–15. Retrieved from http://www.sersc.org/journals/IJSIA/

Cisco. (2014, June 10). *The Zettabyte era: Trends and analysis.* Cisco White Paper. San Jose, CA: Cisco Systems. Retrieved from http://www.cisco.com/c/en/us/ solutions/collateral/service-provider/visual-networking-index-vni/VNI_Hyperconnectivity_WP.pdf

Clarke, E. (2013). *The underground hacking economy is alive and well*. Dell SecureWorks™. Retrieved February 26, 2016 from https://www.secureworks.com/blog/the-underground-hacking-economy-is-alive-and-well

Clements, S., & Kirkham, H. (2010). Cyber-security considerations for the smart grid. In *Proceedings of the IEEE Power and Energy Society General Meeting*. Minneapolis, MN: PES. 10.1109/PES.2010.5589829

Cocks, C. (2001). Lecture Notes in Computer Science: Vol. 2260. *An Identity Based Cryptosystem based on Quadratic Residues*. Springer.

Codes of Ethics Collection. (n.d.). Retrieved September 30, 2015 from http://ethics.iit.edu/ecodes/introduction

Cohen, L. E., & Felson, M. (1979). Social change and crime rate trends: A routine activity approach. *American Sociological Review, 44*(4), 588–608. doi:10.2307/2094589

Combating cybercrime. (2016). *Cybersecurity*. Homeland Security. Retrieved March 7, 2016 from https://www.dhs.gov/topic/combating-cyber-crime

Common Digital Evidence Storage Format Working Group. (2006). *Survey of Disk Image Storage Formats* [PDF document]. Retrieved October 25, 2013 from http://www.dfrws.org/CDESF/survey-dfrws-cdesf-diskimg-01.pdf

Conn, K. (2015). From Student Armbands to Cyberbullying: The First Amendment in Public Schools. Legal Frontiers in Education: Complex Law Issues for Leaders, Policymakers and Policy Implementers (Advances in Educational Administration, Volume 24). New York: Emerald Group Publishing Limited, 35-58.

Cooper, A. (2004). *The Inmates Are Running the Asylum: Why High Tech Products Drive Us Crazy and How to Restore the Sanity* (2nd ed.). Sams Publishing.

Corcoran, L., Connolly, I., & OMoore, M. (2012). Cyberbullying in Irish schools: An investigation of personality and self-concept. *The Irish Journal of Psychology, 33*(4), 153–165. doi:10.1080/03033910.2012.677995

Cowen, D. (2013). *Computer Forensics InfoSec Pro Guide*. New York: McGraw Hill.

Coyne, I., Farley, S., Axtell, C., Sprigg, C., Best, L., & Kwok, O. (2016). Understanding the relationship between experiencing workplace cyberbullying, employee mental strain and job satisfaction: A dysempowerment approach. *International Journal of Human Resource Management*, 1–28. doi:10.1080/09585192.2015.1116454

Craigen, D., Diakun-Thibault, N., & Purse, R. (2014). Defining cybersecurity. *Technology Innovation Management Review, 4*(10), 13–21.

Cranor, L. F., & Garfinkel, S. (2005). Security and Usability: Designing Secure Systems that People Can Use. O'Reilly.

CSMR. (2011). Children and teenagers exposed to negative cyber culture. *Bernama News*. Retrieved on January 28, 2014 from http://www.cybersecurity.my/en/knowledge_bank/news/2011/main/detail/2087/index.html

CSMR. (2014, 2013). *A National Survey Report 2013. Safety net: Growing awareness among Malaysian schoolchildren on staying safe online*. Cyber Security of Malaysia. Retrieved on December 4, 2014 from https://digi.cybersafe.my/files/article/DiGi_Survey_Booklet_COMPLETE.pdf

Cui, Y., Peng, Z., Song, W., Li, X., Cheng, F., & Ding, L. (2014, September). A Time-Based Group Key Management Algorithm Based on Proxy Re-encryption for Cloud Storage. In *Asia-Pacific Web Conference* (pp. 117-128). Springer International Publishing. 10.1007/978-3-319-11116-2_11

Culnan, M. J. (1993). How did they get my name? An exploratory investigation of consumer attitudes toward secondary information use. *Management Information Systems Quarterly, 17*(3), 341–363. doi:10.2307/249775

Culnan, M. J., & Armstrong, P. K. (1999). Information privacy concerns, procedural fairness, and impersonal trust: An empirical investigation. *Organization Science, 10*(1), 104–115. doi:10.1287/orsc.10.1.104

Custers, B. (2013). Data dilemmas in the information society: Introduction and overview. In B. Custers, T. Calders, B. Schermer, & T. Zarsky (Eds.), *Discrimination and privacy in the information society: Data mining and profiling in large databases* (pp. 3–26). New York: Springer. doi:10.1007/978-3-642-30487-3_1

Cyberbullying Research Center. (2015). *Summary of Our Cyberbullying Research (2004-2015).* Retrieved September 10, 2016, from http://cyberbullying.org/summary-of-our-cyberbullying-research/

D'Ovidio, R., Mitnam, T., El-Burki, J., & Shumar, W. (2009). Adult-child sex advocacy websites as social learning environments. *International Journal of Cyber Criminology, 3,* 421–440.

Daim, T., Basoglu, N., & Tanoglu, I. (2010). A critical assessment of information technology adoption: Technical, organisational and personal perspectives. *International Journal of Business Information Systems, 6*(3), 315–335. doi:10.1504/IJBIS.2010.035048

Danaher, B., & Smith, M. (2013). *Gone in 60 Seconds: The Impact of the Megaupload Shutdown on Movie Sales.* Available at SSRN # 2229349.

Danenas, P. (2015). Intelligent financial fraud detection and analysis: A survey of recent patents. *Recent Patents on Computer Science, 8*(1), 13–23. doi:10.2174/2213275907666141101001436

Daramola, J. O., Oladipupo, O. O., & Musa, A. G. (2010). A fuzzy expert system (FES) tool for online personnel recruitments. *International Journal of Business Information Systems, 6*(4), 444–462. doi:10.1504/IJBIS.2010.035741

Darong, H., & Huimin, H. (2010). *Realiation and research of online exam system based on S2SH framework.* Paper presented at the International Conference on Web Information Systems and Mining.

Dash, E., & Zeller, T. (2005, June 18). MasterCard says 40 million files are put at risk. *New York Times.*

Davenport, T. H., Barth, P., & Bean, R. (2012). *How 'big data' is different.* Retrieved from http://sloanreview.mit.edu/article/how-big-data-is-different/

David, L. W., & Andrew, J. (2013). *Digital Forensics Processing and Procedures* (1st ed.). Elsevier.

Davidson, C. J., & Martellozzo, E. (2008). Protecting vulnerable young people in cyberspace from sexual abuse: Raising awareness and responding globally. *Police Practice and Research, 9*(41), 277–289. doi:10.1080/15614260802349965

De Witt, A. J., & Kuljis, J. (2006). Aligning Usability and Security-A Usability Study Of Polaris. *Proc. of the Symp. On Usable Privacy and Security.* 10.1145/1143120.1143122

Decker, M., Kruse, W., Long, B., & Kelley, G. (2011). *Dispelling common myths of "live digital forensics".* Retrieved from http://www.dfcb.org/docs/LiveDigitalForensics-MythVersusReality.pdf

Dehue, F., Bolman, C., Vollink, T., & Pouwelse, M. (2012). Cyberbullying and traditional bullying in relation to adolescents' perceptions of parenting. *Journal of Cyber Therapy and Rehabilitation, 5,* 25–34.

DeLong, R., Durkin, K. F., & Hundersmarck, S. (2010). An exploratory analysis of the cognitive distortions of a sample of men arrested in Internet sex stings. *Journal of Sexual Aggression, 16*(1), 59–70. doi:10.1080/13552600903428235

Den Boer, B. (1993, May). *A. Collisions for the compression function of MD5.* Paper presented at Advances in Cryptology — EUROCRYPT '93 Workshop on the Theory and Application of Cryptographic Techniques, Lofthus, Norway.

Dervin, D. (2011). 2010: The Year of the Bully. *The Journal of Psychohistory, 38*(4), 337–345.

Desmedt, Y., & Frankel, Y. (1990). Threshold cryptosystems. *Lecture Notes in Computer Science*, *435*, 307–315. doi:10.1007/0-387-34805-0_28

Deswarte, Y., Blain, L., & Fabre, J. (1991). Intrusion tolerance in distributed computing systems. *Proceedings of the IEEE Symposium on Research in Security and Privacy*, 110–121.

Dharni, K. (2014). Exploring information system evaluation in Indian manufacturing sector. *International Journal of Business Information Systems*, *17*(4), 453–468. doi:10.1504/IJBIS.2014.065564

Dholakia, N., Dholakia, R. R., & Kshetri, N. (2004). Global diffusion of the Internet. In H. Bidgoli (Ed.), The Internet Encyclopedia (2nd ed.; pp. 38-51). John Wiley & Sons. doi:10.1002/047148296X.tie072

Dinev, T., & Hart, P. (2004). Internet privacy concerns and their antecedents—Measurement validity and a regression model. *Behaviour & Information Technology*, *23*(6), 413–422. doi:10.1080/01449290410001715723

Ding, J. (2004). A new variant of the Matsumoto-Imai cryptosystem through perturbation. In *Public-key cryptography-PKC 2004*. Springer.

Ding, J. (2011). *Method to produce new multivariate public key cryptosystems*. Patents US 7961876 B2.

Doane, A. N., Kelley, M. L., & Pearson, M. R. (2016). Reducing cyberbullying: A theory of reasoned action-based video prevention program for college students. *Aggressive Behavior*, *42*(2), 136–146. doi:10.1002/ab.21610 PMID:26349445

Dodge, D. (2005). *Perspective: Napster's learning curve*. Retrieved February 17, 2014, from http://news.cnet.com/Napsters-learning-curve/2010-1027_3-5901873.html

Doerr, G., & Dugelay, J. L. (2003). A guide tour of video watermarking. *Signal Processing Image Communication*, *18*(4), 263–282. doi:10.1016/S0923-5965(02)00144-3

Doërr, G., & Dugelay, J. L. (2004). Security pitfalls of frame-by-frame approaches to video watermarking. *Signal Processing. IEEE Transactions on*, *52*(10), 2955–2964. doi:10.1109/TSP.2004.833867

Dolev, D., Dwork, C., & Naor, M. (1991). *Non-malleable Cryptography. STOC*, *91*, 542–552.

Dominic, P. D. D., Goh, K. N., Wong, D., & Chen, Y. Y. (2010). The importance of service quality for competitive advantage – with special reference to industrial product. *International Journal of Business Information Systems*, *6*(3), 378–397. doi:10.1504/IJBIS.2010.035051

Donaldson, J. (1992). The Ethics of Risk Management. In J. Ansell & F. Wharton (Eds.), *Risk Analysis, Assessment and Management*. Chichester, UK: John Wiley & Sons.

Dourish, P., & Bell, G. (2011). *Divining a digital future: Mess and mythology in ubiquitous computing*. Cambridge, MA: The MIT Press. doi:10.7551/mitpress/9780262015554.001.0001

Dunhm, W. (2006, May 22). Personal data on millions of U.S. veterans stolen. *Computerworld*.

Dunlap, W., King, S., Cinar, S., Barsai, M., & Chen, P. (2002). ReVirt: Enabling intrusion analysis through virtual-machine logging and replay. *Proceedings of the Symposium on Operating Systems Design and Implementation*, 211-224. 10.1145/1060289.1060309

Durham, M. G. (2016). *Technosex: Precarious corporealities, mediated sexualities, and the ethics of embodied technics*. New York: Springer. doi:10.1007/978-3-319-28142-1

Durkin, K. F., & Hundersmarck, S. F. (2008). Pedophiles and child molesters. In E. Goode & D. Angus Vail (Eds.), *Extreme Deviance* (pp. 144–150). Thousand Oaks, CA: Pine Forge Press.

Dykstra, J., & Sherman, A. T. (2012, August). Acquiring forensic evidence from infrastructure-as-a-service cloud computing: Exploring and evaluating tools, trust, and techniques [Supplement]. *Digital Investigation, 9*, S90–S98. doi:10.1016/j.diin.2012.05.001

Eastlake, D. (2001). *US Secure Hash Algorithm 1 (SHA1)*. Retrieved October 25, 2013 from https://www.ietf.org/rfc/rfc3174.txt

Eek, T. S. (2009). *A big sister helps students cope with bullying*. UNICEF. Retrieved October 4, 2009, from http://www.unicef.org/infobycountry/malaysia_51549.html

Elledge, L. C., Williford, A., Boulton, A. J., DePaolis, K. J., Little, T. D., & Salmivalli, C. (2013). Individual and contextual predictors of cyberbullying: The influence of childrens provictim attitudes and teachers ability to intervene. *Journal of Youth and Adolescence, 42*(5), 698–710. doi:10.100710964-013-9920-x PMID:23371005

Elliott, I. A., & Beech, R. (2009). Understanding online pornography use: Applying sexual offense theory to Internet offenders. *Aggression and Violent Behavior, 14*(3), 180–193. doi:10.1016/j.avb.2009.03.002

Elysee, G. (2015). An empirical examination of a mediated model of strategic information systems planning success. *International Journal of Business Information Systems, 18*(1), 44–66. doi:10.1504/IJBIS.2015.066126

Emami-Tabla, M., Amoui, M., & Tahvildari, L. (2013, August). On the road to holistic decision making in adaptive security. *Technology Innovation Management Review*, 59-64.

Encase Legal Journal. (2014). *Encase Legal Journal*. Retrieved September 22, 2016 from https://www.guidancesoftware.com/docs/default-source/document-library/publication/encase-legal-journal---5th-edition.pdf?sfvrsn=12

Eteokleous, N., & Pavlou, V. (2010). Digital natives and technology literate students: Do teachers follow? *Proceedings of the Cyprus Scientific Association of Information and Communication Technologies in Education*, 113-124.

European Commission, Information Society and Media. (2008). *Internet of Things in 2020: Roadmap for the future. European Technology Platform on Smart Systems Integration*. Version 1.1. Author.

European Commission. (2005). *Special Eurobarometer: Safer Internet*. Retrieved September 10, 2016 from http://polis.osce.org/library/f/3652/2821/EU-EU-RPT-3652-EN-2821

European Commission. (2007). *Qualitative Study: Safer Internet for Children*. Retrieved September 10, 2016, from http://ec.europa.eu/public_opinion/archives/quali/ql_safer_Internet_summary.pdf

European Commission. (2008). *Flash Eurobarometer: Towards a Safer Use of the Internet for Children in the EU—A Parents' Perspective Analytical Report*. Retrieved September 10, 2016 from http://ec.europa.eu/public_opinion/flash/fl_248_en.pdf

European Commission. (2009). *Safer Internet Programme 2005–2008. (Safer Internet Plus)*. Retrieved September 10, 2016, from http://europa.eu/legislation_summaries/information_society/Internet/l24190b_en.htm

European Commission. (2012). *Proposal for a regulation of the European Parliament and of the Council on the Protection of Individuals with regard to the processing of personal data and on the free movement of such data (General Data Protection Regulation), COM (2012) 11 final*. Brussels: European Commission.

European Technology Platform on Smart Systems Integration (EPoSS). (n.d.). *Objectives and mission*. Retrieved from http://www.smart-systems-integration.org/public/about/objectives-mission

Executive Office of the President of the United States. (2012, December 13). *Out-of-Cycle Review of Notorious Markets*. Author.

Fabre, J., & Randell, B. (1992). An object-oriented view of fragmented data processing for fault and intrusion tolerance in distributed systems. *Lecture Notes in Computer Science, 648,* 193–208. doi:10.1007/BFb0013899

Faily, S. (2015). Engaging Stakeholders during Late Stage Security Design with Assumption Personas. *Information and Computer Security, 435*(446).

Family Online Safety Institute. (2013). *Teen Identity Theft, Fraud, Security, and Steps Teens are Taking to Protect Themselves Online.* Retrieved September 10, 2016 from file:///C:/Users/na-saito/Downloads/Teen_Identity_Theft_Full_Report_Nov_13.pdf

Fangere, J., & Spaenlehaner, P. (2010). Algebraic Cryptanalysis of the PKC2010 Algebaic Surface Cryptosystem. Public-Key Cryptography PK- 2010. Springer.

Fanti, K. A., Demetriou, A. G., & Hawa, V. V. (2012). A longitudinal study of cyberbullying: Examining risk and protective factors. *European Journal of Developmental Psychology, 8*(2), 168–181. doi:10.1080/17405629.2011.643169

Favale, M., McDonald, N., Faily, S., & Gatzidis, C. (2016), Human Aspects in Digital Rights Management: The Perspective of Content Developers. *Fourth International Workshop on Artificial Intelligence and Law.*

Felson, M. (2001). Routine activity theory: The theorist's perspective. In C.D. Bryant (Ed.), Encyclopedia of Criminology and Deviant Behavior, Volume I: Historical, Conceptual, and Theoretical Issues (pp. 338-339). Philadelphia: Brunner-Routledge.

Felson, M., & Clarke, R. V. (1997). *Business and Crime Prevention.* Monsey, NY: Criminal Justice Press.

Fessi, B. A., Miaoui, Y., & Boudriga, N. (2013, June). A managerial issues-aware cost estimation of enterprise security projects. *Journal of Information Security Research, 4*(2), 81–89.

Festl, R., & Quandt, T. (2013). Social relations and cyberbullying: The influence of individual and structural attributes on victimization and perpetration via the Internet. *Human Communication Research, 39*(1), 101–106. doi:10.1111/j.1468-2958.2012.01442.x

Festl, R., Schwarkow, M., & Quandt, T. (2013). Peer influence, internet use and cyberbullying: A comparison of different context effects among German adolescents. *Journal of Children and Media, 7*(4), 446–462. doi:10.1080/17482798.2013.781514

Fielder, A., Panaousis, E., Malacaria, P., Hankin, C., & Smeraldi, F. (2014, June 2-4). Game Theory Meets Information Security Management. *Proceedings of the 29th IFIP TC 11 International Conference (SEC 2014),* 15-29.

Filby, M. (2007). Confusing the captain with the cabin boy: the dangers posed to reform of cyber piracy regulation by the misrepresented interface between society, policy makers and the entertainment industries. In *Proceedings of the British & Irish law, education and technology association conference* (pp. 1-47). Stanford, CA: Creative Commons.

Finkelhor, D., Mitchell, K., & Wolak, J. (2001). *Highlights of the youth Internet safety survey.* Juvenile Justice Fact Sheet-FS200104. Washington, DC: US Government Printing Office. Retrieved November 20, 2007 from http://www.unh.edu/ccrc/pdf/jvq/CV46.pdf

Finkelhor, D., Mitchell, K. J., & Wolak, J. (2000). *On-line victimization: A report on the nations' youth.* Alexandra, VA: National Centre for Missing and Exploited Children.

Fiterman, E. M., & Durick, J. D. (2010). Ghost in the machine: Forensic evidence collection in the virtual environment. *Digital Forensics Magazine, 2,* 73–77. Retrieved from http://www.digitalforensicsmagazine.com/

Fitz-Gerald, S. (2014). Everything that's happened in the Sony leak scandal. *Vulture*. Retrieved February 26, 2016 from http://www.vulture.com/2014/12/everything-sony-leaks-scandal.html

Flechais, I., & Sasse, M.A. (2005). Developing Secure and usable software. *OT2003*. DOI doi:10.1234/12345678

Flicker, S., Maley, O., Ridgley, A., Biscope, S., Lambardo, C., & Skinner, H. A. (2008). Using technology and participatory action research to engage youth in health promotion. *Action Research*, *6*(3), 285–303. doi:10.1177/1476750307083711

Flowers, A., Zeadally, S., & Murray, A. (2013). Cybersecurity and US legislative efforts to address cybercrime. *Journal of Homeland Security and Emergency Management*, *10*(1), 29–55. doi:10.1515/jhsem-2012-0007

Forrest, S., Somayaji, A., & Ackley, D. (1997). Building diverse computer systems. *Proceedings of the Workshop on Hot Topics in Operating Systems*. Cape Cod, MA: IEEE Computer Society Press.

Fraser, I., Bond-Fraser, L., Buyting, M., Korotkov, D., & Noonan, S. (2013). Cyber bullying and the law: Are we doing enough. *The American Association of Behavioral and Social Science Journal*, *17*(1), 26–39.

Freed, J. (2007). *Brainerd woman first to go to trial for music sharing: Jammie Thomas at risk for a judgment of millions of dollars*. Retrieved February 17, 2014, from http://brainerddispatch.com/stories/100207/new_20071002025.shtml

Friedman, J., & Hoffman, D. (2008). Protecting data on mobile devices: A taxonomy of security threats to mobile computing and review of applicable defenses. *Information, Knowledge, Systems Management*, *7*(1-2), 159–180.

Gandhi, N. (2014). Study on Security of Online Voting System Using Biometrics and Steganography. IJCSC, *5*(1), 29-32.

Gandhi, R., Sharma, A., Mahoney, W., Sousan, W., Zhu, Q., & Laplante, P. (2011). Dimensions of cyber-attacks: Cultural, social, economic, and political. *Technology and Society Magazine, IEEE*, *30*(1), 28–38. doi:10.1109/MTS.2011.940293

Gao, Q. (2012). Biometric Authentication to Prevent e-Cheating. *International Journal of Instructional Technology & Distance Learning*, *9*(2), 3–13.

Garfinkel, S. (2005). Sanitization and Usability. *Security and Usability: Designing Secure Systems that People Can Use, 293*(317).

Garfinkel, S. L. (2010). Digital forensics research: The next 10 years. *Digital Investigation*, *7*(Supplement), S64–S73. doi:10.1016/j.diin.2010.05.009

Garfinkel, S. L. (2012). The cybersecurity risk. *Communications of the ACM*, *55*(6), 29–32. doi:10.1145/2184319.2184330

Garinger, H. M. (2008). Cyber pox: A look at female adolescent cyber bullying. *Michigan Journal of Counseling*, *35*, 24–32.

Gartner. (2014, November 11). *Gartner says 4.9 billion collected 'Things' will be in use in 2015*. Retrieved from https://www.gartner.com/newsroom/id/2905717

Gavins, W., & Hemenway, J. (2010). Cybersecurity: A joint terminal engineering office perspective. In *Proceedings of the IEEE Military Communications Conference*. San Jose, CA: MILCOM. 10.1109/MILCOM.2010.5679588

Gentile, M., Collette, R., & CISOHandbook.com Team. (2015). Project Management As A Security Touch-Point. In *Project Management and Security*. CISOHandbook.com.

Geradts, Z., & Bijhold, J. (2001). New developments in forensic image processing and pattern recognition. *Science & Justice*, *41*(3), 159–166.

Geradts, Z., & Bijhold, J. (2002). Content Based Information Retrieval in Forensic Image Databases. *Journal of Forensic Sciences*, *47*(2), 40–47.

Gigerenzer, G. (2001). *Decision Making: Nonrational Theories. In International Encyclopedia of the Social and Behavioral Sciences* (Vol. 5, pp. 3304–3309). Oxford, UK: Elsevier. doi:10.1016/B0-08-043076-7/01612-0

Girgenti, R. H., & Hedley, T. P. (2011). *Managing the risk of fraud and misconduct: meeting the challenges of a global, regulated and digital environment.* McGraw-Hill.

Giustolisi, R., Lenzini, G., & Bella, G. (2013). *What security for electornic exams?* Paper presented at the International Conference on Risks and Security of Intrnet and Systems (CRiSIS'13).

Gluhak, A., Krco, S., Nati, M., Pfisterer, D., Mitton, N., & Razafindralambo, T. (2011). A survey of facilities for experimental Internet of Things research. *IEEE Communications Magazine, 49*(11), 58–67. doi:10.1109/MCOM.2011.6069710

Goldwasser, S., & Micali, S. (1984). Probabilistic Encryption. *Journal of Computer and System Sciences, 28*(2), 270–299. doi:10.1016/0022-0000(84)90070-9

Golfarelli, M., & Rizzi, S. (2009). *Data warehouse design: Modern principles and methodologies.* McGraw-Hill, Inc.

Gonzalez & Woods. (n.d.). *Digital Image Processing.* Pearson.

Gordon, L. A., Loeb, M. P., & Lucyshyn W. (2003, May 31). Information security expenditures and real options: A wait-and-see approach. *Computer Security Journal, 19*(2).

Gordon, L. A., & Loeb, M. P. (2002, November). The economics of information security investment. *ACM Transactions on Information and System Security, 5*(4), 438–457. doi:10.1145/581271.581274

Goulding, W. (1960). *Lord of the flies.* London: Faber & Faber.

Government accepts data ethics council proposal. (n.d.). Retrieved on 28 April 2016, from http://www.computerweekly.com/news/450294474/Government-accepts-data-ethics-council-proposal

Goyal, D., & Wang, S. (n.d.). *Steganographic Authentications in conjunction with Face and Voice Recognition for Mobile Systems.* Academic Press.

Gramoll, K. C. (2015). *Development and implementation of a tablet-based exam app for engineering course.* Paper presented at the 122nd ASEE Annual Conference & Exposition, Seattle, WA. 10.18260/p.23850

Greengard, S. (2012, November). On the digital trail. *Communications of the ACM, 55*(11), 19–21. doi:10.1145/2366316.2366323

Grossklags, J., Christin, N., & Chuang, J. (2008, April 21-25). Secure or Insure? A Game-Theoretic Analysis of Information Security Games. *Proceedings of the 17th International Conference on World Wide Web*, 209-218.

GSMA. (2015). *How China is scaling the Internet of Things.* Retrieved from http://www.gsma.com/newsroom/wp-content/uploads/16531-China-IoT-Report-LR.pdf

Guan, S. A., & Subrahmanyam, K. (2009). Youth Internet use: Risks and opportunities. *Current Opinion in Psychiatry, 22*(4), 351–356. doi:10.1097/YCO.0b013e32832bd7e0 PMID:19387347

Guidance Software. (2009). *EnCase Legal Journal.* Retrieved October 29, 2010 (Requires registration) from https://www.guidancesoftware.com/resources/Pages/doclib/Document-Library/EnCase-Legal-Journal.aspx

Gymrek, M., McGuire, A. L., Golan, D., Halperin, E., & Erlich, Y. (2013). Identifying personal genomes by surname inference. *Science, 339*(6117), 321–324. doi:10.1126cience.1229566 PMID:23329047

Haggerty, K. D., & Ericson, R. V. (2006). The new politics of surveillance and visibility. In K. D. Haggerty & R. V. Ericson (Eds.), *The new politics of surveillance and visibility* (pp. 3–25). Toronto: University of Toronto Press.

Hai-yan, L. V., GHong, L. V., Lijun, Z., & Jie, Z. (2014). *Research and design of the common curriculum online examination system that used in military academies*. Paper presented at the 2nd International Conference on Information Technology and Electronic Commerce (ICITEC 2014), Dalian, China. 10.1109/ICITEC.2014.7105585

Hale, J. S. (2013, October). Amazon cloud drive forensic analysis. *Digital Investigation, 10*(3), 259–265. doi:10.1016/j.diin.2013.04.006

Halevi, S., & Krawczyk, H. (1999). Public-key cryptography and password protocols. *ACM Transactions on Information and System Security, 2*(3), 230–268. doi:10.1145/322510.322514

Halsall, F. (1992). *Data Communications, Computer Networks and Open Systems* (3rd ed.). Wokingham, UK: Addison-Wesley.

Han, C., & Dongre, R. (2014). What motivates cyber-attackers? *Technology Innovation Management Review, 4*(10), 40–42.

Hanson, R. K., Bourgon, G., Helmus, L., & Hodgson, S. (2009). The principals of effective correctional treatment also apply to sexual offenders: A meta-analysis. *Criminal Justice and Behavior, 36*(9), 865–891. doi:10.1177/0093854809338545

Hartung, F., & Girod, B. (1998). Watermarking of uncompressed and compressed video. *Signal Processing, 66*(3), 283–301. doi:10.1016/S0165-1684(98)00011-5

Hausken, K. (2014, April). Returns to information security investment: Endogenizing the expected loss. *Information Systems Frontiers, 16*(2), 329–336. doi:10.100710796-012-9390-9

Hayman, S., & Coleman, J. (2016). *Parents and digital technology: How to raise the connected generation*. New York: Routledge.

Heath, T., & Bizer, C. (2011). Linked data: Evolving the Web into a global data space. *Synthesis Lectures on the Semantic Web: Theory and Technology, 1*(1), 1-136.

Heirman, W., & Walrave, M. (2012). Predicting adolescent perpetration in cyberbullying: An application of the theory of planned behavior. *Psicothema, 24*, 614–620. PMID:23079360

Herath, H., & Herath, T. (2011, February 27). Copula Based Actuarial Model for Pricing Cyber-Insurance Policies. *Insurance Markets and Companies: Analyses and Actuarial Computations, 2*(1), 7–20.

Hertzum, M. (2010). Images of Usability. *International Journal of Human-Computer Interaction, 567*(600).

Heuer, R. J. (1999). *Psychology of intelligence analysis*. Washington, DC: CIA.

Higgins, G. E. (2011). *Digital Piracy: An Integrated Theoretical Approach*. Durham, NC: Carolina Academic Press.

Hildner, L. (2006). Defusing the threat of RFID: Protecting consumer privacy through technology-specific legislation at the state level. *Harvard Civil Rights-Civil Liberties Law Review, 41*, 133–176.

Hinduja, S., & Patchin, J. W. (2007). Offline consequences of online victimization. *Journal of School Violence, 6*(3), 89–112. doi:10.1300/J202v06n03_06

Hinduja, S., & Patchin, J. W. (2009). *Bullying beyond the schoolyard: Preventing and responding to cyberbullying*. Thousand Oaks, CA: Corwin Press.

Hinduja, S., & Patchin, J. W. (2010). Bullying, cyberbullying and suicide. *Archives of Suicide Research, 14*(3), 206–221. doi:10.1080/13811118.2010.494133 PMID:20658375

Hinduja, S., & Patchin, J. W. (2013). Social influences on cyberbullying behaviors among middle and high school students. *Journal of Youth and Adolescence, 42*(5), 711–722. doi:10.100710964-012-9902-4 PMID:23296318

Hioki, H. (2010). *A data embedding method using BPCS principle with new complexity measures.* Proc. of Pacific Rim Workshop on Digital Steganography.

Hodge, V., & Austin, J. (2004). A survey of outlier detection methodologies. *J. of Art. Intell., 22*(2), 85–126.

Hoffnagle, G. F. (1999). Preface. *IBM Systems Journal, 38*(4), 502–503. doi:10.1147j.384.0502

Holt, T. J., Blevins, K. R., & Burkert, N. (2010). Considering the pedophile subculture online. *Sexual Abuse, 22*, 3–24. PMID:20133959

Hong Kong Government. (n.d.). *A guide to the EIA (Environmental Impact Assessment) Ordinance.* Retrieved on April 25, 2016, from http://www.epd.gov.hk/eia/english/guid/index1.html

Hong, S. (2009). Queue-based Group Key Agreement Protocol. *International Journal of Network Security, 9*(2), 135–142.

Hong, W., & Thong, J. Y. L. (2013). Internet privacy concerns: An integrated conceptualization and four empirical studies. *Management Information Systems Quarterly, 37*(1), 275–298.

Horwitz, J., & Lynn, B. (2002). Lecture Notes in Computer Science: Vol. 2332. *Toward hierarchical identity-based encryption.* Springer.

House of Commons Science and Technology Committee calls for Data Ethics Council. (n.d.). Retrieved February 13, 2016, from http://www.computerweekly.com/news/4500272963/House-of-Commons-Science-and-Technology-Committee-calls-for-Data-Ethics-Council

HP. (n.d.). *CeNSE.* Retrieved from http://www8.hp.com/us/en/hp-information/environment/cense.html#.Uo1MKMQQZhE

Hua, J., & Bapna, S. (2011). Optimal IS Security Investment: Cyber Terrorism vs. Common Hacking. In D. F. Galletta & T.-P. Liang (Eds.), *ICIS. Association for Information Systems.*

Hua, J., & Bapna, S. (2013). The economic impact of cyber terrorism. *The Journal of Strategic Information Systems, 22*(2), 175–186. doi:10.1016/j.jsis.2012.10.004

Huang, W., & Wang, S. K. (2009). Emerging Cybercrime Variants in the Socio Technical Space. In B. Whitworth, & A. de Moor (Eds.), Handbook of Research on Socio-Technical Design and Social Networking Systems. Hershey, PA: IGI.

Huang, C. D., & Behara, R. S. (2013, January). Economics of Information Security Investment in the Case of Concurrent Heterogeneous Attacks with Budget Constraints. *International Journal of Production Economics, 141*(1), 255–268. doi:10.1016/j.ijpe.2012.06.022

Huang, C. D., Hu, Q., & Behara, R. S. (2008, August). An economic analysis of the optimal information security investment in the case of a risk-averse firm. *International Journal of Production Economics, 114*(2), 793–804. doi:10.1016/j.ijpe.2008.04.002

Huang, N. (2014). Analysis of a multivariate public-key cryptosystem and Its application in software copy protection. *Journal of Software, 9*(8), 8. doi:10.4304/jsw.9.8.2010-2017

Huang, Y., & Chou, C. (2010). An analysis of multiple factors of cyberbullying among junior high school students in Taiwan. *Computers in Human Behavior, 26*(6), 1581–1590. doi:10.1016/j.chb.2010.06.005

Hughes, J., & Cybenko, G. (2013, August). Quantitative metrics and risk assessment: The three tenets model of cybersecurity. *Technology Innovation Management Review*, 15-24.

Hughes, D. (2000). Welcome to the rape camp: Sexual exploitation and the Internet in Cambodia. *Journal of Sexual Aggression, 6*(1-2), 1–23. doi:10.1080/13552600008413308

Husain, F. (2012). A survey of digital watermarking techniques for multimedia data. *Int'l Journal of Electronics and Communication Engineering*, *2*(1), 37–43.

Hussam, U.-D., Ihmaidi, A., Al-Jaber, A., & Hudaib, A. (2006). Securing Online Shopping Using BiometricPersonal Authentication and Steganography. *Proceedings of 2nd International Conference on Information & Communication Technologies*, 233-238. doi: 10.1109/ICTTA.2006.1684376

Huth, A., & Cebula, J. (2011). The basics of cloud computing. *United States Computer Emergency Readiness Team (US-CERT)*. Retrieved from http://www.us-cert.gov/reading_room/USCERT-CloudComputingHuthCebula.pdf

Hvistendahl, M. (2012). China pushes the Internet of Things. *Science*, *336*(6086), 1223–1223. doi:10.1126cience.336.6086.1223 PMID:22679075

IBM. (2008, November). *A mandate for change is a mandate for smart*. Conversations for a smarter planet series, 1. Retrieved from http://www.ibm.com/ smarterplanet/ global/files/us__en_us__general__smarterplanet_overview.pdf

IFPI. (2010, July). *IFPI Response to Commission Green Paper on Creative and Cultural Industries*. IFPI.

Inmon, W. H. (2005). *Building the data warehouse*. New York: John Wiley & Sons, Inc.

International Telecommunication Union. (2005a). *The Internet of Things*. Geneva: International Telecommunication Union.

International Telecommunication Union. (2005b). Privacy and Ubiquitous Network Societies: Background paper. *ITU Workshop on Ubiquitous Network Societies*. Geneva: International Telecommunication Union.

Internet of Things Conference Organizing Committee. (2010). *Internet of Things*. Retrieved from http://www.iot2010.org/outline/

Inthavisas, K., & Lopresti, D. (2012, March). Secure speech biometric templates for user authentication. *IET Biometrics*, *1*(1), 46–54. doi:10.1049/iet-bmt.2011.0008

Ishigaki, Y., Matsumoto, Y., Ichimiya, R., & Tanaka, K. (2013). Development of mobile radiation monitoring system utilizing smartphone and its field tests in Fukushima. *IEEE Sensors Journal*, *13*(10), 3520–3526. doi:10.1109/JSEN.2013.2272734

ISO/IEC. (1998). *ISO/IEC 9241-11 - Guidance on Usability management*. ISO.

ISO/IEC. (2012). *ISO/IEC 27002:2007 - Product quality*. ISO.

Itkis, G., Chandar, V., Fuller, B. W., Campbell, J. P., & Cunningham, R. K. (2015, September). Iris Biometric Security Challenges and Possible Solutions: For your eyes only?Using the iris as a key. *IEEE Signal Processing Magazine*, *32*(5), 42–53. doi:10.1109/MSP.2015.2439717

Iyengar, S. G., Varshney, P. K., & Damarla, T. (2011). A Parametric Copula-Based Framework for Hypothesis Testing Using Heterogeneous Data. *IEEE Transactions on Signal Processing*, *59*(5), 2308–2319. doi:10.1109/TSP.2011.2105483

Jain, A. K., & Uludag, U. (2003). Hiding Biometric Data. IEEE Transactions on Pattern Analysis and Machine Intelligence, 25(11).

Jain, A. K., Duin, P. W., & Jianchang Mao. (2000). Statistical pattern recognition: A review. *IEEE Transactions on Pattern Analysis and Machine Intelligence*, *22*(1), 4–37. doi:10.1109/34.824819

Jaiswal, P., Kumar, A., & Tripathi, S. (2015). Design of Queue-Based Group Key Agreement Protocol Using Elliptic Curve Cryptography. In *Information Systems Design and Intelligent Applications* (pp. 167–176). Springer India. doi:10.1007/978-81-322-2250-7_17

James, J. I., Shosha, A. F., & Gladyshev, P. (2013). Digital forensic investigation and cloud computing. In K. Ruan (Ed.), *Cybercrime and cloud forensics: Applications for investigation processes* (pp. 1–41)., doi:10.4018/978-1-4666-2662-1.ch001

Jang, H., Song, J., & Kim, R. (2014). Does the offline bully-victimization influence cyberbullying behavior among youths? Application of general strain theory. *Computers in Human Behavior, 31*, 85–93. doi:10.1016/j.chb.2013.10.007

Jarrett, M. H. (2016). *Prosecuting computer crimes*. Office of Legal Education Executive Office for United States Attorneys. Retrieved February 26, 2016 from http://www.justice.gov/criminal/cybercrime/docs/ccmanual.pdf

Jha, S., Katzenbeisser, S., Schallhart, C., Veith, H., & Chenney, S. (2007, May). Enforcing semantic integrity on untrusted clients in networked virtual environments. In *Proceedings of the IEEE Symposium on Security and Privacy*, (pp. 179-186). IEEE.

Jiansheng, M., Sukang, L., & Xiaomei, T. (2009, May). A digital watermarking algorithm based on DCT and DWT. In *International Symposium on Web Information Systems and Applications (WISA'09)* (pp. 104-107). Academic Press.

John, H., David, J., & Lamb, M. (2011). *A Framework for the Forensic Investigation of Unstructured Email Relationship data. International Journal of Digital Crime and Forensics, 3(3)*.

Johnson, J. (2007). *Common User Interface Design Don'ts and Dos*. Interactive Technologies.

Jones, L. M., Mitchell, K. J., & Finkelhor, D. (2012). Online harassment in context: Trends from three youth Internet safety surveys (2000, 2005, 2010). *Psychology of Violence, 3*(1), 53–69. doi:10.1037/a0030309

Joye, M., & Neven, G. (Eds.). (2009). *Identity-Based Cryptography*. IOS Press.

Jung, I. Y., & Yeom, H. Y. (2009). Enhanced security for online exams using group cryptography. *IEEE Transactions on Education, 52*(3), 340–349. doi:10.1109/TE.2008.928909

Kahn, D. (2005). The History of steganography. Chapter Information Hiding. *Lecture Notes in Computer Science, 1174*, 1–5.

Kainda, R., Flechais, I., & Roscoe, A. W. (2010). Security and Usability: Analysis and Evaluation. *ARES '10 International Conference on Availability, Reliability, and Security, 275*(282). DOI: 10.1109/ARES.2010.77

Kalita, M., & Tuithung, T. (2016). A comparative study of steganography algorithms of spatial and transform domain. In *National Conference on Recent Trends in Information Technology NCIT2015 (*pp. 9-14). IJCA Press.

Kamali, A. (2015). Assessing cyber-bullying in higher education. *Information Systems Education Journal, 13*(6), 43.

Kamau, G.M., Kimani, S., & Mwangi, W. (2013). A general Purpose Image-Based Electors Smart Card Using an Enhanced Least Significant Bit Steganographic Method for Information Hiding: A case study of the Kenyan Electoral Process. *International Journal of Computer Science Issues, 10*(2).

Kapezynski, A., & Banasik, A. (2011). Biometric Logical Access Control Enhanced by Use of Steganography Over Secured Transmission Channel. *The 6th IEEE International Conference on Intelligent Data Acquisition and Advanced Computing Systems: Technology and Applications*. 10.1109/IDAACS.2011.6072859

Kapur, P. K., Gupta, A., Jha, P. C., & Goyal, S. K. (2010). Software quality assurance using software reliability growth modelling: State of the art. *International Journal of Business Information Systems, 6*(4), 463–496. doi:10.1504/IJBIS.2010.035742

Karim, N. A., & Shukur, Z. (2015). Review of user authentication methods in online examination. *Asian Journal of Information Technology, 14*(5), 166–175.

Kasprzak, W., Stefańczyk, M., & Wilkowski, A. (2015). Printed steganography applied for the authentication of identity photos in face verification. *2nd International Conference on Cybernetics (CYBCONF)*, 512-517. 10.1109/CYB-Conf.2015.7175987

Kassner, M. (2014). The New Phenomenon report shows cybercrime is on the rise. *TechRepublic*. Retrieved March 7, 2016 from http://www.techrepublic.com/article/new-ponemon-report-shows-cybercrime-is-on-the-rise/

Katiyar, S., Meka, K. R., Barbhuiya, F. A., & Nandi, S. (2011) Online Voting System Powered By Biometric Security Using Steganography. *2011 Second International Conference on Emerging Applications of Information Technology*, 288-291. 10.1109/EAIT.2011.70

Kenda, M. (2014). *Internet Society Global Internet Report 2014: Open and sustainable access for all.* Global Internet Report. Retrieved July 2, 2014, from http://www.Internetsociety.org/map/global-Internet-report/

Keramati, A., & Behmanesh, I. (2010). Assessing the impact of information technology on firm performance using canonical correlation analysis. *International Journal of Business Information Systems*, 6(4), 497–513. doi:10.1504/IJBIS.2010.035743

Kerr, O. S. (2010). Vagueness challenges to the Computer Fraud and Abuse Act. *Minnesota Law Review, 1561*. Available at SSRN: http://ssrn.com/abstract=1527187

Khan, R., Khan, S. U., Zaheer, R., & Khan, S. (2010). Future Internet: The Internet of Things architecture, possible applications and key challenges. *10th International Conference on Frontiers of Information Technology*, 257-260. DOI: 10.1109/FIT.2012.53

Kimball, R., & Ross, M. (2011). *The data warehouse toolkit: the complete guide to dimensional modeling.* John Wiley & Sons.

Kim, E., & Tadisina, S. (2010). A model of customers initial trust in unknown online retailers: An empirical study. *International Journal of Business Information Systems*, 6(4), 419–443. doi:10.1504/IJBIS.2010.035740

Kim, Y., Perrig, A., & Tsudik, G. (2004). Tree-based group key agreement. *ACM Transactions on Information and System Security*, 7(1), 60–96. doi:10.1145/984334.984337

Kittler, J., Hatef, M., Duin, R. P., & Matas, J. (1998). On combining classifiers. *IEEE Transactions on Pattern Analysis and Machine Intelligence*, 20(3), 226–23. doi:10.1109/34.667881

Knuth, D. (1998). The Art of Computer Programming: Vol. 3. *Sorting and Searching* (2nd ed.). London: Addison-Wesley.

Kowalski, R. M., Giumetti, G. W., Schroeder, A. N., & Lattanner, M. R. (2014). Bullying in the digital age: A critical review and meta-analysis of cyberbullying research among youth. *Psychological Bulletin*, 140(4), 1073–1137. doi:10.1037/a0035618 PMID:24512111

Kowalski, R. M., & Limber, S. P. (2007). Electronic bullying among middle school students. *The Journal of Adolescent Health*, 41(6), 22–30. doi:10.1016/j.jadohealth.2007.08.017 PMID:18047942

Kowalski, R. M., Morgan, C. A., Drake-Lavelle, K., & Allison, B. (2016). Cyberbullying among college students with disabilities. *Computers in Human Behavior*, 57, 416–427. doi:10.1016/j.chb.2015.12.044

Kraft, E. (2006). *Cyberbullying: A worldwide trend of misusing technology to harass others.* WIT Transactions on Information and Communication Technologies. Retrieved on June 19, 2014 from http://www.witpress.com/elibrary/wit-transactions-on-information-and-communication-technologies/36/16302

Krichene, J., Boudriga, N., & Guemara, S. (2003). SECOMO: An estimation cost model for risk management. *Proceedings of international conference on Telecom (ConTel'03).* 10.1109/CONTEL.2003.176966

Kritzinger, E., & von Solms, S. H. (2010). Cyber security for home users: A new way of protection through awareness enforcement. *Computers & Security, 29*(8), 840–847. doi:10.1016/j.cose.2010.08.001

Krug, S. (2005). *Don't Make Me Think: A Common Sense Approach To The Web Usability.* New Riders Pub.

Ktoridou, D., Eteokleous, N., & Zachariadou, A. (2012). Internet uses and threats for students: Investigating parents' awareness. In T. Bastiaens & M. Ebner (Eds.), *Proceedings of World Conference on Educational Multimedia, Hypermedia and Telecommunications 2011* (pp. 179-188). Chesapeake, VA: Association for the Advancement of Computing in Education (AACE). Retrieved January 25, 2015 from http://www.editlib.org/p/37862/

Kumari, S., Khan, M. K., & Li, X. (2016). A more secure digital rights management authentication scheme based on smart card. *Multimedia Tools and Applications, 75*(2), 1135–1158. doi:10.100711042-014-2361-z

Kumar, K., Sofat, S., Jain, S. K., & Aggarwal, N. (2012). Significance of Hash Value Generation in Digital Forensic: A Case Study. *International Journal of Engineering Research and Development, 2*(5), 64–70.

Laftman, S. B., Modin, B., & Ostberg, V. (2013). Cyberbullying and subjective health: A large-scale study of students in Stockholm, Sweden. *Children and Youth Services Review, 35*(1), 112–119. doi:10.1016/j.childyouth.2012.10.020

Lai, C. C., & Tsai, C. C. (2010). Digital image watermarking using discrete wavelet transform and singular value decomposition. *Instrumentation and Measurement. IEEE Transactions on, 59*(11), 3060–3063.

Lakshmi, V. J., Vineka, P., & Anbarasu, V. (2014). Biometrics and Steganography based Secure Online Voting System. *International Journal of Research in Engineering & Advanced Technology, 2*(2).

Lallie, H., & Pimlott, L. (2012). Challenges in applying the ACPO principles to cloud forensic investigations. *Journal of Digital Forensics Security and Law, 7*(1), 71–86. Retrieved from http://www.jdfsl.org/

Lamport, L., Shostak, R., & Pease, M. (1982). The Byzantine generals problem. *ACM Transactions on Programming Languages and Systems, 4*(3), 382–401. doi:10.1145/357172.357176

Langelaar, G. C., Setyawan, I., & Lagendijk, R. L. (2000). Watermarking digital image and video data. A state-of-the-art overview. *IEEE Signal Processing Magazine, 17*(5), 20–46. doi:10.1109/79.879337

Langheinrich, M. (2001). Privacy by design: Principles of privacy-aware ubiquitous systems. In *Proceedings of the 3rd International Conference on Ubiquitous Computing* (pp. 273-291). London: Springer-Verlag. 10.1007/3-540-45427-6_23

Lanning, K. V. (2010). *Child molesters: A behavioral analysis.* Washington, DC: National Center for Missing & Exploited Children.

Latha, T. J., & Suganthi, L. (2015). An empirical study on creating software product value in India - an analytic hierarchy process approach. *International Journal of Business Information Systems, 18*(1), 26–43. doi:10.1504/IJBIS.2015.066125

Lavanya, N., Manjula, V., & Rao, N. V. K. (2012). Robust and Secure Data Hiding in Image Using Biometric Technique. *International Journal of Computer Science and Information Technologies, 3*(5), 5133–5136.

Lawrence, D. (2014). Christmas Shopping for Cybercriminals. *BloomsbergBusiness.* Retrieved March 7, 2016 from http://www.bloomberg.com/bw/articles/2014-12-15/current-hacker-underground-markets-are-booming

Lee, S., Kim, Y., Kim, K., & Ryu, D. H. (2003, October). An efficient tree-based group key agreement using bilinear map. In *International Conference on Applied Cryptography and Network Security* (pp. 357-371). Springer Berlin Heidelberg. 10.1007/978-3-540-45203-4_28

Lee, W. W. (2015a). Ignorant of ethical pitfalls can hurt information security: Implications for IT users & Information Security Professionals. Special Seminar on Information Security, the Hong Kong Jockey Club.

Lee, W. W., & Chan, K. C. C. (2008). Computer Ethics: A Potent Weapon for Information Security Management. *Information Systems Audit & Control Journal*. Retrieved from www.isaca.org/jonline

Lee, W.W. (2014-15). *Ethical, Legal & Social Issues*. Postgraduate Diploma in eHealth Informatics, The University of Hong Kong.

Lee, W.W. (2015c). *e-Crime & understanding Risk & Ethics in cyberspace*. Inaugural e-Crime Congress, Hong Kong.

Lee, W.W. (2015d, September 11). *Ignorant of ethical pitfalls can hurt information security – Implications for IT users & Information Security Professionals*. The Hong Kong Jockey Club.

Lee, W. W. (2014). Why Computer Ethics Matters to Computer Auditing. *ISACA Journal*, 2, 48–52.

Lee, W. W. (2015a). Ethical Computing. In M. Khosrow-Pour (Ed.), *Encyclopedia of Information Science and Technology* (3rd ed.; pp. 2991–2999). doi:10.4018/978-1-4666-5888-2.ch292

Lee, W. W. (2015b). Ethical Movement: An alternative anti-crime mechanism in cyberspace. *Trusted Computing – A Security Oxymoron or The Future? 16th Info-Security Conference.*

Lenhart, A., Madden, M., & Hitlin, P. (2005). *Teens and technology. Youth are leading the transition to a fully wired and mobile nation. 2005*. Pew Internet and American Life Project. Retrieved from: http://www.pewInternet.org/pdfs/PIP Teens_Tech_July2005web.pdf

Lenhart, A., Madden, M., Smith, A., Purcell, K., Zickhur, A., & Rainie, L. (2011). *Teens, kindness and the cruelty on social network sites*. Pew Internet and American Life Project.

Lew, P., Li, Z., & Olsina, L. (2010). Usability and user experience as key drivers for evaluating GIS application quality. *International Conference on Geoinformatics, 1*(6). 10.1109/GEOINFORMATICS.2010.5567803

Leymann, H. (1990). Mobbing and psychological terror at workplaces. *Violence and Victims, 5*, 119–126. PMID:2278952

Li. (2011). *Gröbner Bases in Ring Theory*. World Scientific Publishing.

Lianos, M. (2000). Dangerization and the end of deviance - The institutional environment. *The British Journal of Criminology, 40*(2), 261–278. doi:10.1093/bjc/40.2.261

Li, F., Wu, K., Lei, J., Wen, M., Bi, Z., & Gu, C. (2016, February). Steganalysis Over Large-Scale Social Networks With High-Order Joint Features and Clustering Ensembles. *IEEE Transactions on Information Forensics and Security, 11*(2), 344–357. doi:10.1109/TIFS.2015.2496910

Lifeng, L., Ho, S. W., & Poor, H. V. (2011). Privacy-Security Trade-Offs in Biometric Security Systems - Part I: Single Use Case. *IEEE Trans. Inf. Forensics Security, 6*(1), 122–139. doi:10.1109/TIFS.2010.2098872

Light, B., & McGrath, K. (2010). Ethics and social networking sites: A disclosive analysis of Facebook. *Information Technology & People, 23*(4), 290–311. doi:10.1108/09593841011087770

Li, J., & Su, X. (2007), Making Cost Effective Security Decision with Real Option Thinking. *International Conference on Software Engineering Advances (ICSEA)* (p. 14). IEEE Computer Society. 10.1109/ICSEA.2007.50

Lin, Y. R., Huang, H. Y., & Hsu, W. H. (2006, August). An embedded watermark technique in video for copyright protection. In *Pattern Recognition, 2006. ICPR 2006. 18th International Conference on* (Vol. 4, pp. 795-798). IEEE.

List of Virtues and List of Vices. (n.d.). Retrieved September 30, 2015 from http://www.virtuescience.com/vicelist.html

Liu, X., Zhang, Y., Wang, B., & Yan, J. (2013). Mona: Secure multi-owner data sharing for dynamic groups in the cloud. *IEEE Transactions on Parallel and Distributed Systems, 24*(6), 1182–1191. doi:10.1109/TPDS.2012.331

Livingstone, S., Haddon, L., Gorzig, A., & Olafsson, A. (2011). *Risks and safety on the Internet: The perspective of European children: Full findings.* London, UK: EU Kids Online.

Livingstone, S. (2012). Critical reflections on the benefits of ICT in education. *Oxford Review of Education, 38*(1), 9–24. doi:10.1080/03054985.2011.577938

Livingstone, S., Bober, M., & Helsper, E. (2005). *Inequalities and the digital divide in children and young people's Internet use: Findings from the UK Children Go Online project.* London, UK: The London School of Economics and Political Science.

Livingstone, S., & Gorzig, A. (2014). When adolescents receive sexual messages on the Internet: Explaining experiences of risk and harm. *Computers in Human Behavior, 33*, 8–15. doi:10.1016/j.chb.2013.12.021

Livingstone, S., & Haddon, L. (2009). Risky experiences for children online: Charting European research on children and the Internet. *Children & Society, 22*(4), 314–323. doi:10.1111/j.1099-0860.2008.00157.x

Livingstone, S., Haddon, L., & Görzig, A. (2012). *Children, risk and safety the Internet: Research and policy challenges in comparative perspective.* Bristol: Policy Press. doi:10.1332/policypress/9781847428837.001.0001

Lokhande, S., Sawant, D., Sayyad, N., &Yengul, M. (2012). YE-Voting through Biometrics and Cryptography- Steganography Technique with conjunction of GSM Modem. *International Journal of Computer Applications.*

Lu, Y., Li, X., Qi, M., Li, J., Fu, Y., & Kong, J. (2008). Lossless and Content-Based Hidden Transmission for Biometric Verificaion. *Intelligent Information Technology Application, 2008. IITA '08. Second International Symposium on,* 462-466. 10.1109/IITA.2008.351

Luby, M. (1996). *Pseudorandomness and Cryptographic Applications.* Princeton University Press.

Lu, R., Lin, X., Liang, X., & Shen, X. S. (2010, April). Secure provenance: the essential of bread and butter of data forensics in cloud computing. *Proceedings of the 5th ACM Symposium on Information, Computer and Communications Security,* 282-292. 10.1145/1755688.1755723

Lutgen-Sandvik, P., & Tracy, S. J. (2012). Answering five key questions about workplace bullying how communication scholarship provides thought leadership for transforming abuse at work. *Management Communication Quarterly, 26*(1), 3–47. doi:10.1177/0893318911414400

Maity, S. P., & Kundu, M. K. (2002, December). Robust and Blind Spatial Watermarking. In *Digital Image.* ICVGIP.

Maity, S. P., & Kundu, M. K. (2011). Performance improvement in spread spectrum image watermarking using wavelets. *International Journal of Wavelets, Multresolution, and Information Processing, 9*(01), 1–33. doi:10.1142/S0219691311003931

Majumder, S., & Das, T. S. (2013). *Watermarking of Data Using Biometrics, Handbook of Research on Computational Intelligence for Engineering, Science, and Business.* IGI Global.

Malhotra, N. K., Kim, S. S., & Agarwal, J. (2004). Internet users information privacy concerns (IUIPC): The construct, the scale, and a causal model. *Information Systems Research, 15*(4), 336–355. doi:10.1287/isre.1040.0032

Malkhi, D., & Reiter, M. (1997). Byzantine quorum systems. *Proceedings of the ACM Symposium on Theory of Computing.* El Paso, TX: ACM Press.

Malwade, N., Patil, C. Chavan, S., & Raut, S. Y. (2013). Secure Online Voting System Proposed By Biometrics And Steganography. *International Journal of Emerging Technology and Advanced Engineering, 3*(5).

Manolis, T., & Panos, V. (2003). *Architecture for Pattern Base Management Systems*. Department of Electrical and Computer Engineering. National Technical University of Athens.

Mao, E., & Zhang, J. (2013). The role of privacy in the adoption of location-based services. *Journal of Information Privacy and Security, 9*(2), 40–59. doi:10.1080/15536548.2013.10845678

Marcum, C. (2007). Interpreting the intentions of Internet predators: An examination of online predatory behavior. *Journal of Child Sexual Abuse, 16*(4), 99–114. doi:10.1300/J070v16n04_06 PMID:18032248

Marthandan, G., & Tang, C. M. (2010). Information systems evaluation: An ongoing measure. *International Journal of Business Information Systems, 6*(3), 336–353. doi:10.1504/IJBIS.2010.035049

Martin, L. (2008). *Introduction to Identity-Based Encryption*. Artech House.

Mason, K. (2008). Cyberbullying: A preliminary assessment for school personnel. *Psychology in the Schools, 45*(4), 323–348. doi:10.1002/pits.20301

Maughan, D. (2010). The need for a national cybersecurity research and development agenda. *Communications of the ACM, 53*(2), 29–31. doi:10.1145/1646353.1646365

McCabe, K. A. (2008). The role of Internet service providers in cases of child pornography and child prostitution. *Social Science Computer Review, 26*(2), 247–251. doi:10.1177/0894439307301438

McCarthy, A. M., Schoorman, F. D., & Cooper, A. C. (1993). Reinvestment decision by entrepreneurs: Rational Decision-making or escalation of commitment? *Journal of Business Venturing, 8*(1), 9–24. doi:10.1016/0883-9026(93)90008-S

McKenna, P. (2010). Rise of cyberbullying. *Reader's Digest Asia*. Retrieved on April 3, 2014 from: http://origin-www.rdasia.com/rise_of_cyber_bullying/

MCMC. (2014). *Internet users survey 2014*. Retrieved on November 13, 2014 from http://www.skmm.gov.my/Resources/Statistics/Internet-users-survey/Hand-Phone-Users-Survey-2014

Mendola, C. E. (2015). Big Brother as parent: Using surveillance to patrol students' Internet speech. *British Columbia Journal of Law & Social Justice, 35*, 153.

Meng, J., & Chang, S. F. (1998, October). Embedding visible video watermarks in the compressed domain. In *Image Processing, 1998. ICIP 98. Proceedings. 1998 International Conference on* (Vol. 1, pp. 474-477). IEEE.

Merton, R. K. (1968). *Social Theory and Social Structure*. Glencoe, IL: The Free Press.

Miaoui, Y., Boudriga, N., & Abaoub, E. (2015a). Insurance Versus Investigation Driven Approach for the Computation of Optimal Security Investment. *Proceedings of the 19th Pacific Asia Conference on Information Systems (PACIS 2015) on IT and Open Innovation*.

Miaoui, Y., Boudriga, N., & Abaoub, E. (2015b). Economics of Privacy: A Model for Protecting Against Cyber Data Disclosure Attacks. *Proceedings of the 3rd Information Systems International Conference (ISICO 2015)* (pp. 1-15). Surabaya, Indonesia: Procedia Computer Science, Elsevier (Scopus Indexed). 10.1016/j.procs.2015.12.165

Mikkonen, S., & Astikainen, T. (1994). Database classification system for shoe sole Patterns - identification of partial footwear impression found at a scene of crime. *Journal of Forensic Sciences, 39*(5), 1227–1236.

Milosevic, T. (2015). Cyberbullying in US mainstream media. *Journal of Children and Media, 9*(4), 492-509.

Ming-Ming, F., & Yan, M. (2013). The online examination system of distance education. *Applied Mechanics and Matrials, 411-414*, 2901–2905. doi:10.4028/www.scientific.net/AMM.411-414.2901

Mishna, F., Bogo, M., & Sawyer, J. L. (2015). Cyber counseling: Illuminating benefits and challenges. *Clinical Social Work Journal, 43*(2), 169–178. doi:10.100710615-013-0470-1

Mitchell, K. J., & Jones, L. M. (2011). *Youth Internet Safety Study (YISS): Methodology Repot*. Durham, NH: Crimes against Children Research Center University of New Hampshire. Retrieved on May 2, 2014 from: http://www.unh.edu/ccrc/pdf/YISS%20Methods%20Report%20formatted%20(final).pdf

Mitchell, M. S. (2011). *Cyberbullying and academic achievement: research into the rates of incidence, knowledge of consequences, and behavioral patterns of cyberbullying* (PhD Thesis). University of Connecticut.

Mitchell, K. J., Finkelhor, D., & Wolak, J. (2005). The Internet and family and acquaintance sexual abuse. *Child Maltreatment, 10*(1), 49–60. doi:10.1177/1077559504271917 PMID:15611326

Mitchell, K. J., Jones, L. M., Finkelhor, D., & Wolak, J. (2011). Internet-facilitated commercial sexual exploitation of children: Findings from a nationally representative sample of law enforcement agencies in the United States. *Sexual Abuse, 23*, 43–71. PMID:20852011

Mitchell, K. J., Ybarra, M., & Finkelhor, D. (2007). The relative importance of online victimization in understanding depression, delinquency, and substance abuse. *Child Maltreatment, 12*(4), 314–324. doi:10.1177/1077559507305996 PMID:17954938

Mohammad, R., Keivan, K., Reda, A., & Mick, J. (2009). *Data modeling for effective data warehouse architecture and design. International Journal of Information and Decision Sciences, 1(3)*, 282–300.

Mohanty, R., Ravi, V., & Patra, M. R. (2010). The application of intelligent and soft-computing techniques to software engineering problems: A review. *International Journal of Information and Decision Sciences, 2*(3), 233–272. doi:10.1504/IJIDS.2010.033450

Montague, D. A. (2010). *Essentials of online payment security and fraud prevention*. Wiley.

Moore, P. G., Thomas, H., Bunn, D. W., & Hampton, J. M. (1976). *Case Studies in Decision Analysis*. Penguin Books.

Murugesan, S. (2009). *Social issues and web 2.0: A closer look at culture in e-learning. Handbook of Research on Web 2.0, 3.0, and X.0: Technologies, Business, and Social Applications, Information Science*. New York, NY: Prentice Hall.

Mustaine, E. E., & Tewksbury, R. (2000). Comparing the lifestyles of victims, offenders, and victim-offenders: A routine activity theory assessment of similarities and differences for criminal incident participants. *Sociological Focus, 33*(3), 339–362. doi:10.1080/00380237.2000.10571174

Myers, J. J., McCaw, D. S., & Hemphill, L. S. (2011). *Responding to cyber bullying. An action tool for school leader*. Corwin Press, a Sage Company. doi:10.4135/9781483350516

Nagurney, A., & Nagurney, L. S. (2015, August). A game theory model of cybersecurity investments with information asymmetry. *NETNOMICS: Economic Research and Electronic Networking, 16*(1-2), 127–148. doi:10.100711066-015-9094-7

Nansel, T., Overpeck, M., Pilla, R., Simons-Morton, B., & Scheidt, P. (2001). Bullying behaviors among U.S. youth: Prevalence and association with psychosocial adjustment. *Journal of the American Medical Association, 285*(16), 2094–2100. doi:10.1001/jama.285.16.2094 PMID:11311098

Natale, S., & Balbi, G. (2014). Media and the imaginary in history. *Media History*, *20*(2), 203–218. doi:10.1080/1368 8804.2014.898904

Natarajan, M., & Makhdumi, G. (2009). Safeguarding the digital contents: Digital watermarking. *DESIDOC Journal of Library & Information Technology*, *29*(3), 29–35. doi:10.14429/djlit.29.249

Nathan, M. J., & Petrosino, A. (2003). Expert blind spot among preservice teachers. *American Educational Research Journal*, *40*(4), 905–928. doi:10.3102/00028312040004905

National Institute for Information and Communications Policy. (2012a). 「青少年のインターネット・リテラシー指標（指標開発編）」 [Internet Literacy Indicator for Youth—Development of Indicators]. NICT. Retrieved September 10, 2016 from www.soumu.go.jp/iicp/chousakenkyu/data/research/survey/telecom/2012/ilas2012-report-build.pdf

National Institute for Information and Communications Policy. (2012b). 「青少年のインターネット・リテラシー指標（実態調査編）[Internet Literacy Indicator for Youth—Investigation of actual conditions]. NICT. Retrieved September 10, 2016, from www.soumu.go.jp/iicp/chousakenkyu/data/research/survey/telecom/2012/ilas2012-report-survey.pdf

National Institute of Standards and Technology. (2010). *Introduction to NISTIR 7628: Guidelines for smart grid cyber security*. Gaithersburg, MD: NIST.

National Post. (1999, August 13). *Eight computer resellers face lawsuits after latest Microsoft anti-piracy sweep: Computers allegedly loaded with unlicensed software*. Retrieved from www.lexisnexis.com/hottopics/lnacademic

Neging, P., Musa, R., & Abdul Wahab, R. (2013). The determinants and outcomes of pathological Internet use (PIU) among urban millennial teens: A theoretical framework. World Academy of Science, Engineering and Technology, 74, 2-21.

Neumann, P. G. (1995). *Computer Related Risk*. New York, NY: ACM Press /Addison-Wesley.

Neumann, P. G., & Weinstein, L. (2006). Risks of RFID. *Communications of the ACM*, *49*(5), 136. doi:10.1145/1125944.1125971

Newswire, P. R. (2009, March 31). *BSA settles lawsuit against Nevada-based engineering company for $205,000*. Retrieved from www.lexisnexis.com/hottopics/lnacademic

Niemela, M., Ikonen, V., Leikas, J., Kantola, K., Kulju, M., Tammela, A., & Ylikauppila, M. (2014). Human-Driven Design: A Human-Driven Approach to the Design of Technology. *ICT and Society*, *431*, 78–91.

Nik Anis, N. M., Abdul Rahim, R., & Lim, Y. (2012). Najib: Cyberbullying a serious threat to kids. *The Star Online*. Retrieved on January 28, 2014 from http://www.thestar.com.my/News/Nation/2012/10/10/Najib-Cyber-bullying-a-serious-threat-to-kids/

Nishimura, K. (2005). The Need for Evidence-Based Policy . *Economic Review (Federal Reserve Bank of Atlanta)*, *1*, 4–7.

NOFR. (2010). *Global insights into family life online*. Retrieved from http://us.norton.com/content/en/us/home_homeoffice/media/pdf/nofr/Norton_Family-ReportUSA_June9.pdf

Nordahl, J. K., Poole, A., Stanton, L., Walden, L. M., & Beran, T. N. (2008). A review of school-based bullying interventions. *Democracy & Education*, *8*(1), 16–20.

Norman, D. A. (2002). *The Design of Everyday Things*. Basic Books.

Nosko, S., Wood, E., & Molema, S. (2010). All about me: Disclosure in online social networking profiles: The case of FACEBOOK. *Computers in Human Behavior*, *26*(3), 406–418. doi:10.1016/j.chb.2009.11.012

Odelu, V., Das, A. K., & Goswami, A. (2015, September). A Secure Biometrics-Based Multi-Server Authentication Protocol Using Smart Cards. *IEEE Transactions on Information Forensics and Security*, *10*(9), 1953–1966. doi:10.1109/TIFS.2015.2439964

OECD. (2004). *Statics, Knowledge and Policy: OECD World Forum on Key Indicators*. Retrieved September 10, 2016 from http://www.oecd.org/site/worldforum06/36422528.pdf

OECD. (2007). *Knowledge Management: Evidence in Education—Linking Research and Policy*. Paris: OECD Publishing.

OECD. (2012). *The Protection of Children Online: Risks Faced by Children Online and Policies to Protect Them*. Paris: OECD Publishing.

Ogura, N. (2012). *On multivariate public-key cryptosystem* (PhD Dissertation). Tokyo Metropolitan University.

Ogut, H., Menon, N., & Raghunathan, S. (2005). Cyber Insurance and IT Security Investment: Impact of Interdependence Risk. *Proceedings of Fourth Workshop on the Economics of Information Security (WEIS 2005)*.

OHalloran, E., & Quayle, E. (2010). A content analysis of a boy love support forum: Revisiting Durkin and Bryant. *Journal of Sexual Aggression*, *16*(1), 71–85. doi:10.1080/13552600903395319

Okamoto, T. (2006). On Pairing Based Cryptosystems. *Lecture Notes in Computer Science*, *4341*, 50–66. doi:10.1007/11958239_4

Olweus, D. (1999). Sweden. In K. Smith, Y. Morita, J. Junger-Tas, D. Olweus, R. Catalano, & P. Slee (Eds.), *The nature of school bullying: A cross-national perspective* (pp. 7–27). New York, NY: Routledge.

Olweus, D. (2002). A profile of bullying at school. *Educational Leadership*, *60*, 12–17.

Online Bullying Is a Top Concern Among Youth. (2012, June 25). *Microsoft global youth online behavior survey*. Microsoft News Center. Retrieved from http://www.microsoft.com/en-us/news/press/2012/jun12/06-25youthbehaviorpr.aspx

Oravec, J. A. (1996). *Virtual individuals, virtual groups*. New York: Cambridge University Press. doi:10.1017/CBO9780511574986

Oravec, J. A. (2000). Countering violent and hate-related materials on the Internet: Strategies for classrooms and communities. *Teacher Educator*, *35*(3), 34–45. doi:10.1080/08878730009555233

Oravec, J. A. (2012a). Bullying and mobbing in academe: Challenges for distance education and social media applications. *Journal of Academic Administration in Higher Education*, *49*, 46–58.

Oravec, J. A. (2012b). *The ethics of sexting: Issues involving consent and the production of intimate content. In Digital Ethics: Research and Practice* (pp. 129–145). New York: Peter Lang.

Oravec, J. A. (2013). Gaming Google: Some ethical issues involving online reputation management. *Journal of Business Ethics Education*, *10*, 61–81. doi:10.5840/jbee2013104

Panaousis, E. A., Fielder, A., Malacaria, P., Hankin, C., & Smeraldi, F. (2014, November 6-7). Cybersecurity Games and Investments: A Decision Support Approach. Lecture Notes in Computer Science: *Vol. 8840. Proceedings of the 5th International Conference (GameSec 2014)* (pp. 266-286). Springer. 10.1007/978-3-319-12601-2_15

Parker, D. B. (1986). Computer Crime. *Financial Executive*, *2*(12), 31–33.

Patarin, J. (1996). Hidden fields equations and isomorphism of polynomials: Two new families of asymmetric algorithms. In *Advances in Cryptology-EUROCRYPT 1996*. Springer.

Patchin, J. W., & Hinduja, S. (2006). Bullies move beyond the schoolyard: A preliminary look at cyberbullying. *Youth Violence and Juvenile Justice, 4*(2), 148–169. doi:10.1177/1541204006286288

Patrignani, N., & Whitehouse, D. (2014). Slow Tech: A quest for good, clean and fair ICT. *Journal of Information, Communication and Ethics in Society*, 78-9.

Patrignani, N., & Whitehouse, D. (2014). Slow Tech: The Bridge between Computer Ethics and Business Ethics. In K. Kimppa, D. Whitehouse, T. Kuusela, & J. Phahlamohlaka (Eds.), *ICT and Society* (Vol. 431, pp. 92–106). doi:10.1007/978-3-662-44208-1_9

Pawar, S., El Rouayheb, S., & Ramchandran, K. (2011). Securing Dynamic Distributed Storage Systems Against Eavesdropping and Adversarial Attacks. *IEEE Transactions on Information Theory, 57*(10), 6734–6753. doi:10.1109/TIT.2011.2162191

PDPO (1966). *The Personal Data (Privacy) Ordinance*, Chapter 486 (amended 2012 and 2013). Retrieved February 13, 2016, from https://www.pcpd.org.hk/english/files/pdpo.pdf

Petersen, H. (1998). How to convert any digital signature scheme into a group signature scheme. In Security Protocols. Springer.

Petzoldt, A., Bulygin, S., & Buchmann, J. (2010). A multivariate signature scheme with a partially cyclic public-key. *Proceedings of the 2nd international conference on symbolic computation and cryptography (SCC 2010)*, 229-235. 10.1007/978-3-642-17401-8_4

Pew Research Center for the People and the Press. (2013). *Few see adequate limits on NSA surveillance program*. Retrieved from http://www.people-press.org/ files/legacy-pdf/7-26-2013%20NSA%20release.pdf

Pew Research Center. (2012). Parents, Teens, and Online Privacy. The Berkman Center for Internet & Society at Harvard University.

Pfanner, E. (2009, April 18). Four convicted in Sweden in Internet piracy case. *The New York Times*, p. 2.

Pfleeger, C., & Pfleeger, S. (2002). *Security in Computing* (3rd ed.). Prentice Hall.

Phan, D. H., & Pointcheval, D. (2004). On the Security Notions of Public Key Encryption Schemes. *LNCS, 3352*, 33–47.

PI&ALP. (2013). *The Demographic of Media Social Users-2012*. Washington, DC: Pew Internet and American Life Project. Retrieved from http://pewInternet.org/Reports/2013/Social-media-users.aspx

Pieschl, S., Kuhlmann, C., & Porsch, T. (2015). Beware of publicity! Perceived distress of negative cyber incidents and implications for defining cyberbullying. *Journal of School Violence, 14*(1), 111–132. doi:10.1080/15388220.2014.971363

Podilchuk, C., & Delp, E. J. (2001). Digital watermarking: Algorithms and applications. *Signal Processing Magazine, IEEE, 18*(4), 33–46. doi:10.1109/79.939835

Poor, H. V. (2012). Information and inference in the wireless physical layer. *Wireless Communications, 19*(1), 40–47. doi:10.1109/MWC.2012.6155875

Portney, P. R. (2008). Benefit-Cost Analysis. In D. R. Henderson (Ed.), *Concise Encyclopedia of Economics* (2nd ed.). Indianapolis, IN: Library of Economics and Liberty.

Potdar, V. M., & Chang, E. (2004). Gray level modification steganography for secret communication. *Proc. of 2nd IEEE International Conference on Industrial Informatics*, 223–228.

Potkar, A. N., & Ansari, S. M. (2014). Review on Digital Video Watermarking Techniques. *International Journal of Computers and Applications, 106*(11).

Prabakaran, G., Bhavani, R., & Kanimozhi, K. (2013). Dual transform based steganography using wavelet families and statistical methods. *Proc. of the 2013 International Conference on Pattern Recognition, Informatics and Mobile Engineering,* 287–293. 10.1109/ICPRIME.2013.6496488

Pranjic, N., & Bajraktarevlc, A. (2010). Depression and suicide Ideation among secondary school adolescents involved m school bullying. *Primary Health Care Research and Development, 1*(l), 349–362. doi:10.1017/S1463423610000307

Prensky, M. (2001). Digital natives, digital immigrants part 1. *On the Horizon, 9*(5), 1–6. doi:10.1108/10748120110424816

Prichard, D., & Theiler, J. (1994). Generating surrogate data for time series with several simultaneously measured variables. *Physical Review Letters, 73*(7), 951–954. doi:10.1103/PhysRevLett.73.951 PMID:10057582

Project Management Institute. (2013). *A guide to the project management body of knowledge (PMBOK' Guide)* (5th ed.). Author.

Pronin, E., Lin, D. Y., & Ross, L. (2002). The bias blind spot: Perceptions of bias in self-versus others. *Personality and Social Psychology Bulletin, 28*(3), 369–381. doi:10.1177/0146167202286008

PwC. (2016). *The global state of information security survey 2016.* Industry Report. Retrieved from PricewaterhouseCoopers website: www.pwc.com/gsiss

Quayle, E., & Taylor, M. (2002). Pedophiles, pornography, and the Internet: Assessment issues. *British Journal of Social Work, 32*(7), 863–875. doi:10.1093/bjsw/32.7.863

Rackoff, C., & Simon, D. R. (1991). Non-interactive zero-knowedge proof of knowledge and chosen ciphertext attack. *LNCS, 576,* 433-444.

Rahman, M. (2013). *A dwt, dct and svd based watermarking technique to protect the image piracy.* arXiv preprint arXiv:1307.3294

Rane, S., Wang, Y., Draper, S. C., & Ishwar, P. (2013, September). Secure Biometrics: Concepts, Authentication Architectures, and Challenges. *IEEE Signal Processing Magazine, 30*(5), 51–64. doi:10.1109/MSP.2013.2261691

Raschke, R. L., Krishen, A. S., & Kachroo, P. (2014). Understanding the components of information privacy threats for location-based services. *Journal of Information Systems, 28*(1), 227–242. doi:10.2308/isys-50696

Rashid, R. D., Jassim, S. A., & Sellahewa, H. (2013). Covert exchange of face biometric data using steganography. *5th Computer Science and Electronic Engineering Conference (CEEC),* 134-139. 10.1109/CEEC.2013.6659460

Raskauskas, J., & Stoltz, A. D. (2007). Involvement in traditional and electronic bullying among adolescents. *Developmental Psychology, 43*(3), 564–575. doi:10.1037/0012-1649.43.3.564 PMID:17484571

Reid, B. (1987). Reflections on some recent widespread computer break-ins. *Communications of the ACM, 103*(105). doi:0.1145/12527.315716

Renugadevi, N., & Mala, C. (2014). Tree based group key agreement–a survey for cognitive radio mobile ad hoc networks. In Advanced Computing, Networking and Informatics (vol. 2, pp. 85-94). Springer International Publishing. doi:10.1007/978-3-319-07350-7_10

Report, C. (2011). *Norton.* Retrieved March 7, 2016 from http://www.symantec.com/content/en/us/home_homeoffice/html/cybercrimereport/

Rhea, S., Eaton, P., Geels, D., Weatherspoon, H., Zhao, B., & Kubiatowicz, J. (2003). Pond: the OceanStore Prototype. *Proceedings of the 2nd USENIX Conference on File and Storage Technology*, 1-14.

Richtel, M. (2001, February 13). The Napster decision: The overview; appellate judges back limitations on copying music. *The New York Times*, p. 1.

Riley, C., & Pagliery, J. (2015). Target will pay hack victims $10 million. *CNN Money*. Retrieved March 2, 2016 from http://money.cnn.com/2015/03/19/technology/security/target-data-hack-settlement/

Riley, M., Elgin, B., Lawrence, D., & Matlack, C. (2014). Missed alarms and 40 million stolen credit card numbers: How Target blew it. *Bloomberg Business*. Retrieved February 26, 2016 from http://www.bloomberg.com/bw/articles/2014-03-13/target-missed-alarms-in-epic-hack-of-credit-card-data

Rivest, R. (1992). *The MD5 Message-Digest Algorithm*. Retrieved October 25, 2013 from https://www.ietf.org/rfc/rfc1321.txt

Rivest, R., Shamir, A., & Adleman, M. (1978). A method for obtaining digital signatures and public key cryptosystems. *Communications of the ACM, 21*(2), 120–126. doi:10.1145/359340.359342

Rizk, N. J., & Choueiri, E. M., & Insticc. (2006). The concept of ethics in electronic qualitative research. *ICEIS 2006: Proceedings of the Eighth International Conference on Enterprise Information Systems: Information Systems Analysis and Specification*, 126-134.

Rizzi, S., Bertino, E., Catania, B., & Terrovitis, M. (2003). Towards a logical model for patterns. *Proceedings. ER Conference*.

Roberts, L., & Samani, R. (2013). *Digital deception: The online behavior of teens*. McAfee: An Intel Company. Retrieved on May 5, 2014 from http://oxfordhandbooks.com/view/10.1093/oxfordhb/9780199561803.001.0001/oxfordhb-9780199561803-e-019

Robson, C., & Witenberg, R. T. (2013). The influence of moral disengagement, morally based self-esteem, age, and gender on traditional bullying and cyberbullying. *Journal of School Violence, 12*(2), 211–231. doi:10.1080/15388220.2012.762921

Romero, Oscar, & Abelló. (2010). A framework for multidimensional design of data warehouses from ontologies. *Data & Knowledge Engineering*, 1138-1157.

Ruan, K., Carthy, J., & Kechadi, T. (2012, May). NIST cloud computing reference model and its forensic implications. *Journal of Digital Forensics, Security and Law, Conference Proceedings*. Retrieved from http://www.digitalforensics-conference.org/ subscriptions/proceedings_2012.htm

Sa'ari, J. R., Wong, S. I., & Roslan, S. (2005). Attitudes and perceived information technology competency among teachers. *Malaysian Online Journal of Educational Technology, 2*(3), 70–77.

Sabbah, Y., Saroit, I., & Kotb, A. (2011). *An interactive and secure e-examination unit (ISEEU)*. Paper presented at the 10th Roedunet International Conference (RoEduNet2011). 10.1109/RoEduNet.2011.5993713

Sahin, M. (2010). Teachers perceptions of bullying in high schools: A Turkish study. *Social Behavior and Personality, 38*(1), 127–142. doi:10.2224bp.2010.38.1.127

Saito, N. (2015). *Internet Literacy in Japan*. Paris: OECD Publishing. doi:10.1787/18151965

Saito, N., & Aragaki, M. (2012). *Analysis on political direction of non-formal parental education to develop a safer Internet environment for adolescents* (Vol. 23). Tokyo: Japan Society of Research and Information on Public and Co-operative Economy.

Sajedi, H., & Jamzad, M. (2009). Contsteg: Contourlet-based steganographymethod. *Wireless Sensor Network, 1*(03), 163–170. doi:10.4236/wsn.2009.13022

Salazar, A. (2013). *On Statistical Pattern Recognition in Independent Component Analysis Mixture Modelling.* Berlin, Germany: Springer. doi:10.1007/978-3-642-30752-2

Salazar, A., Safont, G., Soriano, A., & Vergara, L. (2012). Automatic credit card fraud detection based on non-linear signal processing. *46th Annual IEEE International Carnahan Conference (ICCST)* (pp. 207-212). Boston, MA: IEEE. 10.1109/CCST.2012.6393560

Salazar, A., Safont, G., & Vergara, L. (2014). Surrogate techniques for testing fraud detection algorithms in credit card operations. *48th International Carnahan Conference on Security Technology (ICCST2014)* (pp. 1-7). Rome, Italy: IEEE. 10.1109/CCST.2014.6986987

Salazar, A., Vergara, L., Serrano, A., & Igual, J. (2010). A General Procedure for Learning Mixtures of Independent Component Analyzers. *Pattern Recognition, 43*(1), 69–85. doi:10.1016/j.patcog.2009.05.013

Sallee, P. (2003). Model-based steganography. Proc. of the 2nd International Workshop on Digital Watermarking, 2939, 154–167.

Saltzer, J., & Schroeder, M. (1975). The protection of information in computer systems. *Proceedings of the IEEE, 63*(9), 1278–1308. doi:10.1109/PROC.1975.9939

Sankar, L., Rajagopalan, S. R., & Poor, H. V. (2013). Utility-Privacy Tradeoff in Databases: An Information-theoretic Approach. *IEEE Trans. Inf. Forens. Sec., 8*(6), 838–852. doi:10.1109/TIFS.2013.2253320

Santhi, K., & Kumar, A. M. N. (2013). Biometrics based Steganography using Circular Folding in DWT Domain. *International Journal of Computer Applications, 61*(10).

Sari, S. V. (2016). Was it just a joke? Cyberbullying perpetrations and their styles of humor. *Computers in Human Behavior, 54*, 555–559. doi:10.1016/j.chb.2015.08.053

Sasse, M. A., Brostoff, S., & Weirich, D. (2001). Transforming the 'Weakest Link' - a Human/Computer Interaction Approach to Usable and Effective Security. *BT Technology Journal, 122*(131). doi:10.1023/A:1011902718709

Satoh, N., & Kumamoto, H. (2009). Estimation model of labor time at the information security audit and standardization of audit work by probabilistic risk assessment. *International Journal of Computers, 3*(3), 311-320.

Savulescu, C., Polkowski, Z., & Alexandru, A. I. (2015). *The online and computer aided assessment.* Paper presented at the ECAI 2015-International Conference on Electronics, Computers, and Artificial Intelligence, Bucharest, Romania. 10.1109/ECAI.2015.7301226

Schneider, F. (1990). Implementing fault-tolerant services using the state machine approach: A tutorial. *ACM Computing Surveys, 22*(4), 299–319. doi:10.1145/98163.98167

Schneier, B. (1996). *Applied Cryptography: Protocols, Algorithms and Source Code in C* (2nd ed.). Chichester, UK: John Wiley.

Schneier, B. (2003). *Beyond fear: Thinking sensibly about security in an uncertain world.* Copernicus Books. doi:10.1057/palgrave.sj.8340200

Schreiber, T., & Schmitz, A. (2000). Surrogate time series. *Physica D. Nonlinear Phenomena, 142*(3-4), 346–382. doi:10.1016/S0167-2789(00)00043-9

Schulz, A., Bergen, E., Schuhmann, P., Hoyer, J., & Santtila, P. (2015). Online Sexual Solicitation of Minors How Often and between Whom Does It Occur? *Journal of Research in Crime and Delinquency, 53*(2), 165–188. doi:10.1177/0022427815599426

Schwartz, A. (2016). Critical blogging: Constructing Femmescapes online. *Ada: A Journal of Gender, New Media, and Technology*, (9).

Schwartz, P. M., & Solove, D. (2011). The PII problem: Privacy and a new concept of personally identifiable information. *New York University Law Review, 86*, 1814–1894.

SecureWorks competitors - CB insights. (2016). Retrieved February 23, 2016, from http://www.cbinsights.com/company/secureworks-competitors

Seema, S. S. (2012). DWT-SVD based efficient image watermarking Algorithm to achieve high robustness and perceptual quality. *International Journal of Advanced Research in Computer Science and Software Engineering, 2*(4), 75–78.

Seto, M. (2010). Child pornography use and Internet solicitation in the diagnosis of pedophilia. *Archives of Sexual Behavior, 39*(3), 591–593. doi:10.100710508-010-9603-6 PMID:20182786

Seto, M. (2013). *Internet sex offenders.* Washington, DC: American Psychological Association. doi:10.1037/14191-000

Seto, M., Hanson, K. R., & Babchishin, K. M. (2011). Contact sexual offending by men with online sexual offenses. *Sexual Abuse, 23*, 124–145. PMID:21173158

Shafer, G. (1976). *A Mathematical Theory of Evidence.* Princeton University Press.

Shaikh, H., Khan, M. I., & Kelkar, Y. (2012). A Robust DWT Digital Image Watermarking Technique Basis On Scaling Factor. *International Journal of Computer Science. Engineering and Applications, 2*(4), 63.

Shamir, A. (1979). How to share a secret. *Communications of the ACM, 22*(11), 612–613. doi:10.1145/359168.359176

Shamir, A. (1984). *Identity-Based Cryptosystems and Signature Schemes.* CRYPTO.

Shanthini, B., & Swamynathan, S. (2012). Multimodal Biometric-based Secured Authentication System using Steganography. *Journal of Computer Science, 8*(7), 1012–1021. doi:10.3844/jcssp.2012.1012.1021

Shapiro, J. N., & Cohen, D. K. (2007). Color bind: Lessons from the failed homeland security advisory system. *International Security, 32*(2), 121–154. doi:10.1162/isec.2007.32.2.121

Shariff, S. (2008). *Cyberbullying: Issues and solutions for the school, the classroom and the home.* New York: Routledge.

Shariff, S., & Hoff, D. (2007). Cyber bullying: Clarifying legal boundaries for school supervision in cyberspace. *International Journal of Cyber Criminology, 1*(1), 76–118.

Sharma, S., Mukherjee, S., Kumar, A., & Dillon, W. R. (2005). A simulation study to investigate the use of cut-off values for assessing model fit in covariance structure models. *Journal of Business Research, 58*(7), 935–943. doi:10.1016/j.jbusres.2003.10.007

Shejul, A. A., & Kulkarni, U. L. (2010). A DWT Based Approach for Steganography Using Biometrics, Data Storage and Data Engineering (DSDE). *2010 International Conference on*, 39-43. doi: 10.1109/DSDE.2010.10

Shejul, A. A., & Kulkarni, U. L. (2011). A Secure Skin Tone based Steganography Using Wavelet Transform. *International Journal of Computer Theory and Engineering, 3*(1).

Shende, J. (2010). Live forensics and the cloud. *DFI News*. Retrieved from http://www.dfinews.com/article/live-forensics-and-cloud-part-1

Shi, H., He, M., & Qin, Z. (2006, December). Authenticated and communication efficient group key agreement for clustered ad hoc networks. In *International Conference on Cryptology and Network Security* (pp. 73-89). Springer Berlin Heidelberg. 10.1007/11935070_5

Shin, D. H. (2013). User centric cloud service model in public sectors: Policy implications of cloud services. *Government Information Quarterly*, *30*(2), 194–203. doi:10.1016/j.giq.2012.06.012

Shinder, D. (2011). Cybercrime: Why it's the new growth industry. *IT Security*. Retrieved March 7, 2016 from http://www.techrepublic.com/blog/it-security/cybercrime-why-its-the-new-growth-industry/

Shor, P. (1994). Algorithms for quantum computation: Discrete logarithms and factoring. *Proceeding 35nd Annual Symposium on Foundations of Computer Science*, 124-134. 10.1109/SFCS.1994.365700

Shoup, V. (2000). Practical threshold signature. *Lecture Notes in Computer Science*, *1807*, 207–223. doi:10.1007/3-540-45539-6_15

Shukai, L., Chaudhari, N. S., & Dash, M. (2010). Selecting useful features for personal credit risk analysis. *International Journal of Business Information Systems*, *6*(4), 419–443. doi:10.1504/IJBIS.2010.035745

Sibert, R. W. (1994). DRUGFIRE revolutionizing forensic firearms identification and providing the foundation for a national firearms identification network. *USA Crime Lab Digest*, *21*(4), 63–68.

Simon, H. A. (1976a). From Substantive to Procedural Rationality. In S. J. Latsis (Ed.), *Method and Appraisal in Economics*. Cambridge, UK: Cambridge University Press. doi:10.1017/CBO9780511572203.006

Simon, H. A. (1976b). *Administrative Behaviour* (3rd ed.). New York: The Free Press.

Singer, P. W., & Friedman, A. (2014). *Cybersecurity and cyberwar: What everyone needs to know?* Oxford University Press.

Singh, A., Jain, S., & Jain, A. (2013). A Survey: Digital Video Watermarking. *International Journal of Scientific & Engineering Research*, *4*(7), 1261–1265.

Singh, P., & Chadha, R. S. (2013). A survey of digital watermarking techniques, applications and attacks. *International Journal of Engineering and Innovative Technology*, *2*(9), 165–175.

Singh, S. K., & Tiwari, A. K. (2016). Design and implementation of secure computer based examination system based on B/S structure. *International Journal of Applied Engineering Research*, *11*(1), 312–318.

Sinha, S., Bardhan, P., Pramanick, S., Jagatramka, A., Kole, D. K., & Chakraborty, A. (2011). Digital video watermarking using discrete wavelet transform and principal component analysis. *International Journal of Wisdom Based Computing*, *1*(2), 7–12.

Sipior, J. C., Ward, B. T., & Connolly, R. (2013). Empirically assessing the continued applicability of the IUIPC construct. *Journal of Enterprise Information Management*, *26*(6), 661–178. doi:10.1108/JEIM-07-2013-0043

sKyWIper Analysis Team. (2012). *sKyWIper (a.k.a. Flame a.k.a. Flamer): A complex malware for targeted attacks.* Retrieved September 22, 2016 from http://www.crysys.hu/skywiper/skywiper.pdf

Slonje, R., Smith, P. K., & Frisé, N. A. (2013). The nature of cyberbullying, and strategies for prevention. *Computers in Human Behavior*, *29*(1), 26–32. doi:10.1016/j.chb.2012.05.024

Smith, A. D. (2007). Identity theft and e-fraud driving CRM information exchanges. In A. Gunasekaran (Ed.), *Modeling and Analysis of Enterprise Information Systems* (pp. 110–133). Hershey, PA: IGI Publishing. doi:10.4018/978-1-59904-477-4.ch005

Smith, A. D., & Rupp, W. T. (2002). Issues in cybersecurity; understanding the potential risks associated with hackers/crackers. *Information Management & Computer Security*, *10*(4), 178–183. doi:10.1108/09685220210436976

Smith, H. J., Milberg, J. S., & Burke, J. S. (1996). Information privacy: Measuring individuals concerns about organizational practices. *Management Information Systems Quarterly*, *20*(2), 167–196. doi:10.2307/249477

Smith, P. K., Mahdavi, J., Carvalho, M., Fisher, S., Russell, S., & Tippett, N. (2008). Cyberbullying: Its nature and impact in secondary school students. *Journal of Child Psychology and Psychiatry, and Allied Disciplines*, *49*(4), 376–385. doi:10.1111/j.1469-7610.2007.01846.x PMID:18363945

Smokowski, P. R., & Kopasz, K. H. (2005). Bullying in school: An overview of types, effects, family characteristics and intervention strategies. *Children & Schools*, *27*(2), 101–110. doi:10.1093/cs/27.2.101

Sokouti, B., Rezvan, F., & Dastmalchi, S. (2017). GPCRTOP v.1.0: One-step web server for both predicting helical transmembrane segments and identifying G protein-coupled receptors. *Current Bioinformatics*, *12*(1), 80-84. doi:10.2174/1574893611666160901122236

Sokouti, B., Church, W. B., Morris, M. B., & Dastmalchi, S. (2015). Structural and Computational Approaches in Drug Design for G Protein-Coupled Receptors. In M. Khosrow-Pour (Ed.), *Encyclopedia of Information Science and Technology* (pp. 479–489). Hershey, PA: IGI Global. doi:10.4018/978-1-4666-5888-2.ch046

Sokouti, B., Rezvan, F., & Dastmalchi, S. (2015). Applying random forest and subtractive fuzzy c-means clustering techniques for the development of a novel G protein-coupled receptor discrimination method using pseudo amino acid compositions. *Molecular BioSystems*, *11*(8), 2364–2372. doi:10.1039/C5MB00192G PMID:26108102

Sokouti, B., Rezvan, F., Yachdav, G., & Dastmalchi, S. (2014). GPCRTOP: A novel G protein-coupled receptor topology prediction method based on hidden Markov model approach using Viterbi algorithm. *Current Bioinformatics*, *9*(4), 442–451. doi:10.2174/1574893609666140516010018

Sokouti, M., Sokouti, B., & Pashazadeh, S. (2009). An Approach in Improving Transposition Cipher System. *Indian Journal of Science and Technology*, *2*(8), 9–15.

Sokouti, M., Sokouti, B., Pashazadeh, S., Feizi-Derakhshi, M.-R., & Haghipour, S. (2013). Genetic-based random key generator (GRKG): A new method for generating more-random keys for one-time pad cryptosystem. *Neural Computing & Applications*, *22*(7), 1667–1675. doi:10.100700521-011-0799-8

Sokouti, M., Sokouti, B., Pashazadeh, S., & Khanli, L. M. (2010). FPGA Implementation of Improved Version of Vigenere Cipher. *Indian Journal of Science and Technology*, *3*(4), 459–462.

Sokouti, M., Zakerolhosseini, A., & Sokouti, B. (2014). Improvements over GGH Using Commutative and Non-Commutative Algebra. In M. Khosrow-Pour (Ed.), *Encyclopedia of Information Science and Technology* (3rd ed.; pp. 3404–3418). IGI-Global.

Som, C., Hilty, L. M., & Kohler, A. R. (2009). The Precautionary Principle as a Framework for a Sustainable Information Society. *Journal of Business Ethics*, *85*(S3), 493–505. doi:10.100710551-009-0214-x

Soon, J. N. P., Mahmood, A. K., Yin, C.-P., Wan, W.-S., Yuen, P.-K., & Heng, L.-E. (2015). Barebone cloud IaaS: Revitalisation disruptive technology. *International Journal of Business Information Systems*, *18*(1), 26–43. doi:10.1504/IJBIS.2015.066130

Soriano, A., Vergara, L., Ahmed, B., & Salazar, A. (2015). Fusion of Scores in a Detection Context Based on Alpha Integration. *Neural Computation, 27*(9), 1983–2010. doi:10.1162/NECO_a_00766 PMID:26161815

Sotirov, A., Stevens, M., Appelbaum, J., Lenstra, A., Molnar, D., Osvik, D. A., & de Weger, B. (2011). *MD5 considered harmful today*. Retrieved September 22, 2016 from http://www.win.tue.nl/hashclash/rogue-ca/

South China Morning Post. (2013). Retrieved April 17, 2016, from http://www.scmp.com/news/hong-kong/article/1259422/edward-snowden-let-hong-kong-people-decide-my-fate

Sowaki, H. (2010). The Development of an Evidence-Based Education Policy in England. *National Institute for Educational Policy Research, 139*, 153–168.

Srinivasan, S. (2010a). *New Security Notions for Identity Based Encryption* (Ph.D thesis). Royal Holloway, University of London.

Srinivasan, S. (2010). *Identity-Based Encryption: Progress and Challenges. Information Security Technical Report*. Elsevier.

Stahl, S., & Pease, K. A. (2008). *A Success Strategy for Information Security Planning and Implementation*. Los Angeles, CA: Citadel Information Group, Inc.

Stallings. (n.d.). *Cryptography and network security*. Pearson.

Stanbrook, M. B. (2014). Stopping cyberbullying requires a combined societal effort. *Canadian Medical Association Journal, 186*(7), 483–483. doi:10.1503/cmaj.140299 PMID:24664656

Steiner, M., Tsudik, G., & Waidner, M. (2000). Key agreement in dynamic peer groups. *IEEE Transactions on Parallel and Distributed Systems, 11*(8), 769–780. doi:10.1109/71.877936

Stepien, T. (2010). Transcultural and transdisciplinar competences. Technological transformations of society and education. *3rd International Conference of Education, Research and Innovation (Iceri2010)*, 4815-4824.

Stewart, K. A., & Segars, A. H. (2002). An empirical examination of the concern for information privacy instrument. *Information Systems Research, 13*(1), 36–49. doi:10.1287/isre.13.1.36.97

Stocco, J. A., Otsuka, J. L., & Beder, D. M. (2012). *Logical and physical sensor-based online assessment security support*. Paper presented at the 12th IEEE International Conference on Advanced Learning Technologies.

Subhedara & Mankarb. (2014). Current status and key issues in image steganography: A survey. *Computer Science Review, 13–14*, 95–113.

Subrahmanyam, K. & Greenfield, P. (2008). Online communication and adolescent relationships. *The Future of Children, 8*(1), 119-146.

Sukamol, S., & Markus, J. (2008). Using cartoons to teach internet security. *Cryptologia, 32*(2), 137–154. doi:10.1080/01611190701743724

Sundarambal, M., Dhivya, M., & Anbalagan, P. (2010). Performance evaluation of bandwidth allocation in ATM networks. *International Journal of Business Information Systems, 6*(3), 398-417.

Svetcov, E. (2011). *An introduction to cloud forensics*. Retrieved from http://blog.datacraft-asia.com/2011/01/an-introduction-to-cloud-forensics/

Taleb, N. N. (2012). *Antifragile: Things that gain from disorder*. Random House.

Tambe, S.A., Joshi, N.P., & Topannavar, P.S. (2014). Steganography & Biometric Security Based Online Voting System. *International Journal of Engineering Research and General Science, 2*(3).

Tassabehji, R. (2005). Principles for managing information security. Encyclopedia of Multimedia Technology and Networking, (pp. 842-848). doi:10.4018/978-1-59140-561-0.ch119

Tatsumi, K. I., & Goto, M. (2009). Optimal Timing of Information Security Investment: Real Options Approach. In *The 8th Annual Workshop on the Economics of Information Security (WEIS 2009)*. University College London.

Tax, D., & Duin, R. (2001). Uniform object generation for optimizing one-class classifiers. *Journal of Machine Learning Research, 2*, 155–173.

Taylor, M., & Quayle, E. (2006). The Internet and abuse images of children: Search, pre-criminal situations and opportunity. In R. Wortley & S. Smallbone (Eds.), *Situational Prevention of Child Sexual Abuse* (pp. 169–195). New York: Criminal Justice Press.

Thakur, M. K., Saxena, V., & Gupta, J. P. (2010, July). A Performance analysis of objective video quality metrics for digital video watermarking. In *Computer Science and Information Technology (ICCSIT), 2010 3rd IEEE International Conference on* (Vol. 4, pp. 12-17). IEEE. 10.1109/ICCSIT.2010.5564962

The Daily Record of Baltimore. (2008). *News Summary - 3/21*. Retrieved from www.lexisnexis.com/hottopics/lnacademic

Thurow, L. C. (2000). The product of a knowledge-based economy. *The Annals of the American Academy of Political and Social Science, 570*(1), 19–31. doi:10.1177/000271620057000I002

Tiwari, V., & Thakur, R. S. (2015b). Contextual snowflake modelling for pattern warehouse logical design. *Sadhana, 40*(1), 15-33.

Tiwari, V., & Thakur, R. S. (2015c). P²MS: a phase-wise pattern management system for pattern warehouse. *International Journal of Data Mining, Modelling and Management, 7*(4), 331-350.

Tiwari, V., & Thakur, R. S. (2015a). *Improving Knowledge Availability of Forensic Intelligence through Forensic Pattern Warehouse (FPW). In Encyclopedia of Information Science and Technology* (3rd ed., pp. 1326–1335). IGI-Global.

Tiwari, V., Tiwari, V., Gupta, S., & Tiwari, R. (2010). Association rule mining: A graph based approach for mining frequent itemsets. *2010 International Conference on Networking and Information Technology*, 309-313. 10.1109/ICNIT.2010.5508505

Tobias, K., Claus, V., & Marcus, L. (2011). *Automated Forensic Fingerprint Analysis: A Novel Generic Process Model and Container Format. In Biometrics and ID Management* (Vol. 6583, pp. 262–273). Springer.

Tokunaga, R. S. (2010). Following you home from school: A critical review and synthesis of research on cyberbullying victimization. *Computers in Human Behavior, 26*(3), 277–287. doi:10.1016/j.chb.2009.11.014

Tsai, H. Y., & Chen, W. C. (2013). Exploring Intelligent Information Communication Services: A Case of Corporate Social Responsibility. In X. H. Liu, K. F. Zhang, & M. Z. Li (Eds.), Manufacturing Process and Equipment, Pts 1-4 (Vol. 694-697, pp. 3636-3641). doi:10.4028/www.scientific.net/AMR.694-697.3636

Tsutani, K. (2000). The Cochrane Collaboration and Systematic Review—Its Role in the EBM Movement. *Journal of the National Institute of Public Health, 49*(4), 313–319.

Turow, J. (2012). The daily you: How the new advertising industry is defining your identity and worth. New Haven, CT: Yale University Press.

Tzikas, D. G., Likas, A. C., & Galatsanos, N. (2008). The variational approximation for Bayesian inference. *IEEE Signal Processing Magazine, 25*(6), 131–146. doi:10.1109/MSP.2008.929620

Uckelmann, D., & Harrison, M. (2010). Integrated billing mechanisms in the Internet of Things to support information sharing and enable new business opportunities. *International Journal of RF Technologies: Research and Applications, 2*(2), 73–90.

Uckelmann, D., Harrison, M., & Michahelles, F. (2010). An architectural approach towards the future Internet of Things. In D. Uckelmann & ... (Eds.), *Architecting the Internet of Things*. Berlin: Springer-Verlag Berlin Heidelberg.

Ullah, A., Xiao, H., Barker, T., & Lilley, M. (2014). Evaluating security and usability of profile based challenge questions authentication in online examinations. *Journal of Internet Services and Applications, 5*(2), 1–16.

Ullrich, C. (2013). Valuation of IT Investments Using Real Options Theory. *Business & Information Systems Engineering, 5*(5), 331–341. doi:10.100712599-013-0286-0

Underground, H. M. R. (2014). *SecureWorks*. Retrieved February 27, 2016 from https://www.secureworks.com/assets/pdf-store/white-papers/wp-underground-hacking-report.pdf

United Nations News Centre. (2013). *General Assembly backs right to privacy in digital age*. Retrieved from http://www.un.org/apps/ news/story.asp? NewsID=46780&Cr=privacy&Cr1=#.UuW_5hB6dD8

Upturn. (2014). *Civil rights, big data, and our algorithmic future*. Retrieved from https://bigdata.fairness.io/

Urbas, G. (2010). Protecting children from online predators: The use of covert Investigation techniques by law enforcement. *Journal of Contemporary Criminal Justice, 26*(4), 410–425. doi:10.1177/1043986210377103

USC ASCDF. (2005). *The digital future report 2005: Surveying the digital future: Year five*. Los Angeles, CA: University of Southern California.

USC ASCDF. (2008). *2008 Digital future report*. Los Angeles, CA: University of Southern California.

Vaccaro, A., & Madsen, P. (2009). Corporate dynamic transparency: The new ICT-driven ethics? *Ethics and Information Technology, 11*(2), 113–122. doi:10.100710676-009-9190-1

Vaidhyanathan, S. (2011). *The Googlization of Everything: (And Why We Should Worry)*. Berkeley, CA: University of California Press.

Van den Eijnden, R., Spijkerman, R., Vermulst, A., Rooij, T., & Engels, R. (2010). Compulsive Internet use among adolescents: Bidirectional parent-child relationships. *Journal of Abnormal Child Psychology, 38*(1), 77–89. doi:10.100710802-009-9347-8 PMID:19728076

van Dijk, J., & Terlouw, G. (1996). An international perspective of the business community as victims of fraud and crime. *Security Journal, 7*, 157–167. doi:10.1016/0955-1662(96)00168-3

Van Royen, K., Poels, K., Daelemans, W., & Vandebosch, H. (2015). Automatic monitoring of cyberbullying on social networking sites: From technological feasibility to desirability. *Telematics and Informatics, 32*(1), 89–97. doi:10.1016/j.tele.2014.04.002

Vergara, L., Soriano, A., Safont, G., & Salazar, A. (2016). On the fusion of non-independent detectors. *Digital Signal Processing, 50*, 24–33. doi:10.1016/j.dsp.2015.11.009

Verissimo, P., Neves, N., & Correia, M. (2003). Intrusion-tolerant architectures: Concepts and design. *Lecture Notes in Computer Science, 2677*, 90–109. doi:10.1007/3-540-45177-3_1

Vermesan, O., Friess, P., Guillemin, P., Gusmeroli, S., Sundmaeker, H., Bassi, A., ... Doody, P. (2011). Internet of Things strategic research roadmap. In O. Vermesan & P. Freiss (Eds.), *Global technological and societal trends from smart environments and spaces to green ICT* (pp. 9–52). Aalborg: River Publishers.

Viega, J., & McGraw, G. (2002). *Building Secure Software: How to Avoid Security Problems the Right Way*. Addison-Wesley.

Vignoli, E., & Mallet, P. (2004). Validation of a brief measure of adolescents parent attachment based on Armsden and Greenbergs three-dimension model. *Revue Europeene de Psychologie Appliquee*, *54*(4), 251–260. doi:10.1016/j.erap.2004.04.003

Villani, M., Tappert, C., Ngo, G., Simone, J., Fort, H. S., & Cha, S.-H. (2006). *Keystroke bimetric recognistion studies on long-text input under ideal and application-oriented conditions*. Paper presented at the IEEE Proceedings of the 2006 Conference on Computer Vision and Pattern Recognistion Workshop (CVPRW'06). 10.1109/CVPRW.2006.115

Vivolo-Kantor, A. M., Martell, B. N., Holland, K. M., & Westby, R. (2014). A systematic review and content analysis of bullying and cyber-bullying measurement strategies. *Aggression and Violent Behavior*, *19*(4), 424–434. doi:10.1016/j.avb.2014.06.008 PMID:26752229

Voloshynovskiy, S., Pereira, S., & Pun, T. (1999). Watermark attacks. *Erlangen Watermarking Workshop 99*.

Wade, A., & Beran, T. (2011). Cyberbullying: The new era of bullying. *Canadian Journal of School Psychology*, *26*(1), 44–61. doi:10.1177/0829573510396318

Wang, X., Yin, Y. L., & Yu, H. (2005, August). *Finding Collisions in the Full SHA-1. In* Advances in Cryptology – CRYPTO 2005, Paper presented at the 25th Annual International Cryptology Conference, Santa Barbara, CA.

Ward, W. (2011). Technology correspondent. *BBC News*. Retrieved 24 January 2014 from http://www.how-the-web-went-worldwide

Warren, J. (2015). Why US small businesses should worry about cybersecurity and how to act. *IT Governance*. Retrieved March 2, 2016 from http://www.itgovernanceusa.com/blog/why-us-small-businesses-should-worry-about-cybersecurity-and-how-to-act/

Watson, L. (2015). Crime soars 107% as cyber offences included for the first time – as it happened. *Crime*. Retrieved March 7, 2016 from http://www.telegraph.co.uk/news/uknews/crime/11932670/Cyber-crime-fuels-70-jump-in-crime-levels.html

Watts, S., & Wyner, G. (2011). Designing and theorizing the adoption of mobile technology-mediated ethical consumption tools. *Information Technology & People*, *24*(3), 257–280. doi:10.1108/09593841111158374

Weber, R. H. (2010). Internet of Things: New security and privacy challenges. *Computer Law & Security Report*, *26*(1), 23–30. doi:10.1016/j.clsr.2009.11.008

Weber, R. H., & Weber, R. (2010). *Internet of Things: Legal perspectives*. Berlin: Springer-Verlag Berlin Heidelberg. doi:10.1007/978-3-642-11710-7

Weiser, M. (1991). The computer for the twenty-first century. *Scientific American*, *265*(3), 94–101. doi:10.1038cientificamerican0991-94

Wells, J. T. (2011). *Corporate fraud handbook: prevention and detection* (3rd ed.). Wiley.

Wells, M., Mitchell, K. J., & Ji, K. (2012). Exploring the role of the internet in juvenile prostitution cases coming to the attention of law enforcement. *Journal of Child Sexual Abuse*, *21*(3), 327–342. doi:10.1080/10538712.2012.669823 PMID:22574847

Werner, D. (2011). *Wake-up call*. Retrieved from: http://www.defensenews.com/section/C4ISR/C4ISR-Journal C4ISR

Werrett, D. J. (1997). The national DNA database. *Forensic Science International*, *88*(1), 33–42. doi:10.1016/S0379-0738(97)00081-9

Westin, A. F. (1967). *Privacy and freedom*. New York: Atheneum.

West, R. (2008). The psychology of security. *Communications of the ACM, 51*(4), 34–40. doi:10.1145/1330311.1330320

Wharton, F. (1992). Risk Management: Basic Concepts and General Principles. In J. Ansell & F. Wharton (Eds.), *Risk Analysis, Assessment and Management*. Chichester, UK: John Wiley.

Whitten, A., & Tygar, J. D. (1999). Why Johnny can't encrypt: a usability evaluation of PGP 5.0. *USENIX Security Symposium*. Retrieved from http://dl.acm.org/citation.cfm?id=1251421.1251435

Wiederhold, B. K. (2014). The role of psychology in enhancing cybersecurity. *Cyberpsychology, Behavior, and Social Networking, 17*(3), 131–132. doi:10.1089/cyber.2014.1502 PMID:24592869

Wierzbicki, A. (2006). Trust enforcement in peer-to-peer massive multi-player online games. Lecture Notes in Computer Science: vol. 1180. On the Move to Meaningful Internet Systems 2006: CoopIS, DOA, GADA, and ODBASE (pp. 1163-1180). Springer Berlin Heidelberg. doi:10.1007/11914952_7

Willard, N. (2007). *Cyberbullying and cyberthreats: Responding to the challenge of online social aggression, threats and distress*. Research Press.

Williams, K. (1997). Safeguarding Companies from Computer/Software Fraud. *Management Accounting, 78*(8), 18.

Wilson, S. (2016). The Panama Papers scandal. *MoneyWeek*. Retrieved April 17, 2016, from http://moneyweek.com/the-panama-papers-scandal

Winter, J. S. (2008). Emerging policy problems related to ubiquitous computing: Negotiating stakeholders visions of the future. *Knowledge, Technology & Policy, 21*(4), 191–203. doi:10.100712130-008-9058-4

Winter, J. S. (2013). Surveillance in ubiquitous network societies: Normative conflicts related to the consumer in-store supermarket experience in the context of the Internet of Things. *Ethics and Information Technology*. doi:10.100710676-013-9332-3

Winter, J. S. (2015). Algorithmic discrimination: Big data analytics and the future of the Internet. In J. S. Winter & R. Ono (Eds.), *The future Internet: Alternative visions*. New York: Springer. doi:10.1007/978-3-319-22994-2_8

WIP. (2013). International Report (5th ed.). Prentice Hall.

Wittek, P., & Darányi, S. (2012). Digital preservation in grids and clouds: A middleware approach. *Journal of Grid Computing, 10*(1), 133–149. doi:10.100710723-012-9206-7

Wolak, J., Finkelhor, D., & Mitchell, K. (2009). Trends in Arrests of "Online Predators". Durham, NC: Crimes Against Children Research Center.

Wolak, J., Finkelhor, D., & Mitchell, K. J. (2012a). Trends in Arrests for Child Pornography Possession: The Third National Juvenile Online Victimization Study (NJOV-3). Durham, NC: Crimes against Children Research Center.

Wolak, J., Finkelhor, D., & Mitchell, K. J. (2012b). Trends in Law Enforcement Responses to Technology- Facilitated Child Sexual Exploitation Crimes: The Third National Juvenile Online Victimization Study (NJOV-3). Durham, NC: Crimes against Children Research Center.

Wolak, J., Mitchell, K., & Finkelhor, D. (2006). Online victimization of youth: 5 years later. National Center for Missing and Exploited Children, 7, 6-25.

Wolak, J., Evans, L., Nguyen, S., & Hines, D. A. (2013). Online predators: Myth versus reality. *New England Journal of Public Policy, 25*, 1–6.

Wolak, J., Finkelhor, D., & Mitchell, K. (2011). Child pornography possessors: Trends in offender and case characteristics. *Sexual Abuse*, *23*, 22–42. PMID:21349830

Wolak, J., Finkelhor, D., Mitchell, K., & Ybarra, M. L. (2008). Online predators and their victims: Myths, realities, and implications for prevention and treatment. *The American Psychologist*, *63*(2), 111–128. doi:10.1037/0003-066X.63.2.111 PMID:18284279

Wolak, J., Liberatore, M., & Levine, B. N. (2014). Measuring a year of child pornography trafficking by US computers on a peer-to-peer network. *Child Abuse & Neglect*, *38*(2), 347–356. doi:10.1016/j.chiabu.2013.10.018 PMID:24252746

Wolak, J., Mitchell, K., & Finkelhor, D. (2007). Does online harassment constitute bullying? An exploration of online harassment by known peers and online-only contacts. *The Journal of Adolescent Health*, *41*(6), 51–58. doi:10.1016/j.jadohealth.2007.08.019 PMID:18047945

Wong, C. K., Gouda, M., & Lam, S. S. (2000). Secure group communications using key graphs. *IEEE/ACM Transactions on Networking*, *8*(1), 16–30. doi:10.1109/90.836475

Woodward, J. D. (1997, September). Biometrics: Privacys foe or privacys friend? *Proceedings of the IEEE*, *85*(9), 1480–1492. doi:10.1109/5.628723

Wright, M. F. (2013). The relationship between young adults beliefs about anonymity and subsequent cyber aggression. *Cyberpsychology, Behavior, and Social Networking*, *16*(12), 858–862. doi:10.1089/cyber.2013.0009 PMID:23849002

Wright, M. F. (2014a). Predictors of anonymous cyber aggression: The role of adolescents beliefs about anonymity, aggression, and the permanency of digital content. *Cyberpsychology, Behavior, and Social Networking*, *17*(7), 431–438. doi:10.1089/cyber.2013.0457 PMID:24724731

Wright, M. F. (2014b). Longitudinal investigation of the associations between adolescents popularity and cyber social behaviors. *Journal of School Violence*, *13*(3), 291–314. doi:10.1080/15388220.2013.849201

Wright, M. F. (2015). Adolescents cyber aggression perpetration and cyber victimization: The longitudinal associations with school functioning. *Social Psychology of Education*, *18*(4), 653–666. doi:10.100711218-015-9318-6

Wright, M. F. (in press). Cyber victimization and perceived stress: Linkages to late adolescents' cyber aggression and psychological functioning. *Youth & Society*.

Wright, M. F., & Li, Y. (2013). The association between cyber victimization and subsequent cyber aggression: The moderating effect of peer rejection. *Journal of Youth and Adolescence*, *42*(5), 662–674. doi:10.100710964-012-9903-3 PMID:23299177

Wu, D., & Tsai, W. H. (2003). A steganographic method for images by pixel value differencing. *Pattern Recognition Letters*, *24*(9-10), 1613–1626. doi:10.1016/S0167-8655(02)00402-6

Xue, K., & Hong, P. (2014). A dynamic secure group sharing framework in public cloud computing. *IEEE Transactions on Cloud Computing*, *2*(4), 459–470. doi:10.1109/TCC.2014.2366152

Yang, B., & Chen, J. (2003). A more secure and efficacious TTS signature scheme. In *Information Security and Cryptology-ICISC 2003*. Springer.

Ybarra, M. L., Diener-West, M., & Leaf, P. (2007). Examining the overlap in internet harassment and school bullying: Implications for school intervention. *The Journal of Adolescent Health*, *1*(6), 42–50. doi:10.1016/j.jadohealth.2007.09.004 PMID:18047944

Ybarra, M. L., & Mitchell, K. J. (2004). Online aggressor/targets, aggressors, and targets: A comparison of associated youth characteristics. *Journal of Child Psychology and Psychiatry, and Allied Disciplines*, *45*(7), 1308–1316. doi:10.1111/j.1469-7610.2004.00328.x PMID:15335350

Yeo, B. L., & Yeung, M. M. (1997, October). Analysis and synthesis for new digital video applications. In *Image Processing, 1997. Proceedings, International Conference on* (*Vol. 1*, pp. 1-4). IEEE.

Yin, J., Martin, J., Venkataramani, A., Alvisi, L., & Dahlin, M. (2003). Separating agreement from execution for Byzantine fault tolerant services. *Proceedings of the ACM Symposium on Operating Systems Principles*. Bolton Landing, NY: ACM Press. 10.1145/945445.945470

Young, A., & Yung, M. (2004). *Malicious Cryptography: Exposing Cryptovirology*. Indianapolis, IN: Wiley Publishing.

Young-Jones, A., Fursa, S. F., Byrket, J. B., & Sly, J. S. (2015). Bullying affects more than feelings: The long-term implications of victimization on academic motivation in higher education. *Social Psychology of Education*, *18*(1), 185–200. doi:10.100711218-014-9287-1

Yuksel, S. E., Wilson, J. N., & Gader, P. D. (2012). Twenty Years of Mixture of Experts. *IEEE Trans. On Neural Networks and Learning Systems*, *23*(4), 1177–1193. doi:10.1109/TNNLS.2012.2200299 PMID:24807516

Yusuf, S., Osman, M. N., Hassan, M. S. H., & Teimoury, M. (2014). Parents influence on childrens online usage. *Procedia: Social and Behavioral Sciences*, *155*, 81–86. doi:10.1016/j.sbspro.2014.10.260

Zamaria, C., & Fletcher, F. (2007). *Canada online: Year two highlights, 2007*. Canada Internet Project.

Zhang, H., Zhao, W., Moser, L. E., & Melliar-Smith, P. M. (2011). Design and implementation of a Byzantine fault tolerance framework for non-deterministic applications. *Software, IET*, *5*(3), 342–356. doi:10.1049/iet-sen.2010.0013

Zhang, X., & Wang, S. (2004). Vulnerability of pixel-value differencing steganography to histogram analysis and modification for enhanced security. *Pattern Recognition Letters*, *25*(3), 331–339. doi:10.1016/j.patrec.2003.10.014

Zhao, W. (2007). Byzantine Fault Tolerance for Nondeterministic Applications. *Proceedings of the 3rd IEEE International Symposium on Dependable, Autonomic and Secure Computing*, 108-115. 10.1109/DASC.2007.11

Zhao, W. (2008, December). Integrity-preserving replica coordination for byzantine fault tolerant systems. In *Proceedings of the 14th IEEE International Conference on Parallel and Distributed Systems* (pp. 447-454). IEEE. 10.1109/ICPADS.2008.45

Zhao, W. (2008, May). Towards practical intrusion tolerant systems: a blueprint. In *Proceedings of the 4th Annual Workshop on Cyber security and information intelligence research: developing strategies to meet the cyber security and information intelligence challenges ahead* (p. 19). ACM. 10.1145/1413140.1413162

Zhao, W. (2013, April). Towards practical intrusion tolerant systems. In *Proceedings of the IET International Conference on Information and Communications Technologies* (pp. 280-287). IET.

Zhao, W. (2014). *Building dependable distributed systems*. John Wiley & Sons. doi:10.1002/9781118912744

Zhao, W. (2014, August). Application-Aware Byzantine Fault Tolerance. In *Proceedings of the 12th IEEE International Conference on Dependable, Autonomic and Secure Computing* (pp. 45-50). IEEE. 10.1109/DASC.2014.17

Zhao, W., Moser, L., & Melliar-Smith, P. (2005). Deterministic scheduling for multithreaded replicas. *Proceedings of the IEEE International Workshop on Object-oriented Real-time Dependable Systems*. Sedona, AZ: IEEE Computer Society Press. 10.1109/WORDS.2005.26

Zhao, X., Xue, L., & Whinston, A. B. (2013, March 11). Managing Interdependent Information Security Risks: Cyber-insurance, Managed Security Services, and Risk Pooling Arrangements. *Journal of Management Information Systems*, *30*(1), 123–152. doi:10.2753/MIS0742-1222300104

Zheng, S., Manz, D., & Alves-Foss, J. (2007). A communication–computation efficient group key algorithm for large and dynamic groups. *Computer Networks*, *51*(1), 69–93. doi:10.1016/j.comnet.2006.03.008

Zheng, S., Wang, S., & Zhang, G. (2007). A dynamic, secure, and efficient group key agreement protocol. *Frontiers of Electrical and Electronic Engineering in China*, *2*(2), 182–185. doi:10.100711460-007-0034-7

Zhou, L., Schneider, F., & Renesse, R. (2002). COCA: A secure distributed online certification authority. *ACM Transactions on Computer Systems*, *20*(4), 329–368. doi:10.1145/571637.571638

Zhou, X., & Mao, F. (2012, August). A semantics web service composition approach based on cloud computing. *Fourth International Conference on Computational and Information Sciences (ICCIS)*, 807-810. 10.1109/ICCIS.2012.43

Zhou, Z., Tang, H., Tian, Y., Wei, H., Zhang, F., & Morrison, C. M. (2013). Cyberbullying and its risk factors among Chinese high school students. *School Psychology International*, *34*(6), 630–647. doi:10.1177/0143034313479692

Zickhur, A., & Smith, A. (2013). *Digital differences*. Washington, DC: Pew Internet and American Life Project. Retrieved from http://www.pewInternet.org/2012/04/13/digital-differences/

Zou, X., Ramamurthy, B., & Magliveras, S. S. (2005). Dynamic Conferencing Schemes. *Secure Group Communications over Data Networks*, 91-103.

Zou, X., Ramamurthy, B., & Magliveras, S. S. (2005). Tree Based Key Management Schemes. *Secure Group Communications over Data Networks*, 49-89.

About the Contributors

Mehdi Khosrow-Pour, D.B.A., received his Doctorate in Business Administration from the Nova Southeastern University (Florida, USA). Dr. Khosrow-Pour taught undergraduate and graduate information system courses at the Pennsylvania State University – Harrisburg for almost 20 years. He is currently Executive Editor at IGI Global (www.igi-global.com). He also serves as Executive Director of the Information Resources Management Association (IRMA) (www.irma-international.org), and Executive Director of the World Forgotten Children Foundation (www.world-forgotten-children.org). He is the author/editor of more than 100 books in information technology management. He is also the Editor-in-Chief of the *International Journal of E-Politics, International Journal of Responsible Management Education, International Journal of Social and Organizational Dynamics in IT, International Journal of Handheld Computing Research,* and *International Journal of Information Security and Privacy*, and is also the founding Editor-in-Chief of the *Information Resources Management Journal, Journal of Electronic Commerce in Organizations, Journal of Cases on Information Technology,* and the *Journal of Information Technology Research*, and has authored more than 50 articles published in various conference proceedings and scholarly journals.

* * *

Madoka Aragaki got her Ph.D degree in Graduate School of Medicine, University of Tokyo. After that, she has engaged in online education in several universities. She is interested in psychosocial aspects that internet affects on children and students.

Andrea Atzeni is a Senior Research Assistant at the Dipartimento di Automatica e Informatica, Politecnico di Torino, in the TORSEC Security group. In last twelve years participated in a number of large scale European research project, even as Politecnico di Torino's technical leader. His work addresses definition of security requirements, investigation and modelisation of user expectation on security and privacy, specification of functional and security architectures, development of cross-domain usable security, risk analysis and threat modeling for complex cross-domain systems, legal and technical issues for using cross-border authentication services.

Tony Bailetti is the Director of Carleton's Technology Innovation Management program (www.carleton.ca/it), Chair of the Lead to Win Council and Executive Director (Acting) of the VENUS Task Group. He holds a joint appointment in the Eric Sprott School of Business and the Department of Systems and Computer Engineering at Carleton University, Ottawa, Canada. Tony was presented with the 2011 Ottawa Innovation Community award from the Ottawa Centre for Research and Innovation (OCRI). Tony's research, teaching, and community contributions support the ecosystem approach to innovation for the purpose of creating technology jobs, launching and growing technology companies, and attracting investment. Tony has published in Research Policy, IEEE Transactions on

Engineering Management, Journal of Product Innovation Management, and R&D Management. He has supervised over 60 graduate level theses and projects. Tony Bailetti was born and raised in Peru. He received his M.B.A. and Ph.D. degrees in 1973 and 1976 respectively, from the University of Cincinnati. Tony joined Carleton University in 1979. Today he is a proud 34-years Carleton veteran and Ottawa resident. Tony has four children and six grand children. They are the treasures of his life.

Kannan Balasubramanian received a PhD degree in Computer Science from University of California, Los Angeles, and the M.Tech degree in computer Science and Engineering from IIT Bombay India and his Msc(Tech) degree in Computer Science from BITS, Pilani, India. He is a Professor at Mepco Schlenk Engineering College, Sivakasi, India. His research interests include Network Security, Network protocols, applications and performance.

Diane Barrett holds a PhD in business administration with an information security specialization from North-central University. She is a Certified Information Systems Security Professional (CISSP), and Digital Forensic Certified Practitioner holding many additional industry certifications including, ISSMP, NSA IAM/IEM, Paraben Certified Mobile Examiner, and many CompTIA certifications. Dr. Barrett has an extensive background and has been involved in the IT industry for over 20 years, spending 7 years in software development before becoming involved in security and forensics. She is the President of NextGard technology, LLC and has done contract forensic and security assessment work for numerous years and held positions such as manager of research and training for Kroll's cyber division and forensic training director for Paraben Corporation. Dr. Barrett is the conference co-chair for the Conference on Digital Forensics, Security and Law as well as the President of the Digital Forensics Certification Board. Diane has been involved in collegiate-level forensic education through the development of curriculum and teaching at Bloomsburg University of Pennsylvania, American Military University, and the University of Advancing Technology. She has been a volunteer for ISC2 since 2007 in the areas of item writing and review for the CISSP and ISSMP exams. She has co-authored several security and computer forensics books including Security + Exam Cram, Virtualization and Forensics, and Cybercrime and Cloud Forensics: Applications for Investigation Processes.

Noureddine Boudriga received his Ph.D. in Algebraic topology from University Paris XI and his Ph.D. in Computer science from University of Tunis. He is currently a full Professor of Telecommunications at the University of Carthage and the Director of the Communication Networks and Security Research Laboratory (CN&S, University of Carthage). He was involved in active research in communication networks and system security. He authored and co-authored many chapters and books on information security, security of mobiles networks, and communication networks. His research interests include networking and internetworking security, security management of electronic services, and security-related theories and formal methods.

Tomas Cahlik received his degree in Economics from the University of Economics in Prague in 1979, where he completed his CSc. (equivalent of PhD.) in 1984. From 1979 to 1984 he worked as Assistant Professor at the Department of Econometrics of this University. From 1985 to 1992 he worked at the Institute of Computer and Information Science, Czechoslovak Academy of Sciences (CAS), where he headed the Department of Information Systems. In 1993, he became the Director of the Institute of Information Systems of the CAS. In 1994, he joined the Institute of Economic Studies at Charles University- Faculty of Social Sciences where he nowadays teaches "Ethics and Economics" and "Comparative Economics". Since 2011, he teaches part-time "Econometrics" at the University of Economics in Prague. The main area of his expertise is comparative economics, economic development and growth and analysis of research and development activities. He has had lectures about different economic topics at Cornell University, University of Arizona, Schevtschenko University in Kyiv, University of Cairo, University of Pretoria and University of Cape Town, Waseda University, Doshisha University and Chuo University (Japan), East China Normal University and Fudan University in Shanghai (among others).

Aruna Chakraborty is an Associate Professor in the department of Computer Science and Engineering at St. Thomas' College of Engineering and Technology, Kolkata, India.

Sharon Cox is Professor of Information Systems at Birmingham City University. She gained practical experience of the challenges of managing information from working in international manufacturing organizations. Her recent book, 'Managing Information in Organizations' published by Palgrave Macmillan, provides practical guidance to manage the information resource in a changing environment. Sharon's research interests relate to exploring and structuring contexts within which information is given meaning. She has worked on a number of funded research projects and published in areas such as e-business and knowledge management. Sharon's current work relates to using organizational architectures to support strategic planning of organizational transformation.

Dan Craigen is the Director of Carleton University's Global Cybersecurity Resource. Mr. Craigen was with the Government of Canada (as a science advisor) and previously was President of ORA Canada, a company that focused on High Assurance/Formal Methods and successfully distributed its technology to over 60 countries. His research interests currently lie at the intersection of cybersecurity, open source software and entrepreneurism. He was the chair of two NATO research task groups pertaining to validation, verification, and certification of embedded systems and high-assurance technologies. He received his BScH and MSc degrees in Mathematics from Carleton University.

Ronald L. DeLong has been involved in the evaluation and treatment of sexual offenders throughout the State of Ohio. His services to agencies and courts consist of sexual offender evaluations, risk assessments, evaluations for predator status, forensic and psychological evaluations, and individual and group treatment strategies. Dr. DeLong has over 25 years of experience working with juvenile and adult sexual offenders and other forensic populations. He has also completed advanced training with the Academy Group, Inc., (former FBI profilers and crime scene evaluators) regarding crime scene analysis, violent crime behavior, and profiling dynamics of sexually violent/deviant offenders. He has taught forensic psychology, psychosexual assessments, counseling techniques, and other psychology courses. He also has published articles regarding Internet Sex Offenders, and currently is conducting research on sexual offenders to include residency restrictions, registration, and risk-based vs. statue-based risk classifications.

Keith F. Durkin is a Professor of Sociology at Ohio Northern University. He holds a B.A. in Sociology from Marywood University, and an M.S. and Ph.D. in Sociology from Virginia Tech. His work has appeared in a variety of journals such as Deviant Behavior, Sociological Spectrum, Federal Probation, Journal of Offender Rehabilitation, Journal of Sexual Aggression, Journal of Applied Psychology in Criminal Justice, and Seminars in Integrative Medicine. He has also contributed to a number of edited volumes including Extreme Deviance, Readings in Deviant Behavior, Theories of Deviance, Deviance and Social Control, Handbook of Death & Dying, and Handbook of Deviant Behavior.

Shamal Faily is a Senior Lecturer in Systems Security Engineering at Bournemouth University (BU). His research explores how both security and usability can be designed into software systems. In doing so, Dr Faily's work not only provides assurance that security is incorporated into the design of software, but that the software will continue to be secure when used in different physical, social, and cultural contexts of use. Before joining BU, Dr Faily was a post-doctoral researcher at the University of Oxford, where he completed his DPhil in Computer Science in 2011.

Boutheina A. Fessi received his PhD in Computing Applied to the Management from Higher Institute of Management (ISG) in 2012. She is a member of the Communication Networks and Security (CN&S) research Laboratory (University of Carthage, Tunisia), where she is conducting research activities in the area of intrusion detection, strategic intelligence and digital security, big data and security project management. From September 2013, she has worked as an assistant professor teacher in Computing Applied to the Management in the Faculty of Economic Sciences and Management of Nabeul (FSEGN), Tunisia.

Ruggero Galloni has been working in the field of usability by innovating digital services and engaging final users in design and testing. His experience ranges from coding websites to graphic design, passing along the way through usability testing of UI prototypes and project management. In his job he creates proposals for the company's customers; manages, conducts and reports on user-centered research methodologies such as usability testing and creates user experience deliverables, including usability testing reports, sitemaps, task analysis, click-through prototypes, mockups and other artifacts to describe the intended user experience.

Md. Salleh H. Hassan is a professor at the Department of Communication, Universiti Putra Malaysia and previously served as the Director, Institute for Social Science Studies of UPM (2006-2011). His research interests are in the area of mass communication, development communication and new communication technology. He has been active at the international level presenting papers at conferences and publishing in international journals. Currently he serves as the Vice President of the World Communication Association (WCA). He is also a member of the Asian Mass Communication Research and Information Centre (AMIC), International Association of Agricultural Information Specialists (IAALD), life member Society for International Development and Malaysian Association of Social Sciences. His current research is on the use ICT for agricultural and rural development.

Adamkolo Mohammed Ibrahim did his Master degree programme in Development Communication at Universiti Putra Malaysia in 2017 and received his BA Mass Communication certificate from University of Maiduguri, Nigeria in 2007. He is a lecturer at his Alma Mata department and university where he teaches Mass Communication studies. He conducts research and writes in ICT adoption/e-adoption for socio-economic development and social media. He has published book chapters and journal articles.

Manashee Kalita is currently working as a research scholar, pursuing her PhD from the Dept of Computer Science and Engg, North Eastern Regional Institute of Science and Technology (NERIST) a Deemed University under MHRD, Govt of India since 2014. Prior to this she had completed her M.Tech from the Depertment of CSE, Rajiv Gandhi University, a central university of Arunachal Pradesh. Her interests includes Stegenography, security and Image Processing.

Jan Krasniewicz is a lecturer in computing and has taught on the BSc Forensic Computing course since 2009 contributing to the course design and content. He has taught in the areas of operating system and file system forensic analysis, and currently teaches mobile phone forensics. Jan is trained in using computer forensic software such as Guidance Software's EnCase and MSAB's XRY mobile device forensic software. Jan also teaches in the area of programming and teaches C++ programming and 3D graphics programming with DirectX on the BSc Computer Games Technology course. He has been active as a consultant for the university in the areas of programming and web development, and has worked on a number of successful funded projects. Prior to joining the course Jan was a researcher and successfully achieved a PhD in the area of artificial intelligence.

Wanbil Lee is currently Principal, Wanbil & Associates, Non-Executive Director of Worldcam Ltd., Advisory Board Member, European Centre for eCommerce & Internet Law, and Member of International Experts Network, Nous Global. He is also Founder and President, The Computer Ethics Society, and Co-founder, The Hong Kong Computer Society. He was Foundation Head, Department of Computing Studies, Lingnan University, and Adjunct Professor, Hong Kong Polytechnic University, and held technical line and staff positions in the Commonwealth of Australia Government and international banks. Two university prizes in Ethical Leadership and Ethical Use of Technology, respectively, were established in his name. His research and publication focus is in recent years in Computer Auditing and Ethical Computing; he sits on several professional/learned societies and government committees.

Swanirbhar Majumder completed his BTech in ECE from NEHU, Shillong in 2004 followed by his MTech in 2006 from Dept of Applied Physics University of Calcutta. Since then he has been working on Biomedical and Image Processing research area as well as a faculty in the Dept of ECE NERIST, a CFTI and a Deemed University in Arunachal Pradesh since 2006. He recently completed his PhD from Dept of ETCE Jadavpur University in 2015. He has authored 50+ publications as journals and conferences and publishe a few book chapters and 2 books till date. His areas of interest are image and biomedical signal processing, soft computing and embedded systems.

Jouni Markkula is Senior Research Fellow at the University of Oulu, Finland. He received his Ph.D. in Computer Science from the University of Jyväskylä in 2003. Before the University of Oulu, Dr. Markkula was working at the Information Technology Research Institute of the University of Jyväskylä as a Research Director. His main research areas are data intensive system and service design, software engineering, knowledge management, decision making, and information privacy. He has published more than 80 international peer-reviewed journal and conference articles and book chapters on these topics. He has also lead and managed several research projects in these fields, in co-operation with industry.

Jeremy McDaniel is a 2012 alumnus of the University of South Florida, St. Petersburg, Florida, with a B.A. degree in Criminology. While attending the University of South Florida, he worked as a teacher's assistant and research assistant with a special interest in Cyber Crime for Dr. Shun-Yung Wang. He currently resides in Minnesota with his wife and is a Disability Claims Analyst with Principal Financial Group. In his spare time, Jeremy continues to stay informed in the Criminology field of Cyber Crime.

Yosra Miaoui is a PhD student at the Faculty of Economic Sciences and Management of Tunis, University of Tunis El Manar, Tunisia. She received her Master Diploma in Finance from the Faculty of Economic Sciences and Management of Tunis, Tunisia. Mrs. Miaoui is currently working as an assistant lecturer at the Higher Institute of Technological Studies in Communications of Tunis. She is also a member of the Communication Networks and Security Lab, where she is conducting research activities on determinants and consequences of financial reporting quality, network security economics, and security risk issues in financial decision.

Jo Ann Oravec is a full professor in the College of Business and Economics at the University of Wisconsin at Whitewater in the Department of Information Technology and Supply Chain Management; she is also affiliated with the Robert F. and Jean E. Holtz Center for Science, Technology, & Society Studies, University of Wisconsin at Madison. She received her MBA, MS, MA, and PhD degrees at the University of Wisconsin at Madison. She taught computer information systems and public policy at Baruch College of the City University of New York; she also taught in the School of Business and the Computer Sciences Department at UW-Madison as well as at Ball State University. She chaired the Privacy Council of the State of Wisconsin, the nation's first state-level council dealing with information technology and privacy issues. She has written books (including "Virtual Individuals, Virtual Groups: Human Dimensions of Groupware and Computer Networking," Cambridge University Press) and dozens of articles on futurism, artificial intelligence, disability, mental health, technological design, privacy, computing technology, management, and public policy issues. She has worked for public television and developed software along with her academic ventures. She has held visiting fellow positions at both Cambridge and Oxford and was recently a featured speaker at conferences in Japan and Australia.

M. Rajakani is currently an Assistant Professor in the Department of Computer Science and Engineering at Mepco Schlenk Engineering College, Sivakasi. His interests are in Information Security and Data mining.

Alberto Rodriguez is Associate Professor at the Miguel Hernández University of Elche (UMH). He qualified in Telecommunications Engineering from the University of Vigo (Spain) in 1998. In 2011 obtained a doctorate degree in Telecommunications from the Polytechnic University of Valencia (Spain) with a thesis on time-to-frequency methods for the analysis of ultrasonic signals in the field of non-destructive testing. He develops its research activities in the field of signal processing, particularly in time-to-frequency analysis techniques. He collaborates with the Signal Processing Group at the Polytechnic University of Valencia, participating in national and international research projects. He also participates in international research projects in the field of Ultrasonic Non-Destructive Testing together with the Kaunas University of Technology in Lithuania, where he teaches seminars as guest professor in Doctoral and Master courses of Bioengineering and Electronics studies.

Anna Rohunen works as a researcher at the University of Oulu. She received her M.Sc. degree in 2005 in process engineering, with automation and information technology as the area of specialization. Since then, she has worked for several research projects at the Oulu Southern Institute and in the Department of Information Processing Science at the University of Oulu. She is preparing her doctoral dissertation on information privacy, and her research interests are currently focused on understanding and evaluation of individuals' personal information privacy concerns in the context of personal data intensive services. Specifically, she is interested in privacy behavior models and instruments for evaluating individuals' personal information concerns. Her research is largely based in applying quantitative methods (such as user surveys) and data analysis tools.

Gonzalo Safont received his B.Eng. and his Ph.D. degrees in Telecommunications Engineering from the Universitat Politècnica de València (UPV), Spain, in 2008 and 2015, respectively. He is currently working as a researcher at the Signal Processing Group, a member group of the Institute of Telecommunications and Multimedia Applications (iTEAM) of UPV. His main interests concentrate in the signal processing field. He has worked in advanced methods for data mining, prediction, and dynamic modeling based on mixture of independent component analyzers and decision fusion techniques. He has worked in different applied problems including financial data mining, non-destructive testing, and biomedical diagnosis. He has published 3 papers in JCR-indexed journals, 1 book chapter in an international publisher, and 14 international conference papers. He has also participated in several national and international projects and industry contracts.

Nagayuki Saito is a former Policy Analyst of OECD, Directorate for Science, Technology and Industry, Special Appointment Senior Research Fellow of Ministry of Internal Affairs and Communications, Institution for Information and Communication Policy and visiting researcher of Aoyama-Gakuin University Human Innovation Research Center. He is instructor of Ochanomizu University Interdisciplinary liberal arts. He graduated from a Doctorate Program of Keio University Graduate School of Media Design and had a Master's degree of Economics at Chuo University Graduate School. He is a committee Member of the Committee for Information, Communications and Consumer Policy Division, Working Party on Information Security and Privacy in OECD. His research theme is making a safer Internet environment for the youth. It focuses on awareness of education, making collaborative e-learning system based on theory of social constructivism; information and communication policy.

Addison Salazar received the B.Sc. and M.Sc. degrees in Information and Systems Engineering from Universidad Industrial de Santander, the D.E.A. degree in Telecommunications from Universitat Politècnica de València (UPV) in 2003, and the Dr. in Telecommunications degree from UPV in 2011. He is a senior research official in the Institute of Telecommunications and Multimedia Applications at UPV since 2007. His research interests include statistical signal processing, machine learning, and pattern recognition with emphasis on methods for signal classification based on decision fusion, time-frequency techniques, and mixtures of independent component analyzers. The application of his research has been focused on data mining, nondestructive testing and biomedical problems.

K. John Singh received PhD degree in the Faculty of Information and Communication Engineering from Anna University, Chennai, India in 2013. He received M.S degree in Information Technology from Manonmaniam Sundaranar University, Tirunelveli, India in 2002 and M.Tech degree in Computer and Information Technology from Center for Information Technology and Engineering of Manonmaniam Sundaranar University, Tirunelveli, India in 2004. Currently, he is working as Associate Professor in the School of Information Technology and Engineering, VIT University, Vellore, India. His research interests include Network Security, Cloud Security and Image Processing. He has published several papers in journals and conferences.

Alan D. Smith is presently University Professor of Marketing in the Department of Marketing at Robert Morris University, Pittsburgh, PA. Previously he was Chair of the Department of Quantitative and Natural Sciences and Coordinator of Engineering Programs at the same institution, as well as Associate Professor of Business Administration and Director of Coal Mining Administration at Eastern Kentucky University. He holds concurrent PhDs in Engineering Systems/Education from The University of Akron and Business Administration (OM and MIS) from Kent State University, as well as author of numerous articles and book chapters.

Amber A. Smith-Ditizio is presently a doctoral student in the Department of Kinesiology from Texas Woman's University in Sports Administration. While acquiring strong analytical and professional skills after completing MS in Sport Management, BSBA and MBA from Robert Morris University, with BS from Kent State University in athletic training and related studies, she also holds various personal certifications in the sports performance and athletic areas. She is the author of several academic articles in the sports performance and athletic fields and plans to pursue an academic teaching/research career upon graduation.

Babak Sokouti has over 17 years IT technical management and consulting experience, including managing and maintaining sophisticated network infrastructures. He has obtained Bachelor of Science in Electrical Engineering with a specialization in Control from Isfahan University of Technology, Isfahan, Iran; a Master of Science in Electrical Engineering with a specialization in Electronics (with background of biomedical engineering) from Tabriz Branch, Islamic Azad University, Tabriz, Iran; a Master of Science in Information Security with Distinction from Royal Holloway University of London, London, UK; and obtained PhD in Bioinformatics from Biotechnology Research Center, Tabriz University of Medical Sciences, Tabriz, Iran. In addition, he has obtained IT industry certifications including MCP, MCSA 2003, MCDBA 2000, MCSE 2003, and MCTS 2008. His research interests include cryptographic algorithms, information security, network security and protocols, image processing, protein structure prediction, and hybrid intelligent neural network systems based on genetic algorithms.

Massoud Sokouti obtained a Master of Science in Computer Engineering with a specialization in Computer Architecture from Department of Electrical and Computer Engineering at Shahid Beheshti University, Tehran, Iran and a Bachelor of Science in Information Technology Engineering with a specialization in IT from University of Tabriz, Tabriz, Iran. Currently, he is a PhD student in Nuclear Medicine with a specialization in Meta-Analysis at Nuclear Medicine Research Center, Mashhad University of Medical Sciences, Mashhad, Iran, and an excellent member of Computer Society of Iran. He has been awarded the first prize of scientific and technical innovation in 6th National Conference on Electronic Commerce and Economy and in National Conference in New Ideas in Electrical Engineering. He has worked on Microsoft SQL Server 2005, Net beans, Eclipse, MATLAB, and C++ programming. His main research is in the area of statistics and meta-analysis, m-/e-commerce, cryptographic algorithms, network security, information security, wavelet, and genetic algorithms.

Vaishali Ravindra Thakare is a Research Associate in the School of Information Technology and Engineering, VIT University. She received Bachelor of Engineering in Information Technology from Rashtrasant Tukdoji Maharaj Nagpur University, Nagpur in 2012. She has published many research articles in peer-reviewed journals and in international conferences. Her area of interests includes cloud security and virtualization, security protocols in cloud computing, cloud computing architectures.

Vivek Tiwari (PhD), Assistant Professor in Computer Science and Engineering at International Institute of Information Technology (IIIT-NR), Naya Raipur (C.G.). He is the recipient of Young Scientist Fellowship ((MPYSC_2014_814)) for the year 2014–2016 by Govt. of M.P. He has published more than 25 research papers, books and book chapters in the area of data science, machine learning and pattern management in leading international journals (Springer, Inderscience, ACM, Elsevier, IGI Global) and reputed conferences. He is Editor-in-Chief of book Handbook of Research on Pattern and Data Analysis in Healthcare Settings, Pattern Engineering System Development for Big Data Analytics, published by IGI-Global, USA. He is associated with National Mission on Education through ICT (NMEICT) supported by IIT Bombay and MHRD, India since 2012.

Uruemu (Agwae) Uzamere, Meng, is a graduate of the Technology Innovation Management Engineering program at Carleton University in Ottawa, Canada. She also holds a Bachelor's Degree (BSc Honours) in Electrical Electronics Engineering from University of Ibadan, Nigeria. Uruemu's master's project on mitigating blind spots in cybersecurity She has several years cognitive work experience in IT Management; Network and Desktop support, Quality Assurance, Research, Technical Support and Administration, having worked at different organizations including VENUS Cybersecurity Corporation. As a competent Engineer, an astute proponent of Cybersecurity and a brilliant Communicator, Uruemu has excelled in all her Educational and Professional endeavours. She is particularly exceptional in the areas of contemporary Research, proficient Time Management and organizational skills Uruemu's experience enhances her ability to contribute towards improving Organizations' global business outcome, by means of technical research whilst providing support through engineering best practices. She uses a well-thought-out and modern approach to synthesize her practice with the values and organizational objectives for preferred outcomes.

Luis Vergara received the Ingeniero de Telecomunicación and the Doctor Ingeniero de Telecomunicación degrees from the Universidad Politécnica de Madrid (UPM) in 1980 and 1983 respectively. Until 1992 he worked at the Departamento de Señales, Sistemas y Radiocomunicaciones (UPM) as an Associate Professor. In 1992 he joined the Departamento de Comunicaciones (Universidad Politécnica de Valencia UPV, Spain), where he became Professor and where it was Department Head until April 2004. From April 2004 to April 2005 he was Vicerector of New Technologies at the UPV. He has been coordinator of the Information Technology area at the spanish National Agence for Evaluation and Prospective (1996-99). He is now responsible of the Signal Processing Group of the UPV, a member group of the Institute of Telecommunication and Multimedia Applications (I-TEAM) of UPV. His research lines concentrate in the digital signal processing, more in paticular in statistical signal processing. Currently, his main interests are in algorithms for the detection and classification of events, including fusion of detectors and classifiers. Those algorithms are applied in very diverse problems like quality control in industrial processing, acoustic monitoring, infrared and video surveillance, biomedics, and fraud detection in credit cards. He has published 52 papers in journals indexed in JCR, 5 book chapters in international publishers and more than 130 international conference papers. He is co-author of 6 patents and has supervised 14 PhD theses. He has participated in a large number of projects and industry contracts, both at national and international levels.

Shun-Yung Kevin Wang is an Assistant Professor of Criminology in College of Arts and Sciences at University of South Florida St. Petersburg. He earned his doctoral degree from the College of Criminology and Criminal Justice at Florida State University at Tallahassee and a specialist degree in Information Science from the College of Information at Florida State University at Tallahassee. His research interests include cybercrime, identity theft, juvenile justice, program evaluation, and data analysis. His peer-reviewed publication can be found in Internet Journal of Criminology, Journal of Criminal Justice Education, UCLA Law Review, and book chapters carried by IGI Global and Sage.

Mika Westerlund, DSc (Econ), is an Associate Professor at Carleton University in Ottawa, Canada. He previously held positions as a Postdoctoral Scholar in the Haas School of Business at the University of California Berkeley and in the School of Economics at Aalto University in Helsinki, Finland. Mika earned his doctoral degree in Marketing from the Helsinki School of Economics in Finland. His current research interests include open and user innovation, the Internet of Things, business strategy, and management models in high-tech and service-intensive industries.

Jenifer Sunrise Winter is an Associate Professor in the School of Communications at the University of Hawai'i at Manoa and Co-Director of the Pacific Information and Communication Technology for Development Collaborative (PICTDC). Her research examines algorithmic discrimination, digital inequalities, privacy, and data governance in the context of big data and the Internet of Things. She co-edited The Future Internet: Alternative Visions and has authored dozens of works addressing emerging information policy issues.

Michelle F. Wright is postdoctoral research fellow at Masaryk University. Her research interests include the contextual factors, such as familial and cultural, which influence children's and adolescents' aggression and victimization as well as their pursuit, maintenance, and achievement of peer status. She also has an interest in peer rejection and unpopularity and how such statuses relate to insecurity with one's peer standing, aggression, and victimization.

Sarina Yusuf, MSc. Communication Technology, Universiti Putra Malaysia, 2015. She is currently a PhD candidate in Youth Studies at Institute for Social Science Studies, Universiti Putra Malaysia. Her area of academic interest includes new media study, mass communication and factors affecting youth online behaviours. She has conducted several research studies and authored some articles and book chapters on criminology, children's online safety, social media and ICT for children development.

Wenbing Zhao received the Ph.D. degree in Electrical and Computer Engineering from the University of California, Santa Barbara, in 2002. Currently, he is an associate professor in the Department of Electrical and Computer Engineering at Cleveland State University. His current research interests include distributed systems, computer networks, fault tolerance and security, and smart and connected health. Dr. Zhao has more than 120 academic publications.

Index

R

S

T

U

V

Ensure Quality Research is Introduced to the Academic Community

Become an IGI Global Reviewer for Authored Book Projects

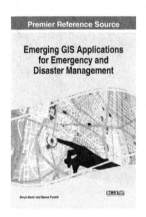
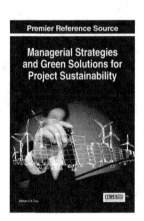

The overall success of an authored book project is dependent on quality and timely reviews.

In this competitive age of scholarly publishing, constructive and timely feedback significantly expedites the turnaround time of manuscripts from submission to acceptance, allowing the publication and discovery of forward-thinking research at a much more expeditious rate. Several IGI Global authored book projects are currently seeking highly qualified experts in the field to fill vacancies on their respective editorial review boards:

Applications may be sent to:
development@igi-global.com

Applicants must have a doctorate (or an equivalent degree) as well as publishing and reviewing experience. Reviewers are asked to write reviews in a timely, collegial, and constructive manner. All reviewers will begin their role on an ad-hoc basis for a period of one year, and upon successful completion of this term can be considered for full editorial review board status, with the potential for a subsequent promotion to Associate Editor.

If you have a colleague that may be interested in this opportunity,
we encourage you to share this information with them.

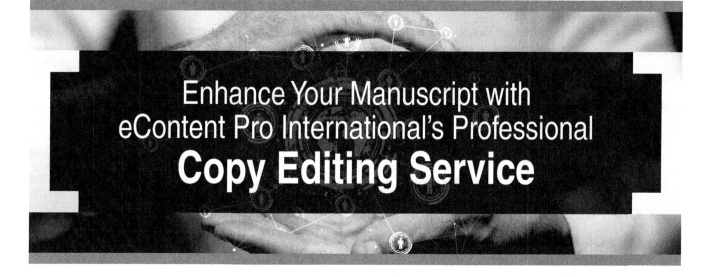

Printed in the United States
By Bookmasters